Other books by Roger F. Duncan

A Cruising Guide to the New England Coast *(with John P. Ware)*
Sailing in the Fog
The Story of Belmont Hill School
Eastward
Friendship Sloops
The Practical Sailor

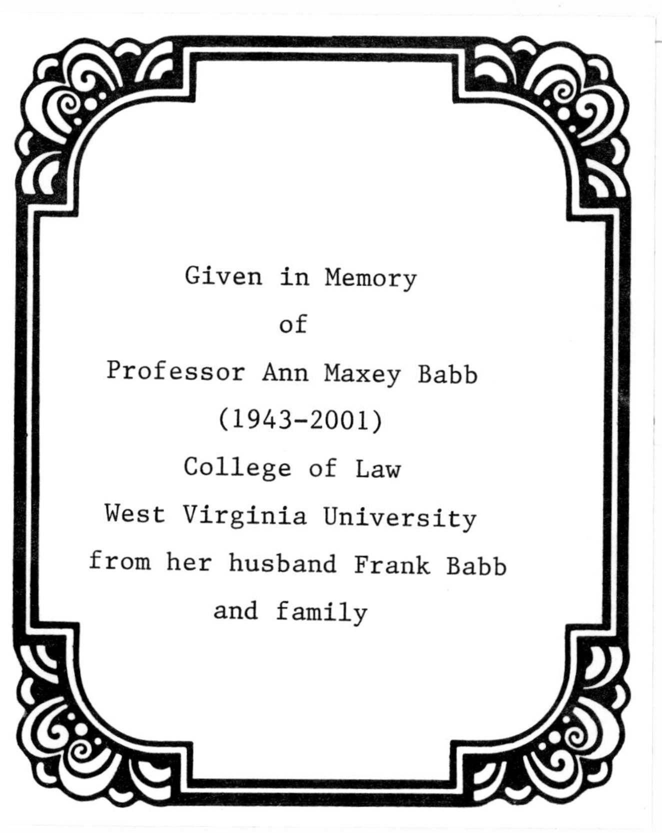

Coastal Maine

W · W · NORTON & COMPANY · *NEW YORK* · *LONDON*

Coastal Maine

A MARITIME HISTORY

Roger F. Duncan

Illustrated by Earle G. Barlow, Kathy Bray, and Consuelo E. Hanks

The drawing on the title page is by Leonard Vosburgh. The maps on pages 32, 109, 207, 211, 231, 269, 273, and 335 are by Kathy Bray.

FIRST EDITION

The text of this book is composed in Galliard, with the display set in Garamond. Manufacturing by the Maple-Vail Book Manufacturing Group. Book design by Marjorie J. Flock.

Library of Congress Cataloging-inPublication Data

Duncan, Roger F.

Coastal Maine / Roger F. Duncan; illustrated by Earle G. Barlow, Kathy Bray, Consuelo E. Hanks.

p. cm.

Includes bibliographical references and index.

1. Atlantic Coast (Me.)—History. 2. Atlantic Coast (Me.)—History, Naval. 3. Atlantic Coast (Me.)—Commerce—History. 4. Fishing—Maine—Atlantic Coast—History. I. Title.

F19.D86 1992

974.1'00946—dc20 91-27534

ISBN 0-393-03048-2

W.W. Norton & Company, Inc., 500 Fifth Avenue, New York, N.Y. 10110

W.W. Norton & Company Ltd., 10 Coptic Street, London WC1A 1PU

1 2 3 4 5 6 7 8 9 0

For Mary Chandler Duncan

Contents

MAPS

Illustrations

Acknowledgments

I SHOULD BEGIN by acknowledging my obligation to the late Professor Robert G. Albion, whose course in maritime history stimulated my interest in the subject in 1962. The late Admiral Samuel Eliot Morison, through his many books and one personal interview, provided a model in good historical writing. My late neighbor, Harold Clifford, author and teacher, was a great encouragement.

Many others have helped more actively in the writing of this book. Arthur Monke, librarian of the Bowdoin College library, and his staff generously permitted me to borrow books and helped to locate obscure information. Their Special Collections room was a valuable resource.

The librarians Joan Greenleaf and Barbara Harvey at the Boothbay Harbor library opened their archives for me and through inter-library loan found books otherwise difficult to locate.

Muriel Sanford and her staff in the Special Collections room at the University of Maine Library in Orono found the Coffin manuscript for me as well as other pertinent material.

The Maine State Library in Augusta and the Harvard College library came to my aid several times. The staffs of the National Archives in Waltham and in Washington and of the Blunt-White library at Mystic Seaport responded generously to my inquiries. My visit to the Mariners' Museum in Newport News was productive, as was a visit to the Jamestown, Virginia, museum where two replicas of seventeenth-century vessels were kept afloat.

Nathan Lipfert, librarian at the Maine Maritime Museum in Bath, made the museum's collection available to me.

Also a number of individuals contributed materially. Among them were: George E. Hall, Captain W. J. Lewis Parker, James P. Stevens, George I. Hodgdon, Jr., Verna and Paul Luke, Admiral William Royall, Gladys and Farnham Butler, William Pattison, Lewis and Sally Iselin, Angie Ferris, Stillman Kelley, Professor Charles B. McLane, Robert C. Brooks, Ralph Stanley, Robert Hinckley, Bert Howe, Hugh Williams, Donald and Robert Duncan, John P. Ware, Charles Chianchiaro, Spencer Apollonio, Evelyn Waite, Carmen Wilder and the staff of Senator Mitchell's office in Rockland, Abbott Fenn, Ted Hanks, and Professor Ben Schneider.

Barbara Schueler typed and criticized part of the manuscript and Ann Foskett put the rest of it on her word processor with the advice and assistance of her husband, Roger Foskett.

I have mentioned elsewhere the contributions of the artists Earle G. Barlow, Kathy Bray, and Consuelo Hanks, but I wish here to underline my appreciation of their talent and commitment, both of which far exceeded my expectations.

Jane Crosen, painstaking copy editor, did much to improve the original manuscript.

My wife, Mary, has supported me materially and critically. She got me into this project to begin with and has stood by me stoutly all the way.

Foreword

THIS BOOK is about people, real living people, who lived on the coast of Maine, who trod the land we tread today, who sailed the same bays and sounds, who fished the same waters and landed on the islands. Each used the resources at hand to make a living in his own way. Conflicts arose, and men fought each other with what weapons they could find, from tomahawks to submarines. Each generation built on what went before and left a foundation for what came after. The story has no beginning and no end.

Here is an attempt to put some of the incidents in context, to give day-to-day life some pattern and significance, to help the reader in this century see the islands, the capes, the coves and harbors not as mere geographical features but as signs and reminders of what real people did here.

You will not find the usual academic machinery of footnotes, *ibid.*s, and *op. cit.*s. Each chapter is followed by chapter notes which give the sources for that chapter and occasionally add supplementary information which does not fit the plan of the chapter. In the back of the book is a bibliography listing the books mentioned in the chapter notes and other books which might be of interest. The scholar will notice considerable reliance on secondary sources. I am not a professional historian and am not expecting to discover much new truth. I have used what others have done where it suits my purposes. Little is to be gained, for instance, in digging into clipper ship logbooks and custom-house records. Responsible historians have done this and done it thoroughly. In other cases, particularly in accounts of early voyages, the writing and research were often done by people who did not know the coast or the problems of coastal navigation in sailing vessels. In chapters on more recent events, I have relied on my recollections and those of people who were there, for very little has been written. I have left ample room for the professional historian.

I have included a few passages of fiction because in no other way could I seem to bring to life the times of which I was writing. Captain Pattishall was a real person, and his ghost has been reported not long ago. His rum jug is purely fictional. Taffy and his crew are fiction, but with a solid basis in fact.

I am deeply indebted to three artists: Earle Barlow, Kathy Bray, and Consuelo Hanks. Each has taken great pains to represent accurately the details of the scene. The sails are such sails as these vessels carried. Each line goes to its proper belaying pin. Scale, hull form, and background are consistent with what we know of vessels of that time. Yet, these drawings are more than blueprints. There is motion, living quality, in each scene. Kathy Bray's technical drawings and the maps are done with the same care and are equally necessary to the success of the work.

I owe an apology to the descendants of those inhabiting the coast when the Europeans first came. I should, perhaps, have spoken of them as Native Americans, which indeed they were. Unfortunately, the term is an awkward one and its meaning a bit hazy because all of us born on this continent are native Americans. The term "Indian" is even less accurate but through consistent misuse has acquired a meaning, and this is about the best we can do.

Let us, then, turn the page and launch ourselves into Chapter 1 to meet those who first told of a new continent.

ROGER F. DUNCAN

East Boothbay, Maine
December 1991

Coastal Maine

ONE

Early Visitors

E DO NOT KNOW who was the first European to tread the shores of Maine, and we probably will never know. For literally centuries before any extant records were kept, Europeans had sailed northern and western Atlantic waters. If we can accept the argument of Professor Barry Fell in *America B.C.,* Phoenicians landed on Monhegan and left an inscription in Ogam carved into a ledge on Manana Island reading, "Ships from Phoenicia. Cargo platform." Pytheas, a Greek navigator and astronomer from Marseilles, in the fourth century B.C. sailed far enough north in the Atlantic to find pack ice and persistent fog. Saint Brendan, an Irish monk of the sixth century A.D., tells in his *Navigatio* a fantastic tale of a voyage to the westward in which he found an island inhabited by birds singing in Latin; the holy man was attended by a friendly whale named Jaconius that surfaced when the saint needed an island. Admiral Samuel E. Morison, as meticulous a historian as ever trod in sea boots, wrote, "Saint Brendan was a real person, and in my opinion his *Navigatio* is based on a real voyage or voyages, enhanced by Celtic imagination."

We know that Norsemen colonized Greenland, Iceland, and the islands north of Scotland, and spent at least one winter on the northern peninsula of Newfoundland at Anse aux Meadows in about 1000 A.D. We know that John Cabot visited Newfoundland in 1497. Between these voyages are numerous more or less legendary accounts of Atlantic voyages. Madoc the Welshman in the twelfth century, the Italian Zeno brothers in the fourteenth century, the Danish pirates Pening and Pothorst in the fifteenth century and the Polish Johannes Scolvus at about the same time, and anonymous Irish fishermen are all credited by various of their countrymen as having sailed the Atlantic and as having discovered America before Columbus. In 1436 Andrea Bianco drew a map showing Stoxafixa, an island where Newfoundland lies. (Codfish in northern lands is still called stockfish.) Although careful historians have blown out of water the literal truth of these stories, the very existence of such tales suggests strongly that Europeans have sailed the Atlantic since the earliest days. Some of them, or some of their contemporaries of whom we never have heard, could have visited Maine.

However, the first European to leave us an historically credible and verifiable account of a visit to the Maine coast was Giovanni Verrazano in 1524. By that time, the Spanish and the Portuguese had explored the coasts of Central and South America from Florida to Tierra del Fuego in search of a strait leading to the Pacific and the wealth of China and the Spice Islands, but they had found no passage north of the Strait of Magellan. The Portuguese and English had visited Newfoundland and Labrador before 1524, found them rich in fish and timber, but had found no navigable passage.

Backed by a syndicate of bankers and silk merchants and probably with a commission from Francis I, King of France, Verrazano sailed from Dieppe, France, in 1524 with two ships, *La Dauphine,* borrowed from the French navy, and *La Normande*. After taking several prizes off the coast of Spain, Verrazano left *La Normande,* presumably to escort the prizes to a French port, and continued alone in *La Dauphine*. He crossed the Atlantic in the northern edge of the trade winds in January and February 1524 and made the American coast near Cape Fear, North Carolina, far enough north to be more or less safe from Spanish ships of war. After a brief sortie southward, he coasted north and east, finding pleasant and friendly natives but no strait. He identified the Hudson as a river and no strait, and continued eastward to Block Island and Newport, where he found the Wampanoag Indians friendly and fearless, eager to trade for bells and beads but not much interested in iron or steel tools. He located Newport in latitude 41° 30′ north, only ten miles off, showing that he was a competent navigator. He rounded Cape Cod, saw the White Mountains over the low shore, and continued north to Maine.

Verrazano found the natives of this coast hostile and rude, unlike those farther south. They would accept in trade "nothing but knives, fishhooks, and tools to cut withall" and were willing to trade only by lowering a basket over a cliff to the white men below. When the transactions were completed, the Abenakis derided the white men in loud, vulgar, and abusive ways from the top of the cliff. One might reasonably assume that they had encountered whites before either as slave traders or as dishonest merchants. Verrazano's encounter happened, according to his reckoning, in latitude 43° 40′ north. Allowing for the same ten-mile error as he made at Newport, the scene could have been any steep promontory between Cape Elizabeth and Monhegan, of which there are many; Admiral Morison favors Cape Small.

Continuing to the eastward, Verrazano passed thirty-two islands "lying all near the land, being small and pleasant to the view, high, and having many turnings and windings between them, making many fair harbors and channels, as they do in the Gulf of Venice and Illyria." East of these islands, at the head of one of the inlets on his map, he wrote "Oranbega," labeling himself as the first to fall for the Abenakis' tall tales of a beautiful City of Gold, later called Norumbega, on the site of the present city of Bangor. Not until Champlain sailed up the Penobscot in 1604 was this ghost laid to rest.

Verrazano returned to France and reported to his backers. However, Francis I was much occupied with a war in Italy and gave him little attention. The silk merchants, disappointed at his failure to find a strait, withdrew their support. Backed then by Jean Ango, merchant prince of Dieppe, and Phillipe de Chabot, admiral in the French navy, Verrazano opened up a logwood trade with Brazil. On a follow-up voyage the next year, still seeking a strait, he called at a Caribbean island, perhaps Guadeloupe, where he was murdered and eaten by cannibal Caribs.

While Verrazano, sponsored by the King of France, was fitting out in Dieppe in 1523, the King of Spain, Charles I, freed Estévan Gomez from the prison in which he had languished since 1518. Gomez had been in command of *San Antonio,* the largest vessel in Magellan's fleet, had deserted his commander in the Strait of Magellan, and had come home. He was imprisoned for mutiny. Nevertheless, after the return of *Vittorio,* Magellan's one surviving ship, under Sebastian del Cano in 1522, Gomez pleaded that the Strait of Magellan was too cold, stormy, and tortuous a passage to be practical and declared he could find a better passage in more temperate climes. The only part of the American coast unknown to Spanish and Portuguese navigators lay between Florida and Newfoundland. There must lie the strait if strait there was. Distressed lest France forestall him, with Verrazano's expedition already fitting out, Charles sent out Gomez, the best and most persuasive navigator he had, to seek the passage to China for Spain.

He was not in time, for Gomez did not sail from Corunna until after Verrazano had returned to France in July 1524. Indeed, Gomez did not leave until September, a miserable time of year in which to cross the Atlantic. He made the Gulf of St. Lawrence in February. With his dislike for cold weather and icy seas established in Tierra del Fuego, he headed south at once, convinced that if there was a strait in that latitude, it would be no better than Magellan's. By June 1525 he was in Passamaquoddy Bay. He saw the hills of Mount Desert Island and Somes Sound, crossed Blue Hill Bay, worked his way through the islands of Jericho Bay and up Eggemoggin Reach to the Penobscot River. He got as far as Bangor and realized he was in a river, not a passage to the Indies. The Indians who greeted him were more friendly than the Casco Bay Indians who had greeted Verrazano the year before. If they told him tales of Norumbega, the City of Gold, he did not believe them, for he wrote on his map "No gold here."

Gomez continued across Muscongus Bay and Casco Bay, saw the White Mountains, noted the Piscataqua and Merrimac rivers and Cape Cod. He continued down the coast, and after kidnapping a number of Indians, returned to Spain, arriving in August 1525. Be it said to the Spanish government's credit that they ordered him to release the captives, but there is no evidence of any attempt to return them to America.

The Spanish, convinced that there was no passage to the Pacific through temperate North America and being very busy with the development of Florida, the Caribbean, and South America, paid no more attention to Maine. The

French, however, followed up Verrazano's voyage with three voyages by Jacques Cartier to Newfoundland and the St. Lawrence between 1534 and 1538. Although Cartier never came as far west as Maine, it is significant to note that early in the century, French fishermen were active in the Strait of Belle Isle between Newfoundland and the mainland. In 1534 Cartier hailed a vessel from La Rochelle off the coast of southern Labrador. In 1560 more than thirty fishing vessels sailed from Saint-Malo and Cancale for Newfoundland, and by 1586 there were 300 fishermen of all nationalities in Newfoundland ports.

In 1555, André Thevet, a friend of Cartier's, a seagoing monk, and the one who introduced tobacco to France, in the course of a cruise from Florida to Canada spent five days partying with the Abenakis on the shore of Penobscot Bay. He writes: "Here we entered a river [Penobscot Bay] which is one of the finest in the whole world. It is marked on some charts as the Grand River. The natives call it Agoncy. Several beautiful rivers flow into it. Upon its banks the French formerly erected a small fort about ten leagues from its mouth. It was called the Fort of Norumbega, and was surrounded by fresh water. As you enter this river there appears an island [Vinalhaven] surrounded by eight small islets. These are near the country of the Green Mountains. About three leagues into the river, there is an island four leagues in circumference which the natives call Aiayascon [Islesboro]. It would be easy to plant on this island, and to build a fortress, which would hold in check the whole surrounding country. Upon landing, we saw a great multitude of people coming down upon us in such number that you might have supposed them to be a flight of starlings. The men came first, then the women, then the boys, then the girls. They were all clothed in the skins of wild animals.

"Considering their aspect and their mode of advancing, we mistrusted them, and retired aboard our vessel. They, perceiving our fear, made signs of friendship."

Several Indians came aboard with presents of provisions, for which they were given "trinkets" with which they seemed well pleased. The next morning, Thevet went ashore with a party to trade for badly needed provisions. Chief Peramick was very friendly, invited them into his house, and had started to cook a generous feast, when warriors came in bearing six newly severed heads of local enemies. The Frenchmen shortly afterwards departed without saying farewell or thanking their hosts. The chief was much distressed and came aboard the next morning with his three children, hoping that he had not offended his visitors. Accordingly, the Frenchmen went ashore again, strained relations were patched up, and the party went on.

"Having remained in this place for five days, we weighed anchor, and, parting from them with marvelous contentment on both sides, went out upon the open sea."

The coast of Maine had been thus far a great disappointment to its discoverers. No gold, no spices, no precious stones, and above all, no passage to the Pacific to rival the Portuguese route around the Cape of Good Hope. There was nothing of value in North America but timber and fish. Accordingly, the

Spanish and Portuguese governments abandoned attempts to explore the coast and left it to the fishermen.

The French and English continued their search for a passage in the voyages of Cartier, Roberval, Frobisher, and Davis, but none of them came as far south as Maine.

The next visitor to the Maine coast, a man about whom we have only the vaguest knowledge, is the almost incredible David Ingram. He sailed from Plymouth, England, in October 1567 with John Hawkins and Francis Drake in a fleet of six ships with 408 men bound for Guinea to pick up a cargo of slaves, contrary to Portuguese law, and sell them in the West Indies, contrary to Spanish law. Both laws were circumvented by Hawkins with the connivance of local officials.

In the fall of 1568, the fleet put into the port of San Juan d'Ulua near Vera Cruz [Mexico] to refit for the voyage home. While they were there, a Spanish naval force arrived to escort the annual shipment of silver to Spain. Aboard the flagship was Don Martín Enriquez, the new viceroy of Mexico, a man who could not afford to have dealings with a foreigner trading illegally in Spanish waters. However, after considerable negotiation followed by a treacherous Spanish surprise attack, Hawkins escaped from the harbor with only two ships, *Judith* and *Minion,* both of which had been roughly handled. Drake, in command of *Judith,* headed for home at once, leaving Hawkins with two hundred men, only one ship, and inadequate supplies. One hundred of these men he set ashore, more or less at their own request. The party divided, most going south and the others north. Hostile Spaniards, hostile Indians, disease, and desertion thinned the northern group to three: Ingram, Browne, and Twide. They walked north and east, following the coast, passed from Indian tribe to tribe, sometimes on foot and sometimes afloat, and in 1571 reached the Maine coast and continued on to New Brunswick, where they were picked up by a French fishing vessel and taken to France.

Ingram returned to England, spoke with Hawkins, and for years told and retold his tale in pub and tavern. In 1579 Sir Humphrey Gilbert heard of him. Gilbert, then projecting a voyage to America, called him in and, with a stenographer to take down his words, bade him tell his tale.

Ingram obliged with the truth, but the truth badly confused and well varnished with imagination. Some of the animals he described no doubt he saw in Africa. His description of a moose is barely recognizable. He speaks of rubies four inches long and of sheep with red wool and red meat. He makes no geographical distinctions but tells of a great Indian city, Norumbega again, with wide streets, roofs of gold on pillars of crystal, and a king on a throne of pearls. Fantastic as his tale is, it is certain that he was set ashore in Mexico; it is certain that he was picked up near what is now Saint John, New Brunswick. He must have traversed Maine.

His account was published verbatim by Richard Hakluyt in his 1589 edition but was omitted from subsequent editions as "a tissue of lies."

Perhaps partly in response to Ingram's account, Gilbert sent out Simón

Ferdinando in the pinnace *Squirrel* in 1579 and then John Walker in 1580 to explore Norumbega and the Penobscot as a possible site for a colony. Walker found Penobscot Bay, climbed one of the Camden Hills, where he claimed to have found a silver mine—probably mica in the granite—and brought home deer and moose hides stolen from an Indian wigwam. He did not get as far up the river as Bangor but described the country as "most excellent both for the soyle, diversity of sweete woode and other trees."

Having assembled what information he could and having obtained a grant from Queen Elizabeth to settle anywhere north of Florida, Sir Humphrey Gilbert set out in June 1583 with a fleet of five vessels to establish a permanent settlement in America, of which he would be the viceroy. He hoped to locate it on the shore of the northwest passage near a gold mine, but his intention was to settle in what is now Maine. It was the first serious attempt at English colonization in America.

One vessel gave up early and ran back to England. The others made St. John's, Newfoundland, of which island Gilbert took formal possession in the name of the Queen and with the consent of the fishermen from various nations present at the time.

With some of his crew sick, Gilbert abandoned one vessel and with *Delight, Golden Hind,* and the little 10-ton pinnace *Squirrel* he headed south to spend the winter on the Maine coast. He took personal command of *Squirrel* because he found the smaller vessel "most convenient to discover upon the coast, and to search into every harbor or creeke, which a great ship could not doe." Unfortunately, he overloaded the little vessel with guns "to make a shew." *Delight* was wrecked on the shoals off Sable Island, and most of her crew drowned. The others, in a shallop with only one oar, got back to Newfoundland.

With the loss of *Delight,* her crew and supplies, and it being already late August, Sir Humphrey decided they had done enough for that year. He gave up the idea of spending the winter in America and, with *Golden Hind,* and *Squirrel,* headed for home, resolved to try again the next year.

On September 2 he went aboard *Golden Hind* to have the surgeon attend to an infection on his foot. The master and crew urged him to stay aboard the larger vessel, but he refused, saying, "I will not forsake my little company going homeward, with whom I have passed so many storms and perils."

North of the Azores they "met with very foule weather and terrible seas, breaking short and high, Pyramid-wise," wrote Hayes, master of *Golden Hind.* "In the afternoone the Frigate *Squirrel* was neere cast away, oppressed by waves, yet at that time recovered; and giving foorth signes of joy, the Generall sitting abaft with a booke in his hande, cried out unto us in the *Hind* (so oft as we did aproch within hearing) 'We are as neere to heaven by sea as by lande'. Reiterating the same speech, well beseeming a souldier, resolute in Jesus Christ, I can testifie he was. . . . The same Monday night, about twelve of the clocke, or not long after, the Frigat being ahead of us in the *Golden Hind,* suddenly

"We are as neere to heaven by sea as by lande."
Drawing by Consuelo E. Hanks

her lights were out, whereof as it were in a moment, we lost the sight, and withall our watch cryed, 'The Generall was cast away' which was too true. For in that moment the Frigat was devoured and swallowed up by the Sea."

Gilbert was lost, but his project was significant in that it was the first effort to establish a colony in Maine. Every expedition before Gilbert's had been in search of a passage to the Pacific with gold, silver, and spices as a sideline. Gilbert had hoped to establish a colony politically, economically, and militarily self-sufficient as an outpost of what was already being called the British Empire.

NOTES

Shadowy suggestions that at a very early date people were sailing the Atlantic Ocean may be derived from the discovery by Norwood Bakeman of two ceramic jugs on the bottom of Penobscot Bay off Castine. "Dr. Barry Bell," says a photocopy of a clipping in my possession, "head of the Department of Comparative Zoology at Harvard, believes they could have come from Phoenician sailing vessels that may have visited the Maine Coast centuries before Christ's birth." *Bell* must be a misprint for *Fell*. There is reference to this find on page 100 in *America B.C.* by Dr. Fell.

Another suggestive note appears in Peter C. Newman's *Company of Adventurers* in a footnote on page 179: "According to H. Lamb's *Climate, History and the Modern World* [London, Methuen 1982], 'A bizarre occurrence—serious for the individuals concerned—presumably resulting from the great southward spread of the polar water and ice was the arrival about the Orkney Islands a number of times between 1690 and 1728, and once in the river Don near Aberdeen, of an Eskimo in his kayak.' " Even allowing for a long extension of the ice on the west coast of Greenland, a rugged constitution and an adventurous spirit on the part of the Eskimo, this is an almost incredible incident. But, "There are more things in heaven and earth, Horatio, / Than are dreamt of in your philosophy."

Admiral Morison's *Northern Voyages* is the basis of most of this chapter. The account of Thevet's visit to Penobscot Bay is translated and quoted in John Abbott's *History of Maine*. Rayner Unwin's *The Defeat of John Hawkins* gives an exhaustive and scholarly account of Hawkins's voyage to Africa and the Caribbean, his defeat at San Juan d'Ulua, and the experiences of many of those set ashore after the battle. David Ingram's march to Saint John, New Brunswick, is studied at length. The transcription of Ingram's interview with Sir Humphrey Gilbert and Walsingham is found in a facsimile of Richard Hakluyt's first edition, edited by De Golyer and titled *Across Aboriginal America: The Journey of Three Englishmen Across Texas in 1568*. The piece which Ida S. Proper claims to quote from Ingram in *Monhegan, The Cradle of New England* is most charitably described as imaginative material inserted by Herbert W. Sylvester in *The Land of St. Castin,* from which Proper is quoting.

Additional details have been quarried from Henry S. Burrage's *Early English and French Voyages,* Abbott's *History of Maine,* James Phinney Baxter's *Documentary History of the State of Maine,* Erroll Bruce's *Challenge to Poseidon,* and Charles M. Andrews's *The Colonial Period of American History*.

TWO

Gosnold, Pring, Waymouth, Gilbert, and Popham

CARTIER IN 1534 had met French fishermen in the Gulf of St. Lawrence. Ingram's Indian friends in 1571 accurately described European vessels, and a French fisherman picked Ingram up in Saint John, New Brunswick, and took him back to France. Gilbert in 1583 found thirty fishing vessels at St. John's, Newfoundland. Gosnold in 1602 met Indians who had been in contact with French fishermen, and Raleigh Gilbert in 1607 met Indians far up the Kennebec River who spoke English. There can be little doubt that by the latter part of the sixteenth century, fishing on the Maine coast was a profitable and well-established business.

I find it difficult to document this assertion directly, for it is well known that when a fisherman finds a profitable fishing ground, he does not publish its latitude and longitude. Also, few of these fishermen could read or write, and pilots who knew the marks and ranges on the New England coast shared their knowledge only within the profession. The importation of salt and pickled fish to Europe was a very profitable business. While adventurers were restlessly seeking a route to the riches of China, fishermen were quietly taking fortunes from the coastal waters.

However, in the opening years of the seventeenth century, the situation changed. Instead of making separately financed annual fishing trips, efforts were made to establish permanent bases. The first recorded evidence of it was in 1602 when merchants of Bristol, England, raised a fund to send out Bartholomew Gosnold with the avowed purpose of establishing a settlement on the New England coast. This would serve as an operating base for fishermen and a center for fur trading. It was no secret. Indeed, the voyage was recorded by two men, John Brereton and Gabriel Archer, with the idea of attracting colonists.

Gosnold made the coast in 43° latitude according to his reckoning, which would be near the Isles of Shoals. Brereton describes their landfall, probably

The Nubble off Cape Neddick, and their first meeting with the local inhabitants:

"And standing fair along the shore, about twelve of the clock the same day, we came to an anchor, where eight Indians in a Basque-shallop with mast and sail, an iron grapple, and a kettle of copper, came boldly aboard us, one of them apparelled with a waist-coat and breeches of black serge, made after our sea-fashion, hose and shoes on his feet; all the rest (saving one that had a pair of breeches of blue cloth) were naked. . . . It seemed by some words and signs they made, that some Basques of St. John de Luz have fished or traded in this place, being in latitude 43°."

Gosnold sailed south and west, leaving Maine waters to attempt a colony on Cuttyhunk Island. The colonists refused to be left on the island, however, so he loaded his vessel with cedar and sassafras, then in demand as a cure for syphilis, and returned to England. He joined the Jamestown colony in 1607 but died in Virginia during that colony's first summer. Gosnold's voyage, while it accomplished little of permanent significance, showed that planting a colony was a much larger undertaking than it had been assumed to be.

In the following year, 1603, Martin Pring was sent out by the Bristol merchants to load his two small vessels, *Speedwell* of 50 tons and *Discoverer* of only 26 tons, with sassafras and to explore farther in search of a site for a colony. Pring made the coast in what he declares to be 43° north latitude. He sailed between two islands where he saw numerous foxes and continued to the mainland where he found deserted campsites and deer, wolves, more foxes, and dogs. On the strength of this rather slim evidence, North Haven and Vinalhaven have been named the Fox Islands, the name surviving in the name of the channel between them, Fox Islands Thorofare. However, these islands are north of 44°. It may be that Pring's instrument was badly bent or broken, for later he located Plymouth [Massachusetts] in "41° and odde minutes" when actually it is in 42° north latitude.

Pring, like Gosnold, sailed south along the coast, in search of sassafras, and left Maine waters before he found it. He loaded his vessels at Plymouth and returned with an accurate and circumstantial account of his voyage.

Gosnold's and Pring's voyages were publicized with the purpose of raising money and attracting settlers to establish colonies. The accession of James I in 1603 ended the long war with Spain, which had smoldered and blazed for over twenty years. Not included in the Treaty of 1604 but apparently understood by both sides was the Policy of Effective Occupation. This had been proposed by England in 1600, and Spain had neither accepted nor rejected it. King James acted on it, not planting English settlements within one hundred miles of lands already effectively occupied by the Spanish. However, he rejected the papal bulls of 1493 and 1494, dividing between Spain and Portugal to the exclusion of all other nations, all lands uninhabited by Christians. James regarded as open to English colonization all of what was loosely called Virginia, the North American coast from Florida to Newfoundland. England's

West Country merchants were eager to invest capital in such an enterprise, and the King was eager to encourage colonization. His personal income depended heavily on customs duties. Increased imports from American colonies would increase trade, hence increase customs receipts. He could impose no other taxes without calling Parliament, which he was reluctant to do; for he resented and feared their incursions on what he regarded as his Divine Right to rule.

At the same time, increasing friction between Catholics and Protestants created international problems. France had emerged from thirty years of religious and political strife as a Catholic country with a strong Protestant Huguenot presence. Spain was strongly Catholic and despite the treaty with England in 1604 was regarded by Englishmen as a source of corruption and treachery. Although King James did not persecute English Catholics at first, pressure from the Church of England and from dissenters forced him to discriminate against Catholics.

Consequently, in 1605, combining commercial and religious interests, the Earl of Southampton, a Protestant, and Sir Thomas Arundel, a Catholic, combined to send out George Waymouth in *Archangel* to find a site for a colony which would be both a profitable commercial venture and a refuge for English Catholics. Aboard *Archangel* was James Rosier, a Catholic who had been with Gosnold in 1602. Rosier's business was not only to record the events of the voyage but to promote the colony that was to follow. His book, *A True Relation of the Most Prosperous Voyage Made this Present Year, 1605, by Captain George Waymouth In the Discovery of the North Part of Virginia,* does both.

Archangel sailed from Dartmouth on March 31, 1605, made Corvo and Flores in the Azores on April 14, and early in May came on soundings on Nantucket Shoals. On May 14 they saw Sankaty Head on Nantucket, became entangled in shoals, and sent a boat ahead to sound out a safe passage to the southward. However, "we found ourselves embaied with continuall showldes and rockes in a most uncertaine ground, from five or sixe fathoms, at the next cast of the lead we should have 15 and 18 fathoms. . . . Thus we parted from the land, which we had not so much before desired, and at the first sight rejoiced, as now we all joifully praised God, that it had pleased him to deliver us from so imminent danger." Finding no way to work south against a southwest wind, they ran northerly and, being short of wood and water, "we stood in directly with the land, and much marvelled we descried it not, wherein we found our sea charts very false, putting land where none is."

On May 17 they saw Monhegan, but because "it blew a great gale of winde, the sea very high and neere night, not fit to come upon on unknowen coast," they stood offshore and the next day anchored north of the island "about a league from the shore." That seems a long way off and in very deep water. Rosier is a very poor judge of distance, but it is understandable.

Waymouth and twelve men rowed ashore, found firewood and fresh water; also fir, birch, oak and beech trees, gooseberries, strawberries, wild peas, wild roses, and "much fowle of divers kinds." The men left aboard tried the fishing and got "above thirty great Cods and Hadocks." However, they found, as later visitors have found, that Monhegan affords at best an uneasy anchorage. "From hence we might discern the maine land from the West-South-West to the East-North-East, and a great way (as it then seemed, and as we after found it) up into the maine we might discerne very high mountains." Accordingly they sailed toward the mountains, the Camden Hills, and with Thomas Cam, the mate, sounding ahead in a small boat, made their way into what we call today Georges Harbor, ". . . a most safe birth defended from all windes, in an excellent depth of water for ships of any burthen in six, seven, eight, nine and ten fathoms upon a clay ooze very tough." Probably Waymouth anchored first on the east side of Allen Island north of the Dry Ledges.

Rosier describes a paradise, and he did not have to exaggerate a great deal to do so, for an island harbor in June is not far removed from the Kingdom of Heaven. The crew went ashore to explore, finding fireplaces, eggshells, bones of fish and animals, but no inhabitants. They brought ashore the parts of a pinnace, later referred to as the "light horseman," carried knocked down in the hold, and they set her up under the direction of the carpenter and the cooper.

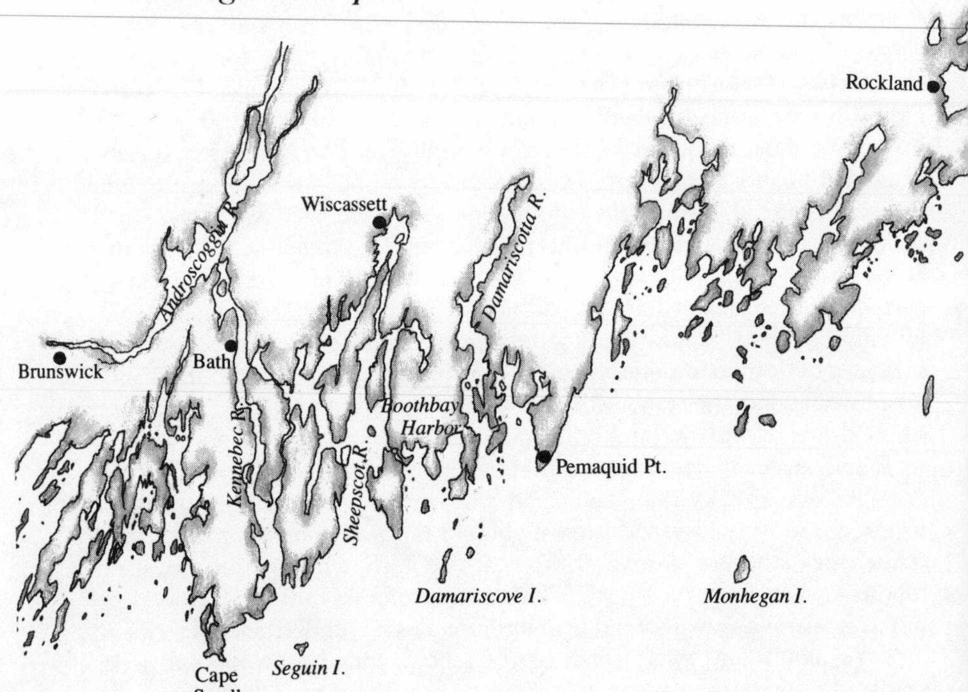

They dug a well and set a cask in it, delighting in the good fresh water, and they found the clay they dug out good for brick and tile. They cut firewood and trees for spare spars, went fishing outside and caught cod, haddock, and "thornebacke" (dogfish?). With a net close to shore they caught lobsters, plaice, rockfish (cunners?), and lumpfish. They planted peas and barley, which sprouted to a height of eight inches in sixteen days. The spruce trees oozed spruce gum "which smelled like Frankencense" and which seemed a profitable source of tar, pitch, and turpentine. They picked up mussels abounding in pearls, fourteen in one shell "all glistering with mother of Pearl." Georges Harbor looked so attractive in this week in May "insomuch as many of our Companie wished themselves settled heere, not expecting any further hopes or better discovery to be made." Through all this, Rosier says of Waymouth, "Heere I cannot omit (for foolish imputation of flattery) the painfull industry of our Captaine, who as at sea he is always most carefull and vigilant, so at land he refuseth no paines; but his labour was ever as much or rather more than any mans: which not only encourageth others with better content, but also effecteth much with great expedition."

On May 29 they set up a cross on Allen Island as a monument to the presence of Christian men and named the harbor Pentecost.

On May 30, the light horseman having been completed, Waymouth and thirteen men departed on an exploring expedition, leaving fourteen men aboard *Archangel* with Rosier. That same afternoon, Indians in three canoes landed on one of the islands and presently came aboard. "They seemed all very civill and merrie; shewing tokens of much thankefulnesse for those things we gave them. We found them then (as after) a people of exceeding good invention, quicke understanding and readie capacitie." An active trade in furs was opened, and the white men and red visited each other ashore and afloat. The next day, Waymouth returned with enthusiastic reports of a great river running 40 miles up into the land. This must have been the St. George River, but it runs no 40 miles inland. However, Rosier in his account is trying to sell the region as a place to settle, and he shows himself in several places to be a very poor judge of distances and excessively enthusiastic.

It rained that afternoon, so no trading took place. However, three Indians came aboard, were presented with knives, a shirt, combs, mirrors, a drink of aqua vitae, which they did not like, sugar candy and raisins, ". . . and some of everything they would reserve to carry to their company. Wherefore we pittying their being in the raine, and therefore not able to get themselves victuall (as we thought) we gave them bread and fish. . . . This because we found the land a place answerable to the intent of our discovery, viz. fit for any nation to inhabit, we used the people with as great kindnes as we could devise, or found them capable of."

They showed the Indians how to fish with a net, giving away most of the catch. "Then on the shore I learned the names of divers things of them: and when they perceived me to note them down, they would of themselves, fetch fishes, and fruit bushes, and stand by me to see me write their names." Rosier touched his sword with a lodestone to magnetize it and with it picked up a knife and needles. He laid a knife on a block and with the magnetized sword made it turn without touching it. "This we did to cause them to imagine some great power in us; and for that to love and feare us." Rosier describes their bows of witch hazel and beech, their arrows of ash tipped with bone, and darts likewise tipped. He threw a dart against a rock and was surprised that it did not break.

Waymouth invited two Indians to dinner "who behaved themselves very civilly, neither laughing nor talking all the time, and at supper fed not like men of rude education, neither would they eat or drinke more than seemed to content nature; They desired peas to carry ashore to their women, which we gave them, with fish and bread, and lent them pewter dishes, which they carefully brought again."

Rosier admired their women and children. "They [the women] were well favoured in proportion of countenance, though coloured blacke, low of stature, and fat, bare headed as the men, wearing their haire long: They had two little male children of a yeare and a half old, as we judged, very fat and of good countenances, which they love tenderly, all naked, except their legs, which were covered with thin leather buskins. . . ." On several occasions Indians slept aboard the ship. Owen Griffin, a sailor who slept ashore, described an Indian dance in which "the men all together fall a stamping around the fire with both feet, as hard as they can, making the ground shake, with sundry outcries and changes of voice and sound." They beat on stones with "fire sticks" and then pounded the stones on the ground as hard as they could. Thus they continued trading, feasting, and "drinking" tobacco through the broken claws of lobsters.

On June 3, Waymouth, Rosier, and about fifteen men went with the Indians to New Harbor, the canoes of the Indians easily outrunning the light horseman. At the entrance to New Harbor, however, Waymouth grew suspicious and suggested that the chief come aboard and remain a hostage while Rosier went ashore to investigate their numbers, trade goods, and intentions. The chief refused and offered a young warrior instead. Waymouth accepted and sent Owen Griffin. Griffin returned, having counted 283 men armed with bows and accompanied by their dogs but with no trade goods. These, they said, were farther up the harbor. Waymouth then withdrew, assuming these Indians were no better than other savages who are "very treacherous; never attempting mischiefe untill by some remisnesse, fit opportunity affourdeth them certaine ability to execute the same."

Two days later, however, Waymouth perpetrated similar "mishchiefe" himself. He kidnapped five Indians to take home as a live exhibit. Three Indians were trapped below decks aboard the vessel. Then Rosier and half a dozen Englishmen went ashore with three others, ostensibly to trade and to eat peas around their fire. One Indian, "feareful of his owne good," went into the woods. The Englishmen jumped the other two and with difficulty got them into the boat. "For they were strong and so naked as our best hold was by their long haire on their heads." Rosier shows no remorse for this treacherous behavior, adding, "We would have bene very loath to have done them any hurt, which of necessity we had been constrained to have done if we had attempted thim [sic] in a multitude, which we must and would, rather than have wanted them, being a matter of great importance for the full accomplement of our voyage. Thus we shipped five Salvages, two Canoas, with all their bowes and arrowes." All but one of these Indians eventually returned to Maine.

On June 6 the Englishmen explored the nearby islands, finding in a cove on one island a stream and pond capable of driving a mill. They took extensive soundings on the four entrances to the harbor and with great success tried the fishing again. The same day two canoes arrived with seven Indians, one of whom was the man who had refused to be a hostage at New Harbor. He bore an invitation from the chief to the eastward to bring the vessel to his village and trade for furs and tobacco. Waymouth, his suspicions sharpened by the fresh war paint on the faces of the Indians and perhaps by his own guilty conscience, refused and hustled the deputation away lest they get wind of the five men he had tied up below.

On June 11 they sailed up the St. George River 26 miles. Again Rosier's estimate of distance is much exaggerated, for it is only 13 miles from Georges Harbor to Thomaston. He is ecstatic about the beauties of the river.

"The first and chiefest thing required, is a bold coast and faire land to fall with; The next, a safe harbor for ships to ride in." Monhegan provides an excellent landmark, and "heere are more good harbours for ships of all burthens, than England can affoard. . . . And on both sides [of the river] every halfe mile very gallant Coves. . . ." He found excellent places for docks and beaches on which to ground out and careen ships. He estimates 18 to 20 feet of tide, an estimate double what actually exists. The woods are not "shrubbish fit only for fewell but goodly tall Firre, Spruce, Birch, Beech and Oke," growing far enough apart to be easily cleared for pasture, "being plentifull like the outward Ilands with fresh water, which streameth downe in many places."

On June 12 ten men in armor "with a boy to carry powder and match" marched inland toward the Camden Hills, which they estimated lay no more than a league away. Actually, the nearest of these mountains is about seven miles from the head of the St. George River. However, after four miles of marching and after climbing three hills on a hot June day, they felt they had done all that could be expected of men in armor.

They returned, Rosier not too tired to observe that in many places the land might be easily cleared for cultivation but even as it was, it would make good pasture. "The sode is blacke, bearing sundry hearbs, grasse, and strawberries bigger than ours in England." He saw trees suitable for masts of vessels of 400 tons. At the bottom of every hill ran a stream, some big enough to drive a mill. "We might see in some places where fallow Deere and Hares had beene, and by the rooting of ground we supposed wild Hogs had ranged there, but we could descrie no beast, because our noise still chased them from us."

On their way back to the vessel in the light horseman, they were again accosted by the same Indian of whom they had been suspicious at New Harbor. Waymouth refused his invitation to send a man ashore to see the chief.

On June 13 they took the light horseman, well armed, past the site of Thomaston for what Rosier estimates as 20 miles, claiming a vessel drawing 18 feet might go as far. This passes the limit of overestimation and crosses the border of prevarication. All one can say in Rosier's defense is that he was trying to sell the land to future colonists. Promotional literature for real estate is subject to such exaggeration even three centuries later. A sample of Rosier's lyric prose for the consumption of prospective colonists shows little restraint:

"The excellencie of this part of the River, for his good breadth, depth, and fertile bordering ground, did so ravish us all with variety of pleasantnesse, as we could not tell what to commend, but only admired; . . . we all concluded . . . that we should never see the like River in every degree equall, untill it pleased God we beheld the same againe." He goes on to observe that the oarsmen who had been rowing since before daylight with no food but a little bread and cheese wanted to keep rowing upstream after the tide turned against them; but Captain Waymouth thought they had done enough. On the way back to the ship, they set up a cross near the present site of Thomaston, and then dropped down to the mouth of the river where they took extensive soundings. They returned to Pentecost to fill water casks and take careful observations with astrolabe and cross staff, and departed for England on June 16. On the 18th, 30 leagues from Allen Island, they came on shoal water and in 24 fathoms caught a great many large codfish, "some they measured to be five foot long, and three foot about." They must have been on Cashes Ledge.

On July 18 they anchored in Dartmouth, England, having beyond question fulfilled their mission.

The five Indians Rosier lists as Tahanedo, Amoret (later called Tisquantum by Gorges), Skicowares (later spelled Skidwarres), Maneddo, and Saffacomoit. Rosier recognizes that at first they "made their best resistance," but after they realized that their captors meant them no harm, "they have never seemed discontented with us, but very tractable, loving and willing by their best means to satisfie us in anything we demand of them." They soon learned English, described the beauties and the products of their country, how they made bread from "Indian wheat" and how they made butter and cheese from the milk of deer. Here either there was a failure in communication or Rosier the real estate promoter is at work again. They were not enslaved in any sense nor were they ill treated. In fact, they were made much of in English society, and all but one of them eventually were returned to their homes.

On Waymouth's return to England, Sir John Zouche, probably a Catholic, agreed on a plan with Waymouth to establish a colony in Maine. Zouche was to be "lord paramount" of a feudal seignory, under whom Waymouth was to be "chief commander," holding such land as he might choose for himself under Zouche. However, the plan never materialized, for Sir Ferdinando Gorges, Sir John Popham, and other West Country merchants interested in

America read Rosier's account. They "adopted" Waymouth's five Indians, continued their English education, and used them to promote their own scheme and defeat that of Waymouth and Zouche.

Gorges and Popham quickly assembled a distinguished group of London and West Country merchants, including Sir Thomas Gates and Sir George Somers, who later were wrecked on Bermuda; Richard Hakluyt, author of *The Principal Navigations;* Edward Maria Wingfield, later president of the Jamestown colony; Raleigh Gilbert, son of Sir Humphrey and later the leader of the colony on the Kennebec; and others. They petitioned the King for a charter incorporating two companies: The London Company and The Plymouth Company. Over the objections of Zouche and Zuñigo, the Spanish ambassador, the petition was granted, no doubt expedited by the exposure of the Gunpowder Plot on November 5, 1605, whereby Guy Fawkes and a group of Catholic extremists planned to blow up the King and Parliament and seize power in the ensuing confusion. With Catholics regarded as enemies of the state, the Protestant petition was granted on April 10, 1606. Under its terms The London Company could settle anywhere between 34° north latitude, near the present southern border of North Carolina, and 41°, the latitude of New York. The Plymouth Company could settle as far south as 38°, about the latitude of Washington, and as far north as 45°, the latitude of Passamaquoddy Bay. Neither was to settle within 100 miles of the other.

Waymouth, disappointed in his scheme to be chief commander on the St. George River, tried to go to Spain, "with intent as is thought to have betrayed his friends and showed the Spaniards a means how to defeat this Virginia attempt," as Sir Dudley Carlton put it in August 1607. Waymouth's attempt was foiled, however. He was given a pension by the government of three shillings fourpence a day, later given a job in the shipyard in Woolwich, and died about 1612.

Both the London and Plymouth companies hastened to establish themselves on the land granted them. Gorges and Popham, perhaps doubting the accuracy of Rosier's account, sent two ships to explore farther for a proper site. Henry Challons, taking two of Waymouth's Indians, Saffacomoit and Maneddo, sailed in August 1606 with instructions to leave a party ashore for the winter if he found a suitable place for settlement. He was instructed to go directly to the Maine coast, but instead held far to the south, made the Windward Islands, and was captured by a Spanish naval force. Challons and his men were taken to Seville, interrogated at length, and then Stoneman, Tucker, and several others of Challons' crew were freed. Most of the crew were sent to the galleys. Saffacomoit later returned to Maine. Maneddo we do not hear of again.

Shortly after Challons sailed, Thomas Hanham and Martin Pring sailed in October and, guided by Tahanedo, more generally known as Nahanada, made a thorough survey of Maine's mid-coast. Pring's account, wrote Gorges, was "the most exact discovery of that coast that ever came into my hands."

Unfortunately, the account has been lost, but, in light of subsequent events it probably recommended a settlement at the mouth of the Kennebec, perhaps because that river extends farther into the interior than the St. George. The London Company had sent its first expedition to Jamestown in December 1606, before Hanham and Pring returned, so Gorges and Popham were eager to get started, despite the Challons disaster. Accordingly, at the end of May 1607, Captain George Popham commanding *Gift of God* and Captain Raleigh Gilbert commanding *Mary and John* sailed for Maine by way of the Azores.

With the expedition sailed an observant and articulate writer whose unsigned account of the voyage was filed with Sir Ferdinando Gorges's papers in the Lambeth Palace library. In 1875 Benjamin Franklin Da Costa discovered it and published it with modernized spelling in Volume 18 of the Proceedings of the Massachusetts Historical Society in 1881. The quotations in the following pages are from Da Costa's version.

Near Flores the expedition met a Dutch ship, whose captain was known to one of Gilbert's crew. Gilbert invited the Dutch captain to come aboard "and take a can of beer, which he thankfully accepted." However, when Gilbert and several others returned the visit, the Dutchmen accused them of piracy, put them in irons, "using some of his gent in most wild manner," and threatened to throw them overboard and seize *Mary and John*. When several Englishmen in the Dutch crew took Gilbert's side, threatening "to either end their lives in his defence or suppress the ship," the Dutch captain let them go. Meanwhile, despite signals of distress from *Mary and John,* Captain Popham, being to windward of the other two, disappeared over the horizon.

On July 31, *Mary and John* made the shore of Nova Scotia where they met a shallop with eight Indians and a small Indian boy, all of whom spoke some French. Gilbert's crew landed, filled water casks, caught many large codfish, and gaffed up fifty big lobsters. "You shall see them where they lie in shoal water, not past a yard deep, and with a great hook made fast to a staff, you shall hitch them up there, a great store of them; you may near load a ship with them, and they are of great bigness; I have not seen the like in England."

Mary and John then coasted along the Nova Scotia shore with a fair northeast breeze and rounded Cape Sable at 5:00 A.M. on August 4. At 3:00 P.M. on August 5 they raised the Camden Hills and stood in for them. About noon on August 6 they passed outside Matinicus. They "saw three other islands lying together being low and flat by the water, showing white as if it were sand, but it is white rocks making show afar off almost like unto Dover cliffs." The weather was calm, so doubtless they saw the shores of Seal Island, Wooden Ball, and Matinicus through a mirage, a common phenomenon on a still summer day.

They continued west-by-north another 8 leagues, about 20 miles, saw three islands, possibly Monhegan, Allen Island, and Burnt Island, sounded and got 40 fathoms. At ten o'clock that night, having sent a small boat ahead to sound, they crept into a cove and anchored in 12 fathoms. Judging by the soundings alone, they might have come in on the north end of Monhegan and anchored in the cove behind Seal Rocks. In the morning they found a cross, which they assumed was Waymouth's, and "you might have told near thirty islands round about us from aboard our ship." Of course, the cross might not have been Waymouth's. Someone else might well have put a cross on the north end of Monhegan, but from the deck of a ship behind Seal Rocks, one could never count thirty islands. Soundings to the contrary, they had probably anchored in the cove behind Little Burnt Island where the chart shows 44 feet at low water.

That day, August 7, as *Mary and John* was sailing around to Georges Harbor, she met *Gift of God* coming in from Monhegan, and the two crews were joyfully reunited.

On August 8, guided by Skidwarres, another of Waymouth's Indians, Gilbert and a crew of thirteen men in the ship's boat rowed across Muscongus Bay "in amongst many gallant isalnds," landed at New Harbor, and marched across the Pemaquid peninsula to the Indian town at Pemaquid Harbor, ". . . where we found near a hundred of them, men, women, and children, and the chief commander of them is Nahanada.* At our first sight of them, upon a howling or cry that they made, they all presently issued forth towards us with their bows and arrows, and we presently made a stand, and suffered them to come near unto us. Then our Indian Skidwarres spoke unto them in their language, showing them what we were, which when Nahanada, their commander, perceived what we were, he caused them all to lay aside their bows and arrows, and came unto us and embraced us, and we did the like to them again." That night the Englishmen, with Skidwarres, returned to Georges Harbor.

On Sunday, August 9, Reverend Richard Seymour, standing under Waymouth's cross, gave thanks for their safe arrival and preached the first Protestant sermon in New England.

On Monday, August 10, Popham in *Gift*'s shallop with thirty men and Gilbert in his ship's boat with twenty men again visited Pemaquid, apparently rounding Pemaquid Point, held further parley with Nahanada and his people, who were still suspicious of the white men, and camped on the north shore of the harbor, leaving Skidwarres ashore with his people.

From Georges Harbor on August 12 the two vessels rounded Pemaquid Point, passed the islands off Boothbay, and made Seguin Island, a mark which Pring had mentioned. Although they were only a mile or so outside Seguin, the pilots missed the mouth of the Kennebec River and stood on to the westward seeking it. When they found they had overshot it, they turned back, *Gift of God* sending her shallop ahead to guide her into the river, but *Mary and John* didn't make it and remained outside.

That night it blew up from the south, putting *Mary and John* on the

* Nahanada had been returned to Pemaquid by Pring in 1606.

dangerous lee shore of Cape Small, a shore beset by ledges and scoured by tide. With an ebb tide and a strong southerly wind, the mouth of the Kennebec can be a furious place. All night they beat back and forth among the ledges, tacking at the cry of "breakers ahead" seen dimly through the murk, carrying more sail than they wanted in order to make an offing against the steep seas. Their ship's boat towing astern was swamped. They didn't want to cut it adrift and lose it and they couldn't bail it out, so towed it half submerged, a serious drag on their progress. At daylight they found themselves close on the lee shore and thought of running the vessel ashore in the forlorn hope of getting safely through the surf, but at the last moment they saw two little islands, probably either Seal Island under Cape Small or the Fox Islands. These are not Pring's Fox Islands but are so called on modern charts. Between the islands they found some shelter and good holding ground. Here they spent the day at anchor repairing their small boat and talking with "four salvages and an old woman." The next day the wind was northwesterly, as it often is after a gale; and although it calmed the sea considerably, they could not get into the Kennebec against it. Even in a modern boat, one cannot sail up the river against the wind and tide. Accordingly, they anchored east of Seguin Island under its lee. *Gift of God,* already safely anchored in the river, sent out her ship's boat with codfish and encouragement. The next day, August 16, in a flat calm, her crew towed *Mary and John* into the river and anchored next to *Gift of God.*

On August 17, Popham with thirty men in his shallop and Gilbert with eighteen in his ship's boat explored up the Kennebec for what they estimated to be 14 leagues. As a league is three miles, this distance must be overstated. It is only 36 miles from the mouth of the river to Augusta, where there are considerable rapids. It is doubtful if they got much beyond Bath, for they found it to be "a most gallant river very broad and of a good depth." Had they passed The Chops or seen Merrymeeting Bay, they doubtless would have mentioned it. Also they were looking for suitable sites for a permanent settlement and would not have wanted to be an unreasonable distance from the sea. The explorers were all likely to overestimate distances, especially if rowing against the tide.

After a rest and a meal ashore, the two parties returned to their vessels the next day. On August 19, after a sermon and a formal reading of the patent and the laws under which they were to live, they took the rest of the day off. On August 20 they went to work in earnest to build a fort, dwelling houses, and a storehouse on Atkins Bay behind the peninsula on which Fort Popham now stands. On August 21 the ships' carpenters started to set up the first vessel built by Englishmen in New England. She was the pinnace *Virginia* of about 30 tons.

During the late summer and fall, while most of the men worked on the fort and buildings, Gilbert explored Casco Bay as far west as Cape Elizabeth and Richmond Island, ascended the Sheepscot River, and crossed over to the Kennebec through the Sasanoa River. The colony was visited by Nahanada and Skidwarres and their friends from Pemaquid several times and a party returned the visit, intending to continue as far as the Penobscot, but were held back by head winds. Their most interesting exploration was an attempt to find the headwaters of the Kennebec. Gilbert with nineteen others sailed upstream for two-and-a-half days until they came to a low, flat island where Augusta now stands. The island, Cushnoc, is now only a shoal spot at low water, but then had "great store of grapes exceeding good and sweet of two sorts, both red, but one of them is a marvelous deep red." They had to haul their boat up the shoal rapid around the island with a line. About a league above Cushnoc, they camped and were visited by four Indians who spoke English. Their leader, Sabenoa, suggested an exchange of hostages as a guarantee of good faith. The Indians took one of the Englishmen in their canoe and paddled away upstream as fast as they could go, leaving Sabenoa in the shallop. The Englishmen rowed valiantly in pursuit until they came to shoal water again, possibly Bacon's Rips. Sabenoa guided the Englishmen to the Indian village where they were confronted by fifty newly painted warriors, very strong and tall. However, Sabenoa talked the Indians out of their hostility, the English hostage was returned unharmed, and the atmosphere warmed. Gilbert suggested that the Indians come down to the boat where he had trade goods. Sixteen men came but brought little to trade. Gilbert, suspicious, got his men aboard and made to cast off. Some of the Indians seized the boat's painter and held her to the shore while another leaped aboard, took up the slow match* kept alight to fire muskets, pretended to light his pipe with it, threw it overboard and jumped after it, knowing the muskets could not be fired without it. Gilbert ordered his men to aim their muskets. The Indians, not so sure they were harmless, fled into the woods and put arrows to their bowstrings. In this moment of tension, no one shot. The shallop backed off and crossed to the other side of the river. "So the shallop departed from them to the further side of the river, where one of the canoes came unto them, and would have excused the fault of the others." They parted friends, and the white men dropped down the river to where they had camped the night before and lay at anchor overnight. The anonymous author notes an abundance of spruce trees fit for the masts of the biggest ships in the Royal Navy and also oak, walnut, and "pineapple." There were also many fish in the river, and on the shore grapes, hops, "chiballs" (a sort of wild onion), and "certain cods in which they supposed the cotton wool to grow, and upon the banks many shells of pearl."

Mary and John was sent home in December to report the colony's success and to return with supplies in the spring. The colonists kept busy through the winter finishing *Virginia,* trading for furs with the Indians, and gathering "sassaparilla." This cannot be the true sarsaparilla, which is a tropical plant, but must have been another aromatic root supposed to be of medicinal value.

* A slow match was a wick of hemp or tow (short fibers of hemp, flax, or jute) treated to burn very slowly, glowing at the end. It was used to fire muskets and cannon before the invention of the flintlock, much as punk is used on the Fourth of July.

The colonists found it a cold winter, much colder than they expected, for they were in the latitude of southern France. Nevertheless, in spite of a fire that burned their storehouse, they had enough to eat and were not afflicted by scurvy, which had killed half the colonists on St. Croix Island two winters before. Captain George Popham died during the winter at the age of seventy-six, but although he was almost the only fatality, his loss was significant. He and Gilbert had been enthusiastic and energetic leaders. When Captain Davies returned in the spring with a cargo of tools and supplies, he brought news that Sir John Popham, the original promoter and backer of the expedition, had died and that Captain Gilbert's half-brother had also died, leaving an inheritance that required Raleigh Gilbert's attention. This left the new colony without a leader. No natural leader arose. The discouraged colonists boarded *Virginia* and *Mary and John* and returned to England.

Thus ignominiously ended England's best chance to colonize North America. The expedition had come to a location already explored by Waymouth and Pring. It was well financed, well equipped, and led by enthusiastic, bold, determined men. It had a secure economic base, if not in sarsaparilla, then in fish, furs, and timber. The local inhabitants were reasonably well disposed toward the colonists; at least Nahanada and Skidwarres were friendly. Had not Sir John Popham and George Popham both died and Raleigh Gilbert been called home, the colony could have survived under any one of the three.

It is ironic that Jamestown, founded at the same time, with no economic base at first, badly led, badly financed, badly situated in an unhealthy swamp in a land of Indians soon turned hostile, and, composed of what Captain John Smith called soft-handed second sons of country squires, should have survived when the Kennebec colony failed.

Yet in spite of its failure, Sir Ferdinando Gorges wrote: "As for the coldness of the clime, I had had too much experience in the world to be frightened with such a blast, as knowing many great kingdoms and large territories more northerly seated, and by many degrees colder than the clime from which they came, yet plentifully inhabited and divers of them stored with no better commodities from trade and commerce than those parts afforded, if like industry, art, and labor be used, for the last I had no reason to despair of means when God should be pleased, by our ordinary frequenting the country, to make it appear, it would yield both profit and content to as many as aimed thereat. . . ."

NOTES

Admiral Morison's *Northern Voyages* again is a useful source of information on Cartier and some of the earliest visitors, but the book concludes with the mystery of the Roanoke colony in 1587 and does not get into the seventeeth century.

Charles Knowles Bolton's *The Real Founders of New England* gives a brief account of the voyages of Gosnold, Pring, Waymouth, and Gilbert. However, the original accounts of these voyages have been often reprinted and are well worth reading. *A Brief and True Relation of the Discovery of the North Part of Virginia,* by John Brereton, "one of the voyage," if it is as true as it is brief, is an excellent account of Gosnold's voyage. Very little of it deals with Maine, however. The account of Pring's first voyage is very sketchy insofar as it deals with Maine, and the account of his second voyage has unfortunately been lost. Rosier's account of Waymouth's voyage has been reprinted by the Massachusetts Historical Society, Third Series, Volume 8, pp. 126–129. It also appears in Dr. Henry S. Burrage's *Gorges and the Grant of the Province of Maine.* The account of Gilbert's 1607–08 voyage to Sagadahoc was written by Sir Ferdinando Gorges, according to Burrage. It was discovered in the Lambeth Palace library, London, in 1875 by Reverend B. F. Da Costa and was printed by the Massachusetts Historical Society in 1881, Volume 18. James Phinney Baxter's exhaustive *Sir Ferdinando Gorges and the Province of Maine* prints the same text with helpful notes, and Dr. Burrage includes it in his book.

These early accounts become much more interesting if read with a modern chart and a cruising guide at hand. An even better way to understand a seventeenth-century writer is to sail the same courses in your own boat. The scholar-skipper will at once discover that the "inexact science" of navigation was a lot less exact in the seventeenth century than it is today. Without a precise timepiece, longitude could not be calculated. Latitude depends upon the altitude of the celestial body when it is on the observer's meridian. The astrolabe and cross staff were not suited to providing an accurate altitude at sea. The instant of meridian passage was difficult to estimate, and declination tables were sketchy at best. (Gosnold and Pring both claim to have made Maine landfalls in 43° but may have been many miles apart.) Estimation of distance sailed was also inexact, distances with a light breeze, a headwind, or a foul tide seeming much longer than they really were. For example, an early map of the Strait of Magellan shows it over twice as long as it is.

Indian names were necessarily spelled phonetically by early writers. The results lead to confusion in identifying natives. The same man, for instance, is called Amoret by James Rosier, Tisquantum by Sir Ferdinando Gorges, Tantum by Captain John Smith, and Squanto by William Bradford.

Charles McLean Andrews's *The Colonial Period of American History* offers an excellent account of the economic, social, and political forces in seventeenth-century England, especially interesting as they affected the Waymouth project.

OVERLEAF: Detail of the Simanca map of 1610. This map was given to Philip II of Spain by James I of England at the time when he was promoting a marriage between his son and a Spanish princess. A close study of the map reveals remarkable accuracy and implies knowledge of French and English explorations of which we have no record. *Courtesy Admiral William Royall*

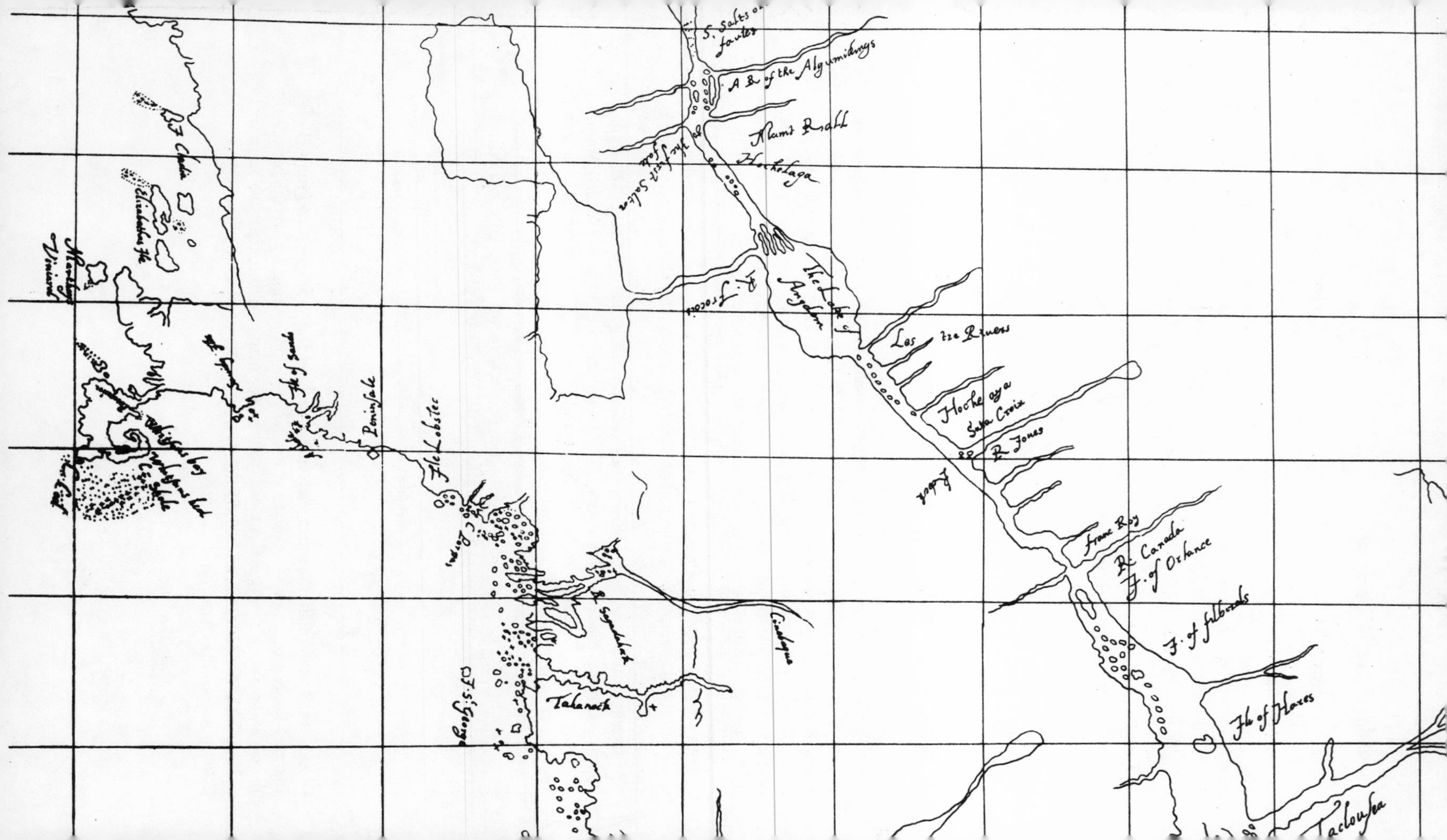

S. Salts or fautes
A B. of the Algumickings
Hochelaga
The Lake of Angolem
Los tre Rivers
Hocke aya Sata Croix
R. Jones
France Roy
R. Canada
I. of Orleance
Isle of Flores
Tacloufea
Cinebaque
R. Sagadahok
Talanock
I. S. George
C. Porpas
Ile Lobster
Peninsule
Ile of Sands
Elizabethas Ile
Marthays Viniard
C. Cod

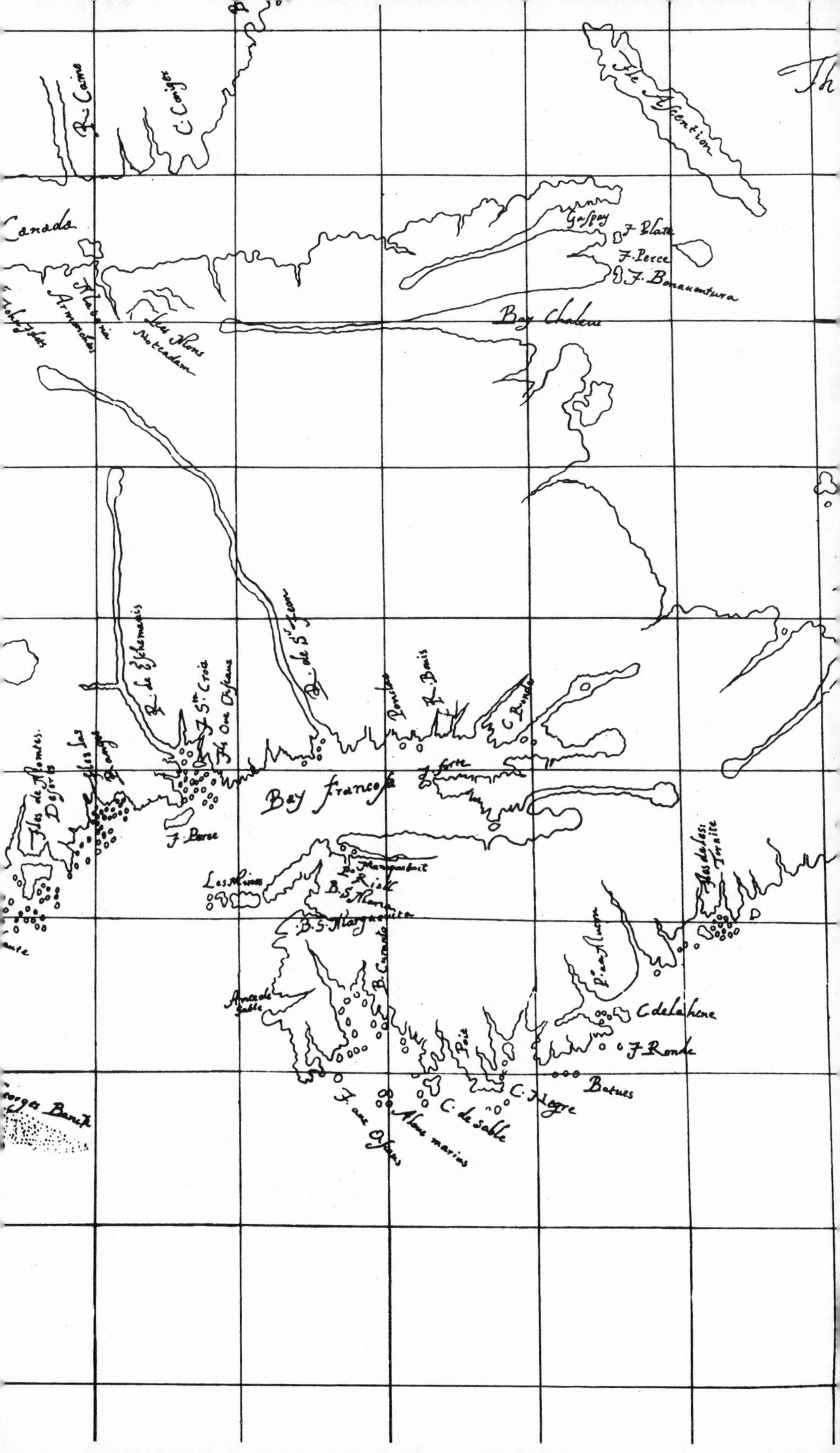

Canada
Gaspay
F. Perce
F. Bonaventura
Bay Chaleur
Les Monts Notredam
R. de St. Jean
R. de Etchemanis
Bay francoise
C. Ronde
Les Mines
B. S. Margarita
C. dela hene
F. Ronde
Batues
C. Negre
C. de Sable
F. Perce

THREE

Captain John Smith, Dermer, and Rocroft

THE ABANDONMENT of the colony at the mouth of the Kennebec in 1608, disappointing as it was, was not significant in the developing economy of the coast. Fishermen from England, France, Spain, and Holland came every summer to salt and pickle highly profitable cargoes. It is not surprising that there is little formal record of permanent settlement, indeed little record of any sort, for those already in the fishery had no motive to attract others. It is only when a group wished to raise money or assemble a company of colonists that we find published descriptions of the coast. One of these documents, a milestone in the maritime history of both England and Maine, is Captain John Smith's *Description of New England.*

Occasionally there rises a man with unusual physical energy, exceptional charisma, and a clear head. Such a man was John Smith. He lived a life of incredible adventure, wrote an incredible autobiography which has been proven accurate in most details, and then he spoke and wrote a clear, accurate, and convincing argument for the intelligent use of New England's resources. Smith was born in 1580, the son of a prosperous Lincolnshire farmer. After a good schooling, a brief apprenticeship to a merchant, and a short trip to France as a servant-companion to a young lord, he retired to the woods to study the military profession with a horse, a lance, and two books: Machiavelli's *Art of War* and Marcus Aurelius' *Diall of Princes.* Later Smith wrote of this brief period in his life, "His diet was thought to be more of venison than aught else." He was next invited to study horsemanship under Pololaga, the Italian rider to the Earl of Lincoln.

By 1600, with a rudimentary military education, "growing tired of seeing Christians slaughter Christians," John Smith set out for Hungary to fight the Turks by way of France, Italy, and Austria. He joined the regiment of Kisell sent to relieve the Hungarian town of Oberlimback, closely besieged by the Turks. Smith signaled the town's commander by a code of lights: "On Thursday night I will charge on the East, at the alarum, sally you." Smith then, in the dark, stretched a long rope around one side of the Turkish camp and tied in it a series of slow matches to simulate a regiment of musketeers with firelocks at the ready. Kisell attacked from the other side, the garrison sallied, and the Turks fled. For this, Smith was given a commission as captain, a title which he proudly held, even after he was made Admiral of New England. He then joined in the siege of another town, firing a rudimentary form of mortar shell over the wall. After further skirmishes, he was serving under Prince Sigismund Bathory at the siege of "Regall," a city held by the Hajdus, an assemblage of renegade Turks and soldiers of fortune. The Christian siege works advanced slowly. The Turks within the city taunted the Christians, urging them to fight. Finally one Lord Turbashaw challenged any Christian to come forth and fight him in single combat. Smith, now an experienced soldier at the age of twenty-two, accepted. The combatants charged each other on horses after the manner of medieval knights. Smith drove his lance through helmet and head of Turbashaw, dismounted, cut off his head, and took his horse and armor. A friend of Turbashaw challenged Smith and received a dose of the same medicine. Smith then challenged the Turks and, after a fierce encounter, decapitated a third Turk. Prince Sigismund awarded Smith a coat of arms with three Turks' heads. Later Sigismund gave him a Latin document confirming the award, accepted as genuine by The Garter King at Arms in England and preserved in The Herald's College.

Shortly after this, Prince Sigismund's small army was overwhelmed by the Turks at the battle of Rotenthurn. Smith was badly wounded, but was rescued from the bloody field and sold as a slave to Bashaw Bogall, who gave him to a young lady named Charatza Tragabigzanda in Constantinople. There may have been a romantic relationship developing here, but Smith was taken off by Charatza's brother up the shore of the Black Sea and north into Russia. Here he was roughly treated as a "slave of slaves." In the fall of 1603, he was set to threshing grain at some distance from the farm buildings. His master beat him, so Smith turned on him, beat his brains out with the threshing bat, took the master's clothes, mounted his horse, and galloped westward. Smith made his way in due course back to the river Don, to the Dnieper, across the Ukraine to Poland and south to Transylvania. Thence he crossed Germany and found Prince Sigismund in Leipzig. The prince gave him 1,500 ducats and the document confirming his coat of arms of three Turks' heads. In search of employment as a soldier, he continued through France and Spain to Morocco, where he visited Marrakesh in the summer of 1604. At Safi he joined a French privateer and, after a hazardous and unsuccessful cruise, made his way at last to England in 1604.

After several attempts to join colonizing expeditions, late in 1606 Smith joined The London Company's expedition to Jamestown on the James River. That colony soon encountered serious trouble, partly through disease but principally through very poor leadership. At length, however, the weak were winnowed out, Captain Smith took command, and he put the colony on a sound basis. In 1608 he was captured by Powhatan's Indians and saved by Powhatan's daughter Pocahontas, only another incredible event in an incredible life. In 1609 he was made "president." Later in that same year he was badly burned when a keg of powder blew up in a shallop in which he was coming down the James River.

Badly hurt, he returned to England late in 1609. During the next few years he was busy clearing his name of the calumnies heaped upon him by people returning from Virginia, and finding out all he could about the new continent. He had talked about the Maine coast with Gosnold in Virginia. Henry Hudson, whom he knew personally, had visited the Penobscot River in 1609. In 1610 Samuel Argall had coasted from the Kennebec River to Virginia. Francis Popham was sending fishing vessels every year to Damariscove Island, Pemaquid, and Sagadahoc. To succeed, Smith concluded, after carefully considering his Virginia experience, a colony needed first a sound financial backing, something more than one man's fortune could provide. It must be established in a land that afforded marketable staple products. The colonists must be carpenters, masons, farmers, fishermen, people experienced in the skills necessary to survive in an uncultivated land. Finally, vigorous, intelligent, disciplined leadership was the *sine qua non*. To Smith, the Maine coast seemed the ideal location for a colony. In 1613 and 1614 he set himself to raising money for a pilot expedition to prove that fish and fur would provide a sound economic base for a colony.

At first he had trouble raising money for a mere fishing expedition. However, through the master of his ship, Michael Cooper, the word leaked out that this was no fishing trip, that Captain Smith knew of a gold mine on the coast. Accordingly, he was supplied with two ships, sailed from England early in the spring of 1614, and landed on Monhegan in April. With him came the Indian Tisquantum who had been abducted by Waymouth, and who had been in England since 1605. Smith spent no time seeking gold, tried whaling without success, and at once set his men to fishing and planting gardens. Smith himself saw to the assembling of a small boat in which he and several others explored and mapped the coast from Penobscot Bay to Nauset, improving the voyage by buying beaver, marten, and otter furs from the Indians. He first visited Matinicus and sailed up Penobscot Bay but found the French in control there. Turning westward, he sailed some miles up the Kennebec, explored Casco Bay, and continued down the coast, mapping and naming promontories, islands, and harbors as he went. The map is surprisingly accurate. Penobscot Bay is clearly shown. Although the islands are sketchy, Isle au Haut, Deer Isle, Little Deer Isle, and Eggemoggin Reach are easily identified. Islesboro is a bit east of its true position, but the Camden Hills, Rockland Harbor, and Owls Head are obvious. Matinicus, Metinic, and the islands of Muscle Ridge Channel are marked. Monhegan, of course, is obvious, as is Pemaquid Point and the islands off Boothbay. The Kennebec River and Seguin are shown, but

Cape Small is labeled Cape Elizabeth. Casco Bay, the promontory now known as Cape Elizabeth, Portland Harbor, and Richmond Island are drawn in. Mount Agamenticus is shown too close to Wells Harbor, and the Isles of Shoals are labeled Smith's Isles. Other names on the map were assigned by Prince Charles when Smith showed him the map in England. Smith had named Cape Ann after (Charatza) Tragabigzanda, and the islands off it—Milk Island, Thachers Island, and Straitsmouth—he named The Three Turks' Heads. Smith's names, unfortunately, failed to stick.

On his return to Monhegan, Smith found one ship loaded with salt cod and the other nearly so. Accordingly he headed for England, stopping at Provincetown on the way to leave Tisquantum close to his home in Plymouth. Captain Thomas Hunt, captain of the second ship, is described by Gorges as "a worthlesse fellow of our Nation, set out by certaine Merchants for love of gaine." He finished loading the second ship at Monhegan and also stopped at Provincetown. Here he lured sixteen Indians aboard, including the unfortunate Tisquantum, with whom he was of course familiar, clapped them in irons, and sailed for Spain, where he tried to sell them as slaves. Tisquantum was rescued and cared for in a monastery and presently made his way to Newfoundland.

After this successful voyage, The Plymouth Company promptly sent out several more ventures. Michael Cooper, captain of Smith's ship, was sent fishing on the New England coast with four ships. Captain Hobson was sent, carrying Saffacomoit, another of Waymouth's captives, to explore the country south of Cape Cod for a site for a colony, and Sir Richard Hawkins, president of the company, undertook a voyage which came to nothing. The Plymouth Company had exhausted its capital. However, Gorges and Matthew Sutcliffe backed Smith with two vessels, the necessary supplies and tools, and a nucleus of sixteen men to start a permanent settlement. Among the sixteen were Dermer and Rocroft, both of whom had parts to play in subsequent years. Smith sailed in March of 1615 with high hopes of establishing a really successful colony.

However, he was dismasted in a gale, and limped back to Plymouth, his crew pumping desperately to keep the vessel afloat. A new vessel was found, and in June, Smith sailed again. This time he was captured by a French privateer, spent the summer aboard her, more or less a prisoner, and in November escaped in a French port and was back in England in December 1615.

He spent the rest of his life trying to organize a permanent settlement in New England, talking, writing, promoting, begging, without success.

Another colonizing expedition was planned for 1617 but never left Plymouth, although in the course of the preparations The Plymouth Company

---

OVERLEAF: Note the close connection between the Kennebec River on page 64 and the Chaudière River in Champlain's map. Examination with a glass shows remarkable accuracy. *Smith Collection, University of Southern Maine*

316
NEW E
The most remarqueab
by the high and migh
Prince of great Bri
THE PORTRAICTUER OF CAPTAYNE IOHN SMITH ADMIRALL OF NEW ENGLAND
These are the Lines that shew thy Face; but those
That shew thy Grace and Glory, brighter bee:
Thy Faire-Discoueries and Fowle-Overthrowes
Of Salvages, much Civilliz'd by thee
Best shew thy Spirit; and to it Glory Wyn;
So, thou art Brasse without, but Golde within.
If so; in Brasse, (too soft Smiths Acts to beare)
I fix thy Fame, to make Brasse Steele outweare.
Thine, as thou art Virtues,
John Dauies. Heref:
43
42
Schooten
Sandwich
Dartmouth
Ipswich
Snadoun hill
Boston
Hull
Poynt Dauies
Smith Iles
South Hampton
Cape ANNA
Bristow
Bastable
Talbotts Bay
Fawmouth
Fullerton Ils
The River CHARLES
Cary Ils
Cheuyot hills
P. Murry
London
Oxford
Poynt Suttliff
Poynt George
Cape IAMES
Plimouth
Milford hauen
STUARDS Bay
Barwick
Vincere est Viuere
Simon Passeus sculpsit.
316
315

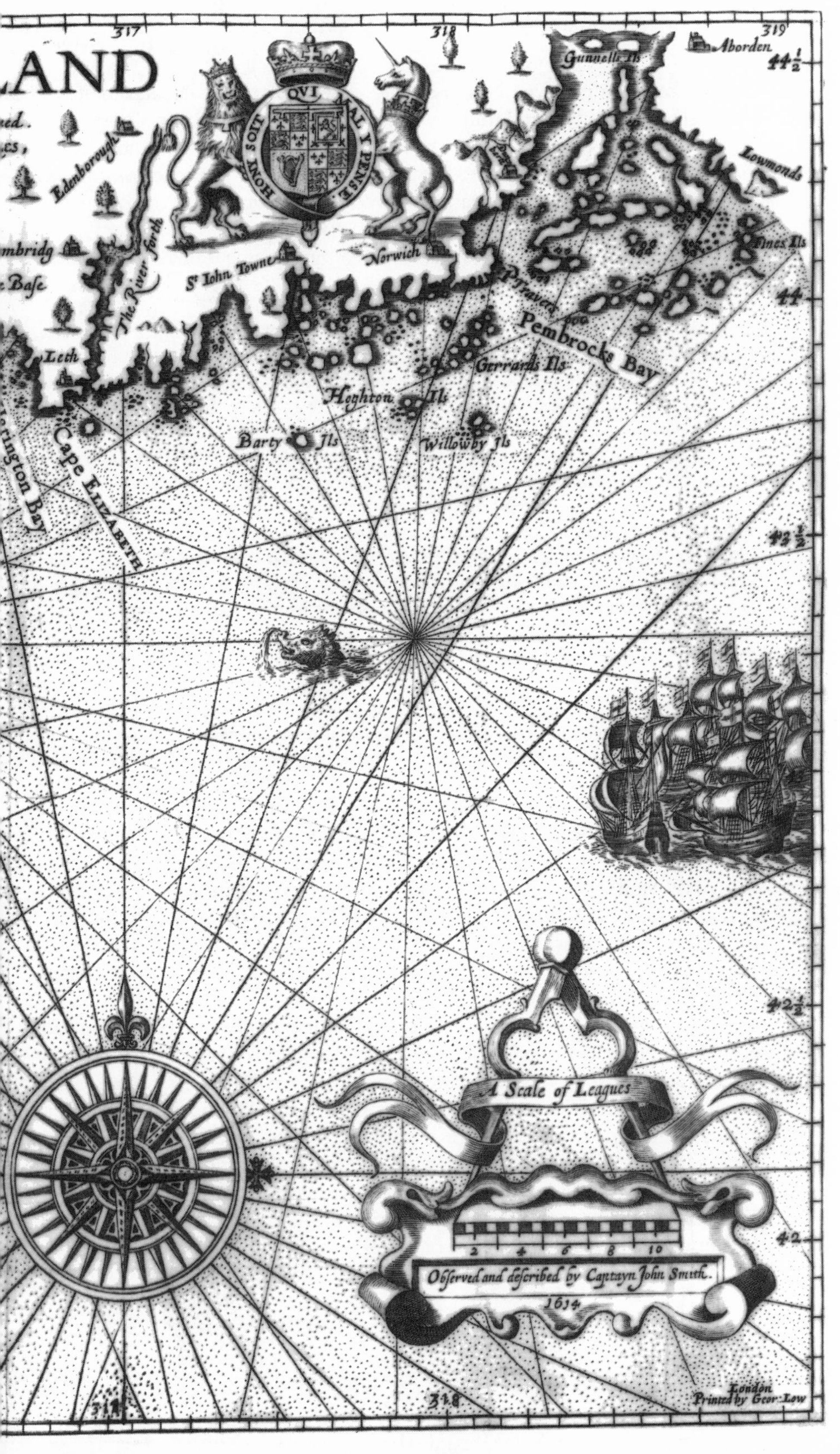

317
318
319
AND
Aborden
Gunnells Ils
HONI SOIT QVI MAL Y PENSE
Edenborough
Loumonds
The River Forth
St Iohn Towne
Norwich
Fines Ils
P Travers
Pembrocks Bay
Leth
Gerrards Ils
Hoghton Ils
Barty Ils
Willowby Ils
Cape ELIZABETH
44½
44
43½
42½
42
A Scale of Leagues
2 4 6 8 10
Observed and described by Captayn John Smith.
1614
318
London
Printed by Geor: Low

named Smith Admiral of New England. He applied to the Pilgrims for a position as their guide and military leader. He would have been a good one, for he had been to Plymouth (Massachusetts) and knew the whole coast. However, the Pilgrims preferred to take Smith's map instead of Smith and employed Miles Standish as their military leader. Despite the disappointment, Smith's efforts continued until his death in 1631.

John Smith's influence, however, affected the settlement not only of Maine but of all British America. He wrote:

> Who can desire more content that hath small meanes, or but onely his merit to advance his fortunes, then to tread and plant that ground he hath purchased by the hazard of his life? What to such a minde can bee more pleasant than planting and building a foundation for his posterity, got from the rude earth by God's blessing and his own industry without prejudice to any; . . . what so truly sutes with honour and honesty, as the discovering of things unknowne, erecting Townes, peopling Countries, informing the ignorant, reforming things unjust, teaching vertue, and gaine to our native mother Country a Kingdome to attend her, find imploiement for those that are idle because they know not what to do: so farre from wronging any, as to cause posterity to remember thee; and remembering thee, ever honour that remembrance with praise. . . . Here are no hard Landlords to racke us with high rents . . . no tedious pleas in law to consume us with their many years disputations for Justice. . . . Here every man may be master and owner of his owne labour and land.
>
> My purpose is not to persuade children from their parents, men from their wives, nor servants from their masters, only such as may by free consent be spared; but that each parish or village in the country or city, that will but apparell their fatherless children of thirteen or fourteen years of age, or young married people that hath small wealth to live on, here by their labor may live exceeding well.

Smith's vision of America saw no feudal seignories, no vast incorporated holdings, but a society of self-reliant independent people drawing their wealth from their own labor and the resources of the land and the sea.

After Smith's capture by the French privateer, Dermer and Rocroft returned to England with Smith's ship. Then Dermer went to Newfoundland. Just when he went, we do not know, for neither Gorges nor Dermer is very clear about dates. From Newfoundland, Dermer wrote Gorges, saying he had met an Indian in Newfoundland who had arrived on a ship from Malaga, probably a ship carrying wine and salt. This Indian was Tisquantum, who had been kidnapped in Provincetown by Hunt, carried to Spain to be sold as a slave, redeemed by some charitable monks, and was on his long way home. Tisquantum gave Dermer such a glowing report of Maine as a base for a colony, that Dermer wrote Gorges suggesting that he go to Maine at once and that Gorges send Rocroft to meet him with supplies and men to stay the winter. However, before Dermer left for Maine, Mason, then Governor of Newfoundland, persuaded him to return to England to talk further with Gorges. So Dermer and Tisquantum went back to England.

Meanwhile, Rocroft had been sent to Sagadahoc, the site of the 1607 colony at the mouth of the Kennebec River, to meet Dermer and spend the winter. He found a Frenchman from Dieppe there, trading with the Indians. He seized the French vessel, sent the crew home in his own ship, and kept the French ship, still planning to spend the winter there. His crew was less than enthusiastic about the plan and cooked up a plot to murder Rocroft and go pirating. Rocroft got wind of the plot, trapped the mutineers as they were about to act, and marooned them at the mouth of the Kennebec with enough supplies to last them until they could find a way to live off the land. He then sailed south to spend the winter at Jamestown, where he was killed in a brawl. The mutineers made their way to Monhegan, where they passed the winter "with bad lodging and worse fare, yet all came safe home except one sickly man which died there." Evidently there were people staying year-round on Monhegan at that time.

In the spring, Gorges, thinking Rocroft had spent the winter at Sagadahoc, sent Dermer with supplies for him. When Dermer got to Sagadahoc and found Rocroft gone, he picked up the mutineers at Monhegan and left his ship there to be loaded with fish. In a five-ton pinnace, he took a few of his men and Tisquantum and headed west on an exploring trip. After stopping at Provincetown to leave Tisquantum, and at Martha's Vineyard, where he found Saffacomoit and Epenow, another Indian who had been in England, Dermer continued to Jamestown. From here he wrote Gorges, bringing him up to date on Rocroft's death and his own actions thus far. He set his crew to building a deck on the pinnace, a project which went slowly, for he and his crew all contracted fevers.

With the pinnace decked, Dermer headed north again to pick up his vessel at Monhegan. On the way he talked with the Dutch in New York and stopped again at Martha's Vineyard. Here Epenow captured him and held him hostage. Dermer's men paid a ransom in hatchets, but Epenow would not let him go. Dermer fought his way out, suffering fourteen wounds. He headed south again to be cured of his wounds at Jamestown, but he succumbed and died there in 1619.

So ended Gorges' first efforts to establish colonies in New England. Before we go on to his next effort, we should review the fates of the five Indians seized by Waymouth on Allen Island in 1605.

Nahanada was returned to Pemaquid by Pring on his second voyage in 1606.

Maneddo and Saffacomoit sailed for home with Challons in 1606 but were captured by the Spanish and imprisoned. Maneddo probably died in prison or in the galleys, for we hear no more of him, but Saffacomoit returned eventually to England, was taken back to America by Hobson in 1614, and died soon after.

Skidwarres returned to Pemaquid with Gilbert and Popham in 1607. He and Nahanada remained friendly with the English and visited them during the winter of 1607–08 at Sagadahoc.

Tisquantum, called Amoret by Rosier, stayed in England with Gorges until 1614, when he returned to Monhegan with Captain John Smith. However, he had come from Plymouth, not from Maine, and had been visiting his friend Samoset in Muscongus Bay when he was captured. Smith, on his way home in 1614, left Tisquantum at Provincetown just across Massachusetts Bay from Plymouth, but before he went home, Hunt arrived in Provincetown with Smith's other ship and invited a party of local inhabitants aboard. Tisquantum, who had spent the summer with Hunt on Monhegan, joined the party. Hunt clapped down the hatches and took the Indians to Spain to be sold as slaves. Tisquantum was rescued, made his way to Newfoundland, met Dermer, returned to England with him, and in the summer of 1619 was again landed in Provincetown.

He returned to his home in Plymouth and found the town deserted, its inhabitants dead of a white man's disease, probably the plague. He joined the Wampanoag Indians on Cape Cod for the next two winters. When the Pilgrims landed at Provincetown in 1620, it is easy to understand the Wampanoags' hostility to the white men, for they had not forgotten Hunt. However, Tisquantum harbored no grudge against the Pilgrims, although they settled on the spot where his people had died. It was Tisquantum and his friend Samoset who walked into the Pilgrim town in 1621 and said, "Welcome, Englishmen." Tisquantum, nicknamed Squanto by the Pilgrims, could be credited with playing a large part in saving the Pilgrim colony. He stayed with the Pilgrims until his death two years later.

NOTES

The story of Captain John Smith's life is told in his own autobiography, written in the third person. It is available in Arber's edition of Smith's collected *Works*. Ever since it was published in the seventeenth century, Smith has been accused of being one of history's biggest liars, for the story is indeed hard to believe. However, in 1953 Bradford Smith, ably assisted by Dr. Laura Polanyi Striker, an expert in Hungarian and Transylvanian history, wrote a biography of the Admiral of New England. Between them, they have documented and confirmed the principal events of Smith's life, incredible as it seems.

The story of Rocroft and Dermer is told by Sir Ferdinando Gorges in *A Discovery of New England,* which James Phinney Baxter reprinted with editorial comment in *Sir Ferdinando Gorges and the Province of Maine*.

William Bradford's *Of Plimoth Plantation,* as interpreted by George F. Willison in *Saints and Strangers,* gives an account of Squanto's history.

FOUR

Champlain, De Monts, and Poutrincourt

THE FRENCH established a presence in Maine at about the same time as the English. After the failure of Cartier and Roberval to establish a colony on the St. Lawrence in 1543, France was torn by a succession of wars, foreign and civil, of political and religious origin. No formal attempt was made at colonization; nevertheless, the fishermen of Brittany and Normandy annually voyaged to Newfoundland and the Gulf of St. Lawrence, curing their fish ashore and engaging in a highly profitable fur trade with the natives.

Henry of Navarre became Henry IV, King of France, in 1589, and under his stern rule the economic life of the country began to recover. The first to petition for the right to colonize America was the Marquis de la Roche, who was granted almost unlimited powers without geographical boundaries. In 1598 he deposited forty criminals on Sable Island, a grass-grown sandbar off the Nova Scotia coast. Five years later the twelve survivors were rescued, de la Roche died, and the patent was given to Chauvin and Pontgravé, who tried a settlement at Tadoussac at the mouth of the Saguenay River. This, too, failed. Then in 1603 the patent was passed to Aymer de Chastes, governor of Dieppe and a staunch supporter of King Henry in the civil wars. De Chastes sent Pontgravé and Samuel de Champlain in two very small vessels of only 12 and 15 tons, no larger than a modern cruising yacht, to explore the St. Lawrence in 1603. They went all the way to Montréal. Champlain, who had been on a voyage to the West Indies and who had taught himself drawing and map sketching on that voyage, made careful and accurate sketches of many of the harbors and landmarks. He was an energetic and eager learner and here was introduced to what became his life's work. It was his next voyage that touched Maine.

When Champlain returned from what is now Montréal, he found that de Chastes had died. The next petitioner for the right to colonize was Pierre du Guast, Sieur De Monts. He was granted not only the broad powers assigned to previous patentees but specific geographic limits, 40° to 46° north latitude, the North American coast from New Jersey to Cape Breton Island. He also was given the right to impress prisoners from the jails and, most important, was given a monopoly of the lucrative fur trade.

Early in 1604 De Monts assembled a crew composed of thieves and ruffians as well as men of character and quality, including among the latter Samuel de Champlain and the Baron de Poutrincourt. In neither of these categories were several Catholic priests and Huguenot ministers, among whom so little light and so much heat was generated by their friction that fierce fistfights broke out among them. Later, surviving colonists buried a priest and minister in the same grave to see whether they would lie quietly together in death as they never had in life.

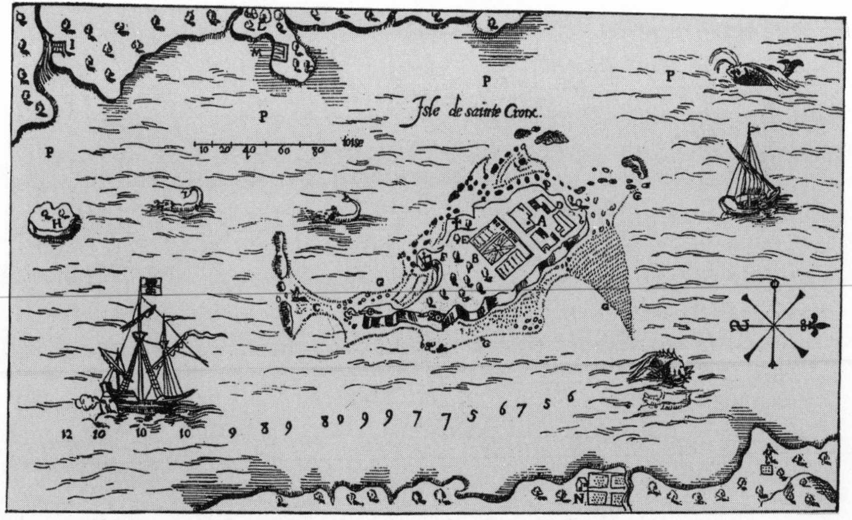

Champlain's sketch of St. Croix Island.

Leaving Pontgravé in another vessel to follow with winter stores, De Monts crossed the Atlantic, made the coast of Nova Scotia, and sought a site for his colony to the south; he had spent one winter at Tadoussac with Chauvin and had no wish to face another arctic experience. He rounded Cape Sable, circumnavigated the Bay of Fundy, stopping at Digby, which he named Port Royal, and at Saint John, where Champlain made a chart of the reversing falls, entered Passamaquoddy Bay, and chose St. Croix Island in the St. Croix River above the present site of St. Andrews for the site of his colony.

He fortified the little island with guns from his ships and built elaborate barracks, storehouses, and a chapel. The settlers also assembled a 17-ton pinnace which they had stowed, knocked down, in the hold.

In September, De Monts sent Champlain on a cruise of discovery to the westward in the pinnace with twelve seamen and two Indian guides, an assignment Champlain said "que j'eus fort agréable." He sailed outside Grand Manan Island through the rough, shoal, and tide-scoured waters east of the island. On the islands to the southeast he saw flocks of puffins, so named the islands Iles des Perroquets. He sailed to the westward outside Libby Islands, Head Harbor Island, Steele Harbor Island, and Great Wass Island, naming them Les Iles Rangés, perhaps because their outer cliffs lie in an almost perfect line.

He continued by Petit Manan and sighted Mount Desert Island. "It is very high, and notched in places, so that there is the appearance to one at sea, as of seven or eight mountains extending along near each other. The summit of most of them is destitute of trees, as there are only rocks on them. The woods consist of pines, firs, and birches only. I named it Isles des Monts Deserts" or 'Islands of the Barren Mountains' in English."*

Champlain sailed along the shore of the island, in one place grounding on a flat ledge. Admiral Morison is convinced Champlain struck just east of Otter Cliffs on a ledge now marked by a bell. They repaired the vessel, probably on the beach in Otter Cove, and here met two Indians who had come beaver hunting and fishing. The Frenchmen traded biscuits and tobacco for fish, and become so friendly with the Indians that the latter agreed to guide Champlain and his men to the Penobscot River, where Bessabez was chief. They called the river Pentagoet. Evidently they sailed up Blue Hill Bay, for Champlain discovered that Mount Desert is an island separated from the mainland by a strait only 100 paces wide—a good estimate.

Probably the Indians took Champlain up Eggemoggin Reach into the upper part of Penobscot Bay. On the way, he saw and named *Ille Haulte,* now called Isle au Haut,† another corruption.

Since the time of David Ingram and perhaps before, Indians had told visitors of Norumbega, a great town on the Penobscot River with roofs of gold, pillars of crystal, rubies as big as pigeons' eggs—and so on. The Indians apparently made a good story of it, and the story gained momentum in the accounts of European visitors. Champlain wrote:

"It is related also that there is a large, thickly settled town of savages who are adept and skillful, and who have cotton yarn. I am confident that most of

*Here is simply one example of the English, and American, tendency to corrupt foreign names. Properly, we should call the island either Mont Désert in French or Mount *Des*ert in English. Indeed, local people for many years did call it Mount *Des*ert. When college-educated summer people invaded the island in the nineteenth century, President Eliot of Harvard called it Mount *Des*ert, but Bishop Doane of Albany called it Mount De*sert*—perhaps, suggests Admiral Morison, because he was unwilling to take orders from a Unitarian. At present the Bishop's pronunciation seems to be the illogical and accepted one.

†Champlain named the island *Ille Haulte,* "high island," on his earliest map. The final *e* on *Ille* was probably pronounced in Champlain's French and was corrupted to *au*. *Ille* was Anglicized to Isle, and in early English deeds the island's name was written as *Aisle au Holt*—and so it is pronounced on the wharves in Stonington today. In an effort to return to the French, summer people have written it Isle au Haut and pronounce it "Eel-a-Ho." One Deer Islander, in an effort to ape the summer people, called it "Eely-Oley."

those who mention it have not seen it, and speak of it because they have heard persons say so, who knew no more about it than they themselves. I am ready to believe that some may have seen the mouth of it [the Penobscot River] because there are in reality many islands, and it is, as they say, in latitude 44° at its entrance. But that anyone has ever entered it there is no evidence, for then they would have described it in another manner. . . . I will accordingly relate truly what I explored and saw, from the beginning as I went."

Champlain gives sailing directions for entering the Penobscot from outside Isle au Haut, but as he was outside on his second voyage in 1605, he could have made the observations then. The directions, while not detailed, are fundamentally correct. Go a mile beyond Isle au Haut and head up the bay, first toward the northernmost of the Camden Hills, then toward the place where you see no islands, "sure of having water enough although you see a great many breakers, islands, and rocks to the east and west of you."

He noticed Fort Point Ledge on his way up the river, and near the present site of Bangor on September 16 found no golden city but an Indian camp where he met the sachems, Bessabez and Cabahis. He established the latitude as 45° 25′. It is actually 45° 48′, but we don't really know exactly where on the river Champlain took his observation.

Champlain must have been a remarkably open, friendly, and attractive person with a genuine respect for the local inhabitants, for he got on famously with them, enjoyed trading and feasting, and took Cabahis for a sail in his ketch.

After the party, Champlain continued down the west side of Penobscot Bay under the Camden Hills and anchored in Rockland Harbor. Thence he continued among the islands some 8 leagues to the west, to an island 10 leagues from the Kennebec. He notes that the ledges and islands make far out to sea, as indeed do the islands now called Two Bush, the Green Islands, and Metinic. He found a good harbor near a navigable river, possibly Georges Harbor, and laid over there during a September storm. He guessed he was about 10 leagues from the Kennebec. Inasmuch as he had not yet seen the Kennebec, we must assume that he edited his account of the cruise after he had visited the coast again the next year.

The season was getting on, so he swung off and sailed back to St. Croix Island, arriving October 2. He found all snug for the winter, with a number of dwellings and storehouses constructed. Poutrincourt had gone back to France, and the pinnaces had been hauled out. However, it was a cold and rugged winter. Like the English, the French assumed that temperature was a function of latitude. St. Croix Island is about in the same latitude as Bordeaux, France, so sub-zero temperatures, heavy snow, and drifting ice floes were a shocking surprise. The settlers suffered much from cold in their drafty buildings, for there was not much wood on the small island and they could not get ashore through or across the drifting ice to the mainland forests. Also, they suffered from scurvy, unaware of its cause or cure, and thirty-five of the seventy-nine people died of it. However, in March some Indians appeared with fresh meat which cured the disease, and in June, Pontgravé returned with supplies from France. De Monts, having found St. Croix a poor site for a colony, took Champlain and a crew aboard the larger of the two pinnaces, and cruised westward in search of a better site in a warmer clime.

De Monts, Champlain, "some gentlemen and 20 sailors" embarked with the Indian Panounias and his wife, on June 18, 1605. They sailed west, inside Grand Manan this time, and anchored probably in the Cow Yard on Head Harbor Island, naming it Ile aux Corneilles for the many crows. They passed outside Mount Desert and Isle au Haut and spent a night in Rockland. On July 1, with what must have been a fine, fair wind, they sailed 25 leagues to the mouth of the Kennebec. Champlain named a high island off the mouth of the river, a prominent landmark, La Tortue, the Tortoise. The modern charts call it Seguin, the Abenaki word for turtle. Champlain located Seguin in 44° north latitude. He was 18 nautical miles too far north, about the same error as he made at Bangor. *(See pages 60 and 61.)*

Both on entering the Kennebec and again on leaving it, Champlain mentioned the dangerous ledges outside: Ellingwood Rock, Seguin Ledges, the Whaleback, the Sisters, and others, but observed that there was plenty of water if the channel were properly buoyed.

The pinnace was anchored west of Stage Island. On July 5, the fog lying thick outside, the expedition, guided by local Indians, went up the narrow Back River on the tide. The banks are steep and rocky, the channel narrow. Champlain thought it unprofitable country, but his view may have been jaundiced by their grounding on a rock in a narrow place. At last, however, they came out into Hockamock Bay and continued through Cowseagan Narrows to the site of Wiscasset, where they met a local chief. Their guides then apparently took them down the Sheepscot River, up the Sasanoa River, and again into Hockamock Bay. As they passed the precipitous and dramatic Hockamock Head, the Indians left an arrow at the foot of the cliff as a sacrifice to ensure good fortune. With a fair tide and a fair wind, they approached Upper Hell Gate. Here the Sasanoa River flows through a narrow gorge, its passage partly obstructed by an island. The current runs very hard by the island, so hard that the river has a perceptible slant to it, and at the full run of the tide it runs over the ledges with a roar and a cloud of spray. A modern auxiliary yacht finds the passage a challenge. Despite the fair tide below the rapids, they found the current running strongly against them. Even with a fair wind, the pinnace could not stem the current, so they ran lines to trees ashore and, with all sails drawing and all hands hauling, got the pinnace through. Above the rapids they found the tide again favorable. This phenomenon occurs near the turn of the tide when the level of the water in Hockamock Bay is lower than that in the Kennebec River but the flood tide is running up under the fresh water above it.

They continued up the Kennebec to Merrymeeting Bay, where the Indians said they would meet Marchin, a powerful chief. He failed to appear, so they ran back down the Kennebec to Stage Island and went fishing with great success.

This penetration of the mainland was significant because in the course of his conversation with the Indians, Champlain found out that by following up the Kennebec, and portaging across the Height of Land, one could descend the Chaudière and come out on the St. Lawrence. Also he discovered that a fort at Sabino at the mouth of the Kennebec did not control access to the river, as one could get into the Kennebec through the Sasanoa. Perhaps the most lasting result of the excursion was Champlain's happy relationship with the Indians. This, in contrast with the contemptuous and often dishonest and cruel attitude of the English, laid the foundation for a century of conflict between the English and the French and Indians.

On July 8, the fog having cleared, they continued to the westward, across Casco Bay, past Cape Elizabeth, and anchored behind Stratton Island in Saco Bay. The White Mountains stood out clearly over the low shore, an inspiring sight in any century. They anchored behind Stratton Island, about two miles off Old Orchard Beach. Indians on the beach danced, shouted, and made welcoming demonstrations. While Champlain and several Frenchmen went ashore, were kindly received, and exchanged hostages with the natives, De Monts landed on Richmond Island. He found it delightful. Champlain wrote, ". . . an island which is very beautiful in view of what it produces, for it has

Champlain's sketch of the mouth of the Kennebec River. Compare with the modern NOAA chart of the Kennebec River on the next page.

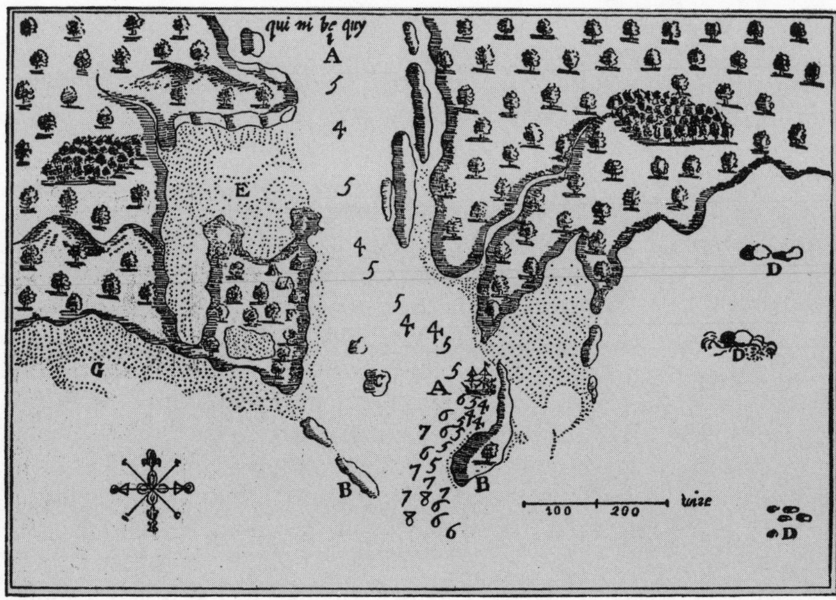

fine oaks and nut-trees, the soil cleared up, and many vineyards bearing beautiful grapes in their season, which were the first we had seen on all these coasts from Cap de la Hève [Nova Scotia]. We named it Isle de Bacchus."

The next day at high water they crossed the bar and anchored in the Saco River. Chief Honemechin appeared, and lively trading ensued. The keen observer Champlain wrote, "These savages shave off the hair far up on the head, and wear what remains very long, which they comb and twist behind in various ways very neatly, intertwined with feathers which they attach to the head.

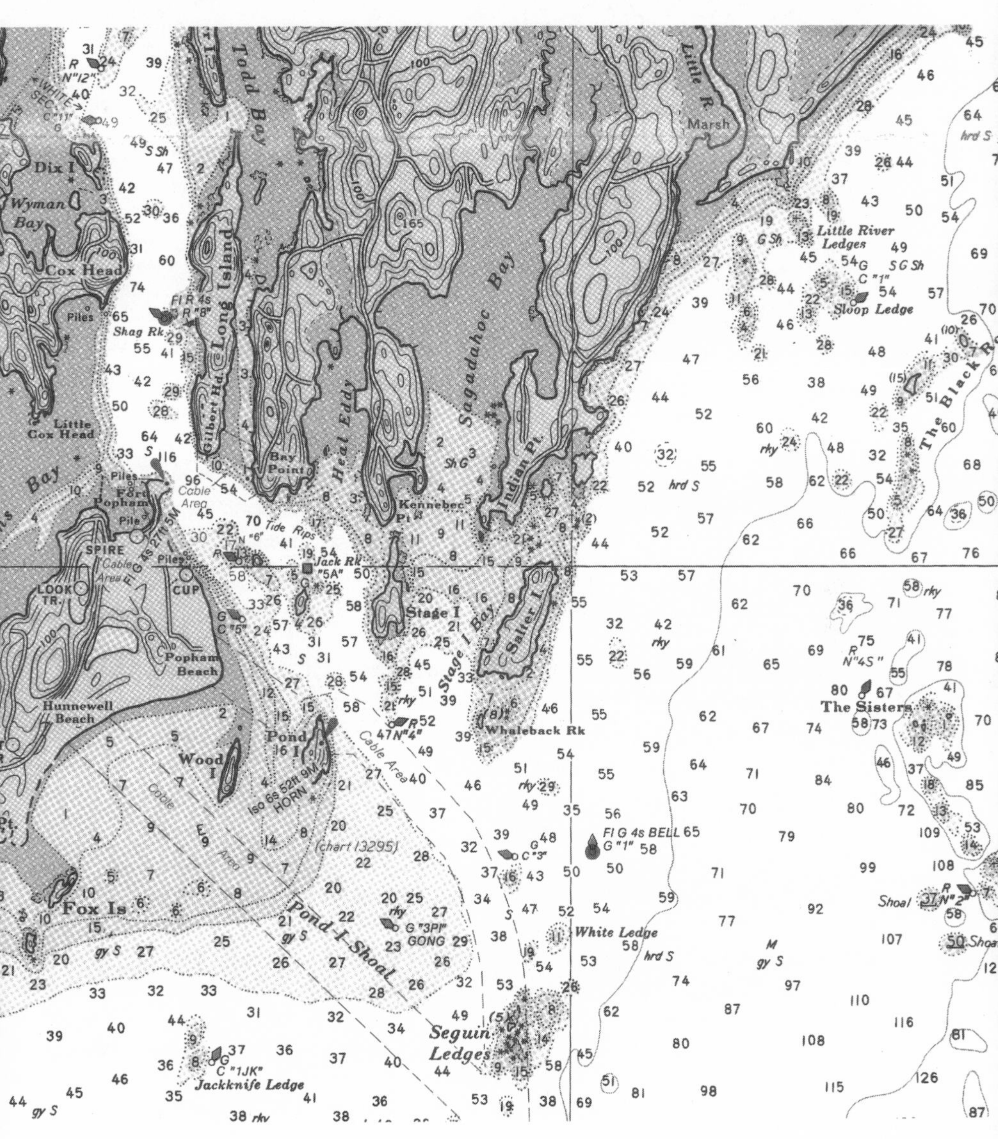

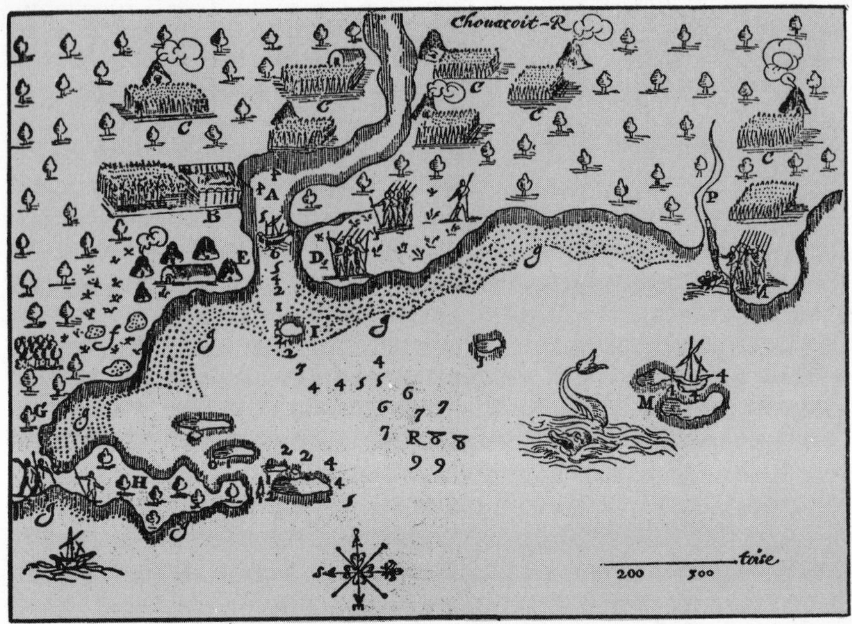

Compare Champlain's surprisingly accurate sketch of the mouth of the Saco River with the Saco River on the NOAA chart on the next page.

They paint their faces black and red like the other savages we have seen. They are an agile people with well-formed bodies. Their weapons are pikes, clubs, bows and arrows. . . . The points of the arrows are horseshoe crab tails, or bone, or plain wood. They plough the soil with a wooden spade. They plant corn in hills with a horseshoe crab for fertilizer and beans to keep the weeds down. They also plant squash, pumpkins and tobacco."

This Indian community, unlike those farther east, was a permanent settlement, not just a summer camp. The tribe lived in a long cabin surrounded by a stout palisade. Champlain determined the latitude to be 43° 45′ north. This is 17 miles too far north—about the same error as those he made at Seguin and Bangor.

On July 12 they continued south along the coast beyond Fletcher Neck "6 or 7 leagues." This would take them into Wells Harbor off Ogunquit. Two Indians on the shore waved, so they sent a boat in, visited a short while, saw red-winged blackbirds, grapevines, and nut trees. The wind coming ahead, they ran back to Cape Porpoise and worked their way in through the ledges to a quiet anchorage. They noted another shelter northeast-by-north from Cape Porpoise, either Stage Island Harbor or Goosefare Bay, but wisely stayed where they were. They found red currants growing there and many pigeons, some of which they shot.

On July 15 they continued southward for 12 leagues and could find no

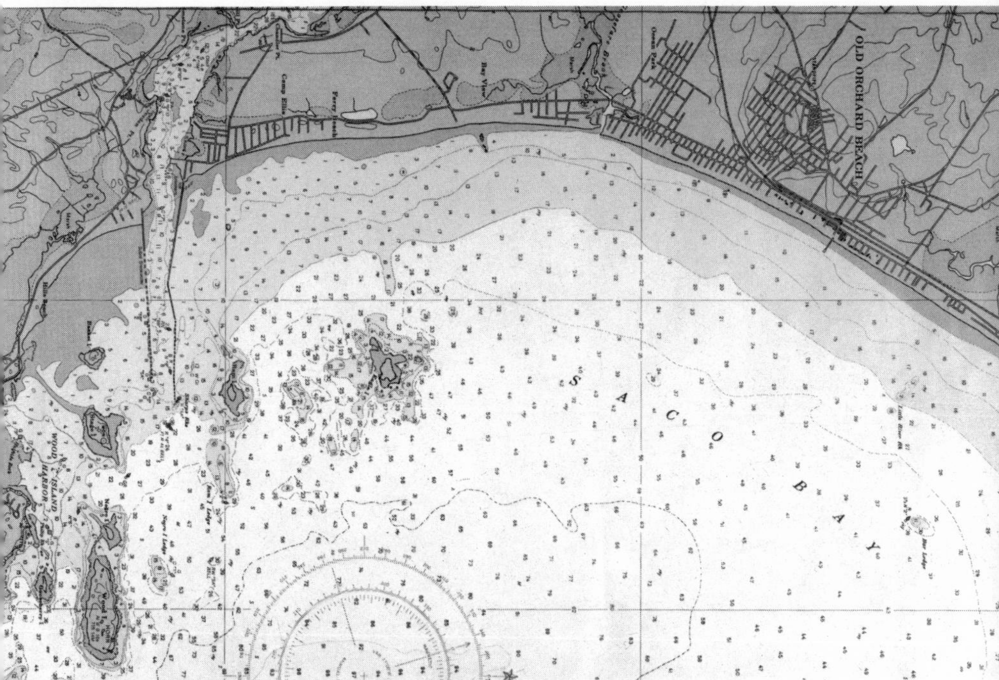

harbor on that stretch of desolate beach. Evidently they failed to notice the York River, the Piscataqua River, and the Isles of Shoals. They continued all night and in the morning made Cape Ann. They went in to Gloucester Harbor and Boston Harbor, and visited Plymouth, Provincetown, and Nauset.

On the way back, they rounded Cape Cod, sailed straight across to Cape Ann and on to Saco. Here they visited with their old friends and met Marchin, the chief whom they had expected to meet at Merrymeeting Bay. He proved very friendly and eager to trade and asked them to take east with them an Abenaki boy, a prisoner, whom he was sending home.

They pushed on east to the Kennebec. Here Sassenou, a local sachem, pointed eastward and said that Englishmen fishing near the island he pointed to had killed five Indians. He doubtless was referring to Waymouth, who had kidnapped five Indians from Allen Island earlier in the summer. Champlain named the island to which the chief pointed La Nef because it looked like a ship.

Historians have assumed that Champlain and his friend were looking at

---

OVERLEAF: Note the close connection between the Kennebec River on page 64 and the Chaudière River in Champlain's map. Examination with a glass shows remarkable accuracy. *Smith Collection, University of Southern Maine*

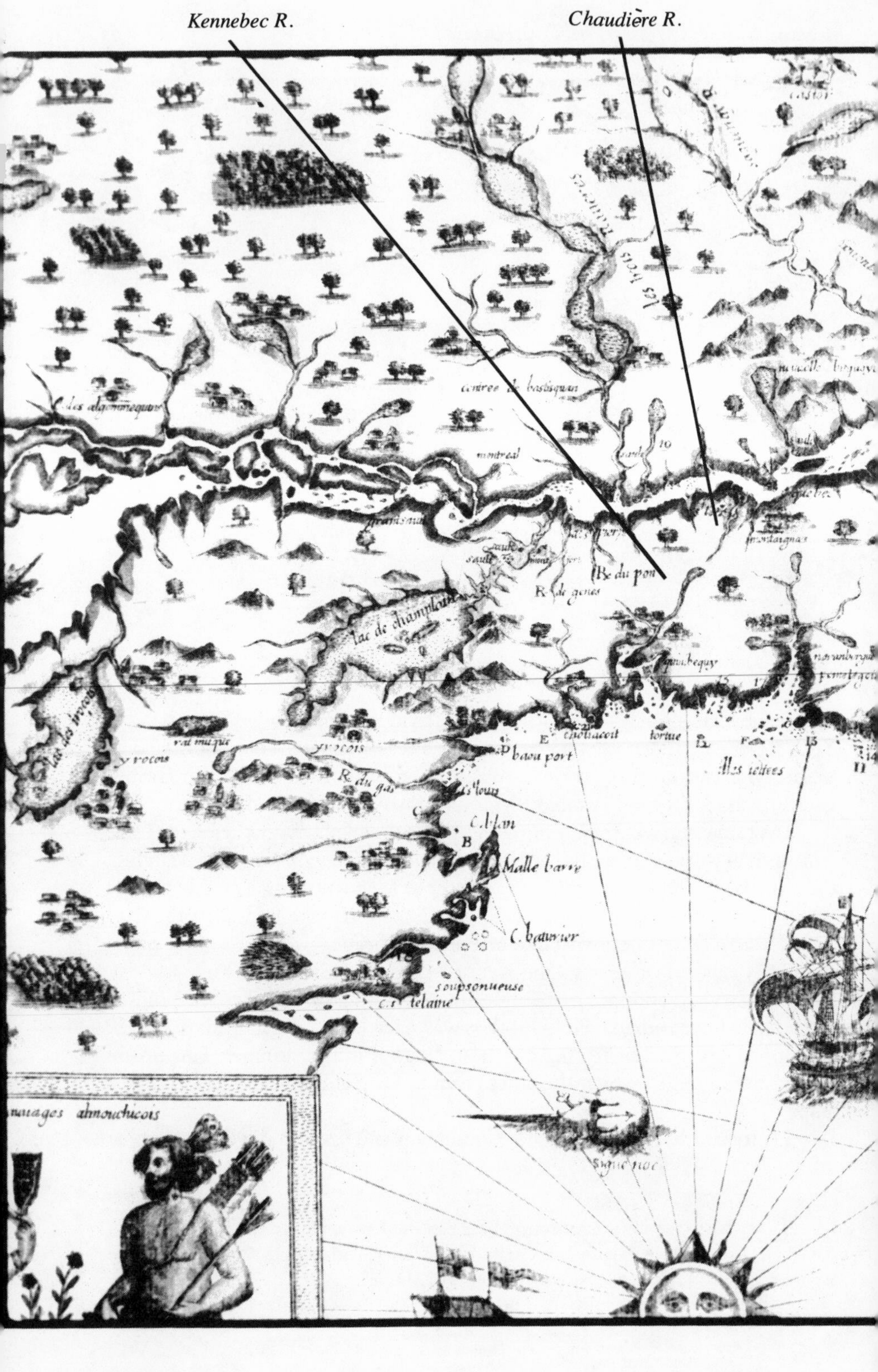

Kennebec R.
Chaudière R.
montreal
lac de champlain
baau port
tortue
Illes ieltees
Malle barre
C. batturier
soupsonueuse
sauuages almouchicois

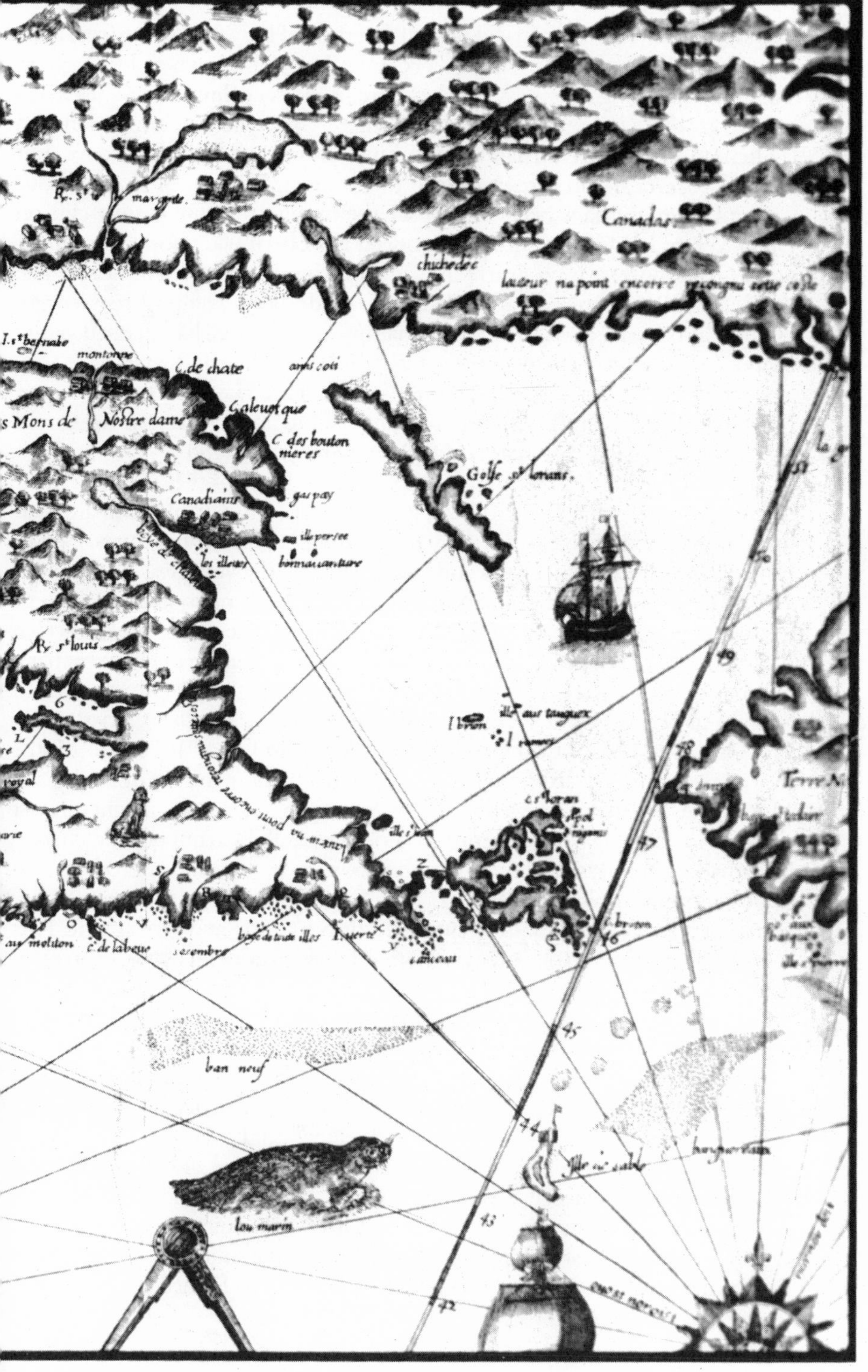

Monhegan, for Englishmen did indeed fish there. However, Monhegan is 20 miles from the mouth of the Kennebec, invisible from anywhere but high on a hill on a sparkling clear day. Furthermore, it looks nothing like a ship when seen from the west. And finally, from where Champlain stood, Monhegan lay behind Damariscove Island. Englishmen fished out of Damariscove, but Damariscove bears little resemblance to a ship. Just north of Damariscove Champlain might have been able to see the triangular white granite cliff on Outer White Island, and this could indeed have been taken for a ship under sail. Furthermore, it is on nearly the same bearing as Georges Harbor, where the five Indians were captured. Had the guide been pointing to Georges Harbor, also too far away to be seen, Champlain might well have named White Island, La Nef. On his map, however, he named Monhegan, La Nef.

From the Kennebec, the expedition made Isle au Haut and the Cow Yard (off Great Wass Island) without stopping ashore and thence ran up Grand Manan Channel and Passamaquoddy Bay to St. Croix Island.

It had been a thoroughly profitable cruise. De Monts had seen a great deal of the coast which he had been granted. He, with Champlain's aid, had made friends and established trade with a number of influential chiefs. Champlain had made excellent charts and had written up the voyage as documentation of De Monts' presence in his domain. It is interesting to note that except for the one reference to Waymouth, no notice is taken of the presence of English or Dutch or indeed anyone else on the coast. Yet we can be sure that a number of vessels were fishing there at the time. Doubtless De Monts wanted his king to believe that New England was inhabited by no other Christians.

On his return from the second voyage in the fall of 1605, De Monts moved the settlement from St. Croix to Port Royal, now the site of Digby. De Monts and Poutrincourt went back to France to defend the patent against enemies in court, leaving Champlain, Pontgravé, and Champdoré in charge. They had a much easier winter than the previous one, and much too early in 1606 set out to explore more of the New England coast in the pinnace. They sailed up Passamaquoddy Bay, checked out St. Croix, and returned to Port Royal, half frozen. No one in his right mind goes cruising in Maine in an open boat in March.

On April 9 they tried again, but in getting out of Digby Gut, Champdoré set only his mizzen, was unable to stem the tidal current, and was wrecked on Man-of-War Rock. All hands got ashore safely with the help of Indian friends, but the pinnace was lost. Champdoré was tried and convicted of barratry—intentionally wrecking the vessel to avoid a New England cruise. He was put in irons but was soon released to assist in building another and bigger pinnace. Champdoré was evidently a very capable ship carpenter and bosun, but as a navigator or seaman he was less effective. With the new pinnace completed, all but two of the colonists set out for Cape Sable and the southeast coast of Nova Scotia in search of a fishing vessel to take them back to France, for De Monts had left orders that if he had not returned by mid-July, they should abandon the colony and return to France.

De Monts had been delayed, but he was on his way. He had chartered *Jonas,* loaded her with supplies and workmen, had crossed the Atlantic, and had run into heavy fog off the Nova Scotia coast. He sent a boat ahead to investigate—rather questionable judgment, perhaps—but the boat met the pinnace, and they all returned to Port Royal to find *Jonas* already at anchor there.

By this time the summer of 1606 was nearly gone, but on September 9 Champlain, Poutrincourt, and Champdoré sailed west again on the Maine coast. With them was Messamouet, an Indian chief from La Have, Nova Scotia. They must have had a fine, fair wind, for after stops only at St. Croix and Rockland, they anchored at Saco. Here Messamouet, seeking an alliance with chiefs Marchin and Onemessin, made generous presents to them. The Saco chiefs responded with gifts of corn, beans, and pumpkins. Messamouet was so resentful at the poor return gifts that the following summer he raided the Saco encampment. Panounias, a Port Royal Indian who had guided Champlain the previous summer, was killed in the battle. Therefore Membertou, the Port Royal chief, perhaps wanting a piece of the action and using Panounias as a *cause de guerre,* led a fleet of 200 canoes across the Bay of Fundy the following summer, attacked the Saco camp, and killed both Marchin and Onemessin. The incident is significant principally because it shows that Indians made long offshore voyages in canoes. The Bay of Fundy can be a formidable stretch. The tides run as much as 5 knots at times and 3 to 4 knots frequently. Such a tide setting against a southwest breeze raises a short, steep sea made even shorter and steeper in the shallow waters over the banks and around Grand Manan. It is about 40 miles from Digby Gut to Grand Manan, a long day's journey in a canoe, a voyage in which a sea dangerous to a canoe could build up. One would need a compelling reason and a serene faith in the weather to chance such a voyage in a canoe.

The party of Frenchmen continued south to what is now Gloucester, Massachusetts, and returned to Port Royal for the first jolly winter in the New World. The Order of the Good Time was established, food and wine were plentiful. The Indians were friendly and contributed deer, moose, and other game to the Good Time; the weather was less severe than in other winters, and the future looked bright. However, the first vessel from France in the spring of 1607 brought news that De Monts' monopoly on the fur trade had been rescinded, and De Monts was unable to support the colony without it. So, in the fall of 1607, Port Royal was abandoned, although Champdoré was sent on another Maine cruise to the Saco.

Champlain turned his attention to the St. Lawrence and Québec, but Poutrincourt, who had been granted the land around Port Royal by De Monts, refused to give it up. After considerable negotiation, he persuaded Henry IV to confirm his grant. One of the terms, however, urged by Father Coton, a Jesuit* adviser to the King, was that in order to justify the expense, Poutrincourt should take with him a Jesuit missionary to save the souls of the savages. Poutrincourt did not want to do this. He, like King Henry, was a sound Catholic, but he was no extremist and had no use for the militant attitude of the Jesuits. Furthermore, he knew, respected, and liked the Indians. They were not an amorphous band of savages bound for eternal torment without the intervention of the black-robed Jesuits; they were his friends. However, Coton appointed Father Biard to accompany the expedition, and in February 1610 Poutrincourt sent Biard to Bordeaux to meet his vessel. Biard went to Bordeaux, found no vessel, waited about the wharves for awhile, and returned to Paris to discover that Poutrincourt had sailed from Dieppe, taking with him Father LaFleche, a priest but no Jesuit.

Poutrincourt reestablished the French presence at Port Royal, was welcomed by his Indian friends, and opened a busy fur trade. Father LaFleche instructed the Indians so effectively in Christianity that he baptized first Chief Membertou, then his son and family and several leaders of the tribe. Influential converts were named after the French royal family and influential members of the French nobility. Sufficient provision was on hand for a proper celebration in honor of such distinguished personages, and more conversions followed rapidly. Clearly the souls of the savages were being saved without recourse to the Jesuits, and the fur trade flourished.

Poutrincourt's son, Biencourt, was sent back to France in the fall of 1610 for further supplies but found on his arrival that Henry IV had been assassinated and the court was in the hands of the Queen, Marie de Medici, acting as regent for Louis XIII. She was much under the influence of the Jesuits and insisted that if Poutrincourt was to continue to enjoy his patent and a monopoly of the fur trade, Biencourt must take back with him Father Biard and Father Masse. Reluctantly, Biencourt agreed, went to Dieppe, and boarded his ship with the two Jesuits. When the Huguenot merchants of Dieppe, who had financed about half the voyage in return for a share in the profits, saw the Jesuits board the ship, however, they were outraged, declared they would have no part of a voyage in which the Jesuits had any stake whatever, and demanded their money back unless the Jesuits went ashore. Biencourt could not refund the money, and Biard, once aboard a ship bound for America, refused adamantly to go ashore. Biencourt returned to Paris to talk with the Queen.

One of the Queen's ladies of honor, the Marquise de Guercheville, was a woman of unimpeachable virtue and considerable wealth. She was also deeply committed to the Jesuit program. She agreed to buy out the merchants' shares

*Jesuits were members of The Society of Jesus, a Roman Catholic order founded by Ignatius Loyola in 1533. Its members were wholly dedicated to defending their church against the Protestant heresy and to winning new Catholics from among the heathen. Many Jesuits were ruthless in their methods and far from ingenuous. In Maine they supported the Catholic French against the Protestant English.

and lend a sum in addition to Biencourt. So at last Biencourt returned to Port Royal in 1611.

Poutrincourt was distressed by the arrival of the Jesuits and went back to France to sell the vessel's cargo of furs and bring further supplies. Meanwhile, Biencourt, accompanied by Father Biard, set out on another Maine coast cruise. They first visited Saint John, where they found Pontgravé's son conducting an illegal fur-trading business in defiance of Poutrincourt's monopoly. Then they dropped in on St. Croix Island, where they found Captain Palatrier. He had had a hard summer, for, some time before, he had been captured at Monhegan by an English ship for illicit trading. He was released on payment of a ransom and a promise not to trade on the Maine coast. He had gone to St. Croix, where he was accosted by Biencourt and fined for encroaching on the Poutrincourt monopoly.

Biencourt and Biard continued westward to the mouth of the Kennebec, their purpose being to trade for corn, necessary in case Poutrincourt failed to return in time, and to see to what extent the English were encroaching on French control of the coast. At the mouth of the Kennebec they visited the abandoned Gilbert and Popham fort of 1607 and camped on the west bank of the Kennebec a little farther upstream. Six canoes filled with Indians came down the river and camped opposite. In the evening the Indians began to dance and sing. Biard, not wanting to leave these imps of hell to sing unchallenged, had the French sing *Ave Maria, Te Deum,* and all the religious songs in their repertory. When they ran out of religious songs, the French continued with increasingly secular contributions until these too were exhausted. As the Indians were still in excellent voice, the French listened and began to mimic the Indians, which they did very well indeed. When the Indians realized what they were doing, a sort of two-part chorale developed in Abenaki, to the delight of both sides of the river. Biard's reaction is unrecorded.

The Indians told Biencourt that a party of Englishmen had been at the Kennebec in 1609, had set dogs on the Indians and abused them, and that the Indians had killed them all. This could not have been the Gilbert colony, but is merely another shred of evidence showing that there was a strong English presence in mid-coast Maine.

From the Kennebec, Biencourt went to Monhegan and set up a French cross as evidence of French claim to the area. Contrary to Biard's advice, he did not burn the fishing sloops in the harbor. That there were fishing sloops in Monhegan harbor in November of 1610 suggests year-round occupation of the island by that date.

Biencourt then returned to Port Royal for the winter. It was a hard, cold winter, but in January 1611, a vessel from France arrived with provisions sent by Poutrincourt, with another Jesuit, Du Thet, and with news of financial and political trouble.

The Jesuits had picked a legal battle with Poutrincourt, had had him jailed, and had attached the cargo of his ship. When he got out of jail, he had no money to send supplies to his son at Port Royal. He was trying to finance a fur trading post; the Jesuits were trying to finance a mission. The Jesuits won. They appealed again to the Marquise de Guercheville. She agreed to finance the voyage if the King, now ten years old, would grant her the whole North American continent from Florida to the Saint Lawrence except for Poutrincourt's small grant around Port Royal. Thus, little Louis, with the Marquise as a cover, gave the Jesuits an enormous kingdom that was not his to give away and of whose people, wealth, and extent he had not the slightest idea. Nevertheless, the Jesuits, by this grant, justified their penetration of the continent, not only up the St. Lawrence, through the Great Lakes, and down the Mississippi, but down the Saint John, Penobscot, Kennebec, Saco, and Connecticut rivers to the coast of New England. Their efforts to Catholicize the Indians were inextricably entangled with the fur trade in competition with the English and with the massacres of villages and towns, both red and white.

So, Poutrincourt got his ship and supplies but had to send with it back to Port Royal another Jesuit, Du Thet. Du Thet, the missionary, quarreled with Poutrincourt's agent on the trip across the Atlantic. The quarrel spread at Port Royal. Finally the three priests, Du Thet, Biard, and Masse, went aboard the vessel and refused to come ashore. Biencourt, afraid of what would happen when they told their biased story at the French court, ordered them ashore. They excommunicated him, thus relieving themselves of the necessity of obeying his orders.

After a stalemate of several weeks, at last they came ashore with no very good grace. When it came time for the vessel to return, Du Thet and Biencourt went with it, neither trusting the other. In France, Poutrincourt had lost any influence he had had, and the Jesuits were in control. They planned a mission on the Penobscot River as a check to the English. Accordingly they raised a large sum at court, outfitted *Jonas* with forty-eight colonists, two Jesuits, and a number of horses, cattle, and goats. La Saussaye was the leader of the expedition, Fleury was master of the ship, and Bailleul the pilot. Du Thet and Biencourt also went along.

Jonas made La Hève on May 16, 1613, proceeded to Port Royal, left Biencourt, picked up Biard and Masse, and crossed the Bay of Fundy. They made the Maine coast in the fog on the southeast corner of Mount Desert Island and anchored perhaps off Otter Cove. The fog cleared, and Indians came aboard. The Jesuits asked to be guided to the Penobscot, but the Indians urged a better place nearby. Also they said Chief Asticou was sick and wanted to be baptized before he died. The Indians guided the party to the mouth of Somes Sound, where Chief Asticou was found suffering the usual agonies brought on by a bad cold. The Jesuits agreed that here indeed was an ideal spot for a mission in an open field protected on the north by Flying Mountain and sheltered from the sea by Greenings, Sutton, and Cranberry islands. There was a spring on the beach below the high-water mark which bubbled out fresh water as soon as the tide left it. They went ashore at once and set up a cross with the French arms, thus establishing the St. Sauveur mission.

Meanwhile, in Virginia, the English had heard of the French presence in New England. Governor Dale was determined to counter the move before it gained momentum. Ready to his hand was the ideal instrument, Captain Samuel Argall. This energetic, ruthless, and acquisitive captain had turned up in Virginia after a privateering cruise, had sailed up the James River, captured Pocahontas, the Indian princess who had saved John Smith's life, and lay off Jamestown ready for another expedition. Dale sent him to dislodge the French. Upon his arrival in Maine, Argall learned from Indians the location of the French mission, sailed up Western Way under the British flag, rounded up, and gave *Jonas* a broadside which killed Du Thet. La Saussaye fled into the woods, and Bailleul fled in a small boat. Fleury shouted "Fire," seized a match, and fired a gun, which, not having been aimed, did no execution.

Argall took possession of *Jonas,* went ashore, picked the lock of La Saussaye's sea chest, and stole the documents signed by the King giving him the right to set up a mission. The next day, when La Saussaye came out of the woods, Argall demanded his commission. Of course, he could not find it, so Argall looted the place, and set fourteen of the colonists adrift in an open boat. They were joined by Bailleul, made their way across the Bay of Fundy, around Cape Sable, and were taken back to Saint-Malo by French fishermen. Argall took the others to Jamestown.

Dale breathed fire at the captives, threatening to hang them as interlopers and pirates. Argall produced the commission, thus saving their lives, and they were at length sent back to France.

Dale then sent Argall back to New England to erase all French presence there. With Biard, who had evidently changed sides, to guide him, Argall first returned to Mount Desert, where he burned the remains of the St. Sauveur mission, cut down the French cross, and set up an English one. He went on to St. Croix Island, where he "liberated" a cargo of salt and destroyed the remains of De Monts' buildings. He crossed the Bay of Fundy and anchored off Port Royal, by this time an active and successful community. Biencourt was away on a visit to some Indians, and most of the colonists were reaping in a field six miles up the river. Argall plundered the place thoroughly, burned all the buildings, including a mill and a forge, butchered or carried off the cattle, horses, and goats, then went up the river and destroyed the crop. Biard, said Poutrincourt later, tried to persuade the reapers to desert the French and join Argall. The French hated Biard for betraying them, and the English hated him because he was a Jesuit. The French ashore hailed the English on Argall's vessel, urging them to kill Biard. The English master of the vessel wanted to set Biard ashore and let the French do it. However, Argall protected Biard, put him aboard *Jonas,* and on November 13, 1613, the three vessels sailed for Virginia.

They sailed right into a North Atlantic gale. The smallest vessel was lost. Argall at last got to Virginia, where soon after he was made deputy governor, succeeding Dale, and ran the colony with an iron hand. *Jonas* finally made the Azores and thence England and was then sent back to France. Biard later went to Québec and played a leading part in the Christianizing of the Indians at St. Francis.

The French colonists at Port Royal after Argall's departure spent a miserable winter living on whatever they could salvage from the ashes of Port Royal: lichens, buds of trees and bushes, and small game. Poutrincourt returned in the spring of 1614 and took his countrymen home. He was given command of the force attacking Méry and was killed in the battle.

Thus concluded for a time the French effort to colonize Maine. However, throughout all this period, 500 French ships sailed each year to Newfoundland, Nova Scotia, and Maine for the fishing and fur trading. Both French and British presences were still strong on the coast, although no year-round community, whose residents planned to make their livelihood in Maine permanently, had yet been established.

NOTES

Admiral Morison's *Samuel de Champlain* gives a quick summary of the explorations of Cartier and Roberval. Francis Parkman's classic *Pioneers of France in the New World* is much more detailed and interesting, as well as being a monument of good historical prose which Admiral Morison and I have both tried to emulate. Parkman continues with an account of Champlain's explorations. Morison's biography extends Parkman's account. Champlain's own account adds authenticity and color and gives us a first-hand glimpse of that remarkable man's personality.

The canoes in which the Nova Scotia Indians raided the Maine coast were not the small, light birchbark canoes used on rivers, lakes, and coastal waters. These were stout, well-formed dugouts constructed from the enormous pine trees that then grew in America. They were as much as 40 feet long, 6 feet wide, and 3 or 4 feet deep, carrying twenty to thirty men, enough to spell each other at the paddles and bail when necessary. If such a craft were swamped, it would not sink but could be bailed out and paddled on.

The accounts of Poutrincourt's, Biencourt's, and the Jesuits' machinations and adventures comes from Parkman.

FIVE

Seventeenth-Century Ships and Their Navigation

IT IS TRADITIONAL to speak of the ships of early navigators as "cockleshells," to suggest that they were unseaworthy, that a successful Atlantic crossing was a feat of great skill, courage, and unusual good fortune. True, by modern commercial standards they were small vessels, most of them under 100 feet long and some probably less than 50 feet. However, seaworthiness is not measured in feet. To keep a vessel afloat, the water must be kept out of her. A bottle, while not a handy rig, will not sink in the wildest gale. Therefore, the early seagoing vessels were entirely decked over, the main deck being built at the point of greatest breadth only a little above the waterline and running unbroken from stem to stern except for two or three small hatches to provide access to the hold. Here were stowed, on top of a layer of stone and sand ballast, sea stores and cargo. About 5 feet above the main deck was another, upper, deck, also running from stem to stern and pierced with only a few hatches. In the " 'tween decks" lived the ship's crew and passengers. Each man had a sea chest lashed to ring bolts or chocks in the deck and a straw mattress or perhaps just a blanket. He slept wherever he could find room to stretch out.

The atmosphere was far from pleasant here. In rough weather when hatches were battened down, the twice-breathed air was thick with the stink of bilgewater, seasickness, and refuse thrown below on the ballast. The galley was a box of sand with a chimney over it. In good weather it smoked. In bad weather it could not be used. The upper deck usually leaked; the *Mayflower*'s leaked distressingly.

Food was traditionally salt fish, salt beef, salt pork, hard bread, and beer. Water did not keep well at sea. There was also a small weekly allowance of cheese and butter. Such a diet, deficient in vitamin C, brought on scurvy after about six weeks. No one in the seventeenth century knew what caused the disease, but they knew that about half a crew might die of it on a long voyage. Of course, after the crew got ashore in America, if they continued the same

A seventeenth-century ship. The "castles" on bow and stern were very lightly constructed. *Consuelo E. Hanks*

diet, the disease continued. Half of De Monts' people died of scurvy the first winter on St. Croix Island. However, at Port Royal there is no mention of scurvy, as there was plenty of fresh meat. Not until Captain Cook's voyages in the latter part of the next century was scurvy controlled. Captain Cook ascribed the health of his crew to his insistence on keeping the fo'c's'le clean and ventilated, but he also insisted on a ration of lime or lemon juice daily.

Over the after third of the upper deck was built a quarterdeck with accommodations for officers and, over the after half of the quarterdeck, a narrow poop deck. Forward, just aft of the bow, was the forecastle, or fo'c's'le, a house built on the upper deck in which spare gear was kept. Probably in these ships it was not regularly used as crew's quarters, for it was likely to be wet in any kind of a head sea. Cannon mounted here and on the quarterdeck could command the waist between as well as pepper an enemy seeking to board.

If the quarterdeck and fo'c's'le were taken off, a seventeenth-century ship would look not unlike a rather stubby and burdensome vessel of any century before the mid-nineteenth. As it is, she looks awkward and topheavy. However, the planking and timbering of the vessel above the main deck were not as heavy as they were below, and the superstructures were very lightly constructed. The vessel's principal weight was below the main deck, and at the main deck was her point of greatest beam. Above that, there was an exaggerated tumblehome or narrowing of the vessel. The rig, while ample, was comparatively low. In hard weather, with the hatches battened tight on the main deck and the upper deck, no water could get below and seriously threaten flotation. Water that came on deck might wash out fo'c's'le and quarterdeck but ran overboard again through scuppers.

The steering arrangements we would consider very awkward. The rudder was hung outboard, both on double-enders and on vessels with flat sterns. The rudderhead came just above the main deck, and a long, heavy tiller worked through a hole in the stern planking, quite a wide hole to allow for the swinging of the tiller. With a following sea, or indeed in any kind of rough weather, water came in through this hole and washed across the main deck around the feet of the helmsman or the men at relieving tackles, before it ran overboard through scuppers in the side. A helmsman on the main deck could not see the sails or where he was going. He was literally in the dark. As a partial solution to this problem, a vertical stick was lashed to the tiller, extending through the upper deck and pivoted on the upper deckbeam. The helmsman could stand, then, on the upper deck and control the tiller with this whipstaff. He could not move the tiller more than a few degrees with this awkward mechanism, but at least he was nearer the officer conning the vessel from the poop deck, he was provided with a compass in a candlelit binnacle, and his feet were out of the wet. In some vessels he stood on a platform and poked his head through a hatch so he could see the sails. When radical changes of course were necessary, men were sent to the main deck to man relieving tackles attached directly to the tiller and responded to commands shouted down the hatches.

The rig on a typical seventeenth-century transatlantic vessel appears to us excessively complicated. She was ship rigged; that is, she had three masts with squaresails. Such a vessel commonly had a mainsail and main topsail, foresail, a sprit sail under the highly steeved bowsprit, and a lateen mizzen on a short mast stepped through the quarterdeck with its heel on the upper deck. The mainsail was the largest and was the principal driving sail, its main yard being nearly as long as the keel and its area increased with bonnets laced to its foot. It was hoisted with a halyard and in heavy weather or in port could be lowered on deck. Before the wind it was a powerful sail, its area sometimes increased by studding sails, or stun' sails, rigged temporarily on extensions of the yard. Going to windward, when the yard was braced as nearly fore-and-aft as the standing rigging would permit, its weather leech, or leading edge, was hauled down tight at the tack and stiffened with bridles and a tackle called a bowline to provide some sort of aerodynamically efficient airfoil. To control the sail, it was provided with clew lines running through blocks on the yard to pull up the lower corners, and buntlines to bag up the middle of the sail to the yard. With the sail thus gathered up, the yard was lowered all or part way and men went aloft to tie the sail down tightly with gaskets. The same rigging was used

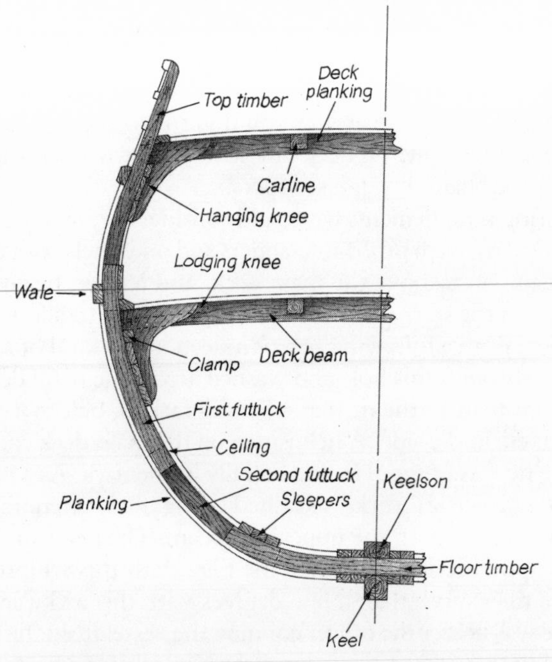

Above: Construction detail of a seventeenth-century ship. *Below:* Cross section of hull. *Drawings by Kathy Bray from Baker's* Colonial Vessels

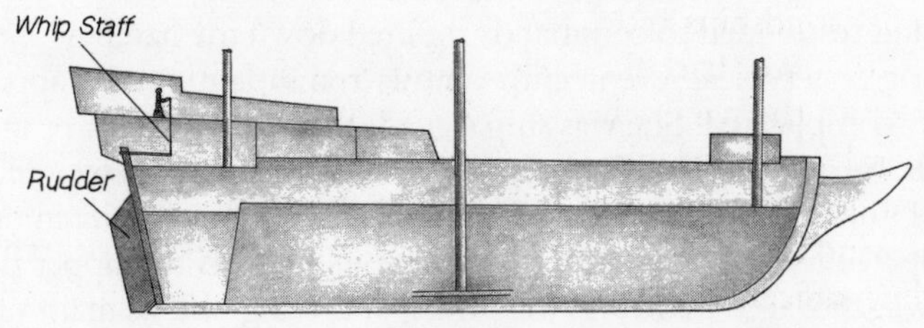

Rig of a seventeenth-century vessel. All the running gear is not shown. Each sail had a halyard to hoist it, a pair of braces to swing the yards, a pair of sheets to control the lower corners of the sail, and clew lines and buntlines to subdue it in a breeze. *Kathy Bray*

on the smaller foresail. The topsail was much smaller than the lower sails and was set from the top or crow's nest at the head of the lower mast. The sprit sail was an awkward rig used principally in light or moderate weather and as a means of balancing the rig to make steering easier. The lateen mizzen was an important sail inherited from Mediterranean and Spanish sailors. It was a fore-and-aft sail—that is, it pivoted on the mast inside the shrouds so that it could be hauled flat amidships and kept full when the vessel was headed so close to the wind as to luff or back the squaresails. Thus it was a great help in holding the vessel up to the wind when going to windward and in turning her bow into the wind when tacking. Its yard, extending forward of its mast, had a tackle at its heel to pull it back around the foot of the mast when tacking. Before the wind it must have had a great proclivity for jibing without warning and startling officers on the poop. Like the mizzen on a modern yawl, it probably was little more than a nuisance before the wind and was probably taken in at such times.

The mainmast was supported with anywhere from five to *thirteen* shrouds on each side, each tightened with deadeyes and lanyards. Each mast had a stout stay leading forward and was supported from aft by the after shrouds. The masts were often sprung forward and held thus by the bowsprit and forestays against the pull of the after shrouds.

In light weather with the wind abeam or abaft the beam, with one or two bonnets laced to the foot of the big mainsail, the vessel slipped along at four or five knots remarkably well, the foresail and sprit sail helping as they could, the mizzen perhaps brailed up. As the wind increased, the topsail would be taken in first, its yard lowered to the cap of the mainmast and the sail handed from the top. As the sea built up, it is likely that the sprit sail would be taken in before Father Neptune took it away, and then the main yard would be lowered and bonnets unlaced from the foot of the mainsail. If wind and sea increased further so that the mainsail was too much, the yard was lowered, the sails gathered up with clew lines and buntlines and then furled, and the vessel run off before the wind under foresail. If still the wind increased, even the foresail was taken in and the vessel lay "a-hull," riding under bare poles. The windage of the high stern held her bow up toward the wind, and the fo'c's'le held her off a bit so she lay sideways, hove to perhaps six or seven points—67 to 80 degrees—from the wind, drifting to leeward, making a bit of a slick to windward. She was small enough to slide down one sea and be lifted by the next, so she did not have to be supported by two crests at once, and as she drifted to leeward could give to the forces of the wind and the breaking crests of the seas. She lay like a duck, in the sea and part of it, any water that came aboard running out through scuppers in the upper deck. As long as she held together under the strains of passing seas, she was safe, however wet and uncomfortable she might be. There was, though, some question of her hanging together, for the frames or ribs of seventeenth-century ships were made up of several pieces of naturally curved wood scarfed together and held together only by the planking on the outside and the ceiling within.

One of the principal dangers lay in the quality of the hemp standing rigging. Hemp shrinks when wet and stretches when dry, requiring frequent setting up with the lanyards. The violent strains produced by a gale or even by slatting in a calm could develop enough slack in the rigging to dismast the vessel.

With the wind anywhere abaft the beam, such a vessel was fairly efficient, but with the wind forward of the beam she was slow and awkward. The yards could not be braced really sharply to windward because of the shrouds, and the baggy squaresails, even stiffened by bowlines from the weather tack to the rail and bowsprit, made at best poor airfoils. Her bluff bow was pushed away to leeward by each sea in spite of the pressure of the lateen mizzen holding her to windward. Her round bottom and comparatively shoal draft gave her scant grip on the water when she was heeled. The seas beating her weather bow and the pressure of the foresail pushed her bow to leeward, while the mizzen, although it helped to balance the foresail, pushed her stern to leeward. The result was considerable leeway. In smooth water she might head six points, 67 degrees, from the wind, but in rough going she might not be able to gain at all. Consequently, vessels were often windbound for weeks waiting for a fair wind down the English Channel. For this reason, many voyages to America started in February or March, sometimes even in January, when easterly winds were much more frequent than in the spring and summer.

Maneuvering a square-rigged ship required good judgment, careful timing, and precise execution of orders. Suppose a high-pooped, bluff-bowed little vessel of about 65 feet to be sailing hard on the wind on the starboard tack heading north. The wind is from the east-northeast. She is carrying foresail, mainsail, main topsail, and lateen mizzen. Her yards are braced as far forward as they will go, hard against the forward shrouds on the lee side, and the bowlines on her starboard side, the forward edge, of her squaresails are hauled down as tight as may be. Her pilot wishes to turn her through the eye of the wind, to fill the sails on the other side; he will then be sailing about southeast. He gets all hands on deck to stand by sheets and braces, and calls down the hatch to the man at the whipstaff to bear off a little and get her going as fast as possible. When the pilot sees a comparatively smooth space coming in the unbroken succession of seas marching against him, he commands "Hard a-lee." The steersman, perhaps helped by a crew on the main deck, pushes the tiller to leeward, to port, and the little vessel turns toward the wind, ramming her bow into a sea and dousing the crew forward. The mizzen is hauled flat aft. The squaresails shiver, shake, and as she swings into the wind are taken aback, pressed against the masts by the wind blowing on their forward sides. The vessel slows suddenly and stops as the wind pushes her backwards, but she keeps swinging. As she comes through the eye of the wind, heading east-northeast, bowlines, sheets, and tacks are cast off and the main yard is swung so its port end is forward. The mizzen sheet is slacked. The foresail, still aback, is pushing her bow to starboard. As the mainsail and topsail come edge-to-the-wind, they flap and fill on the port tack and begin to move the vessel ahead again. Then the fore yard is pulled around, tacks and bowlines hauled down, sheets pulled aft, the yards braced hard against the shrouds on the port tack, and the vessel is headed southeast.

Lots of things can go wrong. One steep sea hitting the bow as it swings toward the wind can slow the vessel down, kill her momentum, and push her back on the starboard tack. If she loses way when she is head-to-wind and is blown backwards, she is said to be in irons, stuck, unable to turn either way as the rudder is ineffective. If commands are not executed precisely, the sails will fill before tacks and bowlines can be taken in, and it will require tackles and lots of heaving to get the leading edges of the sails down tight. If the ship is in a tight spot with land close aboard, she may well go ashore if she misses stays.

Imagine the situation aboard *Mary and John* beating about all night off the mouth of the Kennebec in a southerly gale, tacking every time the loom of breakers glimmered white through the murk, all hands alert, knowing that to miss stays once could mean shipwreck and probable drowning.

Of course, in open water with plenty of room to leeward, a vessel could wear ship, go around the other way from north to west-southwest with the wind astern and then to south and southeast, bracing the yards around, shifting bowlines, tacks, and sheets as she came. This maneuver is much easier but in heavy weather lays the vessel twice in the trough of the seas where a big steep sea might overwhelm her, and in the course of wearing, a ship may lose as much as half a mile to leeward.

How a square-rigged vessel tacks in any century. The foresail aback helps her bow around. As she comes through the eye of the wind, the main yard is swung to port to give her steerage-way on the new tack. *Kathy Bray*

One advantage, however, of the square-rigged vessel was that she could stop. If she braced her main yard around so the big mainsail and topsail were taken aback, she would be balanced between the fore and mizzen driving her ahead and the mainsail and topsail holding her back. Among ledges or sandbanks, or entering a strange harbor, she could thus creep along, taking soundings as she went, and perhaps send a small boat ahead to find a safe channel.

The traditional seventeenth-century compass was divided into thirty-two points, each clearly marked and usually labeled with Latin names. The bowl, unlike that of a modern compass, was dry. The card, balanced on a pivot and without gimbals, gyrated wildly in a rough sea. *Kathy Bray*

We find Waymouth's *Archangel* acting thus off Sankaty Head and again on entering Georges Harbor. Champlain speaks of going up Penobscot Bay *sonde en main,* lead in hand, ready to back his main yard and sound frequently.

Navigation, while not a precise science even today, was in the seventeenth century pretty much by guess and by God—"I guess it is, and by God it ain't." On transatlantic voyages the principle was latitude sailing; that is, one sailed southward from England to reach the latitude of one's destination, usually making the Azores, and then west until a large continent appeared. By the seventeenth century, all oceangoing vessels carried a compass. This consisted of a magnetized needle, with a lodestone to remagnetize it frequently, attached to a card marked off in thirty-two points and balanced on a pivot in a bowl. Most compasses at this time had a lubber line marked on the forward edge of the bowl and lined up with the vessel's keel so the course could be read off even if the helmsman could not see the masts, the bow, or the sails. The compass was lit by a candle. Gimbals had not been invented, so the card tipped and swung wildly, and a course was approximate at best.

The variation of the compass due to the discrepancy between the geographic pole and the magnetic pole had been understood in 1581, but tables were far from accurate. It is interesting that Waymouth took observations of the "declination of the magnetic needle," variation, with great care at Allen Island in 1605. Late in the century, Edmund Halley charted variation for the Atlantic Ocean.

The course and speed were recorded every half hour on a traverse board, a compass rose with holes into which pegs were stuck to indicate the course and time. Here was also a series of holes at the bottom to record speed. Time was kept with a thirty-minute sandglass, at every turn of which a bell was struck. Watches traditionally started at eight bells—four, eight, and twelve o'clock. At the first turn of the glass, the ship's bell would be struck once. At five, nine, and one o'clock, it would be struck twice, two bells—and so on, an additional bell with each half hour. At eight bells the watch changed. Speed was estimated by looking over the side, a process acceptable by an experienced pilot, in moderate weather and familiar waters where position could be frequently checked by landmarks. However, in rough water and heavy winds even experienced skippers are likely to overestimate speed, and at sea or in

A traverse board, used to keep track of course and speed during each watch. Although the photograph is unclear, for the first two hours of the watch the course appears to have been west-southwest and for the last two hours, southwest. The pegs at the bottom were used to record speed each time the log was hove. *Peabody Museum of Salem*

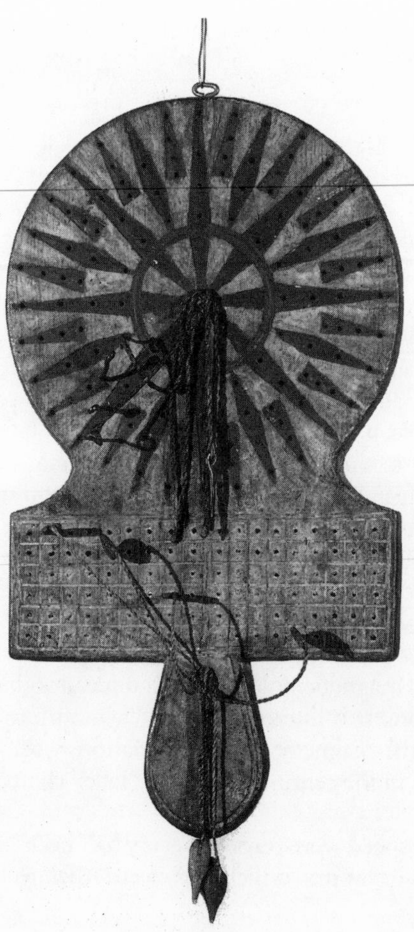

unfamiliar waters the error is cumulative. Both Rosier and Champlain grossly overestimated distances. The Dutchman's log, which was simply timing how long it took the vessel to pass a chip dropped overboard, was little better, for there was no accurate method of measuring seconds or fractions of seconds. The chip log was invented in the mid-seventeenth century. When accurately calibrated, this device is highly reliable. It consists of a pie-shaped "chip" about a foot on a side, ballasted to float upright in the water. To this is attached a line wound on a reel so that it will run out freely. If a fourteen-second sandglass is used, knots are tied in the line every 23.6 feet in accordance with the proportion:

14 seconds in the sandglass: 3,600 seconds in an hour = x (feet between knots): 6,080 feet in a nautical mile

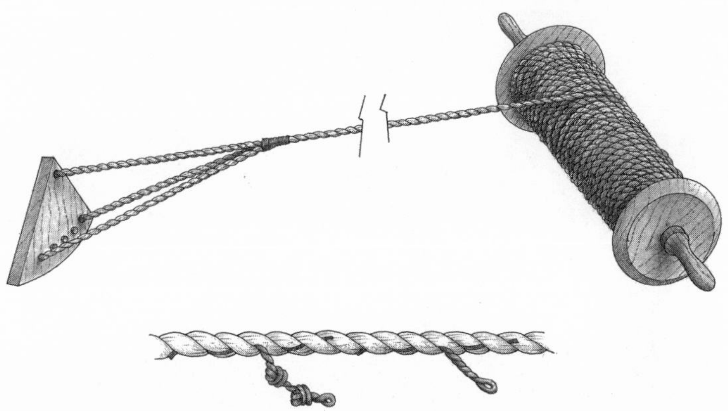

The chip log. As finally developed, it is a very accurate method of determining speed through the water. *Kathy Bray*

If four knots run out in fourteen seconds, then the vessel is traveling four nautical miles per hour. However, when the chip log was first invented, a thirty-second sandglass was used, and seven fathoms as measured by seven stretches of the arms was counted for each nautical mile of speed. Seven fathoms is 42 feet, but for a thirty-second glass the distance per mile should be 50.6 feet. Hence, speeds and distances were overestimated by about 16 percent, assuming that the fathoms were measured accurately.

In water of less than 100 fathoms, the sounding lead was a very valuable aid. Not only did it give the depth of water, but it was armed with tallow stuffed into a hole in its bottom and thus brought up a sample of the bottom.

The pilot's principal aid was his rutter, a book of sailing directions giving courses, distances, soundings, bottom characteristics, and descriptions of landmarks. To this the pilot added his own experience and observations and thus made his way in more or less familiar and well-traveled European waters.

Offshore, the navigator was dependent on the sun and the North Star to fix his latitude. There was no way, before the invention of the chronometer in the mid-eighteenth century, to determine longitude. Consequently, on a voyage to America, the navigator went south from England, which lies in about 50° latitude, made the Azores in about 40°, and then ran west until he found America, working northerly or southerly until he was in the latitude of his intended landfall. To determine his latitude, he took the altitude of the North Star with astrolabe, quadrant, or cross staff. The astrolabe was a disc of brass marked off in degrees around its circumference. It was suspended by a ring at its top. A rotating arm with a peep sight was pointed at the star. The early

Astronomer's astrolabe. The peep sights do not show clearly; they are on the arm directly over the circle illustrating the signs of the zodiac. A degree on the circumference of an instrument 14 inches in diameter is about ⅛ inch. This is an Italian instrument, but the arms of the city of Gloucester, England, are engraved on it. *Peabody Museum of Salem*

quadrant was even simpler: a quadrant, a quarter of a circle, graduated in degrees with a string hung from the apex. The navigator sighted along one edge at the star, while his assistant read off the angle where the plumb line crossed the scale.

A considerable improvement on the astrolabe and quadrant was the cross staff. This was a stick with a sliding stick perpendicular to it. The observer,

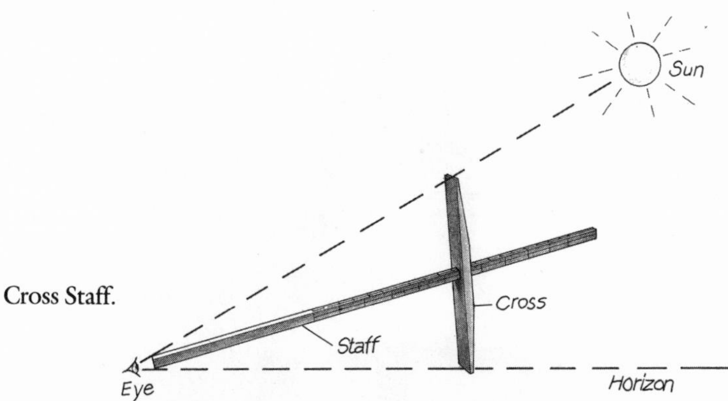

Cross Staff.

Below: Backstaff, or Davis quadrant. The smaller arc is set to an even degree somewhat less than the sun's altitude. The staff is held so that the shadow of the slider (A) falls on the screen (H), which has a slit in it. The observer adjusts the slider on the larger arc (E) so that he sees the horizon through the slit at the same time the shadow falls on it. The altitude is the sum of the angles between the staff and the sun and between the staff and the horizon. A degree on the larger arc might be ½ inch. The altitude could be estimated to within a quarter or an eighth of a degree. *Kathy Bray*

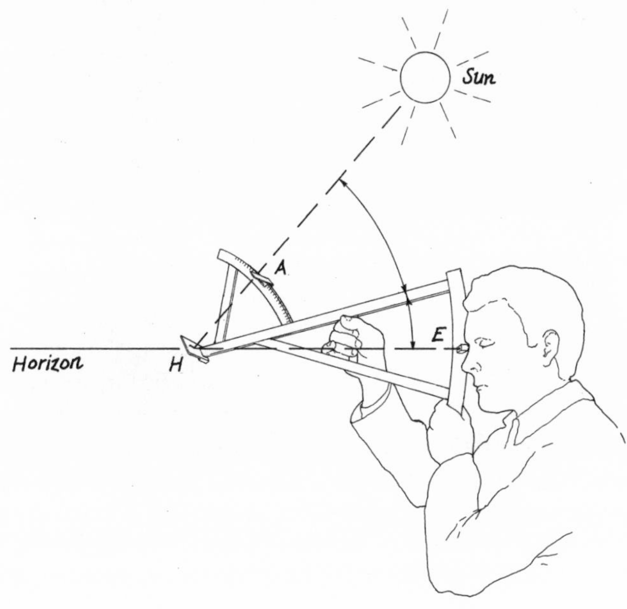

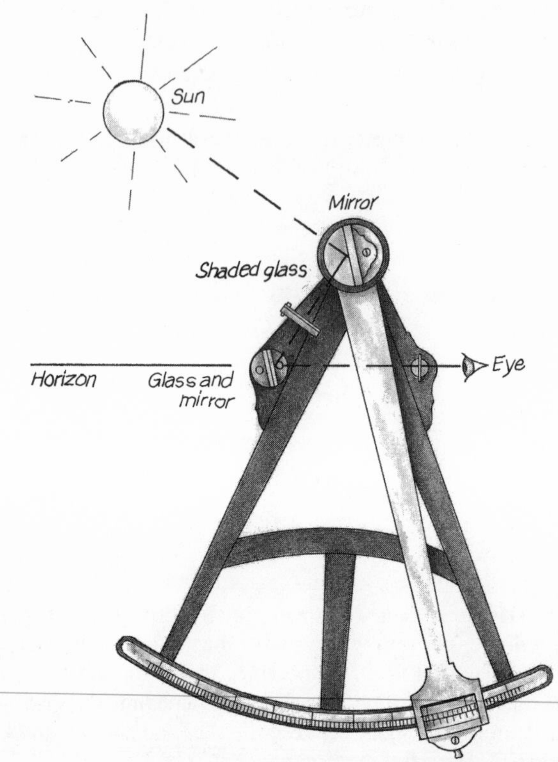

Octant.

with his eye at the inboard end of the longer stick, slid the cross stick to the point at which its upper end touched the star and its lower end touched the horizon. The tangent of half the angle between the star and the horizon was half the length of the cross piece divided by the distance from the observer's eye to the intersection.

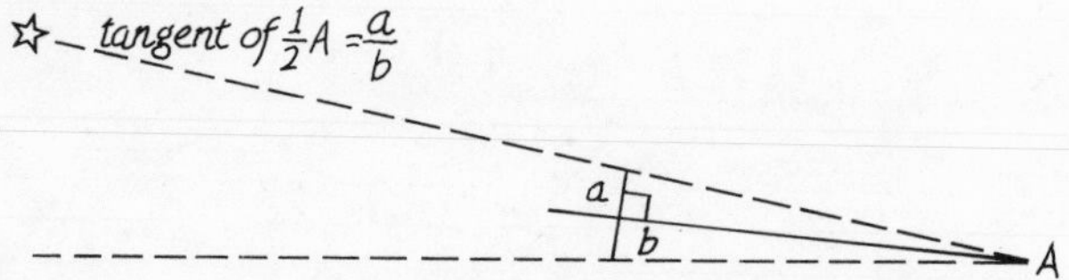

The longer stick could thus be graduated in degrees by the instrument maker and the angle simply read off by the observer at whatever was the position of the cross piece. Sometimes the names of various ports were marked on the staff at whatever was the position of the cross piece according to the altitude of the North Star at that port.

Theoretically, the altitude of the North Star is the latitude. However, the star wandered as much as 3.6° from the Earth's axis in the seventeenth century, so every navigator carried a diagram showing the error according to the position of Kochab, the brightest star in the Little Dipper.

Latitude could also be determined from an observation of the sun when it was on the observer's meridian—that is, when it reached its highest point in the sky, when it bore due south. The astrolabe, quadrant, or cross staff could be used for such an observation, but it meant looking directly at the sun—a difficult, not to say dangerous, procedure. A more effective, accurate, and less dangerous instrument was invented by the Arctic navigator John Davis in the sixteenth century. He called it a backstaff. With this, the observer turned his back to the sun and sighted at the horizon through a slit in a screen at the end of the staff. Then he moved the vertical piece until its shadow fell on the slit. The horizontal staff was graduated proportionally to the tangent of the altitude and could be read directly.

Davis's quadrant was a refinement of the backstaff to achieve greater accuracy. The observer stood with his back to the sun, sighted along the horizontal staff, and moved the lens on the small arc until the image of the sun struck the slit in the screen at the end. Then, to achieve a more precise adjustment, he moved the peep sight down the big arc until he had the bright spot of the sun focused by the lens exactly on the horizon. This instrument was accurate to fractions of a degree. As a degree of altitude is equivalent to a degree of latitude, 60 nautical miles, precision is important. Determination of latitude by this means requires application of a simple formula:

$$\text{Latitude} = 90° - \text{altitude} \pm \text{declination}$$

The declination is the sun's distance north or south of the equator—0° at the equinoxes and $23\frac{1}{2}°$ at the solstices. Tables of declination were easily available in the seventeenth century.

Most of the vessels were too small to carry more than a skiff on deck, so they often carried a shallop knocked down in the hold to be assembled on arrival in America. Waymouth, Smith, Gilbert, and Bradford all speak of doing this. A shallop was a rough, stoutly built workboat, double-ended and usually open, beamy and of rather shoal draft. A small three-ton shallop would be about 26 feet long, $5\frac{1}{2}$ feet wide, and might draw 3 feet. A 12-ton shallop, a big one, might be 39 feet long with a beam of 8 feet 7 inches and a draft of perhaps 4 feet. Shallops were propelled primarily by oars, but also carried a mast and sails. They were used for exploration, for fishing, and sometimes for quite long coastal voyages. Dermer went from Monhegan all the way to Jamestown, Virginia, in a five-ton shallop. We remember that she was an open boat and that he found it important at Jamestown to have her decked before he started back.

On such a trip, the shallop would be rigged to sail, usually with a square mainsail stepped about amidships, and a small square foresail stepped far forward supported by a short bowsprit. A popular variation for coastal work was a spritsail just forward of amidships and a jib or forestaysail, a rig developed by the Dutch. According to William A. Baker, Popham's *Virginia* was

A colonial ketch. *Kathy Bray*

rigged this way. Also, the ketch rig became popular with fishermen in the last half of the century. Rigged usually with a sprit or a square mainsail and with a lateen mizzen astern and later a square main topsail, ketches usually had round sterns and ranged from 10 to 70 tons.

Going to windward, the forward edge of the shallop's mainsail was pulled down tight to the rail with a bowline. The forward edge of the foresail was pulled down to a short bowsprit or braced with a fargood. Although they were probably not very successful going to windward, shallops did well reaching and running.

The line between a shallop decked over and rigged to sail and a pinnace was not clearly defined. However, Baker tells us the pinnace, unlike the double-ended shallop, had a square stern with a single deck and low superstructure forward and aft. Pinnaces ranged from fifteen to two hundred tons and carried a variety of rigs, from sprit mainsail and forestaysail to a full three-masted ship rig. Pinnaces were used in open water, often making transatlantic voyages. In this case, they probably carried square mainsails. Champlain much preferred a pinnace for exploring because she was so much handier than a ship.

In the course of the century, improvements in construction, rig, and navigation were made, but seamen are so conservative and so independent that one never knows in the case of a particular vessel how far the improvements have come. Frames were doubled, made of two pieces overlapping at the joints and fastened together like modern double-sawn frames so they were independently strong and did not depend solely on planking and deckbeams. We see pictures of vessels in the latter part of the century with a fore topmast staysail set from the head of the fore topmast to the end of the bowsprit and eventually with a light extension of the bowsprit, the jib-boom, on which was set a jib on a stay from the masthead. This required a bobstay, martingale, and bowsprit shrouds, which interfered with the sprit sail and led to its disappearance.

Also, the awkward lateen mizzen was replaced with a gaff mizzen and a square mizzen topsail set above it. Fore topsails became common, and top-gallants were added in bigger vessels on fore- and mainmasts. The size of the mainsail was decreased and the size of topsails increased with the abandonment of bonnets and the introduction of reefpoints whereby topsails could be easily reefed. All this work aloft led to the installation of footropes under the yards for sailors to stand on while reefing and furling.

Navigation, too, was improved. The backstaff was developed by Davis into a quadrant before 1600 but only slowly came into use. In 1731 Halley invented the octant, in principle the same as a modern sextant using two mirrors to reflect the image of the sun or star so it appears to the observer to sit on the horizon. The angle between the mirrors is measured on an arc with a vernier, producing accuracy to the order of tenths of a minute.

The chip log was refined to a greater degree of accuracy, and the compass was much improved with the invention of gimbals to keep the bowl more or less level. Halley, in advance of Maury, two centuries later, made a study of the wind system in the Atlantic, reducing the amount of windward work for square-rigged vessels.

Going to sea in any age is hard work and fraught with peril. Eternal vigilance is our only defense. However, during the seventeenth century, a seaman had a reasonable chance of making a transatlantic voyage successfully and, at the end of the century, a much better chance.

NOTES

The best source of information on the rig and construction of seventeenth-century ships is William A. Baker. He did a great deal of research at the time *Mayflower II* was built and wrote *Colonial Vessels* and *Sloops and Shallops*. He also wrote a book specifically on *Mayflower II*. Alan Villiers, who sailed *Mayflower II* across the Atlantic, wrote articles for the May and November 1957 issues of *National Geographic* magazine. *A History of Seamanship,* by Douglas Phillips-Birt, was also very helpful in describing the development of design and rig from medieval to seventeenth-century vessels, essentially the transition from coastal to oceanic seafaring. The sections on navigation were helpful, too. Especially interesting is *The Lore of Ships,* produced by A. B. Nordbok, with articles by a brilliant constellation of marine authorities. Of particular value are the sharp, detailed lithographs of rigging details and old-time navigational instruments.

Information on handling square-rigged vessels came from Alan Villiers' *Way of a Ship,* from his *National Geographic* article on *Mayflower II*'s voyage, and from D'Arcy

Lever's *The Young Sea Officer's Sheet Anchor,* second edition, 1819. This was republished in 1963, a replica of the 1819 edition.

Admiral Morison's *Northern Voyages* continues to be of interest to students of the seventeenth century, particularly with respect to his discussion of living conditions aboard oceangoing vessels. His account of John Davis's contributions to navigational instruments is useful because Davis's inprovements were not made universally and instantaneously but filtered through the marine community during the seventeenth century.

It is interesting that English navigators were scornful of charts, regarding them as merely visual aids to their rutters. Not until the eighteenth century and the development of Mercator projection were charts widely used by the British. The French, however, were much more interested in charts, as Champlain's excellent drawings indicate.

The modern yachtsman in his bottle-tight fiberglass boat—tacking on a dime, rigged with one stick, two sails, and four pieces of running rigging, steered with a powerful destroyer-type wheel, equipped with an engine and electronic navigational gear little short of the miraculous—will profit by imagining the experience of a seventeenth-century navigator exploring an unmarked coast in a bluff-bowed, square-rigged little vessel in the hope of making a profitable voyage out of fish and furs.

SIX

National Politics and High Finance

ALTHOUGH the Plymouth Company continued to send vessels to Monhegan and Damariscove islands annually, no more efforts were made to establish permanent settlements after Dermer's failure in 1619. Sir Ferdinando Gorges, seeing the growing prosperity of The London Company on the Chesapeake, of the Bristol merchants in Newfoundland, and of The Bermuda Company, applied for a new charter, as The Council for New England. It was granted on November 3, 1620, but was held up until June 1621 because it granted the Council a monopoly on trade and fishing. The London Company objected strenuously. They had sent fishing vessels every year to the Maine coast and depended heavily on the catch. They maintained that the sea, like the air, is free to everyone, a position maintained by many nations through subsequent centuries. They took their case to the Privy Council, which decided in favor of Gorges, and then to Parliament, where the issue was kept hot until 1628 when Charles I dissolved Parliament. The monopoly was dropped in 1639 when the charter of The Council for New England was surrendered.

The Council for New England was very different indeed from the old joint stock company. It was composed not of merchants seeking trade but of noblemen seeking dukedoms. The original roster included a duke, two marquises, six earls, a viscount, three barons, nineteen knights, seven esquires, and the dean of Exeter, but no merchants. Its territory ran from 40° to 48° north latitude, from Philadelphia to and including the south coast of Newfoundland, and "from sea to sea." It overlapped the grants both of The London Company on the south and The Bristol Company on the north. Furthermore, King James in his innocence—or ignorance—had no concept whatever of what lay between the Atlantic and Pacific oceans or even how far it was.

The vast area was held "in free and common socage after the manor of East Greenwich." That is, the Council owned it as one might own any estate in England. It remained part of the realm, subject to the King's authority, and its inhabitants were Englishmen still and retained all the rights of English citizens. However, within this territory the Council was granted broad and specific powers: The Council could divide and subdivide the land, making grants to whomever it wished. It could erect a government, appoint a governor with "martial powers," appoint other officials, make laws, set up courts, exercise a monopoly on trade and fishing forbidding outsiders "to visit, frequent, trade or adventure to traffick into or from the said territories, lands, rivers, and places aforesaid," and it could even found other colonies. The territory was to be free of customs for seven years and all taxes on imports to England for twenty-one years except for the usual 5 percent which the King levied on gold, silver, and copper coming from his lands. In short, the Council could divide the northern part of what is now the United States and the southern part of what is now Canada into a number of practically independent nations, subject only to the King of England. Sir Ferdinando Gorges saw himself as governor general of this feudal empire. He planned to appoint an admiral for marine affairs, a master of ordnance, a bishop, chancellor, treasurer, and such other offices as were necessary. This would be a council consisting of those patentees resident in New England and a general assembly of representatives from the various sub-grants called at the pleasure of the governor to make laws.

Almost the first thing the Council did in 1621 was to release the land from the St. Croix River to the St. Lawrence. King James I of England, who was also King James VI of Scotland, acting in his capacity of Scottish King, granted this territory to Sir William Alexander, a Scot with grand ambitions to found an empire in America to be named Nova Scotia, and so it is today.

In the same year the Council received an application from the Pilgrims resident in Plymouth. When they left England in 1620, they had a grant from The London Company to settle south of the Hudson River, but they had landed north of that so had no legal right to their land. The Council granted a charter to John Pierce and associates, the associates being the Pilgrims, but the charter specified no boundaries to their land. John Pierce and associates could settle at Plymouth or anywhere else they chose. The Pilgrims, of course, were already established at Plymouth, but Pierce, in 1623, made two attempts to establish a colony in Maine. He did not make it across the Atlantic, but his son, Richard Pierce, probably the next year established a settlement at Broad Bay, the upper part of Muscongus Bay. In 1625 John Brown of New Harbor bought from the Indian Samoset a large tract on the east side of the Pemaquid peninsula including Richard Pierce's settlement. Then Pierce married Brown's daughter and, with Brown's agreement, purchased the land on which he (Pierce) was settled from Samoset in a separate deed. Overlapping this pleasant family arrangement, in 1631 the Council granted Robert Aldworth and Gyles Eldridge 12,000 acres bounded by a line from the headwaters of the Damariscotta River to the headwaters of the Medomak, including the land granted to John Pierce, bought by Brown from Samoset and sold by Brown to Richard Pierce. It was known as the Pemaquid Grant.

The Council proceeded at once to make other grants to its members and friends. Possibly Weston, Wollaston, and Morton had grants for their attempts to settle on the shores of Massachusetts Bay. In 1622 John Mason was granted land on Cape Ann and northward, and in the same year Sir Ferdinando Gorges and Mason were granted the land from the Merrimac to the Kennebec. Later, in 1629, Mason took the land from the Merrimac to the Piscataqua and called it New Hampshire, while Gorges kept the coast from the Piscataqua to the Kennebec and called it New Somerset. In December of the same year Robert Gorges, son of Sir Ferdinand, was given land on Massachusetts Bay. In 1623 Christopher Levett was given a grant within New Somerset, Gorge's territory, and made governor general of New England.

After this flurry of action, the Council did almost nothing until 1629. Most of its members were involved in the war with France declared in 1626 and in the conflict between Charles I and his Parliament. Sir Ferdinando himself was military governor of the port of Plymouth in England and was personally involved in naval expeditions. However, in 1629, after Parliament was dissolved and peace was made with France, the Council turned its attention again to New England.

Robert Gorges' effort to settle on Massachusetts Bay had been unsuccessful, so a grant was made, overlapping his grant and that of Mason on Cape Ann, to a group of Puritans called The New England Company. This grant extended from three miles south of the Charles River to three miles north of the Merrimac, thus establishing the present southern border of New Hampshire. These Puritans, viewing the many conflicting grants, went over the head of the Council and applied directly to the King for a charter, including the territory of The New England Company, setting up the Massachusetts Bay Company and in 1630 came to Boston with their charter, thus making themselves independent of the Council.

In 1629 the Council granted to the Plymouth Pilgrims land on the upper Kennebec above Swan Island for a fur-trading post.

In 1630 the Council made the Muscongus grant to John Beauchamp and Thomas Leverett of Boston, England, or land from Pemaquid to the Penobscot, where the French were established. This grant was later taken up by Samuel Waldo, who settled on the Medomak River. It was then called the Waldo Patent.

Also in 1630 two other grants were made. One was to a group who planned to settle on the Kennebec but who sold out in 1643 to Alexander Rigby and George Cleeves, their land becoming part of Lygonia, a semi-independent province extending from Casco Bay to Cape Porpoise which lasted from 1646 to 1652. Gorges named it Lygonia after his mother, whose maiden name was Lygon. It was also called the Plough Grant because the occupants came over on the ship *Plough*. The other grant was of land on the Saco River to Lewes, Boynthon, Oldham, and Richard Vines.

In 1631 Aldworth and Eldridge were granted the Pemaquid patent mentioned above and Ferdinando Gorges, grandson of Sir Ferdinando, received 12,000 acres on both sides of the York River. Robert Trelawney received Richmond Island and Cape Elizabeth.

In 1632 Acadia was given to France. When Charles I had married Henrietta Maria, sister of Louis XIII, in 1625, she had brought a dowry of 800,000 crowns, only half of which was paid. When peace was made with France in 1629, it was agreed that Acadia would go to France as soon as the outstanding 400,000 crowns were paid. In 1632 the payment was made, and at the Treaty of St. Germain English claims to Acadia were surrendered. However, no boundary to Acadia was mentioned. The French claimed to the Kennebec, the English to the Penobscot. The English were driven out of trading posts at Pentagoet (Castine) and Machias. Sir William Alexander was ousted from Nova Scotia. To make up for his loss of this territory, the Council gave him the territory from Pemaquid to the St. Croix River, thus giving him land already given to France by the Treaty of St. Germain and to Beauchamp and Leverett in the Muscongus grant. The Marquis of Hamilton was granted from Pemaquid to the Kennebec, partly overlapping the Pemaquid patent of only four years previous.

Things had now reached such a state of confusion that the Council appealed to the King, declaring the Massachusetts Bay Charter illegal and asking that the King take over the government of New England. The King agreed and in May of 1637 ordered the Massachusetts Bay Charter surrendered. The Boston Puritans did not surrender their charter. They had taken it to Boston and were in no hurry to let it go. However, the King, assuming that they had surrendered it, accepted the surrender of the charter for The Council for New England, confirmed all the grants made by the Council including that to Robert Gorges, thus voiding the Massachusetts Bay Charter, and appointed Sir Ferdinando governor general of New England.

This radical move, however, was no solution. Mason had exhausted his resources trying to colonize New Hampshire and had died. Sir Ferdinando Gorges had spent almost all of his fortune on America. The ship he was building to carry himself and his entourage to his new domain "broke" on launching, and finally in 1638 the Scots rebelled against the King, requiring both his and the King's attention; and New England was left, officially, with no government at all.

In 1639 Charles I gave Sir Ferdinando a new charter to the Province of Maine,* now extending from the Piscataqua to the Kennebec. This charter made the territory practically an independent feudal empire. Any lands granted were to be held under Gorges, not under the King, although Gorges was still nominally subject to the King. Maine was now on the same political basis as Maryland, and Gorges held the same status as did Lord Baltimore. This was at

* Sir Ferdinando Gorges appears to be the first to have used the name Maine in an official, formal sense. It was a common term used to distinguish the mainland from the islands. Rosier writes, "From hence [Monhegan] we might discern the maine land from the West-South-West to the East-North-East, and a great way . . . up into the maine we might discerne very high mountains." Gorges established his capital city, Gorgeana, on the maine. Also Queen Henrietta Maria, wife of Charles I, inherited the Province of Maine in France. Gorges was a Royalist, a loyal supporter of King Charles, and may have named his new state as a compliment to his queen.

last what Gorges had wanted from the beginning, and in his remaining years he made the most of it, even though he never crossed the Atlantic.

Gorges established his capital at the mouth of the York River, chartering a "city" in 1642 to be called Gorgeana (now York). It was to be complete with a bishop, a mayor, and twelve aldermen. As deputy governor general of the whole province, Sir Ferdinando appointed his cousin, Thomas Gorges.

Meanwhile, dispute arose between the heirs of Robert Trelawney on Richmond Island and Cape Elizabeth and George Cleeves, who with Thomas Cammock had settled at Black Point at the mouth of the Spurwink River without a charter. The grants to Christopher Levett on Casco Bay and to Richard Vines at Saco were also involved in the dispute. Cleeves secured the help of Alexander Rigby, a member of the powerful Puritan Parliament, and secured from Parliament the right to purchase Lygonia, which extended from the Kennebec to Cape Porpoise. Vines, now deputy governor general of the Province of Maine, protested. The matter was referred to the Commissioners of Foreign Plantations, who decided in 1647 in favor of Cleeves, thus leaving the Province of Maine only the land from the Piscataqua to Cape Porpoise, including the towns of Kittery, Gorgeana, and Wells.

In 1647 Sir Ferdinando died, well along in his eighties, never having seen the land which he had worked so hard to govern. On his death, inasmuch as he owned the entire region, there was no legal government. Accordingly, the local inhabitants very sensibly set up their own government, proclaiming themselves a body politic and electing Edward Godfrey governor "by most voysses." This was a solution entirely satisfactory to the inhabitants, but Massachusetts, casting a covetous eye on the fish, fur, and timber resources of Maine, resurveyed its borders and found that their charter extended to the Presumpscot River just east of Portland. This included all of the Province of Maine and much of Lygonia. Godfrey appealed to the King for redress, but the King by this time was deeply involved in the Civil War in England and had neither time nor authority to settle the dispute. The Parliament, dominated by Puritans, was unlikely to support the heirs of Gorges, who had been steadfastly loyal to the King, and decided in favor of Puritan Massachusetts.

In 1652 the Great and General Court of Massachusetts sent commissioners to Maine, accompanied by an impressive military escort, and received the submission of Kittery and York (formerly Gorgeana) and, in the next year, of Wells, and of Lygonia as far as Saco. In 1658 the settlers east to the Presumpscot submitted. Having previously taken over New Hampshire, Massachusetts now controlled all of New England west of the Presumpscot River. The coastal communities east of the Presumpscot were still without official government.

On the restoration of the Stuart monarchy in 1660, King Charles II ordered Massachusetts to give up New Hampshire to the Mason heirs and sent commissioners to establish royal government in Maine, a task which they found impossible. Sensing the political vacuum, Massachusetts again sent commissioners to Maine with an impressive escort in 1667 and established a government. In 1677, to clear the title, the Great and General Court bought out the interest of the Gorges heirs for £1,270. Thus, Maine to the Kennebec became part of Massachusetts. The Sagadahoc territory from the Kennebec to the Penobscot remained a disputed territory between the English and the French.

This prolonged argument litigation and awarding of grants, counter-grants, and charters is of relatively little ultimate significance. The "men of blood and substance" who formed The Council for New England and those to whom they made grants were seeking to perpetuate in America a feudal society, which was to suffer a mortal blow in the Puritan Revolution and which was to expire rapidly in the succeeding century. These men were not farmers, fishermen, lumbermen, traders; they were gentlemen born to rule the middle and lower classes. They saw themselves, when suitable places had been made for them, living in manor houses, presiding over councils which they appointed, making laws, administering justice, and collecting rents from the peasantry and taxes from the traders. They had no conception even of the size of their territories and much less of the Atlantic gales that lay between them and a virtually unknown and unexplored continent, heavily forested for the most part, penetrated by rivers far greater than England's placid streams, and inhabited by an intelligent, proud, native people well adapted to their environment. The proprietors, signing papers, drawing lines on inaccurate maps, were building paper empires, and the papers were all in England. Not even their shadows fell on the wilderness of Maine.

On the western shore of the Atlantic along what is now the coast of Maine grew up small settlements of fishermen, at first just summertime visitors, who filled their holds with salt fish, topped off with such furs as they could purchase from the Indians, and departed. By the early 1620s groups were staying over the winter at Damariscove, Monhegan, Pemaquid, and possibly elsewhere. These were not permanent colonies in the sense that Plymouth was permanent. Vessels would cross the Atlantic loaded with provisions, salt, fishing gear, and several shallops knocked down in their holds. Once here, the shallops would be assembled, fish flakes built, and perhaps a shed in which to store gear. The crew would catch and cure the fish until a cargo was assembled. The vessel would then sail for an English or European port, leaving a small crew ashore to continue fishing through the winter. When the vessel returned with provisions, a good start would have been made on a return cargo. On the next trip, some of those who had stayed the winter might return and others might stay over. Although no families were thus early established and people did not abandon their property in England to make a new home in Maine, year-round settlements grew in population and number through the 1620s.

These were rough and ready people. They faced the cold, the fog, the gales, and the rough seas to get cargoes of fish ashore. They cured fish, and they ate, drank, roughhoused, and fought. They paid no attention to The Council for New England and its declared monopolies, prohibitions, governors, and charters. In these practically anarchic fishing settlements, maritime Maine was born.

NOTES

This rather dessicated chapter is derived from Andrews's *Colonial Period of American History* and Hatch's *Maine, A History*. The chapter's principal significancés are first, that coastal Maine became part of Massachusetts, and second, that the inhabitants of Maine, those who lived and worked on the coast, became independent of the nominal owners and rulers of Maine. Shadows and echoes of their independent spirit are evident through the succeeding chapters of this work and are even discernible today to the alert observer.

SEVEN

The French in Acadia

WHILE THE ENGLISH were establishing fishing and farming communities on the coast of western Maine, the French were tightening their hold from the Penobscot River east. When the Baron de Poutrincourt was killed at Méry in 1615, his son, Biencourt, took his father's title and maintained his father's commitment to Acadia. He rebuilt Port Royal, established a fort at Cape Sable, and maintained a fur trade with the Indians. In 1618 he wrote a letter to Autorités de la Ville de Paris urging support of the fur trade and the fortification of Acadia against the incursions of the English.

About this time Claude La Tour and his fourteen-year-old son Charles appeared in Acadia, and so impressive was Charles's behavior that Biencourt, now Baron de Poutrincourt, left him all his claims in America.

King James I of England, however, had granted to Sir William Alexander in 1621 the territory between the St. Croix and St. Lawrence rivers. This, of course, included all of Acadia, claimed by France. Alexander, eager to colonize his new domain, sent out "Admiral" Kirke and his brothers to capture Québec and drive the French out of Canada. They did indeed capture Québec in 1629, and thus it was assumed in England that all of Acadia was British. Kirke also captured Claude La Tour at sea and took him to England.

His son, Charles La Tour, having been left in command of the fort at Cape Sable, had appealed to Louis XIII in 1627 for help against Alexander and Admiral Kirke. To make his position stronger, Charles also asked to be made commander of French forces in Acadia.

When the elder La Tour, Claude, arrived in England a prisoner of Kirke, he smoothly renounced his French citizenship, married a "lady of honour" in the English court, and was made a baronet of Nova Scotia by Alexander. He was granted a baronial tract of land at Cape Sable, land held by his son Charles, under the French king. Alexander sent Claude to Cape Sable with two ships to dislodge Charles and take possession of the estate he had been granted.

See chronology for this chapter on page 105.

Claude offered Charles very generous terms if he would abandon the fort and change sides. This he refused to do. Claude attacked, and Charles beat off the assault. Claude, having failed in his mission, could not return to Scotland but was allowed by his son Charles to stay at Cape Sable if he would agree never to enter the fort. A house was built for him nearby, and there he settled.

However, Charles, "a chameleon where principles took the color of his interests," in 1630 appealed to Alexander, was himself made a baronet of Nova Scotia, and was, like his father, granted generous acreage to be held under the Scottish crown. At the same time he was granted by Louis XIII land on the St. John River and, ever the chameleon, got a grant to the same land from Alexander.

In 1632, however, by the Treaty of St. Germain concluding the smoldering conflict during which Charles I of England tried to support the French Huguenots, Acadia was returned to France, its boundaries uncertain. The British acted as if Acadia extended no farther than the St. Croix River, and the French assumed that the coast as far west as the Kennebec, or at least as far as Muscongus Bay, was theirs. Razilly, sent by Louis XIII to take possession of Acadia, took over Port Royal in August 1632, and with the help of his lieutenant, d'Aulnay, assumed control of Nova Scotia and Maine. Charles La Tour, responding immediately to the change in the political climate, went to France and received from the King a confirmation of his grant of land at Cape Sable, and the titles of Lieutenant General at Fort Loméron and Commander at Cape Sable, the latter from The Company of New France.

Hardly had he returned to Cape Sable than Razilly died suddenly, leaving d'Aulnay in charge, claiming authority over all Acadia. But La Tour declared himself independent of d'Aulnay by virtue of his grant from King Louis, thus drawing the lines for nearly twenty years of conflict marked with violence, betrayal, and deceit.

At the same time in England, Gorges and The Council for New England, assuming that the Treaty of St. Germain left them in possession of the coast to the St. Croix River, sold to the Pilgrims at Plymouth the right to trade with the Indians on the Maine coast. Richard Vines set up a trading post on the Machias River, probably at Clarks Point, in 1633. Charles La Tour at Saint John heard of it, came to investigate, and after harsh words with Vines, agreed that he could trade off the remainder of his stock and depart if he would promise to set up no post and make no fortifications east of Pemaquid. Vines agreed, but reestablished the post with five men, two small cannon, and a small vessel loaded with trade goods and considerable "strong water." La Tour came to inspect in Vines's absence, alleged that some of the merchandise had been stolen from his post at Saint John, killed two of the five men—"by accident," he later claimed—seized the vessel and the other three men, and sent all to France.

D'Aulnay visited the Pilgrims' trading post at Pentagoet (later named Castine), seized all trade goods there, gave a note for them, redeemable at his convenience and at such time as the bearer would come to Port Royal to collect.

D'Aulnay had asked for La Tour's help in dislodging the English, but La Tour refused, hoping that d'Aulnay would return to France and forget about Acadia. In 1638 d'Aulnay did return to France but only to marry Jeanne Motin and return with a number of colonists to live at Port Royal. Meeting the challenge, La Tour wrote to his agent, Desjardins, in France to send him a wife. He sent Marie Jacquelin, a loyal, energetic, and resourceful support to her opportunistic spouse.

Shortly after the marriages, La Tour, with two armed pinnaces, attacked an expedition of d'Aulnay's on its way back from reinforcing the fort at Pentagoet. La Tour was defeated, captured, taken to Port Royal, and cast into d'Aulnay's new dungeon. He was shortly released on promise of good behavior, and d'Aulnay took the case to court in France. He won; La Tour's commission was revoked, and he was ordered to return to France. However, believing that the King's arm was not long enough to reach from Paris to the St. John River, La Tour ignored the summons. The King sent six soldiers to help d'Aulnay apprehend La Tour. When La Tour defied d'Aulnay's second summons, d'Aulnay returned to France for further authority and, in 1642, sent three gentlemen and four sailors to capture La Tour. La Tour crumpled up the King's warrant for his arrest, threw it on the floor, and cast the posse of seven into his dungeon. Then, seeking help where he could get it, he sailed for Boston, where he arrived in June 1643.

Showing Governor Winthrop his old commission from King Louis XIII, La Tour admitted that he had made off with the vessel and trade goods belonging to Vines at Machias ten years before, made restitution, and persuaded Winthrop to charter him four armed vessels. In July he drove d'Aulnay's ships, which were still at Saint John, back to Port Royal, burned a mill there, and stole a pinnace loaded with furs.

The next summer, 1644, La Tour again went to Massachusetts for help, but this time in vain. Madame La Tour, who had been back to France, had been forbidden to leave that country. However, she escaped and took passage for Saint John, but the vessel made Boston instead of Saint John. She chartered three vessels in Boston and returned to Fort La Tour on the banks of the St. John River.

In October of 1644, d'Aulnay sent an envoy to Boston with proof that La Tour was a rebel against the King of France and against his own duly constituted authority. The envoy made peace with the Puritans and concluded a trade agreement.

While the envoy was in Boston, d'Aulnay tried again to arrest La Tour but was again refused, Madame La Tour in particular carrying on like a madwoman against him. He returned to Port Royal. Madame La Tour advised her husband to go back to Boston, renounce Catholicism, and agree to divide Acadia with Massachusetts in return for help against d'Aulnay. While he was gone, eight soldiers from Fort La Tour defected to d'Aulnay, not wishing to support a rebel. They told d'Aulnay that La Tour had gone to Boston and that the fort's garrison was depleted. D'Aulnay scratched together every man he could and sailed for Saint John, On the way, he captured Captain Grafton, who had been hired by La Tour to carry supplies from Boston to resupply his fort. D'Aulnay sent Grafton and his crew back to Boston in a leaky shallop and kept his vessel. He then attacked Fort La Tour.

Madame La Tour put up a fierce defense; but at last, several of her few soldiers having been killed, she had to surrender to superior numbers. D'Aulnay paraded her on the wall of the fort with a rope around her neck while most of her surviving garrison were hanged as rebels. Three weeks later she died in prison of hate, pain, rage, disappointment, and humiliation.

While his wife was stubbornly defending his fort in vain, La Tour lived on Noddles Island in Boston Harbor with Samuel Maverick. Unable to get help in Boston, he went to Newfoundland to seek help from Kirke, who almost twenty years before had captured his father. Failing in this endeavor, La Tour returned to Boston and persuaded a merchant to charter him a ship loaded with trade goods for Indians. He cruised down to his old home at Cape Sable, set the Boston crew ashore, and went off with the ship.

With La Tour out of the way, d'Aulnay went to France in 1647 and told the whole story to Mazarin, then regent for nine-year-old Louis XIV. Mazarin, acting for the King, generously gave d'Aulnay the continent of North America from Virginia to the North Pole for his own private domain, any grants he made to be held in fief to him, not to the French crown.

D'Aulnay moved his headquarters from Port Royal to Saint John and, among other things, strengthened the fort and the garrison at Pentagoet.

By this time Pentagoet was a solid bastion of French rule. The fort controlled the entrance to the Penobscot River and all its tributaries as well as the route from the Penobscot through Smith Cove, across a short carry to Orcutt Harbor through what is now Brooksville and down Eggemoggin Reach to the eastern country, making it an ideal center for the fur trade of the Penobscot River valley and the coastal country eastward. Here stood a solid stone fort mounting eighteen cannon and surrounded by a stout palisade. It had a garrison of eighteen soldiers, and there was a small settlement with farmland and an orchard. D'Aulnay also had a farm, a mill, and cattle on the west side of Penobscot Bay, near South Cushing. At Pentagoet there was a boatyard that in 1636 launched several small sloops and a 60-ton pinnace, *Saint Francis de Pentagoet*. She is known to have visited La Rochelle in 1641 and 1646. Later, two small ships, three-masted, square-rigged vessels of about seventy tons each, were built. Pentagoet was not self-sufficient, however, and imported supplies from France. Supplies were purchased also in Boston and from Abraham Shurt at Pemaquid, evidence that enterprising Massachusetts traders ventured east of Pemaquid and that despite the machinations of kings, cardinals, and boards of directors, the French, English, and Indians traded where it was easiest and where it was most profitable.

Despite the strength of the French presence at Pentagoet, however, the white population of the coast, both French and English, was sparse, widely scattered, and shifting.

There may have been a French trading post at Machias, and a few isolated French families lived along the Maine coast. In 1650 the population of Acadia was said to be about 500, most of them at Cape Sable, Port Royal, Saint John, and Pentagoet.

On May 24, 1650, d'Aulnay and his valet capsized in a canoe. The valet survived long enough to be rescued, but d'Aulnay died of exposure clinging to the bottom of the capsized craft. At this point Charles La Tour came to the surface again, appealed to Mazarin, acting for Louis XIV, now twelve. Mazarin reversed his previous decisions and gave Acadia to La Tour in defiance of the claims of Madame d'Aulnay, her eight children, and d'Aulnay's agent Le Borgne, to whom d'Aulnay had been heavily in debt.

To protect and provide for her children, Madame d'Aulnay now married La Tour. Le Borgne got a piece of Acadia, as did La Tour's former partner, Denys.

In 1654, Cromwell, Lord Protector of England, sent Robert Sedgewick to attack the Dutch colony at New York. However, when he reached Boston on his way to New York, he found that Cromwell had made peace with Holland. Reluctant to go home with nothing done, he improved the occasion by attacking Acadia, for England was still at war with France. Sedgewick captured Port Royal, Saint John, and Pentagoet, leaving England to assume ownership of all Acadia by right of conquest.

For one last time La Tour again changed sides, went to England, and claimed Nova Scotia as a baronet under the old Alexander grant of 1630. The Council of State in England granted Acadia to William Crowne, Sir Thomas Temple, and La Tour in 1656. La Tour sold out his interest to Temple for one-twentieth of the annual income of Acadia, and died in 1663. Crowne and Temple divided Acadia, Crowne taking from Muscongus Bay to the St. Croix River. He moved to Pentagoet and began energetically to develop it and encourage trade with Massachusetts, and built a fur-trading post at Negew, the site of Bangor. However, in 1660 Crowne leased both posts and his whole grant to Temple. The agreement lists the equipment of Pentagoet as an active little town including an orchard, sheep, cows, swine, boats, shallops, and canoes.

In 1660 Charles II came to the throne of England, and in 1661, on the death of Mazarin, Louis XIV assumed personal reign of France. Their commercial, religious, and political rivalries and those with Sweden and Holland led to years of warfare punctuated by treaties in which colonial claims and possessions were bargaining chips, Acadia with the rest.

In 1667, by the Treaty of Breda among England, Holland, France, and Denmark, Acadia to the St. George River was returned to France, but not until 1670 was Temple persuaded by the direct and peremptory command of Charles II to turn the fort at Pentagoet over to the new French governor of

Acadia, Grandfontaine. He had come from France with thirty men, thirty women, tools, supplies, and trade goods to populate Acadia. He made his headquarters at Pentagoet. Grandfontaine's 1671 report showed the total white population of Acadia east of the Penobscot to be 389. At Pentagoet he reported twenty-five soldiers and one family but no domesticated animals or cultivated land. He recommended a fort on the St. George River as a deterrent to the English, whose easternmost house was John Brown's at New Harbor. He reported twelve or fifteen houses at Pemaquid and twenty-five to thirty on the Kennebec.

In the same year, 1671, a nineteen-year-old ensign, Vincent de l'Abadis, Baron de St. Castin, was made Grandfontaine's second in command, a man who, with his sons after him, was to have a strong influence on French Acadia and was to leave his name on the town on the Bagaduce River, hitherto Pentagoet.

Grandfontaine and Castin, temporarily at least at peace with England, worked to build the fur trade with the Indians, and with the English at Boston and particularly with Thomas Gardiner at Pemaquid and Silvanus Davis on the Kennebec. English fishermen were permitted to fish in Acadian waters under license. One has reason to suspect that French efforts to encourage trade met with instant success. There can be little doubt that the French at Pentagoet, Port Royal, Saint John, and trading posts between had been trading with the English for years and that fishermen, regardless of nationality, had been fishing where they found fish and selling in the most profitable market. Furthermore, the colonists had been enticing the Catholic, feudalistic French with notions of Protestantism and democracy.

In 1673 Grandfontaine returned to France, leaving Pentagoet, now no more than an isolated fort, in the hands of Chambly. Discouraged, Chambly reported to Frontenac, governor of Canada in Québec, that Pentagoet was not fit for human habitation but agreed with Frontenac that it must be held as a check to English encroachment.

In the previous year, 1672, in accordance with a secret agreement between Louis XIV and Charles II involving more skulduggery than I have time or inclination to explain, England declared war on Holland. In 1674, as a sideshow to that war, the Dutch captain Jurrien Aernouts in *Flying Horse* was sent from Curaçao to expel the English from New York. However, like Sedgewick before him, when he reached New York, he found that a treaty had been signed making peace between England and Holland. At New York he met John Rhoades, a Boston merchant, who suggested that inasmuch as the Dutch were still fighting the French, an unemployed warrior would do well to attack Pentagoet, key to French control of the Maine coast. Piloted by Rhoades, Captain Aernouts attacked and captured the fort on August 1, 1674, with Chambly and Baron de St. Castin. As an inducement to join the Dutch, Aernouts burned a slow match between Castin's fingers, but Castin refused. Aernouts destroyed the fort and went on to sack Machias, Jemseg, and Saint

John, adding Marson, commander at Jemseg on the St. John River, to his captives. Unable to persuade Castin to join him, Aernouts sent him to Frontenac at Québec to collect 1,000 pounds of beaver as ransom for Chambly and Marson, whom he took to Boston.

I find no record that the ransom was ever delivered, but Chambly was released after some time. Castin went to live with the Indians. (More of Castin's story is told in Chapter 10.) The Dutch claimed Acadia from Saint John to the Penobscot River and temporarily occupied Pentagoet. It developed rapidly into a base for pirates of all nationalities and became such a threat to New England trade that an expedition from Boston recaptured it in 1676. However, the outbreak of King Philip's War and the subsequent European wars between France and England, each of which country enlisted the help of Indians, almost entirely drove white settlers out of Maine until the fall of Québec in 1759.

In summary, the seventeenth century saw the "discovery" of the coast, already doubtless well known to fishermen, by voyagers seeking opportunities for colonization by joint stock companies in England and by royal grantees in France. The monarchs of both countries chartered companies and gave grants freely, grants which overlapped not only those of the rival nation but those that they made themselves. Meanwhile the English, maintaining a presence as far as Pemaquid, set up fishing and fur-trading stations, established farming communities, and began a trade in lumber and naval stores. The French, controlling the coast as far west as Pentagoet and the Penobscot River, established a few strong forts, the westernmost at Pentagoet, as centers for the fur trade. Informally, recorded in the most desultory fashion, individual families and small groups, no doubt some of them fugitives, settled in widely scattered communities, few of them of any permanence. Traders, buccaneers, privateers, and fishermen sailed the coast, making profits as they could. An Acadian officer, Sieur Bergier, in 1685 describes the inhabitants as "mostly fugitives from England, guilty of the death of their late King, and accused of conspiracy against their present sovereign; others of them are pirates, and they are all united in a sort of independent republic." In 1665 a commission sent out by the Duke of York—in vain, as it developed—to establish government east of the Kennebec, reported: "Upon 3 rivers east of the Kennebec, the Shipscot, Damariscotta, and Pemaquid, there are three plantations; The greater hath not more than 20 houses, and they are inhabited by the worst of men. They have hitherto noe government, and are made up of such as to avoid paying their debts and being punished have fled hither; for the most part they are fishermen, and share in their wives as they do in their boats."

Francis B. Greene, author of a history of the Boothbay region, takes a more understanding view.

"There is little doubt but that the general condition of this first settlement was, at the date of these transactions, wretched in the extreme. Without church or school privileges, no government, no market, no improvement, fifty years of this kind of life had told upon these people, who were simply the worn-out result of vanished schemes."

NOTES

A chronology of this complex chapter may be welcome:

1618 Poutrincourt is established at Port Royal and Cape Sable.

1621 James I of England, James VI of Scotland, grants Sir William Alexander Nova Scotia and New Brunswick.

1627 Charles La Tour, heir of Poutrincourt, petitions Louis XIII for help from Alexander and Kirke.

1629 Kirke captures Québec and Claude La Tour.

1630 Claude La Tour, made a baronet of Nova Scotia under Alexander, attacks son Charles at Cape Sable and is repulsed. Charles is made a baronet of Nova Scotia under Alexander and given land on Cape Sable, and is granted land at Saint John by Louis XIII and by Alexander.

1632 The Treaty of St. Germain gives Acadia to France. Razilly takes over Port Royal and rest of Acadia as governor. Louis XIII confirms Charles La Tour's title to Cape Sable and Saint John. La Tour moves to Saint John and builds a fort there.

1633 La Tour attacks Pilgrim trading post at Machias.

1635 Razilly dies, leaving d'Aulnay as governor. D'Aulnay attacks Pentagoet and builds a fort there. La Tour refuses to accept his authority.

1638 D'Aulnay returns to France, marries, and comes back to Port Royal.

8–1642 La Tour attacks an expedition of d'Aulnay's to reinforce Pentagoet, is defeated and captured himself.

French court decides in favor of d'Aulnay. La Tour is ordered to report to France and refuses three summonses.

1643 La Tour goes to Boston, gets help from Puritans, and attacks Port Royal.

1644 Madame La Tour goes to France and returns to Saint John via Boston. Charles La Tour goes to Boston for help, in vain.

D'Aulnay, by an envoy, discredits La Tour in Boston; d'Aulnay again attempts to arrest La Tour.

1645 La Tour goes to Boston again. A party of soldiers and friars defects from La Tour to d'Aulnay.

D'Aulnay captures La Tour's fort, despite Madame La Tour's resistance.

1647 D'Aulnay is granted North America from Virginia north.

1650 D'Aulnay dies.

1651 La Tour is made governor of Acadia.

1653 Madame d'Aulnay marries La Tour.

1654 Sedgewick captures Pentagoet, Saint John, and Port Royal for the British.

1656 Council of State in England grants Acadia to Crowne, Temple, and La Tour. The latter sells his interest.

1660 Charles II succeeds to the English throne.

1661 Louis XIV assumes personal rule in France.

1667 The Treaty of Breda restores Acadia to France.

1670 Grandfontaine is made governor of Acadia and takes over Pentagoet.
1673 Chambly takes over Pentagoet under Frontenac.
1674 Aernouts captures Pentagoet for the Dutch.
1676 Massachusetts recaptures Pentagoet.
King Philip's War breaks out in Maine.

This long and complicated story is found in Francis Parkman's *The Old Regime in Canada* and *Pioneers of France in the New World.* Valuable supplementary information comes from *The French at Pentagoet* by Alaric and Gretchen Faulkner. This is a well-documented and well-illustrated history of the fort at Castine, which was excavated by archaeologists. The "dig" was concluded in 1984. Admiral Morison's *The Story of Mount Desert Island* and *Narrative of the Town of Machias,* by George W. Drisko, have also been helpful and will be referred to in later chapters.

Unfortunately, these authorities disagree at various points, not only with reference to their attitudes and interpretations but as to their facts. Aernouts is a pirate in Parkman's account but holds a commission from William of Orange in Faulkner's. Pentagoet is a prosperous if not self-sufficient community when Crowne leased it to Temple in 1660, but it had no domesticated animals and only one family in Grandfontaine's account in 1671 and was not fit for human habitation two years later. Certainly we may guess that the population was temporary and shifting and that the census in each case served the needs of the census taker.

When this complicated tale is all told, however, like the story of English land grants in the previous chapter, it turns out to be of but passing interest and little ultimate significance. It emphasizes the difference between the French attitude toward colonial expansion and the British-American attitude. The French traded, fished offshore, and regarded Acadia as a source of raw materials. A few towns, a few widely separated forts, an occasional isolated trading post, were all that marked French occupation. Very few French families came to America to make it their permanent home. This activity encouraged a symbiotic relationship with the Indians. Trade was to the advantage of both parties. The Jesuit effort, in many cases deeply sincere, to convert the Indians, and the military effort to use them against the English, still encouraged close relationships.

The English, on the other hand, curing their fish ashore, cutting off the forests for lumber and ship timber, and establishing permanent family farms and villages, offended and alarmed the Indians but established a solidly based society which produced a hardy, independent progeny impossible to root out.

We now proceed to study how these settlers lived and how they fared in 100 years of Indian wars.

EIGHT

The Fishing Settlements, 1620-1675

HILE THE KINGS of England and France were distributing paper duchies and seignories among their aristocratic friends, rougher, tougher men were building fragile communities, clinging to the edges of a continent of whose majesty they were yet ignorant.

Fish was their immediate and most easily realized source of wealth. During the first two decades of the century, merchants from the west counties of England sent ships annually to the Maine coast, sailing with the spring easterlies in late winter, landing at the Isles of Shoals; Richmond Island; Casco (near the present site of Portland); Sagadahoc, at the mouth of the Kennebec; Cape Newagen; Damariscove; Pemaquid; Monhegan; and Matinicus. Here they built light platforms called stages on which to spread fish to dry, and rough camps in which to sleep, eat, and store dried fish and gear. They set up shallops, which had been brought across the Atlantic, knocked down, in the holds of their vessels, and went to fishing at once.

As described in Chapter 5, a shallop was a rough, heavily built open boat from about 20 to as much as 35 or 40 feet long, double-ended, beamy and of rather shoal draft. She was moved primarily with oars but also carried a mast and sails. The smaller boats carried a spritsail and a jib or foresail, a rig developed by the Dutch. Others carried a square mainsail on a mast stepped about amidships and a small square foresail stepped far forward.

At first, there were four men in a fishing crew: a master or steersman, a midshipman, and a foreshipman. The fourth man stayed ashore, built drying stages, dressed and salted the fish, spread them to dry, and covered them in case of rain. He also cooked for the crew. Later it is reported that the crew was increased to five, another man staying ashore.

As a general rule, the crews fished by the day, returning at night to land their fish and sleep ashore; although, late in the season, when fish were scarcer, they stayed out for two or three days at a time, cleaning and salting the fish at sea. The shore man then washed them, salted them lightly, and dried them in the sun.

The best quality of fish—large codfish, lightly salted, well dried, neither frost burned, sunburned, or salt burned, and "clear as lantharn horn"—was sent to the Canary Islands, Madeira, Spain, and France. Inferior grades, called refuse fish, were the less desirable codfish and slack-salted pollock, called dunfish, a favorite in the West Indies. Dunfish was brown in color and cured after drying in a dark place. Hake, called poorjohn, and haddock, which did not take salt well, were sold in the West Indies as food for slaves and in Europe and England to those who could not afford the better grades. Shakespeare mentions both dunfish and poorjohn shortly after 1600.

Corfish, the finest cod, pickled, was considered a delicacy. Salt mackerel,

Richmond Island to Penobscot Bay

bass, salmon, and alewives were carried pickled, in barrels. Sturgeon were occasionally caught in the rivers. Eels and lobsters were so common that Josselyn reports being cloyed with them. But the principal resource was cod. Salt mackerel was used for bait, eight hogsheads being sufficient to carry the Richmond Island settlement from September to April. Herring seems to have been a little-used fish. Although attempts were made to make salt from ocean water, it was more economical to import salt from Spain than to make it in America.

Each season there was a rush for the best camps and drying stages, so it was not long before it became the practice to leave a small crew on the coast to hold the site, to guard what equipment was left ashore, and to improve the time by accumulating at least part of a cargo of fish. It soon became apparent that the best season for fishing was from January to May. Therefore, since the ships from England did not arrive on the Maine coast before late March, it became profitable to leave an industrious crew in America, rather than to transport the fishermen back and forth across the Atlantic merely to spend their substance in riotous living at home during the late fall and winter. Also, as the fishermen went on shares, they found it profitable to stay over the winter. Consequently, more or less permanent settlements of fishermen were established at Richmond Island, Damariscove, and Pemaquid. The character of these communities depended heavily on the quality of the leadership.

Abraham Jennings, who was granted Monhegan by The Council for New England, never came to America, managed his business from England, lost heavily, and sold out cheaply to Aldworth and Eldridge of Pemaquid. Monhegan was a desirable location, handy to the fishing grounds and with a good place to dry fish, although the harbor was then, as it is now, wide open to the south and rough in heavy weather. In about 1631 twenty vessels were reported as being at Monhegan. Abraham Shurt, as agent for Aldworth and Eldridge, transferred his headquarters to Pemaquid, but Monhegan maintained a year-round community and was thronged by visiting fishermen in the summer. One July the ship *Jacob* took 173,700 dried fish to Bordeaux, France. That would be roughly the catch of ten boats for five months.

Abraham Shurt was one of the least aggressive leaders and one of the most successful. He came in 1626 as agent for Aldworth and Eldridge and bought Monhegan for them. He recorded the deed by which John Brown of New Harbor bought land of Samoset in 1625. Although he was not a lawyer or an officially sanctioned justice of the peace, the recording stands as legal, and its simple and direct wording has become the standard form for American legal conveyances. Apparently it was Shurt who, quite unofficially, performed what governmental services were required, engineered the discipline and the compromises necessary for law and order, and supervised trade with Indians—so fairly that he was respected by them and could deal with them as respected individuals rather than as savages through the evil times of King Philip's War in 1675–78. Under Shurt's guidance, Pemaquid became the principal trading center for the mid-coast.

Shurt's influence actually extended far beyond Pemaquid, for he was engaged in trading ventures up and down the coast. In 1631 a party of eastern Indians raided Ipswich, Massachusetts, and captured, among others, the wife of a chief known to Shurt. He knew the captors well enough to persuade them to return the lady to her husband. When Vines and Wannerton journeyed to Castine to try to persuade the French to pay for the supplies they had confiscated from The Plymouth Company there and at Machias, d'Aulnay put them in jail. However, Shurt persuaded d'Aulnay to release them, partly as a result of the trade which Shurt had encouraged between French and English. In one case, even the devil respected Shurt. He was off the mouth of the Piscataqua in a shallop bound for Boston. Aboard the boat was a keg of gunpowder. One of the sailors, suffering for a smoke, declared, survivors stated, that he would light his pipe "if the devil dragged him quick [alive] to hell." The devil made good on the offer. There was an immediate explosion, in which the smoker was killed, but the others and Shurt were unharmed.

Besides Pemaquid and Monhegan, Damariscove was another important fishing harbor. Lying off Boothbay Harbor, Damariscove is a long, narrow island with a snug cove on the southern end protected by a sunken rock in its entrance. There is another cove on the eastern side and a pond of fresh water in the middle of the island. Shoals with 3 to 15 fathoms extend to the south and east, providing rich and easily accessible fishing grounds. Humphrey Damerill, a member of the Gilbert-Popham colony of 1607, on the collapse of that venture came to Damariscove in 1608 and set up a store on the island for the convenience of the fishing fleet.

By 1622 thirteen people were reported as living on the island over the winter; two shallops were also kept over. A maypole was erected in the spring by the summer fishermen. Over thirty vessels were reported as fishing there that summer. Considering the size of the harbor, the "vessels" must have been mostly shallops, or, if there were thirty seagoing ships, many of them must have been moored in the cove on the eastern side. By fall, the fishermen had built a stout palisade and a fort mounting a gun. They also had a good supply of small arms and ten big dogs, of whom the Indians were afraid. Apparently Indians frequently visited the island to trade furs for muskets, shot, powder, swords, and "most deadly arrowheads." The Indians had French shallops "which they can manage as well as any Christian."

In the spring of 1622, Edward Winslow was sent east to Damariscove and the the Isles of Shoals for supplies to relieve the Plymouth colony, then in dire need. At Damariscove he was well received and generously supplied, the fishermen refusing proferred payment.

Silvanus Davis of Sagadahoc reported that in about 1631 there were fifteen vessels at Damariscove and two at the Hypocris Islands, now called Fishermans Island, and Damariscove Island was specifically mentioned as being included in the Pemaquid Grant of 1631. Shurt's influence certainly extended to Damariscove.

In 1645 one Packer sued Robert Nash for coming into Damariscove harbor in a bark described as a walking tavern. Nash gave the fishermen a few free drinks and then opened the bar. Everyone, including Nash, was drunk for several days, unable to go fishing, and causing a loss to Parker of £40 to £50. Nash's was probably not the first and certainly not the only floating tavern on the coast. Josselyn reports in 1660 that when the fishermen were £8 or £9 ahead, the merchants sent in a ship loaded with wine from Fayal, Madeira, or the Canaries, carrying also brandy, rum, "Barbados strong water," and tobacco. This led to a week-long party that left the fishermen with heavy heads and light purses, indebted to the merchant and in economic servitude.

In 1676 the court at York charged William Arise of Boston of selling wine and liquor to fishermen, rendering them too drunk to go to sea. Perhaps we need dwell no longer on the weaknesses of the fishermen—weaknesses shared, no doubt, by the farmers, merchants, and every thirsty convivial soul who sought some release from a bleak and rugged life.

On the nearby Hypocris Islands (Fishermans Island), named for hypocris wine, imported with the salt from Spain, there was a small settlement. The name, perverted by a later generation, still sticks to the ledges east of the islands, labeled The Hypocrites on modern charts. On the mainland across a narrow channel from the islands was another small settlement, inhabited by the Grimes and Bennett families.

There was also a settlement at Cape Newagen, a small, snug harbor at the end of Southport Island. Christopher Levett visited here in 1623 looking for a good place at which to settle. He found nine ships fishing out of there and spoke with several Indian sagamores, among them Samoset. He exchanged gifts and made plans to open trade. However, Levett found a place he liked better on House Island, off what is now Portland, built a substantial house there, and returned to England. He became involved in a naval expedition to Spain and never returned.

The next year, 1624, a vessel from Plymouth, Massachusetts, was driven ashore at Newagen and wrecked. ". . . Ye seas broak over such place in ye harbor as was never seen before, and drive her against great rocks, which beat such a hole in her bulke, as a horse and carte might have gone in, and after drive her into deep-water, wher she lay sunke." However, with the help of one Mr. Cook and his friends, then residents at Newagen, her crew raised her, repaired her, and returned to Plymouth.

At Sagadahoc at Atkins Bay at the mouth of the Kennebec, where Fort Popham stands today, was another small settlement with "many families" and ten boats, as reported by Silvanus Davis. There was also a settlement at House Island, in the house Levett built, and another at Casco, which was probably near the mouth of the Presumpscot River.

Just south of Cape Elizabeth on Richmond Island was one of the largest and most successful settlements. This island was described by Champlain and visited by De Monts in 1605. They named it Isle de Bacchus because of its fertile soil and abundance of wild grapes. Its present name came from its first settler, John Richmond, of Bandon Bridge, Ireland. The region around the Bandon River in Ireland had been largely depopulated by the Geraldine Rebellion in Queen Elizabeth's time and had been resettled by English Protestants, mostly Puritans. They had not all been happy in Ireland, and the names of several of them are found on the *Mayflower*'s passenger list and in John Winter's accounts. John Richmond apparently settled on the island in the early 1620s but shortly afterwards moved to the mainland, probably near the mouth of the Saco River. In 1638 John Winter, agent at Richmond Island, reports having bought out the establishment of John Richmond of Bandon Bridge.

In 1628 Walter Bagnall, one of Morton's Merrymount colonists, established himself on Richmond Island and carried on a lucrative trade with the Indians: furs for trinkets, liquor, powder and shot. He is said by Morton to have accumulated a fortune of £1,000. Part of it was found buried in a pot near the shore in 1854, the latest coin bearing the date of 1625.

In 1631 Bagnall's settlement was destroyed by Indians, and Bagnall was killed. In the same year, The Council for New England granted to Robert Trelawney Cape Elizabeth and Richmond Island. Trelawney sent over Thomas Cammock as agent in 1632, but Cammock fell and dislocated his shoulder and was superseded by John Winter in March 1633. Cammock established himself at Black Point, and John Winter became Trelawney's agent. Winter was an efficient agent and a demanding boss, running the establishment with great energy and an iron hand. In addition, he was an excellent businessman, keeping careful records and reporting frequently to Trelawney by letter on the state of the colony.

Richmond Island was an ideal place for a settlement. It is connected to Cape Elizabeth by a narrow, steep-sided bar, bare at low water, thus providing access to the mainland and protection for the deepwater anchorage on its western side, and it is easily defended. Also, it is close to the productive fishing grounds off Cape Elizabeth and to the rivers of Saco Bay, particularly the Spurwink, in which were caught herring, alewives, eels, and bass. Furthermore, the soil both on the island and the adjacent mainland was sufficiently fertile to grow crops to support the settlers. So desirable was the location that when Winter arrived in March 1633, he found four vessels from Barnstable, England, already established, with camps and drying stages ashore.

Although it was late in the season for fishing, Winter set his fishermen to work at once. By July 11 he wrote Trelawney that he was sending home a shipload of dried fish and corfish.

In June 1634, Winter reported astonishing progress. He had built a house 40 feet by 18 feet with a big chimney and a shed adjacent. Near the mainland end of the bar he had built a pig house, cleared a field, built a stockade around it, and harvested a crop of corn, the best of which supported his crew and the rest of which he fed to the pregnant pigs. The other pigs grubbed in the woods for acorns and soon learned to root on the flats for clams. Winter traded with the Indians for furs but found the trade unprofitable. ". . . Their be so many traders that one spoyleth the other." He also sent a trader eastward and inland, but to little profit. His comments on the quality of his supplies tell a good deal about his circumstances. The shoes, stockings, hats, and coats were too small to fit the Indians, and the shoes shrank in the snow. The beer went sour on the voyage, and the barrels leaked. Send malt and meal, advised Winter, and the colony can make its own bread and beer. His shopping list to be sent by the next supply is extensive, including blankets, food, clothes, "2 butts sacke and 2 hogsheads aqua vitae," canvas, findings for shoe repair, hoes, axes, and knives. Also he needs a good cow and a couple of goats. Of the two goats previously sent, a dog killed the "yew" and a boar chased the ram goat into the woods, whence he, the goat, never returned.

Winter's spirit is shown by his reply to Trelawney's suggestion that the settlement be abandoned if there should be no profit in sight. Winter replied that he had food enough to last the next fishing season, a crop of corn coming, "good store of piges against another yeare," trade goods yet unsold, and some debts to collect. Furthermore, there was no one to whom he could quickly sell what he had. "The most parte of the dwellers heare are good buyers but bad payers." His intention to stay was reinforced by his request for more fishermen, ". . . and for the bootes marsters and fishermen. The must be good plyable men. . . . This is no Contry for Loyterers."

Certainly, Winter's establishment was no place for the lazy. Winter found that the best fishing was from January to April, and he kept his men at sea every day that was fit to fish. He lost one crew in a February cold snap. Their boat swamped in a squall. They managed to get an anchor down but were unable to bail out the boat and died of exposure. Another boat was capsized in a squall. The master clung to an oar and was rescued, but the other two men were lost. Fishing for John Winter was a rugged life; it took tough men to make a living in Maine.

Subsequent letters to Trelawney ask for a cannon "for our defence from those that wish us harme heare," not only Indians but pirates, specifically Dixy Bull, who raided Pemaquid about this time. Also, Winter asked for metalwork and rigging to build three more shallops.

During the next few years, Winter built a thirty-ton bark and a hundred-ton ship, both of which made frequent trading voyages coastwise to Boston and Jamestown and transatlantic to Spain, France, and the wine islands, the Canaries and Madeira. More fishermen and more farmers were employed, apparently receiving passage, board and lodging and a stated wage in return for a three-year commitment. By 1635 eight shallops were fishing and there was a brewer, a baker, and a man whose job it was to watch the hogs lest wolves, bears, or Indians eat them.

In June 1636 Winter asked Trelawney to send his wife over, ". . . for she may be a great helpe to me heare in the house, as well as her Company, in lokinge over the household provisions. I do lacke a good Carefull husbandman to overloke our husbandrye, very much to governe the rest, for I cannot be in every place & servants will do but little worke heare if therbe not an eye over them." Apparently, the Winters were birds of a feather. Mrs. Winter arrived in May 1636. A year later she was asking for a firken of gray soap, rennet to make cheese, six brass pans, and a woman servant. Her then present maid was lazy and complaining, and Mrs. Winter, wrote her husband, ". . . is fain to do it all herself."

In response to the request of his brother Edward, Robert Trelawney sent over a minister, Reverend Gibson. Of him Winter writes, ". . . a very fair Condition man—and Instructs our people well, yet please God to give us the grace to follow his Instruction." Gibson stayed several years but fell out with Winter over his salary and moved to Saco, whence his wife had come.

Winter had considerable trouble over men who ran away before their times were up. Sometimes they charged Winter with underpaying or underfeeding them, and although they apparently violated their contracts, several settled at Kittery, York, Saco, or on Strattons Island, worked hard, became solid citizens, and traded their fish with Winter for supplies.

In 1637 he had forty-seven men working on the plantation and several women, either wives of fishermen or girls as indentured servants. One of these was Priscilla, of whom Winter writes as being fat and lazy, dirty and shiftless, that she lies abed in the morning and runs off and hides in the woods. One can imagine the distress of the poor girl, who probably had not been enthusiastic about New England in the first place and found herself under the domination of the determined Mrs. Winter, herself in no happy condition, for the men criticized her bitterly for refusing to give them as much bread or milk as they wanted. Send over a steward, asks Winter.

In 1639 another girl, Tomson, was drowned. She had gone across the bar to the mainland to bring back the cattle. There was only half a foot of water on the bar, but when her hat blew off, she reached to fetch it and slipped off the side of the bar into deep water. People on the island ran to her aid but arrived too late to save her. Winter regretted her loss, as she was worth twice what Priscilla was.

By 1640 Winter had a profitable fishing operation going and enough farmers raising corn, wheat, peas, oats, barley, and vegetables to feed his plantation and provide a surplus. He had pigs, goats, cattle, and several asses, producing enough meat and milk to eat and young ones to sell. He had a gang ashore on the north side of Cape Elizabeth cutting lumber to make clapboards and pipe or barrel staves. These were not, apparently, sawn boards, but "clawboards." The logs were split in halves and then quarters, and the quarters split into many narrow pieces wider on one side than the other, like our milled clapboards.

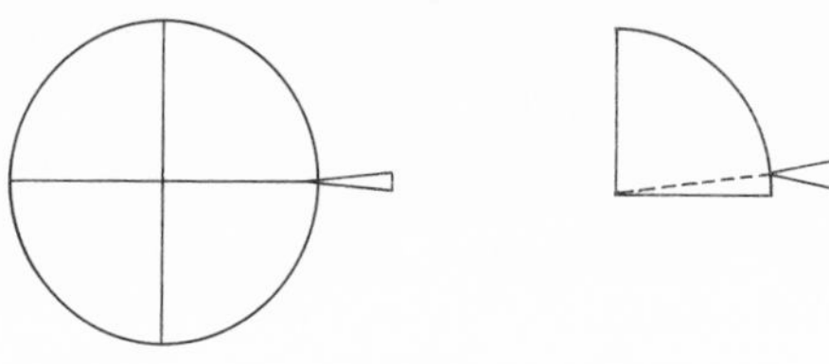

Besides these businesses, Winter imported clothes, tools, wine, and aqua vitae, which he traded to other settlers and to Massachusetts Bay and Connecticut merchants for fish or money, of which they had little. The fish, clapboards, and staves he sent to France, Spain, the Canaries, Antigua, and Jamaica, buying wine, taking the profit in money, and sending it to England. With others doing the same thing, the colonies were drained of hard money, and barter was the only recourse. However, if there is any money available at all, says Winter, they will spend it on sack.

In 1640 another problem surfaced for Winter. Although he had complained earlier that there was no law or law enforcement in the country, he was sued by George Cleeves in the court at Saco for extortion. Winter had bought aqua vitae at £7 per hogshead (52½ imperial gallons) and sold it at 20 pence per quart, a profit of about 300 percent. He bought gunpowder at 22 pence per pound and sold it for 3 shillings, 36 pence—a profit of about 50 percent. After considerable litigation, he was declared guilty, and on October 19 a "martiall" with thirty armed men came in a boat to take him and the value of the court's judgment.

Winter was away, having left Sargent in command. Sargent had three or four men carry the "martiall" back to his boat and hailed, "I charge you come no neare or take that comes." The boat lay off the island for three days, Sargent's men patrolling the shore day and night. Finally, Winter had to go to court and pay up.

If we have spent over-long on the fortunes of the Richmond Island plantation, it is because it sheds considerable light on conditions prevalent all along the coast in the mid-seventeenth century and because the letters of Winter to Trelawney are so specific.

West of Richmond Island there were fishing stations at Kittery and the Isles of Shoals. The Kittery operation was comparatively small and had other interests, too, both farming and lumbering, but the Isles of Shoals were inhabited shortly after John Smith visited them in 1614. By 1622, when Winslow sought help for the distressed Pilgrim colony, there was an active community. In 1623 The Laconia Company set up a saltworks and sent fishermen out. Although the saltworks failed, fishing prospered. Christopher Levett reported the drying stages crowded in that year of 1623. The Laconia Company collapsed shortly thereafter, in 1633. The population of the Isles of Shoals had increased to 600, with a meetinghouse, courthouse, school, bowling alley, and brewery. Fish were cured here for export, and also cargoes of fish, furs, clapboards, and staves were collected and sent to the West Indies, Spain, France, the wine islands, and England.

Besides the fishing communities, there were other settlements on the coast. Kittery, York, and Saco, while no doubt to some extent concerned with fishing, were principally agricultural, lumbering, and fur-trading communities. The Plymouth Company opened a trading post on the Kennebec River at Cushnoc, near the present site of Augusta, and Clark & Lake had another on the southeast side of Arrowsic Island. Also there were occasional independent traders on the coast, muddying the waters by selling the Indians liquor, defrauding them or stealing from them, and disappearing, never to return. Pirates preyed on colonial commerce, not only on the coast but in the mouth of the English Channel. Winter mentions Dunkerkers, pirates from Dunkirk, who took one of his vessels, and Turks, who took another.

East of the Penobscot River were the French. However, the French approach to fishing and to fur trading was different from that of the English. The climate in France was better suited than that of England for making salt from seawater. Also, because French were driven off the Newfoundland coast, they soon developed the technique of heavily salting their fish wet aboard the vessels and taking them back to France, where they were washed out and dried. Thus, the French did not require extensive shore settlements. What few settlements they had, such as Pentagoet and Saint John, were partly military and largely trading posts. The fur trade was to the mutual advantage of French and Indians on the Maine coast, and there were few, if any, French settlers to threaten the Indian way of life. Consequently, the French and Indians lived at peace, and the French were easily able to bring the Indians to their side as allies against the English in the years of more or less constant warfare from 1675 until 1759.

DAMARISCOVE FISHERMEN, 1635

THREE FISHERMEN IN A SHALLOP row out of Damariscove harbor in the chilly dawn of a March morning. Against the brightening sky, the steep eastern shore of the harbor stands stark and black. On the western shore the early light reveals a straggle of rough camps and sheds, in a few of which flicker rush lights. The calm waters of the narrow cove, open to the south, breathe gently with the heave of the sea outside. A dozen shallops lie at moorings in the cove, their skiffs above high-water mark on the shore. A rattle of pebbles and a splash tell of another crew pushing off. A nanny goat bleats forlornly.

The shallop, a heavily built, double-ended boat about 25 feet long, is rowed by two silent men, mere bulks in the dawn light. Their long oars squeak against the tholepins. The third man stands in the stern, steering, watching successive waves check, hump up, and slide over the rock at the harbor's entrance.

As the shallop passes the rock and the protecting arms of the cove, she rises to each smooth sea and drops into the trough beyond. The light strengthens. The steersman, a tall, strong, frosty-bearded Welshman, is called Taffy, not because it is his name but because he is a Welshman. He is the shallop's master, clearly in charge, one big hand on the tiller, the other in the pocket of his heavy, slack, woolen pants. He watches the big roll left over from yesterday's gale breaking heavily on the ledge to the west.

The shallop is an open boat with a small deck at bow and stern. Amidships is a heavy thwart through which is stepped a stout mast with a sail wrapped around it. Aft of the thwart stands the midshipman, Giles, wearing the traditional high-crowned, wide-brimmed hat of his Cornish fisherman forebears. Aft of his standing room is a fish hold, open and empty now except for a barrel of salt mackerel for bait. It has been kept much too long, since last August, but no one seems to mind it. It is just part of the world in which they live.

Forward of the mast is another fish hold, its hatches piled on one side, and the standing room for Robbie, the foreshipman. He is a stout lad of sixteen, almost a man but still a boy. He gazes east, watching for the first crumb of the sun over the horizon, far beyond which lies his home in England.

As dawn becomes day, a light, southerly air ripples the glassy sea. Taffy orders the sail set. Giles ships his oar, unwraps the mainsheet from around the furled spritsail, picks up the long sprit from its place on the port rail. He grabs at the gently flapping peak of the sail, shoves the end of the sprit into a pocket sewn in it. Robbie pushes the butt of the sprit aft, and together they heave it up into the snotter, a loop of rope spliced around the mast with an eye in it. Taffy gathers in the sheet attached to the after lower corner of the sail, eases the tiller to port, and the sail fills. Robbie scrambles forward and ties the tack of the jib to the stem head. Giles hoists the sail and climbs aft to sheet it home. The shallop heels to the breeze, chuckles under her bow, and heads to the westward.

"You like this Dutchman's rig?" asks Taffy. "A lot easier when you tack."

"Flying on one wing," answers Giles. "I like to see that big square mainsail full of wind and the big square foresail to balance her. She scuds, then."

"And how do you like hauling down the tack and bowlines every time you come about with that big square mainsail, and rigging the fargood on that fine, big floppy foresail? And how do you like sailing back and forth in the same rut all afternoon when you want to get to windward? And how do you like those two heavy yards taking charge on a rough day? Me for the spritsail, every time. . . ."

The boy, Robbie, sits forward and shivers, watching the sun rise. He signed on the Bristol fishing vessel in January for three years because he had discovered that the Mousehole was not the world. Now he has been gone less than three months and has found that the New World looks a good deal like the Mousehole but colder, rougher, and a long way from old friends. It was a cold, rough, and wet passage across the Atlantic in an 80-ton vessel heavily loaded with salt, fishing gear, and supplies. With predominantly fair winds, they made the Nova Scotia coast and then Monhegan in late February and slipped into the crowded harbor at Damariscove. He was assigned as foreshipman in Taffy's shallop and given a bunk in a shed ashore with Taffy, Giles, and a swarthy Frenchman called Pierre. Also part of the household is an Indian woman with an unpronounceable heathen name whom they call Queen Bess. When she feels inclined, she cooks, keeps a little garden in the summer, and digs a few clams. Taffy treats her with rough affection and Giles treats her with considerable respect, partly because they value her services and the cheerful atmosphere she brings, partly because she returns from frequent visits ashore with beaver and otter skins which she trades with Taffy for knives, hatchets, beads, and gunpowder, supplies which he acquires after his own fashion—and partly because she has been known to drive Giles out of the camp with an iron skillet. She seems to like the three white men, especially Taffy; and Robbie is beginning to get used to her.

"Why go to the westward?" asks Giles. "We did well down to the southeast last week, and all the others are headed off there."

"They won't be back tonight," says Taffy. "Wind's going to shift northerly and blow cold. They won't be able to claw to wind'ard with that square rig, nor they can't row to wind'ard against the sea. They'll be lucky to scud for Monhegan. We'll fish off Manwegan and fly home on one wing—and one wing will be all the wing we'll need."

"Spring's here. Can't you smell it? Blow, hell!"

Robbie looks at the soft blue sky, the sea just rippling with the southerly breeze, and feels the warmth of the spring sun. He doesn't believe it will blow, but Taffy has seen five winters come and go, and Robbie is learning to keep his mouth shut.

Other shallops now have rowed out of the harbor and made sail, most of them to the east and south, but a few, following Taffy, haul up to the westward.

They sail for half an hour, the spring sun beginning to feel warm on their backs. The big spritsail with a bonnet laced to its foot drives the heavy shallop over the smooth seas with a pleasant rush of wind and water. Taffy watches the distant island of Seguin and the breakers on the nearer ledges, lining up ranges that will tell him where to fish. He has left Wales for good, barely escaping from the shadow of the debtors' prison, and has no intention of ever going back. This is his country now, and he is getting to know it well. Taffy is not his real name, but he has no desire to be called by any other. He has been five years on the coast, has been learning to know and like the weather, the fishing grounds, Queen Bess and her red relations. It's getting to be his country.

Giles rattles on about the weather, the likelihood of setting up a maypole again on the island this year, of the skinflint ways of Parker, the agent, and of the anticipated arrival of the "sack ship," a vessel loaded not only with supplies but with a generous cargo of sack, rum, and brandy. Self-restraint is clearly not one of Giles's virtues.

At last Taffy slips the jibsheet off the tholepin. Giles, silenced, hauls the weather sheet to back the jib. Taffy hauls the clew of the mainsail flat aft, and the shallop stops, lifting easily to the swell.

"Sound," says Taffy.

Robbie drops a line over the side with a five-pound lead on it, lets it run until it stops, then stands up and hauls it in, measuring it with the full spread of his arms.

"Eleven fathom."

"Good enough. Anchor."

Robbie rolls the heavy killick over the side, lets the rode run out. The killick is the forked branch of a tree embracing a long, flat rock, which is held in the fork by a cross-piece of wood acting like the fluke of an anchor. Giles drops the jib, slips the butt of the sprit out of the snotter, stands the sprit up alongside the mast, and passes the end of the mainsheet around sail, sprit, and mast. Each then takes up a reel of stout line with a lead and two hooks. Giles tosses a handful of the stinking salt mackerel forward to Robbie and another aft to Taffy. Each baits up and drops the lines overboard, Taffy and Robbie to starboard, Giles to port.

As the lines run out, each man puts on woolen mittens and a barvel, a long apron of oiled leather. The barvels, literally oiled skins, stink of oil and fish gurry, but they shed water. Soon the fish strike on, and one after another the men haul them aboard. They are fat fifteen- and twenty-pound codfish, green spotted with white on the back, with a white line down each side, a white belly, and two chin whiskers. They make little fight, "coming up like an old boot," says Giles, but heavy to haul over the side.

The exercise warms the crew, once the sun has taken off the chill. The light southerly increases to a moderate breeze, and a chop builds up over the old roll; but the buoyant bow of the shallop rises easily over it. The three bait and haul in silence. By noon the two holds are about half full and the shallop lies more heavily in the water. Taffy hefts a codfish over the rail into the after hold, twists out the hook, and reaches into the cuddy for the water jug. The other two haul up, pass the jug, and gnaw at the hard biscuit.

"Here she comes," says Taffy, jerking his thumb over his shoulder. Robbie looks to the westward toward Seguin, so named by the Abenaki because it looks like a turtle with his neck out. But Seguin has been there all morning. Several shallops from Manwegan are anchored to the west and south, but they are not moving.

"No bigger than a man's hand," says Giles; and Robbie sees now the fast-rising edge of the northwest squall.

"Time for a few more," says Taffy, "to keep Pierre busy." They return to fishing but with one eye out to the north as the clouds pile up, white on top, black underneath. The southerly breeze dies out. The sun is smothered. A dark line races along the surface from the north, a cold puff running ahead of it, swinging the shallop on her anchor.

"Reel up," says Taffy. "Rig the hatches, and get that bonnet off." By the time they have reeled up, the water is slate gray, and a frizzling little chop is driving before the wind. Giles slams the heavy hatches over the holds and climbs forward to help Robbie with the anchor rope as the shallop seems to brace her feet against it with the new wind. Taffy ships an oar over the port side to steady her and take some of the strain. The killick breaks out with a jerk, and the rode comes in more easily. Giles leaves it to Robbie and heaves the sprit up into the snotter, makes it fast. The sail thrashes as Giles stumbles aft to trim the sheet. The shallop turns on her heel, lies over on her port side, slides her length to leeward, and heads for home. Robbie, straining on the anchor rode, can just gain on it, but when the killick comes up under the lee bow, he can't get it over the rail. He looks aft, sees Taffy with both hands on the tiller and Giles straining back against the pull of the mainsheet. He will just have to get the anchor aboard by himself. He takes a turn around his mittened hand, braces again, and heaves up and out with all he has. Taffy luffs a mite, and the killick comes in over the rail as Robbie and the killick fall back against the thwart together.

The shallop heels heavily, even without the jib, as the wind picks up, her lee rail right in the water, a roaring wave under her bow and Taffy well up to windward holding the tiller hard up to keep her to her work. Giles is aft holding the mainsheet with both hands, both feet braced and his high hat pulled down hard against the wind. As the wind blows colder and harder, it nips ears and numbs hands in wet mittens. The shallop rams her bow into the cresting waves and slashes the icy water aft. Robbie, sitting farthest forward, gets the best of it, shivers with cold. As the puffs come stronger, the little vessel is borne down under the weight of the wind and ships water heavily over the lee side of the standing room. Taffy lets her up a little, Giles eases the sheet,

Tabby at the tiller. *Consuelo E. Hanks*

the sail luffs a bit, and before she loses way, Taffy bears off again, and down she goes again. Robbie's shivering is not all cold. The island, as much as he will see of home for a long time, seems a very long way off. The seas charge malevolently, and now the mainland far to windward dims and vanishes as the snow comes down upon them.

"Bail," says Taffy.

Giles, still straining at the sheet, kicks a bucket toward Robbie.

Robbie doesn't want at all to get down in the lee side of the bilge, dip hands and bucket in the icy water stinking with spilled bait, but there is no help for it. He bails as if his life depends on it, as indeed it does. When he looks up, even the island is lost in the driving snow.

After twenty minutes of rushing through thick nothing, and disposing of a number of rotten mackerel and soggy biscuits, things seem a bit easier. Robbie looks up again to see that they have slipped into the lee of the ledge and are out of the worst of the sea. Giles trims the sheet, Taffy heads up, and presently they tack.

"Flies pretty well on one wing, don't she?" says Taffy. As they draw in under the island, they take in sail and row up the cove in the smooth water under the lee of the hill, the wind whistling over their heads. The snow stops, and by the time they have come alongside the spindly staging, the sun shines across the cove. Pierre takes their line, and they heave out the fish, Taffy keeping count, for their pay depends on the number.

By dark that night they are snugged down in their camp, the fire in the stick-and-clay chimney giving light, heat, and smoke enough to add to the smells of wet wool and leather, unwashed people, and fish in various stages of preservation and decay.

Pierre dips out of the pot a thick mixture of ground corn, dried peas, and salt pork boiled in goat's milk—welcome, warm, and nourishing.

"Where's Queen Bess?" asks Taffy.

"Went ashore with her brother this afternoon before it snowed. Maybe back tomorrow. Maybe not."

After dinner, Taffy goes to the door before turning in, to look out into the bright moonlight across the cove. The wind still roars overhead in heavy puffs, and the winter cold has clamped down again, but not for long, thinks Taffy as he sees Orion marching to the westward. The shallops lie quietly at their moorings in the lee of the hill, but nearly half the moorings in the cove are empty. Taffy thinks bleakly of the men offshore, unable to beat back against the heavy wind and sea, hove to, bailing to stay afloat, wet, hungry, and chilled to the bone.

NOTES

The material for this chapter was not easily assembled. The best and most interesting primary sources are John Winter's letters to Robert Trelawney on the progress of the Richmond Island colony. These are detailed accounts of specific events, tales of Winter's troubles with employees, abuttors, Indians, bears, wolves, and visiting vessels. His accounts are painstaking, extending to measuring the leakage in barrels of wine, beer, and oil. The Trelawney Papers are published in Baxter's *Documentary History of the State of Maine*.

Christopher Levett, who sailed from the Isles of Shoals to Newagen in 1623, also left a good account, and John Josselyn, a curious visitor to the coast in 1638 and again in the 1670s, recorded his observations in detail, including the stomach contents of a wolf he shot at Black Point. The wolf had dined on goat.

John Pory from Virginia was sent to observe the coast during this time, and although I have not read his report, I have seen many quotations from it. The commission sent by the Duke of York in 1665 is also much quoted.

One of the best secondary sources is an unpublished manuscript in the Boothbay Harbor library by Charles Griffin, Jr., *A History of Fishing in the Boothbay Region*. Raymond McFarland's *History of the New England Fisheries* skims the surface quite effectively. McFarland relies heavily on Sabine's *Report of the Principal Fisheries of the American Seas,* published in 1853. This report is brief, condensed, statistical, but useful, particularly with reference to the Isles of Shoals. John Scribner Jenness's *The Isles of Shoals, An Historical Sketch* is a little more colorful. Francis Greene's *History of Boothbay, Southport, and Boothbay Harbor,* John Johnston's *History of Bristol and Bremen in the State of Maine Including the Pemaquid Settlements,* and Arlita Dodge Parker's *Pemaquid* all seem to depend on the same sources and dwell too much on legal affairs rather than on the actual experiences of the inhabitants. Ida Sedgewick Proper's *Monhegan, Cradle of New England* assembles considerable useful material but is too quick to make assumptions based on insufficient evidence.

William A. Baker's *Colonial Vessels* and *Sloops and Shallops* were the sources for most of the information on matters nautical. Baker was the naval architect who designed *Mayflower II* and her shallop. He did a great deal of painstaking research. Some information, too, was acquired by visiting Jamestown, Virginia, where reconstructions of seventeenth-century vessels are afloat. Particularly interesting was their pinnace.

None of the writers on this period regard Indians as people; they are referred to as "the Indians" or "savages." There are a few exceptions. Christopher Levett liked Samoset and the other chiefs he spoke with, and Abraham Shurt, while he wrote nothing extant, appears to have dealt with Indians as people. Yet at Pemaquid, Damariscove, and Newagen, for instance, Indians must have been coming and going all the time, trading, fishing, feasting, swimming, playing games, and doing what people do. Certainly, the English with whom they traded must have gotten to know the Indians as individuals, even though they were suspicious of them.

Johnston, in the *History of Bristol and Bremen,* etc., says of Samoset, "He appears not only to have been destitute of the jealousies and petty vices of his race; but at the same time to have manifested on all occasions a love of justice and truth, a generous confidence in others, and an elevation of soul far superior to very many of the Europeans with whom he was brought in contact." With leaders like Samoset and Abraham Shurt, despite prejudices on both sides, natives and immigrants seem to have got on pretty well together until the wars began in 1675.

NINE

King Philip's War, 1675-1678

A QUICK LOOK at a general history of New England suggests that the fire of Indian warfare smoldered from 1675 to 1763, bursting into smoky flame when European conflicts fanned the coals. However, this is at best an oversimplification; for, although there were fundamental problems in America that were not settled until the Abenaki were practically destroyed and the French were expelled from North America, there were intervals of peace during which coastal Maine was repopulated and continued to develop.

The three groups of people in Maine—with three different backgrounds, three different ambitions, and three different attitudes toward the land—came into inevitable conflict. The local Indians believed that as the first inhabitants they had primary rights to the land, the rivers, and the coastal waters. They were stone-age people to whom metal tools were unknown before the coming of Europeans, but the epithet "stone-age" should not imply lack of intelligence, character, ideals, or wisdom. The behavior of those of their leaders of whom we have records, records kept only by their enemies, suggests that they were people of honor and conscience. The native Indians were comparatively few in number and lived on the land as they found it, using its soil, fish, and animals for their subsistence and leaving it to their children much as their fathers had left it to them. That they were proud, resentful of injuries, vengeful, cruel in warfare, and treacherous is undeniable. However, the same deplorable qualities were shared by both French and English, as their own histories clearly show, and the Indians were fighting a desperate losing battle for their homes and their lives.

The French, unlike the Indians, did not live on the land to any great extent. They came from France to America to make money and, in most cases, with the intention of returning to France to spend it. Fish and furs were their primary interests. Their fishing methods involved no considerable American establishment. They came from France in ships loaded with supplies and an ample supply of salt. They anchored, then fished, dressed and salted the catch aboard the vessel, and returned to France. Of course, they went ashore occasionally for wood, water, fresh provisions, and to repair damages, but they were in no great measure dependent on the shore.

The fur traders came from France with trade goods: knives, hatchets, guns, gunpowder, lead, pots and kettles, clothes, blankets, and cloth, as well as bells, mirrors, ribbon, "notions," and rum. They set up trading houses ashore, usually fortified, and welcomed Indians who came in with furs. They also sent out traders among the Indians and established inland trading posts as they went. They got on well with the Indians, for trade was to their mutual advantage; and although communities were established and subsistence farms grew up, most of the French who lived on the coast were traders who intended to return to France or soldiers sent to protect the trade.

Another very influential group of Frenchmen were the Jesuits. Since 1610, when Henry IV ordered Poutrincourt to take Father Biard with him to Port Royal, the Jesuits had maintained a strong interest in saving Indian souls. In 1611 the Marquise de Guercheville bought the Jesuits into the Port Royal expedition, and in 1612 the Jesuits, through the Marquise, were granted the whole North American continent from Florida to the St. Lawrence. Although later grants, conquests, and treaties superseded this grant, the Jesuits, once they had a foothold in French Canada, played a powerful role in keeping it French and Catholic.

Most of the Jesuits were sincere believers in the importance of bringing the Indians into the Christian fold, and to this end they were imaginative and self-sacrificing, and remarkably successful. They lived among the Indians, accustoming themselves to a way of life often revolting to them. They preached a simple doctrine and backed up their preaching with presents of clothing, tools, powder and shot. The French fur traders often accompanied the Jesuits, and together secured the allegiance of many tribes, particularly of the Abenakis living between the St. Lawrence River and the Maine coast.

The source of conflict between French Indians and English colonists lay partly in the militant nature of the Jesuit message. Protestants were regarded by the Jesuits as children of the Antichrist, enemies, a species with only the appearance of human beings. They were to be extirpated, root and branch. This attitude was encouraged by the French government, which cooperated with the Jesuits in providing the Indians with welcome gifts, and in paying liberally for English scalps and English captives. Consequently, the French-supported Indians made devastating raids down the Connecticut, Merrimac, Piscataqua, and Kennebec rivers. One of the principal bases for these attacks was at Norridgewock at the confluence of the Kennebec and Sandy rivers above Skowhegan, where Father Rasle established a mission in 1695. Another base was Pentagoet, where Baron de St. Castin had a fort and a trading post. The third important base was at St. Francis, on the St. Francis River, now on the border between Maine and New Brunswick.

The principal opponents of the French and Indians were the Massachusetts Puritans. To oversimplify a very complex situation, the Puritan believed that the Roman Catholic church, and through it the state-supported Churcl of England, had dangerously corrupted the original Christian church as or dained by Christ and explained in the New Testament. The Puritan wanted t go back to a Bible-ordained commonwealth. His opposition to the Church o England led to his persecution in that country and to his deep determinatio to build a Kingdom of God in a new world. America, he believed, was reserve by God for this purpose.

Accordingly, those who emigrated to Massachusetts left their homes their jobs, their established lives to build this Kingdom in Massachusetts While seeking freedom to practice their religion as they saw it, they wer fiercely intolerant of any whom they saw as instruments of the devil seeking t interfere with their holy purpose. Catholics, Quakers, Ariminians were perse cuted, banished, or executed. Indians, unless quickly converted to Purita Christianity, were children of evil. Jesuits were instruments of the Antichrist.

The Puritan came to America to build a Kingdom of God in the wilder ness. He had no intention and indeed no possibility of returning to Englan He was committed. Therefore, the English and their few Indian allies fough the French Catholic Indians fiercely, and the English paid as handsome bounty for French scalps as did the French for English scalps.

To the French and Indians, who could live together without seriousl interfering with each other's established patterns of living, the English were serious menace. English people came to Maine at first as itinerant fishermen and as long as they inhabited offshore islands and a few points on the coast they were no serious threat to the Indians. But when the English, pushed ou of England by the conversion of farmland to sheep pasture, by growing infla tion, and by religious persecution, came in ever-increasing numbers, the spread rapidly inland and along the coast. They cut the forests for logs to fee their sawmills and cleared land for farms. They brought their families and cam to stay. As more and more towns were built, sawmills established, and farm cleared, the game on which the Indians subsisted and which provided furs fo their trade with both the English and the French was driven out. Some Indian accepted the inevitable, adopted Christian ways, and joined the English. Oth ers retreated northward and were easily provoked by the French to attack thos who had driven them out of the homes of their ancestors.

Fishing rights presented another important source of conflict betwee England and France. Salt codfish—whether caught by Frenchmen, salted taken home wet and then dried, or whether caught by English fishermen an cured on the shores of Newfoundland, Nova Scotia, and Maine—were a tre mendous source of wealth. Both nations made laws to favor their own fisher men—two meatless days a week were the law in England—and they used thei navies to distress their opponents. Every treaty between France and Englan mentions fishing rights.

Lumber, particularly masts, spars, ship timber, and naval stores, wa of vital importance to the maintenance of navies, as will be discussed i Chapter 13.

Finally, the fur trade, a source of great wealth to the French, was being gradually choked off by English settlement.

Add to this explosive situation in America the international tension between France and England over the status of Holland, Malta, Gibraltar, certain West Indian islands, and parts of India, as well as the tension between French-supported Jacobites seeking the crown of England and disagreement as to the proper succession of the crowns of Spain and Austria, and it can scarcely be wondered at that hostility was nearly continuous through the seventeenth and eighteenth centuries.

Until King Philip's War in 1675, relations between the English and Indians on the Maine coast had been more or less peaceful. English fishermen, traders, and pirates had occasionally defrauded or done violence to Indians, and the Indians had responded in revenge by burning houses, murdering white people, and pillaging English settlements. However, these atrocities on both sides were limited in extent and under no organized leadership.

In 1675 an Indian known to the English as King Philip organized the Pequots and their neighbors in southern Massachusetts and Rhode Island in a concerted effort to drive the English into the sea. He was too late. The English hunted King Philip down and killed him in August 1676, but the conflagration, once started, spread rapidly eastward and grew into nearly 150 years of the intermittent French and Indian Wars.

Several level-headed people on both sides sought in vain to avert trouble. Silvanus Davis, agent at Arrowsic, sent a messenger to a gathering of Indians at Teconic on the Kennebec River above Vassalboro offering peace and protection at Arrowsic; but the messenger delivered his message as a threat rather than as a friendly offer. The leader of the Pemaquid settlement, perhaps Abraham Shurt, negotiated a temporary truce, but it failed to hold; too many influences were working against it. The inhabitants of Monhegan offered £5 for any Indian, dead or alive.

In September 1675 a gang of twenty-five white men from Falmouth on Casco Bay sailed up the Androscoggin River in a sloop towing two shallops to raid an Indian village and steal the corn crop. The Indians defended their property, drove off the raiders, and captured the two shallops.

In retaliation, the Indians crossed the Saco River in "English canoes" and attacked the town of Winter Harbor at the river mouth with some success but were driven off. Wells and Falmouth were also attacked.

A party of English fishermen on the Saco, doubtless on a holiday excursion, were arguing as to whether Indian babies were born able to swim. The wife of Squando, a Sokaki chief, paddled by with her baby. The whites, in order to settle their argument, splashed into the river and capsized the canoe. The mother rescued her son and got him safely ashore, but the shock was too much for him, and the child died. From then on, Squando and his tribe made no peace with white men.

Probably the most serious cause of conflict was the strict long-standing policy of the Massachusetts General Court, reiterated in 1675, that no guns or ammunition were to be sold to Indians. By this time, the Indians were depen dent on their muskets to kill the game they needed for food. Unable to ge powder and lead from the English, they turned to the French, who were eage to supply them and to encourage attacks on the English, although France an England were not at war.

A brief truce was arranged in the fall of 1676, but the English, not trustin the Indians, issued warrants for the arrest of those Indians they considere disloyal. Several unscrupulous shipmasters, taking no pains to distinguish on red man from another, used the warrants as licenses to kidnap any unwar Indians and sell them abroad as slaves. The agent at Pemaquid tried to war the Indians of this danger and met with chiefs at Teconic to try to aver retaliation. Chief Squando was not present, but his shadow hung over th conference, and when Chief Madockawando's plea for powder and shot ha to be refused, the conference broke up. Madockawando was a Penobscot chie at least one of whose daughters married Castin.

In the summer of 1676, the Indians devastated the mid-coast. The settle ment at the mouth of the Kennebec was destroyed, two men were killed, an sixteen people were captured. One girl escaped and ran twelve miles throug the woods, doubtless swimming to cross the Sasanoa River, and brought th word to the settlement at Sheepscot, near the present village of Alna abov Wiscasset, where a vessel was being finished by William Phipps, later Si William Phipps. The entire population embarked at once, sailed down th Sheepscot River, alarming settlers on the way, and took temporary refuge i the fort at Newagen. From there they and settlers from Damariscotta, Pema quid, and Corbin's Sound (probably what is now Christmas Cove) went o to Damariscove Island. The Indians destroyed Woolwich and attacked th Clark & Lake fort and trading post on Arrowsic by night, killing or capturin thirty-five people. Among the dead was Lake, Clark's partner. Silvanus Davi was wounded but crawled into a cave in the rocks, from which he escaped tw days later.

Some reports state that the 300 fugitives on Damariscove fled to Mon hegan, whence they sent a boat to salvage what they could from their aban doned homes. Scarcely had the boat returned than the people saw the smok of their burning houses rising from the mainland. Most of those taking refug on Monhegan later sailed westward to Boston, Salem, and Portsmouth. How ever, Damariscove Island was not totally abandoned, for later in the year th Indians attacked again, killing one man and seizing a sloop.

Jewell Island (in Casco Bay) was attacked in September, but the attac was repulsed. Black Point, Wells, and Cape Neddick were attacked. Finally, i November 1676 another truce was concluded with Mugg, an educated, inte ligent Indian who spoke English well and represented Chief Madockawand

The English, not trusting to the good faith of the "savages" who signe the truce, sent eastward a force of 200 men under Majors Frost and Waldro At Dover, New Hampshire, they treacherously betrayed and captured abo

200 of the "savages" who had met with the English in good faith, and continued eastward to Pemaquid. Here they met several chiefs, started to patch up a peace, ransomed three captives, and agreed to meet again in the afternoon unarmed. At this meeting Major Waldron saw the point of a lance under a board, seized it, and brandished it aloft, accusing the Indians of treachery. A squaw fled with a bundle of weapons. Waldron called for reinforcements from his ships, and a battle ensued. One chief, Megunaway, was captured and summarily executed and four others were kept prisoner, among whom was a sister of Chief Madockawando. A canoe was capsized, drowning five Indians, and considerable booty was captured, including a thousand pounds of beef. Waldron and Frost left forty men to garrison the Arrowsic fort on the way and returned to Boston, having effectively demolished the peace treaty.

One does not ordinarily think of Indians as sea fighters, but several incidents in the course of the Indian wars indicate that they were at home on salt water and could fight there.

In September 1676, Black Point had been attacked. A 30-ton ketch, probably about 36 feet long, belonging to a Mr. Fryar, was armed, heavily manned, and sent to Black Point to salvage whatever remained. The ketch anchored on October 12 behind Richmond Island, and several men were sent ashore. The situation deteriorated rapidly. The men ashore were seized by a party of Indians. The wind shifted to the northwest and breezed up, swinging the ketch toward the shore and close to the wharf. The Indians on the wharf fired down on the ketch, driving the crew below. Several other Indians came off in a canoe, and cut the anchor rode so that the ketch drifted ashore.

The Indians demanded that the crew surrender, threatening to burn the ketch and shoot the survivors as they fled the flames. All hands surrendered. It then appeared that Mugg, known to the English as Rogue Mugg, was in command and had developed a definite plan of action.

He had the ketch refloated and, keeping John Abbott, the sailing master, with an Indian crew sailed the vessel up the Sheepscot, where she was laid up for the winter. In February 1677, with Abbott (but not Mugg) still aboard and a crew of ten Indians, an Indian baby, and a white baby, she set off to the westward. Hubbard, in *Indian Wars,* tells what happened.

In the mouth of the Sheepscot River, always a rough spot with a southerly wind and an ebb tide, Abbott drove the ketch into the steepest seas he could find, shipped a few big ones over the bow, soaked the Indians thoroughly, and held her to it until his crew was seasick and entirely without enthusiasm for the voyage. He then put into Newagen at the southern tip of Southport Island. Eight of the ten Indians departed at once, having had quite enough.

The next day, Abbott, with the two remaining Indians and the white baby, set out again. Again it was blowing quite fresh. We can imagine Abbott standing at the tiller, looking terribly worried, telling tales of disaster at sea while he looked to windward seeking the steepest cresting seas, driving the ketch into them with the icy spray slashing aft over his frightened, seasick crew. At length he ran into Damariscove harbor. The Indians wanted nothing as much as they wanted dry land and a warm fire, which they sought ashore, urging Abbott to come with them. Abbott declared that the anchorage was a dangerous place and he must remain on the ketch to be ready for any emergency, and he and the white baby stayed aboard.

Then Abbott rubbed the ketch's mainmast, as high as he could reach, with a piece of greasy salt pork so he could hoist the mainsail alone. Choosing a propitious moment when the shore party was otherwise occupied and believing that they had had quite enough of salt water, he made sail, slipped out of the harbor, and with the baby as his only crew, sailed the ketch to the Isles of Shoals.

Previously, the Indians had acquired several shallops and we know not how many larger vessels. Francis Card, a settler captured earlier up the Kennebec, stated that Mugg's plan had been to assemble a fleet, attack and destroy the island settlements, and blockade the coast, thus effectively cutting off all white settlements. Then, according to Card, Mugg had intended to seize the islands in Boston Harbor, blockade Boston, and burn the town. The Fryar ketch may well have been a key part of the plan.

In the same spring, 1677, Mugg again attacked Arrowsic, which had been fortified by Major Waldron, killing six of a party sent to bury the dead from the attack the previous fall, and seizing their boat.

The Indians then went farther to sea and attacked every fishing vessel they could find. The principal encounters were off the Nova Scotia coast, where by August 1 the fishing port of Salem alone had lost twenty ketches. On August 18, Madockawando, in another effort to make peace, surrendered four prisoners at Pemaquid. The effort to assemble an organized Indian navy fell apart, for in another raid on Black Point, Mugg was killed. Without leadership, without heavy artillery or sufficient powder to supply what cannon they could capture, without supplies of rope and canvas, and, finally, without enough men capable of handling larger sailing vessels, Mugg's plan could not have succeeded. However, with his leadership, many difficulties might have been overcome, and the coast of Maine might have been without white men for a long time.

In the same year, 1677, Edmond Andros, the governor of New York under the Duke of York and through him governor of Maine east of the Kennebec, visited the coast and had a new fort built at Pemaquid, to be called Fort Charles, and he left a strong garrison to protect the settlement there. The Indian attacks ceased, although there was no formal treaty until the Treaty of Casco was signed in April 1678 between the Indian sagamores and the English, thus ending King Philip's War. At the close of the war, 260 white people had been killed or captured, 150 captured and returned, and almost every settlement on the Maine coast had been burned.

This summary of the Indian destruction during King Philip's War would suggest that the Maine coast was practically abandoned by the close of the war, but this does not appear to be the case. Pemaquid was fortified, and apparently there were still people living on Damariscove. These settlers, and those driven out of Maine to Massachusetts, were no longer itinerant fishermen but permanent inhabitants. They had bought land, cut fields and pastures out of the wilderness, built homes, wharves, and boats, and put down stout roots. Their salt-water farms were all they had in the world. When they were driven off of those, they had nothing, so they came back to them just as soon as they could.

NOTES

This chapter was extracted mostly from Mary Calvert's *Dawn Over the Kennebec.* It is somewhat enriched by incidents from *The American Indian as Sea Fighter,* by Horace Beck, and by a long, detailed, and exciting account of the capture and recapture of Fryar's ketch in John Johnston's *History of Bristol and Bremen in the State of Maine Including the Pemaquid Settlements.* Unfortunately, the account is too long to include in its entirety here. The mention of Abbott's greasing of the mast comes from another account in *A Narrative of the Indian Wars in New England* by Reverend William Hubbard.

Madockawando was a chief of the Penobscots, a wise and forbearing statesman who realized that his people could never win a war between the French and the English. He tried for peace, but the situation was insoluble politically. He went with the French ultimately, for several of his daughters were married either officially or unofficially to Baron de St. Castin at Pentagoet, and it was only from the French that he could buy the powder and shot his people needed to survive.

TEN

The Interim Years and King William's War, 1678-1698

BY THE END of King Philip's War, the political control of the Maine coast was tangled at best. Massachusetts, despite the claim of James, Duke of York, brother of King Charles, to govern east of the Kennebec, claimed under her charter the coast east at least as far as Matinicus. The French claimed that Acadia, awarded to France by the Treaty of Breda and subsequent negotiations between King Charles and King Louis, extended west to the Kennebec. The French were firmly established at Pentagoet on the Penobscot River, the English at Pemaquid. Massachusetts had sent commissioners to Maine to secure the allegiance of the inhabitants of the mid-coast, who much preferred the more or less benign neglect of Massachusetts, with which they traded extensively, to the meddling rule of Governor Edmond Andros and the New York Council, governing for the Duke of York.

After the burning of Pemaquid by the Indians in 1676, Andros had Fort Charles built at Pemaquid and well garrisoned. It was finished in 1677, unfortunately without including the great boulder to the west. King Philip's War ended in 1678, and settlers and fishermen immediately began returning. Cotton Mather reports the English "stocked their farms and tilled their fields . . . their lumber and fishing became a considerable merchandise . . . continual accessions were made unto them until ten or a dozen towns in the County of Cornwall east of the Kennebec and the Province of Maine the Piscataqua to the Kennebec were started up into something of observation."

That a substantial population of farmers and fishermen soon returned to the Pemaquid area is indicated by the action of the New York Council, which governed the region under the Duke of York. The rules were made to defend the region against French and possible Indian attack, to prevent foolhardy acts by the settlers, to foster a profitable fishery, and to prevent encroachment by unlicensed traders. Some of the rules were:

All fishermen and old inhabitants to be restored and protected.
Constables to be appointed to the fishing islands and Indyans to have equall Justice and Dispatch.
Fishermen . . . not to trade with the Indyans to the prejudice of the fishery. . . .
Indyans not to go to the fishing islands.
. . . no trade to bee at any other place than Pemaquid and none at all with the Indyans. . . .
All vessels if they come to trade and fish shall enter at Pemaquid.
No coasting vessel shall trade on the coast as BumBoats [itinerant general stores] . . . from Harbor to Harbor.
No straggling farms shall be erected nor no houses built anywhere under the number of twenty.
No rum to be dranke on that side the fort stands and after sunset no one on the peninsula where the fort stands.
An ordinary [tavern] to be set up at everey island and fishing place, but no one to tipple to excessive drinking.
No one to range the woods or sail on the creeks.
The Duke's sloop now sent upon the King's service to remain all winter to enforce the revenue laws.

There was further evidence of vigorous activity on the coast between 1678 and 1690. Six families were living at Long Cove (now Chamberlain) and also there were several families at New Harbor, Muscongus, Round Pond, and Monhegan.

There must have been a considerable number of fishermen, for they were prohibited from fouling harbors with offal and "gutts." The fishermen, in turn, petitioned the Council for regulation of prices charged them by merchants.

Between 1680 and 1685, William Pepperrell of Kittery, father of Sir William Pepperrell, the hero of Louisbourg, was sending vessels to Newfoundland from Kittery selling pork, lumber, and rum. The lumber may have come down the Piscataqua River, but the pork came from colonies to the westward and the rum from the West Indies; Pepperrell traded for these with salt fish. Pepperrell had a fishing station at the Isles of Shoals, but surely that was not his only source of fish.

In 1685 Richard Pattishall bought Damariscove Island. In the same year, the governor of Massachusetts cautioned Baron de St. Castin at Pentagoet not to interfere with English fishermen on Matinicus.

In 1686 John Dollen was given a deed to a fishing station on Monhegan including a house, a barn, outhouses, a stable, an orchard, a cornfield, and one-third of the marsh. It also included fishing stages. There must have been a considerable population on the island then, for Dollen was also appointed sergeant of the militia. In October 1689, as King William's War broke out between France and England, the French raided Monhegan and drove out twenty families. Dollen and at least some others later returned.

In 1687 William Sturt petitioned the governor of Massachusetts for possession of Squirrel Island in Boothbay Harbor. He wanted to build a house on the Hypocris Islands (Fishermans Island), which were then, as now, bare of trees. Squirrel Island was unoccupied and heavily wooded.

In 1689, at the beginning of King William's War, not only was Pattishall killed at Damariscove "as he lay in his sloop," but later in the summer thirteen Indians attacked the island and were repulsed, presumably by a substantial number of fishermen living there. In the same year a frigate and a sloop were assigned to patrol the coast to protect the fishing fleet and the valuable fishing settlements from French and Indian attack.

Meanwhile, wheels far from the Maine coast had been turning. Puritan Massachusetts resented the rule of Charles II and the claim of his brother James to govern east of the Kennebec. Massachusetts merchants, supported by their government, ignored the Navigation Acts, laws enacted by Parliament to restrict Colonial commerce, and declared them invalid inasmuch as Massachusetts was not represented in Parliament. Charles and James resented the stiff-necked independence of Massachusetts and in 1684 revoked the Massachusetts Bay Charter and made Massachusetts a royal colony. Within months, in early 1685, Charles II died and his brother became James II, uniting the English settlements from the Hudson to the St. Croix into the royal Dominion of New England. James appointed Edmond Andros, previously governor of New York, as governor of New England.

Andros, who had built and garrisoned Fort Charles at Pemaquid, was an active and intelligent governor, but the Massachusetts government, deprived of its charter, resented him, and did all it could to block his administration. The Maine fishermen, resentful of the decrees of his New York Council, ignored them.

Andros also incited the resentment of the French and their Indian friends.

In 1687 a shipment of wine consigned to Baron de St. Castin was landed at the fort at Pentagoet within a quarter of a mile of Castin's house, but Palmer and West, English revenue officers, sent an agent to seize the wine because it had not been entered in the customhouse at Pemaquid. This irritated the Baron, who, it will be remembered, was a loyal subject of Louis XIV. Also, he had married one or more of Chief Madockawando's daughters and, through his father-in-law and the fur-trading business, was very influential with the Penobscot Indians. The Baron was outraged at this invasion of his privacy and possessions.

Irritation rose to more serious levels when in 1688 Governor Andros, trying to enforce England's claim to eastern Maine as far as the St. Croix, came personally in the frigate *Rose* to Pentagoet and in Castin's absence took aboard his vessel all Castin's property except his chapel altar. Andros sent a messenger to tell Castin he could have it all back by coming to Pemaquid and swearing allegiance to King James. This, of course, Castin refused to do.

Chief Madockawando and Castin's Indians, angered by the insult and alarmed at Governor Andros's increased zeal in building forts, especially those on the Royal River, attacked North Yarmouth, Sheepscot, and New Dartmouth, now Newcastle.

Andros responded pacifically by releasing Indian captives, calling on the Indians to release white captives, and seeking peace. The Indians failed to respond, so he raised a company of 800 men, raided Indian towns, destroying canoes, houses, and everything he could find. Andros spent the winter at Pemaquid and in the spring left garrisons at the forts in Pemaquid, New Dartmouth, Sheepscot, Arrowsic, and Falmouth.

Events in the spring of 1689, however, swept away all efforts to keep the peace. James II (Catholic) was deposed, and William of Orange (Protestant) and his wife Mary, daughter of James II, became King and Queen of England. In April, when the news reached Boston, Andros, despised governor under James, was imprisoned and authority resumed by those who had governed before the Massachusetts Bay Charter was revoked. This government at once withdrew the garrisons left by Andros, leaving only a small force at Pemaquid under Lieutenant James Weems.

When King James II felt himself so unwelcome in England that he fled to France disguised as a washerwoman, dropping the Great Seal of England into the Thames on the way, he was welcomed by Louis XIV and given a pension. Louis promised to restore Catholic James to the English throne in opposition to Dutch Protestant William, and for other reasons concerned with a tangle of royal family inheritances in central Europe, declared war on England.

On the Maine coast, it was merely the old conflict renewed. The English sought to expand the area of settlement, with fishing their primary resource and lumbering only slightly behind it. They cut the forests, tilled the fields, raised hay for their animals, and made the land untenable for the Indian way of life.

The French, still mostly transient fishermen and fur traders, dwelt in a few fortified posts and depended for their survival on Indian good will.

From the Maine coast, Boston was far more accessible than Québec. Two or three days in decent weather would get a vessel and cargo to Boston, whereas the voyage around Nova Scotia and through the difficult shoals of the St. Lawrence might take weeks. Consequently, both the French and Indians on the coast traded extensively and illegally with Boston, and English vessels fished in Acadian waters. The French government and the Jesuits strongly resisted these associations with the English, for they feared the infiltration of Protestant ideas and democratic ambitions. The French government went to great expense to keep the loyalty of the Indians with supplies of arms, powder, lead, food, clothes, and tools, making it more profitable for the Indians to raid

the English settlements than to live by hunting. The Jesuits were hand-in
glove with the French government, even going so far as to tell their conver
that Jesus Christ and the Virgin Mary were French and that Christ had bee
crucified by the English. Granted, some of the Jesuit fathers were sincere i
their efforts to Christianize the Indians; nevertheless, they used whatever influ
ence they could bring to bear to persuade their converts to extirpate th
English heretics.

Therefore, when Louis XIV declared war on England, the French an
Indians, already angered by Andros, were eager for conflict.

In May 1689 the fort at Falmouth was taken by Indians from the Penob
scot, only a few of the garrison escaping in a shallop. Then a party of English
men from Arrowsic sailed across the Kennebec in a sloop to pick up som
cattle. They were attacked by Indians in canoes, and, after a desperate fight i
which six of the nine on the sloop were killed, the sloop outsailed the cano
and escaped. On August 10 the Indians captured the Arrowsic fort.

On August 2 and 3 the Indians, urged on by Father Thury and led b
Moxus and Chief Madockawando, attacked Fort Charles at Pemaquid, killing
capturing, or driving the settlers into the fort. By climbing the great bould
that Andros had not included within the fort, the Indians were able to fi
down on the defenders. (The boulder is now enclosed by the reconstructe
round tower.) At last, Weems, with half his small garrison dead, and badl
wounded himself, surrendered on condition the defenders be allowed to leav
in the two sloops in the harbor. However, the Indians killed the disarme
English. Father Thury, as quoted in Baxter's *Pioneers of New France in Ne
England,* takes pride in his Indians. He reports that there was no drunkenne
and no torture, although the Indians killed those whom they wished to kill—
all Protestants, no doubt.

The fort was leveled, and the assailants returned in triumph to Pentagoe
This left the country east of Falmouth quite without defense. All the inhabi
tants—without exception, according to a number of authorities—fled to Fa
mouth and thence westward. The coast was left to the Indians, as it had bee
a century before.

King William's War was essentially a French victory on the mid-coas
leaving the French and Indians in control as far west as York, but at sea
continued vigorously. French privateers appeared on the coast, preying o
English merchantmen and fishermen. The British colonials fitted out priva
teers to cruise in the Gulf of St. Lawrence, preying on French supply ship
Indians in big canoes capable of crossing the Bay of Fundy attacked the colo
nial fishing fleets, and the British Admiralty sent the frigate *Nonsuch,* the sloo
of war *Mary,* and the brigantine *William and Mary* to patrol the coast.

In 1690 a forty-man garrison was established by the British at the Isles o
Shoals, again to protect fishermen. That same year, two sloops in Penobsco
Bay were attacked by Indians, but got clear—further evidence of naval activity
if not fishing.

In 1695 several ketches from the Isles of Shoals were captured by the French, evidence that the fishing settlement was surviving.

Representatives of the colonies east of the Hudson met in New York early in 1690 and developed a grandiose plan for attacking Canada. An army of colonials and Iroquois Indians was to attack Montréal via Lake Champlain, while a naval force principally composed of Massachusetts, Connecticut, and Rhode Island vessels was to attack Québec. The first plan foundered for lack of leadership and coordination coupled with an epidemic of smallpox. The second plan achieved a strong start under Sir William Phipps, a rough colonial diamond, indeed.

William Phipps was born in 1651 in what is now Woolwich, across the Kennebec River from Bath. He was one of twenty-six children, all with the same mother. Until he was eighteen, he kept sheep, but then ambition stirred him to become a ship carpenter. Phipps was just finishing a vessel on the Sheepscot River in 1676 when Indians attacked the town, and the inhabitants fled aboard his vessel. After this he moved to Boston and married a widow whom he promised he would someday live with "in a fair brick house in Green Lane in North Boston."

Phipps learned to read and write, apparently not very well, for historian Francis Parkman says his signature was that of a peasant. Resolved to make his fortune at one step, he went to England and persuaded the Admiralty to lend him a frigate in order to salvage a treasure in a foundered Spanish galleon. In 1687, after quelling three mutinies by force of fists, arms, and character, he returned to England with gold, silver, and gems worth £300,000. After paying off all who had claims on it and dividing the rest among his crew, he had a fortune of £16,000 and a knighthood. Sir William Phipps returned to Boston in 1689 and in 1690 was put in charge of the force to assault Québec.

In April 1690 he sailed eastward, intending to subdue Acadia first. In May he took Port Royal, captured the French governor Mineval and a number of other important officials, looted the fortifications and the private property of those who would not swear allegiance to King William, and the property of some of those who did so swear, and left a provisional government of local residents in charge. He dispatched Captain Alden, who had already taken Pentagoet, to seize La Hève and Chedabucto, and returned to Boston in triumph.

The French governor was released after a while, but Phipps kept much of his personal property.

Despite Phipp's success against the French in Acadia, the Québec project stalled. Massachusetts, bereft of its charter in 1684, had no legally recognized government. Requests to the British government for military supplies were refused. Private subscription failed to provide sufficient money. Prayer and fasting failed to secure divine assistance. However, Massachusetts borrowed against the booty expected from Québec, collected thirty-two vessels of various types, including one West Indian merchantman heavily armed with forty-four guns—caliber not stated—and numerous smaller vessels. Volunteers were called for, and, their number being insufficient, other men were impressed. Phipps, with no military experience whatever beyond the parade through Port Royal, was put in command. On August 9 the fleet sailed with 2,200 seamen and soldiers, "rustic warriors," as Parkman calls them. They were brave and determined men but untrained and ignorant of how to make war.

When they had arrived at Québec, Phipps sent a letter to Count Frontenac demanding surrender. Frontenac refused, with no little emphasis. Phipps mounted a noisy bombardment. The French replied vigorously, shooting away the British flag at the stern of Phipps's ship. The colonials spent much ammunition firing at the French flag on the citadel, quite in vain. Major Walley, in command of the troops, landing below the St. Charles River, attempted ineffectually a crossing of that river and an assault on the city. Several thousand French soldiers from Montréal arrived to support Frontenac's garrison, and within the week poor communications and lack of powder forced Phipps to retreat with nothing accomplished. Massachusetts, unable to pay its debt, was forced to issue paper money and was left financially exhausted and discouraged in spirit. Frontenac, meanwhile, urged King Louis to send a fleet to capture Boston and New York, thereby to secure North America and the Grand Banks fisheries for France.

Both Louis XIV and William of Orange were far too busy in Ireland and on the European continent to pay any attention to America. The war in Maine, then, continued, largely at sea.

The French rebuilt Port Royal in 1691, for Massachusetts was quite unable to send a force to hold it. In August 1691 two sloops bound up Penobscot Bay were grounded out. The French Indians attacked the English crews ashore, a hot skirmish took place, the crews retreated to the grounded vessels, which they defended until the tide came and floated them off.

Late in the summer, near Boon Island off York, an English sloop and a shallop cruising in company captured a shallop "with a great gun" manned by French and Indians. The shallop had been harassing the English fishing fleet.

The French, alarmed by a conference of Abenaki chiefs with the English as a preliminary to peace, put forth extra efforts to hold Abenaki allegiance. Their generous gifts of arms, ammunition, food, and clothing, as well as spiritual massage by Jesuit priests Bigot and Thury, led to a savage Indian attack on York in February 1692. The town was devastated and a number of people killed or captured, but four blockhouses held out, and the town was not abandoned. Nevertheless, the French made much of the victorious Indians and urged them on to further depredations.

In June 1692 an even larger band of Indians, led by French officers and accompanied by Castin and several priests, descended upon the town of Wells. On June 9 two English sloops had just entered the tidal river at Wells with supplies and fourteen soldiers to reinforce the settlement. The next morning, the Indians attacked the palisaded blockhouse after being urged on by a French officer. While the blockhouse was resisting stoutly, a party of Indians occupied a point at the entrance to the river, blockading the sloops inside, and an all-out attack was mounted. Musketry, however, was ineffective against the thick bulwarks of the vessels, whose crews gave as good as they received and quickly quenched what blazes were started by fire arrows. As the tide fell and the flats bared out, the Indians built a breastwork of boards on a two-wheeled cart, piled hay in front of it, and pushed it out toward the vessels, firing from behind it. As they approached, they set the hay ablaze; but just before they got close enough to set the nearest sloop afire, one of the cart wheels sank in the soft mud. A Frenchman dashed out and tried to lift the wheel, but was shot dead. The fire died down and the attack stalled.

Then the tide began to rise, making the rudimentary fort on the cart untenable. Several of the French and Indians were shot down as they ran for their lives across the flats, which must have been already knee deep.

The attack on the blockhouse continued ineffectually all day. Shortly after high water, a raft loaded with hay was drifted down on the tide to set the sloops afire. It was barely carried clear of the sloops by wind and current. Shortly thereafter, the attackers departed, leaving the sloops and the blockhouse in English hands.

The war at sea continued vigorously between French and English naval vessels and privateers, with fishermen and traders on both sides the victims. The English naval patrols convoyed merchantmen, and Salem sent out an armed shallop to protect fishermen from Indian attack.

In 1692 the English government found time to grant Massachusetts a new charter under which was included all of Maine, Nova Scotia, and Canada to the St. Lawrence. Sir William Phipps was named the first governor. He came east in August, picked up the guns still lying in the ruined fort in Falmouth, and built a new stone fort at Pemaquid, which he named Fort William Henry. It was armed with at least fourteen guns, of which six were eighteen-pounders. Fort William Henry was a powerful influence in controlling the Indians and establishing a strong barrier to French conquest. The French, of course, could not allow this fort to stand unmolested. Late in the year, Count Frontenac sent two armed vessels to Pentagoet, where they picked up 200 Indians to join with another force of Indians under Villebon, governor of Acadia, to attack Pemaquid, and then York, Wells, and the Isles of Shoals. However, John Nelson, a Massachusetts captive in Québec, bribed two French soldiers to defect to Boston with the news of the impending attack. When the French ships arrived at Pemaquid, they found an armed vessel from Massachusetts lying under the heavy guns of Fort William Henry and gave up the attack.

In 1693, the war on salt water continuing, Convers, the hero of the defense of Wells, built a fort on the Saco River. The Indians, impressed by the impregnable nature of this fort and that of Pemaquid, made solemn peace with Massachusetts in August 1693.

The French, of course, resisted this course of action. They assembled a force of Indians in the spring of 1694 at Pentagoet, where Villebon and the Jesuits Bigot and Thury, with generous gifts of powder, lead, and flattery, stirred them to attack Pemaquid. However, news came that Sir William Phipps was patrolling nearby in a frigate, had feasted Chief Madockawando and other Indians aboard, and that the Indians had thrown overboard the hatchet. Accordingly, the Indian expedition bypassed Pemaquid and attacked Durham, New Hampshire, and Groton, Massachusetts.

The war on fishermen and traders continued, with British patrols attempting to stand off French privateers and marauding West Indian pirates. In 1695 several ketches from the Isles of Shoals were captured, probably by Indians, and taken up Casco Bay.

A large force, including Villebon, Villieu, d'Iberville, Castin, and Father Thury, proceeded westward from Pentagoet in June 1694, but, perhaps impressed by the strength of Fort William Henry, made no attack. Disguised as a friendly Indian, Villieu entered the fort and made a plan of it, which he later sent to France. The expedition continued westward and destroyed the settlement at Oyster River, New Hampshire.

In November, Chief Bomazeen, one of those who had signed the treaty made at Pemaquid in 1693, appeared at Fort William Henry under a flag of truce. There was no parley, however, as he and his party were instantly made prisoners and sent to Boston. The others were released, but Bomazeen was kept because of the treachery of the savages—a strange excuse from the English.

The Indians so wanted Bomazeen freed that they assembled for another parley in May 1695, but the English refused to release the chief and made unreasonable demands. The Indians retaliated on whatever English they could find, including Sergeant Hugh March and three other soldiers stationed at Fort William Henry.

There now followed an example of English treachery. In February 1696 three chiefs, Toxus, Egeremet, and Abenquid, appeared at the fort under a flag of truce to arrange for an exchange of prisoners, although warned by Father Thury not to do so. The new commander of the fort, Pascho Chubb, after several days of friendly discussion and trade, suddenly and without provocation attacked and murdered Egeremet, Abenquid, and two others.

In 1696 the British frigate *Nonsuch,* in an action with a Frenchman, lost her foretopmast and was taken, thus severely weakening British control of the sea off the coast. This opened the way for an all-out attack on Pemaquid. Madockawando and the chiefs who had signed and kept the 1693 treaty were persuaded that breaking faith with heretics was no sin.

The French took instant advantage of this to set up an attack on Fort William Henry, long a thorn in their flesh from both a military and an economic point of view. In August 1696 Pierre Le Moyne d'Iberville, with two French ships, captured another English patrolling vessel, *Newport.* He picked up at Pentagoet Castin, Villieu, a force of French soldiers, some 200 Indians, and Fathers Thury and Simon. They attacked the fort by land and by sea on August 14, to no effect. Chubb boastfully refused to surrender. The French then set up cannon and mortars ashore and urged Chubb to surrender lest his whole force be slaughtered should the fort be taken by assault. Chubb had ninety-five men and ample supplies of food and ammunition; but, after a few mortar shells had exploded inside the fort, he surrendered.

The French hastily removed Chubb and the garrison to a nearby island under the guns of d'Iberville's ships. The Indians found one of their friends in irons in the fort, and, enraged, destroyed the fort as much as lay in their power to do so and would have killed the garrison, especially Chubb, had not d'Iberville protected them. Chubb was imprisoned in Boston for having surrendered the fort, but even that did not save him, for he was later captured by the Indians at Andover, Massachusetts, and was killed picturesquely.

After further raids, depredations, naval engagements, and attacks on the fishing fleet, the three parties to the war in America, all heartily sick of it no doubt, laid down their arms. France and England had resolved their tangled conflicts in Europe at the Peace of Ryswick in 1697, and there was nothing more to fight about. Conquests, such as they were, were mutually restored, and an exhausted peace settled on Maine leaving nothing significant accomplished by eight years of bloody war. Neither side won, and the Indians lost.

NOTES

The first part of this chapter is drawn from Arlita Dodge's *Pemaquid.* She quotes from Cotton Mather. Ida S. Proper in *Monhegan, the Cradle of New England* gives Andros's rules for the conduct of Maine's inhabitants in detail and in the original diction, and she adds a good deal more about John Dollen than appears here. Material on Damariscove and the Boothbay region comes from Charles Griffin's thesis, *A History of Fishing in the Boothbay Region,* including the reference to Squirrel Island as a source of timber. James P. Baxter's *Pioneers of New France in New England* opens a window on French involvement from a Yankee point of view, particularly on the machinations of Castin and the Jesuits. Francis Parkman in *Count Frontenac and New France* takes a more thorough and more objective point of view. By unduly condensing it, I have done violence to Parkman's brief biography of Sir William Phipps; it is a story a novelist would hesitate to offer for publication. Mary Calvert's *Dawn Over the Kennebec* continues to be useful to the student of Maine history. Most of the marine events in this chapter come from *The Indian as a Sea Fighter,* by Horace P. Beck, a small book which has never been appreciated as it should have been.

This tale of fragmented, disoriented, badly managed conflict is at best inconclusive and at worst a tale of betrayal, arson, murder, piracy, and pillage to no purpose whatsoever. Still, it is the story of what really happened to real people who lived before us on the same coast we inhabit today.

ELEVEN

Queen Anne's War and Lovewell's War, 1703-1725

SIGNIFICANT AS the Treaty of Ryswick may have been in Europe, by the French and Indians of the Maine coast it was largely ignored. The French still claimed the coast as far west as the Kennebec and urged on the Indians to drive out the English. Partly because Chief Bomazeen was still a prisoner in Boston and partly because the basic cause of conflict remained unresolved, the Indians were not hard to persuade. They burned houses, killed settlers and livestock, attacked fishing vessels, and interrupted the coastal trade on which the few remaining English settlements depended.

The English claimed the coast as far east as the St. Croix, fished in Acadian waters, traded illegally with French and Indians, sent out naval patrols to protect fishermen and coasters, and tried to defend their isolated forts and settlements.

Finally, in January 1699, Indians and English met at Mare Point, now called Mere Point, below Brunswick and agreed to a treaty which settled nothing but at least brought an end to the fighting and returned captives on both sides, including Bomazeen.

Both English and Indians had suffered serious losses during King William's War. The Abenakis were virtually eliminated as a nation, not only by the death and capture of many of their warriors and by raids on their unprotected villages, raids which destroyed gardens and food stores and killed women and children, but also by disease and famine. The Indians were susceptible to diseases against which the Europeans seem to have built up some genetic immunity so that measles, for instance, was very often fatal to Indians yet was often no more than an incident in the life of a European child. Smallpox, too, which wiped out whole Indian villages, was a disease from which many Europeans recovered. John Josselyn, who visited Maine in 1663, mentions plague, smallpox, and syphilis among others.

Although the English settlements in Maine had been destroyed except for Wells, York, Kittery, and the Isles of Shoals, although their coastal trade was cut off, and although they had 450 people killed and 250 taken captive, the English had vast resources in Massachusetts virtually untouched by the war. Settlers soon began to return, trade was reestablished, and fishing resumed.

In the brief period of peace between 1697 and the beginning of Queen Anne's War in 1702, Colonel Romer, sent by Massachusetts to report on the condition of the eastern country, recommended a fort on Wood End, the north end of Damariscove Island, to protect the growing trade in that area.

This brief and uneasy peace was broken by the death of King William in 1702 and the accession of Queen Anne, daughter of James II. She at once renewed the war on France, giving the French in America an excuse to urge on the Indians again to raid English settlements.

Governor Dudley of Massachusetts, in an effort to conciliate the Maine Indians, called a conference at Falmouth on June 20, 1703, at which, with feasting, dancing, and song, the treaty of Mare Point was reaffirmed. However, the French moved vigorously behind the scenes to incite further violence. One of their principal supports was Father Rasle, a Jesuit priest. After an apprenticeship in Canada and Illinois, he was sent in the last years of the seventeenth century to the Indian town of Norridgewock at the confluence of the Kennebec and Sandy rivers to establish a mission. He soon won the respect and loyalty of his Indian congregation by his sincerity and willingness to share their lives and take their part in the defense of their lands. By the French and Indians he was regarded as a saint. Seen through English eyes he was a devil, an agent of the French government and the hated Catholic church inciting the Indians to arson and murder. It is reported that he was present at Falmouth but took no active part in the negotiations.

French influence was soon sufficient to turn the Indians against the English again. The fort at Casco was attacked in August 1703 and resisted strongly until relieved by Captain Southack in the *Province Galley,* a vessel built in Massachusetts especially to patrol and protect Maine waters. Southack captured and destroyed over 200 Indian canoes and recaptured a vessel previously taken by the Indians.

In spite of Southack's efforts, however, Indian canoes again interrupted the coastal trade on which the settlers depended. Governor Dudley beat the drum for 150 volunteers to man the coasting fleet. This must have consisted of a considerable number of vessels and suggests a growing coastal population. One might observe that the presence of any settlers at all in coastal Maine east of Wells is evidence of the energy and courage of those who pressed eastward even in the midst of war. It also suggests that there were considerable intervals between attacks and that possibly commercial relations were established informally among settlers and local Indians to their mutual advantage, only to be interrupted by French-inspired attacks by northern Indians. Indeed, Horace Beck in *The American Indian as a Sea Fighter in Colonial Times* writes, "1705, 1706, and 1707 appear to have been relatively peaceful years, in which trade pursued its normal course, with about the only 'news from eastward' concerning itself with the mast fleet, occasional visits to Piscatua [Piscataqua, now

Portsmouth] by the Governor and lists of vessels clearing from the above port to various parts, principally the West Indies and Boston." This in spite of the continuing European war.

At least until 1707, Governor Dudley and his son carried on a lucrative trade with the Indians in powder, lead, rigging, and naval stores. It may be that the Governor did this as a means of persuading the Indians to remain on the English side. Certainly, if he did not provide them with these military supplies, the French would—and did.

It is especially interesting to notice the inclusion of rigging and naval stores in the list, for it suggests that the Indians had captured or built sailing vessels and intended to maintain them. In 1702, for instance, Indians in canoes captured three fishing vessels in Port La Tour. In 1703 they attacked unsuccessfully a sloop in Casco Bay, and in 1704 they attacked another. In August 1711 there were reports of French and Indian privateers and of "Pyrates" on the coast. A French privateer was captured with a number of Indians in her crew, and one Captain Carver was captured by privateers. Governor Dudley considered sending the *Province Galley* east again to put out the fires, but nothing was done.

Queen Anne's War appears to have been more devastating than the preceding conflict. In 1704 Colonel Church was sent with a fleet to attack the French in Maine. He makes no mention of a settlement at Monhegan, where he stopped, nor at Matinicus. However, at Matinicus he got word of a French family "on a neighboring island." He captured them and continued eastward all the way to Passamaquoddy Bay, making a thorough search of the coast and finding only a few poor French families struggling to cling to the edge of the continent. Church concluded his expedition with the murder of several Frenchmen who had surrendered and a futile demonstration before Port Royal.

In 1707, 150 Indians attacked the town of Winter Harbor at the mouth of the Saco River. They first went for two shallops in the harbor manned by eight fishermen. The fishermen held their fire until the Indians were at point-blank range, then fired a volley that did enough execution to stall the attack temporarily. They abandoned the slower of the two shallops, cut the anchor rode of the faster one, and made sail in a light breeze. The Indians came on again, manned the abandoned shallop, and, to increase her speed, towed her with their canoes. The English rowed. At one time the Indians got close enough to grab at the shallop's oars, but were driven back by musketry. The Indians returned the fire. Benjamin Daniel, mortally wounded, cried, "I am a dead man, but give me a gun to kill one more before I go." But he had not strength enough to fire. The battle lasted for three hours. At last the shallop got clear, with the loss of Daniel on one side and thirty Indians on the other.

After several futile efforts early in the war to take Port Royal, in 1710 Colonels Nicholson and Vetch, with an overwhelming landing force, seven naval vessels, and a motley fleet of transports manned by impressed sailors, easily captured the fort. Nicholson renamed it Annapolis Royal in honor of Queen Anne. As it was the only major fort in Nova Scotia, its capture assured British control of Acadia and for practical purposes concluded Queen Anne's

War in America—although the next year, a shallop was captured off Monhegan and "Pyrates" landed at Damariscove and careened two vessels.

In March 1713 the muddled European war came to an end with the Treaty of Utrecht. By this treaty France ceded to England all of Acadia, Nova Scotia, Newfoundland, and the Hudson Bay Territory, voiding, on paper at least, all French claim to any part of the Maine coast. In July 1713 peace was made with the Indians at Portsmouth. The treaty required the Indians to swear allegiance to Queen Anne and to give hostages for their good behavior. Furthermore, they had to pay the board and lodging for these hostages.

However, at sea, hostilities continued. In 1715 Nova Scotia Indians attacked the fishing fleet in such force that the armed ship *Rose,* the *Mary Galley,* two frigates, and two sloops were sent to recapture the vessels and to warn the rest of the fishermen to return to home ports. Such a force suggests a fleet of Indian privateers far more formidable than a number of canoes. It is probable that the Indians, after the manner of Caribbean buccaneers, seized small vessels and fitted them out as privateers to seize larger ones.

Ashore, the English continued to press into lands the Indians believed to be theirs. In 1715, twenty-six houses had been built on Arrowsic Island, Fort William Henry was being rebuilt at Pemaquid, and a stone fort was built at Cushnoc just below the present site of Augusta. The Kennebec Proprietors were selling land on the river. Governor Shute called a conference in Arrowsic in August 1717. The Indians, advised by Father Rasle, declared their resolve to fight for any land east of the Kennebec and objected to the building of English forts. Shute took a hard line; the Indians granted concessions. Again, in 1721, a conference was held at which the Indians, again advised by Rasle and also by a son of Baron de St. Castin, objected to English encroachment. Although the Indians had made as yet no significant hostile move, in December 1721 the younger Castin was seized, taken to Boston a prisoner, and sharply questioned. As a grandson of Chief Madockawando and a leader of the Penobscots, he declared he was doing and would do all he could to preserve peace, and he was released. In an attempt to seize Father Rasle, Colonel Westbrook attacked Norridgewock in January 1722. Rasle escaped, but Westbrook seized letters from the governor of Canada, Vaudrevil, urging Rasle to incite the Indians against the English. Westbrook also seized the dictionary of the Abenaki language that Rasle had compiled.

In the spring of 1722, the Indians, resenting the seizure of Castin and the attempt on Rasle, burned Brunswick and Georgetown as well as isolated houses along the Kennebec. The English retaliated by shooting fifteen sleeping Indians and offered a bounty of £15 for the scalp of an Indian male over twelve years old and £8 for any captive woman or child. In July 1722 Governor Shute issued a formal declaration of war on the Indians.

There was a maritime aspect to this war, called Lovewell's War. On June 14, 1722, six Indians attacked a fishing schooner in Fox Islands Thorofare. The story is told in a broadside ballad of the time written by "W. G." The schooner was manned only by Lieutenant Jacob Tilton, his brother Daniel, and a boy. The six Indians, led by Captain Sam and Governor Penobscot, boarded the schooner as she lay at anchor in "Fox Bay," probably Fox Islands Thorofare. One Indian sat down on each side of Tilton and one behind him. It is interesting to note that neither brother suspected the Indians of hostile intent at first. Conversation turned to the hostages held by Governor Shute. Tilton said he was just a fisherman and hostages were none of his business. The discussion heated up. The Indians seized Tilton and tried to bind him. He got out the cuddy door and almost escaped, but they finally subdued him and tied him up. Daniel, on deck, was also bound.

Both were beaten and threatened, but talk continued. Tilton objected that France and England were at peace and asked the reason for the attack. Captain Sam replied that they intended to kill and capture Governor Shute's men, capture Colonel Westbrook's fort, and drive the English from their lands. French and English treaties were none of their concern. Then they made the boy hoist their flag over the schooner, and two of the Indians went ashore.

Daniel persuaded one of the remaining four to untie his legs and ease the lashings on his hands a little. Then the Indians went to rummaging about in search of loot. Daniel saw a splitting knife on deck, managed to back up to it and cut his bonds. Pretending still to be tied, keeping his hands behind his back, he waited until the Indians were busy in search of booty and then cut loose his brother. The Indians, perceiving this, "Like roaring lyons with an axe and knives, Made violent assault to take their lives."

Swinging his splitting knife with furious energy, Daniel cut up Captain Sam about the face and head and flung him overboard while Jacob went for Governor Penobscot, punched him bloody, and threw him overboard. Jacob then went for another Indian and quickly put him over the side. The Indian swam for shore but drowned on the way.

Captain Sam and Governor Penobscot climbed into a canoe alongside. Jacob aimed a musket the Indians had brought aboard, but the musket misfired. He seized a setting pole lying on deck and beat the Indians lustily about their heads until the canoe capsized and both drowned. The last Indian jumped overboard and swam for his life, the only survivor of the four.

Then three more canoes appeared, crowded with warriors. Daniel cut the anchor rode, they made sail, and escaped, landing the next day at Matinicus. The part played by the boy is not mentioned except that he much relieved the pain of the two brothers by binding up their wounds.

On June 22 the Indians attacked another fisherman, and so much concern was felt for the fishing fleet that ten whaleboats were sent by the Massachusetts government to patrol the coast. There was also considerable activity on the Nova Scotia coast, with Indians attacking fishermen and fishermen retaliating. The information gleaned from Boston newspapers is fragmentary, and abounds with references to events not previously described or described in earlier issues now lost. However, it is evident that fishermen were active on the coast and that the Indians were making a determined effort to capture their vessels and drive them away.

The Indians often operated from canoes, probably dugouts, bigger and with more freeboard than the traditional bark canoe. In April 1724, Captain

Josiah Winslow and seventeen men set out from St. George in two whaleboats to shoot Indians if possible, and birds at least, on the Green Islands. They were attacked by thirty or forty canoes. One whaleboat was shot full of holes, beached, and her crew captured. The other was captured, and Winslow and three men were killed.

Fragmentary reports indicate that the Indians had learned how to handle sailing vessels and naval guns and had fitted out a number of the captured vessels as privateers or pirates, the distinction depending more on one's point of view than on the actions involved. Privateers are on our side; the others are pirates.

In June 1724, the Indians captured eleven fishing vessels, killed twenty-two of their crew, and held twenty-three captive. They offered to return the men for a ransom of £30 apiece and the vessels at £50 apiece. Four heavily armed and manned vessels were sent out from Massachusetts in response; there is no report of their success or lack thereof.

In July word came to Boston of several privateer schooners on the coast attacking shallops and other fishing vessels. A number of armed vessels were sent in pursuit, among them an armed schooner under Dr. George Jackson and a shallop under Sylvester Lakeman, both manned by men from Maine. Off Penobscot Bay these two vessels met a large schooner armed with swivel guns and manned by Indians. Jackson apparently fired on the schooner. She did not reply until close aboard, when she opened fire with muskets and artillery, shot away Jackson's shrouds and mainsheet, and wounded Jackson, his mate, and two others. Lakeman came up too late to do more than help Jackson's men repair their rigging, while the Indians escaped up Penobscot Bay.

Two others of the Massachusetts "navy" sent to capture the Indian pirates met an Indian-manned schooner in a Mount Desert harbor and fought a four-hour battle with her before recapturing her. Clearly, the Indians were a serious threat afloat as well as ashore.

The climax of Lovewell's War, and probably the telling blow, was delivered in August 1724 when Captain John Harmon and Captain Jeremiah Moulton with 208 men attacked Norridgewock. As they approached the town, thus far unobserved, they surprised Chief Bomazeen with his wife and child on the river below the town. They shot the child and fired at Bomazeen. Running to alarm the town, Bomazeen was pursued by the soldiers, who knew that if he succeeded, their mission was lost. He tried to cross the river but was shot on a ledge in midstream. The next day the soldiers quietly surrounded the village, burst from ambush, and killed every Indian whom they could, men, women, and children. Father Rasle was killed in defense of his Indian friends. One story tells of his attempt to distract the English from killing others by showing himself plainly. Another tells of an Englishman bursting into a house Rasle was defending. Rasle was in the act of dropping a musket ball into the barrel of his gun when the Englishman demanded his surrender. Rasle refused and was shot dead and scalped.

With the destruction of Norridgewock and the death of Father Rasle,

Lovewell's War wound down. There were still attacks on the fishing fleet, and some Indians apparently took to living aboard captured vessels, subsisting on fish and seals; but without a secure base and without supplies of powder, shot, and naval stores, they were doomed to eventual defeat.

In the summer of 1725 there occurred what may have been an isolated incident, but it may suggest the rough and lawless character of coastal seafarers. Baron Castin's son by one of Madockawando's daughters, leader of the Penobscot Indians and one who had tried hard to preserve peace with the English, was anchored in Naskeag Harbor near the eastern end of Eggemoggin Reach in a sloop. With him was his young son and Samuel Trask, a Salem boy whom Castin had ransomed. An "English" sloop, probably a colonial vessel, came up Jericho Bay, saw an Indian and two boys aboard, and fired on Castin. Castin and the boys fled ashore. The skipper of the sloop raised a white flag, hailed Castin, said the shooting was a "mistake," and invited him aboard. The skipper then seized Trask and declared that Castin and his son were his prisoners. All hands went ashore. When one of the sloop's crew seized the Indian boy, evidently with the intention of taking him away from his father, Castin shot the man dead and with his son disappeared into the forest. Clearly, there was no military value to be gained. But Indian scalps and Indian captives were worth hard money in Boston. Finally, in December 1725, Dummer's Treaty was signed; it was ratified the following July. There were still a few Indian attacks on colonists, and the mast fleet carrying spars to England was "annoyed," but conflict between English and Indians was essentially at an end.

Thus, one of the three forces in the wars was eliminated. The Indians surviving either remained and lived more or less a white man's life or moved to St. Francis and joined the French. No longer were they a factor in the war. The French, for the time being, were at peace with the English, but the conflict would smolder and blaze up until the French were finally driven from the continent.

The raids and counter-raids, scalpings, burnings, and massacres on both sides during King William's War and Lovewell's War had driven out most of the former inhabitants of the Maine coast. "They had given up and gone by 1725, leaving a few hardy, watchful souls brooding behind the thick walls of fortified houses." In 1720 there was no house east of Georgetown except a fisherman's camp on Damariscove, reports Patrick Rogers, writing his reminiscences in 1773.

However, even before the ratification of Dummer's Treaty in 1726, we find evidence that settlers and fishermen were filtering back to the Maine coast. Lovewell's War held back only briefly the rising tide of immigration.

• In 1714, twenty families had settled in Falmouth.

• In 1715, as mentioned before, there were twenty-six houses on Arrowsic Island, and the Kennebec Proprietors built a fort at Cushnoc below what is now Augusta to protect their settlers.

• In 1716 fishermen complained to the governor of Massachusetts that Indians were demanding payment for the privilege of fishing off Damariscove.

The town of Georgetown on the lower Kennebec was incorporated in the same year.

• In 1717 a fort was built across the Kennebec from Swan Island.

• In 1718 Samuel Annis of Round Pond lived on Monhegan, and several others from Round Pond spent the summer fishing from the island. In the same year the Pejepscot Proprietors, who owned thousands of acres north of Casco Bay, built a fort at Brunswick and settled three families at Topsham.

• In 1720 the sloop *Maquoit* was built at Brunswick, and settlers came to Harpswell.

• In 1721 Reverend Richard Baxter visited Monhegan and found several families who had moved over from Muscongus in fear of Indians.

• At about this time William Pepperrell had sawmills, gristmills, and shipyards in Kittery and Saco and had vessels trading to Boston, Nova Scotia, Cape Breton, and the West Indies.

• In 1722 Lovewell's War broke out and the Indians burned Brunswick, attacked vessels, and scalped settlers. Many others were driven out but, after the peace, returned in ever-increasing numbers. Relations with the Indians improved markedly. There were no more French on the coast to inflame the Indians against the English, and after peace was made, the English at last gave the Indians a fair deal in trading houses at Saco, Pemaquid, and Thomaston. John S. C. Abbott writes in his history of Maine, referring to the early eighteenth century, "In very many cases the Indians and the white families had been well acquainted with each other. They had often met in familiar intercourse, called each other by name, and had apparently cherished for each other sincere friendship."

Down east on Matinicus, a band of Indians hunting seals was unable to return to the mainland because of bad weather and, needing food, they killed a cow and some pigs belonging to local inhabitants. The Indians stood ready to pay for what they had taken in their distress.

• In 1726, forty vessels were counted taking refuge from a storm in Falmouth.

• In 1727 sixty-four families lived in Falmouth and thirty vessels lay at anchor in what is now Portland Harbor.

• In 1729 there were 200 families in Falmouth. The British Admiralty, seeing the rapid advance of civilization inland, instituted the "broad arrow" policy to save mast trees. This will be dealt with more fully later, but mention is made of it here simply to indicate that increasing numbers of people were living and working on the coast.

One of the most energetic and enthusiastic settlers on the coast was William Vaughan.

In 1726 he bought land on Damariscotta Lake and built a stout garrison house, sawmills and gristmills, and houses for farmers who cultivated his land. He established a fishing station on Matinicus, which prospered until 1728 when a fierce winter storm wiped out boats and wharves. However, he was undiscouraged, for in 1730 he had a fishing station on Monhegan. In 1745 he was a mainspring of the Louisbourg campaign, as we will see in Chapter 12.

At about the same time, 1729–30, David Dunbar, a former colonel in the British Army and Lieutenant Governor of New Hampshire, persuaded the British government to commission him also as Governor of Sagadahoc from the Kennebec to the St. Croix, to rebuild Fort William Henry at Pemaquid, and to be Surveyor of the King's Woods. We will hear of his career as Surveyor in Chapter 13. Dunbar claimed that because the coast east of the Kennebec had been conquered from France and conveyed to the Crown of England by the Treaty of Utrecht, Massachusetts no longer had a claim on it and all deeds and grants made prior to 1713 were null. Dunbar therefore brought in 150 families, mostly Scotch-Irish farmers, to the Pemaquid region and granted them land. The fathers and grandfathers of these people had moved from the barren hills of Scotland to the slightly less barren hills of northern Ireland in the time of King James I, when that unhappy land had been largely depopulated by the Irish wars. They found Ireland a hard and inhospitable country and, driven out by famine and persecution about 1718, came to America.

Most of those who came with Dunbar had been in Massachusetts or New Hampshire and welcomed the chance to own their own land in Maine. Dunbar set up Townsend in what is now Boothbay, Walpole in what is now Bristol and Damariscotta, Newcastle in what is now Newcastle and Edgecomb. He rebuilt the fort at Pemaquid and had it garrisoned by the governor of Nova Scotia, not of Massachusetts. Each settler, after building a house and clearing at least two acres, was given a deed to 140 acres more. The deeds were from the governor of Nova Scotia but were not stamped or recorded there, only signed by Dunbar, who promised to put his official seal on them when the King sent it to him.

Dunbar's commission as governor and the seal never arrived. This led, of course, to serious conflict with the original settlers and their heirs in later years. In 1732 Dunbar was ousted after vigorous complaint from Waldo, Shem Drowne, and the government of Massachusetts to the King, claiming that the 1692 charter giving Massachusetts authority over Sagadahoc and Nova Scotia was still valid despite Dunbar's claim that it was Crown land. The King decided in favor of Massachusetts.

Few of these settlers were fishermen. Most of them were farmers who worked hard to wring a living from a stony soil in a short season. When food failed, they lived on clams and "shore-greens" salted down in a crock with a board and a rock on top to keep them under the pickle. They supplemented this meager fare by cutting firewood, which they shipped to Boston in sloops, for by this time Boston had used up all the firewood growing for miles around. Hay was also a cash crop in Boston, for horses and oxen, "hay burners," were the prime movers.

In 1735 Samuel Waldo took up the old Muscongus Grant and settled a number of German farmers on the Medomak and St. George rivers. East of Penobscot Bay, in what had been French territory, there appears to have been little settlement, but from Kittery to Waldoboro the coast prospered.

Salt fish was still a staple export. William Williamson reported 600 men fishing in western Maine in 1736. Lumber was also a valuable export. Struggling farmers cut firewood, but others cut mast timber—tall white pines exported under permit to England and illegally to France and the West Indies for masts and spars. Also there was a booming market in the West Indies for building lumber, shingles, shooks, and staves. Shooks were sugar boxes, knocked down and tied in bundles. The staves were barrel staves—white oak for rum, red oak for sugar hogsheads—bundled with heads and hoops. While it is likely that a few sloops, schooners, and brigs traded directly from the Maine coast to the West Indies, probably most of Maine's fish and lumber went to Portsmouth, Newburyport, and Boston to be shipped thence to the West Indies. The subject will be dealt with more fully in a later chapter.

Shipbuilding, too, was getting a start. Shallops, ketches, and pinkies were needed by fishermen in considerable numbers but unfortunately were seldom registered, so we have no record of them. However, we know that in 1742 there were forty topsail vessels a-building in Maine and that Kittery, York, Saco, and Casco Bay had made healthy starts on building oceangoing vessels. With fish, lumber, the remains of a fur trade, subsistence or sub-subsistence farming with exports of firewood and hay, and the beginning of a shipbuilding trade, Maine's coastal population was healthy and growing. In 1742 the population of the District of Maine was about 12,000 courageous and determined people with increasingly strong roots.

NOTES

Mary Calvert in *Dawn Over the Kennebec* gives a summary of King William's War. John Abbott's *History of Maine* gives colorful details of Queen Anne's War, particularly the naval battle with the Indians at Winter Harbor. Charles Griffin's thesis has a few nuggets concerning Damariscove. William D. Williamson's *History of the State of Maine* is very detailed; incidents significant to maritime history must be sifted out. Again, Beck's *The Indian as a Sea Fighter* deals with specific incidents and includes the complete text of the ballad describing the attack on Tilton's schooner. *The Skolfields and Their Ships*, by Reynolds and Martin, deals with the last of the Indian wars in describing the settlement of Harpswell.

Dawn Over the Kennebec continues with Lovewell's War and the story of Father Rasle. It is revealing to read Mary Calvert's view of Rasle, including his two long letters to his brother and his nephew in France, in comparison with Baxter's view of him in *Pioneers of New France in New England*. Both writers agree on the fundamental facts but differ on emphasis and interpretation. Francis Parkman in *A Half-Century of Conflict* gives a blow-by-blow account with transcripts of some of the conferences. From this, one can come to his own conclusions.

The attack on the son of Castin at Naskeag is found in John Abbott's book.

Most of the statistical details of the growth of Maine in the eighteenth century are from Williamson. The account of Dunbar's settlement at Pemaquid is from Greene's *History of Boothbay*.

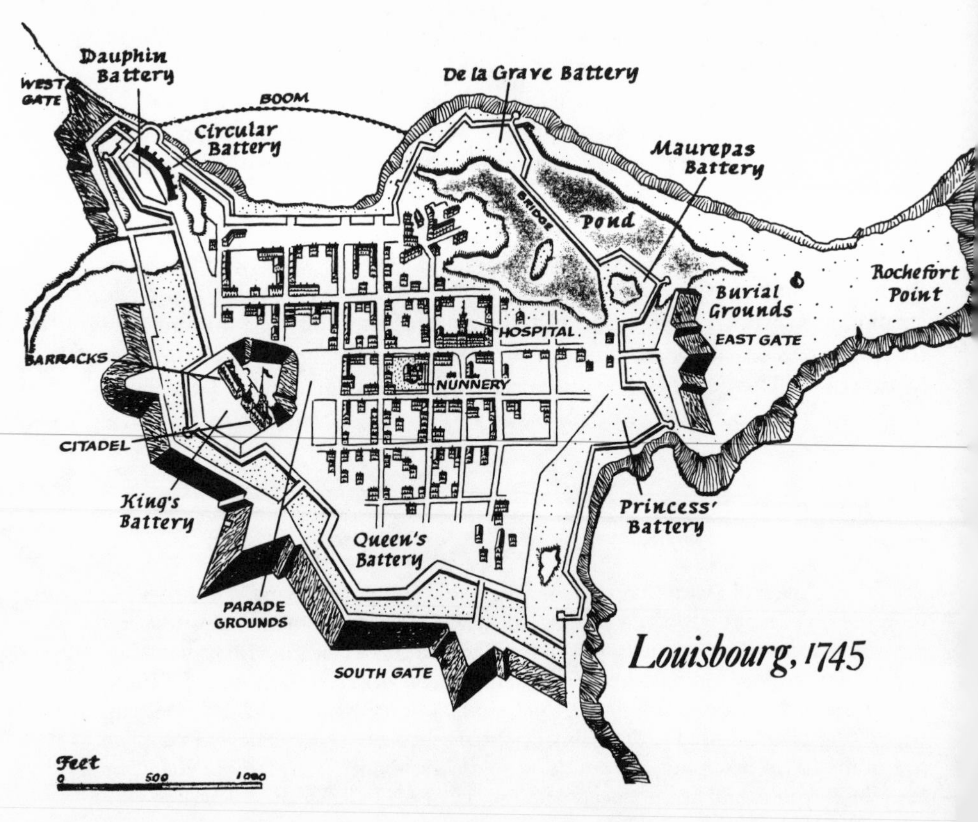
Dauphin Battery
WEST GATE
BOOM
Circular Battery
De la Grave Battery
BRIDGE
Pond
Maurepas Battery
Burial Grounds
Rochefort Point
EAST GATE
HOSPITAL
BARRACKS
NUNNERY
CITADEL
King's Battery
Princess' Battery
Queen's Battery
PARADE GROUNDS
SOUTH GATE
Feet
0
500
1000

Louisbourg, 1745

TWELVE

The Siege of Louisbourg, 1745

IN 1744 Maine's growth was interrupted by another European war. The War of the Austrian Succession was fought from 1740 to 1748 over complex political problems in central Europe. England was drawn into it through King George II's interest in his home electorate of Hanover, and in March 1744 France declared war on England, the news arriving at Louisbourg in May.

Louisbourg on Cape Breton Island was a formidable fortress, built at such vast expense that King Louis XV is reported to have said that if he looked out to sea from the shores of Brittany he would be able to see it. The story of its capture by the combined operations of colonial troops and the Royal Navy is so dramatic, so dependent on the characters of the leaders, and so bent and twisted to their advantage by pure luck, that it is worth telling in detail. It has an important part in the history of Maine inasmuch as Maine men led the expedition, and Maine supplied almost half of the assailants. Maine vessels were heavily involved, and the protection of Maine commerce and fishing was one of the principal reasons for attacking the fortress in the first place.

The Treaty of Utrecht in 1713 had given England all of Acadia, Nova Scotia, Newfoundland, and the Hudson Bay territory, leaving France only the islands in the Gulf of St. Lawrence including Cape Breton Island and the right to dry fish on the northeast coast of Newfoundland without either settling or fortifying it. However, there was no provision in the treaty against fortifying the islands. The English commissioners were later accused of having accepted French gold in return for this apparently inadvertent omission.

The French made the most of it. In order to protect their communication with Québec, Montréal, and their empire in the Great Lakes and the Mississippi valley, they needed a naval base at the mouth of the St. Lawrence. They chose Cape Breton Island, renamed it Isle Royale, moved their Newfoundland colonists to it from Placentia, and at once commenced to build a fortress and naval base at a harbor near the island's northeastern tip. They named it Louisbourg after King Louis XV, who was going to have to pay for it.

Construction began in 1718. The plan was ambitious. The entrance to the harbor was protected by a walled battery on an island, by the Circular Battery inside the wall on the west side of the town, and by thirty heavy guns in the Grand or Royal Battery on a hill overlooking the head of the harbor. On the land side, attackers would have to cross about two miles of swamp. They would then face an open glacis, a ditch 80 feet wide and 30 feet deep over which towered a vertical wall of earth 60 feet thick faced with stone with embrasures for 148 guns. The works were substantially complete in 1738.

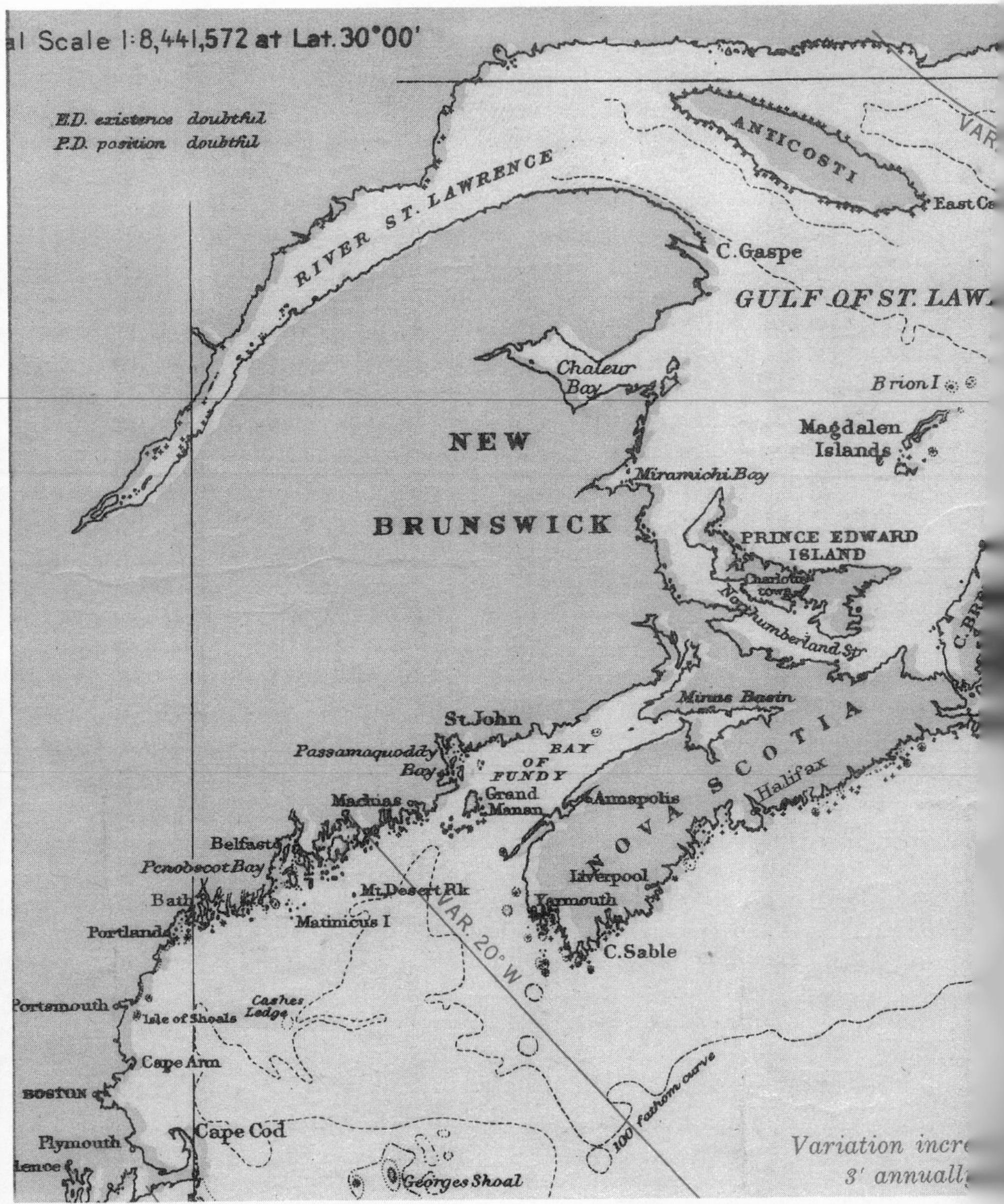

On May 3, 1744, the word reached Louisbourg that war with England had been declared in March. With the news came orders from Maurepas, the French minister, to fit out privateers and to attack Canso and Annapolis Royal. He promised two naval vessels, more food and munitions, and permission to buy food from New England. The latter was badly needed, for by mid-May people were living on clams. Nevertheless, Louisbourg's governor, DuQuesnel, sent DuVivier with the schooner *Succes,* another small vessel com-

Nova Scotia, Newfoundland, and the Gulf of St. Lawrence. *U.S. Hydrographic Office*

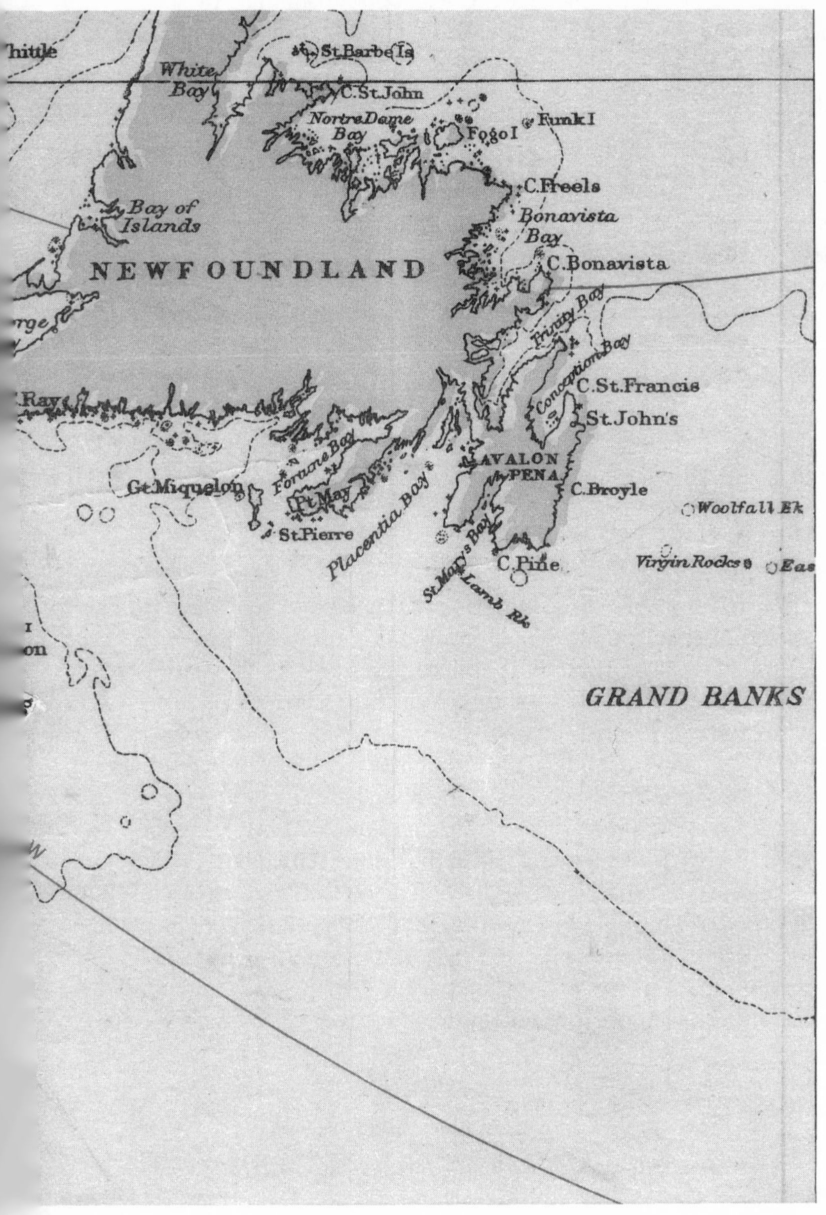

manded by DuChambon, a privateer commanded by Doloboratz, and a force of 139 officers and soldiers in a fleet of 14 fishing vessels to attack Canso on May 29. It was an easy victory over a fishing town protected only by a neglected blockhouse. The blockhouse, the dwellings, and the fish houses were burned and the inhabitants taken captive to Louisbourg.

Later in the summer DuVivier attacked Annapolis Royal, which had been strengthened by a detachment of Massachusetts soldiers in the province snow *Prince of Orange* under Captain Edward Tyng of Falmouth, Maine. DuVivier and his Indians burned some powder, killed two men, parleyed, and finally, when forty men arrived to reinforce the defenders, abandoned the siege. They returned to Louisbourg to find that DuQuesnel had died and left the less resolute DuChambon in command—"Notably lacking in experience as well as judgment, deficiencies that even the great wall of the fortress could not conceal," wrote a resident of Louisbourg.

When a sixty-four-gun ship, *Ardent,* arrived from France in September, there was talk of another attack on Annapolis Royal, but it was abandoned. *Ardent* sailed for France, convoying fifty-two merchant vessels. The convoy was scattered by gales, and *Ardent* finally arrived in France having accomplished nothing.

While these ineffective hostilities were developing in Louisbourg, events were moving with increasing momentum in Massachusetts.

News of the declaration of war arrived in Boston in late May 1744. Governor William Shirley, an active, ambitious, and imaginative governor, swore publicly that he would do nothing against the French unless they attacked first; but if they so much as harmed a child, he would retaliate quickly and forcefully. When news arrived of the destruction of Canso, he moved at once.

He dispatched support for Annapolis Royal. He contracted for the immediate construction of a new vessel for the defense of the coast, probably *Boston Packet,* of sixteen guns. He appropriated £1,500 for repairs to Castle William protecting Boston Harbor, bought 500 muskets, 150 cutlasses, and 10 harquebuses, and provided for the defense of the western borders. He kept the province's snow *Prince of Orange* busy patrolling the coast in search of French privateers and encouraged the fitting out of colonial privateers. Fifteen privateers from Massachusetts harassed the French fishing fleet and practically cut off trade from the French West Indies to Canada. HMS *Kinsdale* (44)* captured ten French privateers and raided the fishing settlements on the shores of Cape Breton Island and Newfoundland. The ketch *Comet,* after a five-hour battle, captured and brought in a much larger French privateer. By September 28, 1744, Governor Shirley reported that Massachusetts privateers and the two Massachusetts warships had captured forty French vessels and devastated the French fisheries. Another Massachusetts privateer sacked the French fish-

* A number in parentheses after the name of a vessel denotes her rated number of guns.

ing towns, took 17 ships, sunk 1,000 boats, and took nearly 700 prisoners.

Perhaps the most significant of these cruises was that of Captain Edward Tyng in the snow *Prince of Orange,* 180 tons, armed with sixteen 6-pounders. Off Cape Cod on June 23 he fell in with the French captain Doloboratz who had been at the attack on Canso and had been privateering since then, in a sloop of 80 tons carrying eight guns and ten or twelve swivels. Since the action at Canso in May, Doloboratz and Captain Morpain had taken ten vessels. Seeing Doloboratz approaching as if he thought *Prince of Orange* was a

Prince of Orange takes Doloboratz's sloop. *Earle G. Barlow*

merchant vessel, Tyng kept his gunports closed and showed no colors. Doloboratz bore down and fired a gun. Tyng replied with a broadside. Doloboratz, seeing his mistake, tried to escape by resorting to his oars in the very light air. Tyng ordered out his oars, too, and for twelve or thirteen hours kept up the chase, at last gaining enough to fire a broadside and a volley of musketry. Anticipating what was coming, the French crew ran below. The broadside cut up the French sails and rigging badly, one ball striking the mast just below the hounds. Doloboratz surrendered with compliments to Tyng's gunner as the top of the Frenchman's mast crashed down on his deck, bringing all the rigging with it and disabling the vessel completely. Tyng towed her into

Boston where he was received with great acclaim. Nobody on either side was hurt in the battle.

Tyng's reward for this successful action was to be commissioned to find another vessel for the provincial navy. He found a 400-ton brig under construction, had her finished as a frigate, armed her with twenty guns, and launched her on February 20, 1745, under the name *Massachusetts*. In her as commodore he commanded the provincial fleet against Louisbourg.

In September 1744, DuChambon, unwilling or unable to feed the captives taken at Canso, paroled them and sent them to Boston. One, John Bradstreet, a merchant who had often visited Louisbourg, reported that the garrison consisted of only 500 regulars and they were on the verge of mutiny, demanding better rations, clothes, which the officers should have issued to them but which they were selling, and sufficient firewood. "Rugged fishermen, sharp merchants and fortune-seeking military officers and government officials made up the bulk of the fortress's population," concludes William Pepperrell's biographer. Indeed, the troops did mutiny in December. Parts of the city wall were in need of repair, and there were no French naval vessels in the harbor or on the coast. Furthermore, the season was so far advanced that no more ships from Québec or France could be expected until the ice cleared in the spring. This news revived what had heretofore been considered mad schemes for the capture of the fortress.

Surely there were good reasons for the British to seek control of Louisbourg. It was a base from which French naval vessels and privateers harried the British fishing fleet on the Nova Scotia coast, Newfoundland, and the Gulf of St. Lawrence and from which they could cruise against British vessels making for Boston and for Maine and New Hampshire ports. From Louisbourg the French could protect their commerce up the St. Lawrence from British privateers. Finally, Isle Royale was a base for a rapidly growing French fishery which competed seriously with British and colonial fisheries.

An assault on Louisbourg was not a new idea. Since 1740 it had been proposed. Two successive governors of New York had proposed it. Judge Auchmuty had written a pamphlet, *The Importance of Cape Breton,* in 1743; an anonymous London merchant had written another in 1744. Kilby, Massachusetts agent in London, had proposed a plan, and Captain Warren, serving as commodore on the North American station, had proposed such an attack as of the greatest service to the King. Even St. Ovide, governor of Louisbourg before DuQuesnel and DuChambon, had written to the ministry in France a detailed account of what would likely be the British plan of attack. He was quite right. However, it remained for William Vaughan of Damariscotta in the fall of 1744 to take quick and aggressive action.

Vaughan was the son of the former lieutenant governor of New Hampshire. In 1726 he bought a large tract on Damariscotta Lake, built a garrison house, storehouses, a gristmill, and a sawmill and houses for those who would cut timber, catch salmon and alewives, and farm the land. He was energetic, not to say precipitate. In 1725 he sent a party to Matinicus to set up a fishing station. When it was wiped out by a storm three years later, he lost no time in setting up another on Monhegan. His intentions were never "sicklied o'er by the pale cast of thought"; action followed hard upon conception. The attack on Canso, the interruption of trade, and the prospect of removing France forever from the fisheries led Vaughan to interview John Tufton Mason, John Bradstreet, and others who had recently been prisoners at Louisbourg. In December 1744 he presented a plan to Governor Shirley suggesting a surprise attack in winter over the snowdrifts that pile up to the top of the Louisbourg walls. Shirley regarded the plan as too dependent on precise timing, luck, and the weather, but he too was eager to see Louisbourg conquered, for he believed that there could be no peace or prosperity in Massachusetts until the French were driven from North America. The destruction of Louisbourg would be a first and necessary step.

Governor Shirley wrote to the Duke of Newcastle, then prime minister of England, that a force of six or seven warships and 1,500 to 2,000 men would be sufficient, and he offered Massachusetts's help. Before he received an answer, however, on January 9, 1745, he called a session of the Great and General Court of Massachusetts, swore the members to secrecy, and proposed that Massachusetts undertake the campaign. A committee of fifteen members was appointed, and on January 12 that committee advised that the project was too big for Massachusetts but that Massachusetts forces should assist Britain's. Shirley was disappointed, but wrote Newcastle again, explaining the advantages to be gained by taking Louisbourg. Vaughan, when he heard that the committee had rejected the plan, at once rode a circuit through Maine, New Hampshire, and Massachusetts towns, carrying a petition to the General Court to reconsider. Also James Gibson, a Boston merchant, carried a petition among the merchants and fishermen of Boston, Marblehead, and Salem. Shirley, who welcomed Vaughan's petition and who had stirred Gibson to circulate his petition, called other sessions of the court on January 19 and 22. This time William Pepperrell of Kittery was among the members present. He was made chairman of a new committee which on January 25 reported enthusiastically in favor of such an expedition. The committee recommended raising an army of 3,000 men, assembling supplies, munitions, and transports by early March, and assaulting the fortress at once before help could come from France.

It appeared that the vote of the Great and General Court on the committee's recommendation would be a close one. One member, hurrying to vote against the expedition, slipped on the ice and broke his leg. The measure passed by just one vote. Other members may have absented themselves, not wishing to vote against the measure because of the power of the Boston merchants, who, of course, were very much in favor. The court voted that 3,000 men be raised, that each man receive 25 shillings per month, a blanket, a half pound of ginger, a pound and a half of sugar, and all the plunder he could find. Other colonies were to be invited to help. Shirley named William Pepperrell as commander in chief with the rank of lieutenant general.

Pepperrell was a resident of Kittery. His father had come to the Isles of

Shoals as a boy, amassed a bit of capital in the fishing industry, moved ashore to Kittery, married the daughter of a shipbuilder, and embarked on a career as a merchant, trading to Nova Scotia, Newfoundland, the Southern colonies, and the West Indies. He invested his profits in land. In 1694 he was made a selectman, and in 1695 was appointed a judge. In 1696 he was elected to the General Court of Massachusetts and again in 1708, for Maine until 1820 was part of Massachusetts and was represented in the Great and General Court.

His son, William, in association with his father by 1723, owned 10,000 acres of Maine land, had a gristmill, a sawmill, and a shipyard as well as a prosperous trading business with Boston merchants. He owned a number of ships engaged in trading, legally and illegally, to Ireland, Madeira, Martinique, and Nova Scotia.

William Pepperrell became a selectman in 1720, was elected to the General Court, and in 1728 became a member of the Governors Council. He was an easy person to talk with, attractive, tactful and persuasive, accustomed to getting what he wanted by making others want it with him.

Although he was a captain of militia in the District of Maine, he had had no military education or experience. However, writes Francis Parkman, he was a good choice, ". . . for Pepperrell joined to an unusual popularity as little military incompetency as anybody else who could be had." It was largely through his and Vaughan's personal enthusiasm and influence that over one-third of the 3,000 men raised in Massachusetts came from Maine.

Maine men volunteered for the expedition for a variety of reasons. Probably first among them was resentment against French attacks on colonial fishermen and what they believed to be the necessity of eliminating French competition.

Secondly, and primarily for many, was the religious motive. The old Puritan enmity toward Roman Catholics died hard. Of Reverend Samuel Moody of York, Parkman writes, "The old Puritan fanaticism was rampant in him," and when he sailed for Louisbourg, he took with him an axe, as he said, "to hew down the altars of Antichrist and demolish his idols."

The famous evangelist George Whitefield, then preaching the Great Awakening through Maine, replied to Pepperrell, who was reluctant to take command, that if Pepperrell would undertake it, he (Whitefield) would beg of the Lord God of Armies to give him a single eye; that the means to take Louisbourg in the eye of human reason were no more adequate to the end than the sounding of rams' horns to blow down Jericho; but that if Providence really called him, he would return more than conqueror. Whitefield gave the expedition the watchword "Nil Desperandum, Christo Duce," thus making the expedition something of a crusade.

Benjamin Franklin was less sanguine. From Philadelphia he wrote to his brother in Boston, "Fortified towns are hard nuts to crack, and your teeth are not accustomed to it; but some seem to think forts are as easy taken as snuff." J. S. McLennan sums up the motives thus: "The expedition against Louisbourg to the fanatic was directed against Romanism; to the timorous as a preventive invasion; to the greedy a chance for plunder; and to all an object for the self-sacrifice of every patriotic Briton."

With the invasion thus authorized and Pepperrell appointed commander, Shirley moved with astonishing speed. He wrote to the governors of New Hampshire, Rhode Island, Connecticut, and New York asking for troops and armed vessels. Governor Benning Wentworth in New Hampshire sent 350 men plus 150 more to be paid by Massachusetts, and he added an armed vessel. Roger Woolcott of Connecticut, in consideration of 500 men and a vessel, was made a major general and second in command. Rhode Island sent the sloop *Tartar,* and New York sent ten cannons and £5,000. New Jersey sent £2,000 in July, and Quaker Pennsylvania sent £4,000 for provisions and clothing.

Vaughan, with his characteristic enthusiasm, rushed off to Maine, enlisted a company of soldiers, and on February 8 wrote Pepperrell urging that they be ordered to march at once to Boston "to give life and spring to ye affair . . . for dispatch is ye life of business." Vaughan declined command of a regiment, preferring to be unencumbered, but asked and obtained a seat in the Council of War.

Samuel Waldo of Waldoboro, Maine, was commissioned a brigadier general. Edward Tyng, another Maine man, was made commodore of the fleet, which at last consisted of three Massachusetts vessels: *Prince of Orange* and *Boston Packet* (16), and the flagship *Massachusetts* (24). There were also the Rhode Island sloop *Tartar* (14), the privateer *Shirley* (20), under Captain Rous, and eight other vessels, mostly sloops and for the most part lightly armed. They were to escort a mosquito fleet of small unarmed transports.

Shirley knew very well that his naval force was quite incapable of fighting even a French frigate, not to mention heavier vessels. Accordingly, he at once wrote the Duke of Newcastle, Prime Minister of England, for naval support and sent a fast vessel to the West Indies with a letter to Commodore Warren in command of the British Navy's North American squadron. Warren was willing to help, but his captains, thinking that Louisbourg was a strong fortress with no good anchorage nearby and that planning had been too hasty, advised sending *Mermaid* (40) to New York and *Launceston* (40) to New England as was previously planned and keeping the rest of the squadron in the West Indies lest the French fleet appear at Martinique. Warren wrote Shirley that he could do nothing without orders from the Admiralty. Then, just as *Mermaid* and *Launceston* were heading north and Warren with the rest of his squadron was starting on a cruise, a vessel arrived from England with orders for Warren to go to Boston with *Mermaid, Launceston, Weymouth, Hastings,* and the flagship *Superbe* (60) to protect the colonies and the fisheries and "as occasion shall offer, attack and distress the enemy in their settlements and annoy their fisheries and commerce."

That was enough for Warren. He sailed for Boston on March 13 with his squadron. On April 10 he met a Marblehead schooner whose pilot told him Pepperrell had already sailed for Canso. Warren changed course at once for Canso and sent word to Shirley, who was much relieved, for his fleet had gone to sea under the doubtful protection of Tyng's scratch squadron. Warren also sent orders to *Eltham* (40), which had wintered in Boston and was to escort a fleet of mast ships to England, to join him at Canso.

Meanwhile, in England, the Duke of Newcastle ordered two vessels to sail for Cape Breton the day he received Shirley's letter and six more vessels soon after.

In Boston, events had moved with incredible speed—incredible, at least, to those accustomed to combined land and sea operations.

Within sixty days of the General Court's affirmative vote, Governor Shirley assembled a force of about 3,000 men with transport and convoy to move them to Nova Scotia. To pay for provisions, clothing, munitions, and artillery, he and Governor Benning Wentworth of New Hampshire issued a flood of paper money. Finally, on March 24, 1745, the fleet sailed from Nantasket Roads.

The fleet immediately ran into a northeast gale, which drove them into the Sheepscot River on the Maine coast for two days. Pepperrell described the voyage from Sheepscot to Canso merely as "rough and somewhat tedious." Another diarist wrote, "Our men was exceeding sick and did vomet very much as they would dy the sea running mountaining." The fleet arrived off Canso on April 4 and found the coast eastward to Louisbourg blocked with drift ice. Tyng took his fleet east at once to blockade Louisbourg. He was fortunate enough to capture two French merchantmen loaded with rum, molasses, and coffee, commodities of great value to the army in the prevailing cold, wet spring weather. Within a few days *Massachusetts* and *Shirley* intercepted the French frigate *Renommée* (36), loaded with supplies and munitions for Louisbourg and capable of blowing both colonial vessels sky high. However, they engaged her in a running battle and drove her off to the southwest. She ran into the fleet of transports carrying the Connecticut troops convoyed by the Rhode Island sloop *Tartar* and a Connecticut sloop. The two small warships lured *Renommée* into chasing them away from the transports and that night eluded the frigate in the dark. *Renommée* went into Baie des Castors (now Beaver Harbor) for a few days, tried to beat back the 140 miles to Louisbourg, gave it up, and went back to France. In the meantime, the rest of Tyng's fleet captured and sent to Canso four more provision ships.

Ashore at Canso, Pepperrell, while he waited for the ice to go out, kept the soldiers busy drilling, making cartridges, and setting up a prefabricated blockhouse, which he armed with 8-pounders.

On April 22 *Eltham* came in from Boston, and during the next two days Warren came in with *Superbe, Launceston,* and *Mermaid*. With these heavily armed ships, Warren sailed at once to blockade Louisbourg with a force capable of engaging anything short of a French battle fleet. The next day the

Connecticut convoy came in, and within the week news came that the ice was out of Gabarus Bay. With the first fair wind, on April 24, the fleet sailed eastward, intending to arrive in the early evening and land by surprise during the night. However, the wind was light, and not until the morning of April 30 did the fleet anchor.

Although DuChambon had been warned in March by an Indian who had visited Boston in February that an attack was planned, and although his predecessor, St. Ovide, had written a detailed account of what form the British attack would take, DuChambon had comforted himself with the assurance that no assault would come that year. When the transports anchored in Gabarus Bay in sight from the walls, he hesitated to send out a force to resist the colonial landing lest his mutinous troops desert. However, Morpain, now ashore from his privateering expedition, and de la Boularderie organized a force of thirty soldiers and fifty volunteers. By the time this force reached the landing place, 1,000 colonials were ashore and the guns of the ships covered the beach. The small French force was routed, a number were killed, de la Boularderie was wounded and captured, and Morpain, although wounded, was brought off by his black slave, whom he freed at once. By the end of the day, 2,000 men were ashore with a considerable quantity of supplies and munitions.

Vaughan, who had come to capture Louisbourg, proceeded that same day to set about it. With about 400 men he marched around the swamp, and camped behind the Grand (Royal) Battery. The next day, May 1, he burned a number of buildings and naval stores on the northeast arm of Louisbourg Harbor. The smoke drifted down over the Grand Battery. Chassin de Thierry, in command, was unnerved by the smoke and the sight of a large body of assailants. He rushed to the town and told DuChambon that because part of the wall had been leveled for repairs, he could not defend the battery. He advised blowing it up. A council of war hastily agreed that the battery could not be defended, but an engineer who had helped build it, Verrier, strongly objected to blowing it up. That same evening, de Thierry returned to the battery, had its guns spiked rather inexpertly by hammering spikes into the touch holes, and abandoned the battery. He and the garrison were back in Louisbourg by midnight.

On the morning of May 2, most of Vaughan's force had dispersed in search of plunder. Making his way back to the camp with only thirteen men, Vaughan noticed that no flag flew over the battery and all was silent. A Cape Cod Indian agreed to investigate the battery for a flask of brandy. He cautiously approached, found a port unsecured, entered the deserted battery, and opened the gate. Vaughan took possession of Louisbourg's most powerful battery and sent a message to Pepperrell: "May it pleasure your Honour, to be informed that with ye Grace of God and ye courage of about thirteen men I entered this place about nine a clock and am waiting here for a reinforcement and flag."

William Tufts, an eighteen-year-old from Medford, Massachusetts, solved the flag problem temporarily by shinning up the pole and tying his red coat to the top. Pepperrell sent Colonel Bradstreet with a few men at once, followed by Samuel Waldo with a larger force and an armorer who at once began drilling out the spikes. However, before these men arrived, the French counterattacked in four boats. Vaughan, with the help of a few "moroders" who had been plundering the countryside, stood on the open beach swept by ineffective cannon fire from the town, and drove off the landing force with musket fire. Vaughan's courage and impetuous character had secured for the attackers a fort commanding the harbor and town, a fort armed with twenty-eight 42-pounders and two 8-pounders, 280 bombshells, a number of cannon cartridges, and a supply of powder and cannonballs. Pepperrell had brought a number of 42-pound cannonballs to use in captured French guns, although he had brought no gun bigger than a 22-pounder. The guns of the Grand Battery were drilled out, and on the evening of May 3, two of them opened fire on the town.

Meanwhile, Pepperrell and the troops at Gabarus Bay lightered the artillery ashore in flat boats brought from Massachusetts. These guns were 22-pounders weighing about two-and-a-half tons each. They were carried ashore from the boats on the heads of men wading waist deep in *cold* water. The first gun ashore was set in its carriage and rolled toward Louisbourg, but it went—not far. In the soft ground of the swamp, it sank over the rims of the wheels, to the hubs, over the gun itself, and at last completely disappeared under mud and water. Yankee ingenuity in the person of Lieutenant Colonel Meserve of New Hampshire devised sledges—something like a stone boat. Two hundred men harnessed themselves to each sledge and, wading through icy mud and water, hauled those stubborn masses of metal by main strength and ignorance to where others had constructed batteries commanding the town. The whole operation had to be done by night, for the hauling parties were within range of the French guns. Nevertheless, within four days Green Hill battery opened fire on the city. The attackers set up two batteries to hammer the west gate, one at a range of only 250 yards of the target. The gunners were somewhat protected by trenches but were partly exposed when loading. French and English exchanged insults and rude gestures between shots until the French were "beat from their guns."

It was the tremendous enthusiasm of this volunteer force, building momentum with each success, that swept aside obstructions and difficulties. However, there were setbacks. One result of this excess of enthusiasm was a tendency to overload the guns and double-shot them. A number of guns blew up, killing and wounding crews and bystanders. Pepperrell had to borrow from Commodore Warren a corps of gunners from the fleet to teach the impetuous colonials how to serve the guns effectively.

Pepperrell had other problems, too. The weather in Nova Scotia in May is far from balmy. Men who had been wet to the waist for hours had to sleep in wet clothes in shelters constructed from old sails through cold and foggy nights. Many were sick, and not a few died. Even this did little to discourage others. Parkman writes, "While the cannon bellowed in the front, frolic and confusion reigned at the camp, where the men raced, wrestled, pitched quoits, fired at marks—though there was no ammunition to spare—and ran after the French cannonballs, which were carried to the batteries, to be returned to those who sent them." One observer compared the scene to a Cambridge commencement, in those days a disorderly if not riotous celebration. Others went fishing and lobstering, while a number ravaged the countryside in search of plunder. Occasionally a party of looters was surprised by French or Indians. Not a few lost their scalps, and several were tortured to death. Nevertheless, writes Parkman, "Barefoot and tattered, they toiled on with indomitable pluck and cheerfulness, doing the work which oxen could not do, with no comfort but their daily dram of New England rum, as they plodded through the marsh and over rocks, dragging the ponderous guns through fog and darkness."

Pepperrell had to drive this team of independent and enthusiastic warriors with a loose rein, for they were as impatient of discipline as they were of delays. Furthermore, lurking in the back of his mind was always the fear that the governor of Canada might send a force overland to take him in the rear and relieve the city. Actually, Lieutenant Colonel Marin with 1,200 men was besieging Annapolis Royal, and DuChambon had already summoned him to help defend Louisbourg.

On May 7, only eight days after dropping anchor in Gabarus Bay, with the Grand Battery under Waldo firing on the town and with other batteries in place hammering the walls, Pepperrell sent DuChambon a summons to surrender. DuChambon replied, ". . . nous n'avons de response à fair à cette demande que par le bouche de nos cannons."

While the colonials were busy ashore, Commodore Warren was blockading the harbor, constantly concerned lest a French fleet take him in the rear. He could not enter the harbor while the channel was swept with heavy fire from the Island Battery and the Circular Battery. He proposed an attack on the Island Battery on May 8, but it was too rough to land through the surf. On the morning of May 9 the Council of War determined to storm the walls that night. However, the soldiers objected so forcefully that the council met again in the afternoon and canceled the attack. The colonial guns battered the walls and gates for day after day while Warren's ships maintained the blockade.

At last, on May 20, Warren scored an important success. The French ship of the line *Vigilant* (64) under Captain Maisonfort, heavily loaded with supplies and munitions, approached Louisbourg. She first encountered the smaller, more lightly armed frigate *Mermaid* (40). *Mermaid* fled toward Warren's fleet. *Vigilant* followed, and soon found herself facing *Eltham* (40), *Superbe* (60), and swift little *Shirley* (16) of the Massachusetts navy. *Vigilant* now fled, and a running fight ensued in which *Shirley* "Ply'd his Bow Chase very well." Finally *Mermaid, Eltham,* and *Superbe* overpowered the Frenchman after a heroic defense. Maisonfort struck only after his spars and rigging were so cut up that he could make no sail and sixty of his crew were dead or wounded.

The loss of *Vigilant* was a serious blow to the defenders, for she carried not only food, powder, and shot but a force of men and guns which, under the bold leadership of Maisonfort, could very well have raised the siege. *Vigilant*'s cargo gave the besiegers a big lift, for they were already short of powder and food.

Warren grew increasingly impatient, sending Pepperrell several proposals, one after another, for attacking the town by land and by sea.

On May 24 Commodore Warren submitted another plan, a plan that involved putting 1,000 soldiers aboard the warships, 600 soldiers aboard *Vigilant,* sailing up the harbor in the face of the Island Battery and the Circular Battery, and, led by British Marines, attacking the town in boats. The remainder of the army would attack at three places ashore. Pepperrell's Council of War objected to this for the stated reasons that it was not always easy to get men aboard warships and get them ashore quickly, that the soldiers would soon get seasick and thus prove ineffective if kept aboard for long, and that with 1,600 men afloat, the army would be wide open to attack from the rear by Marin and his French Indians, whose whereabouts were unknown. An unstated reason was that if 1,600 soldiers were transferred to Warren's command and led by his marines, and the colonial navy was placed under Warren's command, the credit for the victory would go to Britain and not to Massachusetts. The council submitted an alternate plan whereby only 500 men would go aboard the warships.

Warren replied to the alternate plan in a note beginning, "For God's sake let us do something, and not waste our time in indolence." He then continued more politely, "I sincerely wish you all the honour and success imaginable, and only beg to know, in what manner I can be more serviceable, than in cruizing, to prevent the introduction of succours to the garrison. I fear that if that is all that is expected from the ships, or that they can do, Louisbourg will be safe for some time. For my part, I have proposed all that I think can be done already, and only await your answer thereto."

Probably the most serious obstacles to a direct attack from the sea were the Island Battery and the Circular Battery. The latter, although damaged by fire from ashore, was still dangerous. The Island Battery stood squarely in the mouth of the harbor where its heavy guns could rake any ship entering the channel. Regardless of Warren's impatience, his captains advised very strongly against any attempt to enter the harbor until that battery was reduced.

On the night of May 26, after several earlier efforts frustrated by a bright moon, the northern lights, and heavy surf, 300 volunteers with scaling ladders paddled quietly down the harbor in whaleboats. The surf on the island was still heavy. There were only two places where whaleboats could land, and then only three at a time. Stealthily the boats crept in, and when about half the attackers had landed, they impetuously gave three cheers and rushed the walls.

The French, of course, responded at once with musketry and cannon fire. There was a scene of frightful confusion in the dark, but some reports say that colonials scaled the walls and that Brooks, their leader, was in the act of hauling down the French flag when he was cut down by a Swiss grenadier with a cutlass.

The attack failed. The rest of the whaleboats drew off, and the attackers were left exposed before the walls which sheltered the French marksmen. At dawn the survivors surrendered; 189 men were killed or captured, and Warren still could not enter the harbor.

However, on the same day, May 26, Samuel Waldo had been exploring the point opposite the island where stood the lighthouse. He found an excellent site from which a battery could fire effectively on the island. In the next week several 42-pounders were moved by boat from the Grand Battery, hauled up the cliff, and set up within easy range of the island. While this heavy work was being done, a scout explored the carénage where French ships were grounded out and cleaned. He found, lying in shallow water, thirty-five French 18-pounders. These were soon in position at the Lighthouse Battery, and they were shortly supplemented by a big mortar.

Pepperrell replied on May 28, after the assault on the Island Battery: "In answer to yours of 26th inst. I beg leave to represent to you that this is now the 29th day since the army first invested the town of Louisbourg, and drove the inhabitants within their walls. That in this time we have erected five fascine* batteries, and with hard service to the men drawn our cannon, mortars, balls etc.; that with 16 pieces of cannon, and our mortars mounted at said batteries, and with our cannon from the royal battery, we have been playing on the town, by which we have greatly distrest the inhabitants, made some breaches in the wall, especially at the west gate, which we have beat down, and made a considerable breach there, and doubt not but that we shall soon reduce the circular battery. That in this time we have made five unsuccessful attempts on the island battery, in the last of which we lost 189 men, and many of our boats were shot to pieces, and many of our men drowned before they could land; that we have also kept out scouts to destroy any settlements of the enemy near us, and prevent a surprise in our camp . . . that by the services aforesaid and the constant guard kept night and day round the camp, at our batteries, the army is very much fatigued, and sickness prevails among us, to that degree that we now have but about 2,100 effective men, six hundred of which are gone in quest of two bodies of French and Indians we are informed are gathering, one to the eastward, and the other to the westward."

Meanwhile, the batteries north and east of the town were hammering the west gate, the Circular Battery, and the walls of the town and of the citadel. DuChambon was trying to rebuild and repair the damage as fast as it was done, and he made two ineffective sorties. Warren and Pepperrell carried on a

*The fascine batteries were gun emplacements protected by bundles of sticks.

vigorous and polite correspondence, each frustrated by the delays and each apprehensive of attack from the rear, Pepperrell by Marin and his Indians, Warren by a French fleet cruising under the command of Perier de Salvert. The entire operation could have foundered here on the rocks of disagreement and jealousy between the commanders. However, each had genuine respect for the other, and each knew that neither could take Louisbourg alone. Furthermore, Pepperrell was not a jealous military man with a lifetime reputation to build.

Early in June, the campaign regained momentum. On June 10 *Chester* (50) arrived from England, followed two days later by *Sunderland* (60) and *Canterbury* (60) with supplies and munitions. June 14, the anniversary of the accession of George II, was celebrated by the simultaneous firing of all the guns in all the batteries, including the new Lighthouse Battery. The barrage continued all afternoon. At the same time the warships put ashore all their spare gear, soldiers ashore gathered moss to stuff the ships' hammock nettings to protect men on deck from musketry, and the army was paraded before Pepperrell and Warren. Six hundred men were told to go aboard the ships. Warren addressed the colonial army, saying that neither army nor navy could take Louisbourg alone but that together they were irresistible. An all-out attack was planned by land and sea for the next day, June 16.

Meanwhile, the guns had been battering Louisbourg unmercifully. The west gate and its battery had been destroyed. The Circular Battery had only three guns operational. The west flank of the King's Battery was in ruins, and the walls were breached in several places. There was not an undamaged house in town. Powder was short, there being only forty-seven barrels left in the city. The inhabitants were busy all night trying to repair damage and could find no secure place in which to sleep by day. Their water supply, a shallow dug well on the slope above the harbor, was polluted and was spreading dysentery. Most significant of all, the Lighthouse Battery demolished the Island Battery. The big mortar dropped seventeen of its nineteen shells inside the walls, one of which blew up the magazine. Balls from the cannon drove through and through the walls and buildings. The garrison fled to the water for shelter.

In the afternoon of June 15, with the invaders poised to attack, DuChambon asked for a cease-fire. June 16 was spent in negotiation, and on June 17 the city was surrendered, the French troops marching out with flags flying and bands playing to lay down their arms and go aboard transports to be taken to France.

Victory raises as many problems as it solves, not all of which we need discuss in a history of Maine. However, we should note that the Maine men and the colonials generally were disappointed that by the terms of surrender they were not allowed to pillage the town. Plunder was part of their pay.

Reverend Moody could not be restrained from using the axe he had carried from Maine to smash the altar and statues in the Catholic church and to preach over the wreckage a proper Puritan sermon. Protocol required that he be asked to say grace at the victory dinner, something which the guests dreaded, for Moody had a reputation for long orations. On this occasion, however, he gauged correctly the attitudes and appetites of his audience. He said: "Good Lord, we have so much to thank Thee for that Time will be too short and we must leave it to Eternity. Bless our food and our fellowship on this joyful occasion for the sake of Christ, our Lord. Amen."

The French flag was kept flying over the citadel, luring in four richly laden French East Indiamen. Their capture raised hard feelings between soldiers, who were not allowed to plunder private property ashore, and sailors who received generous prize money from the capture of the merchantmen.

The French had sent a fleet to relieve Louisbourg under de Salvert, but de Salvert heard that the city had capitulated and he returned to France. In June 1746 another fleet was sent, but it was scattered by gales, was irresolutely commanded, and came to nothing.

The only other naval action was the Battle of Tatamagouche (see chapter notes). DuChambon had belatedly summoned Marin, who was besieging Annapolis Royal, to attack Pepperrell in the rear. Marin left Annapolis Royal in early June and hurried toward Louisbourg by sea. Captain David Donahue in the colonial privateer *Resolution* (10) met Marin's fleet: a sloop, two schooners, a "shalloway," and fifty canoes. The wind died, and Marin attacked. Donahue fought furiously. "My stern by force of firing is down to the water's edge, round house all to pieces, but bold-hearted." A little air came in, and with it to the rescue came *Tartar* (26) and *Bonetta* (6), the Rhode Island sloops. The three pursued Marin's vessels until they ran aground. The Indians deserted him, and his force disbanded.

In the summer of 1745, when the news reached England, England needed a victory. England and her allies in Europe had been defeated at Fontenoy in May and were retreating across Flanders. Prince Charles Edward had landed in Scotland, proclaimed his father King of England, and was marching on Edinburgh with an army of Jacobites. The victory at Louisbourg was therefore celebrated extravagantly.

General Pepperrell was made a baronet, was repaid the £10,000 he had spent on the expedition, and was given command of a regiment. There were no soldiers in the regiment, but nevertheless, a colonel received perquisites.

Captain Rous of *Shirley* was given command of a ship in the Royal Navy.

Governor Shirley, who had been instrumental in mounting the campaign, received a regiment. The British government paid Massachusetts £183,000, which Shirley wisely used to buy in the paper money and reestablish Massachusetts credit. Other colonies were reimbursed proportionately.

Edward Tyng and William Vaughan apparently received no reward whatever. The latter went to London, lobbied with influential people, and wrote a long "memorial" to the King outlining his contribution to the success of the siege and urging some recognition. It was all in vain, and he died in London in December 1746 of smallpox.

Two unplanned results of the expedition were far more significant. The campaign showed New England men that their own resolution, dash, and on-the-spot courage could succeed against what appeared to be insuperable formal military odds. They conveniently forgot the contributions of Commodore Warren and the Royal Navy, which, from their view ashore, did not do much, and they went home believing that they had taken Louisbourg and could lick the world.

The other result came at the end of the European war. By 1748 England and France were both exhausted by their European campaigns. While England had eliminated the Jacobite threat in Scotland, her armies were being harried across Europe and defeated in India. It was time to make peace and gird for a new conflict. The Treaty of Aix-la-Chapelle settled nothing, but in exchange for Madras in India it restored Louisbourg to France.

The American colonies were shocked, Massachusetts was insulted, and Maine was outraged. Maine men, Pepperrell, Vaughan, Waldo, and Tyng, had initiated and led the campaign. Maine soldiers and seamen had made up an undue proportion of the force. Now all they had fought for and all that many had died for was being thrown away by the British ministry. The Louisbourg "incident" not only gave Americans confidence that they could win a war, but fostered a bitter resentment against the British government.

NOTES

There are three very good sources for the information in this chapter. Francis Parkman's *Half Century of Conflict,* Volume II, tells the story briefly and dramatically. J. S. McLennan's *Louisbourg from Its Foundation to Its Fall* is told largely from the Canadian point of view. It is particularly strong on the building of the fort and on the weaknesses of the French administration in supplying and controlling the soldiers, the officers, and the merchants. The third source is Neil Rolde's *Sir William Pepperrell of Colonial New England.* Nearly half the book is devoted to the years 1744–46. Rolde deals in detail and at length with the movements of the colonial troops.

Canso is on a small island close to the mainland of Nova Scotia, assumed to be British under the Treaty of Utrecht. It was a fishing station at first, used jointly and more or less amicably by British and French fishermen. Then in 1717 the French were driven out and it was given a token fortification. It soon developed into a base for illegal trade with Louisbourg and other French settlements on Isle Royale. Pepperrell himself used it before war broke out.

Annapolis Royal was the only strong British fortification in Nova Scotia. DuVivier's attack on it was irresolute at best. The captain of *Ardent* made a feeble move against Annapolis and was ready to go back and attack more vigorously, but the French Indiamen in his convoy had insufficient anchoring gear and refused to venture into the tide-scoured waters of the Bay of Fundy and Digby Gut.

Prince of Orange was a snow—that is, a two-masted vessel square-rigged on both masts. The after mast, the mainmast, had another spar stepped close aft of it on which was set a gaff-rigged sail. She measured 180 tons, a big vessel for the day, and probably was about 80 feet long. She was armed with sixteen 6-pounders, each throwing a ball about the size of a baseball. She also carried a number of swivel guns on her rails, each a bit bigger than a musket and throwing a 1-pound ball.

After her capture of Doloboratz's sloop, she was employed in the relief of Annapolis Royal and joined the Louisbourg expedition. After the surrender of the town, Massachusetts sources assume she was lost in a gale. However, McLennan found that de Salvert captured *Prince of Orange* and from her learned that he was too late to relieve Louisbourg. Parkman, in writing of D'Anville's calamitous expedition of 1746, quotes a writer who was aboard *"Prince d'Orange,"* which could have been the same vessel. Of what happened to her crew we have no word, but the vessel probably survived the expedition, as the writer lived to write about it.

Doloboratz's sloop of 80 tons was about 50 feet long and rigged with a single mast. The ball struck just below the crosstrees. All the blocks for controlling the sails were above the crosstrees, so when the top of the mast went, the whole rig collapsed.

Doloboratz and Morpain were privateers much feared by Massachusetts merchants—hence Tyng's enthusiastic reception in Boston, symbolized by the award of an engraved silver plate. Doloboratz evidently was permitted considerable freedom, for he visited New York and Newport, and other coastal towns as far south as Philadelphia. He reported to DuChambon on his exchange and return to Louisbourg that five or six vessels of war, a fire ship, and some small merchant vessels could take any coastal town except New York.

There is a good deal of disagreement about the number of guns with which a particular vessel is armed. This is partly because a naval vessel's "rating" is not always an accurate statement of her actual armament. *Constitution* was rated 44, but at one time, counting carronades on poop and quarterdeck, she carried fifty-six guns. Smaller vessels carried swivel guns, which sometimes were counted and sometimes were not.

The sad state of the Louisbourg garrison in the fall of 1744 is well described by McLennan but only summarized in our text. The soldiers did indeed mutiny in December. Their lot was somewhat improved, but real relief had to wait for help from France. *Renommée* and *Vigilant* carried this help but were intercepted. DuChambon, therefore, was reluctant to trust his troops outside the walls.

Warren's letter to George Anson in McLennan's book shows he had given the project considerable thought and had also written to Corbet on the same subject.

Vaughan's memorial to King George II describes his part in the campaign from the very beginning. It is printed in the appendix to the original edition of McLennan. Granted that he is writing to persuade the King to reward him, his account is consistent with that of others.

The incident of the broken leg is characterized as "probably legendary" by Rolde.

McLennan characterizes Vaughan as "too unbalanced to be trusted with an executive office," but Vaughan declares that Shirley offered him a regiment, which he declined. Shirley wrote Pepperrell asking that Vaughan be included in the Council of War.

With the exception of Maisonfort, captain of *Vigilant,* the French naval commanders appear to have been indecisive and easily discouraged. *Ardent, Renommée,* de Salvert's fleet, and D'Anville's fleet ran from lighter British vessels or were discouraged by foul weather.

Another account of the capture of the Grand Battery adds about forty "maroders" to Vaughan's bold thirteen immediately after they entered the fort.

DuChambons' reply to Pepperrell's summons to surrender may be bad grammar, but there can be no question of its meaning: "We have no response to make to this demand but by the mouth of our cannons."

One can only speculate on the presence of the French guns at the carénage. Perhaps a vessel grounded out, found the next tide insufficient to float her, and dropped her guns to lessen her draft. Why they were not later picked up is harder to guess. However, omission to perform such a heavy and onerous task is consistent with the behavior of French officers in Louisbourg.

More British ships were present than those listed. Warren dictated the order in which the ships were to sail in the planned assault: *Hector, Vigilant, Eltham, Superbe, Princess Mary, Mermaid, Launceston, Bien Aime, Molineux, Caesar, Boston Packet. Chester, Sunderland, Canterbury,* and *Lark* were also present.

DuChambon had insisted on the French garrison's leaving with "honors of war"—that is, flags flying, drums beating, private property unmolested. Pepperrell, fearing an attack on his rear by Marin, and Warren, fearing the arrival of a French fleet under de Salvert—both legitimate concerns—concluded not to stick at trifles.

The Battle of Tatamagouche poses geographic problems. Tatamagouche Bay is on the north side of Nova Scotia. Why Marin should take that circuitous route to Louisbourg is not clear. Also, how the American vessels happened to find themselves north of Nova Scotia when all the action was on the east coast is difficult to understand. I have been unable to penetrate this mystery, but Rolde tells a very circumstantial story of the battle. He spells the name of the bay Tatmagouche. Could there have been a bay by that name on the east coast?

THIRTEEN

Colonial Development, 1763-1775

A PARTY of Indians attacked Friendship in 1758 but were unable to take the fort, were beaten off, and fled. This was the last organized Indian attack on the Maine coast. The Massachusetts government in 1722 on flimsy pretexts had declared Lovewell's War, a war of extermination on the Indians, and had posted bounties of up to £200 for Indian scalps. Many Indian men, women, and even children who had been living at peace with the settlers and wanted to continue to do so were killed. When the white men had the upper hand, they were without mercy or compunction. The "Indian menace" was eliminated.

The French menace was also eliminated. The English campaigns of the French and Indian War against Ticonderoga, Niagara, Louisbourg, and Québec were all successful. By the close of 1759 the French were powerless, and under the Treaty of Paris in 1763 France ceded to Britain all claims to Newfoundland and Canada except for the islands of St. Pierre and Miquelon in the Gulf of St. Lawrence. Maine fishermen could now fish on the Nova Scotia and Newfoundland banks without fear of molestation or serious competition.

The third powerful influence for change was the determination of the powerful Tory party in England to make the merchants and colonists pay for the eighteenth-century wars that had left the country heavily in debt. The Tory party consisted largely of landholders. Capital invested in land had always been a chief source of income. However, during the seventeenth and eighteenth centuries, capital invested in ships, trade goods, and bills of exchange had become another highly profitable source of income, income that the Tories taxed to lighten the tax on land. These taxes on commerce such as the Navigation Acts interfered with colonial trade, led to widespread smuggling, to desperate efforts to control smuggling by force, to retaliation, fierce resentment, and finally to war.

Maine seafarers' reactions to these changes is the subject of this chapter and the two following it.

Captain Richard Pattishall bought Damariscove Island from the Indians in 1685 and was killed by a war party at the beginning of King William's War in 1689 "as he lay in his sloop." Tradition has it that he was not easily subdued, for, having by him a full stone jug of rum, he laid about him vigorously, flattening several attackers before he was overwhelmed. His ghost, says the tale, still visits the island, jug in hand, and has been seen even in recent years.

On a visit to Damariscove in 1769, eighty years after his demise, Captain Pattishall's ghost found much the same and much changed. The fort was in ruins. The crude huts were now houses. The shore was crowded with wharves and fish flakes (drying stages) where salt codfish lay drying in the sun. As he stood on the hill looking out over the quiet harbor on a summer morning, the Captain could see no ketches, a rig with which he had been familiar, and no shallops with square mainsails and foresails, the foremast cocked forward over the bow. The small shallops, about 20 feet long, that he did see were rigged with a spritsail and jib in the Dutch way, a change he approved of—a handy rig for a small boat. A big sloop—about 45 feet, guessed the Captain—was unloading cordwood to take aboard a cargo of dry salt cod.

He strolled down the hill, passing open kitchen doors, picking his way among the fragrant fish flakes, to a wharf where lay a boat like none he had ever seen before. She was double-ended like a shallop, about 30 feet long, decked over, with standing room for men who would fish along the rail. She had two masts, one stepped a little aft of amidships, the other only a foot or so aft of her bluff, buoyant bow. Her stem was carried a foot above the top plank to act as a mooring bitt. Each mast carried a gaff-headed sail, now on deck, bundled up clumsily. She looked to be a handy rig.

Captain Pattishall hailed a man rigging a handline in the after standing room, asked what kind of a boat this might be. He had trouble being understood, for the West Country speech common 100 years before sounded strange to the Scotch-Irish settler whose parents had come to the coast in the 1730s.

"She's a Chebacco boat." The word was unfamiliar, but the Captain later learned it was named thus after the parish north of Cape Ann where these boats were first built.

"Come aboard, Cap, and bring your jug," hailed the skipper of the Chebacco. Pattishall accepted with enthusiasm. Two teenage boys pelted down the path and leaped aboard. The skipper cast off, and the boys took the long oars and rowed down the cove.

They passed another boat lying to a mooring, one much like their own but with a square stern and a rudderpost working through a counter. "That's called a dogbody," observed the skipper, "but I'm damned if I know why."

The rock in the entrance was just where it had always been. Outside, they set the sails. The loose-footed foresail overlapped the mainsail a yard or so, but the mainsail was laced to a boom.

They stood off to the eastward before the gentle southwest breeze. Pumpkin Rock was still the same bare granite ledge the Captain remembered. The ranges the skipper picked up to locate his fishing spot were ones Pattishall had used many times. He felt quite at home. The killick that one of the boys threw over as an anchor was the same; and the barvel, a long canvas apron the skipper tossed the Captain "so you don't get all beglammed with salt alewives," was like his own. The lines, leads, reels, the snoods, gangings, and hooks were familiar, and so was the tug of the first 30-pound codfish on his line.

As they rolled at anchor outside Pumpkin Rock, the Camden Hills showing round and blue over the distant land, a sail appeared outside Seguin, came rapidly up over the horizon, and, headed toward Monhegan, passed close aboard. She was a lovely thing. Old Captain Pattishall had never seen anything like her before. Like the Chebacco boat, she had two masts, each with a gaff-headed sail, but she was much bigger, about 50 feet long, and both masts were stepped farther aft. On her upward-slanted bowsprit was set a big, loose-footed jib, now hanging slack as she ran before the wind. She was running wing-and-wing, the mainsail out to port, the foresail to starboard, each hard

Pinky schooner. *Earle G. Barlow*

full and straining ahead. She pushed a roll of foam under her bluff bow as she bore down on the fishermen. She had a quick sheer, emphasized by a sharp, upward sweep and so exaggerated that the two rails joined beyond the stern in a crotch to hold the boom. Seated comfortably in the angle between the high rails, one of her crew waved his sou'wester as she slipped by, leaving almost no wake behind her fine stern.

Pattishall stared after her, breathless. "What in hell is that?" he asked.

"That's a pinky, come down east for firewood. Sets on the water like a pintail duck, don't she? She's the latest thing in schooners, Cap."

"Schooner?"

"Seems's though up to Gloucester, some time back, Cap Robinson built a small vessel rigged like this here Chebacco with two masts, but he moved them aft a piece, gave her a bowsprit, and set a jib on her. They had a great launching. She shot off the ways halfway across the harbor. 'See how she schoons!' said Cap Robinson's wife. 'A schooner let her be,' said Cap. Now you know what a schooner is, and pass the jug, Cap."

At the word, the ghost of Captain Pattishall dissolved like fog on a sunny summer morn. No mortal ever drank of that jug.

The offshore fishermen frequented the Gulf of Maine and Nova Scotia banks, salting the fish aboard the vessel. After six or eight weeks, when they had a full cargo, when all the salt was wet, they came home, washed the fish, and dried it.

Count was kept of how many fish each man caught, and, after deducting a proportion for the owner, the proceeds of the voyage were divided in proportion to each man's catch. Customarily, the owner supplied the vessel, the salt, the bait (salt clams and salt mackerel), barrels for water, knives, nippers, and pants for the salter. For this the owner got three-eighths of the proceeds. The fisherman provided his own lines and hooks and his own sea stores, consisting principally in the eighteenth century of salt pork, molasses hard tack, rum, and perhaps some rice, potatoes, or dried peas. Fish was the principal food. The fisherman also provided himself with a stout canvas petticoat or a barvel, which was like an apron extending from the chest to the knees, a sou'wester, and a pair of stout leather boots with thick soles and legs that would turn up to cover the thighs.

When the schooner reached the banks and found fish, she was anchored, and the men went fishing, each man having a "berth" along the rail. It was customary for the skipper to have the after berth on the starboard side. If the fish kept biting after dark, as they not infrequently did, the men fished watch and watch—four hours fishing, then four hours to dress the fish, get a "mug up," and sleep.

A schooner of 50 tons would be perhaps 45 feet long and carry seven men. Marblehead schooners made a trip to Sable Island in March, then to Browns Bank on the Nova Scotia coast, two trips to Georges Bank in the summer, and another to Sable Island in the fall. Such a vessel would bring in about 600 quintals* for the year. It is rather doubtful that many Maine vessels fished that intensively.

Salt was imported, the best coming from Cadiz, Spain, and Lisbon, Portugal. Salt from Turks Island and Tortuga in the West Indies was likely to be more "fiery" and could lead to salt-burned fish.

The best New England salt cod brought a high price in Bilbao, Spain, because it would stand the overland trip to Madrid. A salt fish was not considered merchantable in England unless it measured 18 inches from the first fin to the beginning of the tail. In general, the best fish went to France, Spain, and Italy, the Catholic countries of Europe. Some went to the British Isles, but it was sold there in competition with their own catch.

As was the practice in the century before, the second grade of fish went to the "wine islands"—Madeira, the Azores, and the Canaries—and to the southern American colonies. The so-called "refuse fish," the lowest grade, went to the West Indies as food for slaves on the sugar plantations. This was perfectly good food. It consisted of smaller codfish, hake, and slack-salted pollock. In the early days of the twentieth century, a Maine man might keep such a pollock hanging by the tail in his fish house. He or his guest might cut off a piece with his jackknife and eat it raw as a preliminary to conversation. Savory stuff! It was a favorite with the West Indians, too.

We do not have figures on fish exported from Maine in the colonial period, but it may help to know that in 1747, 300,000 quintals of dry salt fish—16,800 tons—were exported from British North America. In 1748, 32,000 quintals went from Salem, Massachusetts, to Europe and 20,000 quintals of refuse fish went to the West Indies. These figures deal with codfish only. One must remember that quantities of haddock, hake, and pollock were also caught and eaten both at home and abroad. Mackerel were caught, at first for bait only and then salted in barrels for winter food. Some was exported to the West Indies, but plantation workers were said to prefer salt cod.

The fisheries suffered during the first half of the century from the almost continual wars, but after the fall of Québec in 1759 and especially after the Treaty of Paris in 1763, which practically eliminated French competition, the fisheries rapidly increased. Salem had 30 vessels cod fishing in 1762; in 1763, 300 vessels were cod fishing, with an additional 90 vessels catching mackerel. It is doubtful if fishing in Maine increased proportionally, but certainly Salem's figures suggest a rapid increase in demand and in opportunity.

Not all the inhabitants of coastal Maine were fishermen. Many worked in the woods, yet had a close connection with the sea.

The growing towns and cities to the westward were in increasing need of fuel. They relied on wood and had long ago burned all the firewood within easy reach. Accordingly, the Maine coast settlements with large resources of

* Fish were usually measured in quintals, pronounced "kentals," of 112 pounds.

wood close to tidewater shipped great quantities by sloop and schooner to Boston and surrounding towns. Harvard College owned a sloop, *Harvard,* that was kept constantly occupied carrying firewood from Maine. The populations of the new towns established along the Maine coast depended heavily on the exchange of firewood for flour, pork, beef, tools, shoes, cloth, rum, molasses, and other necessities that they were too busy—fishing or cutting wood—to provide for themselves. Many, of course, had farms, but the food raised on stony soil in a harsh climate was insufficient.

Sawn lumber was another staple forest product in great demand both in the American colonies and in the West Indies, a product abundant in Maine close to navigable water. At first, lumber was cut in a saw pit. This was simply a hole in the ground perhaps 6 feet deep. The log to be sawed was laid across it. One man stood on the edge of the pit, his long saw projecting downward. An unfortunate helper stood in the pit, holding the lower end of the saw. The top man pulled up, and the bottom man pulled down, the sawdust filling his mouth, nose, and eyes, his pockets, and his boots. His only respite came at the pause when the log was moved along.

Where there was a stream that could develop a sufficient head of water, however, a mill could be set up. This was merely a mechanical adaptation of the pit saw, for the circular saw was still to be invented. A water wheel turned a shaft on which an eccentric wheel with a crank moved the saw up and down. Where power was sufficient, more blades could be added so that three or four boards could be sawed simultaneously. By this means, sawn lumber could be turned out in quantity. Much of it was shipped as it came from the saw.

An expanding population requires an increasing supply of building material. Nowhere was lumber more abundant, more easily available, and less expensive to deliver than along Maine rivers. Sawn pine and spruce lumber was shipped in deals, each piece or "deal" being about 7 inches wide and 3 inches thick, in large quantity both to England and the West Indies. Some enterprising merchants even shipped prefabricated houses, the pieces cut to shape and ready to assemble. Also, shingles and clapboards were sent in shiploads not only for new construction but to repair buildings damaged or demolished by hurricanes.

Much lumber, especially oak, was used for staves and sugar boxes shipped knocked down in bundles to be assembled when needed. There was a growing demand in Spain, Portugal, and the wine islands for barrels and pipes—long barrels of comparatively small diameter—for shipping wine. New England white oak was a favored material. The staves, heads, and hoops for a barrel would be packaged together and assembled in the islands when needed. If they were to make tight barrels, each stave must be wider in the middle than on the ends, and the bevel on each stave must be the same and sharper at the ends than in the middle. This called for a good eye and a sharp drawknife. The cooper's trade was an important one.

In the West Indies, rum was shipped in white oak casks and molasses in red oak. Rum came from the distillery in casks, but the buyer of molasses was expected to provide his own barrels. Consequently, vessels trading to the West Indies carried a cooper and a supply of staves for themselves as well as staves for sale.

Sugar, too, was shipped in hogsheads but also in boxes, which were sold knocked down to be set up as needed. Thus, besides firewood and sawn lumber, staves and shooks were made and exported in quantity.

Ship timber was another important Maine export in the eighteenth century. The stems and frames, especially the lower ones, of eighteenth-century ships were gotten out from naturally grown crooks called "compass timber." The gnarled oak growing in English hedgerows had supplied much of this, but when sheep raising became widespread, hedgerows were cut down. By the mid-eighteenth century, very little compass timber of English oak was available. Maine had an abundant supply of white and red oak compass timber.

Also needed was "straight timber," the heavy, straight pieces used for keels and sternposts. These came from big forest oaks. The keel of the seventy-four-gun *Thunderer* built from 1756 to 1760 at Woolwich dockyard in England consisted of seven timbers 18 inches square and 26 feet long. The sternpost had to be a piece of clear oak 30 feet long and the same size as the keel. For the compass timber and straight timber alone, exclusive of planking, decking, and ceiling, *Thunderer* used about 2,600 fully grown oak trees. All told, 3,400 oak trees went into her. With about 600 vessels, some bigger, many smaller, in the Royal Navy, the demand for ship timber was enormous.

In addition, these vessels, although very heavily constructed by any standard, were subject to rot. With frames almost touching each other, with 4-inch planking on the outside, 4-inch ceiling on the inside, and numerous knees, deckbeams, and bulkheads, there was little circulation of air. Damp, warm, stagnant air rots seasoned wood quickly and rots green wood while you watch it—almost. Consequently, more wood was needed for replacement and rebuilding.

Much of the timber for the Royal Navy came from the Baltic countries. The Admiralty scorned American ship timber, regarding white oak as inferior to English oak. It is not unlikely that, buying American oak with this attitude, they did indeed get an inferior grade. In 1696, 1700, and again in 1740 they rejected shiploads of American oak. Nevertheless, they purchased a few shiploads of American timber for dockyards in England as well as in Antigua and Jamaica. Very considerable amounts of timber were shipped—illegally, of course—to French islands and to Cuba, where the Spanish had a large dockyard.

Under great pressure for naval vessels, the Admiralty, over the objections of the heavily prejudiced Navy Board, had *Falkland* (54) and *Bedford Galley* built at Portsmouth, New Hampshire, in 1696. Contrary to the predictions of the Navy Board, these vessels lasted as long as comparable English ships yet were condemned as unfit for naval use in prejudiced English dockyards. In

1747 the Admiralty sought to build four frigates in America. The Navy Board contracted for one, *America* (44), built by William Pepperrell in Kittery, but she too was soon condemned.

"The real timber problem with the Royal Navy was the trouble with the wooden heads which guided its policies, and England didn't have to import that kind of timber," observed an enlightened but unidentified British naval official.

Despite the prejudice of the Navy Board, British shipyards used large quantities of American oak in British merchant ships. Many American-built merchant ships were sold to English merchants and to foreign merchants in the West Indies and in Europe. British merchants also contracted for ships built in the Colonies, which were much less expensive than those built in England. This may have been partly because Maine, New Hampshire, and Massachusetts builders began to use live oak from the South. This is excellent ship timber, hard, strong, and resistant to rot. However, the Southerners were more interested in growing tobacco and food crops than in lumbering and did not use live oak themselves. When English oak ran out and Baltic oak became unavailable, the Navy Board turned to teak and mahogany and ignored American live oak.

Another, very important product of Maine forests was masts and spars. White pine is light and, comparatively speaking, limber—ideal for masts. A mast for a seventy-four-gun ship would be 30 yards long and 30 inches in diameter. Eastern white pines of what to us seem incredible size* flourished along the Maine rivers. It is said that the old-growth pines were so big, one could turn a team of oxen around on top of a stump.

James Rosier reports cutting spars on Allen Island in 1605, and Henry Hudson cut a mast for his vessel on the shore of Penobscot Bay in 1609. In 1634 the first cargo of masts was shipped from the Piscataqua River. At first, masts were part of the lumber cargoes and were sold to anyone who would buy. Since England grew no trees suitable for masts, the Royal Navy had been buying masts from Sweden and Norway, but in 1652, during the First Dutch War, the Dutch cut off this supply and the Admiralty sent ships to America for masts. The first two shipments were lost to shipwreck and the enemy, but the third got through in 1653. They were too few and came too late, for although the English won the battle of Scheveningen, they were so slow in replacing damaged spars that Dutch convoys got through and prolonged the war.

The Second Dutch War, from 1664 to 1667, again put pressure on the Royal Navy for masts, especially after the King of Sweden ordered that no more masts be cut in Sweden for seven years. Clerk of the Acts of His Majesty's Royal Navy, Samuel Pepys, sent the frigate *Elias* to America for masts in 1664, but she sank with her cargo. The Four Days' Battle in June 1666 put the British navy out of action for seven weeks for lack of spars. With the navy

*One tree measured 17 feet in circumference.

unable to make sail in its own defense, the Dutch sailed into Chatham on the Thames and towed out several large English warships. In December of 1666, Pepys wrote, "There is also the very good news come of four New England ships come safe home to Falmouth with masts for the King, which is a blessing mighty unexpected and without which, if for nothing else, we must have failed the next year."

After the war, Massachusetts gave the King as a present two mast cargoes to make up for the province's refusal to join an invasion of Canada.

By 1685 the Royal Navy needed masts so badly and so few were available that King Charles II appointed Edward Randolph as Surveyor of Pines and Timber and gave him four deputies to help him mark with a broad arrow all white pines 24 inches in diameter 12 inches above the ground growing within 10 miles of the water. By 1688 Randolph had surveyed the Maine woods as far east as the Sheepscot and Penobscot rivers and was appointed Surveyor General in 1691.

From 1691 until 1729 a series of laws was enacted and reenacted which added up to the Broad Arrow Policy.

- All white pines anywhere in the New England colonies not growing on private property—fenced land—were reserved for the King under a penalty of £100. Later, all white pines not growing in an organized township were included.
- A mast contractor in England bid in the contract for the Navy Board, which set the specifications for navy masts. The contractor could also sell spars to private citizens in England. The contractor appointed agents in America to have the trees cut and shipped after approval by the Surveyor of the King's Woods or his deputy.
- The Royal Navy could preempt any mast within twenty days of its arrival in England.
- No masts, spars, or other ship timber were to be shipped anywhere but to England, although some were delivered to English dockyards in Jamaica and Antigua.
- A bounty of £1 per ton was paid for masts to the mast agent. A mast hewn sixteen-sided might weigh 15 to 20 tons.

The contractor through his agent paid the laborers who worked in the woods, the ox drivers, who owned their own animals, and the adzemen who hewed the logs, but not the man on whose land the tree grew. In 1728 Nathaniel Knight of Falmouth received 7 shillings a day for hewing thirty-two masts. In 1738 a laborer earned £1 per day. A man with four oxen earned £5 10 shillings for four days' work "twitching" masts out of the river; twitching means dragging. In 1754 Nathaniel Knight agreed "to deliver to Samuel Waldo, mast agent, at Presumscot Dam and Stroudwater Landing 15 main masts, 8 fore masts, 10 main yards, and 10 bowsprits at dimensions and lengths aforesaid at 2 shillings fourpence per inch in diameter, which are to be Apple pines [white pines]; all over 20 inches to be hewed 16 squares, and thereunder and yards and bowsprits 8 squares as is customary. To be handsome straight and sound sticks free from Defects of all sorts." The penalty for failure to deliver on time was £200.

John Bridger succeeded Randolph as Surveyor General in 1705 and did such a thorough job of hunting down violators of the law and of pressing the legislators of Massachusetts and New Hampshire to enact laws supporting the Broad Arrow Policy that he became very unpopular and was fired in 1718. His successor, Burneston, never came to America and appointed Armstrong his deputy. Their administration was evidently undistinguished. In 1728, David Dunbar, lieutenant governor of New Hampshire, the same man who as governor of the Sagadahoc Territory brought settlers to the Boothbay and Pemaquid regions in 1729, was appointed. In 1732 he was dismissed as governor of Sagadahoc but evidently continued as lieutenant governor of New Hampshire and Surveyor until Governor Benning Wentworth of New Hampshire bought the position of Surveyor for £2,000 in 1743. He installed as agents his friends and relations, Mark Wentworth, George Tate, Thomas Westbrook, Edward Parry, and Samuel Waldo, who had brought German settlers to the Waldo Grant. Governor Wentworth recouped his purchase price partly by creating and selling "paper" townships on which mast trees grew. The governor could establish an area of wilderness as a township at the request of a private citizen, who then acted as an absentee proprietor until the township was populated and incorporated as a town. The paper township, once granted, became "private property," open to lumbering by the proprietor and exempt from the Broad Arrow Policy, except for such trees as might have previously been marked. In 1766 Benning Wentworth turned over the office of Surveyor to his nephew, John Wentworth, who held it until the American Revolution in 1775 with a deeper respect for the King's Broad Arrow than his uncle had shown.

The Broad Arrow laws were deeply resented and ingeniously evaded. Many of the trees were cut and quickly sawn into boards less than 24 inches wide so it could not be proved that they came from a bigger tree. For this reason, the wide boards found in colonial houses and barns are frequently 23 inches wide and never wider. Anyone who informed the Surveyor of such an infraction was quietly dealt with locally by "swamp law"; and even when a culprit was brought to court, he was neatly acquitted.

People cut down trees that protected the King's trees from the wind, and winter gales blew the mast trees down, to the profit of the neighbors. Another device was to set a fire which scorched the bottom of the tree, making it useless as a mast but marketable as boards.

Some of the deputies tried hard to catch and prosecute offenders. In 1700, Deputy Armstrong seized 25,000 logs, two-thirds of which were over the 2-foot limit. In 1730, David Dunbar came on very strong as Surveyor. He "came with an armed force, turned [the inhabitants] from their lands, seized their timber, burned and destroyed their houses." The people of Exeter expressed their resentment by scuttling his boat, and his very life was threatened at Dover. In 1759 one of Benning Wentworth's deputies was nearly drowned in a millpond. In eastern Maine, settlers and Indians conspired to guide the mast surveyors into parts of the forest where they could do little harm. In 1763, 6,389 logs were seized in Maine, New Hampshire, and on the Merrimac River.

When John Wentworth succeeded Governor Benning Wentworth as Surveyor, he seized a shipment of illegal lumber at Brunswick and watched the wharves at Falmouth. In 1772, as resentment against Britain was growing on other issues besides the Broad Arrow Policy, he called for help from Captain* Mowatt in *Canso,* who with his deputy seized 70,000 board feet of illegal lumber. Surveyor John Wentworth wrote in 1773 that illegal cutting was much reduced and was being done by "only the very lowest and abandon'd among them, who will ever revile and calumniate every Law and its officer that prevents their enormities vainly hoping that thereby they will overcome all government." Wentworth was a Tory, and he might have been right.

Not only were the King's pines cut and sawn up, but many were taken out as masts and sold in the French and Spanish West Indies and in Spain and Portugal. Spain even sent purchasers to Portsmouth, New Hampshire, where Wentworth supplied them. French privateers were fitted with masts as well, even in 1739 as war with England was imminent.

The landowners' resentment was not without reason. Wentworth, himself a Surveyor of the King's Woods, wrote that had the Broad Arrow Policy been strictly enforced, it "would have prevented cultivation and soon put an end to the lumber trade both to the West Indies and England, though the latter was an object of Parliamentary bounty." Most of the pines were unfit for spars, many being rotten at the heart or proving defective on being hewn out. John Wentworth in 1771 found that 102 out of 106 mast trees were defective. However, the trees were valuable as lumber, and in order to clear the land for hay, pasture, or planting, even the King's trees had to go.

In spite of all the obstacles, a great many masts were cut, shipped to England, and stepped in the King's ships. The following table, which continues on page 184, gives an idea of the size of spar with which we are concerned:

	120-GUN SHIP		74-GUN SHIP		28-GUN FRIGATE	
	SPAR DIAMETER	LENGTH	SPAR DIAMETER	LENGTH	SPAR DIAMETER	LENGTH
Mainmast	40″	40 yds	36″	36 yds	20″	24 yds
Bowsprit	37″	25 yds	34″	22 yds	21″	14 yds
Foremast	37″	37 yds	31″	33 yds	19″	22 yds

*Mowatt was a lieutenant. In the eighteenth-century British navy, a lieutenant or a commander in command of a vessel was called by courtesy "Captain" but kept his rank until made a post captain.

	120-GUN SHIP		74-GUN SHIP		28-GUN FRIGATE	
	SPAR DIAMETER	LENGTH	SPAR DIAMETER	LENGTH	SPAR DIAMETER	LENGTH
Main yard	25″	35 yds	23″	33 yds	14″	21 yds
Mizzenmast	24″	27 yds	22″	25 yds	16″	18 yds
Maintopmast	21″	23 yds	19″	22 yds	13″	14 yds
Jibboom	15″	17 yds	14″	16 yds	9″	11 yds
Main top-gallant mast	12″	11 yds	11″	11 yds	7″	7 yds

Getting out a 100-foot mast was a heavy, difficult, and dangerous job that often led to a frustrating conclusion.

With the mast tree located and—if the operation was to be a legal one—permission granted from the Surveyor of the King's Woods and the agent of the mast contractor, a gang moved to the woods. Hovels were built for oxen and a camp for the men. Small trees and brush were cleared away in the direction the tree was to fall to make a level and springy bed for it to land on so it would not be shattered by its own weight. Then, men with the oxen swamped out as straight and level a road as they could to a river big enough to float the spar. Holes, dips, and soft spots in the road were filled with dirt and brush, and high spots were knocked off. When cold weather came, water was poured over the fill and allowed to freeze to make a hard base. Then, after the snow came, axe-men would start cutting a scarf in the tree in the direction it was to fall. On a quiet day, lest a gust of wind twist the tree and lay it the wrong way, the backcut was made, several men swinging their axes in a rhythm timed not to interfere. At last the tree leaned, everyone ran, and down she came, bounced, and lay in her bed.

After the tree was limbed off, the top was jacked onto a sled and chained to the tongue. The butt was loosely chained to another sled so the spar could turn on the sled to get around corners. Several other sleds supported the middle of the spar. Teams of oxen were hitched up, the word was given, and the great spar, weighing 15 to 20 tons, was moved slowly off.

Balking—moving the spar on sled or wheels—was slow enough on the level, but when a hill lay between the log and the river, problems multiplied. As the log was slowly and painfully hauled up the hill, the lead sled and lead oxen might be lifted off the ground and perhaps choked by their yokes, or at least lose traction. Then, when the log, dragged over the top of the hill, balanced and tipped down, the sled might be smashed or the oxen killed while the butt flipped up and hanged the oxen behind.

Going downhill, the runners of the sleds were wrapped with chains, teams of oxen were hitched to hold the log back, and pinch lines were rigged to trees, then slacked off creaking as the log was eased ahead. If the log took charge, the lead oxen might well be run over and killed.

Whatever the difficulties, the King's navy must be served, and the spar went ahead. If it was summertime, the spar was moved on wheels 15 feet in diameter attached to a single axle. One wheel was laid flat, the axle vertical,

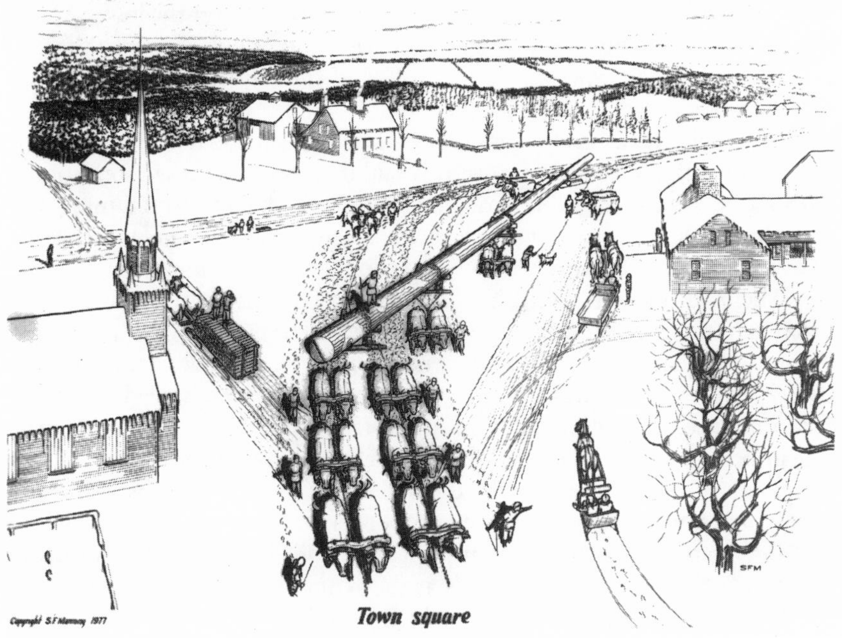

Above: A mast for a king's ship. *Below:* A mast ship loading. *Sam Manning*

and the other wheel in the air. The log was maneuvered over the lower wheel, chained loosely against the axle. Then the wheels were pulled over so the axle was horizontal, the wheels ready to roll, and the log slung under the axle loosely enough to let it turn a corner.

The route was as straight as possible, but where it had to turn a corner, it was a turn with a very wide radius. It is said that town squares in some of the riverside towns in Maine are spacious enough in which to turn a mast, and that some of the very straight stretches of road, generally quite uncharacteristic of country roads, were originally swamped out for the moving of masts.

The great log was rolled into the river at last and floated down to the shipping point where a seagoing vessel could pick it up. Here it was dragged ashore and squared with a broadaxe, then hewn to eight sides and finally cut sixteen-sided with an adze—these tools being in the hands of skilled workmen, for a misplaced cut with a dull tool could start a split that would ruin a spar. The inspectors would condemn a mast even for one rotten knot.

The spar was then returned to the water to lie afloat until a mast ship came for it. Such ships were built for the trade—over 100 feet long, measuring 500 to 1,000 tons—and could carry from forty to one hundred 100-foot masts plus bowsprits, topmasts, and yards as they could be fitted in. These vessels had loading ports cut in the stern which were battened down and caulked before sailing; and, of course, they had no bulkheads, because a bulkhead athwartships would prevent using the full length of the hold for a mast. In a seaway, they were stiff. One observer wrote, "Our old vessel shipped many seas, being bound up with long spars [she] was not nearly as lively as with another cargo."

By the latter part of the eighteenth century, New England was almost the only source of trees large enough for single lower masts for 100-gun ships. Lacking big enough trees, large spars had to be made up of smaller pieces expertly scarfed together—an expensive job, but one that made a strong spar.

The supply of mast trees and indeed of all lumber in western Maine was seriously reduced in 1761 and 1762 when furious fires swept the woods from New Hampshire as far east as Cape Elizabeth. The next year, many inhabitants of Scarborough, principally lumbermen, moved east and established the town of Machias.

In 1772, however, the mast trade was still going strong, as the following table shows. The listing under Portsmouth includes spars cleared from the Portsmouth Custom House cut on the Merrimac and Piscataqua rivers and the surrounding regions. Spars cut near Cape Elizabeth and from there east to the Canadian border are listed under Falmouth.

	FALMOUTH	PORTSMOUTH	NOVA SCOTIA
Masts	382	329	189
Bowsprits	69	80	25
Yards	451	12	285
Small spars (spruce)	476	1,086	—

In 1775 with the beginning of the American Revolution, the Colonies refused to ship more masts to Britain. At first this caused little distress, as most of the British fleet was laid up and rotting quietly. Some masts were cut in Nova Scotia, and one British ship in Halifax sent crews ashore to cut a mast for their own ship. When France joined the United States in 1778 in the Revolution against England, however, masts and spars became an immediate problem for England. Maine mast ships bound for France were intercepted—one on the Sheepscot River in 1777 and another in 1778 loading for France.

When hostilities started in 1778, the French had thirty ships-of-the-line at Brest and twelve at Toulon, the latter with 4,000 soldiers. If either reached America, British Admiral Richard Howe's fleet at New York would be heavily outnumbered. The British navy found that its ships, many built of Baltic green oak fifteen or twenty years before, were badly rotted and their spars were tottering. French Admiral D'Estaing left Brest on April 9 with his fleet and took four weeks to reach Gibraltar. British Admiral Byron with thirteen ships of the line left England on June 9 with an outside chance of catching D'Estaing. On July 3, he ran into a southwest gale which found the weaknesses in his spars. His fleet was dispersed, many ships were dismasted, and after the gale, crews were a long time fishing sprung spars or inventing jury rigs. Some of the fleet returned to England and others limped into American ports.

In a subsequent gale, HMS *Invincible* (74) sprung her bowsprit in three places, and her mainmast was sprung at the gun deck and had to be cut away above the quarterdeck lest it rip up that deck should it fall. The foremast broke in three pieces, killing one man and injuring several others. They cut away part of the bowsprit, rigged jury masts, were lucky to avoid D'Estaing, and limped into Halifax.

Admiral Howe's own ships were few and in equally bad shape for lack of spars. After being blockaded by D'Estaing in New York, then following him to Rhode Island where he could not fight him because of shaky spars, Howe finally sailed for England, leaving Admiral Byron in command with only one of his thirteen ships of the line in seaworthy condition and only seven of his thirty-nine frigates safely operational.

In 1779 Admiral Sir Charles Hardy was ordered to send *Isis* (50) against John Paul Jones, who was then spreading fire and fear on the west coast of England in little *Ranger*. However, Hardy could not leave port because his masts would not stand the strain.

Finally, on September 5, 1781, with General Cornwallis besieged at Yorktown, the French kept Admiral Graves out of the Chesapeake. The battle was indecisive, but Graves wrote that his ships "had not speed enough in so mutilated a state to attack them." General Sir Henry Clinton had 7,000 troops in New York to relieve and reinforce Cornwallis, but Graves did not have the ships to deliver them.

There can be little doubt, then, that Maine masts were essential to the British navy and that one of Maine's contributions to the nation's independence was to deprive Britain of the spars she needed to command the seas.

Other naval aspects of the American Revolution will be described in Chapters 14, 15, and 16.

NOTES

The source for the general history of the period is William D. Williamson's *History of the State of Maine,* Volume II. This is a detailed year-by-year study from which has been gleaned relevant information. The third paragraph in this chapter is digested from many sources but can be clearly inferred from Williamson.

Captain Pattishall was indeed murdered by Indians in 1689 at Damariscove, and his ghost has been reported many times since then—usually at night. Pattishall's ghost appears here in order to make more palatable a heavy dose of important technical information. The rum jug is pure fiction, "corroborative detail, intended to give artistic verisimilitude to an otherwise bald and unconvincing narrative" *(The Mikado)*.

Raymond McFarland's *History of New England Fisheries,* while not primarily concerned with Maine, has useful information. *Goin' Fishin'* by George Wesley Pierce has excellent descriptions and attractive drawings of the early fishing vessels. George Brown Goode's *The Fisheries and Fishing Industry of the United States* is a classic and is excellent on the nineteenth century, with some useful information on the eighteenth.

The skipper's information on Chebacco boats, dogbodies, pinkies, and schooners is all well documented except for the story about Captain Robinson. This is a tradition much quoted and often repeated but a little too neat to be entirely true. It is probable that the schooner rig developed in Holland. A Dutch lady of wide historical knowledge connects the word schooner with *schoen,* the Dutch and German word for *beautiful*. The Dutch word for schooner is *schoener*. The Oxford English Dictionary lists the origin of the word as uncertain.

It is difficult to tell how many vessels from Maine fished on the offshore banks, because the figures that we have are all for Massachusetts, which at the time included Maine; only occasionally is there a separate reference to Maine. Lorenzo Sabine's *Report on the Principal Fisheries of the American Seas* yields these nuggets:

- In about 1700 Massachusetts exported 100,000 quintals (5,600 tons) of dry cod annually to Portugal, Spain, and Italy.
- In 1731 Massachusetts fisheries employed 5,000 to 6,000 men.
- In 1741 Massachusetts took annually 230,000 quintals. There were 400 vessels of 50 tons and an estimated 400 ketches, shallops, and undecked boats.
- From 1741 to 1761 there was a decline in the fisheries of Massachusetts due to emigration to inland Maine from Marblehead, Provincetown, and elsewhere on Cape Cod, and due to wars and to privateering.
- From 1765 to 1775 *Maine* employed annually 60 vessels (1,000 tons of shipping) and 230 men.
- George Washington is reported to have had a Saturday lunch almost every week of creamed salt codfish with egg sauce.

Few authorities emphasize the trade in firewood and hay, necessities of life for Boston. A great many small sloops and schooners were built for this trade, never registered, and long ago wrecked or rotted. The woodcutters, however, learned to build and sail boats and acquired the character that goes with shoestring sailors.

Sawmills appear to have been quite common and to have been quite simple machines to build, given the saw. Four men left Scarborough in April 1763 with their families. They arrived at Machias on May 20, and built a house and mill in what was then a wilderness. More families joined them, and that winter they sawed 1,600,000 feet of lumber. That can't be done with a pit saw! These people did no farming. They depended entirely on Boston merchants. Drisko's *Narrative of the Town of Machias* is our source.

The information on *Thunderer* comes from *Building the Wooden Fighting Ship,* by James Dodds and James Moore, a detailed account of *Thunderer*'s construction as typical of shipbuilding practice of the day. The bulk of the information on ship timber and masts came from Robert G. Albion's *Forests and Sea Power,* an exhaustive study of the subject. Sam Manning's *New England's Masts and the King's Broad Arrow* has a wealth of detail and excellent drawings. *Masts and the King's Navy,* by William C. Carlton in *The New England Quarterly* for March 1939, has a few interesting sidelights, especially on the felling, transporting, and trimming of the trees.

The Captain Mowatt who at John Wentworth's call seized 70,000 feet of illegal lumber is the same man who in 1775 was seized by Thompson and who later burned Falmouth. It appears that already he was much disliked.

Like other laws made by a legislature sitting 3,000 miles away with no constituency among the citizens on whom the weight of penalties fell, the Broad Arrow Policy was an egregious failure. The trees had to go in order that the land be developed. Efforts to enforce the law led merely to increased resentment.

In Chapter VII of *Forests and Sea Power* Albion deals dramatically with the effect of depriving the British navy of new masts.

William Hutchinson Rowe's *Maritime History of Maine* gives a quick and interesting summary of the Broad Arrow Policy.

FOURTEEN

Colonial Shipbuilding and Trading Before the Revolution (1775)

DURING the French and Indian wars there were very few settlements east of Pemaquid except for those of fishermen on Monhegan and Matinicus. However, after the fall of Québec in 1759 and the construction of Fort Pownal at Fort Point on the Penobscot River in the same year, settlers moved in rapidly. In 1761 the population of Maine was about 17,500. In 1764 it was 24,000 and in 1790, 96,000. The following chronology, while far from complete, suggests how quickly the Penobscot Bay region was populated.

- In 1759 Fort Pownal was built.
- From 1760 to 1770 workers from Fort Pownal and families from Rhode Island and Connecticut settled Searsport and Frankfort.
- In 1760 eight families lived at Castine, and a sawmill was built at Carver's Harbor on Vinalhaven Island.
- In 1761, the townships of Bucksport, Orland, Penobscot, Sedgwick, Blue Hill, Surry, Trenton, Sullivan, Mount Desert, Steuben, Harrington, and Addison were legally established. These were townships, not established villages, but their promoters agreed to settle sixty Protestant families in each township, saving a lot in each for a parsonage, for the first settled minister, for a school, and for the use of Harvard College.
- In 1762 more than seven families were living on Deer Isle and about ten families on Mount Desert and adjacent islands.
- In 1763 five families were living at Naskeag, in Brooklin. In the same year, two families, a millwright and a blacksmith, established Machias; by 1775, eighty families and a hundred single men lived there.
- In 1764 Shubael Williams and his five sons were established on Islesboro. Jonathan Buck built the first sawmill on the Penobscot River at Bucksport.
- In 1769 Camden was settled.

• In 1770 settlers came to Belfast. (The town was incorporated in 1772.) A settlement was established at Ducktrap (Lincolnville).

• In 1772 there were twelve families at Bangor, and a group from Cape Cod established Hampden.

• New towns were incorporated at Boothbay, Pemaquid, Walpole, Broad Bay (Thomaston), Georgekeag (Warren), Meduncook (Friendship), Bristol, Cape Elizabeth, Belfast, and Waldoboro by 1773.

Few of the new settlers were fishermen. Most of them were farmers and lumbermen, people who had been driven out of western Maine by severe forest fires that raged as far east as North Yarmouth in 1761 and 1762. As we read in the previous chapter, these new communities survived by sending firewood, sawn lumber, shooks, staves, shingles, clapboards, and hay in sloops and schooners to Portsmouth, Boston, Salem, and other towns to the westward, to be used there or re-shipped to the West Indies. These small vessels were built along the shore wherever a good carpenter could find a level site close to deep water with a supply of timber on the stump. No doubt hundreds of small sloops and schooners were built, sailed, wrecked, rotted, and replaced with no record ever made of their existence. In the cases of those recorded, many of the records were lost or were burned in customhouse fires. However, we have a scattering of evidence that gives a suggestion of the shipbuilding carried on to support the essential coastal trade. Most of the reports come from the western part of the Maine coast, for there was no customhouse east of Falmouth until after the American Revolution.

The Public Records Office in London reports fifty-six vessels built in the Kennebec River region before 1765. They were mostly brigs, schooners, and sloops, with one 180-ton* ship. All were engaged in foreign voyages. William A. Baker in his *Maritime History of Bath* estimates that sixty more foreign-going vessels were built during the ensuing ten years, and he does not even hazard a guess at the number of coastwise traders and fishermen.

• In 1737 a vessel was built at Wiscasset for the lumber trade.

• In 1740 Wyman Bradbury was building boats in Brunswick. In the same year there was a yard at Yarmouth on the Royal River.

• In 1750 Captain Cowing built a sloop at New Meadows.

• In 1752 seven schooners and fifteen sloops totaling 1,367 tons were owned in Falmouth, the largest measuring 80 tons.

• In 1753 sixteen sloops, twelve schooners, and four brigs were owned in the Casco Bay region.

• In 1756-57 forty-nine Maine-built vessels (2,435 tons) entered or cleared New Hampshire ports. Forty-two Maine-built vessels were registered in New Hampshire, six in Boston, and one in Antigua.

• In 1762 Captain William Swanton established a yard at Long Reach

* See the chapter notes for an explanation of tonnage.

(Bath); he built *Earl of Bute* and a vessel a year until the American Revolution.

- In 1764 the Howards had a sawmill on the Kennebec and built two sloops. Christopher Blaisdell built a 25-ton vessel, and at Gardiner there was a double sawmill and a shipyard.
- In 1765 the brig *Betsy* was built for a mast maker.
- In 1766 Abiel Wood was building vessels at Wiscasset.
- In 1770 the 60-ton sloop *Hannah* was built at Bucksport.
- In 1771 the Georgetown assessors reported 588 tons of vessels over 10 tons. A blockmaker, a caulker, and several shipwrights lived in the town.
- In 1772 the sloop *Unity,* of 140 tons, was built for the West Indies trade and also the sloop *Industry,* first to trade from the Kennebec to the West Indies.
- In 1773, 2,020 tons of shipping were owned in Falmouth. In 1774 this figure increased to 2,555.

These vessels were small by modern standards, most of them probably under 50 feet long and measuring less than 30 or 40 tons. There was no need to make them bigger; a small settlement could not load a very big vessel nor could it spare a large crew to sail one. Communities that produced large quantities of sawn lumber either built bigger vessels or shipped their lumber in vessels provided by Boston merchants.

The process of building a typical Maine trading vessel would begin with a "hawk's nest" model. The profile of the vessel was sketched on a board, a stick was tacked to it where the keel was to be, and timbers for stem and stern were put in place. A 'midship frame—that is, a rib—was then set on the model keel perpendicular to the board and to the waterline. Two or three other frames were set forward and aft of the 'midship frame, and then battens made fast to stem and stern were bent around the frames, thus making a model of the finished vessel. If the battens did not lie fairly on the frames, the frames were shaved down or pieced out until they did, for the full-sized frames would be made from the model. Then the shipwright would go into the woods seeking a long, straight tree from which a keel might be got out, either with a pit saw or a sawmill, if one were nearby. He would also look for a curved tree or branch for the stem. The sternpost was often another straight piece.

The ship's keel was laid down on a series of blocks, stern to the shore. Because a vessel, after she is launched, tends to "hog" or sag at the ends, the keel blocks were often higher at bow and stern to build a little rocker into the keel. The keel was let into the blocks about an inch to be sure it did not shift during construction.

Then the stem was scarfed and bolted to the keel. The sternpost, with a counter—a stern projecting aft above the waterline—if she was to have one, was set on the after end of the keel, its lower end with a tenon to fit a mortise in the keel. It was braced in position with a stout knee* cut from a tree where

* A knee is a triangular brace such as might brace a deckbeam against a frame or rib. It is cut from a natural crook in a tree in such a way that the grain runs around the right angle more or less parallel to each side of that angle. See the drawings in Chapter 5.

the root spreads out from the trunk. Next, floor timbers were laid on the keel athwartships. The 'midship frame from the model was marked out full size on a piece with the grain running around the curve of the finished "rib." The frame was set on the keel next to a floor timber and bolted to it where the two pieces overlapped. The other frames taken from the model were cut out full size and set up and battens bent around them. The battens, of course, must lie fairly on the frames. If they did not, the offending frame would be dubbed down, trimmed with an adze to fit. Then intermediate frames would be set on the keel between the original ones and fitted to the battens. A keelson—a heavy timber running fore-and-aft bolted or drifted through floors, frames, and keel to stiffen the vessel—was fitted over the floors on larger vessels.

With the skeleton of the vessel thus established, a rabbet—a groove—was cut in the stem, keel, and stern to take the planking. The two sides of the vessel were planked together. The planks were fastened with treenails, called trunnels—hexagonal or octagonal wooden pegs of oak, ash, or locust cut a little larger than the hole bored through plank and timber. The trunnel was driven through, its ends split, and a wedge driven in each end to spring it out so hard against the plank on the outside and the frame on the inside that it would be watertight. Once the trunnel was well soaked and swelled up, it would never move and would be as strong as a metal screw or a nail. In several places the planks were made doubly thick, especially those at the turn of the bilge. If the frames had to be made in two pieces, the "thick stuff" was planned to cover the joint. These double-thick planks helped to stiffen the vessel longitudinally.

Then the vessel was ceiled inside—that is, she was planked up on the inside of the frames as well as on the outside. This was to provide further stiffening and to keep the cargo dry. In some vessels, salt was packed between

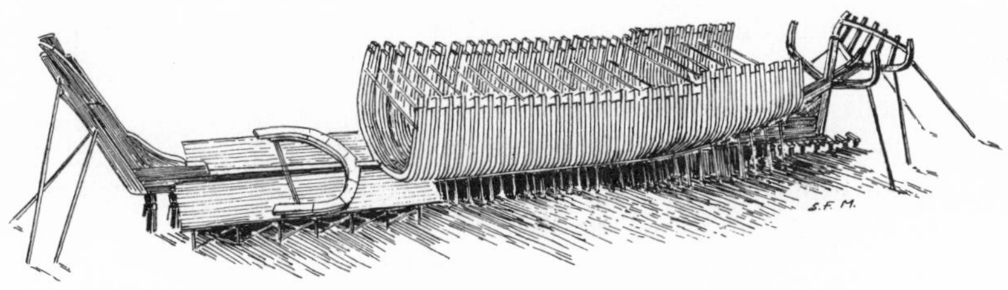

Above: framing. *Below:* planking. *Sam Manning*

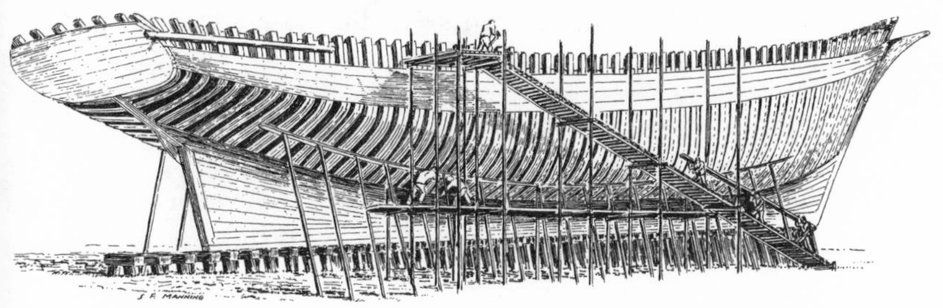

Stepping a mast. *Sam Manning*

the frames to prevent rot, a practice more common in later years. The ceiling had strakes of "thick stuff" in the turn of the bilge and under the place where the deckbeams were to come. They served the purpose of clamp and shelf in modern wooden boats.

Both outside planking and inside ceiling were caulked, the oakum (tarred hemp) driven into the seam with a mallet and iron, then "payed" with pitch. This not only kept the water out but also rammed the planks against each other and stiffened the whole structure.

Deckbeams were then laid athwartships, and on larger vessels fore-and-aft timbers, carlins, were fitted between them. The deck was then laid over the deckbeams. Rails, deckhouses, hatches, bulkheads—whatever was needed for the trade in which the particular vessel was to be used—could be added.

Spars were cut in the woods. What ironwork was needed would be forged on the site.

Standing rigging was tarred hemp, set up with deadeyes and lanyards. Sails of cotton or flax would be sewn under the vessel's shadow, perhaps. Anchors might be imported or forged on the site.

Laid under the new vessel's bilges, leading down as far below low-water mark as necessary to get water deep enough to float the vessel at high water, were the launching ways—heavily greased timbers, with sliding ways laid over the grease and kept from sliding by battens at the top. A cradle was built on these timbers snugly up against the vessel's bilge. Wedges were driven in between the cradle and the sliding timbers to raise the cradle against the bilge and take much of the vessel's weight. Then the keel blocks on which the keel had been laid months before were knocked out so the vessel's weight was on the cradle. At high water on the appointed day, in the presence of every man, woman, boy, and dog in town, the battens holding the sliding timbers were cut and the little vessel slid neatly into the water and fetched up on her anchor, surrounded by broken bits of the cradle and leaving a thin cloud of smoking grease behind her.

At this early date, the mid-eighteenth century, a small vessel would probably be launched without her spars. She would be brought alongside a wharf to be rigged, fitted out, and loaded and be off to Boston with two men and a boy and a mixed cargo of salt fish, sawn lumber, and clapboards, with perhaps a deck load of hay. She might be back a month later with the flour, pork, beef, nails, boots, axes, adzes, bar iron, molasses, rum, and yard goods that the community needed to survive.

As the community grew in population and produced more and more goods to sell, bigger vessels were built. Instead of trading with Boston, a few began to make foreign voyages to the West Indies, the wine islands, the Mediterranean countries, and England.

For longer ocean voyages, not only were the vessels bigger but their rigs were modified. For coastal voyages, considerable windward work was necessary, particularly when bound up to Boston, against the prevailing westerly winds. Coming home to Maine, the vessel would run before the wind, sailing "down east." For windward work, the fore-and-aft rig was a good choice. On a voyage to the West Indies, however, little time was spent going to windward. The skipper would head east or southeast before the prevailing westerly winds until well east of the Gulf Stream, then haul up and go south until he hit the easterlies of the trade winds, which would carry him down the islands to Barbados. There he would be far to windward of any other island he might have to visit. This meant that for most of the voyage he would have a fair wind; at least, he would seldom have to beat. On the return voyage he would get into the Gulf Stream and sail north before the prevailing southwesterly. For a fair-wind ocean voyage, the square rig was favored. The yards were trimmed square to the wind, and, with the same amount of sail on both sides of the mast, the boat ran easily. A fore-and-aft-rigged vessel will yaw as the sail, all on one side, pulls the stern around. She requires a firm and steady hand on the helm. If she yaws too far to leeward, the wind gets on the forward side of the sail and slams it across the boat, fetching up with a frightful jerk on the main sheet and possibly breaking the boom or gaff. So, the sloops and schooners in overseas trade carried square topsails and sometimes topgallants on their foremasts, and frequently a square foresail as well as a fore-and-aft foresail.

It is only a short step from this rig to the brig, a favorite of West Indies traders. This vessel was two-masted and square-rigged on both masts. She was a fast and comfortable vessel with the wind anywhere from abeam to dead aft.

To make the brig more efficient to windward, a small, gaff-headed fore-and-aft sail, called a spanker, was carried on the mainmast below the main yard. A much larger and more efficient spanker could be carried by a variation of the brig called a snow. This was the same as a brig, except that the larger spanker was bent to an auxiliary mast stepped on deck only about a foot aft of the mainmast and secured at the top between the trestletrees, the two fore-and-aft timbers near the top of the lower mast that support the crosstrees. This arrangement allowed the throat of the spanker to be hoisted above the main yard. Also popular was what was later called the brigantine, with squaresails

West Indian trading brig. *Consuelo E. Hanks*

on the foremast and a fore-and-aft mainsail on the mainmast. However, the term was used indiscriminately in the mid-eighteenth century to refer to brigs, brigantines, and topsail schooners.

Trade with the West Indies was not a simple matter of loading a brig or topsail schooner with salt cod, staves, and shooks and setting sail to the south'ard.

The British Parliament, operating on the basic theory that colonies existed primarily for the benefit of the mother country, enacted a series of Navigation Acts beginning in 1661. The laws that most affected the colonial merchant forbade direct importation of any goods originating in other European nations to a British colony without the shipper first paying a customs duty in England and the goods then being trans-shipped. Thus, a merchant could not import Spanish wine to Falmouth, Maine, without first unloading the casks on an English wharf, paying customs, then loading again for Falmouth—obviously an expensive business. Another law forbade the export of "enumerated items" from the Colonies to any country other than Great Britain. These items included tobacco, rice, indigo, sugar, naval stores, i.e., pitch, tar, turpentine, masts and spars. At first there was little serious objection to these laws because they permitted the export of Maine products, fish and lumber, to any West Indian or Atlantic island and the importation of wine, rum, molasses, sugar, and other products of the islands to Maine. The laws also permitted the exchange of West Indian products for the corn, flour, pork, and beef of the Middle American coastal colonies. As Maine had a surplus of fish and lumber and a need for food while Jamaica, for instance, had a surplus of rum, molasses, and sugar and a need for food such as salt cod and for casks and building materials, and as the Middle colonies had a surplus of food and a need for West Indian products and building materials, a profitable trade was possible. Importations of manufactured goods such as cloth, cutlery, and ironware from England could be paid for with molasses, sugar, indigo, masts, and bills of exchange or specie, hard money.

However, in 1733, at the behest of British sugar growers and distillers, the Molasses Act was passed, forbidding the importation of molasses from French and Dutch islands. By this time the demand for molasses in New England was prodigious. Not only were there many rum distilleries producing an inferior but inexpensive product in large quantities, but molasses rather than sugar was the sweetener used in most New England households. This act, could it have been enforced, would have seriously damaged the Maine economy. New England in general and Maine principally and in particular, produced far more fish and forest products than the British islands could absorb. Therefore the fishermen would be unable to sell their refuse fish, and this would so reduce the market as to make it unprofitable to go fishing for the high grade of fish only, the grade acceptable in Europe and England. Furthermore, rum, another export available in quantity, was not popular in France because of a subsidized brandy industry. The French, in an effort to stimulate sales of French flour and other foods, forbade the importation of these products from other countries to French islands. Consequently, the Maine trader had to become a smuggler on both ends of his voyage.

There were ways in which this was accomplished. French merchants sold licenses to trade at French islands if properly approached, and customs agents were not always incorruptible. A ship loaded with fish, lumber, flour, horses, etc., might prove a great temptation to a French merchant. Another alternative was to anchor in the roadstead at St. Eustatius, about halfway between Puerto Rico and Guadeloupe. This was a sort of free-trade zone, not by law but by general agreement. Here a Maine skipper might strike a bargain with a French skipper to trade all or part of his cargo for French rum, molasses, brandy, lace, wine, or whatever product was available. Then, of course, to be admitted at Falmouth he had to have a clearance from a British West Indian port. One method was to call at the little British island of Anguilla where the governor was also the customs officer. He obligingly cleared vessels for New England, exporting from an island only 34 square miles in area enough molasses to have floated the entire island. Corrupt customs officers on both ends of the trade made smuggling profitable, so the fisheries and the carrying trade actually flourished.

In 1763 the Sugar Act reduced the tariff on molasses but increased pressure on enforcement. The customs officers were still pliable, but the British navy was also charged with enforcing the customs laws. Often the naval officers did not really understand the laws they were to enforce and seized vessels almost indiscriminately. Add to this peril the French navy, which seized vessels trading illegally with French islands. Nevertheless, in 1763 Massachusetts imported 15,000 hogsheads of molasses, only 500 of which came from British islands.

Beyond all these complications were the problems of selling a cargo and being paid for it. Most of the business was in the hands of "factors," agents who bought cargoes and sold them to planters on commission. The factors also bought local products and sold them to shipmasters. Should there come a bad crop year or a hurricane, a cash-flow problem would quickly arise whereby the factor would agree to pay for a cargo of fish and lumber—later. The fish did not keep well in the tropics and had to be sold at once. The lumber was badly needed to rebuild after the hurricane. The ship owner could either sell and wait for his money, perhaps for a long time, or let the fish rot while he waited for a cash customer for the lumber.

A Rhode Island shipmaster wrote of the factors, ". . . most of them will bear dunning for years together without any marks of shame, and perhaps promise ten times a day, if you can meet them so often, that they will pay in an hour. It is a very good place to sell a cargo, but if a stranger don't take care, it will be to persons who never expect to pay him."

Ezekiel Edwards of Philadelphia wrote concerning Barbados, "I bleve thair is more honner and honesty in so many highwaymen in England then in the marchants of this place."

This situation militated against the independent ship owner, for the Boston merchant owning a number of ships and doing business with several factors, sometimes through a resident partner of the Boston firm, could exert a deal more leverage on the factor than could the independent trader.

On top of all these difficulties was the volatile demand for fish. A large shipload of salt codfish could entirely glut the market of a small island, especially if another vessel with the same cargo had recently visited. Therefore, it was important to sail with a mixed cargo including perhaps horses from Connecticut, flour from New York, and rice from Charleston.

The case of "Lord" Timothy Dexter of Newburyport will serve as an illustration of the unpredictable nature of the trade. He sent in one of his ships a large consignment of brass warming pans—shallow, covered brass pans with a long handle which a New Englander filled with hot coals to warm his bed on a cold night. Ridiculous as such a cargo seemed, Lord Timothy did very well, for the warming pans commanded a high price as dippers to dip molasses from vats into barrels. On another voyage he carried a shipment of fur mittens. These his skipper traded with the master of a Russian vessel for hemp, canvas, and ironwork.

Add to the legal problems and the economic problems the hazards of the French and British navies, pirates, and the normal hazards of a long voyage through waters occasionally agitated by hurricanes and Atlantic gales, and it is not to be wondered at that most Maine fishermen and lumbermen shipped their products to Portsmouth, Salem, and Boston to be exchanged there with merchants who imported products from England, the Southern colonies, and the West Indies.

The resentment of American colonists toward British rule grew from 1759 to 1775, as the Tory party in control of British Parliament sought to shift the cost of the defense of the Colonies during the previous half-century of wars from the shoulders of the landholders to those of the merchants and colonists, in whose interests the Tories claimed these expenses had been incurred. The colonists regarded this as unfair because they felt that they had done most of the fighting and won the wars in spite of British ineptitude—and largely at their own expense.

One of the first devices used by the British was more effective enforcement of the Navigation Acts and the Molasses Act of 1733, by granting to customs officers writs of assistance in 1760. This gave a customs officer authority to inspect any ship or building at any time on mere suspicion, without a warrant. Not only were the writs of assistance a violation of the Magna Carta and the rights of British citizens, it looked as if they might be effective. James Otis of Boston argued against them in a Boston court in 1761, and some years later a successful plea canceled the writs. Nevertheless, the image of Parliament as an illegal instrument of tyranny was early established.

The Revenue Act of 1764 included the Sugar Act, which lowered the duty on molasses from foreign countries but raised duties on foreign sugar and on wine, silk, and linen. It also added to the list of enumerated items that could be sent only to England and put a heavy tax on the importation of Madeira wine, a favorite beverage of the wealthy.

Maine and Massachusetts were adept at avoiding much of the pain of the new taxes in spite of the writs of assistance, but the Stamp Tax passed in March 1765 created a storm that quickly spread to Maine towns. Unlike customs duties, this was the first direct tax on the citizens of the colonies. It required that almost everything of paper be stamped by a royal stamp officer. This included marriage licenses, deeds, college degrees, customs clearances, bills of sale, even every copy of every newspaper. The fees were collected in hard money, and the citizens had the humiliating duty of appearing before the stamp officer on every occasion. Riots broke out in every seaport city. Falmouth did its share with a notable riot in which stamped paper and stamped clearances were taken from the customhouse and publicly burned. The tax was never effectively enforced and was repealed in March 1766. However, it had given the separate colonies common cause against Britain, and had gathered in one room at the Stamp Act Congress for the first time some of the men who met eleven years later to sign the Declaration of Independence.

Maine's heavy dependence on Boston as a market and source of supply had stimulated a vigorous coastal trade that kept Maine in touch with wider developments. The Declaratory Act of 1766 by which Parliament asserted its right to "bind the colonies in all cases whatsoever" passed more or less unnoticed in Maine, but not the Townsend Acts of 1767 imposing taxes on the importation of glass, lead, paper, paint, and tea and granting cash bounties on the importation into Britain of colonial hemp, flax, and timber. The effect of these acts on Maine was indirect. The bounty on timber applied to oak staves only, for which there was little market in England, and the increased taxes hurt considerably, for they checked overseas trade not only in the enumerated items but in colonial products traded for them. A more serious effect was the increased resentment fanned by the merchants and the Sons of Liberty, first organized at the time of the Stamp Tax. They had something to resent, for besides the new taxes, Parliament set up in Boston an American Board of Commissioners of Customs to abolish corrupt absentee and deputy officers and to appoint new and more energetic officers. Customs cases were to be tried in Admiralty courts without a jury rather than in provincial courts, which had been generous to offenders. The increased customs receipts as a result of the crackdown were to be spent partly to pay the salaries of customs officers and judges and thus to remove them from dependence on provincial legislatures.

Response in Boston, led by Sam Adams, was violent. The Sons of Liberty adopted non-importation agreements to boycott British goods, and finally drove Governor Bernard to resign. The Maine town of Falmouth responded enthusiastically and sent a formal letter of thanks to Boston for "their seasonable and very laudable attention to and concern for the happiness and welfare of this province as well as of the whole continent." Although taxes on glass, lead, paper, and paint were repealed in 1770, the tax on tea remained and the enforcement of customs laws combined with non-importation agreements to diminish seriously the volume of trade in Maine staples. This led to hardship in coastal towns, the blame for which was piled on the back of Parliament.

In 1771 Arthur Savage, the customs officer in Falmouth, ordered the captain of his revenue cutter to seize one of Edward Tyng's schooners. Savage was roughly treated by an angry mob, and the schooner was released.

More violent action followed. John Wentworth, the Tory mast agent, seized illegal lumber in Brunswick and in 1772 called upon Captain Henry Mowatt in HMS *Canso* to seize 70,000 feet of illegal deals (lumber) in Falmouth. Riots, jail deliveries, rescue of seized goods, and violent demonstrations by the Sons of Liberty broke out on small provocation.

In December 1773 the Boston Tea Party expressed colonial resentment at the importation of British tea at a price below that at which it could be smuggled from Holland. Parliament replied by closing the port of Boston, appointing General Gage as governor with power to appoint or dismiss all provincial officers and to convene or dissolve the General Court. This action struck hard at the economy and the freedom of every town in coastal Maine.

The town meeting in Falmouth declared that citizens could not be taxed without their consent and resolved to use no tea, to support Boston, and to maintain a Committee of Correspondence.

Militia companies were organized, armed, and drilled. The First Continental Congress gathered in Philadelphia in September 1774 and recommended non-importation on a national scale, a recommendation which seriously affected coastal Maine commerce and left many communities suffering for lack of food. However, the slide toward war was gathering momentum, and economic hardship could not stop it.

Sheriff William Tyng of Falmouth (not Edward Tyng, hero of Louisbourg) swore before the Cumberland County Convention that he would enforce the laws of the Convention, not those of Parliament. The presence of 500 armed men must have been convincing motivation. Representatives were sent to a Provincial Congress in Concord, Massachusetts, and British government was effectively broken down in Maine.

In the winter of 1774–75, Falmouth, Cape Elizabeth, York, Kittery, Wells, Biddeford, Scarborough, North Yarmouth, Berwick, and Gorhamtown sent firewood, food, and cash for the support of Boston.

In February 1775 Parliament enacted the strictest Navigation Act in their history to punish New England by stifling its trade. It prohibited American fishermen from fishing on the Grand Banks and other offshore banks and the export of all goods from Massachusetts, Rhode Island, and Connecticut to any ports but those in Great Britain and the British West Indies. It was too strict even to be effectively enforced and amounted to a declaration of war.

As spring came, events gathered like a cresting wave for the outbreak of open rebellion. In Falmouth, Captain Coulson had built and launched a big new mast ship of 1,000 tons, *Minerva,* and in defiance of the non-importation agreement had brought from England in another of his ships the necessary rigging, sails, and stores to fit her out. When the vessel carrying these arrived in Falmouth, the Committee of Inspection summoned Coulson and the captain of the English ship to list the cargo. The Committee ordered the captain to return to England without unloading. Coulson claimed that the ship needed repair and must unload so that workmen could get at the leak. The Committee refused, and the situation reached a stalemate. Captain Coulson then went to Boston and returned with Captain Henry Mowatt in HMS *Canso.* Under her protection, the cargo was transferred to *Minerva* and she was rigged and fitted for sea.

At this point came news of Concord and Lexington.

NOTES

Background material for this chapter comes again from William D. Williamson's *History of Maine,* with help from Raymond McFarland's *History of the New England Fisheries.* William A. Baker's *Maritime History of Bath* is an excellent source for the technique of shipbuilding and for information on ships built on the Kennebec. Wasson and Colcord's *Sailing Days on the Penobscot* gives dates of early Penobscot Bay settlements. Robert G. Albion's *Forests and Sea Power* was of peripheral help in this chapter. Information on the Caribbean trade came principally from *Yankees and Creoles* by William Pares. Samuel Eliot Morison's one-volume *History of the American People,* Louis Hatch's *Maine,* and Albion's *New England and the Sea* were also consulted. William Hutchinson Rowe's *Maritime History of Maine* provided a few nuggets not found in other sources. A detailed account of Captain Coulson's effort to fit out *Minerva* is found in "A Lost Manuscript," a paper read by James P. Baxter before the Maine Historical Society, December 18, 1890, published in MHS proceedings, Series 2, Volume 2, page 345. Barbara Tuchman's *The First Salute* gives much of pre-Revolutionary background.

The illustrations should make clear the different rigs of vessels mentioned, but it is more difficult to describe their sizes. The tonnages of vessels are given in their registry documentation, but the tonnage, while an accurate statement of the capacity of a vessel, gives little idea of how big she looks. Tonnage has little to do with weight or displacement. A vessel's tonnage was originally a statement of how many tuns of wine she could carry, a tun being a big barrel. For convenience, it was first figured from the formula:

$$\frac{\text{Length of keel} \times \text{Width} \times \text{Depth}}{100}$$

Later this was modified by substituting 94 for 100 as the divisor. Then it was found difficult to take these measurements with the vessel afloat after the ceiling was in. Consequently, the length of keel was assumed to be the length from the forward side of the stem to the after side of the sternpost less three-fifths of the beam. The beam is the extreme width to the outside to the planking. Depth was figured at one-half the beam for two-decked vessels and was measured from the underside of the deck to the top of the sheathing in the hold in single-decked vessels. The formula can be stated:

$$\frac{(\text{Length} - \tfrac{3}{5}\text{ Beam}) \times \text{Beam} \times \tfrac{1}{2}\text{ Beam}}{94} = \text{Tonnage}$$

Thus, a wide vessel of the same length as a narrow vessel will have a much greater tonnage. A few examples may help to give some idea of the relationships between length and tonnage.

- A 3-ton shallop was 26 feet length overall with a beam of 6 feet 4 inches.
- A 12-ton shallop was 42 feet overall with a beam of 10 feet 0 inches.
- A 37-ton schooner was 58 feet overall with a beam of 12 feet 1 inch.
- A 78-ton schooner was 57 feet overall with a beam of 17 feet 2 inches.
- The schooner *Halifax,* possibly the schooner wrecked off Machias in 1775 from which Midshipman Moore was to save the guns, was 83 tons, 60 feet overall, with a beam of 18 feet 3 inches.
- The sloop *Lady Washington,* which rounded Cape Horn and explored the West Coast of North America, was 90 tons and 60 feet overall.
- John Paul Jones's first command, the sloop *Providence,* was 85 tons, 63 feet overall, with a beam of 19 feet 6 inches.
- *Defense,* a sixteen-gun ship, was 145 tons, 87 feet overall, with a beam of 25 feet.
- *Cabot,* 189 tons, big for a West Indian trader, was 79 feet overall with a beam of 24 feet 8 inches.
- *Alfred,* a twenty-gun ship of 275 tons, was 101 feet overall with a beam of 26 feet. She was the first flagship in the Continental Navy under John Paul Jones in 1776.
- *Ranger,* the ship in which Jones raided Scotland and Ireland, was 304 tons, 104 feet overall with a beam of 29 feet.
- The frigate *Boston,* twenty-six guns, was 574 tons, 128 feet overall, with a beam of 32 feet.
- The frigate *Raleigh,* thirty-two guns, was 697 tons, 140 feet overall, with a beam of 34 feet 5 inches. She was built at Kittery and captured off Matinicus.
- The frigate *Hancock* was 762 tons, 149 feet overall, with beam of 35 feet 2 inches. She was captured in 1777 by HMS *Rainbow.*
- Jones's famous *Bonhomme Richard* was 1,050 tons, 162 feet overall, with a beam of 40 feet. She was built as an East Indiaman.
- *America* was a seventy-four-gun ship of the line, 1,982 tons, 196 feet overall, with a beam of 49 feet. She was given as a present to France after the American Revolution.

Most of these figures come from Millar's *American Ships of the Colonial and Revolutionary Periods.*

A discussion of tonnage measurement is found in *The American Neptune,* Volume 5, 1945, page 226.

FIFTEEN

The Battle of Machias and the Burning of Falmouth

A PARTY of British marines marched to Concord, Massachusetts, on April 19, 1775, to seize guns and ammunition cached there, fired on the minutemen in Lexington, were driven from Concord Bridge, and were harried all the way back to Boston. A combination of unwillingness to buy trouble, traditional loyalty to Britain, and fear of the British army and navy, had held down the safety valve of fierce resentment against increasing excesses of British tyranny. With the British armies on the run, however, the resentment exploded and flashed up and down the Yankee coastline. The shots fired at Concord Bridge were heard, if not around the world, at least as far east as Maine. A company of volunteers marched at once from York, followed on April 21 by companies from Biddeford and Falmouth. Falmouth, among other Maine towns, enlisted companies of minutemen, ready to defend their land against the redcoats. The war was on, although many of the more conservative and influential colonists did not realize it and the British military did not have the least idea what war with Americans meant.

In Falmouth, Captain Coulson of Falmouth had rigged the mast ship *Minerva* under the protection of Captain Mowatt. Mowatt returned to Falmouth in early May to find the town seething, divided between those ready to fight, the conservative patriotic citizens opposed to hasty, dangerous, and expensive action, and a few confirmed Tories who stood loyally for the King. Thus far, no actual hostile action had occurred.

On May 9, Lieutenant Colonel Samuel Thompson, an impetuous patriot, commander of the Brunswick militia, mustered a company of about fifty Sons of Liberty to march on Falmouth and seize *Minerva* and HMS *Canso*. Wearing sprigs of spruce in their caps and carrying for an ensign a young spruce tree stripped of branches but for a tuft at the top, they marched to Falmouth and hid on the north slope of Munjoy Hill. They seized every passer-by in order to keep their ambush a secret. Late in the afternoon Captain Mowatt, his surgeon, and Reverend Wiswell, the Episcopal minister, fell into their hands.

When the sailing master of *Canso,* Lieutenant Hogg, heard of his captain's capture, he sent ashore a message that if Mowatt were not back aboard in two hours, he would burn the town.

This polarized the situation at once. Thompson refused to free his prisoners, and Edward Phinney, colonel of the minutemen, called out his troops in support. Meanwhile the solid citizens of Falmouth, Whig and Tory alike, did two things simultaneously. Some argued and pleaded with Thompson, urging moderation and negotiation; others flew into a panic, sent women and children out of town, commandeered carts and wagons, and began to move their valuables out of reach of Hogg. The minutemen—an undisciplined crowd inflamed with rum and a spirit of righteous and patriotic indignation, and having nothing to lose—marched, drank, ran, and rioted.

Finally, Thompson agreed to free Mowatt and the surgeon on parole if they would appear ashore at 9:00 in the morning. General Preble and Colonel Freeman guaranteed their appearance.

The minutemen and Thompson's company, amounting now to about 600 men, raided houses of suspected Tories, exacted tribute in food and rum, gutted Coulson's house, dragged one of *Minerva*'s boats through town and over into Back Cove, seized Sheriff William Tyng's official hat and a silver dish worth £500, made Preble, Freeman, Tyng, and others crawl publicly, and, in short, made a night of it.

In the morning, Captain Mowatt, having been told of the night's rioting and that if he went ashore, he would be "cut to pieces," broke his parole and stayed aboard *Canso.* He released the hostages taken by Lieutenant Hogg and did not fire on the town, knowing that his captors and the rioters were not the owners of the houses he might destroy but were Sons of Liberty and minutemen from out of town, entirely unauthorized even by the Whig element in town. Neither Mowatt nor the citizens of Falmouth were thinking of the disorders as part of the Revolutionary War and considered themselves all good citizens seeking to reestablish law and order. Thompson and the Sons of Liberty were at war.

After two days, the out-of-town element departed, things settled down, and the town meeting voted to disavow all responsibility for the affair. Mowatt in *Canso,* convoying *Minerva,* sailed for Portsmouth, leaving Falmouth citizens believing that the regrettable incident was behind them. However, the matter of the masts that Coulson was to take to England in *Minerva* was not yet settled.

On June 12, Lieutenant Duddington in *Senegal* (16), with two smaller vessels, convoyed *Minerva* back to Portland to pick up the masts. The Committee of Safety had the masts towed up the Fore River and hidden. This was part of the policy of boycotting English trade previously agreed upon in both the Provincial and Continental Congresses. There was nothing riotous or disorderly about it—just determined. Sheriff Tyng, who had been roughed up and robbed of his hat and silver plate the month before, went aboard *Minerva* and asked that his wife and Coulson's be allowed to join them for their safety. The Committee refused. Duddington parleyed with the Committee, saying he came to protect loyal subjects, not to distress them. The Committee released five of Coulson's men and one of his boats, which they had recently seized, and released the two ladies on Duddington's promise that *Senegal* and *Minerva* would depart without the masts, which they did.

Admiral Graves in Boston was furious at Coulson's being denied the masts. He summoned before him Philip Crandell of Harpswell, who happened to be in Salem, and told him that if the citizens of Falmouth did not give Coulson his masts, he, Graves, would "beat the town down about their ears."

At the same time, down east in Machias, another defeat was about to confront Admiral Graves. Graves had been harried and harassed ever since he had taken command of the North American station in April 1774. He had arrived in Boston on June 30, 1774, and had known scarcely a moment's peace. He was ordered to enforce the Boston Port Act, cutting off all commerce with the city. He had under his command his flagship *Preston* (50), four sloops of war, three schooners, and HMS *Canso,* a converted merchantman hitherto used as a surveying ship. *Preston* was far too big, slow, and deep to be

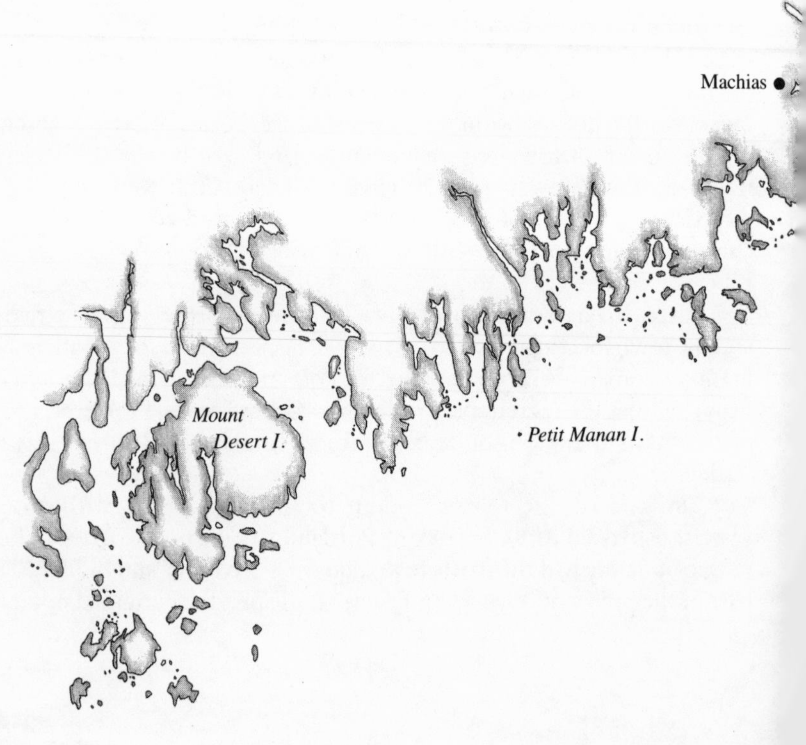

of any use whatever. There were no ships of the line for her to fight, and she could not catch a smart Yankee brig on any point of sailing. The sloops of war, ship rigged with guns on only one deck and armed with 6-pounders, were little better. The schooners were faster, more weatherly, and of shoaler draft and were useful in patrolling the entrances to the harbor, but were little threat to Yankee sloops, whaleboats, and other small craft of shoal draft which could thread the intricate channels among the islands at night. Forty-four cannon

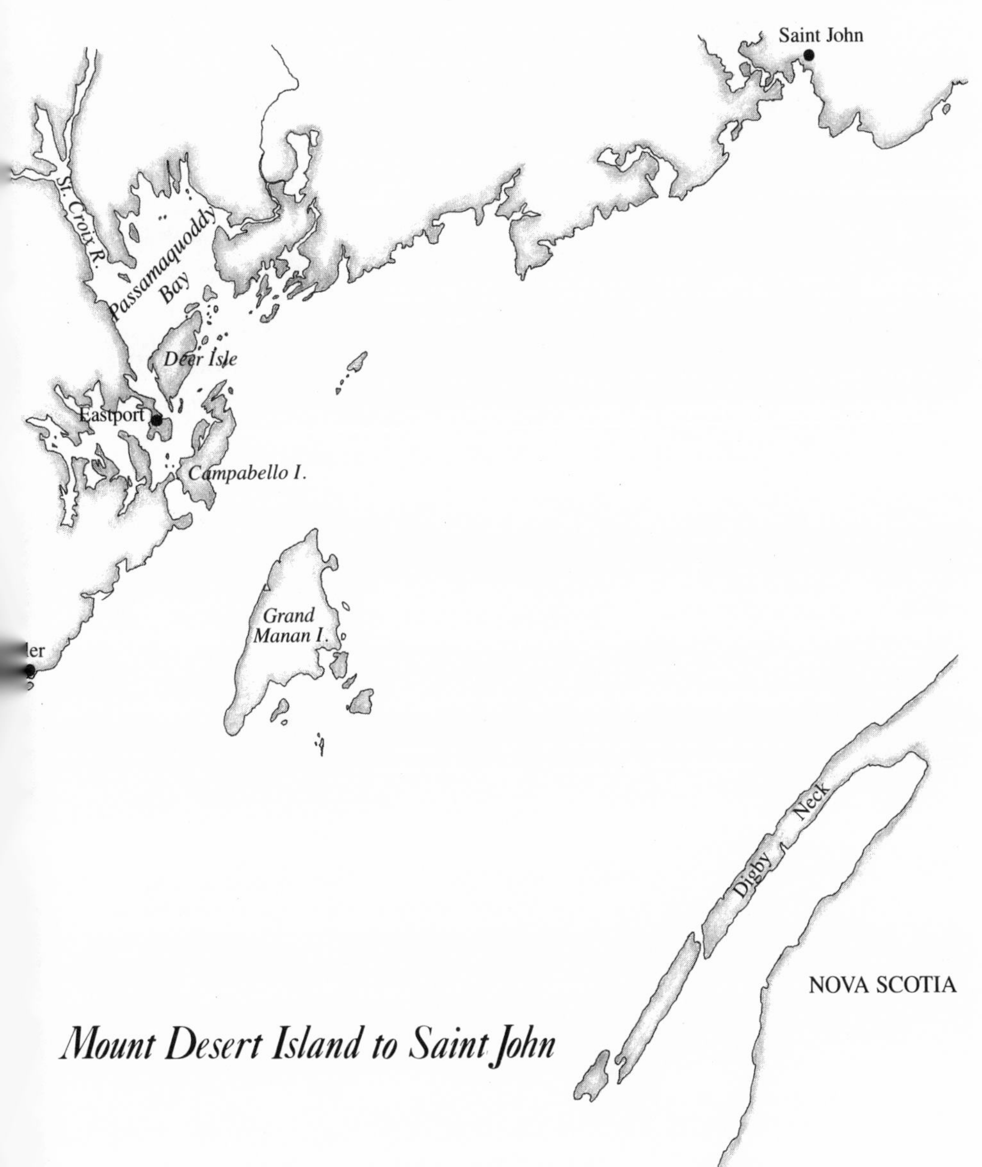

were stolen from the the British arsenal at Newport, and Rhode Island was in open rebellion. Sixteen cannon, powder, and small arms were stolen from Castle William in Portsmouth. The Committee of Inspection in Salem impounded the Admiral's supply of candles.

Although Graves reported the schooner *Halifax* (6) to be leaky and almost useless, he sent her to patrol the Maine coast. Lieutenant Nunn in command was ordered to make random and unscheduled cruises in the hopes of intercepting smugglers bringing in supplies and ammunition for the rebels.

At 3:00 A.M. on February 15, 1775, Lieutenant Nunn sailed from Cranberry Island, Mount Desert, for Machias under the guidance of a local pilot. About noon, with the wind west-southwest, a fresh gale, the vessel was tearing across Englishman Bay south of Roque Island at 7½ knots. The pilot at the helm ordered the squaresail on the foremast taken in and cable ranged on deck, declaring they would anchor in half an hour. Lieutenant Nunn asked the pilot whether they were passing too close to a nearby island, but was assured there was plenty of water. Just then, *Halifax* struck. In the words of her master, "She went over the first rock, came round with her broadside to the wind, fell into a pit among the rocks, and there she lay."

Nunn tried to get her off with the headsails, but she was stove in. He got his crew and some supplies ashore before she broke up that night. In the morning only her masts floated above the wreck.

Nunn sent the master with the pilot and a boat's crew for help. After drifting, bailing, and rowing most of the day, they arrived half frozen in Bucks Harbor, where they hired a schooner to rescue the rest of the crew and bring them to Boston. The pilot escaped despite Nunn's orders to the master to prevent him.

The island off which *Halifax* was lost was called, by Nunn, Sheep Island. There is now no Sheep Island anywhere near Bucks Harbor, but what is now Halifax Island was formerly Sheep Island and was probably renamed for the wreck. One may speculate on whether the local pilot was ignorant or patriotic. He might have mistaken the high, barren Brothers for high, barren Libby Island, but that seems unlikely. His preparations for anchoring suggest that he thought he was nearer Bucks Harbor than he was, and his confusion in piloting the boat to Bucks Harbor the next day suggests ignorance. In either case, he did well to vanish as soon as he got ashore.

Thus Graves lost one schooner and her guns. Then *Asia* (64) and *Boyne* (70), too big and slow to be useful, arrived from England with Pitcairn's marines, for whom Graves must find food and quarters. Another of Graves's schooners was badly damaged by running on the ledges off Cohasset. Graves was trying to kill hornets with a baseball bat. After the defeat at Concord on April 19, 1775, and the subsequent inglorious flight of the soldiers, Graves for one realized that a war was on. He advised Gage to burn Charlestown and to fortify Bunker Hill to prevent the Americans from setting up a battery there that could command his ships and the city of Boston. Gage, more conciliatory, refused.

Meanwhile, Graves had a supply problem. The city of Boston, besieged by the American Continental Army, was painfully short of firewood and in need of lumber to build barracks for the British soldiers already in the city and for those which the Ministry was sending to reinforce Gage.

Graves thought he had found a favorable opportunity when General Gage recommended to him Ichabod Jones of Machias as one who had already performed loyal service to the King and who could supply cargoes of lumber and firewood from Machias in return for permission to carry supplies to that town. Graves willingly gave Jones permission to leave Boston with supplies for Machias and a letter saying that anyone bringing supplies to Boston, then under siege, would have free passage in and out of the port. To be sure that Jones would return with lumber for British barracks, Graves sent to convoy Jones the armed schooner *Margueritta* commanded by midshipman James Moore. Moore's orders also required him to bring back the four 4-pounders that Machias citizens had salvaged from the wreck of *Halifax,* guaranteeing payment to the salvors.

Midshipman Moore was twenty-five years old, the son of an English minister, and had six years' service in the British navy as able seaman and midshipman. He had passed his examination for lieutenant, and his commission waited only on an opening for a lieutenant's position. Because *Margueritta* carried only swivels, not carriage guns, her command was not one for a commissioned officer. Admiral Graves regarded Moore as one of the best midshipmen in *Preston,* his flagship. Second in command of *Margueritta* was Midshipman Stillingfleet.

The merchantmen *Unity* and *Polly* were loaded with barrels of pork and flour for the people of Machias, who were so occupied in cutting, sawing, and shipping lumber that they had little time or energy to grow their own food. The sloops with Captain Jones, convoyed by Moore in *Margueritta,* sailed from Boston in late May and arrived in Machias on June 2.

The news of Concord and Lexington had reached Machias a month before. The Sons of Liberty had at once formed a company of minutemen under a nephew of Ichabod Jones, Judge Jones, known as a firm if conservative patriot. His lieutenant and the practical leader of the company was Benjamin Foster, the only member with any real military experience. He had been at Louisbourg in 1745 and with Abercrombie in the Old French War (1756–1763). Leading members of the company were the volatile O'Brien brothers, John and Jeremiah, of whom Jeremiah had perhaps the lowest flash point.

As Captain Jones rather expected, when he landed at Machias to buy lumber for British barracks, he met considerable resistance. He refused to sell provisions unless he was given permission to load lumber. A town meeting was called, and after much debate it was voted by a narrow margin to sell Jones the lumber. However, Jones, in selling pork and flour, would advance no credit to those who had voted against him at town meeting. This excited a good deal of resentment against the Tory Jones among the patriots.

Moore, for his part, behaved in a polite and reserved manner by which he managed to acquire the guns from *Halifax* and stow them in *Margueritta*'s hold. On Sunday, June 11, while most of the community was in church, Lieutenant Foster held a meeting of the Sons of Liberty in the woods nearby and decided to seize Jones, Moore, and Stillingfleet in church, capture *Margueritta,* and confiscate *Polly* and *Unity.*

Tradition says that to end debate among the Sons on the question of challenging the British navy and finding themselves without provisions in the event of failure, Foster stepped across a small brook, inviting friends of liberty to follow and advising British supporters to stay where they were. Led by the O'Brien brothers, all followed.

As they approached the meetinghouse armed with only a few muskets and with pitchforks and narrow axes, Moore, Jones, and Stillingfleet saw them coming, leaped out a window, and ran for it, Jones to the woods whence he emerged ignominiously two days later, Moore and Stillingfleet to *Margueritta*'s boat, which was sent ashore for them. At this time *Unity* was lying at a wharf below the falls at Machias, *Margueritta* was a quarter-mile down the river, and *Polly* was below her, presumably not yet unloaded, near where the East River joins the Machias River. The Sons seized *Unity,* took out what remained of her cargo, and took ashore her sails. Another group assembled on the shore opposite *Margueritta* and demanded her surrender, which Moore stoutly refused. Further, Moore ordered the Sons to restore *Unity* and to cease and desist from their rebellion or he would fire on the town and beat it down. Inasmuch as *Margueritta*'s armament was six or eight swivel guns, scarcely more than big muskets, each mounted on what looks like a big oarlock on the rail and firing a 1-pound ball, smaller than a ping-pong ball, his threat was not taken seriously. On the contrary, a party of the Sons in three boats seized *Polly* and started to bring her up the river to the town, but, perhaps because the tide turned, they grounded her below *Margueritta.* Then Moore weighed anchor, dropped down the river with the ebb tide, and anchored close to *Polly,* intending to retake her. However, the tide ebbed, *Polly* was hard aground, and the people on the shore again demanded Moore's surrender. Of course, he refused and a brief and sporadic night engagement ensued, Moore's crew firing swivels and muskets at a dark shore and the Sons, with very little powder, firing at the dim outline of *Margueritta.* After an hour or more, Moore, seeing little hope of getting *Polly* off or persuading the aroused Sons to desist, cut his cable, dropped farther down the river, and lay alongside a sloop owned by one Captain Toby.

In the morning, Moore took aboard Toby for a pilot and with a fair wind and ebb tide ran down the river to get to sea. However, probably near the narrows at Machiasport or just below it, *Margueritta* jibed and carried away a boom and gaff. Moore anchored and, seeing a sloop at anchor waiting for the flood tide, brought *Margueritta* alongside and took the sloop's boom and gaff, some supplies, and one Captain Avery.

Meanwhile, the Sons, having discovered that *Margueritta* was underway, determined to pursue her. Jeremiah O'Brien and a group of about thirty Sons rerigged *Unity* and started down the river. Benjamin Foster and another party seized the schooner *Falmouth Packet* at East Machias and joined *Unity* at the confluence of the rivers. *Unity* was the faster vessel and soon drew ahead of *Falmouth Packet*. Moore, having rerigged *Margueritta,* stood down the bay with *Unity* and *Falmouth Packet* in pursuit. Moore set all the sail he could and

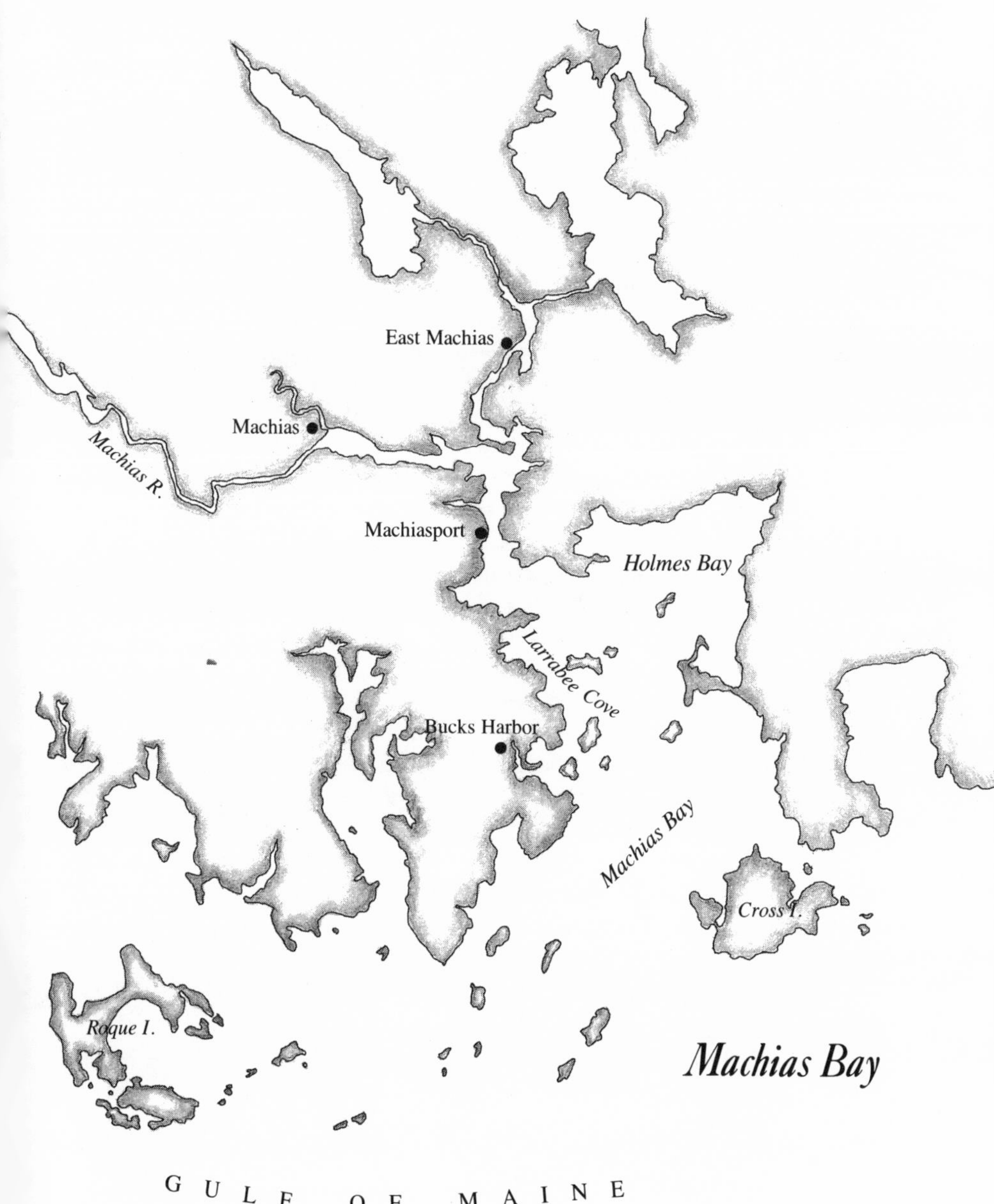

cut his boats away, but *Unity* and *Falmouth Packet* continued to gain. Moore fired his swivels and muskets at his pursuers. O'Brien built a breastwork across *Unity*'s deck to protect his crew and returned the fire, but he was almost out of powder. However, the crew of *Unity* was armed not only with muskets but with a few swords, narrow axes, and pitchforks—the latter being not the delicate, light, narrow-tined forks seen today but heavy, hand-forged and hand-sharpened weapons, lethal in the hands of a determined Son of Liberty challenging British tyranny.

As *Unity,* closely followed by *Falmouth Packet,* overtook *Margueritta,* a shot from one of the Sons killed the helmsman on *Margueritta.* She swung into the wind, toward *Unity,* and *Unity*'s bowsprit drove through *Margueritta*'s rigging and through her mainsail. John O'Brien was the first to board *Margueritta.* He was fired at by four marines, all of whom missed him but immediately charged with bayonets. John leaped over the stern and was picked up by his brother Jerry. Moore, standing on *Margueritta*'s rail, began throwing grenades into *Unity* but was struck with two musket balls and fell, badly wounded. The crew of *Unity* charged over *Margueritta*'s port rail with pitchforks while Foster, having laid *Falmouth Packet* on *Margueritta*'s starboard bow, led a rush down her deck from forward. Wounded and overwhelmed, Stillingfleet fled below, his crew surrendered, and the first naval battle of the American Revolution was over.

Unity and *Margueritta* returned to Machias. Moore was cared for as well as could be and a doctor was sent for, but Moore died the next day. Four others were killed aboard *Margueritta* including the unfortunate Captain Avery, the first Englishman killed in the first naval battle of the American Revolution. Avery Rock in Machias Bay bears his name.

Polly was renamed *Machias Liberty,* fitted with *Margueritta*'s 4-pounders, and in company with Foster in *Falmouth Packet,* cruised in search of *Diligent* (10) and *Tatamagouche* (sixteen swivels), two schooners from Halifax on patrol in the Bay of Fundy. The rebels found the two in Bucks Harbor at the head of Machias Bay, their officers having already been captured ashore. The schooners surrendered without a fight.

Three weeks later a frigate, a twenty-gun sloop of war, a sixteen-gun brig, and several schooners with 1,000 men were sent from Halifax to chastise the rebels. The vessels anchored down Machias Bay, and the brig with 500 men was sent up the narrow, shoal Machias River. She anchored off Scotts Point to set the soldiers ashore. Jerry O'Brien and Foster threw up a breastwork on the point and fought a Bunker Hill battle. The attack was repulsed, the brig went ashore, and the surviving soldiers were driven below by musket fire until the tide came again and floated the brig. The fleet returned to Halifax with the loss of 100 men.

Six weeks later a force was landed in Passamaquoddy Bay to attack Machias overland, but after two days' march over rocky ridges and through tangled swamps, the attempt was abandoned.

Jeremiah O'Brien was hailed in Cambridge as the Machias Admiral. He and John Lambert were commissioned in the Massachusetts navy to command *Machias Liberty* and *Diligent,* respectively, and £160 was appropriated for their support. John O'Brien was Lambert's first lieutenant. They became part of the force patrolling Massachusetts Bay to intercept merchantmen supplying the British in Boston.

After a year and a half, John O'Brien built a letter-of-marque vessel, *Hannibal,* a ship of twenty guns, and took her on a cruise to Santo Domingo. On her return, Jerry O'Brien took her as a privateer. Off New York he was chased by two frigates, which he eluded for forty-eight hours, but finally was overpowered. He was confined in the prison ship *Jersey* in New York and then transferred to the Mill Prison in England. Here he concealed his decent clothes, wore rags, neglected his appearance, became dirty, unshaven, lousy, a repulsive and disgraceful spectacle. Then, when he felt the time was right, he washed, shaved, put on his good clothes, and walked out of the prison, stopping at the bar in the warden's house for a drink with other gentlemen, and took a boat to France.

He returned to America to take command of the privateer brigantine *Hibernia* (10) in 1781. John O'Brien in the meantime had commanded the schooner *Hibernia* (10) in which he took the twenty-gun *General Pattison* and a mast ship.

Joseph Wheeler, standing in his big, flat-bottomed skiff, rowed up Damariscove Harbor on a pleasant September day in 1775, facing forward as was the custom. He had been out picking up driftwood on the western shore since dawn. Night before last there had been thunder squalls, and for a while in the early morning, on the high tide, there had blown a heavy breeze from the northwest which had left dead branches, limbs, and even whole trees and perhaps an odd plank or piece of slab wood stranded on the western shore of the island. It was easier firewood than walking down to the scraggly forest on the north end, cutting green spruce trees and lugging them the length of the island on his back.

As he slid the skiff alongside his spindly wharf and began heaving up his cargo, he realized someone was on the wharf moving the wood away from the edge, stacking it on the shore end. He'd thought he was alone on the island, but he was glad of the help and kept heaving up logs and tossing small stuff.

With the last stick in his hand, he called, "Here's the one we been looking for!", tossed it up, and climbed after it.

His helper, a cheerful old man in rather old-fashioned garb, asked, "You all alone? Where is everybody?"

"They've all got frightened and run up the river to Pleasant Cove. Old Dan Knight went first. That's his house over there. Took his whole tribe with him, whole kit and caboodle. Then my old man got rattled and run us all off and took all the sheep ashore, too."

"What all for?"

"Since the trouble started with the British to the westward, when they hove the tea into Boston Harbor and shot up the soldiers at Concord and then that wild man Thompson from Brunswick raised hell in Falmouth, people are scared the British will take it out on us. We are wide open, but they haven't done anything yet and I don't believe they want to rile up people down here. They got trouble enough in Boston. Say, who are you, anyway?"

"Me? Pattishall. I lived here once, way back."

"Oh, one of them. Dan Knight bought them out. You must be a cousin or something."

"Or something. You say your pa took all the sheep ashore? What are these creatures eating weeds and bleating?"

"The Boothbay town meeting got all excited last March, and John Murray and McCobb and some others got them to set up a rag-tag army and a little stone fort and got them to put all the beasts from the whole town together in one herd so they could drive 'em into the woods if the British came. Well, a herd like that eats right down to the dirt and there ain't enough place for them to graze, so I pulled my sheep out of there and brought 'em back. They're doing fine."

"Seems 's though. What happens if the British do come?"

"The British ain't all that bad. That Cap Mowatt in the *Canso* that Thompson went for, he's been pretty decent. Been on the coast a long time and paid for what he got."

The two had reached Wheeler's house on the island's western ridge where they could see north up Boothbay Harbor, northwest across to Cape Newagen, and westward to Seguin and the mouth of the Kennebec. Two sloops were standing toward the island, beating down from Townsend Harbor against the light southerly breeze. As they watched, one tacked and then the other, their headsails slatting and booming as they came around. They steadied on a course to clear the rocks off Newagen, their decks crowded with men.

"Who are they, Joe, and where are they bound? I saw a gaggle of 'em run into the Kennebec yesterday. These two must've run into Boothbay ahead of those thunder squalls t'other night and laid over yesterday."

"Likely. That one ahead is *Conway* and the other's *Abigail*. Belong up to Newburyport. They come down here pretty often for cordwood and haul it someplace up to the westward."

"That ain't cordwood they got now. Looks like soldiers," observed the old man.

"Well, I'll tell you, Cap," said Joe, "there's a big thing going on up the river. Reuben Colburn up to Pittston has been out straight building bateaus. You know what they are? Flat-bottomed skiffs about 20 feet long. Sides flare out wide. Loaded, they ain't bad, but empty they're the tiddliest thing you ever stepped in. Shift your chew, and you're overboard.

"Them soldiers, they're goin' up to Colburn's, put their supplies in these bateaus, go up the Kennebec, across the Height of Land, down a river on the other side comes out at Québec, and take Québec."

"Take Québec! That's a big order. Who's doing it?"

"Fella named Arnold from Connecticut. Don't know much about him. Say, Cap, what about a pull on that jug you been carryin'?"

At the word, the ghost of Captain Pattishall dissolved like fog on a sunny summer morning. No mortal ever drank of that jug.

Colonel Benedict Arnold had suggested to General Washington early in 1775 that he take a force of 1,200 men up the Kennebec River, across the Height of Land, and down the Chaudière River to Québec. At the same time, General Montgomery would go north up Lake Champlain, down the Richelieu River, take Montréal, descend the St. Lawrence, and join Arnold at Québec. The capture of Québec would exclude the British from any military campaign to the west of the Colonies and would bring all of Canada to the American side.

Arnold's small fleet of ten sloops and schooners sailed from Newburyport on September 19, 1775, was scattered in a night of thunder squalls, heavy rain, and fog off Cape Elizabeth, and reassembled at Reuben Colburn's shipyard in Pittston on the Kennebec River below Gardiner. Here they picked up 200 hastily built bateaux and went on up the Kennebec, finding the going very difficult. A third of the party turned back with most of the food that had survived the rains, the portages, and rapids. After suffering heroically through icy swamps and over rocky hills, about 600 men reached Québec, were joined by Montgomery, and on December 31, 1775, attacked Québec in a snowstorm. Montgomery was killed, Arnold wounded, and the attack failed.

In the spring the British General Burgoyne raised the siege, but Arnold's masterly retreat up the St. Lawrence and down the lakes delayed Burgoyne for nearly two years and led to his defeat at Saratoga in 1777.

The story is part of Maine's history because the expedition sailed up the Kennebec, because Maine men made up much of Arnold's force, and because in the defense of Lake Champlain, Maine shipbuilders and seamen played a significant part.

Admiral Graves, shut up in Boston with his clumsy big ships, was increasingly frustrated through the summer of 1775. In May, while Captain Mowatt was in Falmouth supervising Coulson's *Minerva,* the Admiral sent the sloop of war *Diana* under his nephew, Thomas Graves, to dismantle Fort Pownal at the mouth of the Penobscot River and to bring its guns and ammunition to Boston. Young Graves accomplished his mission, but one of the schooners into which he had loaded round shot and langrage was captured by Edward Emerson of Boothbay along with four other vessels collecting wood and provisions for Boston. Later, *Diana* attempted to prevent Americans from driving off cattle and sheep on Noddles Island. She grounded on a falling tide, was fired on heavily from the shore, fell over on her side, was abandoned, captured by Americans, and burned.

The Admiral was bombarded with orders from the Admiralty to search all vessels for military stores, for flint stones in the ballast, for letters bearing useful information, and to take masts and rudders from laid-up vessels to prevent their use as privateers. Also he was to be reinforced by more useless big vessels and hampered by soldiers that he could not support. It is scarcely surprising that by September 1 he had decided to carry the war to the enemy as vigorously as he could in the time remaining before winter. Graves determined to punish the rebellious seaport towns of New England and prevent their carrying on their naval guerilla war against him. He strengthened the decks of *Canso, Symmetry,* and the sloop *Spitfire* to take field guns and mortars. As the work was being completed on October 4, he received orders dated July 6 by which he was required and directed to "carry on such Operations upon the Sea Coasts of the Four Governments in New England as you shall judge most effective for suppressing, in conjunction with His Majesty's Land Forces, the Rebellion, which is now openly avowed and supported in those Colonies." On October 8, Mowatt sailed with a new schooner, *Halifax,* added to his fleet and with orders from Graves, consistent with Graves's July 6 orders from the Admiralty, to "lay waste burn and destroy such Sea Port towns as are accessible to His Majesty's ships. . . . My design is to chastize Marblehead, Salem, Newbury Port, Cape Ann Harbor [Gloucester], Portsmouth, Ipswich, Saco, Falmouth, in Casco Bay, and particularly Machias where *Margueritta* was taken." He was to "make the most vigorous efforts to burn the Towns and destroy the Shipping in the Harbours." Bearing these stern orders from his exasperated admiral, Mowatt sailed eastward on the mission that was to make his name disgraced in Revolutionary annals next only to that of Benedict Arnold.

Mowatt was probably not a savage, vengeful, or cruel man. In 1759 he had been commissioned a lieutenant in the Royal Navy and in 1764 was put in command of HMS *Canso,* a converted merchantman armed with a few 6-pounders, to survey the coast of New England. If the American Neptune charts published by the Admiralty late in the eighteenth century are his work, he did an outstandingly good job, in the course of which he visited many Maine harbors and made many acquaintances, if not friends. The story is told that he was holding a party aboard *Canso* in Boothbay Harbor attended by a number of local skippers. The wine flowed pretty freely. Mowatt brought out a box of gold coins and a British flag. He offered young Captain Booth a royal commission and a bag of gold if he would run the British flag to the masthead of his schooner. Booth replied, "I am but a poor and obscure man at best, but poor as I am, the King of England is too poor to buy me."

This and the unpleasant confrontation at Falmouth in the spring of 1775 no doubt soured Mowatt's view of the Sons of Liberty and excited his anger, but he had parted from the citizens of Falmouth on good terms and had apparently accepted their apologies, believing that the riot was in no way incited by them.

Captain Daniel Tucker, who was present at the time, wrote later of Mowatt's departure from Falmouth after giving his parole the night of May 9.

"When he [Mowatt] went to his barge he was accompanied by a large number of the most respectable inhabitants to whom he expressed his thanks in most glowing language for their influence in saving his life, as he expressed it, and he lamented the unhappy civil war that had been begun by the battles of Lexington and Bunker Hill. [When he wrote his memoir, Captain Tucker had forgotten that Bunker Hill was not fought until June 17.] What events the war might lead to he could not forsee, but he thought it might be that orders would be sent from the court of Great Britain to burn or destroy every town on the continent that was assailable; and if that should be the case he thought he had influence enough to save the town of Falmouth and with a solemn assurance that his influence should be exerted to the utmost he stepped into his barge, bid the gentlemen 'good night' and went on board and broke his parole."

So, as Mowatt led his fleet eastward in October 1775, he was probably not animated by a spirit of revenge, although no doubt he shared his admiral's frustration and was carrying out his orders willingly enough. As he passed Cape Ann, Mowatt was advised by his Army artillery officer that the houses in Cape Ann Harbor were so widely separated that bombardment would be useless. He continued on to the eastward, anchoring far down Falmouth harbor* on October 16. Citizens were at first alarmed by the sight of four naval vessels in their harbor but soon recognized *Canso,* knew that Mowatt was in command, and assumed that he had come to seek food and fodder from the islands. The militia company was sent to oppose him, but the citizens, Tucker reports, were relieved that Mowatt was in command.

The next day, there being no wind, Mowatt kedged and towed his vessels up the harbor and anchored off the town. He sent Lieutenant Fraser ashore with a proclamation that the people "had been guilty of a most unpardonable Rebellion" and that he had come to "execute a just punishment." He gave the 75citizens two hours "to remove without delay the Human Species out of the said Town."

A deputation visited Mowatt at once, and pleaded for mercy. Mowatt relented to the extent of promising that if they would take an oath of allegiance to King George and deliver to him the town's five carriage guns and all their powder and small arms, he would not fire until he had talked further with Admiral Graves.

They delivered a few muskets but refused the oath and carriage guns. The citizens spent the night removing as much of their property as they could. At 9:00 A.M., the deadline, Mowatt saw several women and children on the shore and held his fire. By 9:40 the town appeared to be deserted. He ran a red flag to *Canso*'s masthead, and the fleet opened fire. All day they blazed away with naval guns, howitzers, and flaming carcasses.† They set several houses afire in

* What is now Portland Harbor.

† A carcass is a hollow iron ball stuffed with combustibles like oil and rags. It is lighted and fired from a gun, spouting flames through three holes in the shell.

the north end of the town and smashed up the courthouse, customhouse, Episcopal church, and a number of dwellings. Destruction appearing to be inadequate, Mowatt sent a party ashore to throw torches into doors and windows. At length he managed to burn about two-thirds of the 300 dwellings in town and most of the public buildings, and the next morning departed. After a brief and ineffective raid on Boothbay, during which he burned Knight's house on Damariscove and stole 100 of Joseph Wheeler's sheep, the punitive expedition fizzled out.

His ammunition was mostly expended. The howitzers had all jumped their carriages, and the strengthening of the decks had proved inadequate, so Mowatt had no recourse but to return to Boston. The season being so late and the needed repairs so extensive, the punitive expedition was abandoned for the year. Admiral Graves was relieved in December, and the project never revived.

Captain Mowatt at first was pleased with his success. He reported to Graves that by 6:00 P.M., "Falmouth with the Blockhouse and battery, the principal wharves and storehouses, with eleven sail of vessels was all laid into ashes, including a fine distillery." He had captured four ships at the cost of one midshipman and one marine wounded by militia resisting a shore party.

Graves, too, was pleased at first with Mowatt's success. He called it "a severe Stroke to the Rebels. Falmouth having long been a principal Magazine of all kinds of Merchandize from whence . . . large quantities of Goods were usually transported in small vessels to Newbury Port and from thence to the Rebel Army round Boston."

The Americans were shocked. They were outraged. They were moved to anger and revenge. As propaganda, the raid backfired on the British with as much force as the sinking of the *Lusitania* in later years hurt the German cause. George Washington, a man not given to overstatement, wrote that the raid on Falmouth had been "effected with every circumstance of Cruelty and Barbarity, which Revenge and Malice could suggest."

James Warren wrote to John Adams describing the "pirates on the Eastern Shore" as "savage and barbarous in the highest stage. What can we wait for now? What more can we want to justifie any step to take, kill and destroy, to refuse them any refreshments, to apprehend our enemies, to confiscate their goods and estates, to open our ports to foreigners and if practicable to form alliances . . . ?" Clearly, he planned to use the raid as propaganda.

When the news of the atrocity reached England, Lord George Germaine wrote to General Howe, "I am to suppose that Admiral Graves had good reasons for the step he took to destroy the town of Falmouth, and that he did not proceed to that extremity without an absolute refusal on the part of the inhabitants to comply with those requisitions stated in the orders he received from the Lords of the Admiralty which however does not appear from any account I have seen of that Transaction."

The orders to which Germaine refers read in part that Graves was to send ships "to demand of the Inhabitants of the Maritime Towns that they do furnish at a reasonable Price such Supplies of Provisions and other Necessaries as may be procured there, for the use of His Majesty's Fleet and Army, and in case of refusal to comply with so just and reasonable a demand to proceed hostilely against such Towns as are in Open Rebellion." However, this gentle order did not reach Graves until some time after Mowatt had sailed from Boston. It was dated September 14, 1775, a little more than three weeks before Mowatt sailed on October 8. Five weeks was considered a reasonable time for a westward-bound Atlantic crossing in September. Therefore Graves, exasperated by American tactics and acting on the July 6 orders from England to do everything he could to suppress the rebellion, had given Mowatt his stern orders to "burn the towns and destroy the shipping." Afterwards, Mowatt was the scapegoat.

To demonstrate that the deed lived in infamy we need only quote the words of James Phinney Baxter, mayor of Portland and one of Maine's most scholarly historians, speaking before the staid Maine Historical Society in 1890: "It is sufficient for us to say that Henry Mowatt ruthlessly and needlessly destroyed a thriving and well ordered town, peopled with men and women of his own race, and scattered them abroad exposed to suffering and death from want, hardship, and exposure."

In later years both Mowatt and Graves suffered for the deed. Graves was relieved of command in December 1775 for having failed to kill wasps with his baseball bat and never held another command. Mowatt was passed over for promotion from commander to captain repeatedly, at one time having to serve under a captain who had once been his own lieutenant. He finally achieved post rank in 1783. In the long letter he wrote describing his achievements in the Royal Navy in order to explain why he should be granted seniority as of 1776, Mowatt did not even mention the destruction of Falmouth.

We may conclude this chapter, then, by observing that Admiral Graves and the British navy, equipped with ships, guns, and men far exceeding the numbers of those possessed by the Americans, through their lack of understanding of the nature of the war and through their ineptitude were unable to achieve control of the sea. By mustering enormous force to destroy two-thirds of one small and defenseless seacoast town they demonstrated not their strength but their weakness.

NOTES

Again, Williamson's *History of Maine* gives an outline of the early events of the American Revolution. J. P. Baxter's "A Lost Manuscript" gives his interpretation of the destruction of Falmouth. The actual manuscript is a long letter to the Admiralty written by Captain Mowatt to explain why his commission as captain should date from 1776 rather than 1783 when he received it. In the eighteenth-century British navy a lieutenant or a commander in command of a ship was called by courtesy Captain.

However, he retained only the insignia and perquisites of his actual rank. Only when promoted to the rank of captain could he wear a captain's epaulette. Mowatt's letter deals with much of his work, especially his actions in the Battle of Penobscot Bay in 1779, but it does not mention his burning of Falmouth. Baxter infers that it was not an action of which either Mowatt or the Admiralty was proud and that it was the reason for his being passed over. Mowatt was the scapegoat.

John A. Tulley's *The British Navy and the American Revolution* is a thorough and interesting review of Graves's problems in Boston. Also it contains detailed accounts of the destruction of Falmouth and of the Battle of Machias. It identifies *Margueritta* as a schooner, although other authorities call her a sloop. Graves bought her into the British navy, so he should have known what he bought. However, the term "sloop" had a variety of meanings and did not necessarily refer to a single-masted vessel. A sloop of war was usually ship rigged. Chebacco boats were called sloops although they carried two masts. The term "sloop" was often used to distinguish a decked vessel from an open shallop. Consult William A. Baker's *Sloops and Shallops.*

Rebels Under Sail, by William A. Fowler, Jr., gives the story of the Machias conflict from an American view but lacks detail.

George F. Talbot's "The Capture of the *Margaretta*"* appears in the same volume of the Maine Historical Society's Proceedings as does "A Lost Manuscript." It contains more information about Foster and also mentions Hannah and Rebecca Weston, who carried forty pounds of powder and shot from the Chandler River to Machias on the day of the battle.

Shipping Days of Old Boothbay, by George Wharton Rice, tells the story of young Captain Booth and of Mowatt's visit to Damariscove. It also preserves a number of other incidents in the region's maritime history that will surface in later chapters.

George W. Driska's *Narrative of the Town of Machias* is a detailed history of the town, including, of course, the battle. It has numerous interesting, if irrelevant, incidents. For example, Reverend Lyon, who came as the first minister in 1771 and who was preaching the sermon on June 11, 1775 was colorblind. He appeared one Sunday in an elegant red robe, having bought it thinking it was black.

The Maine Historical Society has also published in Volume 2, pages 246–249, "Exertions of the O'Brien Family" by Captain John O'Brien, then of Brunswick. This is a colorful account of the battle, of the subsequent British efforts to punish Machias, and of the later careers of Jeremiah and John O'Brien in the American Revolution.

This and most other accounts of the Battle of Machias are based almost entirely on the recollections of members of the O'Brien family and of imaginative supporters of Machias history. In the Maine Historical Society Quarterly for Fall 1975, Edwin A. Churchill published a carefully documented account of the battle based on recollections of Stephen Jones, nephew of Ichabod Jones. Churchill traces to their sources six previously accepted "myths" surrounding the affair. The first was that the O'Briens had erected a liberty pole in Machias which Moore demanded be cut down and that the O'Briens' refusal was a primary basis of the confrontation. The second was that *Falmouth Packet* under Foster went aground in the East River and took no part in the action. Another myth was the story of Foster's Rubicon in which Foster is said to have stopped debate before the attack on the meetinghouse by stepping across the brook.

*A common confusion over the spelling of *Margueritta.* The O'Briens thought they captured *Margaretta.* Graves bought *Margueritta.* It was the same vessel.

The fourth myth says that the alarm was given in the church by London Atus, a negro servant of Parson Lyons. Another myth says two girls to whom Moore and Stillingfleet were attached accompanied them aboard *Margueritta,* and Moore's inamorata, a niece of Ichabod Jones, died of a broken heart after Moore's death. Finally, an attempt was made to cover up Ichabod Jones's Toryism, of which Gage and Graves were convinced.

In support of Churchill, Robert C. Brooks, in an unpublished but extensive study of the accounts of Godfrey, who was aboard *Margueritta;* of Parson Lyons, who wrote responsible reports to the Massachusetts legislature after the battle; of Flinn, master of *Falmouth Packet;* and of Stephen Jones, has assembled an authoritative composite account of the battle which I have used. Much of Brooks's material comes from *Naval Documents of the American Revolution* as well as from British archives. In Brooks's study it is clear that Moore commanded *Margueritta,* not *Margaretta,* and that *Halifax*'s guns were not part of *Margueritta*'s armament but were unmounted in the hold.

The O'Briens' father was as short-fused as his sons. He wanted desperately to sail aboard *Unity,* but his sons physically prevented him. In the attack on *Diligent* and *Tatamagouche* in Bucks Harbor, O'Brien *père* followed *Machias Liberty* (ex-*Unity*) in a small boat with a surgeon in case one of his boys was hurt, and he was ready to fight if necessary.

Samuel Eliot Morison's *Oxford History of the American People* should never be out of reach.

One may speculate that Mowatt decided to attack Falmouth rather than Newburyport or Portsmouth because it was there that he had broken his parole. Psychologists say that we don't like people whom we have wronged.

Mowatt must have known that the terms he offered would be unacceptable, but at least he did give the people a chance to move more than the "Human Species" out of town.

The fascinating account of the wreck of the schooner *Halifax* is found in Harold M. Hahn's *The Colonial Schooner.*

The details in the conversation between Pattishall and John Wheeler are all authentic, as will be seen in the next chapter. Many who were lukewarm or indulging in wishful thinking in 1775 became good patriots later.

John Codman's *Arnold's Expedition to Quebec* supplies the date and the names of the two sloops late at the rendezvous. The book is a careful and well-documented account of the expedition. A more exciting account is Kenneth Roberts's *Arundel,* a work of historical fiction but thoroughly researched.

What is now the city of Portland was first known as Machigonne, then as Casco, and in 1658 as Falmouth. In 1786 Portland was divided from the larger town of Falmouth. The fire set by Mowatt was the first of three devastating fires which the city survived. The other two occurred in 1854 and 1866.

SIXTEEN

Privateering and the Penobscot Expedition

SOMETIME AFTER the Battle of Machias, *Falmouth Packet* was registered in Massachusetts as a privateer by Benjamin Foster and, one might guess, taken to Mount Desert Island by his partner in the lumber business, John Manchester. Manchester had been at Machias at the time of the battle and may have been aboard *Unity*.

By the fall of 1775, anyone living on the Maine coast knew very well that he was fighting a war with Great Britain. The Battle of Machias and subsequent raids, the burning of Falmouth, the demolition of Fort Pownal, Tory raiders, and the ubiquitous British patrols were bringing the war very close. While the only major campaign was the British occupation of Castine and the effort by Massachusetts to re-take the town, until the end of the war in 1783 a strange sail off the coast was probably that of an enemy.

While Manchester was out hunting in the fall of 1775, a British warship attacked his house at what is now Southwest Harbor, killed and stole his livestock, and took his winter provisions. The British skipper told Manchester's wife she could starve, then sailed off to the westward with *Falmouth Packet* in company.

John Bunker, Manchester's brother-in-law, paddled his canoe westward, searching every cove and harbor for the schooner, and at last found her up the Sheepscot River at Wiscasset, loaded with food supplies. On a dark night with an ebb tide when the British crew was ashore, Bunker cut the schooner adrift, floated her down the river, made sail, and took her back to the Mill Pond in Norwood Cove near Manchester's house. The schooner's cargo kept Manchester's and several other families from starvation that winter.

Then, probably the next summer, Bunker took *Falmouth Packet* east to Roque Island. Just south of Roque Island, in Great Spruce Island, there is a tight little cove with high, cliffy shores heavily wooded with tall spruces. At the foot of a cliff is a deep basin where *Falmouth Packet* anchored, probably with lines ashore to trees, her spars completely hidden behind the islands. Bunker established a lookout on top of the island whence with a glass, he could pick out British vessels which he thought vulnerable. He was known locally as Pirate Jack, although he was probably a legitimate privateer.

A privateer was a private vessel of war carrying no cargo, licensed by her government to attack the enemy's commerce. Any vessel captured was manned with a prize crew from the privateer and sent into a friendly port where a court would decide if she were a legitimate prize. If so, she and her cargo would be sold at auction, half the proceeds going to the owners of the privateer and half divided among captain and crew.

During the American Revolution the British were quite unable to deal with American privateers. In European wars they had found a combination of two methods successful. The first was "stopping the earths." Early in a war, small, fast luggers heavily manned by "whiskeradoes in stocking caps" swooped out of French and Dutch Channel ports to pick off unarmed British merchantmen. There were not many ports out of which these could come, so several British frigates assisted by smaller boats capable of operating close inshore could keep the whiskeradoes bottled up.

This did not work in America. There was too much coastline and too many "earths" to stop. The Maine coast has literally hundreds of coves, rivers, harbors, islands, and peninsulas providing safe hiding places. The rest of the New England coast is almost as intricate; and the Chesapeake, the sounds and inlets of North Carolina, and the Sea Islands of Georgia are superb refuges. Furthermore, the British were far from home. To maintain one frigate off the Maine coast required at least one more being refitted in Halifax, Jamaica, or England and several small supply ships in support. Communication with the admiral and with the Admiralty in England was also difficult: an Atlantic crossing could take from five to ten weeks. As Admiral Graves discovered in trying to blockade Boston Harbor, "stopping the earths" was next to impossible.

Britain's other answer to privateering was the convoy system. Larger oceangoing privateers, lightly armed and heavily manned, infested bottlenecks of commerce like the approaches to the English Channel, the passages leading out of the Caribbean, the mouth of the St. Lawrence, and the Grand Banks. A line-of-battle ship or a stout frigate with several smaller, faster corvettes would convoy a fleet of perhaps 100 merchantmen through these dangerous waters.

The Americans soon developed an answer to this defense. They built big, fast topsail schooners, brigs, and ships which, because they carried no cargo, could be built like yachts to outsail any merchantman or stubby frigate. These privateers were armed heavily enough, some of them with over twenty guns, to defeat a corvette or even a small frigate. They would circle a convoy, capture a merchant ship, and get away before the escort could touch them. Because they could stay at sea for long periods, they could catch merchantmen after convoys broke up. They could even raid British harbors and capture prizes off the English coast. Off Banff, Scotland, in 1777 American privateers took eight ships in two weeks.

After the French entered the Revolutionary War in 1777 and America built a small fleet of frigates, the British had to concentrate on fighting warships. The ministry ordered General Sir William Howe to "relinquish the idea of carrying on offensive operations within land and embark troops with orders to attack the ports on the coast from New York to Nova Scotia so as to incapacitate the rebels from continuing their depredations on the trade of this Kingdom." It did not work. A speaker in Parliament estimated that by February 1777, 733 English merchant ships had been captured. Eighteen British warships were taken by privateers between 1778 and 1783.

The privateer *Grand Turk* of 300 tons, built in Hanover, Massachusetts, for Elias Haskett Derby of Salem, carried twenty-four guns and a crew of more than a hundred men. Over 100 feet long, *Grand Turk* was ship rigged, carrying very deep topsails as well as topgallants and royals on all three masts and even two sprit sails under her bowsprit. She cruised the Atlantic and Caribbean and captured in less than two years sixteen British merchantmen along with a well-armed British privateer brig of fourteen guns and a 400-ton ship of twenty-two guns, the latter without opposition. She ran successfully from a fleet of British frigates and left single warships hull down to leeward.

Not only was British commerce intercepted by the capture of merchantmen, but it was further hampered by soaring insurance rates: 30 percent on vessels in convoy and 50 percent on those sailing independently. And commodity prices soared, too. Potatoes were up 500 percent and beef was up 200 percent over pre-war prices.

Although many Maine men sailed on big Massachusetts privateers, Maine did not have the capital to finance many such ventures. However, the experience of Daniel Tucker of Falmouth will show what one Maine man did.

After several adventurous years privateering, in 1780 he shipped on the letter-of-marque brig *Portland* for the West Indies. A letter of marque is a license issued by the government to a cargo-carrying merchantman to take such enemy prizes as come in her way. *Portland* sold her cargo in the West Indies and on the way home was captured by a smaller, less powerful British privateer, as Tucker says in his journal, "wholly for want of courage in our Captain who was unfit for the command of an armed vessel." Confined below deck, the Americans hatched a plan to capture their captors but were betrayed by a "worthless American sailor." They were then put in irons and soon after transferred to a captured Dutch schooner, which took them to St. Eustatius. Here Tucker joined the twenty-gun American letter-of-marque ship *Columbia* with a crew of fifty and sailed to Port-au-Prince where *Columbia* shipped a cargo of sugar, cocoa, and coffee for Spain. She was blockaded for a week by a fifty-gun British ship and then continued her voyage. On the voyage the captain, Greeley, a Casco Bay man, lent Tucker his books and instruments so he could learn geometry, trigonometry, and navigation from a shipmate.

Columbia left Cadiz, Spain, for Boston in May 1781 with a cargo of wine, silks, and "other dry goods," keeping a sharp eye for English merchantmen to capture. Inside Cape Cod, with Boston Harbor in sight, *Columbia* was chased by two British warships. *Columbia* was heavily loaded and foul on the bottom, but Captain Greeley cracked on all sail in an effort to get into Boston with his valuable cargo. *Columbia* made a running fight of it from 4:00 until 8:00 P.M., ". . . and for a part of this time we were within range of musket shot and the number of musket shots that were fired at us were like showers of hailstones flying about our heads, and the cannon at the same time making havoc of our masts and yards. During part of the time of this chase I steered the ship, and the mizzen being brailed up and hanging in folds, it was perforated with musket balls that did not pass more than a foot or two over my head, and the sail was literally cut to pieces." Less than two miles from Boston Light, Captain Greeley was struck in the forehead with a musket ball, the British ship got alongside and boarded *Columbia* with forty men, and the battle was over.* Many were wounded, but Captain Greeley was the only man killed. The British ship was *General Monk* of twenty guns, formerly the American privateer *General Washington,* later recaptured by Joshua Barney's *Hyder Ally* in Delaware Bay. Tucker and the crew of *Columbia* were transferred to a captured Nantucket sloop and set ashore.

Another Maine man, Paul Reed of Boothbay, purchased the brigantine *Warren* in Boston on December 7, 1776. He sailed her to Boothbay, took aboard a cargo of lumber, and headed for the French West Indies on February 7, 1777, to trade his cargo for munitions. On March 12 he was captured, escaped or was exchanged, took over the brig *Reprisal,* and captured the British brig *Nancy* (16). She was lost in the Penobscot Expedition of 1779, after which Reed took over the big sloop *General Wadsworth* (12) and captured more prizes.

For the most part, the Maine coast fitted out small, lightly armed privateers for local efforts. All privateers were supposed to be registered with the Commonwealth of Massachusetts and bonded to be sure they captured only enemy ships or neutrals with military supplies for the enemy and also to be sure they did not ship sailors from the navy or soldiers from the army. Forty-one Maine vessels appear on the list of those bonded. Of these, only two are ships: *Hannibal* (24), registered by Jeremiah O'Brien in 1780, and *Cyrus* (12), registered by John O'Brien in 1782. There are five brigs or brigantines, the most heavily armed being Jeremiah O'Brien's *Hibernia* (10), which he registered in May 1781, after his cruise in *Hannibal.* There are twenty schooners, ranging from *Saco Bob* with three guns and thirty-five men under Solomon Coit of Saco, to *America* with ten guns and eighty men under Captain Isaac Snow of Harpswell. Most of the schooners carried four or six guns. Thirteen

* See chapter notes for a brief discussion of naval ordnance.

sloops or boats are listed. By far the most powerful were the sloop *Retrieve,* carrying twenty guns and eighty men from Falmouth under Joshua Stone, and the sloop *General Wadsworth,* 110 tons, carrying twelve guns and eighty men under Paul Reed of Boothbay. The smallest was *Fly* under John Perry of St. George, carrying nine men and armed with small arms only.

One can guess at some of the exploits hidden in the list. For instance, *Fly* is registered as above in August 1781. In June 1782 John Perry registered *Fly* with one gun and a crew of fourteen. Did he make a capture and move up? Then there was Solomon Coit, who in the schooner *William* out of Pepperrellborough (Saco) on May 3, 1781, captured the schooner *Halifax Bob.* On May 22, 1781, he registered the schooner *Saco Bob* with three guns and thirty-five men out of Saco.

The registered privateers did only a part of the fighting, however. Many coastal people joined either Washington's Continental army or the Massachusetts provincial forces. Many stayed at home, cut firewood and lumber to supply the cities and shipyards, and fought off the British and the Tories. The British, in an attempt to "stop the earths," had at different times a number of big vessels on the coast including *Milford* (32), *Rainbow* (44), *Hope, Canso, Albany,* and others. From these, whaleboats and cutters were sent out, often guided by Tories who fled east of the Kennebec to Lincoln County for British protection. These small boats—"shaving mills," as they were called, shaving in the sense of cheating, defrauding, or robbing—were a constant menace to comparatively unprotected coastal communities.

The town of Boothbay, on a large harbor much used by British vessels, took quick action. On March 21, 1775, before the war actually broke out, the town meeting voted, among other items, to take an inventory of supplies on hand, to estimate supplies needed for the next year, to hire a vessel or vessels to take their lumber and firewood to market, sell it, and buy the requisite supplies, borrowing on the town's credit if necessary. They voted to build a storehouse in the woods in which to store the supplies, and to mount a guard on it day and night. On Mondays the selectmen would issue supplies. Livestock on the islands was to be brought ashore and all livestock kept in one herd, to be driven into the woods on the approach of any enemy. Militia officers were to inspect all firearms in town, have the defective ones repaired at the owners' expense, and see that each man had an effective musket and bayonet. A vessel was to be sent to the French West Indies for powder. A guard of ten men was to stand watch by day and a password was to be given for each night. If an alarm was given, all men were to assemble with arms, ammunition, and two days' rations to await orders. Finally, if the enemy appeared, they were to be told that no hostile action would take place unless they land or "anoy us."

In July 1775, after the battle of Concord and Lexington, the disturbance in Falmouth over Coulson's *Minerva,* and the taking of the *Margueritta* at Machias, Edward Emerson of Boothbay seized five British vessels collecting wood and provisions alongshore, one a 70-ton schooner containing round shot and langrage which Thomas Graves had taken from Fort Pownal in May, and petitioned the Massachusetts General Court that he be permitted to arm her and man her with thirty men to defend the coast.

In October 1775 Mowatt raided Damariscove, burned a house, and took a flock of sheep. Dr. Francis Greene in his *History of Boothbay* writes, "It was ascertained that Mowatt paid [Joseph] Wheeler $2 apiece for the sheep," perhaps suggesting that Wheeler was not as patriotic as others. Edward Emerson petitioned the General Court for more powder because the militia had exhausted their supply on Mowatt in the defense of Damariscove. In 1776 Reverend John Murray petitioned the General Court to fit out idle vessels in Boothbay as privateers because trade with the West Indies was cut off.

A "shaving mill" manned by loyalists approaching a rebel town with obviously hostile intent. *Consuelo E. Hanks*

British raids continued. In 1777 Commodore Collier with *Rainbow* and *Hope* anchored in Boothbay after burning four vessels at Damariscotta, capturing another in the Sheepscot, and stealing livestock. Reverend John Murray of Boothbay went aboard *Rainbow* and negotiated successfully with Collier.

Clark Linekin, a confessed Tory who later fled to St. George and then to Castine, was fishing in his canoe off Fishermans Island when he was captured by a boat from HMS *Rainbow,* taken home, and forced to provide turnips and oxen for $40. He was allowed to keep the hides and tallow. The raiders also stole sheep and hay from one Robinson, who then owned Fishermans Island. On September 5, 1777, McCobb, a leading Boothbay patriot and selectman, accused Linekin of trading with the enemy and had him put in Pownalborough jail, charging him £3 19 shillings 6 pence for transportation. Linekin pleaded that he never was paid for the oxen and turnips, that his family was in distress, and that he was sick. He was released and went to St. George.

A Tory from Friendship, Pomroy, had been a friend of Robert Jameson, a committed patriot in Camden. Pomroy volunteered to guide a Tory shaving mill to Jameson's house at Clam Cove between Rockland and Camden. The party captured Jameson, put him aboard their boat, and looted his house, shot his oxen, killed and stole his pigs, and then freed him. Jameson, who had seen an American privateer coming up the bay from Owls Head as the fog shut down, refused to go ashore and, although told to keep his mouth shut, hailed the privateer. However, she did not respond. Knowing the privateer was nearby, he still refused to go ashore. The party brought his wife aboard to persuade him, but he still refused. They spent the night on the barge. In the morning the fog lifted and revealed no privateer, so Jameson went ashore swearing "his wrath would be forcibly visited upon the head of the base Pomroy."

Pomroy joined the British in Castine, took out a vessel for them, and was captured in August 1781 by the brigantine *Captain* of Salem.

After the Revolutionary War, Pomroy returned to Friendship and was piloting a Waldoboro vessel owned by Paul Jameson, Robert's brother. They happened to anchor in Clam Cove. While Paul was ashore, Robert came aboard with a musket and bayonet. Pomroy pleaded for forgiveness. Jameson, a powerful man, laid aside his musket and gave Pomroy a frightful beating with his fists. As he left, he pinked the unconscious Pomroy with his bayonet to see if he was still alive. He was.

Many other examples could be cited, but these seem sufficient to show that the war along the Maine coast was a matter of British and Tory raids, of burning houses, shooting cattle, destroying shipping, and blockading the coast to prevent trade, while the American patriots strove to defend themselves and to attack the enemy where he could be found.

The only significant naval effort on the Maine coast was the Penobscot Expedition of 1779, probably the worst naval defeat suffered by the United States Navy until December 7, 1941. On June 12, 1779, General McLean and about 800 soldiers in transports escorted by the frigate *Blonde* (32) and three sloops of war landed on the shore of Dice (Dyce) Head at Castine. They had come to establish a British presence in eastern Maine, to provide a rallying point for Tories, to give color to a British demand that the Penobscot River should be the eastern boundary of the United States if it should come to peace negotiations, and to provide a naval base from which to harass coastal communities, attack privateers, and enforce a blockade on New England ports.

Brigadier General McLean, veteran of nineteen battles and an experienced administrator of civilian populations, was an intelligent, energetic, and imaginative leader at a time when there were few like him in the British army. He commanded a contingent of the Royal Artillery, the Argyll Highlanders, and a new regiment, the 82nd Foot, known as the Hamiltonians because it was raised by the Duke of Hamilton. In this regiment served Lieutenant John

Moore, later to become a distinguished British general and, after his death at Corunna, subject of a well-known poem by a little-known poet.*

The fleet was escorted by *Blonde,* which departed after seeing the expedition safely into the Bagaduce River. Captain Henry Mowatt, now with the rank of commander, was left in command of three small sloops of war, *Albany, North,* and *Nautilus,* each carrying about ten 6-pounders. Despite the hard words said of him after the burning of Falmouth, Mowatt was an able, efficient naval officer who put the demands of the service before his own career.

As soon as they got ashore, McLean marked out the site of Fort George on Dice Head and set the soldiers to clearing the trees, digging a ditch, and throwing up earthworks. Numbers of Tories joined him and helped in the work.

The news of the landing reached Boston on June 18. It startled the General Assembly into instant action. From a British base on the Penobscot River the Maine, New Hampshire, and Massachusetts coasts could be effectively blockaded, privateers could be kept in port, trade interrupted, and sources of fish, lumber, and firewood cut off. The Assembly at once appointed Solomon Lovell commander of the land forces, assisted by Peleg Wadsworth. Paul Revere was made commander of the artillery. Dudley Saltonstall, in command of the Continental Navy frigate *Warren* (32), was appointed commodore of the fleet, which included, besides *Warren,* the Navy sloop *Providence,* which John Paul Jones had commanded earlier, and the Navy brig *Diligent.* Five vessels of the Massachusetts navy and one from New Hampshire were joined by twelve chartered privateers and about two dozen unarmed transports. Of the armed vessels, nine were ships, five of them with twenty guns or more, six were brigs of fourteen to sixteen guns, and three were sloops carrying fourteen, twelve, and ten guns. The fleet sailed from Boston on July 19 and anchored in Boothbay Harbor on the 21st.

Lovell mustered his troops, some of whom were marines, and found instead of the promised 1,500, less than 900, of whom Wadsworth wrote, "One fourth part of the troops appeared to be Small Boys & old men & unfit for the service." Nevertheless, they sailed confidently for the Penobscot, supplied with ample munitions, 9 tons of flour and bread, 10 tons of salt beef, and 600 gallons of rum. On July 25 the fleet anchored off Castine.

McLean sent at once to Halifax for help. He was outnumbered and had only the outlines of a fort, the earthworks being scarcely more than knee high, and no cannon were mounted. Mowatt's naval force consisted of only the three sloops, quite unable to resist Saltonstall's armada. Nevertheless, Mowatt moved them down the harbor and anchored them with springs on their cables so they could be swung to command the entrance—with 6-pounders! Saltonstall's ships fired at them ineffectively and withdrew.

The next morning an American who had visited the fort only two days

* "The Burial of Sir John Moore at Corunna," by Charles Wolfe.

before told Saltonstall about the weak state of the fort and of Mowatt's "fleet" and advised him to sail in and "make everything his own." In reply, said the spy telling of it afterwards, "he [Saltonstall] hove up his long chin and said, 'you seem to be damn knowing about the whole matter! I am not going to risk my shipping in that damned hole!' "—and he did not.

Later in the day, the American marines seized Nautilus Island and three guns the British had left there. More guns were landed, and Mowatt was forced to retreat up the Bagaduce River out of range.

Saltonstall still refused to go in with his fleet to cover a landing, so Lovell determined to land on the west side of Dice Head near a huge boulder now known as Trask Rock, named after a fourteen-year-old marine fifer, Israel Trask, who sheltered behind it.

On July 28, after an initial barrage from the ships, about 600 Americans landed on the beach and set out to climb the high bluff. Not only was it so steep that they had to scrabble and scramble, holding on by bushes and rocks, but they had to sling their muskets and could not reply to the brisk fire from McLean's soldiers on top, among whom was Lieutenant John Moore in command of a squad of twenty men. By sheer courage and persistence, about 500 of Lovell's men reached the top by two different paths.

Most of the British soldiers fired once more and ran for it. Moore shouted, "Will the Hamilton men leave me?" His squad returned and kept up their fire. Captain Dunlop reported to McLean that such a large force of Americans had landed, he was obliged to retreat.

"But where is Moore?"

"He is, I fear, cut off."

"What, then, is the firing I still hear?"

Dunlop was sent out again and, with thirteen of Moore's twenty, retreated in good order to the fort.

Meanwhile, the Americans had swarmed up the cliff and pushed ahead through the woods to the edge of the clearing in front of the fort. There was no artillery in the fort, the walls were not high enough to keep anyone out, nor was the ditch deep enough. The Americans outnumbered the British, and McLean knew he could not hold his position against a determined charge. He planned to fire one volley as the Americans came out of the woods, haul down his flag, and retreat to the shore where Mowatt's guns could cover him at least for the time being. Actually, the general had his hand on the flag halyards, ready to haul down and run—but the Americans never came out of the woods. Their plan had been to gain a foothold on the top of the hill, dig in, bring up cannon, bombard the fort, and then rush it. Lovell failed to notice that there was no fort worth bombarding.

From this point, the American fortunes declined with increasing speed. Despite intense pressure from Lovell and Wadsworth as well as his naval captains, Saltonstall refused to sail in and wipe out Mowatt. Lovell and Revere set up batteries to bombard the fort. McLean built up the fort faster than the

Upper Penobscot Bay

Americans could knock it down and soon had guns mounted to return the American fire. There was some skirmishing around a British battery on the south side of the peninsula, but nothing was accomplished, and Saltonstall remained in terror of three guns. A week went by, and except for a large quantity of powder burned, no progress had been made while McLean grew daily stronger.

Wadsworth, seeing this, urged Lovell to send a few men and guns up the Penobscot River to old Fort Pownal or to a narrow place above it in order to set up a place to which to retreat. Lovell did not intend to retreat, but every American knew that the British would send naval reinforcement just as soon as possible—any day. Lovell wrote to Massachusetts for more troops. Saltonstall refused to move.

Finally, on August 14, two weeks after the landing, Saltonstall agreed to move if Lovell would attack from the north and the isthmus at the same time. Lovell moved up his troops, gave the signal to Saltonstall, and Saltonstall had to wait for the tide. Then, late in the afternoon, *Diligent* came up the bay, reporting that Commodore George Collier with seven big vessels was becalmed down the bay.

From here, the decline in American fortunes became precipitate indeed. During the rainy night the American troops and most of the guns were evacuated and put aboard the vessels. In the nearly windless morning, with a flood tide, it was impossible to beat down the bay, so Saltonstall ordered the transports to run up the river while he, very slowly in the light air, deployed the fighting ships in a crescent to protect the transports. As the light southerly increased, the British got underway. They had seven vessels: *Blonde, Raisonable* (64), *Greyhound* (28), *Galatea* (24), *Camilla* (24), *Virginia* (18), and *Otter* (14). The Americans had three times as many ships, many times the number of guns, and enough men to board and overwhelm any but perhaps *Raisonable*. Furthermore, the British vessels were very slowly approaching the American crescent so that the American broadsides would rake the British fore-and-aft and the British could reply only with their few forecastle guns. The situation was not yet hopeless.

About 1:00 P.M. on the 15th Saltonstall hoisted the signal for each vessel to run up the river, to save itself as best it could. Not a shot had been fired. The British, bringing the wind with them, followed rapidly.

Defiance tried to round Turtle Head and beat down between Islesboro and the shore. Mowatt sallied out and drove the brig *Defiance,* Commander Edwards, ashore in Sears Cove, where she burned and sank, to be discovered years later.* *Hampden* (22), the New Hampshire vessel, fought the bigger and more heavily gunned *Blonde* (32) all afternoon and finally surrendered at five o'clock, the only American vessel to fire a shot.

The rest of the fleet ran up the river, the naval vessels passing the trans-

* Much of her equipment is now on display in the Maine State Museum in Augusta.

ports as the tide turned against them and the wind died out. In the course of the night and the next two days, the American fleet was driven ashore and burned, despite efforts by Wadsworth, Lovell, and others to organize resistance. Lovell wrote in his diary, "To attempt to give a description of this terrible Day is out of my Power. . . . To see four ships pursuing seventeen sail of Armed Vessels, nine of which were Stout Ships, Transports on fire, Men of War blowing up . . . and as much confusion as can possibly be conceived." Almost the entire force, soldiers and sailors, completely disorganized, set out to walk westward overland to the Kennebec and from there to proceed to Boston by land or sea. They were ill equipped, and many were without food.

Peleg Wadsworth and a few men went down the west shore of the bay to Camden, where they arrived so hungry that they ate raw green peas from the gardens and drank up a churn of buttermilk by a kitchen door. Here Wadsworth planned to make a stand, to fortify the place, call in militia, and put up resistance to British expansion westward. This is, indeed, what he later did after being reinforced by a regiment of Continental troops.

The others at length got home or back to Boston, those that did not starve in the woods. Of course, there was an investigation. Saltonstall received most of the blame, and quite rightly, for he had acted a cowardly and irresolute part. Lovell was acquitted, his mistakes largely due to inexperience. Wadsworth was commended, and Revere, after prolonged hearings and controversy, was acquitted in a backhanded way: ". . . the Court considering that the whole Army was in great Confusion and so scattered and dispersed that no regular orders were or could be given, are of Opinion that Lieut. Colo. Revere be acquitted with equal Honor as the other Officers in the same Expedition." There was scarcely enough honor to go around.

With the British firmly established at Castine, Tories flocked to that refuge, some even coming back from Halifax and Saint John; the architecture of the town today reflects the Tory trend. Local inhabitants for miles around were forced to work on the fort at Castine, especially the patriots, who were identified by Tories. One of these, Jonathan Eaton, being marched along the top of a steep hill at night, broke away from his captors, sprang and rolled and tumbled down the hill through brush and over rocks, ran home, collected some of his household gear, and departed in his boat for Isle au Haut, where he became one of the island's first settlers.

A Tory detachment from Castine burned Jonathan Buck's sawmill and shipyard at Bucksport, and the patriot population of Belfast evacuated the town. John Long, a Camden Tory, guided a British shaving mill into Camden Harbor. Ashore, Leonard Metcalf beat his drum while Andrew Wells bawled orders to an imaginary company of militia. The British backed off to get more men, landed, and charged up the shore. Metcalf fired and ran. Reloading his gun on the run, he tripped and fell.

"There's one of the damned rebels dead," exulted a soldier.

"That's a lie," shouted Metcalf as he disappeared into the brush.

The party burned one house, found Mrs. Ogier pretending convincingly to be sick in her bed so saved her house, burned the town's sawmill. Then they set fire to the gristmill, which held goods belonging to the inhabitants of Belfast, who had had to abandon their homes. A Belfast cripple named Daw put out the fire. The British set it afire again, threatening Daw ferociously; again Daw put it out. The soldiers beat him and set the fire again, and once again Daw put it out. The soldiers gave up, saying, "Well, we'll let it alone as the damned rebels will starve if we burn their mill." About this time the militia mobilized and fired on the British as they retreated.

After the war, John Long was in Ott's tavern in Camden one cold day. Robert Jameson came in and bade Ott build up the fire, as he wanted to burn someone. Ott thought he was joking but built up the fire. Jameson seized Long like a stick of wood and threw him into the fire. He got out, scorched, blistered, and burned. "There," said Jameson, "burn the harbor village again, will you."

Shortly afterwards, Leonard Metcalf met Long in the street, and Long held out his hand. Metcalf refused to shake it, said "Let every dog shake his own paw," and administered a sound drubbing. The local colonel, coming out to quell the disturbance, gave Metcalf a dollar to drink his health and no more was said.

Henry Mowatt, perhaps still unjustly under a cloud at the Admiralty for burning Falmouth, was not promoted and was left at Castine in *Albany* in command of the small naval force there. He sent out James Ryder Mowatt, probably a relation, in a whaleboat in May 1780 to capture what French, Spanish, or rebel vessels he could. He worked to the westward and soon captured the little schooner *Sukey* just east of Boothbay and sent her on her way back toward Castine as a prize. Between Ocean Point and Fishermans Island he caught the big 90-ton sloop *Ranger* under Joseph Reed. He set the crew ashore and, accompanying *Ranger* in his whaleboat, headed east after *Sukey*. Reed quickly assembled neighbors aboard another sloop in Boothbay, set out in pursuit, and caught Mowatt and his crew of nine in the whaleboat in Penobscot Bay. In triumph he returned with them to Boothbay. James Mowatt was so humiliated at being captured by a mere fisherman that he offered, in exchange for his freedom and that of his crew, to return *Sukey* and *Ranger* and throw in the whaleboat, he to remain hostage until the boats were returned. Inasmuch as Boothbay, like other coastal towns, was short of food and ten hungry men were an embarrassment, Reed agreed.

In the winter of 1781 a British armed brig sailed up the Sheepscot, robbed and set fire to Benjamin Sawyer's house on Sawyers Island, burned two sloops in Campbells Cove (now West Harbor Pond), captured the sloop *Patty,* and attacked the Herrington house in Edgecomb.

Although Maine shipbuilding languished during the war, two fine vessels were built for the Navy at Kittery: *Raleigh* and *Ranger*. *Raleigh* was launched on May 21, 1776, and after considerable trouble in finding and mounting suitable guns, sailed for France in company with *Alfred* in midsummer under Captain Thomas Thompson. They ran into the British West Indian convoy but were driven off. Nevertheless, they took several prizes which were sold in France to pay for refitting and resupply. On the way back to America they ran into the British ships *Ariadne* and *Ceres* on March 9, 1777. Rather ineptly, the two American vessels were so far apart that the two British vessels together overwhelmed *Alfred*. *Raleigh* could not face the victors alone and fled.

In September 1778 Captain John Barry took *Raleigh* out of Boston to hunt British vessels to the eastward. The first day out, he saw two British warships, one a two-decker much more powerful than *Raleigh*. The wind was light northwest, so he stood off to the eastward. In the light morning fog there was no enemy in sight, but as the fog dried up, it appeared that the British vessels had gained on *Raleigh* during the night. Barry kept off to the eastward, and all day the two British followed. At sunset *Raleigh* cleared for action, but nothing happened during the night. In the morning again no British were in sight. By this time Barry was closing in on the Maine coast, perhaps in the broken country between Monhegan and Metinic. He stood offshore to the southeast and again saw the British topsails. The wind breezed up northwest, and with a working breeze on the quarter, *Raleigh* headed east and sailed away from her pursuers, going 11 knots by her log, a breathtaking pace for a frigate. However, the wind died away again, as September northwesters do on the Maine coast, and again the big two-decker and her faster consort crept up. Somewhere between Matinicus and Wooden Ball Island, the smaller vessel, *Unicorn* (22), came within range. Barry took in his light sails and attacked. *Unicorn* shot away *Raleigh*'s foretopmast. *Raleigh* pounded *Unicorn* badly, but the bigger vessel, *Experiment* (50), was coming up fast, and *Raleigh* without her foretopmast was at a serious disadvantage. Barry jammed his vessel ashore on Wooden Ball with the idea of getting his men and a gun or two on the steep shore and holding off the British at least until he could burn *Raleigh*. While he was ashore, the junior officer left in command hauled down his flag and surrendered.

At high water, the British got *Raleigh* off the rocks and bought her into the British navy. She participated in the attack on Charleston, South Carolina, in 1780 and was sold out of the navy at the end of the war in 1783.

Ranger (18) had a more distinguished career. She was built at the same Kittery yard as *Raleigh*, was launched in 1777, and sailed for France under Captain John Paul Jones on November 1. On the way she took two prizes, and shortly after her arrival, as France entered the war, *Ranger*'s stars and stripes were saluted by the French, the first time our flag was recognized officially by a foreign government.

Jones rerigged *Ranger* and set out on a cruise around the British Isles. He took four prizes, raided Whitehaven where he burned ships and spiked cannon, and attacked St. Mary's Isle with the intention of capturing Lord Selkirk, who unfortunately happened to be away. He protected Lady Selkirk from his

U.S. Frigate *Raleigh,* her foretopmast shot away, ashore on Wooden Ball Island. *Earle G. Barlow*

crew, who felt it their right to loot the house. He kept their zeal under some control, but they got some valuable silver; Jones later bought it back and returned it. Outside of Carrickfergus he captured HMS *Drake* (20) and put his lieutenant, Simpson, aboard as prizemaster to cruise in company with *Ranger*. For reasons not exactly clear, Simpson returned to France with Jones following in a rage. After considerable political maneuvering, Jones was given *Bonhomme Richard* for another cruise, and Simpson sailed for Portsmouth in *Ranger* on August 21, 1778.

On March 13, 1779, *Ranger, Warren* (32), and *Queen of France* (28) sailed from Boston and intercepted a fleet from New York bound for Georgia. They took *Hibernia, Jason* (20), and five other ships loaded with military supplies.

In July 1779 *Ranger,* still with Simpson in command, sailed with *Providence* (28) and *Queen of France* for the Grand Banks. In the fog they encountered the Jamaica convoy, took eleven prizes, and returned to Boston triumphantly with the richest haul of the war.

On November 23, 1779, *Ranger* sailed with her former consorts *Queen of France* and *Providence* and with the frigate *Boston* to defend Charleston, South Carolina. The British invested the city by land and sea, captured *Ranger,* renamed her *Halifax,* and sold her in October 1781.

Mention should be made of the brig *Hampden,* built in the same Kittery yard as *Ranger* and the same size, 308 tons, about 116 feet long. She carried twenty-two guns and under Captain Pickering took at least four prizes in European waters in 1778–79. In early 1779 she met a thirty-four-gun converted merchantman. Captain Pickering of *Hampden* was killed and the two ships parted, each badly cut up in rigging. On *Hampden*'s return to Portsmouth, she was bought by New Hampshire for the state navy and sent on the Penobscot Expedition, the only vessel in the whole American fleet to put up a fight against the British. She was overwhelmed and captured by the bigger and more heavily gunned *Blonde* (32).

After the Penobscot Expedition in 1779, the seat of war shifted south from New England, and except for shaving-mill raids, blockading British frigates, and a few surviving privateers, there was little activity off the Maine coast. The American navy was practically wiped out, the French navy was eliminated in the Battle of the Saintes in the West Indies, and Britain maintained a tight blockade on the American coast. Although in 1783 she still occupied Castine, New York, Wilmington, Charleston, and Savannah, Britain was quite incapable of controlling the interior, no matter how many battles she won; and a British army under Cornwallis had surrendered to Washington at Yorktown in 1781. Furthermore, Britain was at war with Spain and the Netherlands as well as with France and the United States. British people, including even the Tories in Parliament, were heartily sick of war. A Whig ministry under Lord Shelburne took office and negotiated a peace at Paris in 1783 which, among other provisions, recognized the United States of America and granted it the North American continent north of Florida, south of Canada, and east of the Mississippi River, including the right to dry fish on the shores of Newfoundland.

When news of the peace arrived in Boston, Daniel Tucker of Falmouth—now Portland—picked up a handbill announcing the good news and, in the old schooner *Dolphin* skippered by Father Barton, headed east at once. He arrived in Portland Harbor at low tide early in the morning and ran aground on the flats just off the wharf. The two men fired guns in the air as quickly as they could load. The people, roused from their beds, rushed to the wharf. Tucker continues in his journal: "The word 'peace' was expressed and echoed over and over again with feelings that were unutterable, and by this time the old skipper had paddled me in the float [skiff] to the wharf. It being low water, the people got part of the way down the wharf and took me by the collar and lifted me on to the wharf where I delivered one of the printed handbills to Parson Hall, and he mounted a hogshead and read it to the people. . . . They spent the day in a frolic drinking and firing guns among the houses."

So ended the American Revolution in Maine, but much remained to be done before the United States became a single nation.

NOTES

The story of *Falmouth Packet* and Pirate Jack comes from Ralph Stanley of Southwest Harbor, a many-times-great-grandson of John Manchester and a careful local historian. Part of the information comes from records in Machias, the home of Benjamin Foster, Manchester's partner, and part comes from records in the Mount Desert region, Manchester's home. The British did raid Manchester's house, but how the British got *Falmouth Packet* is speculation. Bunker did hunt her up, cut her out, and bring her back to Norwood Cove. The rest of the tale is authentic. Cruising men who have anchored in Bunkers Cove know how easily a small schooner might be hidden there.

John A. Tulley's *The British Navy in the American Revolution,* William A. Fowler's *Rebels Under Sail,* and *The Navy,* by Fletcher Pratt, are authorities for the general information on privateering. *The Log of the Grand Turks* by Robert E. Peabody tells of her voyage. *Massachusetts Privateers of the Revolution,* by Gardner Wild Allen, after a long, helpful introduction on privateering, lists the vessels bonded during the American Revolution. The Maine vessels can be identified by the home ports of the owners. There may be other Maine vessels whose home ports are not given, but I can be sure of those I have listed.

Anyone interested in privateering and the informal naval aspects of the Revolution and the War of 1812 should read *Joshua Barney,* by Ralph D. Paine.

The account of Paul Reed's career can be found in Francis B. Greene's *History of Boothbay, Southport, and Boothbay Harbor* along with the account of Boothbay's actions to resist the British and the shaving-mill depredations.

The suggestion that Joseph Wheeler was something less than enthusiastic in the cause of liberty was derived from Greene's statement that Mowatt paid him $2 apiece for his sheep and that Mowatt burned Knight's house and not Wheeler's. However, Greene also credits Wheeler with later serving in the army.

The accounts of the raids on Camden came from *The History of Camden and Rockport* by Reuel Robinson. There is much here that I have not used in this volume.

The most complete account of the Penobscot Expedition that I have seen thus far is in *Rise and Fight Again,* by Charles Braulen Flood.

Lovell is given rather less credit than most accounts of the Penobscot Expedition give him, and Paul Revere emerges as nearly as incompetent as Saltonstall, who, *compared to other officers,* looks not as bad as he is painted. Wadsworth comes out of it the best, and his subsequent career as officer in charge of the defense of Maine at Thomaston reflects great credit on him. The story of his capture, his confinement at Castine, and his incredible escape is found in William D. Williamson's *History of Maine,* pages 489–497.

The story of Lieutenant Moore's exploit is here and also in more complete form in the *Collection of the Maine Historical Society,* Series 2, Volume 2.

Mowatt emerges as a capable officer, alert to cooperate both with McLean before the battle and with Collier during and after it. Collier expressed his appreciation of Mowatt's contribution orally but did not even mention Mowatt's name in his report to the Admiralty and sent not Mowatt's *Albany* but another vessel to England to report the victory. This conspiracy of silence against Mowatt by Graves, Collier, and the Admiralty was perhaps because he was made the scapegoat for the burning of Falmouth.

The account of the American Jonathan Eaton who rolled down the hill is found in *A Historical Sketch of the Town of Deer Isle, Maine,* by George L. Hosmer.

Joseph Reed's story is found in Greene's *History.*

In the early days of the war there were many who were lukewarm at best to taking arms against the world's most powerful army and navy. Later, after the British captured Castine, the country east of the Kennebec was a refuge for Tories. The histories of Boothbay, Bristol, Friendship, and Camden make this evident, although the authors denigrate the Tories whenever they can.

The account of the career of *Raleigh* comes from Fletcher Pratt's *The Navy,* from Howard I. Chapelle's *History of the American Sailing Navy,* and from *Sea Power* by Potter and Nimitz. Also *Rebels Under Sail* and *The British Navy in the American Revolution* contributed details and clarification. The identification of Wooden Ball as the island where *Raleigh* was captured comes from the Kittery Historical Society and was printed on the back of a menu at The Weathervane, a restaurant on Route One.

Ranger's career came from the same sources as *Raleigh*'s. It is interesting to note that *Raleigh* was in the British fleet that captured *Ranger* at Charleston, South Carolina.

The account of *Hampden*'s career is from *American Ships of the Colonial and Revolutionary Periods,* by John F. Millar. You never know where you will find a piece that fits neatly into the puzzle.

One may marvel at the inaccuracy of the musket. In battle, a musket was loaded hastily and often with no wad between powder and ball. Also, the ball was considerably smaller than the bore of the barrel, so as the charge drove the ball out, the ball might take a spin according to which side of the barrel it touched as it left. This gave it the same sort of hook that a pitcher gives a baseball. Also the powder charges were not necessarily uniform nor the balls always perfectly spherical. The Kentucky rifle, using a rifled barrel and patched balls, was much more accurate than the smooth-bore musket.

Naval guns were open to the same infirmities as the musket. There was considerable "windage," space between the ball and the barrel. While extreme range of a 4- or 6-pounder might be a mile, one could expect little accuracy over 200 yards, and most naval battles were fought at closer range than that.

Usually the object of a naval battle was to cut up the enemy's rigging in order to make his vessel unmanageable and to spare the hull so that it could be captured intact. For this purpose, bar shot (two cannonballs connected by a bar) and chain shot (two balls chained together) were often used. One skipper used crowbars with deadly effect. As a defense against boarders, grape shot, canister, and langrage were used at close quarters. These were all types of shrapnel, grape shot and canister consisting of musket balls and langrage being a bag of old iron.

In reading accounts of eighteenth- and early-nineteenth-century naval encounters, one must be wary of the word "sloop." In the navy, a sloop was a vessel of about twenty guns on one deck. She was usually ship rigged. A merchant vessel described as a sloop had one mast with a gaff-headed mainsail, one or more jibs, and often a square topsail or even topgallant.

In most carefully written pre-twentieth-century accounts, the word "ship" refers to a three-masted vessel, square rigged on all three masts. The word is seldom used generically, as it is commonly used today, to refer to anything afloat.

SEVENTEEN

Neutral Trade, French Spoliations, and the War of the Barbary Pirates

PEACE BROUGHT no prosperity. In 1783 the United States was not a single nation, but a loose federation of independent states presided over by a gentleman's club in Philadelphia called the Continental Congress. There was no national army, no navy, no police force, no reliable currency. Each state acted in its own interests, imposing its own taxes, even coining its own money. England, partly as an expression of bitterness brought about by the war and partly to force the Colonies to return to the "empire," prohibited trade with the British islands in the West Indies, insisted that goods imported from America to England travel in English ships, forbade British merchants to purchase American-built ships—in short, took every possible measure to choke off American trade.

France and Spain, anxious to protect their own commerce with their own colonies, prohibited other nations, including of course the United States, from trading with their possessions.

On top of these restrictions, privateers turned pirate, and the pirates of the Barbary States (Tripolitania, Tunisia, Algeria, and Morocco) attacked American vessels, knowing very well that no navy would oppose them.

Finally, the Revolutionary War had destroyed most of America's merchant and fishing fleets. A thousand merchant ships had been lost to enemy action. Most of the rest had been laid up where sun, rain, snow, and drying winds had shrunk their planks, opened their seams, and rotted their timbers. A great many seamen had been killed or had died in prison hulks or British prisons. Many of those who returned came home crippled or broken in health and spirit. Moreover, with currency unreliable and many of the formerly wealthy merchants impoverished, there was no capital available with which to build ships and buy cargoes. The French consul in Boston, Massachusetts, reported that whereas 125 ships had been launched annually before the war, only forty-five were launched in 1784 and twelve of these were for French merchants, who were not satisfied with them. From 1785 to 1787 only fifteen to twenty ships were built in Massachusetts, including Maine, annually. One may cast some doubt on these figures because records were not kept meticulously, and it is quite possible that many small vessels were built alongshore and never registered.

Maine pulled itself up by its bootstraps, a slow process. Fishing vessels were built locally, crews organized, and the industry gradually recovered. In four years after the end of the war it was reported that the fishing fleet was back to 80 percent of its pre-war size.

Firewood and lumber, shooks and staves, were still in demand and could be produced with little capital investment. The coastwise trade recovered as the demand for these products increased to the westward.

Overseas trade, however, recovered more slowly.

Despite all of Britain's restrictions, the West Indies badly needed American salt fish, corn, and lumber. Just as badly it needed a market for its sugar, molasses, and rum. Some American skippers still carried British merchantmen's registry papers issued before the war; a cooperative customs officer might not notice the date. Other American vessels entered West Indian ports "in distress," had to sell their cargoes "to pay for repairs," or "to relieve the starving population," and sailed north loaded with West India goods.

Southern states had surpluses of rice, flour, beef, pork, tobacco, and West India goods. With no commerce to protect, they were glad to sell to British vessels that could legally carry these cargoes to England and return with British manufactures. Northern states imposed heavy taxes on imports from Britain, but they imported Southern products and British manufactures from the South in coastwise vessels or overland.

During the war, under the influence of privateering, Americans had learned to build big, fast, and able vessels and to sail them with judgment, skill, and courage. With the old West Indian trade and trade with Britain much diminished, Americans sought and found new markets in northern European ports, on the Northwest coast, in Hawaii, China, the East Indies, Mauritius, and, while the Portuguese were fighting the Barbary pirates and providing naval protection, in Mediterranean ports. This expansion was largely the work of Boston, Salem, and Newburyport merchants. However, Maine yards built many of their ships, and Maine seamen manned them. Maine coasters carried fish and lumber westward to make up parts of their cargoes and traded farther westward to the Middle and Southern states for other products carried in Boston and Salem vessels worldwide. By 1789 at least forty American vessels were east of the Cape of Good Hope at one time.

This process of slow recovery was much accelerated by the ratification of the Constitution in 1788. At last the nation could act with authority and begin to command the attention of other nations. The First Congress in 1789 levied taxes on foreign ships using American ports and imposed import duties on foreign goods entering American ports in foreign ships. The taxes were heavily slanted in favor of American commerce. For instance, an American-built vessel owned by an American firm on entering an American port paid a tonnage tax of 6 cents per ton; whereas an American-built vessel owned abroad paid 30 cents per ton, and a foreign-built and foreign-owned vessel paid 50 cents per ton. Hyson tea landed from an American vessel paid a duty of 20 cents per pound; from a foreign vessel, the duty was 45 cents per pound. American vessels in the coastal trade paid an annual tonnage fee, but foreign vessels, whether coastwise or not, paid the tonnage fee at every port. These regulations, enforced in all states equally, led to a rapid increase in shipbuilding and commerce. In 1789 American ships carried only 23½ percent of our foreign trade; ten years later, American ships carried 88½ percent. In 1789 United States registered tonnage was 201,562; by 1795 it had increased to 747,965 tons. Massachusetts tonnage, including Maine tonnage, increased from 10,000 tons in 1790 to 62,000 tons in 1807. H. C. Adams, quoted in William A. Fairburn's *Merchant Sail,* writes, "The growth of American shipping from 1789 to 1807 is without parallel in the history of the commercial world."

Much of this expansion happened in Maine. Customhouse records unfortunately are fragmentary, and many of the early documents were destroyed in the Portland fires of 1854 and 1866. However, here are a few indications. James Coffin had a busy shipyard on the Saco River from 1784 to 1806. There was another yard at Biddeford Pool and another at Factory Island five miles up the Saco River. Many vessels were built as much as 25 miles from the river and hauled over the snow by ox teams to tidewater. Others were launched into the river far above the falls, floated downstream, hauled out and around the falls on the snow, and relaunched in salt water.

At Bath six vessels were built from 1783 to 1789, the biggest a 178-ton brig. In 1790 alone, five vessels were built, the largest a 254-ton ship.

Wiscasset built seven vessels between the end of the war and 1789. In 1790 and '91, eight were launched. One Wiscasset citizen, Abiel Wood, built and owned eight vessels between the adoption of the Constitution and 1793.

Maine was further helped by the passage on July 4, 1789, of a bill granting a federal subsidy of 6 cents for every quintal of dried fish or barrel of pickled fish exported. In 1792 Congress transferred the bounty to the vessel, granting $1.50 per ton to vessels up to 30 tons engaged in cod fishing for at least four months of the year. Vessels over 30 tons received $2.50 per ton up to a maximum of $170, which would be awarded to a vessel of 68 tons. Three-eighths of the bounty went to the owners and five-eighths to the crew. This stimulated the building of fishing vessels and the export of fish, for fish and timber continued to be, with shipbuilding, Maine's greatest resources.

Not only was fish traded in the West Indies for sugar, rum, and molasses, but it was traded in the Southern states for rice, flour, pork, beef, cloth, cutlery, and foreign manufactured goods. Fish was carried coastwise to Salem and Boston whence it was traded, along with the Southern and West Indian products brought north, to Russia and Sweden for iron, hemp, cotton duck, and linen.

It was basically by trading fish and timber that Salem and Boston assembled their cargoes for the Northwest coast, China, India, and the East Indies, cargoes that traveled frequently in Maine ships with Maine men on the quarterdeck and before the mast.

In 1793 revolutionary France declared war on England, a war that was to last twenty-three years, until 1815, with occasionally an uneasy truce. This war, which merged into the Napoleonic Wars, was a tremendous stimulus to American trade. As Americans saw it, being neutral, they were at liberty to trade with both parties to the war indiscriminately: a neutral flag exempts a ship from capture. However, the belligerents did not see it that way. Each tried to cut off the other's overseas trade in an effort to deprive its adversary of food and munitions. So the navies and privateers of both nations attacked the Americans.

The French declared that American ships had all the rights of French ships, which opened the French West Indies to American ships. The 1792 harvest had been small in France, so France arranged to convoy American ships carrying 24,000,000 pounds of flour from America to France, along with a number of French West Indiamen loaded with sugar and coffee. Britain attacked and defeated the escort in the Battle of the Glorious First of June but failed to intercept the convoy.

Trading with France under the protection of the French navy was very profitable for Americans. Britain had declared breadstuffs and flour to be contraband as well as military supplies, and her navy and privateers seized American ships so loaded and American ships trading with the French West Indies. The British navy confined its seizures more or less to what they saw as legal limits, but the privateers, many of whom had been pirates until very recently, showed no restraint whatever and seized every American ship they could overpower.

The French, hoping to starve out the British, adopted the same tactics. The French ambassador to the United States in 1793, Citizen Genet, even before he had presented his credentials, began making arrangements to fit out and commission privateers in the United States to attack British commerce, this in spite of Washington's declaration of neutrality and Congress's Neutrality Act. Caribbean pirates, "red-bonneted ruffians," were commissioned freely, and by the end of 1794, American shipping was being enthusiastically captured by both sides.

On top of depredations by French and British privateers and naval vessels, the Barbary States, having made peace with Portugal, could now cruise Atlantic waters and in short order captured ten American vessels. It became obvious that if the United States was to do anything but make whining protests to the powerful combatants and the ruthless pirates, a navy was essential. In May 1794 Congress authorized the construction of six frigates, unless peace were made with Algiers. Three were launched in 1797: *United States* (44), *Constellation* (36), and *Constitution* (44).

The two biggest, *United States* and *Constitution,* were the pocket battleships of their day. At 175 feet long, 20 feet longer than most British frigates, more sharply built below the waterline, heavily sparred and by contemporary standards overcanvased, they could outsail any ship of the line and most frigates. Furthermore, they were heavily armed with thirty 24-pounders on the gun deck and twenty 32-pound carronades on fo'c's'le and quarterdeck. Fo'c-'s'le and quarterdeck were so long that for practical purposes they met and formed an upper deck called the spar deck. Although they were rated as forty-four gun vessels, they carried more than their rated armament. Thus being able to outsail more heavily armed vessels and to overwhelm any frigate, in the hands of determined and skillful commanders they were almost invincible.

Neither *Constitution* nor *United States* was ever defeated, although the latter was driven into New London and blockaded by a much superior British force.

Before these vessels were at sea, however, President Washington sent John Jay to England in 1794 to seek an agreement and reconciliation. Britain, finding herself in need of American food, masts, and ship timber, both at home and in her West Indian possessions, agreed to open her West Indian islands to American ships and to pay for those that had been seized. They even acceded to the "Rule of 1756" permitting neutrals to continue trade with either belligerent, which had been allowed before hostilities broke out. This agreement became known as Jay's Treaty. However, Britain continued to insist that food supplies were contraband. This assumed that Britain had the right to stop and inspect any American vessel and to seize her if she were carrying contraband.

The French, angry at America for agreeing to such a treaty and for admitting that food was contraband, sent home the American minister and in January 1798 declared that any vessel carrying any goods coming from England or her possessions was a fair prize. The French continued to seize American ships, and war seemed imminent.

President John Adams, aware that in 1798 we had a navy of only three unfinished frigates and no line-of-battle ships, sent three envoys to Paris to work out an agreement something like Jay's Treaty. The envoys, on presenting their credentials, were informed quite bluntly by Messieurs X, Y, and Z that before any negotiations could begin, sizable payments were expected—*bribes,* in short, sharp language. The shocked American delegates are reported to have replied, "Millions for defense, but not one cent for tribute." They returned home and found Congress and the nation moved to the brink of war. The three frigates were completed, and *President* (44), *Congress* (36), and *Chesapeake* (36) were authorized and laid down. Subsequently, six 74-gun vessels were authorized and about fifty smaller vessels acquired by purchase, principally through the efforts of Secretary of the Navy, Benjamin Stoddart. No war was declared, but one was fought. In July 1798 President Adams ordered United States vessels to seize all French merchantmen and naval vessels met at sea.

Despite this conflict, trade with the belligerents, who needed American products, was extremely profitable. The device commonly employed was the broken voyage. A Portland vessel might carry a cargo of fish and shooks, a neutral cargo, to Guadeloupe and there load a cargo of rum and sugar consigned to Portland, again a neutral cargo. The rum and sugar would be landed on the wharf at Portland, duty paid, and the cargo then loaded again in the same vessel, having thus become not a French but an American cargo. The duty paid would be refunded and the vessel cleared for Hamburg, again a neutral cargo because American. Variations on this involved loading the cargo on another vessel or making up a mixed cargo for export from several incoming cargoes. A vessel bound for London from Wiscasset, for instance, might carry rice from Carolina, French wine that came coastwise from Savannah, sugar from Martinique, and tea from China. The vessel carrying an "American" cargo would not be subject to seizure by the British. Until 1805 this was a reasonably safe way to deal with England, but the French seized everything that floated.

Maine by 1795 had acquired enough capital through fishing, lumbering, and shipbuilding to get into overseas trade in no small way. Maine lumber in the West Indies was worth seven to ten times as much as it was on the banks of the Kennebec. Here are some examples of Maine cargoes:

- In 1795 the schooner *Peggy* of Brunswick, 126 tons, took a cargo of shooks, fish, and soap to Hispaniola.
- In 1796 the 86-ton sloop *Lucy* of Harpswell took a cargo of apples, beef, bread, candles, fish, flour, lard, staves, pork, and tobacco to Barbados. Notice that here we have products of Southern and Middle states being reexported from Maine.
- Also in 1796 *Mayflower* carried pine boards, laths, wood, and masts to Liverpool, England, a strictly Maine cargo.
- In 1798 *Telemachus,* built in Brunswick, left Boston for New Orleans, then a Spanish port, with anchovies, brandy, capers, silk, vinegar, and Spanish wines. She returned with West Indian rum, coffee, meat, silverware, glassware, and tropical fruit, a clear case of a broken voyage with provision for another.
- In 1799 the schooner *Orange* of Brunswick carried cordage, clapboards, fish, flour, nails, iron, and naval stores to Trinidad, again a mixed cargo assembled from a number of previous voyages.

The trade to the Northwest coast for sea otter, thence to Hawaii for sandalwood and China for tea, silks, and chinaware was highly profitable and centered largely in the hands of Boston merchants. The outward cargoes for trade with the Indians of the Northwest were such things as copper, cloth, nails, blankets, kettles, chisels (6-inch lengths of strap iron), shoes, pants, pea jackets, gimlets, buttons, old muskets and blunderbusses. These cargoes were assembled from voyages to Europe and the Southern states, but the foundation of the trade was fish and lumber. The cargoes were carried in small, handy brigs and schooners built in Maine, and the merchants' offices were warmed by Maine firewood.

Both France and England, at home and in their colonies, became heavily dependent on American food. England, through Jay's Treaty, adopted a more or less friendly approach to America in the last years of the eighteenth century, but France, in a desperate effort to deprive Britain of food, paid high prices for American products exported to French possessions and seized every American vessel bound elsewhere. While the vessels we have mentioned profited hugely from neutral trading, all were not so fortunate.

In March 1797 the Maine brig *Dolphin,* having successfully completed a voyage to Martinique and thence to Savannah, sailed for St. Bartholomew with lumber and rice. She was brought to by the French privateer *Serene* and sent to Guadeloupe, which was much in need of food. Her skipper was told that his cargo would be paid for in sugar and coffee and his vessel would not be attacked. A French prize crew was put aboard. The next day the British frigate *Roebuck* stopped *Dolphin,* took her to Antigua, and charged the skipper £472 for the privilege of being recaptured.

In 1798 the schooner *Favorite* of Boothbay sailed for Barbados with lumber and fish, which Captain William Reed traded for a cargo of sugar and rum. Two days out of Barbados on his way home, he was captured by the French privateer *L'Aigle* and taken to St. John (San Juan), Puerto Rico. Before any prize court proceedings, his cargo was seized, put aboard another vessel, and sent off to Philadelphia, where no doubt it brought a good price. Captain Reed persuaded a Captain Scott, then at St. John, to take his papers to Philadelphia and reclaim the cargo. Unfortunately, on the voyage Captain Scott's vessel was captured and the papers lost.

Meanwhile, *L'Aigle*'s crew was refitting their vessel for another cruise and took *Favorite*'s mainmast to replace theirs. *L'Aigle* sailed on another cruise with most of *Favorite*'s crew. *Favorite* was taken to Santo Domingo and condemned by a prize court on the basis that she had been carrying a British cargo. *L'Aigle* was captured by an English frigate. *Favorite*'s crew was liberated; they all found passage back to Maine on different vessels. Captain Reed made his way to Wilmington, Philadelphia, and at last to Boothbay, bearing the condemnation paper given him by the prize court. At last, in 1824, he was paid for vessel and cargo by virtue of that paper.

The topsail schooner *Columbia,* probably from Ebenecook Harbor on the Sheepscot River, homeward bound from Barbados, was captured by a French vessel, sent into Guadeloupe, the cargo condemned, and the vessel freed at a loss to the owners of $16,000. *Columbia* returned to Wiscasset in ballast. The next year, 1800, she was again seized by the French en route to Antigua, captured by the French, recaptured by the English, sent on to Antigua, and charged $10,000 for the privilege of being recaptured.

The experience of Captain William Clifford, Jr., of the schooner *Apollo* was unusual if not unique. In company with the schooner *Venus, Apollo* was captured by a French privateer. Prize crews were put aboard each vessel with orders to sail in company for a French port. Clifford and his mate, Trask, were left aboard *Venus* with a prize crew of five Frenchmen. The next day, the privateer having departed, the two schooners were sailing in close company. The two prizemasters stood at the rails of their respective vessels in cheerful conversation. Clifford noticed that the prizemaster had left his cutlass and pistols on the binnacle. He tossed the pistols down the companionway to Trask, who was standing on the ladder, seized the cutlass, and bade the helmsman put the wheel hard down. The prizemaster shouted to his friend to shoot the Americans. Clifford replied that if he did, Trask would blow daylight right through the prizemaster. The two vessels parted company; Trask and Clifford battened the prize crew below, and headed for home. They met another American vessel, put two of their captives aboard her, and made their way safely back to Wiscasset to a hero's welcome.

In 1800 the United States schooner *Enterprise,* of which we will hear more later, met the brig *Polly,* which had been taken by a French privateer, and a prize crew of eight had been put aboard. The captain, one man, and a boy, who had been left aboard, re-took the vessel, killing two Frenchmen and "disabling" the rest. *Enterprise* put a crew aboard to help the three to anchor the brig in St. Pierre.

Three Sisters, en route from St. Thomas to Wiscasset, was captured by a French privateer and sent on to Wiscasset with twenty-two prisoners from the Frenchman, the crews of eight vessels the privateer had captured previously.

Examples could be multiplied, but these are sufficient to show that Maine fish and lumber brought in goods and capital to finance a very profitable neutral trade and that from 1798 until 1801 the French attacked this trade with determination.

The new American navy responded. In the battles of Cape St. Vincent, Camperdown, and the Nile, the British navy had dealt the French navy such heavy blows that the French had few naval vessels to spare for the defense of their Caribbean possessions. The Americans had eight new frigates, including *Boston* (28) and *Essex,* built by popular subscription in Boston, the fast schooners *Enterprise* and *Experiment,* and a number of converted merchantmen. Furthermore, they had the very valuable assistance of British naval bases at Dominica and St. Kitts, of another at Cap François, Haiti, then under Toussaint L'Ouverture, and of the Spanish base at Havana. They also had the sympathetic cooperation of the British West Indies squadron, a great help in establishing procedures and traditions in a new navy.

Enterprise, in one cruise, captured five privateers, dismasted a twelve-gun lugger, and recaptured eleven American merchantmen. *Boston* (28) captured *Berceau* (24), convoys were organized and protected, pirates and privateers were captured or kept down, and finally, in 1799 *Constellation* (36) under Commodore Truxton defeated *Insurgente* (40) in a gale of wind off Nevis and went on the next year to beat *Vengeance* (50) into a helpless wreck.

Napoleon Bonaparte, now First Consul of France, saw no point in continuing a conflict that was driving the United States into closer association with Britain and depriving the French of much-needed food. The victor of Marengo and in control of western Europe, in 1802 he concluded the brief Peace of Amiens with Britain. He also made concessions to the United States to end hostilities at sea. The treaty of 1778 by which France had joined the United States in the American Revolution was annulled, and the French decree of 1798 making a fair prize any neutral vessel that had had any dealings with Britain or a British colony was canceled. American ship owners' claims against the French government for vessels and cargoes confiscated were admitted but unsettled. In 1803 the United States government agreed to pay them as part of the price of the Louisiana Purchase.

The war was over. The new American navy had shown that it could sail and fight in a way to command respect at sea and, temporarily, neutral trade proceeded while France and England appeared to be drifting toward peace.

About the time that peace was made with France, new work for the United States Navy boiled up in the Mediterranean. The United States had been paying tribute to the Barbary nations and ransoming American citizens fortunate enough to attract their nation's attention. The going rate was $2,000 for a captain, $1,500 for a mate, and $725 for a sailor. Many who could not find the ransom died in the mines or the galleys.

Maine ships and Maine men suffered their share. The sloop *Squirrel* of Saco was captured in 1783 by an Algerian corsair. Captain Alexander Paine and his crew were offered two choices: become Mohammedan or become slaves. They chose the latter. Captain Paine and his mate were sent to the mines, the crew to the galleys. With no shelter, scant clothing, and a diet of bran bread and goat meat, they toiled at the oars until 1787 when a French frigate exchanged broadsides with the galley, slammed alongside, and boarded. The Algerians, seeing that they were defeated, fell upon the galley slaves with bayonet and cutlass, killing without mercy until they were overrun by the French boarding party. Seven of *Squirrel*'s crew of eighteen survived, were taken to Bordeaux by the French and sent on to New York, whence they walked home to Saco, arriving in 1790. The skipper and mate did not make it. In September 1800 *George Washington* (24) arrived in Algiers with the annual tribute, was commandeered by the Dey of Algiers and sent to Constantinople to deliver the Algerian tribute to the Sultan. While Jefferson was considering what to do about this, the Bashaw of Tripoli chopped down the pole flying the American flag in front of the United States consulate—a declaration of war. He needed a war because he had just made peace with Sweden and needed occupation for his corsairs lest they turn on him. President Thomas Jefferson accepted the challenge. He had written earlier, "Tribute or war is the usual alternative of these Barbary pirates. Why not build a navy and decide on war?"

Commodore Dale was sent to the Mediterranean with frigates *President, Philadelphia,* and *Essex* and the schooner *Enterprise*. Dale accomplished little and was relieved in 1802 by Morris, who, with five frigates, did little more and appealed to Congress for shoal-draft craft. Before these could be built, Morris was recalled and a Portland man, Captain Edward Preble, was appointed commodore. He had only two frigates, *Constitution* and *Philadelphia,* but with them accomplished far more than his predecessors.

Preble was a Maine man, born in Portland in 1761, son of Jedidiah Preble, a veteran of Louisbourg. Edward was sent to Dummer Academy in South Byfield, Massachusetts. Showing convincing evidence that he was unlikely to succeed as a scholar, he went to sea on a letter-of-marque vessel to Bordeaux. He so distinguished himself on that voyage that he was offered a commission as lieutenant aboard the Massachusetts ship *Protector* (26). When she beat the British privateer *Admiral Duff* (36), Preble acted so coolly in charge of the main-deck guns that when his captain, George Little, was given the new Massachusetts vessel *Winthrop,* he took Preble with him as first lieutenant. *Winthrop* captured a tender to a British brig moored in Castine Harbor after the Penobscot Expedition. Little, Preble, and forty men sailed the tender up the harbor at night and slid alongside the brig. Preble with fourteen seamen leaped aboard, but before Little and the others could join them, the tide carried the tender away, leaving Preble's party heavily outnumbered.

"Do you need more men?" shouted Little.

"No, we already have too many," shouted back Preble in the heat of battle. "We stand in each other's way." The fifteen overpowered the crew of the brig and triumphantly sailed her out from under the guns of the fort.

After the American Revolution, Preble became captain of a merchant vessel, and in the French war was first a lieutenant in *Constitution* and then captain of *Essex* protecting American vessels in the East Indies. He was not high on the captains' list in the new navy when made a commodore of a fleet of three frigates, *Constitution, Philadelphia,* and *John Adams,* two brigs, and three schooners. He was not a popular commander. After meeting the captains of his fleet, he burst out: "They have given me a pack of boys." However, to have been one of "Preble's boys" was in later years the highest recommendation.

In 1803 Preble was a crusty veteran of forty-two, harsh, demanding, not given to praise and encouragement. His crew disliked and resented him. However, one incident that lit up the sky and has been remembered verbatim for nearly two centuries changed their minds.

One dark, windy night as *Constitution* approached Gibraltar on her way to take command of the Mediterranean fleet, Preble became aware of another vessel close by to windward, just a looming shape in the dark. Without a sound, he had *Constitution* cleared for action, then hailed the shadowy stranger: "What ship is that?"

The stranger answered with the same question, and neither captain gave a clear answer. Preble hailed: "I now hail for the last time. If you do not answer, I will fire a shot into you."

"If you do, I will answer with a broadside."

Preble then hailed once more: "What ship is that?"

"This is his Britannic Majesty's ship *Donegal,* eighty-four guns, Sir Richard Strachan, an English commodore. Send your boat on board."

Replied the crusty Down-Easter, leaping on the rail: "This is the United States ship *Constitution,* forty-four guns, Edward Preble, an American commodore, who will be damned before he sends his boat on board any vessel." And to his crew, "Blow your matches, boys."

The stranger was not an eighty-four-gun ship of the line but a thirty-two-gun British frigate whose captain had been stalling for time in which to get cleared for action. He sent his boat aboard *Constitution,* and as the two nations were not at war, the vessels parted amicably. However, *Constitution*'s crew knew that they had a fighting commodore with confidence enough in them and in his ship to take on a vessel of at least twice his power.

Having arrived at Gibraltar, Preble took command at once. He found that *Philadelphia* under Captain Bainbridge had captured a Moroccan corsair which had, contrary to treaty, taken a Salem merchant vessel. He mustered his fleet, sailed at once to Tangier, cleared for action in front of the town, and cowed the Dey into submission.

While the details were being arranged, Preble sent *Philadelphia* to Tripoli to blockade that city at the time when grain ships were expected. In chasing one of these close inshore, *Philadelphia,* traveling at 8 knots, fetched up hard on a ledge. When a vessel weighing thousands of tons committed to forward motion at 8 knots strikes something as immovable as a ledge, she runs herself right up on top of it, her forward half well out of water.

Bainbridge lightened his vessel by throwing his guns overboard, pumping out his fresh water, even cutting away his foremast. He set out anchors and hove away in vain. Tripolitan gunboats fired into his stern, the tide dropped, heeling *Philadelphia* so that the few guns she had left could hit only sea or sky, and Bainbridge surrendered.

The Tripolitans got *Philadelphia* off the ledge a few days later when a high tide and a gale piled water against the shore, and they moored her under the guns of their fort.

Preble had lost a powerful ship, and the Tripolitans had gained one. *John Adams* had gone home, so it was *Constitution* and five small vessels against *Philadelphia* and numerous corsairs. Preble, obviously, should have retired to Gibraltar or Malta and sent home for reinforcements, especially as the season of frequent gales was coming on when naval activity ordinarily was suspended. This, however, was not the style of Preble and his "boys."

One of the latter, Lieutenant Stephen Decatur, commanded the schooner *Enterprise* in Preble's squadron. She was built in Baltimore in 1799, with a hull form quite different from the usual merchant ship in that it was more V-bottomed than round-bottomed, was finer forward than the apple-cheeked New Englanders, and had a fine run which left the water astern without a ripple. In the French war she had proven herself fast and lucky. In her, Decatur had already taken one corsair in the Mediterranean and now took another, *Mastico,* loaded with female slaves. Preble, knowing he could not cut out *Philadelphia* under the guns of the fort, renamed *Mastico* as *Intrepid,* put Decatur in command with a selected crew of volunteers, and sent him into Tripoli to burn *Philadelphia.* The story has been told elsewhere in detail, but suffice it to say that *Intrepid* drifted up the harbor looking like any other local vessel, tied up alongside *Philadelphia,* rushed her, set her afire, and departed without losing a man. Lord Nelson, the British fleet, and Congress made much of Decatur. Preble growled that the boys had done only what was expected of them.

In the spring Preble was back, keeping up the pressure, reinforced with six gunboats and two bomb ketches loaned by Ferdinand IV, King of the Two Sicilies. Preble sent in his gunboats under the protecting fire of *Constitution,* his brigs, and his schooners, while the bomb ketches dropped mortar shells over the walls of the city. The Dey's gunboats came out intending to board the American vessels, for these pirates were considered the world's fiercest hand-to-hand fighters with pistol and scimitar. They found themselves boarded and overwhelmed by Yankee seamen, as handy with cutlass, pike, and pistol as any pirate.

Lieutenant Trippe boarded a corsair with ten men. Before he could be supported, the vessels parted and Trippe, although badly wounded, personally slew the pirate captain, and the demoralized pirate crew surrendered. Decatur took two gunboats, one in revenge for the death of his brother, shot by a pirate captain who had previously surrendered.

The other corsairs retreated under the guns of their fort, and the American gunboats withdrew to *Constitution.* Decatur boarded her and reported to Preble, "Sir, I bring you three gunboats." Preble retorted sourly, "Aye, and why did you not bring me more?" He stood a moment and went below, sending a message for Decatur to attend him. When some time later other officers peeped into the silence of the commodore's cabin, they saw both men, seated side by side, in tears.

Day after day, whenever the weather served, Preble hammered away at the fort and the city. The Dey kept lowering his ransom price for *Philadelphia*'s crew, but Preble refused every offer, drove the defenders from their guns, and bombarded the city. *John Adams* rejoined the squadron from America, bringing news that *President, Congress, Constellation,* and *Essex* were on the way. Preble, with weight of metal enough to bring the Dey to surrender, was not one to stand idle waiting for help. He loaded *Intrepid* with 15,000 pounds of powder and sent her into the harbor at night manned by Lieutenant Somers, Lieutenant Wadsworth (another Portland man), Midshipman Israel, and ten other volunteers. They were to get close to the Tripolitan gunboat fleet, light the fuse, and depart, producing an explosion that would wreck the gunboats, the fort, and half the city. However, before she reached a place where the explosion would be effective, *Intrepid* blew up with a tremendous concussion, killing everyone aboard. A Turk who was ashore in Tripoli at the time reported to Ambassador Eaton that two big row galleys had come alongside *Intrepid* and gone up with her when Somers chose rather to blow her up than allow her to be captured.

A few days later the new frigates joined the *Constitution* with Commodore Barron in command. As he was senior to Preble, Congress had ordered Preble home. After Preble had handed over command to Barron, Decatur, now a captain, presented Preble with a scroll reading: "We, the undersigned officers of the squadron late under your command, cannot, in justice, suffer you to depart without giving you some small testimony of the very high estimation in which we hold you as an officer and a commander."

Preble was hailed at home as a hero in 1804. Congress voted him a sword and a gold medal, President Jefferson offered him a seat in the Cabinet, British guns saluted him, and the Pope wrote the President that Preble "in forty days has done more for the cause of Christianity than the most powerful nations in ages."

Commodore Barron was no Preble. However, with the help of Ambassador Eaton, a tough Irish marine named O'Bannon and seven other marines, the jealous brother of the Dey, and a motley collection of North Africans who invaded Tripoli from Egypt, Barron forced the surrender of Tripoli in 1805.

After receiving the surrender and liberating *Philadelphia*'s crew, Barron left for home almost at once, leaving in command Rodgers, one of Truxton's former lieutenants. When the Bashaw of Tunis suddenly demanded higher tribute in defiance of a signed treaty and threatened to attack American ships, Rodgers lined up his fleet before the city, cleared for action. After protests and squirmings, the Bashaw backed off and the War of the Barbary Pirates was over.

Edward Preble, that demanding, tough, vinegary son of Maine, had been the one man without whom the war could not have been won. His determination, in spite of pain and sickness, his insistence on leaving nothing undone to ensure success, his high expectations of his "boys" and the sense of duty and discipline which he instilled by precept and example, not only won the war but gave the new United States Navy a pride, an esprit de corps, a feeling of being winners that has lasted to this day. That is why we include so detailed an account of one Maine man's contribution in a maritime history of Maine.

NOTES

As usual, Williamson's *History of Maine* provides a brief factual background. However, *Merchant Sail,* by William Armstrong Fairburn, provides a great deal of detailed information. Volume I contains the historical outline of the period, and Volume V lists vessels built in various ports year by year with occasional colorful notes. Fairburn admits that the lists are not complete, but certainly they give important indications.

Fletcher Pratt's *The Navy* has excellent chapters on the French war and especially on Commodore Preble. George W. Rice's *Shipping Days of Old Boothbay* has specific incidents concerning Boothbay vessels. *The Skolfields and Their Ships,* by Reynolds and Martin, also is helpful. Potter and Nimitz's *Sea Power* is a concise naval history useful in supporting doubtful statements found elsewhere. Samuel Eliot Morison's classic *Maritime History of Massachusetts* was also useful, although he pays little attention to the District of Maine. William Hutchinson Rowe's *Maritime History of Maine* is a valuable reference and a source of specific detail. Occasionally authorities disagree, and this author does the best he can to resolve questions of doubt, but time does not serve to chase every reference back to disagreeing primary sources.

Most of the stories of neutral trading involve captures of American vessels by French or English privateers. It should be understood that while many were captured, the ones that got through—most of them—made outrageous profits. This fact attracts little attention from historians, but if the trade had not been almost immorally profitable, few would have taken the chance of capture, confiscation, and imprisonment.

As far as I have been able to discover, Maine merchants were not heavily into the Northwest coast–China trade or the Mauritius–East Indies trade, but certainly Maine ships were to be met in Atlantic, Mediterranean, Baltic, and Caribbean ports, whence came cargoes to fit out the Boston and Salem ventures to the Orient.

There seems little evidence that Maine had serious involvement with the slave trade, although there are two instances of it described in Chapter 19.

The schooners *Enterprise* and *Experiment* were of the early Baltimore Clipper type with very considerable deadrise, sharp bows, and enormous spreads of sail. Each carried not only a gaff foresail but also a square foresail, fore topsail, and fore topgallant, with a gaff topsail on the mainmast. *Experiment* was sold to the Swedish navy, but *Enterprise* had a long and successful career in the United States Navy. In 1813 she defeated the British *Boxer,* even though her wings had been clipped. More of this in the next chapter.

Preble in *Protector* and *Winthrop* tangled with Mowatt in Castine. Mowatt had burned Preble's house in Portland in 1775. The account of Preble's confrontation with the British frigate off Gibraltar is quoted in every book about Preble or the Barbary pirates. Potter and Nimitz give the source as the *Autobiography of Commodore Charles Morris, U.S. Navy.* Morris was an eye-witness. Our account of Preble's campaign against the Barbary pirates is shamefully abbreviated.

The Barbary pirates are termed pirates legitimately. The rulers of the Barbary States maintained a series of wars against other naval powers and commissioned their corsairs to capture enemy ships. In this sense they were privateers. However, they did not confine their attacks to the designated enemy but attacked any ship whose government had not paid tribute to the Bey, Dey, Sultan, or Bashaw in question. Even then, they occasionally overstepped. The Moroccan under *Philadelphia*'s lee in Gibraltar had taken a Salem vessel and claimed he was not commissioned but acting on his own. "Then he is a pirate," said Bainbridge. "Hang him instanter." The Moroccan then produced a commission from the Sultan issued in violation of his treaty with the United States. Preble treated him as described in the text.

The note about the Turk who saw row galleys alongside *Intrepid* before she blew up occurs in Fletcher Pratt's *The Navy.*

EIGHTEEN

Embargo and the War of 1812

THE BRIEF RESPITE in the Napoleonic Wars begun at the Peace of Amiens in March 1802 lasted just long enough for Napoleon to consolidate his previous gains and have himself elected First Consul. In May 1803 the war resumed. England's powerful navy blockaded the French navy in Brest and Toulon, while Napoleon's powerful armies dominated Europe and seemed to be preparing for an invasion of England; this was impossible, however, without control of the sea. Thus, neither enemy could get at the other.

England tried to break the deadlock by allying herself with Russia, Austria, and Sweden in the Third Coalition. Spain joined France, and Napoleon moved to consolidate the French and Spanish fleets to attack England. But the efforts of both parties failed. England under Nelson in October 1805 defeated the united French and Spanish fleets at Trafalgar. The remaining French ships were blockaded at Brest, and England retained control of the seas. Napoleon defeated the armies of the coalition at Ulm and Austerlitz, and went on to ally himself with Czar Alexander and become master of all Europe while the English fleet cruised the Channel, blockading the French fleet, and made ineffective raids on European coasts.

England's strongest weapon now was starvation. Britain's Orders in Council declared a blockade of all Europe. There was no longer any such thing as "neutral," for practical purposes. All cargoes to Napoleonic Europe were contraband. Winston Churchill wrote: "The British blockade wrapped the French Empire and Napoleonic Europe in a clammy shroud. No trade, no coffee, no sugar, no contact with the East, or with the Americans! And no means of ending the deadlock!"

Napoleon put his brother Joseph on the Spanish throne and seized Portugal, thus controlling the entire coast of Europe from the Baltic to the Adriatic. Through the Berlin and Milan decrees of 1806 he declared Britain blockaded and shut off all British trade with Europe.

In 1805 the *Essex* case decided by a British court destroyed the "broken voyage" fiction as described in the last chapter whereby a neutral American vessel, forbidden from carrying sugar from the French West Indies to Amsterdam, could land the cargo in Portland, Maine, pay duty, reload it, receive a refund on the duty, and proceed to Amsterdam as carrying an American cargo. After the *Essex* decision, a vessel on such a voyage was a fair prize.

Americans were thus shut off by proclamation from trade with the West Indies, Britain, and all of Europe. New Englanders, Maine men in particular, were not given to obeying paper proclamations and continued the trade as best they could despite the danger of being captured by French privateers and British naval vessels. The American vessels that got through made such handsome profits that merchants could afford considerable losses. In 1798, for instance, Portland handled 5,000 tons of shipping; in 1807, 39,000 tons. In 1806 Portland importers paid $342,909 in duties.

This profit, however, was not without its human price. Britain, absolutely dependent on her navy to enforce a blockade of the French fleet and a commercial blockade of all Europe, needed not only ships but men to man these ships. The British navy was a hard master. Men died of sickness, wounds, and battle casualties. Food at sea was scant and poor, and even water was rationed. Shore leave was a dream, and there was no discharge. In many ships discipline was savage, enforced by flogging with a cat-o'-nine-tails, an instrument of torture comparable to the Russian knout. It is scarcely surprising that desertion was common, although not easy. The comparatively better conditions in the American navy or the American merchant service led many a British seaman to slide down an anchor line on a quiet night and swim to a nearby American vessel.

To replace men lost by sickness, battle, and desertion, the British navy sent press gangs into British waterfront towns and swept up whatever men they could catch: seamen, tailors, farmers, or shepherds. It made no difference. They were all cannon fodder. Also, the British navy, supported by Orders in Council, adopted the policy of stopping American ships, mustering the crews, and seizing naval deserters or any British subjects. Their methods of determining British citizenship were crude. Almost any stout American seaman could be quickly identified as a British subject. On one Maine vessel: "Where are you from?" "Wells" (Maine). "I *thought* you looked like a Welshman." And off he went to the British navy.

The American brig *Ceres* had all but her master, mate, and one man impressed by a British warship.

In 1803 Joseph Emerson was impressed from the Boothbay schooner *Harriet* in St. Kitts. A year later, when the warship again visited St. Kitts, Emerson and two others slipped down the anchor line at night, swam ashore, climbed a wall topped with broken glass, and hid in the hills. When their ship left, they came down and, with the help of a friendly local farmer, arranged passage in a Portsmouth brig. After dark they climbed the wall again, swam off to the brig, and were taken home.

In 1804 Silvanus Snow of Boothbay was impressed aboard HMS *Zea-*

land, was transferred to *Acteon,* was captured by the French, taken to Spain, exchanged as a British seaman, and put back aboard a British naval vessel. He fought at Trafalgar and served in various vessels until 1811. Finally at Minorca he escaped and came home to Boothbay in a Nobleboro vessel.

The British navy sent a squadron to patrol outside New York. Their activity is described by Midshipman Hall serving aboard *Leander* (50): "Every morning at daybreak we set about arresting the progress of all the vessels we saw, firing off guns to the right and left to make every ship that was running in heave to or wait until we had leisure to send a boat on board. . . ." On April 25, 1806, *Leander* fired a shot across the bow of the coastwise sloop *Richard.* Captain Pierce hove to. *Leander* fired two more shots, one of which decapitated the helmsman, John Pierce, the captain's brother. Captain Whitby of *Leander* declared later that it was all a joke—he had meant to fire high and merely frighten the crew of *Richard.* New York and then the nation was aroused. Whitby was indicted for murder. President Jefferson ordered his arrest if he were ever found in American jurisdiction, and closed American ports to British warships, then apologetically explained to the British that he was compelled to do this in order to prevent future incidents that might lead to war. Captain Whitby was tried by a British court-martial, acquitted, and promoted to command a 74.

In June 1807 USS *Chesapeake* had aboard three Americans who had been impressed aboard HMS *Melampus* and who had escaped. The British minister in Washington demanded their return. *Chesapeake* refused and shortly afterwards sailed for the Mediterranean, ill prepared for war, her decks cluttered and her guns unready. HMS *Leopard* met her off the Virginia capes with an order from the British admiral to search *Chesapeake* for deserters. Captain Barron refused. *Leopard* fired three broadsides into *Chesapeake.* Unready for battle in a time of peace, Barron fired one shot and struck his flag. A British lieutenant came aboard and seized the three men in question and one other. Two of the three were condemned to be flogged through the fleet, a punishment to which death might be preferable. The sentence was countermanded from England, but the third man had been immediately hanged as a deserter.

The United States made a whining protest to which England replied that she regretted the score of people killed and wounded by *Leopard*'s fire but could not permit the desertion of her seamen in time of war. In impotent rage, the U.S. Navy fired Barron for not having his ship ready for battle—not his fault—and authorized the construction of 188 shoal-draft gunboats.

Had President Thomas Jefferson called for war in 1807, he might have had enthusiastic support. Instead he resorted to an alternative to war. If the combatant navies were to seize our ships and impress our sailors, they could damned well starve. In December 1807 Jefferson pushed through Congress a total embargo. No American ships whatever were to clear for any foreign ports.

This stirred up a hornet's nest in every New England port. Commerce was the basis not only of prosperity but of survival in New England. In every port from Kittery to Eastport, ships were laid up, rigged down, and rotted as they swung idly at their moorings.

The embargo did not apply to coastal trade and fishing, but with no foreign market for fish, that industry collapsed and even farmers and lumbermen were thrown out of work.

In January 1808 sixteen ships, twenty-seven brigs, and a number of schooners and sloops were laid up at Bath. General King recollected in 1825 that in 1808 he had had five ships and four brigs, loaded and ready to sail, swinging at moorings, a loss of $5,558 per month. While one can feel very sorry for General King, one's grief is somewhat relieved by the information that his ship *Reunion* had earned her full cost on each of three successive voyages to England before the embargo took effect.

Portland's five principal merchants lost their fortunes. The bank failed, and import duties fell from $342,909 in 1807 to $4,369 in 1808. Ships were laid up, and grass grew on the wharves.

Off Wiscasset in February 1809 lay thirty-two loaded vessels.

Castine had a ropeworks, a tannery, saw and grist mills, a sail loft, and a booming business in fish and groceries, all wrecked by the embargo and subsequent British occupation.

The stated purpose of the embargo was to protect American merchants and sailors from capture of their cargoes and impressment into the British navy. However, this purpose was stated by farmers from the South who had never seen salt water and had little understanding of the total dependence of the Eastern states on commerce. The effect was to ruin the merchants and to leave the sailors unemployed ashore.

Fishermen, farmers, and lumbermen with no market for their products felt the pinch sharply as the prices of such staples as molasses, rum, tea, woolen cloth, cutlery, and other manufactured goods rose out of sight. New England became strongly Federalist in opposition to Jefferson and the Republicans of the South. There was even talk of secession.

It is scarcely to be wondered at, then, that there should be efforts made to evade the embargo and escape to sea. The following incidents are illustrative of the determination and ingenuity if not the patriotism of Maine seamen.

The sloop *Ploughboy* of Bangor cleared from Newport in October 1808 for Castine on a legitimate coastwise voyage. However, she was "blown off" all the way to Antigua, finally completing her coastwise voyage to Castine in February 1809.

Some citizens of Bath, feeling that the embargo was an unconstitutional law depriving them of the use of their property without due compensation, loaded the 342-ton ship *Sally* with lumber and ran by the fort at Popham, manned by local militia and built, ironically, to prevent Americans from leaving the river rather than to defend it against invasion. The mouth of the Kennebec is very narrow, less than one-quarter mile wide at the fort, and it would seem that passing it with impunity was practically impossible. Remarkably, *Sally* suffered only minor rigging damage in running by the fort; it has been suggested that the guns of the fort could have been aimed more precisely. On the voyage to England, *Sally*'s crew mutinied, well aware that she had no clearance papers and was on an illegal voyage. The captain mollified their rage with a note for $50 for each man. On approaching the British Isles, he put ashore supercargo* William Richardson who approached the British authorities. When *Sally* arrived at London, the crew were arrested for mutiny but released on payment of $50 each. The cargo was sold at a handsome profit.

The 52-ton sloop *Adoniram* sailed out of the Kennebec River with a partial cargo of fish and hove to off Monhegan where she met the schooner *Washington* with 100 barrels of flour. *Adoniram* stood off and on for a week while boats from Boothbay brought out 200 quintals of fish, and then she bore off for Demerara, where both vessel and cargo were sold for cash.

In response to these escapes, the Collector of Customs at Bath fitted out a revenue cutter armed with six 6-pounders to patrol the Kennebec.

The brig *Mary Jane,* armed with four 4-pounders, was loaded for the West Indies, with spars rigged over her sides to repel possible boarders. An audacious skipper from Bristol was put in command. He added twelve extra Bristol men to the crew, including Peter Carey, a gigantic mulatto. On the night of January 2, 1809, with a strong northerly wind and no moon, *Mary Jane* stood down the river, the face of every man but Carey's blacked as disguise. The revenuers found one of their boats scuttled, but the cutter ranged alongside *Mary Jane* and fired a broadside. *Mary Jane* replied with her 4-pounders. For several miles the two vessels charged through the night down the twists of the tide-scoured river, the scene lit by the lurid flashes of the guns. *Mary Jane* outsailed the cutter, ran by the fort, and emerged with a hole in her fore topsail and some rigging damage. No one in either vessel was hurt. The twelve Bristol men were set ashore at Harmons Harbor on the Sheepscot, and *Mary Jane* was off to Demerara, where she and her cargo were sold for cash at a fine profit.

Waldoboro, which had 18,214 tons of registered shipping, found business so poor that even cordwood was not salable to the westward because people had not the money to buy it. The prices of foreign goods put them out of reach, and smuggling was rife. The Collector of Customs at Waldoboro fitted out the sloop *Income* of Bremen to cruise against smugglers and brought in a sloop loaded with rum.

A Camden skipper got his vessel out of Penobscot Bay with a cargo for the West Indies, sold it at a good profit for cash, and returned in ballast, with the gold coins concealed in holes bored in his rail stanchions and plugged. There was no law prohibiting a vessel's entering without cargo.

*A supercargo is the business manager of a merchant ship, responsible for selling the cargo and buying a return cargo.

At Eastport the legal coastal trade brought in 30,000 barrels of flour in one week and 150,000 barrels in two months. It was estimated that much more than that was actually accumulated in Eastport warehouses and on the wharves. Of course, the residents of Eastport could not eat anything like that quantity of flour. It "leaked" across the border to Campobello and Indian (now Deer) Island at a freight rate of $1 per barrel.

The most interesting leakage in the embargo was in New York. The Honorable Punqua Wingchong, described as a Chinese mandarin, applied to President Jefferson to permit him to charter a vessel to take him back to China where the "funeral obsequies" of his grandfather required his "solemn attention." He was permitted to charter John Jacob Astor's 427-ton ship *Beaver,* to take with him numerous attendants and $45,000 in hard money or merchandise. *Beaver* was also permitted to bring back to New York a cargo of Chinese goods. The proceeds of this voyage brought Mr. Astor an astronomical profit in a city starved for tea, silk, and porcelain. It later appeared that the distinguished mandarin was not of Chinese ancestry at all but was a clerk in Astor's office.

Not only was the embargo ineffective as a means of persuading France and England to recognize America's right to free trade, it ruined many New England merchants and gave British merchants a free hand in the West India and China trades and even in trade with southern United States ports. Furthermore, it strengthened the weakening Federalist party against Jefferson and the Republicans. Federalists regarded Napoleon as the real enemy and wanted to support England against him. One reason was that with Paris, Amsterdam, and Hamburg under Napoleon's control, the only remaining center of international banking was London. Most New England merchants dealt with the Bank of England, depositing proceeds there in return for bills of exchange. One does not go to war with his banker. Feeling ran so high that almost every coastal town in Maine sent town meeting resolutions to Washington urging repeal of the embargo. Finally, on March 3, 1809, his last day as President, Jefferson signed the repeal of the embargo act. The new blockhouse at Edgecomb celebrated the occasion by firing its guns for the first time in salute.

President James Madison substituted for the embargo in June 1809 the Non-Intercourse Act, permitting trade worldwide except with France and England. This was followed up by Macon's Bill #2, which permitted free trade but stated that when either France or England removed its restrictions, the United States would forbid trade with the other. Very profitable trade resumed at once. As of November 1, 1810, Napoleon announced the revocation of the Berlin and Milan decrees against neutral trade with England. Madison agreed to shut off trade with Britain in ninety days. But Napoleon continued to seize American ships and cargoes, a fact which Madison ignored. On March 2, 1811, trade with England was forbidden.

Illegal trade with England continued under British license, and impressment also continued. Early in 1811 the British frigates *Guerriere* and *Melampus* were sent to cruise off New York. They seized any vessel that they thought might be carrying a cargo to a French port and impressed whomever they chose. The captain of *Guerriere* was particularly arrogant, but he had no corner on that quality. He stopped *Spitfire* on a voyage from Portland to New York and impressed John Deguyo, an American citizen. Commodore John Rodgers in *President* (44) was sent to get him back. As Rodgers stood offshore late on the murky afternoon of May 16, 1811, he saw ahead of him a vessel that by the depth of her topsails he recognized as a British naval vessel. About 8:00, after dark, he came up with her and hailed, "What ship is that?"

The strange vessel replied with a shot that struck *President*'s mainmast. Rodgers fired three guns. The stranger fired a broadside. Rodgers returned a broadside, and the action became hot. However, it soon appeared that the stranger was inferior to *President,* and she ceased fire. Rodgers ceased fire. The stranger loosed another broadside, and Rodgers pounded the vessel until the captain hailed that he was sinking. Rodgers ceased fire and found that it was not *Guerriere* whom he was fighting but the equally arrogant captain of *Little Belt* (22). Rodgers stood by until morning when *Little Belt* under jury rig limped off on a course to Halifax.

Americans felt that *Little Belt* got just what she asked for and that *Chesapeake*'s insult had been to some extent avenged. Britain's protest was muffled by Madison's discovery of a British plot to dismember the United States.*

The British government was now under considerable pressure. The winter of 1811–12 had been unusually severe, and both food and fuel were short in Britain. Wellington was winning in Spain but draining Britain of money, food, and munitions. British manufacturers, shut out of Europe by Napoleon's Continental System, had no markets but America and that was shut off by the Non-Intercourse Act—although the Act, like all paper dams, leaked somewhat. Unemployment was high and riot threatened. By the spring of 1812 it was time to repeal the Orders in Council and reopen commerce with an America whose commercial interests were entirely in sympathy with England's. The Prime Minister, Percival, decided to repeal the Orders in Council but was assassinated before he did it. Finally, Lord Castlereagh, foreign secretary, announced on June 16, 1812, that the Orders in Council were repealed. However, he was too late. On June 18 Congress declared war on Britain.

This was a new Congress, elected in 1811. Henry Clay, Speaker of the House, and John C. Calhoun, a firebrand from South Carolina, led a group of back-country farmers and small-town lawyers called "war hawks." They wanted to fight the British in order to annex Canada to the United States, to defeat what they considered to be the Indian menace in the West and Northwest, and to open the country north of the Ohio River to pioneers. They cried "Free Trade and Sailors' Rights" but had never seen salt water. They knew nothing

*This plot is mentioned but not explained in Fairburn's *Merchant Sail,* page 315. I have found no other authority.

of naval affairs or seaborne commerce and cared little. They were prepared to send America's few frigates and a fleet of Jefferson's gunboats, unsafe in any weather, against the world's most powerful navy.

The old-line Federalists, the merchants of Massachusetts, New Hampshire, and Maine, would rather have helped the British to defeat the tyrant Napoleon, if there was to be a war. British armies in Spain were buying all the flour, pork, and beef that ships could carry to them, and Americans were eager to buy manufactures of which the embargo had deprived them. Profits were enormous. War with England was unthinkable. Federalist opposition in Portland, Bath, Wiscasset, and Waldoboro was close to treasonous. The Hartford Convention in 1814 came close to secession.

The war of 1812–14 turned into a comic-opera war in some respects, for each side had interests which took precedence over the usual military purpose of killing the enemy and destroying his armaments. Britain needed American food supplies, particularly in Spain, Canada, and the West Indies. Also she needed the money to be realized by selling her manufactures in America, for her war with Napoleon was a very expensive undertaking. American merchants and farmers were eager to sell their products wherever they could, and the United States government, which got most of its revenue from import duties, needed commerce. Accordingly, the British issued licenses to unarmed American merchantmen to carry American cargoes to Spain, Portugal, Canada, and the West Indies. American naval vessels, regarding this as trading with the enemy, made prizes of fellow Americans carrying British licenses. The American courts repudiated the Navy's captures. Congress did nothing about this until after the crops harvested in 1812 were sold and then was slow to act. In 1813, with the war in Spain practically concluded and Napoleon's armies on the run, the licenses were withdrawn. However, the traffic went on.

Large caches of British goods were assembled on Deer Island and Campobello, while coasters brought American goods to Eastport. The border leaked in both directions.

Peleg Tallman was made Swedish consul in Bath and issued Swedish registration to whomever applied. Any vessel with Swedish papers was neutral. It is reported that "neutral" vessels, flying the Swedish flag, loaded to the scuppers, were so swift that they made two trips to Sweden in one day. At least they could show Swedish clearance papers.

Although war with England was unpopular in Maine, although the British in 1812 did not enforce a tight blockade on the Maine coast in the hope that New England would secede from the United States, and although the principal naval activity of the War was at sea and on the coast to the west and south, Maine saw some picturesque incidents nevertheless. The brig *Grand Turk,* third of her name, was built in Wiscasset and outsailed her pursuers.

Dash was a successful privateer from Portland. *Dart,* after one unsuccessful cruise as a privateer, took out a letter of marque and carried cargo. Nevertheless, she captured a British vessel loaded with excellent rum, and Old Dart Rum became a valued commodity in Portland.

Swift, a replica of an 1812 privateer built by Robinson and Chapelle in Fox Creek, Ipswich, Massachusetts, ca. 1940. *Author's collection*

In 1813 the British clamped down a blockade on the Maine coast. The waters between Seguin and Monhegan were patrolled by the sloops of war *Rattler, Bream* (6), and *Liverpool Packet.* In early 1813 the British vessels captured a number of coasters and fishermen and set their crews ashore on Damariscove Island.

A cracker-barrel committee around a stove in the store at Round Pond hatched up a plan to capture *Bream.* Commodore Tucker of Bremen and forty-five men sailed the sloop *Increase* to Boothbay, borrowed several guns, and headed east in search of *Bream.* Failing to find her after two days and with their food running low, they returned the guns to Boothbay and headed home. In Muscongus Bay, a short way east of Long Cove Point, they met the British privateer *Crown.* The skipper of *Crown* thought *Increase* an unarmed sloop and headed for her. As the two vessels approached each other, Tucker put his helm up and ran down as if to board *Crown.* Aboard *Increase* was "a volunteer of swarthy complexion and gigantic stature." This could have been Peter Carey, the mulatto in *Mary Jane*'s crew when she sailed from the Kennebec during the embargo. His assignment was to hurl *Increase*'s anchor aboard *Crown* to act as a grapple. As *Increase* bore down on *Crown,* the British captain surrendered, saying afterward, "When I beheld a giant standing at the bow with a huge anchor on his back ready to throw on board of us through a space of 20 feet, and heard his awful cry, 'Commodore, shall I heave?', I thought the Devil was coming after my vessel."

Rattler came up Boothbay Harbor and landed a party on Spruce Point one night, but it was driven off.

In April 1813 at least ten American coasters and fishermen were captured between Seguin Island and Owls Head, and during the summer many more were taken. It was not all one-way, however. The American privateer *Young Teazer* took a number of British prizes, among them *Grey Hound* bound from Nova Scotia to the West Indies. A prize crew was put aboard and she was on her way to Portland when *La Hogue,* a British 74, stopped her. The prize crew acted so much like her original crew that the boarding officer did not know she had been captured and let her go.

The lieutenant aboard *Young Teazer* had previously been captured and paroled. When *La Hogue* stopped her, he knew that he would be shot with no questions asked if he were recognized. Rather than face that fate, he blew up the vessel and himself with it.

The Portsmouth privateer *Thomas* brought in the British armed ship *Dromo* to Wiscasset and a brig into Boothbay, both with valuable cargoes. She sailed again and captured *Liverpool Packet*.

The British privateer *Fly* captured three local vessels and held them in a cove at Brimstone Island in East Penobscot Bay. The American privateer *Mary* with two guns attacked *Fly,* but her guns were too light to do much execution. However, *Mary*'s crew drove *Fly*'s crew below with musket fire. One of *Fly*'s men threw the halyards down the hatch and slipped the anchor cable. From below the crew made sail and, steering with a tiller below deck, escaped.

Mary retook the prizes, sailed to the westward, and met HM Brig *Boxer* near Boothbay. *Mary* slipped into Christmas Cove safely. USS *Enterprise* captured *Fly* in August 1813 off the Maine coast. Thus, the two combatants that were to meet in Maine's biggest naval encounter of the War of 1812, HM Brig *Boxer* and USS *Enterprise,* were both on the coast in the summer of 1813.

The reader uninterested in the technical details of this encounter may skip the following pages with small loss. Others, who may find this account too brief, may read an even more detailed account in Sherwood Picking's *Sea Fight off Monhegan*.

HM Brig *Boxer* was a 181-ton brig, 84 feet long, carrying twelve 18-pound carronades and two long 6-pounders. She carried a crew of seventy. She was commanded by Commander Blyth. Blyth at the age of thirty-one had already had an active naval career. As an eleven-year-old midshipman he had served aboard *Bellerophon* in the Battle of the Glorious First of June. After an active adolescence aboard a succession of British ships, he was promoted to master's mate in 1803 and to lieutenant in 1806. In 1812, having fought French gunboats, privateers, and frigates and been twice wounded, he was promoted to commander and given command of *Boxer*. In 1813 he was sent to Saint John, New Brunswick. His mission was to keep privateering down and to interrupt commerce on the Maine coast.

In June 1813 Commander Blyth captured a small boat off Quoddy Head carrying a picnic party of ladies including the wife of Colonel Ulmer, military commander at Eastport. Apparently the ladies had been swept out of Passamaquoddy Bay by the powerful ebb tide; Captain Blyth returned them to the bay on the flood tide. Colonel Ulmer put a note in the newspaper thanking Captain Blyth for his civility. After a summer cruise on the Maine coast, *Boxer* returned to Saint John in late August to refit. Word had come that *Enterprise* was on the coast, and Blyth sought action with her.

USS *Enterprise* was built in Baltimore in 1799 as an 84-foot topsail schooner carrying twelve 6-pounders. She was a very fast vessel, sharp forward, slim aft, and much more V-bottomed amidships than most vessels of her type. She carried a cloud of sail including a square foresail and fore topsail as well as a fore-and-aft foresail, a huge fore-and-aft mainsail, and a gaff main topsail. In the war against the French she fought five actions and took nineteen vessels. She was then sent to the Mediterranean, where in August 1801 she took the polacca *Tripoli*. In 1803 with *John Adams* she defeated a twenty-two-gun corsair, and under Decatur captured the corsair *Mastico*.

In 1811 *Enterprise* was rebuilt, lengthened 12 feet, and re-rigged as a brig. She was then slower to windward but was said to be faster off the wind. She was also more heavily armed, carrying two long 9-pounders and fourteen 18-pound carronades. Captain Blakely commanded her until August 1813, when, after capturing the British privateer *Fly*, he was sent to command the sloop of war *Wasp*. Lieutenant Burrows was then put in command of *Enterprise*.

Burrows had gone to sea as a midshipman in 1800 and was in *Constitution* under Preble in 1803. In another vessel he quelled a mutiny, for which Preble made him a lieutenant. As first lieutenant in *Hornet* he saved her in a heavy gale. He was passed over for promotion and resigned from the Navy. Alexander Hamilton refused to accept his resignation and granted him an extended furlough. Burrows went to China in the merchant service, was captured and paroled on the return trip and exchanged in 1813. He was then given *Enterprise*. His assignment was to keep down British privateers and capture *Boxer*.

The story of the encounter illustrates the Gilbert & Sullivan quality of the War of 1812. In the summer of 1813 a syndicate in Bath headed by a Mr. Tappan had a contract to supply woolen cloth to make blankets and uniforms for the United States Army in Canada. The nearest source of woolen cloth was Saint John—enemy territory. Nevertheless, Tappan went to Saint John and was able to buy sufficient cloth. The British were eager to sell it because they wanted the money more than they wanted the American army to freeze. Tappan was willing to deal with the enemy because he wanted to fulfill his contract.

In order to get the cloth to Bath, he chartered the Swedish brig *Margaretta*, with Captain Kobs. Tappan realized that a British privateer might seize *Margaretta* because she was bound for an American port, and an American privateer might seize her as being loaded with British goods from a British port. It had been the policy of the British government to protect British exports and to issue licenses for trade, although there was some doubt as to whether any policy covered the transportation of cloth for American army blankets.

While *Margaretta* was loading at Saint John, Tappan saw *Boxer* fitting out on the other side of the same wharf. He offered Blyth £100 to convoy *Margaretta* to Bath, an offer which Blyth accepted. The two vessels set off westward in company, a British naval vessel convoying a brig with cloth for the enemy army. When the fog shut down, *Boxer* actually towed *Margaretta* to be sure they did not part company.

On September 3 the two brigs were north of Monhegan. It was a warm, quiet, hazy day with perhaps two miles' visibility. A small boat rowed out from Monhegan and asked if *Boxer* had a doctor aboard, as a fisherman on Monhegan had been hurt and needed medical help—a strange request to make of an enemy ship in wartime. Blyth sent his surgeon, Dr. Anderson, ashore and with him midshipmen Nixon and Pike and Lieutenant J. A. Allen of the British army, who was taking a sea voyage for his health. They carried light shotguns, as it was said that there were pigeons on the island and one might anticipate some sport. This was a strange expedition into enemy territory.

Boxer and *Margaretta* continued across Muscongus Bay, past Boothbay, to the mouth of the Kennebec where *Margaretta* bore off for Bath. Blyth fired several shots after her, as he said, "in case some curious people were looking on" to make it appear he was chasing her in. He then turned east again and anchored behind Johns Island off Pemaquid.

On the same day, about the time that Blyth was talking with the fisherman, *Enterprise* was leaving Portland, working her way out with sweeps in the morning calm. Presently a little air came in from the south, *Enterprise*'s sails filled, and she sailed slowly across Casco Bay. About 3:00 P.M., Burrows heard Blyth firing after *Margaretta,* but in the haze he could see nothing. He kept on to the eastward in light airs, which died out after sunset. About 2:00 A.M. on September 4, the breeze came in light northerly, the haze dried up, and at first light Burrows saw *Boxer*'s masts over the trees on Johns Island. He tacked and stood inshore.

Blyth recognized *Enterprise* and got underway about 7:30. He stood down the Pemaquid shore, firing several guns to let his surgeon on Monhegan know it was time to return.

Burrows had taken aboard a Portland pilot, Captain Drinkwater, who told Burrows that surely the wind would die and come in southerly. He advised standing offshore and waiting for the shift, which would then put *Enterprise* to windward.

At 9:30 both vessels were becalmed about four miles apart between Pemaquid Point and Monhegan. The crew of *Enterprise* was busy moving one of the long nines on the fo'c's'le aft to the port quarter. At 10:00 the southerly struck in, very light; by noon it had grown to a working breeze. Burrows still kept off to the south. Finding that *Enterprise* was faster than *Boxer* on any point of sailing, he cleared for action and at 3:00 P.M. he put his helm up and ran down 200 yards to windward of *Boxer* on the starboard tack headed to the eastward. The British cheered and fired. *Enterprise* fired and fired again before *Boxer* replied. As Burrows was standing on one leg, pushing out the after carronade with his other foot, he was mortally wounded in the groin with a grapeshot. Lieutenant McCall took command. Burrows refused to go below, sat against the bulwark in considerable pain, and encouraged his crew. He lived long enough to know of his victory.

McCall set foresail and jib and ranged ahead of *Boxer,* but the main yard swung aback as the braces were shot away. *Enterprise*'s bow swung to leeward, and she slowed down. *Boxer* ranged up on her, her bowsprit over *Enterprise*'s quarterdeck, but *Enterprise* slipped by, now to leeward of *Boxer,* ahead of her and almost stern to her. Lieutenant Tillinghast, serving the long nine that had been moved aft—now the only gun that would bear—shot away *Boxer*'s main topmast, which came down in a tangle of sails and rigging, dragged over the side, and left her dead in the water. McCall took in jib and foresail, luffed across *Boxer*'s bow, and raked* her four times.

"Do you surrender?" hailed McCall.

"We will never surrender to any damned Shingle Jack," replied someone aboard *Boxer.*

"Yes," shouted someone else.

"Then haul down your colors."

"We can't. They are nailed aloft."

Blyth had been so sure of victory that he had not only nailed his colors aloft but had promised certain members of his crew that they could be in the prize crew to sail *Enterprise* back to Saint John. Now Blyth was dead, killed in the first broadside, and *Boxer* was going to Portland.

Naturally, there was great rejoicing in Portland over the victory. The next day McCall, aboard *Boxer,* was waited upon by a Mr. Kinsman of Bath. Mr. Kinsman asked to go through Captain Blyth's pockets and sea chest. McCall indignantly refused. Kinsman explained that Blyth had a draft on the Bank of England for £100 signed by Mr. Tappan. He explained further that should it come into British hands, it would be compromising to Blyth's heirs and to his reputation. Should it come into American hands, it would lead to Tappan's arrest. Therefore, Kinsman suggested that he put $500 in silver coins in Blyth's chest and tear up the draft.

McCall said, "I trust that this will go no further."

"It will go on further."

Portland held a ceremonious funeral for the two captains, who were buried on Munjoy Hill. Afterwards there was a victory banquet attended by the surviving officers of both vessels. The final toast was: "To the crew of the *Boxer,* by law enemies; in gallantry, brothers."

*To rake an enemy vessel is to sail across its bow or stern so that a broadside travels the length of the enemy. The enemy cannot reply effectively because very few of his guns can be turned directly forward or aft.

Bath
Wollwich
Kennebec R.
Back R.
Damariscotta R.
Westport I.
Sheepscot R.
Arrowsic I.
Boothbay
Harbor
South
Bristol
Linekin Bay
Southport I.
Kennebec R.
Georgetown
Sheepscot Bay
Popham Beach
Small Pt.

Small Point to Allen Island

Dr. Anderson and his party were picked up on Monhegan and joined the other prisoners. It was a little embarrassing because the people of Monhegan did not want to seize them and imprison them as enemies when they had been kind enough to help the wounded fisherman, but they could not just ignore them.

After all the shooting and shouting, poetry and preaching, the battle did not change anything. The big American frigates had been defeated or bottled up in various ports. The British navy thus could blockade the coast tightly, forcing American merchant ships to lay up or be captured. After the battle of Trafalgar in 1805 and Napoleon's exile to Elba in 1814, the British had more ships and men for the American war. They conducted raids alongshore, and captured Castine, Machias, and Eastport with a view to making the Penobscot River the Maine–New Brunswick border.

On April 25, 1814, Admiral Cochrane declared the coast of the United States blockaded from Eastport to the Mississippi—and so far as Maine was concerned, he meant it.

During the month of June, *Bulwark* (74) attacked the mid-coast. On the 20th British troops landed on the shores of the Sheepscot River and marched toward Wiscasset but were driven off. On June 27 and 28 they tried Boothbay, but the militia resisted stoutly and the British marines withdrew. On the 29th, in thick fog, a barge or barges tried to enter Pemaquid Harbor, but the inhabitants heard the oars against the tholepins, fired at the sound, and the barge left without having been seen. Finally, on June 30, the British tried New Harbor and, finding it stoutly defended, sailed away in *Bulwark*. However, *Rattler, Bream,* and others maintained a tight blockade, and very few got by; even fishermen and coasters were swept up. At least fourteen vessels from Bath were captured in 1814.

On July 11, 1814, *Ramilies* (74), with a sloop of war, a brig, two or three armed schooners, and several transports, anchored off Eastport. An officer came ashore with a demand that Fort Sullivan surrender. He insisted on an answer within five minutes. In the face of all those guns, the fort was surrendered. Martial law was established, all public property taken over by the British, but for the most part, private property was respected. The British found customhouse bonds in the names of five residents in the amount of $64,580.27 and tried to collect. The debtors fled and established the town of Lubec.

In August five British naval vessels and several transports anchored off Birch Point in Machias Bay and landed about 1,000 soldiers. Sixteen American militiamen under Colonel Morse manned a fort on Sanborn Point. When the fiery Jerry O'Brien, who knew something about defending Machias against the British, heard of the attack, he mounted his horse, rode up the main street of town, and called for volunteers to help defend Fort O'Brien. No one volunteered. Enraged, he galloped across the bridge and up the hill "uttering imprecations not of gospel tone." Colonel Morse abandoned the fort. One shot was fired by a frustrated militiaman who wanted "one crack at 'em." Morse, having been paroled from a captured privateer, left town and went overland to the Penobscot River.

There was little in Machias for the British, and they left after a week.

On August 8, 1814, the British sloop of war *Tenedos* sailed up the Eastern Way between Cranberry Island and Sutton Island off Mount Desert and anchored off Bear Island. Captain Benjamin Spurling of Cranberry Island had two vessels laid up at the head of Norwood Cove with green spruce trees instead of topmasts for camouflage; apparently he knew that *Tenedos* had come to destroy them. He went aboard *Tenedos,* tried to dissuade the captain, and offered him two oxen, butchered, in exchange. The captain replied, "You shall go with us and see them burn." Captain Spurling warned him that he had three sons at Southwest Harbor who could shoot a duck on the wing.

Meanwhile, two other Cranberry Islanders rowed ashore to Mount Desert Island and called out the militia, which mustered to the number of about seventy. Old Jacob Lurvey, a veteran of the Revolution, was sick in bed, but he got up and headed for Southwest Harbor. His wife objected that he had no musket. He answered, "By this time there'll be some of our men wounded, and there'll be a musket for me." John Richardson, another Revolutionary War veteran, was stone deaf and missed hearing the place of rendezvous. He marched down the north side of Norwood Cove in full view of the British and began firing from behind a rock. They replied with a 4-pounder mounted in the bow of the barge. The ball threw up a shower of dirt and rocks right where Richardson was standing, but when the dust settled, he was still there and still shooting.

As the barge came in by Clarks Point, Rob Spurling begged the British to let his father go. Instead, they pushed Captain Spurling down in the bottom of the boat in a safer position. He couldn't stand that, reared up, and shouted, "Never mind me, Rob. I'm an old man. But give it to these dashed Britishers as hard as you can." The British fired high and hit nothing, but after seven of their soldiers were killed, they withdrew.

The situation at Castine was quite different. On September 1, 1814, *Bulwark,* a frigate, a brig, and fourteen transports appeared off Castine. The Americans spiked the guns at the port, blew up the magazine, and retreated up the Penobscot River. Captain Morris with the corvette *Adams* set his guns ashore and tried to organize a defense, but the pursuing British outflanked him. He burned his vessel and left for the Kennebec on foot.

The British pressed on to Bangor, which was forced to surrender unconditionally. The British burned seventeen vessels and took forty oxen, a hundred sheep, and various geese. They paroled 191 prisoners of war.

The British made Castine a port of entry for the province of Nova Scotia, collected customs (which, incidentally, were used to found Dalhousie University in Halifax), and bought supplies from the neighbors. They rebuilt Fort

George, mounted sixty guns, and dug a canal across the isthmus to prevent surprise and to hinder desertion. In short, they settled in as if they meant to stay forever, and no doubt they did so intend.

They were so friendly to Americans and paid so well that a great deal of food and fuel was smuggled from the United States to Britain via Castine. Also Peleg Tallman, the Swedish consul in Bath, gave Swedish registry to many vessels trading from Hampden to Castine rendering them "neutral" and immune to capture. Foreign goods were plentiful and cheap, especially after November 3, when a fleet came in from Halifax well supplied.

From their base at Castine the British conducted raids on Bucksport, Camden, and Saturday Cove, but without significant damage. At the latter "battle" the British surprised old Amos Pendleton at his breakfast. He departed by the window; they ate his breakfast and took his watch. Several days later, Mr. Pendleton went to the fort at Castine in high dudgeon and demanded his watch. The commander had it returned to him with suitable apologies.

By the summer of 1814 it was time to stop this war which never should have been fought. The American coast was blockaded and her commerce paralyzed. Every port had vessels laid up, topmasts sent down, and tar barrels inverted over lower mastheads to keep the rain out of the wood; these were called "Madison's nightcaps." American troops had failed to invade Canada, and viewed with no little concern large British forces in Bermuda and the West Indies apparently poised for invasion. Britain, defeated on Lake Erie and Lake Champlain, was unable to invade the United States except for the raid on Washington, D.C., and the capture of eastern Maine. The United States Navy was blockaded or defeated, and the federal government was nearly bankrupt.

However, many American privateers were out distressing British commerce. Early in the war, the British, unable to prevent the emergence of American privateers by blockading every American harbor, creek, and sound, convoyed fleets of merchantmen with warships. The American response was to build big, fast, heavily rigged and lightly armed vessels carrying large crews. These vessels could outsail any British war vessel and overwhelm any merchant ship. They caught unconvoyed merchant ships and stragglers from convoys and harried the convoys, outmaneuvering the escort vessels and cutting out merchantmen.

American privateers guarded British trade routes, actually operating in the English Channel, the Irish Sea, and off Gibraltar, Finisterre, and the Azores. They were highly effective. Joshua Barney in *Rossie* captured twenty British vessels on his first cruise. *Midas,* besides taking numerous prizes, captured and burned the town on Harbor Island in the Bahamas in retaliation for the burning of Washington by the British. *Syren* captured a British dispatch vessel in the Irish Sea. *Governor Tomkins* burned fourteen British merchant vessels in the English Channel. *Harpy* cruised for three months off the English and Irish coasts and in the Bay of Biscay, returning to Boston with half a million dollars in hard money. *Prince De Neufchatel* cut off all British coasting trade in the Irish Channel.

Perhaps the most famous American privateer was *Chasseur*, Captain Thomas Boyle. She was a topsail schooner about 115 feet long, 356 tons, and carried sixteen long 12-pounders. Boyle sailed from New York on July 28, 1814, and captured eighteen British vessels on his cruise to the English Channel. On

Great Harbor of Mount Desert Island

several occasions he teased British warships sent specifically to catch him. His crowning achievement, after capturing a number of vessels close to British shores, was to have posted on the door of Lloyd's Coffee House, the insurance center for British merchants, a proclamation over his signature blockading the British Isles, a parody of Admiral Cochrane's proclamation blockading the American coast. On October 24 Boyle returned to New York with a cargo worth $100,000 and about fifty prisoners.

During the war there were at least 517 American privateers at sea. Of these, 15 came from Maine, 150 from Massachusetts, and lesser numbers from other states. These 517 privateers took over 1,300 prizes worth in aggregate about $39,000,000. Not only was this a serious loss to British commerce, but the uncertainty and fear sowed in the British shipping community was even more serious. Insurance rates at Halifax rose 33 percent over prewar rates and rocketed 666 percent for voyages between England and Ireland. The entire British economy felt the pinch of paralyzed commerce.

The merchants of Glasgow met and resolved: "that the numbers of American privateers with which our channels are infested, the audacity with which they have approached our coasts, have proved ruinous to our commerce, humbling to our pride, and discreditable to the British navy; that 800 vessels

An 1814 privateer. *Earle G. Barlow*

have been taken by that Power, whose maritime strength we have impolitically held in contempt, and that there is reason to anticipate still more serious suffering."

The Secretary of the Admiralty announced publicly in 1814 that it was unsafe for any ship to sail from a British port unless convoyed. Although Napoleon was defeated, it was not unlikely that Britain would have to fight some of her former allies. Her best generals and much of her army must be kept at home. The Duke of Wellington and two of his best officers refused to command British troops in America because they believed an overwhelming victory to be impossible.

In short, no one seemed to be winning anything in the war, and both nations needed commerce. Britain was occupied in rebuilding Europe at the Congress of Vienna. Commissioners of Britain and the United States met at Ghent and agreed on a peace on December 24, 1814. The Treaty of Ghent said nothing about neutral rights or impressment, but the two nations agreed to stop fighting, and that was the main thing.

It took some time for the news to reach Maine, but one night in early February a brilliant party at the home of Moses Carlton in Wiscasset was thrown into disarray when a horseman rode jubilantly through the front door announcing peace amid the crash of breaking glass as Pendy, the maid, dropped her tray in the excitement.

One might say that the war had not proven much. Certainly it proved nothing about free trade and sailors' rights. It proved, however, by a series of brilliant single-ship actions, that America could build ships, sail them, and fight them as well as anyone on earth. It proved that American privateers could be built faster and handier, and could be handled more boldly than anything the British or French could put afloat. The war gave America confidence in her maritime heritage.

Finally, in the words of Ralph D. Paine in *The Old Merchant Marine:* "The War of 1812 was the dividing line between two eras of salt water history. On the farther side lay the turbulent centuries of hazard and bloodshed and piracy, of little ships and indomitable seamen who pursued their voyages in the reek of gunpowder and of legalized pillage by the stronger. . . . On the hither side of 1812 were seas unvexed by the privateer and the freebooter. . . . The great trade routes of the world were peaceful highways for the white-winged fleets of all nations."

NOTES

Again, William D. Williamson's *History of Maine* provides the outline of the chapter. On the conflict between France and England, Winston Churchill's *History of the English Speaking Peoples,* Volume III, *Ploetz's Manual of Universal History* by Tillinghast, and Samuel Eliot Morison's *Oxford History of the American People* give different points of view and among them provide the necessary facts. More detailed accounts of local incidents come from William Fairburn's *Merchant Sail,* Volume I; William Baker's *Maritime History of Bath,* Volume I; George W. Rice's *The Shipping Days of Old Boothbay;* Francis Greene's *History of Boothbay, Southport and Boothbay Harbor;* John Johnston's *History of Bristol, and Bremen;* Jacob Jasper Stahl's *History of Old Broad Bay and Waldoborough;* George E. Street's *Mount Desert, a History;* George W. Drisko's *Narrative of the Town of Machias, Maine;* and William Henry Kilby's *Eastport and Passamaquoddy.* Morison's *Maritime History of Massachusetts,* which includes Maine until 1820, also sheds a few gleams of light on the general situation in New England.

A man being flogged through the fleet is lashed to a scaffold in a ship's boat and rowed from one ship to another through the fleet, receiving a specified number of lashes alongside each ship. Seldom does anyone survive such punishment; and if he does, he is physically and mentally crippled for the rest of his life.

The story of *Boxer* and *Enterprise* comes almost entirely from Captain Sherwood Picking's *Sea Fight off Monhegan,* a thoroughly researched analysis of the entire affair based on United States Navy reports, British Admiralty reports, and numerous letters and diaries of participants. William Hutchinson Rowe's *Maritime History of Maine* provided useful details and a sort of road map to the chapter, although I tried to avoid simply duplicating his excellent chapter on the same subject.

Here is the best stanza of a broadside of twelve stanzas of doggerel rhyme on the embargo, each stanza ending with the same word:

> Our ships all in motion,
> Once whiten'd the ocean,
> They sail'd and return'd with their cargo;
> Now doom'd to decay,
> They have fallen a prey
> To Jefferson, Worms, and Embargo.

It appears in many books, but I found the complete poem in Albion, Baker, and Labaree's *New England and the Sea.*

There are many more tales of efforts, successful and unsuccessful, to evade the embargo, but we have here enough to show its unpopularity, the difficulty of enforcing it, and the rewards of evading it. It bred, like Prohibition in the 1920s, a spirit of lawlessness and contempt for government that may have been its most serious negative result; a close second, if it be a second, was the move to nullify federal law and secede from the Union that prompted the Hartford Convention. Fortunately, other events intervened and postponed dissolution of the Union from 1814 to 1861.

The lines and sail plan of *Enterprise* are published in Howard I. Chapelle's *The Search for Speed Under Sail.* His account of *Enterprise*'s career, however, is incomplete. After the battle, she was re-rigged as a brigantine. In 1821 she defeated the pirate Jean Lafitte at Galveston and for the next two years chased pirates in the Caribbean with notable success. She was wrecked in 1823 on Little Curaçao.

Boxer was found too slow to be useful in the United States Navy, was sold as a merchantman, and was still active in 1845.

Captain Blakely had successful cruises in *Wasp,* until she disappeared with all hands in the South Atlantic.

Burrows was assigned to *Enterprise* in June 1813, but Blakely was on a cruise in her until August. Burrows actually took command in Portsmouth in late August.

One may wonder at the willingness of both British and American governments to wink at trade with the enemy. Britain needed money badly, as she was subsidizing the European enemies of Napoleon as well as supporting a large army and navy. She had a glut of manufactures. America also needed money, almost the only source of which was import duties. The Tappan syndicate paid duty on the cloth in Bath.

The Monhegan fisherman's willingness to hail a British naval vessel in time of war suggests that up to that time the blockade had not been rigidly enforced, although privateers on both sides had been active.

One account says *Boxer* had captured or at least inspected another "neutral" Swedish brig in Pemaquid Harbor.

"Shingle Jack" was the British nickname for *Enterprise*.

The situation at Castine in 1814 was the same as that at Eastport in 1812–13. Coastal trade at the time being embargoed or dangerous, great quantities of British goods were transferred westward in wagons—"mud schooners" or "horsemarines" to wits in local papers. Farmers and woodsmen began to prosper from the British need for food and lumber.

The awkward positions of both United States and British governments in 1814 is admirably summed up by C. S. Forester in *The Age of Fighting Sail*. He regards as highly significant the Duke of Wellington's refusal to command a British force in America.

This chapter, long enough already, says nothing of the dramatic single-ship actions of the big frigates and of the fast sloops of war *Wasp, Frolic,* and *Peacock;* nor does it tell much of American deep-water privateering. These actions had little to do with the Maine coast, but the interested reader can find a thorough, readable, and exciting analysis in C. S. Forester's *The Age of Fighting Sail*. Ralph D. Paine's biography of Joshua Barney gives one man's experience, and the flavor of that exciting period can be tasted in responsible fiction. Forester's *Captain from Connecticut* and Kenneth Roberts's *Lively Lady* and *Captain Caution* are good examples.

In the late summer of 1932, the writer and a friend visited Nelson Poland on Louds Island. Although Mr. Poland was in his nineties, he still had a good reputation as a sailmaker. Besides ordering a sail, we heard him sing several ballads of the War of 1812, one of which is quoted below. His father, when a small child, had seen the battle of *Boxer* and *Enterprise* from Pemaquid Point.

Mr. Poland sang this one several times with gusto and a triumphant ring. The song takes liberties with history but bears rereading.

> Ye Parliaments of England,
> You Lords and Commons too,
> Consider well what you're about
> And what you're going to do.
> You're going to fight with Yankees,
> I'm sure you'll rue the day.
> You've roused the Sons of Liberty
> In North Americay.
>
> You first confined our commerce,
> And said our ships shan't trade,
> You next impressed our seamen
> And used them as your slaves;
> You then insulted Rodgers,

While ploughing o'er the main
And had we not declarèd war,
You'd done it o'er again!

And next your Indian Allies,*
You styled them by that name
Until they took their tomahawks
And savages became.

You thought our frigates were but few
And Yankees could not fight,
Until brave Hull your *Guerriere* took
And banished her from sight.
The *Wasp* next took your *Frolic,*
We'll nothing say of that
The *Poictiers* being of the line
Of course she took her back.

And next your *Macedonian*
No finer ship could swim.
Decatur took her gilt-work off
And then he sent her in.
The *Java* by a Yankee ship
Was sunk you all must know;
The *Peacock* fine in all her plume
By Lawrence down did go.

Then next you sent your *Boxer*
To box us all about;
We had an *Enterprising* brig
That beat your *Boxer* out.
We boxed her up to Portland
And moored her off the town
To show the Sons of Liberty
The *Boxer* of renown.

Then next upon Lake Erie
Where Perry had some fun,
You own he beat your naval force
And caused them for to run;
This was to you a sore defeat
The like ne'er known before—
Your British squadron beat complete—
Some sunk, some run ashore.

There's Rodgers in the *President*
Will sink, burn and destroy;
The *Congress* on the Brazil coast
Your commerce will annoy;
The *Essex* in the South Seas
Will put out all your lights.

*This fragment was sung by Nelson Poland but was omitted from the printed version. After so many years, I do not remember the second half of the stanza, if it had a second half. The ballad, with an approximation of the tune Mr. Poland sang, appears in *American Sea Songs and Chanteys* by Frank H. Shay, W. W. Norton, New York, 1948.

The flag she wears at her mast-head
"Free Trade and Sailors' Rights."

Lament ye sons of Britain
For distant is the day
When you'll regain by British force
What you've lost in Americay;
Go tell your King and Parliament
By all the world 'tis known
That British force by land and sea
By Yankees is o'erthrown.

Use every endeavor
And strive to call for peace
For Yankee ships are building fast
Our navy to increase.
They will enforce their commerce
Their laws by Heaven are made
That Yankee ships in time of peace
To any port may trade.

NINETEEN

Foreign Trade, 1815-1860

AFTER THE INCONCLUSIVE Treaty of Ghent ending the War of 1812, details concerning trade and fishing were negotiated. The Reciprocity Treaty of July 1815 permitted British ships to enter United States ports and United States ships to enter British ports; however, it did not permit United States ships to enter British West Indies ports or trade between the British West Indies and Britain. British merchants, eager to sell the surplus of manufactured goods accumulated during the war, found that they could send a shipload of woolen cloth, for instance, to Boston, pick up a cargo of fish, flour, staves, pork, and horses, sell these in Jamaica for sugar and molasses, and carry that to England with no Yankee competition. They could even carry it back to Boston under the Reciprocity Treaty. Therefore, they could afford to sell cloth, and even Irish potatoes and British ham, in America for less than it cost Americans to produce the same things.

France and Spain, eager to build up their own merchant fleets, put restrictions on trade with their ports, particularly their West Indian ports which had taken large quanties of American products before the war. New Brunswick in 1816, in an effort to prevent Maine vessels from taking gypsum or plaster from their ports to the exclusion of their own ships, prohibited the export of those products in any American ship with a home port east of Boston.

In 1817 Congress replied to these restrictions with a Navigation Act saying that no foreign goods could enter the United States except in U.S. vessels or in vessels of the country in which the goods were produced; however, this act would not apply to any country that was open to United States vessels. Spain opened Cuba and Puerto Rico to U.S. vessels in 1818, but not until 1830 did Britain open West Indies trade to the United States.

Another effect of the Reciprocity Treaty, and one favorable to the United States, was to open British and European ports to direct trade with the United States. This provided an opening for the establishment of packet lines. In 1818 the New York papers announced that on scheduled dates, twice a month, a Black Ball Line vessel would sail from New York for Liverpool, whether fully loaded or not; twice a month, other vessels of the same line would sail from Liverpool for New York. The idea met immediate success. Passengers could count on sailing on a certain date, and shippers in a hurry would not have to provide a full cargo.

The owners of the Black Ball Line were eager that their vessels carry full cargoes. There was no problem for the westbound packets, as the surplus of British goods created a steady pressure. Eastbound vessels were not so easy to fill. Britain at this time needed raw cotton to supply her new steam-powered cotton mills. So, packet lines were established from New York south to Charleston and New Orleans to carry British manufactured goods south and to bring cotton north, whence it was carried east to Liverpool. Maine-built ships were used as packets both transatlantic and coastwise.

The growing interest in the packet, China, and East Indies trades called for concentration of capital in Boston and New York, at the expense of smaller ports like Salem, Plymouth, Newburyport, Bath, Wiscasset, and Waldoboro. These trades also called for larger ships of 700 to 1,000 tons rather than the brigs and schooners of 200 to 400 tons. Many of the bigger vessels could not use the smaller shallow harbors, and even if they did get in, they could not, in a small town, assemble a full cargo.

Boston, with its growing rail network and expanding textile factories in the Merrimac valley, and New York, with both the Erie Canal and a rail network, could assemble and distribute large cargoes more effectively than Bath, Wiscasset, Waldoboro, and Thomaston. Therefore, Maine merchants built and owned ships that sailed from Boston, New York, Philadelphia, Charleston, Savannah, and New Orleans. Waldoboro, for instance, in 1860 owned 187,200 tons of shipping and had only $12,000 worth of exports and imports, whereas Boston owned 464,200 tons of shipping with an export-import trade of $54,535,000. Portland, with 131,800 tons, had $3,442,000 worth of trade and was the busiest of Maine ports.

Portland had a large and fairly well protected harbor and early became a distribution center for the back country. Wagons and pungs came down through Crawford Notch all the way from Vermont and New Hampshire farms loaded with pork, beef, butter, cheese, corn, and hay, and driving pigs and cattle before them to trade on the Portland wharves for flour, salt fish, molasses, rum, sugar, coffee, cotton cloth, and various other manufactured goods. Portland had by 1800 two banks and in the 1840s had seven rum distilleries and the Brown sugar refinery, which had a patent process for refining many grades of brown sugar cheaply. Consequently, Portland became the country's second most important molasses port. In 1860 Maine distilled 452,000 gallons of rum, most of it in Portland. One store in Pittston sold ninety hogsheads of rum in one winter. In 1853 the Grand Trunk Railroad from Portland to Montréal was opened so that when the St. Lawrence River froze, Canadian wheat and other food products were exported through Portland in return for the usual imports, and a regular steam packet line ran from Liverpool to

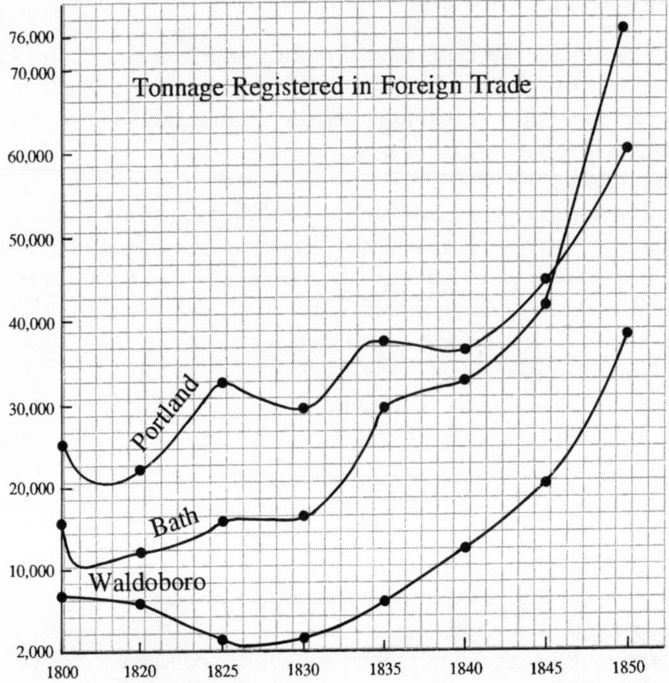

Above: Tonnage registered in foreign trade at Portland, Bath, and Waldoboro, 1815–1850. *Below:* Registered at Boston, same period.

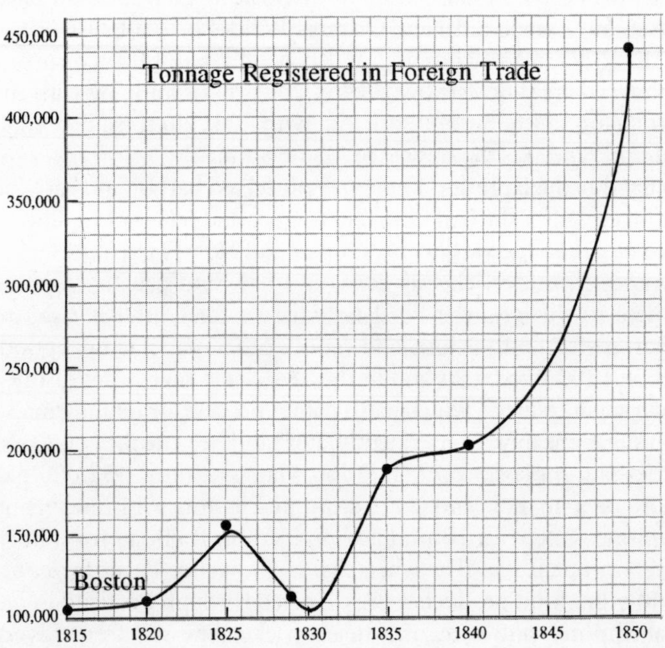

Portland in the winter. In 1807 an octagonal observatory was built on Munjoy Hill, from which a lookout with a good telescope could identify incoming ships and by a code of flags signal the owner. On one day in 1844, 200 vessels were in sight from the tower. The tower still stands and is open to the interested observer.

The accompanying charts showing tonnage registered in foreign trade give an idea of the early slow recovery and subsequent rapid growth of Maine commerce. The precipitate increase in Bath tonnage in relation to Portland tonnage is misleading. Bath was by far the most active shipbuilding town in the state, building 16,800 tons but with exports and imports amounting to only $40,000. Vessels owned in Bath traded out of Boston and New York. The Boston chart also is at first glance misleading. Notice that the scale of tonnage on the side is five times the scale on the other chart. Boston's decline and subsequent growth was explosive compared to those of the Maine ports.

After a slow start, then, Maine's maritime activity picked up, both foreign and coastwise. As it had been in the past, the West India trade was by far the largest in which Maine vessels were involved, in spite of the restrictions laid on by British, French, and Spanish governments—restrictions that changed from year to year, were variously enforced in different ports, and were often evaded by Yankee skippers, with the connivance of local merchants and officials. The islands needed New England goods, and if British vessels could not supply them, they would buy from Yankees.

After 1830, when Britain permitted American vessels to trade legally with the West Indies, trade increased rapidly; this is reflected on the chart showing Maine tonnage. Cargoes bound south consisted of lumber, including boards, shooks, shingles, and masts. Cuba took a great deal of these Maine forest products. From 1856 to 1861, 1,207 cargoes of lumber went to Cuba from Maine; in 1856 eight vessels sailed from Bath alone carrying shooks. Salt codfish, herring, mackerel, apples, potatoes, beef, butter, cider, horses, oxen, and poultry were also staples. Notice that these are all Maine products. Very little was brought in from England and the South for re-export. Cargoes home included the usual West Indies products: rum, molasses, sugar, and coffee.

There were more serious obstructions to the West India trade than paper barriers. The Caribbean was a nursery for hurricanes. Although most of these came in July and August, a hurricane could strike at any time from late May to mid-October. These storms blew sometimes well over 100 knots. Because of their circular nature, the seas they kicked up were violent and irregular, not running in regular mountain ridges but peaking up here and there, falling over, smoothing out, sometimes developing very high and steep rogue waves that could overwhelm a vessel already on her beam ends, held down by the wind. In the days of rope rigging, which stretched under strain, dismastings were common.

On July 26, 1825, a violent hurricane hit Basseterre. The brig *Lydia* of Bath, loaded with molasses and hides, was driven out of the harbor, hove down, and her masts carried away. The captain and four men went overboard. The four men were lost, but the captain, with the help of the mate, got back aboard. The wind suddenly shifted, as is usual in a hurricane, and *Lydia* drifted ashore on Pigeon Island. The captain, mate, and three seamen swam ashore and were later rescued by a passing boat.

In the same hurricane the brig *Eden,* also from Bath, was driven to sea, abandoned, and drifted ashore at Montserrat, a total loss.

After a hurricane in September 1828, four Maine vessels limped into St. Barts more or less disabled:

- On the 9th, *Susan and Jane* came in, having lost her bowsprit, some sails, her deck load, and her small boat.
- On the 11th, *Hunter* came in without her bowsprit and deckload. She had also lost some spars and sails. The galley had been washed overboard and with it her small boat. Worst of all, her plank sheer was split. She was condemned and sold.
- On the 17th *Neutrality* came in having lost both masts, all her sails and spars, her deckload, her small boat, and her mate. She, too, was condemned and sold.
- On the 19th *Rebecca* came in with her masts still standing but with her flag at half-mast for the loss of her mate.

The list could be extended for over 100 years in either direction. One who has never seen a hurricane can have but the vaguest notion of the unmanageable chaos of wind and water.

If a skipper would avoid hurricanes by sailing in the fall and winter, he must still face the North Atlantic gales, particularly furious in the Gulf Stream off Cape Hatteras.

Pirates were another peril to be faced. After the War of 1812 a number of successful privateers found themselves unemployed. Some turned directly to piracy, preying on whatever ships they could find. Others, making a gesture toward legality, took out privateering commissions from the new South American republics then fighting for their freedom from Spain. Of course, these commissions permitted them to attack only Spanish ships or ships carrying contraband to Spanish ports, but in many cases the terms of the commission were badly bent or broken. With the United States strongly in sympathy with the new republics, fighting for their freedom from Spain as the United States had fought for freedom from Britain, the U.S. government did little to curb these privateers. And, besides ex-privateers, some of them still based in United States ports, and the commissioned privateers from South America, there were bands of buccaneers, many of them operating in nothing bigger than whaleboats, which would attack a becalmed brig or schooner, swarm aboard with pistol and cutlass in overwhelming numbers, seize the ship, murder the crew, take money and small valuable cargo, burn the ship, and disappear into the inlets and mangrove swamps alongshore.

These pirates were a ruthless lot. Later times look back on piracy as romantic, but the pirates of the 1820s were as bloody, as dedicated to immediate profit, and as contemptuous of human life as are the drug runners of the twentieth century. In both cases, the motto is: "Dead cats don't mew." Consequently, we have few accounts of pirate attacks. Niles Register for May 24, 1823, reports 3,002 pirate attacks since the end of the War of 1812. Albion and Pope in *Sea Lanes in War Time* estimate 500 vessels captured and a great many more attacked, stopped, or molested by pirates.

Charles Gibbs, an officer on *Chesapeake* under Captain James Lawrence, after spending the remainder of the War of 1812 in Dartmoor prison, joined an Argentine privateer, led a mutiny, turned pirate, and in the West Indies captured more than 20 vessels and murdered more than 400 of their crew. Some time later the British warship *Jearus* raided Gibbs's base near Cape San Antonio, Cuba, found the remains of 12 vessels burned, and ascertained that 150 men of their crews had been murdered. Between 1818 and 1824 Gibbs took at least forty vessels and murdered the crews of at least half of them. Gibbs was later captured, tried, and hanged at New York in March 1831.

In November 1821 the brig *Cobbosseecontee,* almost certainly a Maine vessel by her name, was bound for Boston from Havana. Only four miles on her way she was captured by a pirate sloop and plundered, the mate hanged from the main crosstrees, and Captain Jackson beaten heavily by the flat of a sword and stabbed through the thigh. The pirates sailed off with their booty.

The schooner *Exertion,* with captain Lincoln, sailed from Boston bound for Cuba in November 1821 with the usual New England cargo of fish, lumber, and provisions. Her crew bore names common in Maine such as Brackett and Reed, and the cook, David Warren, came from Saco. On December 17 they were captured by a pirate, perhaps with a commission, flying Mexican colors, and taken into a secluded harbor among the keys called Twelve League Key or Key Largo. The pirates plundered the vessel, taking several loads of the loot to Cuba where they sold it. The crew was marooned on a sandy islet without water or shelter and left to die of starvation. However, they contrived to wade to another island and find enough material with which to build a boat large enough to take six of them. These departed for help, but the next day the men left behind found the boat swamped and adrift. When they were almost dead of thirst, a group of the pirates, who had repented of their evil ways and deserted their leader, returned and rescued the survivors.

The pirates throve on political and economic contradictions. Everyone deplored piracy, but. . . . Many Americans, sympathetic with the South Americans rebelling against their Spanish masters, were not eager to attack the "privateers" from whatever nation. American ex-privateers carried their plunder into their home ports from New York south to New Orleans, where merchants who asked no questions bought their loot and the captains were known to move in polite society. The Spanish resented attacks on their commerce by Americans sailing under South American colors and did nothing to prevent the seizure of American vessels. In Cuban ports American vessels were legally trading New England cargoes for Cuban sugar, molasses, and rum, while at the same time pirates were openly selling New England produce looted from other New England ships.

Of course, English, Spanish, French, and Portuguese merchantmen suffered too, but the United States was at first the only nation to take action. In 1819, Commodore Oliver H. Perry, the hero of the Battle of Lake Erie, was sent to round up the pirates but unfortunately died of fever before he accomplished anything significant. Two years later, in 1821 and 1822, the United States Navy sent *Enterprise, Macedonian, Congress,* and several shoal-draft barges to the Caribbean. In 1823 Commodore Porter arrived with a fleet of seventeen vessels, including one steamer. The Spanish authorities, who had been profiting from pirate loot, cooperated reluctantly. With the assistance of a British naval force and a few warships of other nations, the pirates were generally wiped out by 1825. The last pirate attack occurred in 1832.

The third peril, against which at the time there was no defense, was fever. Yellow fever in particular was endemic if not epidemic in Caribbean and Central American ports and from time to time appeared in epidemic proportions in American ports as far north as Philadelphia. In 1796 Mrs. Joshua Shaw died in Woolwich, Maine, of yellow fever brought by a mosquito from the Caribbean in a cargo of hides. In 1827 the schooner *Orleans* met the brig *Planter* of Bath off Mobile, Alabama, sixteen days out from Jamaica. Her captain was dead, the mate and three men were sick, and only two men and a boy were healthy enough to hand, reef, and steer. Furthermore, a gale had carried away both her topmasts, leaving her no more than enough sail to maintain steerageway. Captain Swiler of *Orleans* gave the surviving crew of *Planter* the course to Mobile and a few supplies. She made it to Mobile, but after her arrival the mate died in the hospital.

In January 1858 the entire crew of the bark *Tonquin* died of yellow fever.

Nevertheless, in spite of hurricanes, pirates, and disease, the West India trade continued to flourish.

Maine shipbuilders and owners found other ports profitable. Johnson Williams & Co. of Bath sent several vessels to the African coast between 1829 and 1836 for a wide variety of local products including ivory, gold dust, turtle shells, goatskins, hides, salt, and donkeys. Fevers of various deadly kinds were serious hazards. In 1833 two United States vessels were found in Rio Nunez, one with no living crew; the other, *Macondy,* was deserted. Several of *Macondy's* crew were still alive but sick ashore. Enough of them recovered to bring *Macondy* home, but other ports soon proved more profitable and less dangerous.

There seems little evidence that Maine people engaged in the slave trade to any great extent. Slavery was outlawed in Massachusetts as early as 1641, but slaves were openly carried from Africa to the West Indies and Southern ports until 1807 when Britain abolished the trade, followed by the United

States in 1808. This abolition had small effect. In 1818 the United States rewarded informers. However, as slaves cost $10 to $20 in Africa and sold in America for $400 to $1,000, the practice continued. In 1820 the U.S. Navy was sent to patrol the African coast in cooperation with the British navy. Slavers were declared pirates who could be hanged. In 1842 Congress required the Navy to keep a force on the African coast "sufficient to suppress the slave trade." This slowed up the ugly business somewhat, but because a ship, to be condemned, must be caught with slaves actually aboard, ships on the outward passage could not be molested; westbound, a Brazilian flag often gave protection. Two famous clippers—*Nightingale,* built in South Berwick, Maine,* and *Sunny South,* built in New York—were caught and condemned. The yacht *Wanderer,* flying the flag of the New York Yacht Club, met the British naval vessel *Medusa,* entertained her officers aboard, then slipped into the Congo and took aboard 750 slaves, which she landed safely at Savannah. However, the story of the voyage leaked out, and the yacht was seized and sold at auction by the government but bought back by her owners. They were severely punished, however, for the New York Yacht Club expelled the owners and forbade the yacht to fly the yacht club flag.

It fell to the lot of Maine to have almost the last slave trader as one of her sons. Captain Nathaniel Gordon of Portland sailed from New York to the Congo, took aboard 890 natives, and four days out was captured by USS *Mohican.* The slaves were set ashore in Liberia; Gordon was tried in New York, found guilty, and hanged in February 1862 for piracy under the 1820 law.

Whaling, a chancy business calling for highly specialized skills and gear, never was very successfully pursued from Maine ports.

In 1833 the 388-ton ship *Science* was fitted out for whaling by a Portland group. They hired an experienced whaling skipper, Captain Whipply, from Nantucket. *Science* sailed in January 1834 and after a slow start and a long voyage returned to Portland in April 1838 with 2,100 barrels of sperm oil, a "saving" voyage. She sailed again in September 1838 and returned in less than three years with 3,100 barrels of right whale oil—not an outstanding success. *Science* was sold to New Bedford owners, and Portland whaling died.

In May 1834 the ship *Wiscasset,* built in Nobleboro and with a Nantucket Macy in command, sailed from Wiscasset and returned in September 1837 with enough sperm oil to pay for the cost of the vessel and the expenses of the voyage. Her second voyage was less successful, and she was sold to Sag Harbor whalers. In 1841 the bark *Massasoit* sailed from Bath on a whaling voyage under Captain Dinsmore, who was guided by occult voices. She took little oil, and went ashore in Fiddlers Reach on the Kennebec almost in sight of home in 1843. The ship and cargo were saved, but the voyage was a loser. In 1851 the schooner *Lively* sailed in search of whales, but in October 1852 was reported capsized off Bermuda.

* See Chapter 20.

Maine yards built ships and barks for New Bedford whalers, and many Maine-built packets and merchantmen were converted to whaling ships after a life of hard driving had loosened them up. And many Maine men went whaling in Massachusetts and Connecticut vessels. However, Maine entrepreneurs had other, cleaner, and more profitable interests.

The increasing demand in England and Europe for American cotton employed a considerable number of Maine merchant ships very profitably until the Civil War. Products of the West that came via the Erie Canal and, later, via the railroads were loaded in New York along with a general cargo of European manufactures and carried to Charleston, Savannah, or New Orleans. Then cotton bales were stowed for Liverpool, Le Havre, Bremen, or other European ports. The ship might return from England to New York with iron, hemp, crockery, cutlery, textiles; from France with wine and brandy; from Italy with fruit, rags, and marble; from Sweden with iron; from Russia with hemp, cordage, duck, leather, feathers, and salt. Quite often emigrants would come as well, from any of these countries. Fare was £5 in the steerage, and bring your own food.

The cotton trade was dependable and profitable, but one from which a vessel seldom returned to the Maine town where she was built. No longer did the owners of the ship own the cargo and charge the captain with the responsibility of selling it profitably. The cargo was carried as freight at a stipulated charge per ton. Although these ships were often built, owned, and commanded by Maine people, their crews were made up of seamen, or what passed as seamen, from the waterfronts of the ports they touched. If enough men were not easily hired, the services of a "crimp" were often used. Many an unfortunate tailor, barber, or farmboy accepted a friendly glass and woke up in a fo'c's'le outward bound. One Baptist minister served involuntarily before the mast, but most of the shanghaied crews were longshore "packet rats." Such mixed crews required tough mates adept with fists, boots, and belaying pins. Gone were the days when eager Maine boys shipped with their uncles on 100-foot schooners hoping to learn navigation on a voyage to Jamaica.

The cotton trade brought about a change in shipbuilding, too, because bigger ships were needed to carry a bulk cargo of cotton available in almost unlimited quantities to be carried to a destination where the demand was insatiable.

In 1840 the 400-ton ship *Monmouth,* built in Bath, was considered to be a very large vessel. Of the thirty vessels built in Harpswell and Brunswick by the famous Skolfield family, none built before 1822 was over 200 tons; the brig *Mentor* built in that year was 212 tons and only 86 feet long. The first Skolfield vessel in the cotton trade was *John Dunlap,* 476 tons, 127 feet long, built in 1835. In 1846, after a number of other vessels, came the ship *H. H. Boody,* 646 tons, 144 feet long, and equipped for passengers as well as cargo. Their first ship over 1,000 tons was *Roger Stewart,* 1,066 tons, 180 feet long, built in 1852; like the others, she was used in the cotton, general cargo, and passenger trade.

The same pattern was followed in other towns. In 1848 Kennebunk built a lock on the river to accommodate vessels over 500 tons built upstream. In 1852 *Golden Eagle* (1,273 tons, 188 feet long) was built above the lock. Bath built *Cleopatra,* a 578-ton ship, before 1825 and as early as 1841 built a ship over 1,000 tons, *Rappahannock,* 1,133 tons. Wiscasset before 1839 built *Ontario* and *Sterling,* both over 500 tons, and in the 1840s Newcastle, Waldoboro, Rockport, Camden, Belfast, Castine, Searsport, and Bangor followed the trend, although still a great many smaller vessels were built as well. Not until the 1850s, with the advent of the clipper ships, did most of the small towns build any vessel over 1,000 tons.

Maine vessels were built for other trades, too, although these were largely conducted by Boston and New York merchants. One route led around Cape Horn to the Northwest coast for sea otter furs, perhaps to the Hawaiian islands for sandalwood, thence to China for tea, silk, and porcelain. Other vessels went east to Mauritius and to the East Indies for pepper, coffee, and other spices, and thence either home or on to China. For a time there was a brisk trade in opium from India to China, a trade which China tried to interdict and which led to the Opium War between China and Britain.

Maine ships carried Maine ice to hot and distant ports. Frederick Tudor of Boston conceived the idea of exporting ice in 1805 and shipped 130 tons to Martinique. The voyage was a commercial failure, but Tudor kept at it, sent shiploads of ice to southern American ports and to South America, sold it at a loss and gave much away in order to build a market. In 1833 he sent 180 tons of ice to Calcutta. The idea caught on. Maine ice was just as cold and cheaper than Massachusetts ice and soon was cooling drinks from Calcutta to Mandalay in exchange for jute, saltpeter, and indigo. Ice also was sent to the West Indies and South America in exchange for hides and raw wool, for the shoe factories of Lynn, Massachusetts, and the woolen mills on the Merrimac and in Brunswick, Maine. Hides also were a staple product of the California coast long before the Gold Rush.

The transatlantic packet trade occasionally used a Maine-built ship. *Roman,* a transatlantic packet on the Savannah–Liverpool run, was built on the Kennebec. The Black Ball packets *William F. Storer* and *Hamilton Fish* were built in Waldoboro in 1856. They were big vessels, 1,628 tons and 200 feet long, with elegant accommodations for cabin passengers.

Some Maine ships were bought or chartered by other countries. *Alfred Storer* of Waldoboro, for instance, sailed from London for Bombay loaded with railroad iron and machinery in October 1856. She ran into a fierce gale on the 27th which in the next three days carried away the main topgallant mast and, of course, everything above it. The mizzen royal mast broke and took with it the top of the mizzen topgallant mast. The main and mizzen crosstrees were broken, the main topsail yard sprung, the fore and main topmast caps broken, and almost an entire suit of sails blown away; the cargo was adrift in the hold, and the ship leaked badly. On the 30th she limped into Vigo.

Compare this catalogue of disaster with the experience of the schooner

John F. Leavitt, abandoned at sea in a gale in the 1980s because a cargo boom was adrift and oil had spilled on deck.

A vigorous trade was carried on with Canada, trading cotton cloth, leather, meat, flour, and tea for gypsum, grindstones, and coal during the 1840s and 50s.

In short, American ships in general and Maine ships in particular were all over the Earth and the seas thereof. In 1836 Maine built 157 vessels, 26 percent of the ships built in this country. By 1855 Maine was building 388 vessels, 35 percent of the total United States production. If we count only barks and ships, the biggest vessels used in long-haul bulk trades, the figures are even more impressive. In 1836 ninety-three of these vessels were built in the United States, of which Maine built thirty, or about one-third. In 1855 the figures had climbed to 381 ships and barks built in the nation, 213 of which, or 56 percent were built in Maine.

Not only did Maine lead the United States, but the United States led the world in ocean commerce from 1830 until the depression of 1857 and the Civil War. America, in two wars, in a century of illegal trade and piracy, had learned to build fast ships and to sail them boldly. The typical British skipper sailed a square-ended, under-rigged vessel, felt 5 knots was speed enough, shortened sail at night, and reefed early and often, his aim being to get his cargo to its destination safely without damage to his vessel. He navigated pretty much as the seventeenth-century navigators did, by getting into the latitude of his port and sailing east or west until he sighted a large continent. American ships were sharper, were far more heavily sparred and canvased, and were sailed with determination. To be sure, they carried away spars, blew out sails, and strained hulls; but they could make five trips a year to the Englishman's three. Shippers preferred the faster ships, insurance companies charged them lower premiums, and passengers were willing to pay for speed.

As early as 1800, Nathaniel Bowditch, a Salem shipmaster, had developed a method of determining longitude by simultaneous observations of the moon and another celestial body, thus using the moon to determine time, when chronometers were still too expensive for general use. He published his method in 1801 in *The American Practical Navigator,* in the course of which work he found and corrected 8,000 errors in the tables used by English shipmasters. As a result of Bowditch's theory of lunar distances, Yankee shipmasters, already adept at dead reckoning, could steer direct courses from port to port, in most cases cutting days from their passages and making their landfalls with greater precision and safety.

Also, by the 1830s American skippers were accustomed to dealing with foreign commercial agents, port officials, and merchants and were often able to unload and take on a new cargo with greater dispatch than their British counterparts whose business was simply to sail and navigate their ships. Consequently, American ships and American officers dominated world ocean-going trade until the Civil War, steam, and steel brought up a whole new set of considerations.

NOTES

William Armstrong Fairburn's *Merchant Sail* is an excellent basis for this chapter. It is concerned with the whole United States, not just Maine; but inasmuch as Maine was the leading shipbuilding state, the book has considerable information on Maine. It deals also with trades with which Maine had only peripheral interests.

The Skolfields and Their Ships, by Erminie Reynolds and Kenneth Martin, has helpful accounts of the building and life histories of a number of Casco Bay vessels.

For specific information on particular towns, William A. Baker's *Maritime History of Bath* is both comprehensive and detailed. *Shipping Days of Old Boothbay,* Francis Greene's *History of Boothbay, Boothbay Harbor and Southport,* John Johnston's *History of Bristol and Bremen,* Stahl's *History of Old Broad Bay and Waldoborough,* and Aubigne L. Packard's *A Town That Went to Sea* give many details of local history which support the thesis developed by Fairburn and Baker. *Sailing Days on the Penobscot,* by George Wasson and Lincoln Colcord, lists vessels built in the various Penobscot Bay towns year by year.

Albion, Baker, and Labaree's *New England and the Sea* is sketchy and lacking in specifics but useful for a view of the forest if you do not care about the trees. Samuel E. Morison's *Maritime History of Massachusetts* has some useful material relevant to Maine. Of course, William H. Rowe's *Maritime History of Maine* is a constant companion but in this period deals only with the West India trade.

The material on Maine whaling comes from Kenneth Martin's *Whalemen and Whaleships of Maine.* Some of the details on piracy come from *The Pirates Own Book,* for which no author is named; it is such a gory book that perhaps no one wants to admit having written it. Another of the same ilk is *Slave Ships and Slavery,* by George Francis Dow. A lucid explanation of the theory of lunar distances can be found in John Letcher's *Self Contained Navigation with HO 208.* Albion's *Rise of the New York Port* does an excellent job on transatlantic and coastwise packet ships.

The developments in design and construction of ships, the important coastal trades, and the impact of steam on Maine maritime life must wait for the next chapter.

TWENTY

Maine Clipper Ships

THE VIRUS of speed-at-any-price that afflicted the American shipping world with a kind of madness in mid-century came to a climax between 1850 and 1854 with the clipper ship, and then it quickly subsided.

As far back as the War of 1812, shipbuilders in the Chesapeake knew that a vessel with a long, fine entrance, a straight run, and considerable deadrise—that is, a cross section amidships like a flattened V—was a fast vessel. If rigged with a huge sail plan and sailed by men who were willing to risk spars and sails for speed, she could catch almost any ordinary craft afloat. But she could carry little cargo, required a large crew, and was expensive to build and maintain.

Nevertheless, a number of these vessels were built in Pennsylvania, Maryland, and Virginia for high-risk trades where speed meant survival. Privateering, slaving, piracy, opium smuggling between India and China, and the legitimate trades in coffee and fruit produced a number of fast brigs and topsail schooners about 75 feet long and a few barks and ships under 100 feet.

With the growth of the tea trade from China to Boston and New York, larger vessels were needed, and speed was important, for tea loses some of its aroma and exotic flavor in the damp hold of a ship. Furthermore, the first cargoes of tea to come on the market in the new season brought premium prices. One of the early successful vessels in the tea trade was the ship *Ann McKim,* built in 1832 for the South American trade and shifted to the China trade in 1839. She was bigger than her forerunners, 138 feet long, but she had the fine ends and considerable deadrise of the Baltimore Clipper brigs and schooners built on the Chesapeake.

Increasingly bigger and faster ships were built for the China trade. *Panama* and *Montauk* were built expressly for the China trade in 1844 and, while less extreme than *Ann McKim* and with a larger cargo capacity, were ahead of the competition and quite successful. In 1845 *Rainbow,* built in New York, 161 feet long, stirred the shipping world. She was not an extreme model, as clippers go. She had a slight hollow in her forward waterlines, a very long, straight run, less deadrise than *Ann McKim,* but she was very heavily sparred and sailed hard. On her first trip to China, under Captain John Land of Edgecomb, Maine, she met the ship *Monument,* a traditionally designed vessel, homeward bound, off Java Head, went on to China, was eighteen days unloading and taking on a new cargo, and was lying alongside her New York wharf when *Monument* arrived. *Rainbow*'s fastest trip was from Hong Kong to New York in eighty-four days.

Rainbow's success led to the building of increasingly longer, faster, and finer vessels. They carried cargoes of light weight and great value whose early arrival was important. *Sea Witch,* built in 1846, 178 feet long, sailed from China to New York in seventy-seven days, a record that still stands, and averaged 10½ knots for ten days. In 1847 came *Samuel Russell,* 173 feet, with slight reverse curves in both entrance and run. She was logged at close to 16 knots.

The question of how much cargo space to sacrifice for speed was now very much in the minds of merchants and marine architects. Subsequent events tipped the decision heavily toward bigger, sharper, and even faster ships.

In 1848 gold was discovered in California, and in 1849 the rush was on. Everything that could swim was chartered for California, and passage on fast ships was at a premium. As people flooded into San Francisco, freight rates skyrocketed, making fast ships profitable, even those with small cargo capacity.

Then in 1849 Britain repealed the Navigation Acts passed in the seventeenth century. No longer must cargoes entering British ports come in British vessels. Therefore, British merchants chartered the bigger, faster American vessels to bring home the season's tea, further escalating the demand for fast ships.

Gold was discovered in Australia in 1851, and another gold rush was on, from England this time. A fast vessel could make sensational profits carrying freight and passengers to California, tea from China to England, and passengers and fast freight to Australia. Or she could return to America with passengers and manufactured goods and then sail again for California.

Boston and New York went mad for speed. Bigger and faster vessels were built, rigged, loaded, and pushed off for San Francisco in record time. English merchants ordered clippers built in America for the tea trade and the Australian passenger trade. Bigger and faster was better and better.

In a history of Maine, it is hardly necessary to repeat the names and records of famous Boston and New York vessels and their builders. Who has not heard of Griffiths, Webb, and Donald McKay, of *Celestial, Comet, Young America,* of *Challenge* and *Ocean Monarch,* of *Flying Cloud, Lightning,* and *Sovereign of the Seas?* Their descriptions, their port-to-port records, the stories of their voyages are easily available, often airbrush colored and over romanticized; and their pictures adorn rope company calendars on many a fish house wall.

Maine, in a characteristic, conservative way, contracted the speed disease less violently than Massachusetts and New York. Before the California Gold Rush, Maine yards sacrificed little cargo capacity to speed, although the response to the cotton and packet trades had led to larger and larger vessels. When the demand for fast vessels came, however, Maine responded. Over sixty clipper ships were built in Maine between 1849 and 1855.

The figure is easy to challenge, for no one knows exactly what a clipper ship is or was. The late Howard I. Chapelle, curator of the National Watercraft Collection in the Smithsonian Institution, gives us a technical definition: ". . . A clipper was a very sharp-ended vessel having a hull form that possessed a high potential speed and that could carry a spread of sail sufficient to drive the vessel at this high potential speed, at least on occasion." A clipper *ship* was ship rigged: she had three masts and was square rigged on all three.

Robert G. Albion comments: "The overworked and badly abused word *clipper* simply implied streamlined construction in which carrying capacity was sacrificed to speed, or at least to the hope for speed."

Captain Arthur H. Clark limited the term to vessels making the voyage from New York or Boston to San Francisco in 110 days or less.

Carl Cutler in *Greyhounds of the Sea* includes many other vessels because they were called clippers and the term was very loosely used.

Howe and Matthews, authors of *American Clipper Ships,* write: "The clipper ship was a sailing vessel of peculiar construction, designed for great speed rather than capacity. It had a long, sharp bow, generally flaring outward as it rose above the water, and a long, clean run aft. The entrance lines were hollow, the masts were set with a great rake, and the yards were very square. A great sheer enhanced the appearance of a beautiful model and in every way the clipper ship ranked among the most beautiful vessels ever put afloat."

Admiral Morison, in a superb chapter on clipper ships in *The Maritime History of Massachusetts,* adroitly avoids a definition but writes: "Never, in these United States, has the brain of man conceived or the hand of man fashioned so perfect a thing as the clipper ship. In her, the long-suppressed artistic impulse of a practical, hard-worked race burst into flower. The *Flying Cloud* was our Rheims, the *Sovereign of the Seas* our Parthenon, the *Lightning* our Amiens, but they were monuments carved from snow."

Admiral Morison is correct, for the economic conditions that made such expensive vessels possible continued for a matter of only five years. When California became more or less self-sufficient, when the British took over the Australian trade, when the panic of 1857 seriously reduced American purchasing power, speed no longer was a marketable commodity and such clippers as remained were forced into transporting coolies from China to Peru or California, into carrying guano from the Chincha Islands for fertilizer, or lumber from Puget Sound.

The development of the clipper ship in Maine, the towns that built them, the records they set, and some of the experiences that surround their memory are worth recounting.

When Sam Brennan, a native of Saco, Maine, and manager of Sutter's store on the American River in California, picked up a gold nugget in the river's millrace in January 1848, the word spread like a prairie fire. People on the East Coast imagined every brook in California to be lined with golden sands. They marched overland, they sailed to Panama, crossed the Isthmus, and sailed to San Francisco, but a very great many got aboard whatever would float, none of them clippers or anything like it, and headed for Cape Horn. Even the little village on Isle au Haut was not immune. Several families joined forces to build a small bark in which they set out for the gold fields. From Belfast the big bark *Suliot,* 266 feet long, sailed for California in January 1849 with fifty passengers and a mixed cargo whose cargo list was 15 feet long and included clothing, shoes, medicines, house frames ready to set up, and a great deal more. As a floor for the cabins and staterooms, several thousand feet of hemlock boards were stowed over the mixed cargo. The boards were worth $10 per thousand feet in Belfast but sold for $300 a thousand when *Suliot* reached San Francisco after a voyage of 171 days.

Suliot was not alone. Whereas only two vessels entered San Francisco from East Coast ports in 1848, 775 entered in 1849. Among these were nineteen from Bath, thirteen from Portland and the same number from Bangor, ten from Eastport, three from Belfast, two each from Saco and Thomaston, and one each from other Maine ports, to make a total of sixty-seven Maine vessels.

In October 1849 *J. A. Thompson,* no clipper, sailed from Bath carrying forty-nine passengers at a fare of $150 to $200 each. The Reverend Amariah Kallock paid no fare so he could preach to the passengers and perhaps seek Almighty favor with reference to the weather. His prayers must have been heard, for the voyage was accomplished in 128 days, good time for a vessel with no pretensions to speed.

The 259-ton bark *Abby Barker* took the Pratt family and a hold full of house frames. Timothy, the father, was skipper, and the mates were his two oldest sons. He had his wife and twins William and Henry, about eleven, as passengers, plus a crew. They had a hard trip, taking eighty days to beat through the Strait of Magellan. Out in the Pacific the father-skipper dropped dead. The eldest son brought the vessel in to San Francisco, but here the family contracted cholera. The crew deserted en masse. All the Pratts died of the disease except little Henry, who was picked up and taken home by Captain Talbot of Freeport.

Late in the year 1849 the ship-rigged *Andrew Scott* sailed with a cargo of lumber purchased by a Portland syndicate, but by May 1850, when she arrived after a long voyage of 160 days, lumber was going begging, the market saturated. However, they had a small boat on deck which was sold at the handsome price of $2,000 and was used on the river between Sacramento and San Francisco to move freight to the gold fields.

Very soon after these hasty departures, clippers—or what were advertised as clippers—were laid down at shipyards from Kittery to Eastport. To list all of them would be tedious, but a few of the most interesting vessels cannot be overlooked.

At least four clipper ships were built in Kittery, if we count Badgers Island as being in Maine, though they were registered in Portsmouth. *Nightingale,* designed and built by Samuel Hanscom, Jr., was launched on the Maine side of the Piscataqua River in 1851. She was named for Jenny Lind, an accomplished singer from Sweden acclaimed as the Swedish nightingale. The figurehead was a bust of the singer, and the vessel's stern was ornamented with a carving of Jenny Lind reclining with a nightingale perched on her finger.

The vessel was designed to carry 250 passengers to the International Exposition in England for a fare of $100–$125 apiece, and so her accommodations were elegantly finished and cargo capacity was not important. She was 185 feet long, registered at 1,060 tons, had a very long, sharp entrance, considerable deadrise, and her long, clean run finished in a deep narrow V as the water left her. Her owners encountered financial reverses and sold her at auction for $43,500 before she sailed for the Exposition.

Nightingale's first voyage was from Boston to Sydney. Her best day's run was 365 miles, and she often attained a speed of 16 knots. She continued in the Australia–China–New York trade while the speed fever lasted, and then she was bought by a slave trader. *Nightingale* was caught with slaves aboard by USS *Saratoga* on the African coast in 1861, was taken to New York as a prize, and was then bought into the Navy as a dispatch and supply vessel attached to the Gulf blockading squadron during the Civil War. She was armed with four 32-pounders. Judged to be infected with yellow fever, a disease not understood then, she was sent to Boston with a crew of sailors whose enlistments were expiring and sold there for $11,000. She sailed to San Francisco in 119 days from Boston, a creditable performance for a vessel no longer new and with speed no consideration, and was chartered by Western Union to explore the possibility of laying a cable under the Bering Sea. She sailed between New York, San Francisco, and China until 1876 when she was sold to Norwegians and used in the Atlantic lumber trade. Finally, in 1893, at the advanced age of forty-two, she was abandoned at sea.

A little bigger than *Nightingale* was *Dashing Wave,* built in 1853 in Kittery, 182 feet long, registering 1,180 tons. She was even more durable than *Nightingale*. After 120 Cape Horn voyages averaging 127 days, the fastest being 107—good time and the record passage for 1858—she carried general cargo around Pacific ports. She made some fast runs from China and India to New York, and then hauled lumber on the Pacific coast. She carried lumber, grain, and rice through the rest of the century, ran ashore, sank and was raised, and in 1920, having been cut down and used as a barge, was surveyed, found sound, loaded with cannery supplies, and towed to Alaska. Here she went ashore in Seymour Narrows and broke up, after sixty-seven years at sea.

Typhoon, another fast Kittery vessel, bigger than the first two at 225 feet, sailed from Portsmouth to Liverpool in thirteen days, twenty-two hours, within hours of *Red Jacket*'s all-time record. She logged 346 miles in one day and posted speeds of over 15 knots. She raced *Raven* and *Sea Witch* from New York to San Francisco; *Sea Witch* made it in 111 days, with *Typhoon* in 108 days and *Raven* in 106 days.

Snow Squall, built in 1851 at Cape Elizabeth, has been resurrected from her grave at Port Stanley, Falkland Islands. Her bow can be seen in the Spring Point Museum in Portland. She was a small clipper, registering only 742 tons, but she had fine lines and was very fast. Beset by bad luck, she scored no fast passages to San Francisco; indeed, she posted one of the slowest at 206 days. In South Atlantic gales she lost all three topmasts and limped into Montevideo for repairs. Ready for sea at last, she was riding out a gale at anchor when a dragging Spanish brig fouled her, holding her up for twenty-one days more. However, she did sail from New York to Melbourne in eighty-one days and from Shanghai to New York in ninety-one days. Her best demonstration of speed was in 1863 when the Confederate raider *Tuscaloosa* (ex-*Conrad*), showing United States colors, got close to windward of her, fired a gun, and hoisted the Stars and Bars. Instead of surrendering, as the Confederates expected, *Snow Squall* under Captain Dillingham ranged enough ahead of *Tuscaloosa* to fill her sails, sheeted everything home, and despite wild shots from the raider, sailed clean away from her and ran her hull-down* before sunset.

In 1864 *Snow Squall* went aground in the inhospitable tide-ridden Strait of Le Maire, between Staten Land and the South American mainland. Her skipper got her off, but she was leaking badly, so he pumped her into Port Stanley where her cargo was transshipped, and she was abandoned as a total loss. In 1987 Peter Throckmorton, Nicholas Dean, and others found her quite well preserved and at great effort and expense brought her bow back to Portland.

Defiance, 240 feet long, 1,900 tons, designed by Samuel Hartt Pook of New York and built by George Thomas in Rockland, became the center of an international incident on August 14, 1853. She was about to sail for home from the Chincha Islands off Peru with a cargo of guano. One seaman was in jail for having shot a pelican, fine $1.00. The captain offered to pay the fine but was refused. On sailing day, thirty indignant captains and officers of other American vessels came aboard to see *Defiance* off. A gun was fired as the usual signal of departure. Before the echo died, a Peruvian gunboat was alongside and demanded payment of a $25 fine for firing a gun in port. The captain paid reluctantly but observed that unless the Peruvian officer left abruptly, there would be another fine to pay. The officer called for reinforcement, and a bloody fight ensued during which the captain was knocked on the head with a carbine butt, put in irons, and jailed. The mate appealed to the American minister in Callao, and at length the Peruvians freed the captain and the murderer of the pelican, promised redress, and fired their officer.

In 1856 in a heavy gale off the Canary Islands, *Defiance*'s cargo shifted, a

* Got so far ahead of her that *Tuscaloosa*'s hull was below the sea horizon from *Snow Squall*'s deck.

water tank burst, the first and second mates were hurt, and she limped into a Spanish port, where she was sold.

Nonpareil, built in Frankfort in 1852 by George Dunham, illustrates how bad luck can hold up a fast vessel. She was 220 feet long, registered at 1,431 tons, a sharp, fast vessel. In 1854 she was only thirteen days from the Delaware capes to Liverpool, very close to *Red Jacket*'s record time. Yet, in the winter of 1855–56 she was sixty-one days from Liverpool to Philadelphia. She ran into violent westerly gales, lost two complete suits of sails, went south as far as 24 degrees north latitude looking for a favorable slant, and for three solid weeks beat to and fro within 250 miles of the Delaware capes. She completed her next voyage from New York to San Francisco in 115 days, showing that she was still a fast ship.

Model of the clipper *Red Jacket*. *Maine Maritime Museum*

Red Jacket, built in Rockland in 1853 by Deacon Thomas, is the one Maine clipper that everyone knows. She was a big vessel, one of the biggest ever built in Maine, 251 feet long, registering 2,305 tons. Samuel Pook, her designer, gave her a very long, fine entrance with only a slight hollow below the waterline and a bit of a hollow in the run. She had only a very moderate deadrise. After her launching, she was towed to New York to be rigged. Uncoppered,* with "a very indifferent crew," she sailed from her wharf in New York, bound for Liverpool. On one day near the end of this passage she ran 413 miles, an average of over 17 knots. When she appeared off the Mersey

* See chapter notes for a discussion of copper sheathing.

a day before she was expected, two tugs hurried out to tow her up the river. They got lines aboard, but under forced draft could not go fast enough to keep them taut. As she approached her wharf, she took in light sails, backed her topsails, got lines ashore, and warped alongside; it had been thirteen days, one hour, and twenty-five minutes from her wharf in New York. Her record stood until some trimaran yacht beat it in the 1980s. *Red Jacket* was chartered by the British for Australia and ran from the Cape of Good Hope to Melbourne in nineteen days, another record. On her return trip she logged 18 knots at one cast of the log. Back in England, she was sold to the British for £30,000, an unusually high figure, and in 1855 under British colors beat *James Baines, Lightning,* and *Invincible* from England to Australia. In 1882 she was still sailing, carrying lumber from Québec to England. She ended her life as a coal hulk at Cape Verde.

White Falcon, a ship built in Pittston by William Stevens in 1853, had a ghastly end. She never was on the New York–San Francisco run, but carried general cargoes, coal, and guano between New York and Pacific ports. In 1864 she was bought by the Peruvian government to carry coolies from China to the Chincha Islands to work the guano deposits—only a notch above the slave trade. In 1866 in mid-Pacific the coolies mutinied. They were driven below and the hatches secured. The desperate Chinese below decks then set fire to the vessel. The crew, unable to extinguish the fire, abandoned the vessel, leaving her to burn and sink with the Chinese still under the battened hatches.

The ship *Wild Rover,* built in Damariscotta in 1853, had one of the most persistent skippers ever to stand in boots—Captain Thomas Crowell. In 1860 he was sixty days beating against head gales and currents trying to weather Cape Horn. On August 11, at the height of the southern winter, he weathered the Cape, but westerly gales drove him back. Again on August 13 he had the Cape under his lee, and again on August 17, but each time was driven back. Many a skipper might have up helm, run off for the Cape of Good Hope, and taken the eastern way around the world, but he persisted and finally got by on September 4. He was 178 days from New York to San Francisco on that voyage.

The ship *Wild Wave,* 207 feet long, 1,547 tons, was built in 1854 by G. H. Ferrin at Richmond, too late for the Gold Rush trade to California. After a guano voyage from the Chincha Islands to Genoa and back to New York she had a hard passage to San Francisco and thence sailed in ballast for Valparaiso in February 1858 with ten passengers, a crew of thirty, and $18,000 in gold. At 1:00 A.M. on the night of March 5, 1858, the lookout saw breakers on the lee bow. Captain Knowles tacked at once, but the vessel missed stays. With the reef close under his lee, his only chance was to wear ship, turning away from the wind, hoping she would turn quickly enough to clear the breakers. She did not make it and crashed ashore on Oeno Atoll, which was charted 20 miles from its actual position. She hit hard and began to break up at once, sheets of her copper sheathing being torn off by the breaking seas and cast on deck. Captain Knowles got all hands ashore on the low, sandy atoll with considerable provisions and enough sails to make tents. Birds, fish, and eggs were plentiful, and a well was dug which provided fresh water. Never one to sit still and await rescue, the skipper set out in one of the ship's boats with mate Bartlett, five men, and the gold for Pitcairn Island, about 80 miles to the southeast.

In three days they made it, but after a difficult and dangerous landing they found the island deserted, the inhabitants having moved to Norfolk Island. Without a safe harbor, their boat was wrecked. However, they found enough tools left behind by the inhabitants to build a 30-foot schooner from trees cut on the island. She was successfully launched on July 23 and, leaving three of her crew on Pitcairn, set off with the gold aboard for Tahiti, about 1,000 miles to the west-northwest. The wind coming ahead and blowing a gale, Captain Knowles bore off for the Marquesas, lying more northerly and about the same distance away. The course took him close to Oeno, but the schooner passed it out of sight. After eleven days they made land, but pressed on despite the enthusiastic invitation of natives they feared were hostile. On August 4 they made Nukahiva and there found USS *Vandalia*. Captain Knowles sold the schooner to a missionary, and *Vandalia* carried him and his crew to Tahiti. From there, Knowles sailed to Hawaii aboard the French naval vessel *Eurydice* and on to San Francisco in the bark *Yankee*. Meanwhile, *Vandalia* with mate Bartlett aboard rescued the castaways on Oeno, finding they had built a boat from the wreck of *Wild Wave* but had found her too heavy to launch. The three on Pitcairn were picked up, and all duly returned to civilization except for one man who had died on Oeno.

Captain Pattishall, surfeited with the delights of the Celestial City, materialized on Damariscove like a vessel coming out of the fog. It was December 1853, one of those mild, hazy December days that comes after a spell of southwest weather. The captain, rum jug in hand, walked slowly along the island's west shore, hearing the swash of the water on the stony beach, the cry of a gull balancing on the wind overhead. With delight he sniffed the sour, salty smell of rockweed and pools left by the ebbing tide. The incense of wood smoke led him southward by the pond to the head of the harbor where a man on a stone wharf hauled in the painter of a dory. Over the edge of the wharf the man lowered a bucket of shucked clams and tossed down several handlines.

The Captain admired the trim dory, much lighter than the shallops he used to row, and longed for the bite of oars in the water, the lift of a sea under his feet, the heft of a codfish on the end of a handline. The man started down the ladder.

"Hi, Cap. Want a hand? I'll be glad to take an oar."

"Sure, Cap. My boy's laid up. Afraid I'd have to go it alone. Bring the jug along."

An hour later, anchored off to the southeast of the island, the end of

Outer Heron Island, just out by Pemaquid Point, each had slatted aboard several big green-and-white codfish. The weather had changed. They had buttoned their jackets, pulled down their caps. The wind had come off northwest and the hazy blue sky, now sharp and clear, was crowded with hard clouds, dark underneath, brilliant white above, marching quickly up the northern sky.

"Goin' to blow some, ain't it?"

"Likely. Pass the gobstick."

"Hard pull home."

"Good you come along. It'll be easier with two. We can hang on awhile, though."

Captain Pattishall took a long look to windward up the Damariscotta River. The cold wind bit through his coat, felt good to him. Far up the river he saw a square of white over the trees on Farnham Point. As he watched, two more squares appeared beneath the first as a square-rigged vessel rounded the distant point and charged down the river by Inner Heron Island. She was black with a gold line along her sheer, a roll of white water now showing under her bow, her jibs hanging slack, blanketed.

"Big vessel coming down."

"Oh, that's the one they been building all summer up to Damariscotta. She's a big one, and some sharp. Built for some company up to New York."

As they watched, the great clipper, bigger than anything the Captain had ever seen in his life or since, bore down upon them to pass only 50 yards to port. Her new duck sails, gray in the cloud shadow, brilliant white as she burst into the sunshine, were taut and hard in the wind. Four men aloft on the fore royal yard were setting the sail, and above them another yard, still bare, crossed the mast.

"A three-skysail-yarder, Cap. She's a flyer."

The clipper rushed down on them, her bowsprit high above them, her sharp bow carrying a feather of foam on the cutwater, building a wave that slipped back to the fore rigging before it creamed white. As she drove down on the first of the ocean swells, her flaring bow thrust deep into the sea, then lifted her, showing gleaming copper sheathing below her waterline. She passed with a rush, the irresistible rush of a huge, graceful hull through the water, the rush of wind in new rigging, the rush of the building northwester in an acre of new cotton duck canvas.

The two fishermen stood open-mouthed at the majesty of her passing. High on her lovely stern stood a man holding the reel of a chip log, rattling as the line ran out. Beside him stood the mate with a sandglass.

"Mark," called the mate. The man checked the reel, called, "14 and two fathoms."

The mate waved to the dory as she dropped astern and shouted, "She's a flyer." The gold-leaf letters on her stern read, "FLYING SCUD, New York."

The last they saw of her as she headed offshore was the splash of color

Flying Scud's maiden voyage. *Earle G. Barlow*

from the ensign at her spanker gaff and the capsized log chip skittering along the surface.

"*That* calls for a—"

"Hold it, Cap. Don't say anything about it till we get in."

They hauled the killick and, with both men rowing, worked into the lee of the island, slipped up the harbor, and came alongside the stone wharf.

"Now, how about a pull at that jug, Cap?"

At the word, the ghost of Captain Pattishall dissolved like fog on a sunny summer morning. No mortal ever drank of that jug.

Metcalf & Norris in Damariscotta built *Flying Scud,* 1,713 tons. She sailed so fast on her trial trip from Damariscotta to New York that the skipper thought her chronometer was seriously out of adjustment. On her first voyage from New York to Liverpool and back *Flying Scud* could not demonstrate her speed, for she ran into headwinds and heavy weather both ways. She was then chartered for Melbourne. On this voyage she was struck by lightning twice on September 30, 1854, and her cargo of iron was temporarily magnetized. Her compasses ceased to show any interest in the Earth's magnetic field and were useless until mounted on a board projecting 10 feet over the port side. By December 7 they, or the iron cargo, had returned to normal. On November 6 in the South Atlantic *Flying Scud* sailed 449 miles in one day, an average of 18.7 knots. Few indeed are the sailing vessels that have done better than 400 miles in a day, and many a steamer butts along at a great deal less than that.

In 1856 *Flying Scud* sailed from New York to Bombay in eighty-one days, a passage seldom beaten. She continued in trade to the Orient, making one voyage from New York to San Francisco in 118 days in predominantly light airs. She was sold to the British in 1863 and was still sailing under British registry in 1871.

One is tempted to sentimentalize over the end of the clipper ship era, and most writers have succumbed to that temptation. Let us look at those years as a happy combination of economics, engineering, craftsmanship, and art a long time in growing, brilliant in its brief flowering, and remembered nostalgically.

After 1855 few clippers were built, and the ones that survived storm, fire, and shipwreck struggled to make a profit with cut-down rigs and smaller crews carrying guano, coal, lumber, grain, and indigent Chinese to the Western world.

The end of the clipper ship era was not the end of American shipping by any means, for new political and economic forces and new technologies already at work brought about changes equally as interesting and significant as the brief flash in maritime history of the American clipper ship.

NOTES

Captain Arthur Clark's *The Clipper Ship Era* and Carl Cutler's *Greyhounds of the Sea* deal in great detail with this period. Octavius T. Howe and Frederick C. Matthews in *American Clipper Ships* have assembled the life histories of a great many clipper ships; from this book I have picked out the vessels built in Maine. Howard I. Chapelle's *The Search for Speed Under Sail* deals effectively with the development of the clipper ship, and William A. Fairburn's *Merchant Sail* adds specific detail. William A. Baker's *Maritime History of Bath* includes material on Kennebec clippers. *Sailing Days on the Penobscot,* by George Wasson and Lincoln Colcord, has information on Penobscot Bay vessels and that nugget about Isle au Haut. Samuel Morison's *Maritime History of Massachusetts* is of some help, although his emphasis is on Massachusetts, not Maine. Robert G. Albion's *Rise of the New York Port* and *New England and the Sea* are useful, although the latter paints the scene with such a wide brush as to be of little specific interest to Maine readers. There is no lack whatever of sentimentalized accounts of the period, of the specific ships and of their architects and captains.

Captain Pattishall reappears in an effort to give some sort of feeling of what a clipper ship really was. *Flying Scud* was indeed built in Damariscotta by Metcalf & Norris and launched in November 1853. She was a big one, 221 feet long, registering 1,713 tons.

It would have seemed unkind to have had the Captain forced to return to Realms Above before helping to row back to Damariscove against a rising northwester.

The following table gives some notion of the time and place in which many Maine clippers were built. Details on most of these can be found in *American Clipper Ships* (Howe and Matthews).

Some have written disparagingly of the weak construction of American clipper ships, stating that they were lightly built of soft wood and were wracked to pieces after a few years of hard driving. There seems little evidence to support this, at least as far as Maine clippers were concerned. Several were captured by Confederate raiders and burned during the Civil War. A number of Maine clippers went ashore and broke up. *Criterion,* built in Damariscotta in 1855, was in good enough shape to be sold foreign in 1882. *Euterpe,* built in Rockland in 1854, was abandoned leaking badly in the South Atlantic in 1871 at the respectable age of seventeen years. *Flying Eagle* was condemned at Mauritius in 1879 at the age of twenty-seven and was still in good enough shape to find a buyer. *Gauntlet,* built at Richmond in 1853, burned at sea in 1878. *Golden Rule,* built at Damariscotta in 1854, was still sailing in 1900. *Monsoon* was sold to Norway in 1870. *Nightingale* lasted until 1893. *Red Jacket* was still sailing in 1882, and *Dashing Wave* was still sound, even though being used as a barge, in 1920.

It is certainly true that the strains on the hull of a clipper were enormous, and it cannot be denied that they were driven hard. These ships were longer, sometimes twice as long, as earlier vessels, thus alternatively supported only in the middle by the crest of a wave and then on the ends as the wave passed aft and another lifted the bow. Furthermore, they were narrow, the beam being about one-fifth of the length. This meant that their lofty rig was supported athwartships on a very narrow base. Thus the sideways force of the wind was largely converted to a downward thrust on the masts, tending to push the keel down through the bottom of the ship. However, the rigging was not rigid because it was composed of Russian hemp, the least elastic natural fiber available, but still not without stretch. This created an additional sideways strain on the deck where the mast came through. The immensely long lever arm of the mast above the deck tended to pry the deck to leeward and the keel to windward.

To meet these strains, here vastly oversimplified, the clippers were heavily constructed of oak and hard pine. The decks, especially in the way of the masts, were braced with natural grown hackmatack knees tightly fitted and firmly bolted. Longitudinal strength was achieved with massive built-up keels and keelsons on top of the frames and floor timbers and bolted through and through. The keelson often stood up 6 feet inside the hold. The ceiling was edge-nailed and its seams caulked, thus jamming the planks against each other to make almost a solid skin inside the frames. Then, there were heavy longitudinal clamps, or extra-thick strakes of ceiling, at the turn of the bilge and under each deck.

An inspection of the remains of *Snow Squall* in the Spring Point Museum in Portland will support many of the above assertions.

William A. Baker writes of *Monsoon,* a small clipper built at Bath in 1851: "The

Monsoon was framed of Virginia oak [white oak] and hackmatack and her outside planking was 4-inch-thick yellow pine and oak, the latter being employed principally where sharp bending was necessary at the bow and stern. Her deck beams were of hard pine 13x15 inches on the lower deck and 10x13 inches on the upper, all strongly fastened with 1½-inch-diameter iron. She was heavily copper fastened and copper sheathed before launching."

About the time of the American Revolution, the Royal Navy began experimenting with copper sheathing to protect the bottoms of their wooden vessels from the attacks

PLACE	1851	1852	1853	1854	1855	1856	OTHER
Kittery	*Nightingale* *Typhoon*		*Dashing Wave*	*Midnight*			
Kennebunk	*Roebuck*						
Cape Elizabeth	*Snow Squall*			*Phoenix*			
Freeport			*Quickstep*				*Tam O'Shanter* (1849)
Harpswell			*Rising Sun*				
ath	*Monsoon*	*Carrier Pigeon* *Peerless*	*Flying Dragon* *Viking* *Undaunted* *Emerald Isle* *Strelna* *Miss Mag*	*Mary Robinson* *Windward*			*Maid of the Sea* (1859)
ennebec R.			*Gauntlet* *Pride of America* *White Falcon*	*Dashaway* *Wild Wave* *Wizard King*			
iscasset				*Golden Horn*			
amariscotta wcastle }		*Flying Eagle* *Levanter* *Queen of the East*	*Flying Scud* *Ocean Herald* *Wild Rover*	*Golden Rule* *Talisman*	*Criterion*		
ldoboro		*Wings of the Morning*					
omaston		*Golden Racer*	*Oracle*	*Crest of the Wave* *Ocean Chief*			
ckland		*Defiance* *Rattler* *Springbok*	*Anglo Saxon* *Live Yankee* *Red Jacket*	*Euterpe* *Yankee Ranger*	*Young Mechanic*		
nkfort		*Flying Arrow* *Ocean Spray*	*Nonpareil* *Spitfire*			*Arey*	
wer							*Golden Rocket* (1858)
ast				*Seaman's Pride*			
port							*Grey Feather* (1850)
binston			*Red Gauntlet*		*Dictator*		

of the teredo worm in tropical waters. The teredo can make a honeycomb of a stout plank in a matter of months. In temperate as well as in tropical waters, weeds and barnacles fouled the bottoms of vessels and made them slow and logy. The copper sheathing proved a great success. Admiral Horatio Nelson's *Victory* was coppered, doubtless a number of years after her launching in 1765, and USS *Constitution* was coppered before her launching in 1797. Her copper was made by Paul Revere.

By the mid-nineteenth century, most seagoing vessels, commercial as well as naval, were coppered. To prevent galvanic action between the copper and the iron fastenings in the vessel, which would quickly eat away the iron, a layer of tarred horsehair felt was laid under the copper. Whaling vessels which sailed on much longer voyages than most merchant vessels were coated with hot pitch, then 1-inch pine sheathing under the copper.

The sheet copper generally used was called yellow metal or Muntz metal after its inventor. It was 60 percent copper and 40 percent zinc. Much of it was manufactured in Manchester, England. It was customary to copper a vessel a year or two after she was launched, although the clipper *Monsoon* and USS *Constitution* were coppered before launching.

Copper sheathing came in four weights, the heaviest used forward, the lightest aft. After forty months the sheathing would be reduced to half its original thickness by friction and by chemical reaction with salt water. In well-maintained vessels it was then renewed. The theory was that any marine growth would be poisoned by copper ions in the water and would be washed off as the copper wore away.

Composite ships, ships with iron frames and wooden planking, were used instead of all-steel vessels; they could be coppered as steel ships could not because of the galvanic action between the copper and the steel. One of the disadvantages of the early steel vessels was that their bottoms quickly became fouled with weed and barnacles. *Dirigo,* Sewall & Co.'s first steel vessel, logged 11 knots at the beginning of her maiden voyage but could not do better than 8 or 9 knots toward the end of it. The return trip, Japan to New York, took 140 days; Captain George Goodwin estimates he would have done it in 20 days less with a clean bottom.

About 1900 copper paint was developed. This was essentially powdered copper oxide in a vehicle that made it stick to the bottom of a vessel and slowly wash away as the copper sheathing had done. With a suitable primer to insulate the copper oxide from the steel, copper paint could be used on steel vessels.

Few small vessels were coppered. Before the invention of copper paint they were tarred. Most of the coasting schooners were copper painted, but a few deepwater wooden vessels were coppered as late as the 1920s. James Stevens of Goudy and Stevens in East Boothbay reports having repaired vessels that had been coppered, and Paul Luke, also of East Boothbay, who built commercial wooden vessels before World War I, reports that boys and girls after school worked in shipyards pounding hundreds of copper tacks, closely spaced, into centerboards before they were installed in order to prevent fouling. It was impossible to paint a centerboard when a vessel was grounded out or hauled on a marine railway.

The scantlings of *Lightning* given in the appendix to Chapelle's *The Search for Speed Under Sail* are massive. Although she was not a Maine-built ship, she might serve as an example of good clipper ship construction.

I once was accosted by Nicholas Dean in a Damariscotta bookstore. Mr. Dean is a man of very considerable physical stature, a really *big* man. He had just returned from the Falkland Islands with the bow of *Snow Squall,* which he had detached from the remains of the vessel. He towered over me, clutching his hands together, and shouted, "Did you ever want to choke a ghost?"

"What ghost?" I stammered.

"Howard I. Chapelle's ghost. He said clippers were lightly built. Twelve by twelves!"

TWENTY-ONE

Maine Steam

LIKE THE EARLY AIRPLANES, the first steamboats were considered but a fad that would soon be forgotten—at best rather dangerous amusement. However, with the success of Robert Fulton's *Clermont* on the Hudson River in 1807, wider possibilities unfolded. Jonathan Morgan of Alna in 1816 built an open scow, equipped her with a wooden boiler banded with iron, a simple steam engine, and a screw propeller and ran her down the Sheepscot, across to Seguin, and up the Kennebec against the tide. It was a triumph of science, but Morgan made no practical application of it.

Two years later, in 1818, *Tom Thumb,* Maine's first practical wood-fired steamboat, owned by a Mr. Dodd, was towed from Boston to Seguin. There she fired up, and puffed up the Kennebec River. She was an open wooden boat about 30 feet long with two paddles on each side connected with rods like the wheels on a steam locomotive. She was at once put on a scheduled run between Bath and Augusta with occasional coastwise excursions, once getting as far east as Rockland. She ran at least until 1828.

In 1822 Captain Seward Porter had the steamer *Kennebec* built for the Augusta–Waterville run, but she soon appears in old records running from Portland to Yarmouth. She was very much an experimental craft. The next year, 1823, Captain Porter established the Kennebec Steam Navigation Company and had the 82-foot *Waterville* built at Bath. He also bought the 80-foot *Patent* from New York. Her engine and boiler were built by Daniel Dod in Elizabethtown, New Jersey. On her trial trip on the Hudson the boiler had blown up, killing Dod and four others, and she was for sale cheap at $20,000. *Patent* was about 80 feet long, measured 200 tons, and could maintain a speed of 10 knots. In conjunction with *Waterville,* in 1824, one could go from Augusta to Boston with comfort and dispatch for $7.00. *Waterville* left Augusta at 1:00 P.M. on Monday for Bath; there the passenger could spend the night and leave at 5:00 A.M. Tuesday on *Patent* for Portland. She left Portland at 6:00 P.M. on Tuesday and landed in Boston on Wednesday. On Friday she left Boston at 4:00 A.M., then left Portland on Saturday at 4:00 for Bath, where *Waterville* waited to run to Augusta.

The value of a steamer as a towboat was at once evident to the master of any sailing vessel trying to get down the Kennebec. In July 1924 *Patent* towed a brig from Bath to sea in 1 hour and 26 minutes, then towed a sloop up to Butler Point, towed the schooner *Maine* almost to Seguin, came back into the river and towed a sloop up to Bath, all in one morning. From this it is evident that *Patent* did not maintain her Bath–Boston schedule consistently.

The Kennebec Steam Navigation Company, still experimenting with steamers, had the 83-foot *Maine* built in 1824. She was a sort of catamaran consisting of two schooner hulls with a paddle wheel between them. She was enough of a success to run from Bath to Bangor with stops at Boothbay, Waldoboro, Owls Head, Camden, Belfast, Castine, Bucksport, and Frankfort. Later in the summer she was based in Portland. *Patent* brought passengers down the river from Bath and met her at Pond Island.

In 1826 the company bought *Legislator,* another boiler-explosion case. She was 115 feet long with a 60-horsepower cross-head engine and ran from Boston to Portland and on to Bath two days a week.

Competition with the company came in 1824 when a Mr. Bartlett of Eastport bought *New York* to run from Boston to Portland and on to Eastport three times each month. In August 1826 she had several hard days. Early one morning, she ran on a rock in the Kennebec; no serious damage was done, and she came off easily on the next tide. A few days later she ran down *Patent* off Owls Head. *New York* towed the crippled *Patent* to Belfast, continued on her way to Eastport, but caught fire off Petit Manan, burned, and sank. All hands were rescued. The next year *Experiment* ran from Augusta to Bath to connect with *Legislator* via stage in Portland for Boston.

Success, however, was limited, for in 1828 the Kennebec Steam Navigation Company was liquidated and its assets sold at auction in Boston. Captain Porter personally bought *Patent* and kept her on the Boston–Portland route until 1830 and then on the Penobscot River until 1835 when she was sold south. In 1829 Porter also ran the 150-foot *Connecticut* from Boston to Portland to Bath.

Profits were marginal because of the then-current economic depression and because wood-burning paddle-wheel steamers required such large quantities of room for fuel that there was little comfortable accommodation for paying passengers and freight. An advertisement in the *Maine Gazette* lists the following wood depots on the Bath–Eastport route: Bath, Boothbay, Herring Gut (Port Clyde), Owls Head, Belfast, Castine, Eggemoggin Reach, Cranberry Island, Moosabec Reach, Haycock Harbor, Lubec, and Eastport.

Nevertheless, there was a real and continuing need for steamboats on the Maine coast. Roads were few, unpaved, and very rough. Furthermore, because the coast lies in a great arc facing southeast from Boston to Eastport, it is much shorter to cut across by water from Cape Ann to Seguin (90 miles) or to Monhegan, than it is to come by road. While sailing packets could take a week or very much longer to beat up to Boston, a 10-knot steamer could make the run overnight and provide passengers with a good dinner and a comfortable bunk. Indeed, some of the later boats were very luxurious.

Maine was gaining rapidly in population, principally along the rivers where water power ran new textile and shoe factories. Lumber was coming down the rivers and being sawn at places like Machias, Bangor, and the Kennebec River towns. Fishing in coastal towns was a big business, too, and provided a source of freight once the fresh-fish market in Boston became active enough to demand fish from Maine. Shipbuilding was booming all along the coast, but especially in the mid-coast region between Casco Bay and Mount Desert. Finally, summer people were coming in increasing numbers, as discussed in Chapter 31.

Steamers were ideal for river transport in smooth water where fickle winds and strong currents made sail navigation difficult. East of Portland there was a well-protected inside passage alongshore almost to Eastport with only a few promontories extending into the open ocean. Therefore, fast and reliable freight and convenient passenger service by water was much in demand by the growing population.

In 1835 the Kennebec & Boston Steam Navigation Company was founded to provide service from Gardiner to Boston. In 1836 the 173-foot wooden paddle-wheel steamer *New England,* built at New York in 1833, was put in service from Portland to Boston, making two round trips a week.

On May 31, 1838, *New England* collided with the stout Thomaston lime schooner *Curlew* off Boon Island. *Curlew* rescued all but one of *New England*'s passengers. The crew, with sufficient lifeboats, stayed aboard to save valuable property including $50,000 in cash. When *New England* filled, she rolled over. The crew escaped, but her heavy engines and wood-burning boilers fell out through the light superstructure. She was towed into Portsmouth bottom up and righted but never rebuilt. *Huntress,* chartered from the New London & Norwich Steamboat Company, took her place with great success.

The early steamers were remarkably simple machines. They used a single-cylinder steam engine set vertically in the bottom of the boat. Steam at low pressure, 20 to 40 pounds per square inch, was admitted first below the piston to drive it up and then above the piston to drive it down, a suitable exhaust port being provided near the middle of the cylinder. The piston rod went up through the boat to one end of a walking beam, a fore-and-aft timber pivoted in the middle and prominent above the upper deck. The other end of the beam was connected by a rod and eccentric to the shaft of the paddle wheels, extending slightly over the sides of the vessel. The boiler, fired at first with wood and later with coal, ran the heat to and fro past pipes full of water to make steam and out through a tall stack to increase draft. Some engines exhausted steam up the stack to increase draft.

Other early steamers employed a cross-head engine. This had the same cylinder, piston, and piston-rod arrangement as the walking-beam engine, but the cylinder lay horizontally in the boat or perhaps slightly inclined and the piston rod drove a steel block back and forth between guides. A connecting rod from the cross-head to the eccentric on the paddle-wheel shaft drove the paddle wheels. When compound and then triple-expansion engines were developed, calling for higher boiler pressures and higher revolutions per minute, the cross-head engine was more generally used, until *Camden* and *Belfast,* built in 1907 and 1909, were equipped with steam turbines.

The smaller coastwise steamers exhausted steam directly or up the stack, but the vessels running continuously for some distance offshore, like those on the Boston–Bangor route, carried condensers to recycle boiler water. Lubrication was provided by oil cups where possible and by an ingenious device for using boiler pressure to mix a spray of oil with steam entering the cylinder.

Although the screw propeller was invented at about the same time as the paddle wheel, the paddle wheel was more generally used at first. In order to protect the paddles from damage against wharves, a guard was built out from the side of the hull, extended forward and aft of the wheel, and faired into the hull at bow and stern. This increased the area of the main deck considerably as well as protecting the paddle wheels.

The screw propeller was tried on the lightly built early steamers—Jonathan Morgan's 1816 vessel used one—but because the hulls were so flexible, and the shaft, going out through a rigid stuffing box in the stern, either leaked or produced numerous other leaks, the simpler paddle wheel with its shaft running above the waterline was generally preferred. The light construction of early hulls led to one steamer's loss on the Hudson. The weight of boiler, engine, paddle wheels, and fuel amidships broke her in two, and she quickly sank. Some of the early vessels were strengthened by a "hog frame," a truss of heavy timber and iron rods extending over two-thirds of the vessel's length and very prominent in photographs.

Steamers were much more lightly constructed than the stout sailing craft that had to bear the enormous strains of tall spars and Cape Horn seas. Also steamers were narrower and of shoaler draft in order to navigate rivers and harbors along the coast and to lie alongside wharves. For instance, *Portland,* the first of that name, built in 1834 in Portland for the Portland–Boston route, was 163 feet long, 27 feet wide, and only 10 feet deep. She registered 400 tons. For comparison, the schooner *Old England,* built in 1849, was 164 feet long, 35 feet wide, 17½ feet deep, and registered 917 tons. The ship *Hellespont,* built in 1856, was 160 feet long, 32 feet wide, and 22 feet deep; she registered 750 tons.

With the development of steel hulls and more rigid wooden hulls, the screw propeller became popular. It was efficient as it was submerged for its full revolution, was less subject to damage, and increased maneuverability as it drove a stream of water by the rudder. Tugboats found the screw propeller far preferable to paddle wheels, and naval vessels soon came to use it exclusively.

Yet after paddle wheels were abandoned, the screw-propelled vessels were still built with guards or sponsons to increase deck area and prevent rolling to some extent. This made the vessels look top-heavy, but one must remember that the upper works were very lightly constructed and the engine, boiler, fuel, and water were all below the main deck.

Sails were rigged on steamers at first as safety devices and later kept to increase speed should the wind be fair but were abandoned in later years.

Some of the passenger steamers, particularly the ones running out of Boston to Maine ports, were elegantly appointed with gold leaf, carved panels, and shuttered staterooms. They took pride in the excellence of their cuisine as well as in their speed and good looks.

Navigation on the offshore routes was largely by clock and compass. Thachers Island off Cape Ann, Seguin, and Monhegan all had powerful lighthouses and fog signals; even in fog or snow a skipper could get close enough to hear them. The skippers on the inside routes knew every island, rock, and buoy intimately and seldom went astray. Running at a known speed on a compass course for a familiar landmark only a short distance away was well within the capabilities of a steamboat skipper.

Early in the history of steamboating the courts made it clear that no state or city could grant any one steamboat line a monopoly on any particular waterway. Consequently, rival lines competed with first-comers and fired up steamboat wars. One of the first of these was on the Gardiner–Bath–Portland–Boston run.

In 1833 "Commodore" Vanderbilt, a successful steamboat entrepreneur on Long Island Sound, came to Maine in *Chancellor Livingston* to challenge Captain Porter. However, Porter bought *Chancellor Livingston,* ran her in 1834 with *Connecticut,* and then put her cross-head engine in the new *Portland.* This was a formidable machine with a bore of 56 inches and a stroke of 6 feet. *Portland*'s boiler burned coal; she was the first coal-burning steamer in Maine. After running from Portland to Boston and then for a time as "connecting boat" on the Bangor line, in 1842 she was sold to James Cunningham for the Boston–Portland route again, where she ran with *Bangor*.

Commodore Vanderbilt tried again in 1838 to capture the Boston–Portland route from *New England*'s replacement, *Huntress*. *Huntress* was 173 feet long, a handsome, fast, and well-appointed vessel. Her main cylinder was 36 inches in diameter with a 12-foot stroke. Vanderbilt challenged with the smaller *Clifton,* running from Hallowell to Portland, and in July with *Augusta,* running from Hallowell to Portland to Boston. Neither could compete with *Huntress,* so the 175-foot *Commodore Vanderbilt* took up the challenge. She had a huge engine with a 41-inch-diameter cylinder and a 10-foot stroke. Competition was keen. Vanderbilt cut the fare to $1.00 and piled on the steam. Finally, the two steamers held a formal race, starting together from Boston. When *Huntress* passed her lines ashore in Bath 9 hours and 10 minutes later, *Commodore Vanderbilt* was emerging from Fiddlers Reach two miles below the city.

The slight difference in speed might not have been significant had the atmosphere on Vanderbilt's boat been more attractive. A passenger wrote a letter to the Bath newspaper in September 1838, saying in part:

"You will scarcely credit it that one hundred and fifty persons, at least, embarked that night on a craft so miserably contrived, or that were they swine instead of human beings their sufferings would not have been more intolerable, their comfort less consulted, nor their lives less endangered. Drunkenness, quarreling, horrid oaths and epithets were the soul-stirring performances throughout the night."

The Commodore tried once more. He bought *Huntress* from New London & Norwich and offered either to sell her to Kennebec & Boston or to run her himself. Kennebec & Boston bought the steamer for $10,000 more than Vanderbilt had paid for her, and Vanderbilt retired from the competition.

Other small steamers were employed from time to time to maintain service with the Kennebec River ports. *Minerva* was one of these, with no great reputation for speed. The Bath newspaper observed that on one occasion, bound upstream against a heavy ebb tide, she had raced a steam sawmill on the bank and been fairly beaten.

The Boston–Portland route was run by the steamer *Portland,* first of that name, built at Portland, and owned by the Cumberland Steam Navigation Company. She was a fine vessel, with the cross-head engines from *Chancellor Livingston* and the coal-burning boiler from the old vessel. This first *Portland* ran successfully from 1835 until 1850 with occasional diversions to Bangor, but usually she connected with *Bangor* at Portland.

Bangor was owned by the Boston & Bangor Steamship Company, founded in 1833, and ran regularly between Portland and Bangor. She was a wood burner, consuming twenty-five cords of wood each trip, and carried fore-and-aft sails to steady her and back up the engines. In 1842 she was sold to a Turkish company to transport pilgrims on their way to Mecca. However, no Moslem would board her, for she was painted white, the color of mourning to Moslems. A coat of black paint met that crisis. Later she was sold to the Turkish government as a military vessel.

The Eastern Railroad reached Portland in 1842. As an encouragement to passengers, the railroad company put *Huntress* and *M. Y. Beach* on the Portland–Penobscot River run, but Captain Memnemon Sanford of the Sanford Independent Line brought on the new *Express* in competition.

Bangor Steam Navigation Company raised its flag in challenge on the Bangor–Boston route by ordering in 1842 a new *Bangor,* the first iron steamer in Maine. She was an elegant vessel, three masted, schooner rigged, with a clipper bow and a figurehead. She was driven by a screw propeller instead of paddle wheels. Unfortunately, this very promising steamer burned on her second voyage, was raised, sold to the government as a military vessel for the Mexican War in 1846, and sold to New Orleans interests in 1849.

In 1845 the Sanford Independent Line built the first *Penobscot,* 196 feet long, registering only 494 tons, for the Boston–Bath service, but transferred her the same year to run from Boston to Bangor. Instead of more or less following the shore, *Penobscot* ran directly from Cape Ann to Monhegan, cutting many miles off the voyage and eliminating a stop at Portland.

As the traffic both in freight and passengers increased, vessels became larger and faster. *Governor,* 203 feet long, built in 1846, ran from Portland to Bangor and other routes. *State of Maine,* built for the Eastern Railroad and Boston & Maine Railroad, 248 feet and 840 tons, was one of the longest steamers. *Daniel Webster,* built in 1853, was 240 feet long but wider and deeper than *State of Maine,* hence registered 50 tons more. In 1882 a new *Penobscot* was built, 255 feet long, 1,414 tons, with a 50-inch cylinder and a 12-foot stroke. She was so long and light that she was supported by a hog frame to prevent her from flexing in rough water. In 1894 came *City of Bangor,* a wooden side-wheeler of 277 feet, and finally *Camden* and *Belfast* in 1907 and 1909, 320 feet long, 2,153 tons, built by the Bath Iron Works and driven by 4,000-horsepower triple-screw turbines.

While this increase in size, power, speed, and elegance was developing in the boats which ran to Boston, inshore coastal lines were fanning out from Portland, Bath, and Rockland to bring freight and an increasing number of summer people to the islands and smaller coastal communities. The Casco Bay Steamboat Company controlled most of the Casco Bay traffic. Their queens were *Sebascodegan* and *Aucocisco,* built at South Portland in 1895. They connected Portland with the inner islands and then with Chebeague Island, Harpswell, and Bailey Island. Besides these two 100-foot ladies, there were many smaller wooden steamers running from Portland among the Casco Bay islands, up to South Freeport, across to Harpswell, Cundys Harbor, and Cape Small. Local people grew emotionally attached to their favorite steamboats and will greet with bitter scorn and harsh words any book that does their beloved less than justice. Little *Phantom,* only 75 feet long, ran up to South Freeport, as did *Alice and Madeleine. Pilgrim* carried commuters to and from Peaks Island. *Pejepscot* ran across to Cape Small. And there were many others carrying freight, island residents, and summer visitors to and from the island communities. The steamboats and the hotels established a symbiotic relationship, each stimulating the other. The steamboat companies advertised excursions, carnivals, illuminations and explosions* on the islands, and the hotels, some of them owned by the steamboat companies, advertised the charms of the local scenery and the elegance of the accommodations to be reached via the boats. All the food and equipment to provide for these visitors, of course, came from Portland by steamer. This applied to mainland as well as island towns, for as yet railroads, trolley lines, and stagecoaches could not carry all who wanted to come nor the food and equipment to support them.

From about 1840, "Uncle Sam" Donnell rowed people from Bath to Boothbay for $1.00 apiece or 50 cents each for two or more, sometimes

* Fireworks.

rowing 60 miles in 24 hours, presumably with the tide. With a fair wind, he set a sail. In 1865 a sailing packet advertised service to Boothbay and way-points, and in April 1866 the steamboat *Spray* made her first trip, from Boothbay to Bath, connecting with the westbound train at Bath. From then on a number of wooden steamers ran up and down the tide-scoured Sasanoa River, sometimes using ringbolts set in the rocks on the shores of Hell Gate to make their way against the current, a practice reminiscent of Champlain's passage up the same stream in 1605. The names of these steamers still provoke memories from oldest inhabitants in mid-coast Maine. *Samoset,* only 67 feet long, renamed *Damarin,* met the Bath–Boothbay steamer at Westport and visited the Isle of Springs, Squirrel Island, Mouse Island, and Sawyer Island, making her last run in 1914. *Nahanada, Wiwurna,* and *Winter Harbor* docked at wharves from Pemaquid and New Harbor to Christmas Cove, South Bristol,

From left to right: Wiwurna, Nahanada, Samoset, and an unidentified steamer at Boothbay. *Boothbay Region Historical Society*

East Boothbay, Ocean Point, Linekin Bay, Boothbay Harbor, and up the Sasanoa to Five Islands, MacMahan Island, Robinhood, Westport, and Bath. *Island Belle, Islander, M & M, Eldorado, Nellie G,* and *Tourist* ran between landings in the Boothbay and Pemaquid regions. *Tourist,* running from Bristol up the river to Damariscotta, got caught in a strong flood tide at Damariscotta, was carried up against the bridge, capsized, and sunk. She was raised, rebuilt, renamed *Sabino,* and plied the waters of Casco Bay and later the Merrimac River. She is now at Mystic Seaport, restored and still carrying passengers.

Brandon, a 200-foot steel vessel, ran from Boston to Portland and continued down east to Boothbay and on to Eastport. *Enterprise, Salacia, Mineola,* and *Monhegan* ran to and from Portland to Penobscot Bay ports, stopping at many waypoints. It was this service, established in the late 1880s, that made it profitable for mid-coast fishermen to supply the Boston fresh-fish market, leading to winter fishing and the development of the Friendship sloop, a subject dealt with in a later chapter.

Captain Ed Archibald's 80-foot *May Archer* was a favorite. Built in 1906, she was used for one summer, running from Portsmouth to the Isles of Shoals, and then brought east. Believing that Monhegan had great possibilities as a summer retreat, Captain Archibald built, or participated in building, the Island Inn in 1907, carrying all the material from Boothbay in *May Archer.* He established a regular service from Boothbay to the island and also carried the mail to Thomaston where it was put on the train. During the winter *May Archer* was used on the Rockland–Northeast Harbor run. In 1913 she was running in Boston Harbor; later she carried the mail to Block Island, and she finally burned alongside a wharf in Quincy, Massachusetts, in May 1934.

Westport and *Southport,* 125-foot twins built in 1921, proved too big and deep for the Bath–Boothbay route. They moved east, met *Camden* and *Belfast* in Rockland, and ran to Mount Desert and Penobscot Bay landings until 1934.

Part of Penobscot Bay steamboat history is the great steamboat war on the Rockland–Vinalhaven (Carvers Harbor) run. In 1873 the Fox Island & Rockland Steamboat Company's *Pioneer* was challenged by *Ulysses,* owned by a rival line, and to meet the challenge the company chartered *Clara Clarita* and cut the fare. The new boat, a converted wooden yacht and then a tug, was fast—she still holds the steamer record across the Bay—but she was expensive to operate. Even so, the fare came down to 25 cents round trip. The Fox Island company won. *Ulysses* was put on the Rockland–Bar Harbor run by the Rockland, Mount Desert & Sullivan Steamboat Company, *Clara Clarita*'s charter expired, and *Pioneer* went back to the Rockland–Vinalhaven run. In November 1891, however, residents of Vinalhaven, dissatisfied with *Pioneer*'s service, agreed with the Frenchman's Bay Steamboat Company that if that company would put on a better vessel than *Pioneer,* they would give her their business.

During the same month the Fox Island & Rockland Steamboat Company contracted for a new steamer and chartered *Forest Queen* from Casco Bay. In April 1892 she replaced the old *Pioneer* and beat *Emmeline,* Frenchman's Bay's new boat, by "several minutes." Indeed, she beat *Emmeline* consistently. However, *Emmeline* had her enthusiastic supporters who would rather row than take *Forest Queen.* The partisans of each vessel became highly emotional. Fistfights were frequent, bets heavy. There were fracases in the poolrooms of Rockland, the Rockland police force was augmented, and a number of enthusiastic poems appeared in the Rockland paper. Despite her loss of the race by four minutes, *Emmeline,* with the support of her partisans, carried more passengers and freight. Spectators counted aloud the passengers coming off the boats, counting those with free passes as "deadheads" (thus: "One, two, three, deadhead, four . . ."), doubtless to the embarrassment of those with passes. Fares stabilized at 50 cents, round trip.

The Vinalhaven Steamboat Company, an offshoot of the Frenchman's Bay Steamboat Company and then running *Emmeline,* was building a new boat to match the Fox Island Company's. In the meantime, they put the fast steamer *Viking* on the line. There was again fierce argument and frenzied betting. On the day of the race, *Viking* appeared to have the advantage, and the Vinalhaven line's supporters made ready to enjoy their triumph—the first in a long time—when *Viking* blew her main steam line. Again the Rockland line won out.

In the spring of 1892 both new steamers were launched. On June 30 the Rockland line's *Gov. Bodwell* took over the Vinalhaven run from *Forest Queen.* A few days later the Vinalhaven line's new *Vinal Haven* appeared, a sad disappointment from her "screech owl whistle" to her ungainly pilothouse, her yellow funnel, and her obsolete machinery. The two new boats did not race. The outcome was never in doubt. What had been an even match now tilted in favor of the handsome *Gov. Bodwell* and the Rockland line.

All of these early steamers were built of wood. On January 13, 1893, *Vinal Haven* caught fire alongside her wharf. The engine and superstructure were badly damaged, but she was scuttled before the hull was seriously hurt. She was entirely rebuilt with an improved power plant and a much better-looking superstructure dominated by a rakish stack of appropriate black. Nevertheless, she was never as fast as *Gov. Bodwell.* Feeling gradually subsided. The Vinalhaven Steamboat Company fell on hard times and sold *Vinal Haven* to W. S. White of the Rockland line. The war was over, and the two boats served Penobscot Bay travelers as far east as Swans Island for many years.

Gov. Bodwell burned at her Swans Island wharf in March 1931, and *Vinal Haven* was condemned in 1938, stripped, and abandoned on the bar between Monroe and Sheep islands. Other steamers replaced them until May 30, 1942, when *North Haven* made her last trip. Now a stout diesel car ferry run by the state provides communication for Vinalhaven residents.

Other steamers ran out of Rockland during the later steamboat years. One of the most popular was *J. T. Morse,* running through Fox Islands and Deer Island Thorofares to Mount Desert. President Eliot of Harvard was a frequent passenger. One day a member of *J. T. Morse*'s crew accosted the president. "We have agreed," he said, "that you are probably the smartest man that travels on this boat. But if you are so smart, why aren't you rich?" President Eliot considered the question fairly from all angles and answered, "Because I never had time."

In September 1915 *J. T. Morse* collided with the steamer *Pemaquid* in the fog off the western end of Deer Island Thorofare. *Pemaquid* backed off, leaving a deep wound in the *Morse*'s bow, and after a decent interval, went on to Rockland. Captain Shute managed to get the *Morse* alongside a wharf at Moose Island before she sank. All passengers and crew got ashore safely except for one Ray Eaton, who was missing. His baggage and even his topcoat were found aboard the wreck, but Mr. Eaton could not be found. It was assumed that somehow he had fallen overboard in the confusion. The company authorities were notified of the sad event, but before the news of his demise could spread far, Mr. Eaton appeared in Rockland alive and well. He had been standing forward on the deck of the *Morse* when the bow of *Pemaquid* came out of the fog right in front of him and cut deep into the deck. Seeing that the *Morse* was badly damaged and the *Pemaquid* apparently unhurt, it seemed the part of wisdom to step aboard the sounder vessel. Or perhaps he did not think at all but just did what seemed to be the thing to do at the time. Almost immediately *Pemaquid* backed off and took Mr. Eaton with her.

Another steamer with a picturesque history was *Norumbega,* running from the railroad terminus at Hancock Point to Mount Desert harbors. It was customary in her fireroom to enter Northeast Harbor with a good head of steam and bank the fires, relying on the steam in the boilers to get her across the short stretch to Southwest Harbor. One foggy morning there was a delay, the steam proved inadequate, the pressure fell, and the engine stopped in the fog off Greening Island. However, *Norumbega,* although out of control, had way enough to slide up on the rocks of Clark Point at the entrance to Southwest Harbor. It is said that a boy and girl, sitting on the rocks in the fog exchanging confidences, were startled beyond belief by the sudden silent appearance of a great steamer which appeared to be chasing them up the shore.

Norumbega struck on the top of the tide, and it was evident she would not come off easily. However, the ingenious Captain Rodney Sadler had her afloat on the next high tide. The only tug available took a line to her stern. *Norumbega*'s twin screws ran full astern, and Captain Sadler in the 2,400-horsepower steamer *Moosehead* steamed at full throttle up the narrow channel between Greening Island and Clark Point as close to *Norumbega*'s stern as he could come. *Moosehead*'s huge stern wave gave *Norumbega* the lift she needed, and she slid smoothly into deep water. *Norumbega* and *May Archer* burned side by side in Quincy in 1934.

The first *Rockland,* built in 1854, ran on the Blue Hill and Bar Harbor lines, connecting with *Daniel Webster* at Rockland for Boston. When the Civil War broke out, Captain Otis Ingraham and the crew volunteered with the steamer and in 1861 sheathed her pilothouse in boilerplate. They were ordered to run up the Rappahannock River past a Confederate battery on Windmill Point. More than 160 projectiles—solid shot and shell—the Confederates fired at *Rockland.* If one had hit her fairly on a paddle wheel or exploded near her boiler, she would have sunk on the spot, but she got through. Later she was lost in the attack on Charleston.

Other steamers served coastal communities east of Mount Desert Island all the way to Jonesport, Eastport, and Calais, bringing few summer people to this cold and often foggy land but affording fast, reliable freight and passenger service for the inhabitants.

The most picturesque vessels, however, ran from Boston to Portland, Bath, and Bangor, where they were met by the smaller ones for local landings. These were big vessels over 200 feet long, and they easily covered the distance overnight. One of the finest on the Bangor run was *City of Cambridge,* a paddle-wheel steamer built in New York in 1867 for the Sanford Independent Line. She was a coal burner built by Engles & Son in New York, 250 feet long, fast and comfortable, a very popular boat. Bound for Boston in September 1869, she ran into a fierce gale southeast of Monhegan. A steam pipe burst and her rudder jammed, leaving her helplessly adrift. She came in toward the ledges west of Allen Island off the St. George River. When the lead showed shoal-enough water, she anchored, and although exposed to the full force of the open ocean, her anchors held through the night. Seventeen years later in February 1886, bound east for Bangor on a clear, moonlit night, she made Monhegan and struck on Old Man Ledge off Allen Island. All passengers and crew were saved, but she broke in half and went to pieces on the ledge, the only Boston–Bangor boat to be lost in 100 years.

A close call was that of *Memnemon Sanford,* a paddle-wheel steamer 237 feet long built in 1856 and pride of the Sanford Independent Line. She ran ashore on Thachers Island off Cape Ann at about 2:00 A.M. in the morning of July 5, 1856. It was a clear, moonlit night with a smooth sea. A passenger declared that Thachers Island was visible three miles away; furthermore, it is protected by two brilliant lighthouses. The steamer struck only about four rods from the southern tower. All passengers and crew got off safely, somewhat disgruntled by having had to pay for their meals while aground and for their passage, which they did not complete. The key to the accident may lie in the date, July 5: the anniversary of American independence may have been unduly celebrated.

Later, in 1862, *Memnemon Sanford* struck on the Dry Salvages, an unmarked rock off Cape Ann, but again was refloated. Taken over by the government in the Civil War as a troop transport, she was run ashore on Caryfort Reef off Florida on December 10, 1862, by a careless or treacherous pilot and lost.

City of Bangor was one of the biggest, fastest, and most luxurious on the route. Built in 1894, she established a speed record from Boston to Rockland, and ran without an accident until 1902 when she hit Monhegan but was grounded safely in Lobster Cove on Sprucehead Island in Muscle Ridge Channel. She ran to Portland, to Bath, and to Boothbay Harbor at various times. She survived a serious fire in 1913 but was rebuilt and carried on until 1927.

Finally, in 1907 and 1909 came *Camden* and *Belfast,* 320 feet long, with steel hulls and triple screws driven by 4,000-horsepower steam turbines. They ran without serious accident on the Boston–Rockland route until 1935 when there was insufficient business to support them, and they were sold to run between Providence and New York. They both were used by the Navy in World War II as transports. After the war, *Camden* was towed to China in

Steamer *Camden,* sister ship of *Belfast,* two of the largest and fastest Maine steamers. *Maine Historical Society*

1948. *Belfast,* under tow to Oregon, parted her tow line and went ashore on the Washington coast, where her wreck still lies.

Many of the Bangor boats either stopped in Rockland or at various times terminated their runs there. *City of Rockland* terminated one run in 1904 on Gangway Ledge off Ash Island in Muscle Ridge Channel. She was refloated and after extensive repairs ran to Bath. After running ashore in the Kennebec in 1923, she was condemned and burned in 1924.

The Boston–Portland run was relatively free of navigational hazards. Fast and dependable service kept the steamers in operation until 1917, with a brief resurgence after the war until 1927.

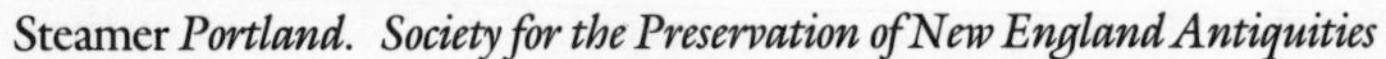

Steamer *Portland.* *Society for the Preservation of New England Antiquities*

The loss of the second *Portland* in the great gale of November 1898 was the worst tragedy in the history of Maine steamboating. *Portland,* owned by the Portland Steam Packet Company, was a handsome, fast wooden vessel built in 1890 by The New England Company at Bath. She was 291 feet long with a beam of 42 feet, but, being a paddle-wheel steamer, she had guards extending 13 feet beyond the hull on each side. She drew only 10 feet 8 inches to enable her to navigate rivers and was rather lightly constructed, but her power was entirely adequate to drive her at 13 knots with a walking beam engine of 62-inch bore and a 12-foot stroke. The walking beam, just aft of her stacks, is clearly visible in her pictures.

At 7:00 on the evening of Saturday, November 26, *Portland* took in her lines at India Wharf, Boston, and headed down the harbor. The weather report predicted snow, and *Bay State, Portland*'s sistership, then at Portland, decided to stay there.

At 7:20 *Portland* passed Deer Island Light at the entrance to Boston Harbor. At 9:30 the schooner *Maude S,* running in for Gloucester, saw *Portland* through the snow and dusk about 4 miles southwest of Thachers Island. The easterly wind backed into the northeast and rapidly increased. The anemometer on Highland Light at the tip of Cape Cod registered 90 before it blew away, and the wind was recorded at 90 on Nantucket.

At 11:00 the schooner *Grayling* saw *Portland* 12 miles south-by-east of Thachers. She had gained little to the north and was being pushed offshore. At 11:15 she was reported by another schooner, *Florence E. Stearns,* as heading to the westward. At 11:45 she was reported 14 miles southeast-by-east of Eastern Point without lights and with damage to her superstructure. She may have been trying to get under the lee of Cape Ann.

During the night *Portland* was driven southward across Massachusetts Bay. Her fuel must have been running low or have been exhausted, and one may guess that with her superstructure damaged she was taking a great deal of water aboard.

About mid-morning on Sunday the snow let up a little, and the schooner *Ruth M. Martin* saw *Portland* and the steamer *Pentagoet* from New York off Peaked Hill Bar, north of the tip of the Cape.

On Sunday evening about 7:00 a life preserver from *Portland* came ashore just east of Race Point Life Saving Station. From then on, for a week, wreckage and bodies came ashore all along the back shore and the tip of the Cape. A large piece of *Portland*'s superstructure came ashore near Peaked Hill Bar Life Saving Station. There were no survivors.

It is probable that the steamer broke up and sank somewhere north of Peaked Hill Bar or perhaps actually struck on the bar. There must have been a frightful sea running with the heavy wind, the tide, and the shoal water.

Pentagoet, a small wooden propeller-driven freighter bound from New York to Rockland, after having been reported off Highland Light and by *Ruth M. Martin* on Sunday morning, was never seen again. No wreckage was picked up and although fishermen all across Massachusetts Bay have brought in wreckage from *Portland* dragged up from the bottom, nothing from *Pentagoet* has ever been found.

Before leaving the story of passenger steamers we must record the brief career of Charles W. Morse of Bath. He was born in 1856, the son of Benjamin Morse, who controlled the towing business on the Kennebec. In 1897 Charles Morse's Consolidated Ice Company controlled the ice business on the Hudson and in 1898 on the Kennebec through the Knickerbocker Ice Company. In 1899 he combined these to form the American Ice Company, which cornered the ice market in Boston, New York, Philadelphia, Baltimore, and Washington. The company sold ice at such a high figure that by 1912 artificial ice became profitable and the trade in natural ice collapsed. Morse sold out before the collapse and in 1901 combined the steamship lines from Boston to Portland, Bath, and Bangor, and the Eastern Steamboat Company, into the Eastern Steamship Company. Mr. Morse became involved in international finance and left the steamboat business in 1909. It was reorganized in 1911 as the Eastern Steamship Corporation and again in 1917 as Eastern Steamship Lines, Inc., controlling steamer travel in Maine, with the exception of a few small lines still running excursions and local boats.

As soon as steam was applied to marine propulsion, the value of the tug became apparent. To move a big vessel around a harbor, she had to be towed with a rowboat, warped, or kedged. A big sailing vessel, particularly a square-rigger, often had to wait days for a fair wind to get out of a river or a harbor with a narrow mouth. At first, any steamer was used as a tug. *Patent,* when not carrying passengers, had towed vessels to sea at Bath as early as 1824. In 1825 the paddle-wheel tug *Rufus King* was active in New York Harbor. In 1838 the tug *Jefferson,* built for towing logs on Damariscotta Lake, was hauled overland to salt water, run around to the Kennebec, and engaged regularly in towing there. She got a bad name when sparks from her boiler set fire to a cargo of hay on a barge which she was towing. In the early 1840s she was joined by the tug *Billingham,* which also served as an excursion boat. All these tugs and their successors were built of wood until 1900.

In 1845 Robert B. Forbes, a forward-looking Boston entrepreneur, had the tug *R. B. Forbes* built for the Boston Marine Underwriters. She was especially constructed as a towboat and driven by twin screws, the propeller being far more efficient than paddle wheels for a towboat. She towed vessels in and out of harbors and rivers as well as alongshore.

In 1850 the first *Seguin* was built, a wood-burning paddle-wheel vessel. She did contract towing and excursions on the Kennebec and alongshore. In 1860 she towed the ship *Col. Adam Mills* to sea from Thomaston.

In 1851 the first tug, *Tiger,* came to Portland Harbor, and Captain Benjamin Willard reports being towed to sea by her in his schooner in 1853. *Tiger* was built in Philadelphia and owned by William Willard. She towed vessels in and out of Portland but also served Kennebunk, Saco, Yarmouth, Freeport, and Brunswick. After the Civil War, tugs regularly towed vessels from Bangor down to Fort Point.

Seguin and *Billingham* were taken south during the Civil War and replaced by *Fearless* in 1864, but she was at once purchased by the government for use at the Charlestown Navy Yard. Another tug, *Popham,* was quickly built the same year, measuring only 69 tons. She had a hard life, much of it spent towing logs. In April 1874 her boiler blew up, killing two of her crew, and in January 1885 she was sunk by ice but raised and repaired. Finally in 1888 she struck a rock off Mark Island in the Sheepscot River and was abandoned as a total loss, although her engines were saved.

Other tugs were added when the ice business called for the towing of large, heavily loaded schooners to sea from the ice houses above Dresden. *Popham, American Union,* and *Resolute* were three of these owned by the Knickerbocker Steam Towage Company, dominated by T. H. Southard and three Morses. When another Morse, Charles W., cornered the ice business, the Knickerbocker company flourished and competition was choked. Nevertheless, other tugs found work to do. In 1880, when Knickerbocker had five tugs with two more coming, the Kennebec Steam Tow Boat Company was organized. In 1883 there were sixteen tugs on the river, Knickerbocker with eight of them. In 1887 Knickerbocker had added two more. *Clara Clarita,* a participant in the Penobscot Bay steamboat war of the 1890s, had been built in Brooklyn in 1864 as a yacht and joined Knickerbocker's fleet as a tug in 1882. In 1898 she was sold to Boston owners and put to towing barges of frozen herring from Newfoundland to Boston.

Captain B. W. Morse, realizing the future in offshore towing, ordered a 147-foot tug for deep-sea work. Unfortunately, he died of blood poisoning before she was launched. Her oak frames were strapped with iron before she was planked and ceiled with yellow pine. She was fitted with a 1,400-horsepower engine and launched in 1887. Later that year she towed a schooner to New York and towed four heavily laden coal schooners from Nantucket Shoals to Boston. She was lost on Charleston Bar in 1893.

Two more big, wooden offshore tugs were built. *C. W. Morse,* built in Bath in 1889 for the Knickerbocker Ice Company, towed six barges, each with over 2,000 tons of coal, against a headwind. She was the first tug built for a special trade, coal and ice. The first real oceangoing offshore tug and the first to tow barges in successful competition with schooners, she towed ice to Cuba and coal from Southern ports to New England.

By the end of the century it was becoming obvious that bulk cargoes could be moved cheaply by tug and barge. In 1900 lime was being towed to New York from Rockland in barges, and by 1906 most of the Kennebec ice was towed out. As early as 1886 the Morses cut down the ship-rigged *Lizzie Moses* to haul coal behind a tug. As a barge she had only lower masts standing, on which could be set steadying sails. Her hatches were much enlarged, as water would seldom come on deck, and a loading port was cut in her side. In

1889 ice was first shipped in barges, and in October of that year the world's largest barge at the time, *Independent,* was built at Bath. She was 251 feet long, 52 feet wide, and 23.8 feet deep; a huge box, she had four masts, set 2,500 yards of sail, and carried 4,000 tons of coal or 4,500 tons of ice. *Independent* was followed by more barges, to the exclusion of square-riggers in 1902 and at the expense of large coastal schooners after 1905.

The tug *Gettysburg,* 158 feet long, with a 1,000-horsepower engine and a crew of nineteen, towed three big manned schooner barges. She would stop outside the harbor to which the barges were consigned. Harbor tugs picked up the loaded barges and brought out empties. The tug then proceeded to the assigned loading port where harbor tugs took the empties in to be loaded. *Gettysburg* entered a harbor only for food, fuel, and water. The quick turn-around was obviously profitable.

Virginia, the last of Maine's small inter-island steamers. *Goudy & Stevens*

The diesel engine at last put an end to the steam tug. *Clyde B. Holmes,* built as *John Wanamaker* for the city of Philadelphia and elegantly appointed for the occasional entertainment of dignitaries, was sold to Eastern Maine Towage in 1956 and used with *Seguin* and *Eugenie Spofford* to dock ships at Sears Island and elsewhere around Penobscot Bay. She was sold in 1977 to be used as a restaurant in Camden. *Seguin,* built in 1884, was given to the Maine Maritime Museum at Bath in 1969 with the hope that she could be rebuilt. She was hauled out at the museum's Percy & Small Shipyard and her deck and engines removed. The hull is under cover, is in very hard shape, and is unlikely to float again.

Steamboats were a very valuable asset in the growth of coastal Maine, but gave way after World War I to the automobile and the truck operating on well-paved roads. To drive down Route 1 may be faster and more convenient than leaning on the rail of *J. T. Morse* with the summer sun on your back, the slow, steady vibration of the big steam engine underfoot, and the islands of Penobscot Bay unfolding before you. But something is lost.

Some people sense this, and today large diesel vessels are beginning to carry passengers on pleasure excursions alongshore, providing staterooms and dining saloons, visiting coastal towns for gift shopping.

NOTES

The principal authorities for this chapter are *Steamboat Days,* by Fred Ewing Dayton (Chapter XIV), *Steamboat Lore of the Penobscot,* by John M. Richardson, and *Windjammers and Walking Beams,* by Fred Humiston. The first is a detailed but rather dry account of the history of Maine steamboating. It has a few glaring inconsistencies, but on the whole I have accepted it as accurate. The second has been written and collected with a real enthusiasm for steamboats and a desire for accuracy overspread with a not unpleasant romanticism. The text is interesting and detailed; the photographs are excellent. Unfortunately, it deals almost exclusively with Penobscot Bay boats. The last book is a series of romantic essays in which boats are given personalities and personal emotions. It has some accurate details and provides leads to others. Humiston's account of the loss of *Portland* has a number of interesting details, especially of sightings on Saturday night and Sunday, not found elsewhere. The book borrows heavily from *Steamboat Lore.*

William A. Baker's *Maritime History of Bath* has two good sections on steamers and an excellent chapter on tugs. Also *On the Hawser,* by Steven Lang and Peter Spectre, has good pictures and in the back a list of tugs from which one can extract those built and owned in Maine. Most of them must be diesel powered, although this is not said.

The paperback *Kennebec Boothbay Harbor Steamboat Album* gives pictures and details on local steamers, as does the *Casco Bay Steamboat Album.*

Special thanks are due Charles Chianchiaro, director of the Owls Head Transportation Museum, for his help with the construction of steam engines.

Jonathan Morgan ran out of money, and his boat was taken over by a creditor with little interest in steam propulsion. She was later used as a lighter in Casco Bay and broke in half with a load of planks laid across her hull.

Apparently there was another *Tom Thumb* at Eastport in use from 1825 to 1836. She was lost on Boon Island.

There are many amateur steam-engineering aficionados about. If the reader wishes more technical information, scratch one of them and get all the intimate details of steam-propulsion anatomy. There are books on steam engineering, but they appear to have been written by people who understand steam engines but do not understand those people who don't understand steam engines.

The emotional attachment of some people, especially older summer people, to particular boats is remarkable. Mention at the Jordan Pond House or Asticou Inn *Norumbega* or *J. T. Morse,* and you will quickly make the acquaintance of some of these steamers' affectionate personal friends.

Many more details might be added about the loss of *Portland.* Edward Rowe Snow deals with this in considerable detail, and Robert P. Tristram Coffin's *Book of*

Uncles describes her departure from Boston—without his uncle. The details included here were culled from Fred Humiston's book *Windjammers and Walking Beams*.

Charles W. Morse had a colorful career after he left the Eastern Steamship Company. He went to prison for shady financial dealings but had little more to do with Maine.

The British navy was one early supporter of steam tugs, believing that a warship in harbor, subject to the vagaries of the wind, was of little use, and the country whose ships first got to sea would have considerable advantage.

TWENTY-TWO

The Civil War

PRESIDENT ABRAHAM LINCOLN'S call for volunteers on April 15, 1861, produced immediate results in coastal Maine. Thousands of Maine men enlisted in the United States Army, although only between 5,000 and 6,000 enlisted in the Navy and the Marine Corps throughout the war. However, both the North and the South started immediate naval action. In the spring of 1861 residents of Deer Isle reported hearing guns offshore as United States warships stopped suspicious-looking merchantmen.

The South, having foreseen war, already had three commissioners—Yancey, Mann, and Rost—in England to buy ships and munitions. The Confederacy commissioned a few privateers, for the South had not the shipyards, machinery, or skilled workers to build or arm ships in any number. Several privateers put to sea immediately. One, *Savannah,* was captured and her crew imprisoned, to be tried as pirates. The South had a number of Union officers in custody and declared that they would get the same treatment, man for man, as the privateers, the victims to be selected by lot. The matter was dropped. However, although at first successful, privateering was deemed an unprofitable trade, for the North clapped a blockade on Southern ports so there was no port to which a privateer could send in prizes. Instead of privateers the South sent out commerce-destroying raiders, commissioned in the Confederate navy, manned by Confederate naval officers, to prey on Union merchantmen. So far as actual destruction was concerned, these raiders did little damage. There were never more than four at sea at any one time. About 200 Northern vessels were captured, 88 of them built in Maine, and this, according to Robert G. Albion, was only about one-hundredth of all Union traders at sea. However, the very existence of the raiders—*Sumter, Florida, Alabama, Tallahassee, Georgia, Shenandoah, Chickamauga,* and *Tuscaloosa*—at sea threw Northern ship owners and insurance companies into a panic. When *Alabama* visited Singapore in 1863 after taking only three ships east of the Cape of Good Hope, her captain, Raphael Semmes, found twenty-two United States merchantmen laid up in terror of his depredations. Insurance rates soared, running 8 percent higher for cargoes carried in United States ships than for those in foreign ships. Finally, with trade thus diminished by fear, many Northern ship owners sold their ships to foreign countries, principally to England, and found after the war that according to United States law, they could not ever be registered again in the United States. Consequently, the damage done to United States shipping by the Civil War was all out of proportion to the number of Confederate warships and to the actual sinkings they perpetrated.

Accounts of a few incidents as they affected Maine may give the reader some feeling for the fear that beset the seamen and merchants of the coast. Although the numbers were comparatively small, the news that filtered home was alarming. The Southern privateer steamer *Calhoun* in ten days in May 1861 took four Bath ships. On May 26, 1861, nineteen Northern ships were held captive in New Orleans, six of them from Maine. Seven Confederate raiders took at least nineteen more Maine vessels in the first year of the war. *Golden Rocket* of Bangor, *Cuba* of Milbridge, *Machias* of Machias, *Maria* of Portland, a Thomaston lime schooner, and *General Knox* of Thomaston loading ship timber in Virginia were victims of privateers and Confederate navy raiders at the very beginning of the war.

Captain Raphael Semmes from Charles County, Maryland, and in the Navy since 1826, was one of the most terrifying Southern names to Northern merchants. In April 1861 he took over the fast bark-rigged steamer *Habana,* which had operated on the New Orleans–Havana run. He strengthened her main deck, mounted an 8-inch shell gun and four 32-pounders, and renamed her *Sumter*. On June 30 he slipped out of the mouth of the Mississippi under sail and steam, and outran the powerful USS *Brooklyn*. It was a few days later, on July 3, that he took *Golden Rocket* of Bangor. An incurable romantic with literary pretensions, he wrote the following account of her destruction.

> The flame was not long in kindling but leaped full grown into the air in a very few minutes after its first faint glimmer had been seen. The boarding officer . . . had applied the torch simultaneously in three places—the cabin, the main hold and the forecastle; and now the devouring flames rushed up these three apertures with a fury nothing could resist. The burning ship, with the *Sumter*'s boat in the act of shoving off from her side; the *Sumter* herself with her grim black sides, lying in repose like some great sea monster gloating upon the spectacle, and the sleeping sea (for there was scarce a ripple upon the water) were all brilliantly lighted. The indraught into the burning ship's holds and cabins added . . . new fury to the flames, and now they could be heard roaring like the fires of a hundred furnaces in full blast. The prize ship had been laid to with her main-topsail to the mast, and all her light sails, though clewed up, were flying loose about the yards. The forked tongues of the devouring element, leaping into the rigging, newly tarred, ran rapidly up the shrouds, first into the tops, then to the topmast heads, thence to the top-gallant and royal mastheads, and in a moment more to the trucks; and whilst this rapid ascent of the main current of fire was going on, other currents had run out upon the yards and ignited all the sails. A top-gallant sail, all on fire, would now fly off from the yard, and sailing leisurely in the direction of the light breeze that was fanning rather than blowing, break into bright and sparkling patches of flame, and

settle . . . into the sea. The yard would then follow, and not being wholly submerged by its descent into the sea, would retain a portion of its flame and continue to burn as a floating brand for some minutes. At one time the intricate network of the cordage of the burning ship was traced as with a pencil of fire upon the black sky beyond, the many threads of fire twisting and writhing like so many serpents that had received their death wounds. The mizzen mast now went by the board, then the foremast, and in a few minutes afterward the great mainmast tottered, reeled, and fell over the ship's side into the sea, making a noise like that of the sturdy oak of the forests when it falls by the stroke of the axeman.

During the remaining months of 1861 *Sumter* took eighteen United States ships, burned seven, bonded the others, and slipped into the neutral port of Gibraltar where she was blockaded by Union warships. Semmes sold *Sumter,* went to England, and later took over *Alabama* at Terceira.

The relationship of the belligerents with England was strictly one of neutrality—legally, but feelings in England ran high on both sides, fanned by Confederate agents. There were several influences bearing on this relationship. First, England needed cotton to supply her mills, and she needed a market, which she found in the South, for her manufactured goods. Many Englishmen were not averse to seeing the United States dismembered before it became any more powerful and even hoped that parts of it, the South in particular, might return to the British empire. Britain's shipyards were eager to build ships and sell munitions to whoever would buy them. And finally, there was a romantic element to the Southern "cavalier"; false as it may have been, it influenced some.

On the other side, Britain needed California wheat to feed her expanding population, wheat carried largely by Northern ships. Also, the United States had a navy, which, although not at first efficient at maintaining a blockade, could be a formidable adversary in battle and could cause terrible damage to British commerce and to the communications that held the empire together. Finally, the notion of slavery was repugnant to a great many Englishmen, particularly to the laboring class. Consequently, the following conditions for British neutrality were promulgated:

1) No British subject was to enlist on either side.

2) No armed ships of war were to be sold to either side.

3) Ships of either side could enter British ports but could not be altered or improved while there.

4) Privateers commissioned by either side would not be treated as pirates.

5) The Northern blockade of Southern ports would be respected if it could be enforced.

6) The Confederate States of America were recognized as a belligerent but not as an independent nation.

This proclamation affected Maine principally in items 2 and 3. England could not build armed ships of war for the Confederacy, but it could build ships. Although they could not be armed in British ports anywhere in the world under item 3, they could be fitted with British-made weapons elsewhere. Captain Bulloch, CSN, representing the Confederacy, proceeded at once to contract more or less secretly for two vessels. In the meantime, there was considerable action on the American coast.

The Union navy was ordered to blockade the coast of the Confederacy. At first glance, this appears very difficult indeed, for it is a long coast from Norfolk all the way around Florida to Texas. However, it is not, like the Maine coast, frequently and deeply indented. There are very few deepwater harbors such as Wilmington, Beaufort, Charleston, Savannah, Mobile, and New Orleans. There are places where shoals and low islands provide lurking places for blockade runners—such as Bogue Sound, the Outer Banks, and the Florida Keys—but these can accommodate shoal-draft vessels only.

The Union navy, ill-prepared for blockade duty, at once sent out every available vessel to patrol off major ports as USS *Brooklyn* watched the Mississippi in a futile attempt to stop Semmes in *Sumter*. At the same time they attacked and captured Hatteras Inlet in North Carolina, Port Royal in South Carolina, and New Orleans as bases for blockading squadrons. These bases had to be supplied with coal, supplies, and reinforcements. For this service Maine schooners and steamers from the coastal routes in Maine were hurriedly purchased and put to work.

The blockade at first was not very effective, and at its best it was never impenetrable. Fast Confederate steamers, built low to the water, painted a neutral gray, and loaded with bales of cotton—a bulky cargo, but not heavy—would wait for a murky night and creep silently, almost invisibly, out of Charleston or Savannah or Beaufort, for instance. If detected by a Union gunboat, they cracked on all steam and sail and ran for it. Once clear, they sailed to Nassau, Havana, or Bermuda where they exchanged the cotton for munitions and luxury goods in which there was great profit. If hotly pursued on the way back, they ran ashore rather than lose the cargo to the North. Two successful voyages could pay for a vessel.

In order to muster a fleet strong enough to make the blockade effective, the Union navy called on Maine. *Kineo,* one of a class of twenty-three 500-ton gunboats, was built in Portland by J. W. Dyer, and *Katahdin* was built in Bath by Larrabee & Allen. They were wooden screw-driven vessels with 300-horsepower coal-fired engines, schooner rigged with a yard on the foremast. Each carried an 11-inch Dahlgren smoothbore mounted on a pivot forward, a 25-pound rifled Parrot gun, and two 24-pound howitzers. *Katahdin* was with Admiral David Farragut in 1862 in the attack on New Orleans.

The Union navy also needed shoal-draft steamers for the shallow Southern sounds and rivers. These used paddle wheels in order to lessen draft and to make them maneuverable. Paddle-wheelers develop full power moving either ahead or astern, and indeed one would have trouble telling which end was which, as these vessels were double-ended like a ferry, had rudders at both ends, and could go in either direction without having to turn around.

During the Civil War, Maine shipbuilding was sharply curtailed. In the four years from 1853 through 1856, 301 new vessels were registered at Bath, the most active shipbuilding district in the state. Yet from 1861 through 1864, only 147 were registered. A Bath newspaper wrote with as much enthusiasm and gave almost as much type to the launching of the 30-foot fishing schooner *Oceola* in May 1864 as it might have given to a big vessel. *Iosco,* a 974-ton wooden, paddle-wheel gunboat, built under contract for the Union navy by Larrabee & Allen in Bath, was delayed over a year. The delay was caused partly by expensive change orders and partly, as stated by another Bath newspaper, because of ". . . the difficulty of getting workmen, as the demand for the services of the men in the Army and Navy was so great, and also on account of the number of vessels being built by the Government making it impossible with the scarcity of labor, to fulfill the contracts within the given time. During the delay, the prices of labor and materials advanced rapidly, causing greater expense than if the machinery had been promptly erected."

The Confederates were active in England from the beginnings of the war. Captain Bulloch, formerly captain of a New York–New Orleans steamer—a naval officer, a man who knew intimately the shipping business and the ship construction business, and a man of great tact and energy—set out to circumvent the British neutrality act and to supply the Confederacy with a navy. Almost as soon as he arrived in England, he conferred with an excellent lawyer and then ordered a vessel laid down at the yard of Miller & Sons in Liverpool. She was called *Oreto,* whatever that might mean, and later *Manassas,* which as their first victory of the war meant a great deal to Southern sympathizers. She was not armed. While she was being built, he contracted with the Laird yard across the Mersey in Birkenhead to build another vessel known only as Hull 290. This was *Alabama,* most famous of Confederate raiders, whose career we will come to shortly.

Leaving these two hulls under construction, Bulloch bought the steamer *Fingal* in Greenock, Scotland, and secretly had her loaded with military supplies, rifles, ammunition, artillery, uniforms, and medical equipment. She was under British registry with a British captain and crew, all strictly legal, with a cargo destined for Bermuda. Bulloch himself was still in Liverpool.

The United States consul in England could not prevent *Fingal*'s departure but did manage to send home a description of the vessel and her cargo and a photograph, copies of which were distributed to captains of Union blockading vessels.

On October 10, *Fingal* left Greenock for Holyhead on the northwest tip of Wales where Bulloch was to come aboard. On the night of October 14–15, in a gale of wind, *Fingal* entered the harbor, ran down and sank an Australian brig, picked up Bulloch, and departed before dawn. *Fingal* stopped at Terceira in the Azores for water, then went on to Bermuda. Here she met CSS *Nashville* on her way to England and picked up a Savannah pilot. She left on November 7 despite the efforts of the United States consul. Bulloch took command, hoisted the Confederate flag, mounted guns, distributed small arms, and headed for Savannah. He crept in during a foggy spell, left *Fingal* to be converted into an ironclad ram, later sunk by the monitor *Weehawken. Fingal* was raised, repaired, and used by the Union navy as a blockade ship in the Chesapeake.

Bulloch returned to England on March 10, 1862, to find *Manassas* afloat and ready to sail. She left on March 22 for Nassau where she picked up Captain John Moffit, CSN, and met the British vessel *Bahama,* loaded with guns and ammunition. This cargo was transferred to a schooner—all legally—which met *Manassas,* now *Florida,* at Green Key and installed her guns. Moffit headed for Mobile and ran in past the blockading squadron, unable to return their fire for lack of rammers, sponges, and quoins which had never been put aboard. She was badly shot up, but she made it safely, was repaired, and took aboard a full complement, among whom was Lieutenant Charles W. Read, an officer described by Moffit as "daring beyond the limits of martial prudence." He had distinguished himself aboard the CSS *McRae* in the defense of New Orleans and was to lead one of the most daring raids on the Maine coast.

Florida, repaired and resupplied, left Mobile on January 16, 1863, eluded the blockaders, and called at Nassau for coal. She then cruised in the South Atlantic, capturing a number of United States merchant ships including *Jacob Bell* with $2,000,000 worth of tea and firecrackers from China. On March 28 she captured *Lapwing,* armed her, and commissioned her as a Confederate naval vessel. On May 6 Moffit captured the brig *Clarence* and put Charles Read in command with twenty-one men and one 12-pound boat howitzer. Lieutenant Read asked for *Clarence* because she was bound for Baltimore and had papers that would let her into Chesapeake Bay where, once by the capes,* he could cause tumult, alarm, panic, and confusion in Hampton Roads and the Norfolk Navy Yard before escaping to the Confederate lines in Virginia. It was certainly a daring scheme. When Captain Moffit gave Read his commission as commander of a Confederate naval vessel, he wrote: "The proposition evinces on your part patriotic devotion to the cause of your country, and this is certainly the time when all our best exertions should be made to harm the common enemy and confuse them with attacks from unexpected quarters. I agree with your request and will not hamper you with instructions. Act for the best and God speed you. . . ."

Clarence was renamed *Florida No. 2* and headed north. Read captured and burned four merchant vessels, but when he arrived off the capes, he found Hampton Roads very closely guarded, open only to vessels carrying military supplies. So he cruised off the coast, looking for such a vessel and in the meantime causing as much destruction as possible.

On June 12, pretending to be in distress, he captured the bark *Tacony* and found her a better and faster vessel than *Clarence.* Before he could transfer to *Tacony,* the schooner *M. A. Shindler* fell into his hands. He was in the act of

* Capes Charles and Henry.

transferring his little howitzer to *Tacony* when the schooner *Kate Stewart* appeared. Threatening her with a spar masquerading as a gun, Read captured her too, set fire to *Clarence* and *M. A. Shindler,* and went in chase of another vessel, the brig *Arabella.* He bonded her and let her go. He was by this time overwhelmed with prisoners, so he put them all aboard *Kate Stewart* and bonded her. The bond stated that within thirty days of a peace treaty between the Confederate States of America and the United States, the captain would pay the Confederate States $150,000. This was, of course, under the assumption that the Confederacy would win.

While *Kate Stewart* was heading for Philadelphia, Read captured two more vessels. The moment Captain Munday, formerly of *Tacony,* got ashore, he informed Gideon Wells, Secretary of the Navy, of the situation. Reaction was immediate. Every Union vessel that could be kept afloat was sent out, including the yacht *America,* the slow *Dai Ching,* which could not make more than 5 knots, and *Seminole,* whose three steam pumps could not quite keep up with her leaks.

But it is a big ocean. Although at least twenty-four vessels, most of them steamers, were looking for *Tacony,* only one, a Union gunboat, found her. Her skipper hailed: "Bark ahoy, what and where bound?" Read answered, "Bark *Mary Jane* from Sagua La Grande bound for Portland." The gunboat captain warned Read to keep a sharp lookout for a Confederate raider. Read thanked him, and the gunboat steamed off to the south, alert for a Confederate raider. Yet, despite Union watchfulness, Read took fifteen vessels between June 12, when he took *Tacony,* and June 24, when he captured *Shatemuc,* loaded with emigrants for Boston. He put all captives aboard her, bonded her for $150,000, and set her free.

About suppertime on the same day, *Tacony* came up with the fishing schooner *Archer,* under Captain Robert Snowman of Southport, Maine. Evidently Read moved very softly, for Captain Snowman invited the visitors to supper, an excellent meal of chowder, cods' tongues and sounds.* Afterwards, however, Read decided to transfer his crew to *Archer,* because the hunt for *Tacony* was getting hot and his howitzer ammunition was used up. He put *Archer*'s crew aboard the *Shatemuc,* which must have been still nearby, and headed in for the Maine coast with the intention of cutting out a steamer or at least raiding some coastal towns.

Off Damariscove Island, Read found two fishermen, Bibber and Titcomb, fishing in a sloop. Read ordered them aboard *Tacony.* They did not realize to whom they were talking and refused to cut their gear. However, they soon found they had no choice but still failed to understand that they were up against the Confederate navy. From them Read learned that the New York–Portland steamer *Chesapeake* was in Portland and also the armed revenue cutter *Caleb Cushing,* a topsail schooner. Two unfinished gunboats were at the wharves.

* A delicacy among fishermen are the tongues, cheeks, and swim bladders of codfish.

Read persuaded one of the captive fishermen to pilot *Archer* into Portland, with most of his crew below busily engaged in making balls of oakum soaked in turpentine to set fire to the two gunboats. *Archer* was a familiar sight in Portland, and the forts took no alarm.

Chesapeake was alongside a wharf, and anchored out in the harbor was the revenue cutter *Caleb Cushing,* armed with a 32-pounder amidships and a 12-pounder on the forecastle. Read's plan was to seize *Chesapeake,* run out of the harbor, return, and burn the two gunboats, *Caleb Cushing,* and anything else he could. However, *Chesapeake*'s boilers were cold, and Eugene H. Brown, the engineer whom Read had brought along for just such an opportunity, said that without help he could not get the engine running in time to get out before dawn. Accordingly, Read decided to cut out *Caleb Cushing.*

At first the plan went well. The captain of the *Cushing* had died recently and most of the crew were ashore, leaving only Lieutenant Davenport and a few men aboard. Shortly after midnight the Confederates swarmed aboard, overwhelmed the watch, and handcuffed the crew. From that point things went crosswise. First, the topsail and topgallant sheets had been unrove and awnings put up. All this gear had to be cleared away. Second, they were unable to slip the anchor cable and had to haul the anchor and 25 fathoms of chain. And then they found that the vessel was aground. They ran a line to another vessel and, with the first of the flood tide, hauled her off and set sail. By this time the light, fair wind had died, so Read ordered two boats out ahead to tow the *Cushing* to sea as dawn came.

As they towed her down the harbor, the paddle-wheel steamer *Forest City,* the overnight boat from Boston, came in and at first saw nothing unusual in *Caleb Cushing* being towed to sea in the morning calm.

A light breeze came in. As *Caleb Cushing* gathered way, Bibber was brought aboard from *Archer* and, more or less tacitly, he piloted the vessel out between Hog and Cow islands, down Hussey Sound, and off to the southeast. Bibber was then released, and he rowed away in a small boat.

When *Forest City* landed in Portland on the morning of June 26, Reuben Chandler was surprised to see the *Cushing*'s master-at-arms on the wharf and asked him what he was doing there when his vessel was on her way down the harbor. At once it was assumed that Lieutenant Davenport, known to be a Southerner, had defected to the Confederacy and run off with the schooner.

Jedidiah Jewett, the customs collector, and Mayor Jacob McLellan of Portland started wheels spinning at once. They chartered—or commandeered—*Chesapeake* and *Forest City* to go in chase. The tug *Tiger* and the island steamer *Casco* brought soldiers, artillery, and ammunition from the harbor forts. Provided with guns, ammunition, soldiers, enthusiastic volunteers, bread, beef, and powder, *Forest City, Chesapeake,* and *Tiger* started in pursuit. Time had been taken to pile cotton bales along *Chesapeake*'s rails and around her boilers as protection from Confederate shot.

As the pursuers approached, the Confederates cleared for action. They found plenty of powder in the magazine but only one 32-pound shot. The Confederates failed to find the rest of the ammunition stowed in a locker behind a mirror in the captain's cabin, and Davenport gave them no help.

The pursuers, with *Forest City* in the lead, were now only about 2 miles astern. With scarcely more than steerageway in the light air, the *Cushing* luffed and, as the 'midship gun bore, fired on *Forest City*. The shot missed, but *Forest City* slowed and swung around. The Confederates fired several more shots, using what odd bits of iron they could find and a few ballast stones. It was said later that they had even fired a cheese, but one of the men on *Forest City* doubted it, saying that what flew over his head was a lot less digestible than cheese.

Portland Harbor

Fearing that one good shot in paddlebox, boiler, or engine would disable her, *Forest City* held back, but the propeller-driven *Chesapeake* came up from behind with a bone in her teeth, determined to ram *Caleb Cushing* or take her by boarding.

However, the Confederates, now out of ammunition, pushed their prisoners over the rail, still handcuffed, into a small boat towing alongside and tossed a bunch of keys after them. They then set the *Cushing* afire, dropped into another boat, and rowed away.

There was considerable confusion aboard *Chesapeake* as she bore down on the *Cushing* and the two boats. The one with the cutter's original crew was nearest, waving Lieutenant Davenport's white shirt as a symbol of peace, but eager volunteers shouted, "Shoot. They're going to board us." The crew in the boat held up their handcuffed hands and replied, "Don't shoot." Colonel Mason of the 7th Maine Volunteers, sword in hand, threatened to run through the first man to fire, and the crew was hustled aboard *Chesapeake.* Still handcuffed, they were driven below and confined, it being assumed that Davenport had planned to sail the *Cushing* south.

Forest City picked up the other boat with the Confederates aboard and brought them over the side, one man at a time, searched each man and tied him up, and put them all below with no very kind words.

Meanwhile, with *Caleb Cushing* still burning, three volunteers took one of *Chesapeake*'s boats and rowed for the *Cushing,* intending at first to save her and then to salvage a small boat towing alongside. They received plenty of advice from *Chesapeake,* the gist of which was to keep away from the schooner as she was about to blow up. They would not be dissuaded, got alongside, and after a few panicky moments untying the painter—they had no knife—began to tow the small boat away. They had not gone far when *Caleb Cushing* blew up with a most satisfactory explosion. No one was hurt.

Forest City picked up *Archer* off Jewell Island with Titcomb aboard and brought her back to Portland.

After the dust settled, one man was hurt and one man killed accidentally. With *Archer* alongside the wharf in Portland, thirty loaded muskets found in her salt room were laid on deck, their muzzles on the break. John Sidney, out of curiosity, picked one up, cocked it, and snapped the lock, not thinking it loaded. The ball passed through both of Daniel Gould's thighs and wounded another man. Gould did not survive the amputation.

The material result of the raid was small. The Confederate navy had destroyed one Union revenue cutter. However, the panic effect was much larger. First, the City Marshall of Portland insisted that the Confederates be in his charge in the Portland jail as criminals rather than in the Army's charge as prisoners of war in Fort Preble. After considerable furor, the prisoners remained in Fort Preble.

Then about 3:00 in the morning of June 27 alarm bells rang and kept ringing and ringing. It was reported that a party of Confederates had landed on Cape Elizabeth and was marching on Portland. Troops at Fort Preble were turned out to repel the invaders. A crowd of eager volunteers piled aboard the steamer *Montreal,* ready to attack by sea. At length the bells stopped, and it appeared that a small tug had been seen close inshore. Some panicky observer had reported it as Confederate, and the scare was on.

A week later, with everyone still nerved up, a small coastal survey steamer charged up the main channel of Portland Harbor under full sail, passing by Fort Preble without making any of the carefully planned recognition signals. The lieutenant on watch ordered a blank cartridge fired to call the steamer's attention. She disregarded it. The lieutenant then ordered a solid shot fired across her bow. As the steamer now was passing between Forts Preble and Scammell, the shot ricocheted off the water, bounced ashore, and demolished the outhouse at Fort Scammell. The steamer at last got the message, hove to, and another supposedly Confederate raid was frustrated.

The Portland newspaper demanded that the federal government issue letters of marque to private vessels in order to bring the pirates quickly to justice. More importantly, fortifications were erected or at least guns emplaced at Belfast, Boothbay, and Calais, and massive Fort Popham was built at the mouth of the Kennebec to protect Bath, a sincere compliment to the Confederate navy.

The Confederate prisoners were shortly sent to Fort Warren in Boston Harbor, from which they at once made plans to escape. They were confined in a casemate adjacent to a pumproom pierced for musketry. Lieutenant Alexander found he could squeeze through the 8-inch slit. On the next dark night, Alexander, Read, Sanders, and Thurston slipped out but found the water too rough to swim to nearby Lovells Island. They climbed back into the fort undetected. The next night they took with them Pryde and Sherman, good swimmers, who were to swim to Lovells Island, find a boat, and return for the others. They struck out into the dark, cold water and were never seen again.

At length the other four got tired of waiting, so Sanders and Thurston, using a pine board to help them, struck out for Lovells Island, narrowly avoiding being caught by patrolling guards. At the edge of exhaustion, they made it. When they had drawn breath, dressed in the clothes they had piled on the board—less pants, which were lost—they found a small schooner-rigged boat and pushed her off. But by then dawn was coming. They sailed as close to the fort as they dared, but it was obviously too late for Read and Alexander to swim out to them, so they headed east for New Brunswick.

Read and Alexander were caught trying to return to prison, and the alarm was given for Pryde, Sherman, Sanders, and Thurston. The United States Navy at once went into action and sent two sailing vessels and a steamer to scour the coast. The fugitives made slow progress in light airs across Massachusetts Bay and landed briefly on Cape Ann. Some boys whom they asked for food alarmed the town, and a body of citizens rushed to the shore to find the Confederates gone. About dark they spoke with a man at Rye Beach, New Hampshire, who gave them some food, pants, and tobacco.

There was little wind during the night, and the next day off Boon Island they were accosted by the revenue cutter *Dobbin*. Their story of being Eastport fishermen bound for home was accepted until they were searched and found to be carrying a gold watch and a wad of Confederate money. That did it. They were recaptured and taken to Portland. The steamer *Brunswick* carried advance notice of their arrival. A considerable crowd watched their arrival, handcuffed together, and followed them to the Portland jail where they were kept for several days, stared at by throngs of curious citizens come to view the "rebel pirates." Eventually Read and all his crew were exchanged.

While little damage was done beyond the destruction of *Caleb Cushing*, the soldiers, sailors, and vessels employed, the panic among the citizens, and the fortification constructed amounted to considerable expense and diversion valuable to the Confederate cause.

Another desperate Confederate adventure in December 1863 caused the Union little damage but extensive disturbance and diversion of forces. An accomplished con-man, John Clibbon Brain, and a Nova Scotian with Southern sympathies, Vernon Locke, alias John Parker, hatched a plot in Saint John to seize the New York–Portland steamer *Chesapeake,* the same vessel that had pursued *Caleb Cushing* out of Portland, and either use her as a privateer or take her to a Southern port. As a shred of legality they had a letter of marque from Jefferson Davis issued to the ex-tug *Retribution,* which Locke had once owned. Legally worthless on any other vessel, it was an impressive document. Parker, with no authority whatever and in defiance of Britain's declaration of neutrality, gave Brain, masquerading as a Confederate naval lieutenant, "orders" to go to New York with three "officers" and eleven men, seize a steamer, and take her to Grand Manan Island. Parker issued an impressive commission as lieutenant to David Collins, who will appear later.

Brain and his men went to New York and took passage for Portland on *Chesapeake,* Captain Isaac Willett. About midnight on December 7, 1863, they seized control of the steamer, killing second engineer Schaffer and wounding mate Johnson and the chief engineer. Brain took *Chesapeake* to Seal Cove at Grand Manan and then up the Bay of Fundy to the mouth of the St. John River, where Parker came aboard from a pilot boat and where Captain Willett, most of his crew, and five passengers were released. Willett got ashore in Saint John and, via the United States consul in Canada, reported to the Navy that *Chesapeake* had been seized.

Again the United States Navy went into action along the Maine coast. USS *Agawam,* one of the gunboats under construction during the *Cushing* scare, sailed from Portland; and the steamer *Ella and Annie,* commanded by a Searsport captain, left Boston in search of *Chesapeake*.

Meanwhile, *Chesapeake* rounded Cape Sable in vile weather and anchored off Shelburne, Nova Scotia, for coal and wood, which they paid for by selling some of *Chesapeake*'s cargo, thus violating Nova Scotia revenue law. The United States agent in Shelburne, suspecting that the steamer was *Chesapeake,* telegraphed Halifax. Brain went ashore in Shelburne.

The Navy dispatched USS *Acacia* from Boston, USS *Niagara* from Gloucester, and USS *Ticonderoga* from New York. They ran into a heavy gale which forced *Acacia* into Portland in a sinking condition and blew *Ticonderoga* 200 miles offshore. *Niagara* rode out the gale anchored off a lee shore on the Nova Scotia coast. *Ella and Annie* was at Eastport and left in pursuit when the gale cleared. Meanwhile *Chesapeake,* now under the name *Retribution,* cleared from Lunenburg for La Have,* where Brain rejoined the vessel and sold more cargo. He absconded with $400 worth of "captured" jewelry, was arrested in Liverpool, Nova Scotia, produced his impressive Confederate commission, and was released.

USS *Dacotah* sailed from Kittery and the steamer *Cornubia* from Charlestown, both in pursuit of *Chesapeake. Ella and Annie,* searching along the Nova Scotia shore, grew short of coal and headed for Halifax. *Chesapeake,* also short of coal, eluded *Ella and Annie* and entered Mud Cove close to Halifax where *Ella and Annie,* after a futile chase to Lunenburg, caught up with her at last. The hijackers fled in a small boat, and the crew of *Ella and Annie* swarmed aboard. The fleet in pursuit and *Chesapeake* finally gathered at Halifax where, after legal discussion and the dramatic escape of Wade,† who was accused of murdering Schaffer, the "pirates" dispersed and *Chesapeake* returned to the United States. The incident had led to the death of one man and the wounding of two, but had involved seven United States naval vessels in a wild two-week chase, had entangled numerous diplomatic officials in the United States and Canada in vigorous telegraphic exchange, and had severely inconvenienced commerce in New York Harbor for some time by causing the authorities to require that all her passengers and baggage be inspected before any vessel could leave the harbor. And no Confederates were caught!

The Confederate agents had been busy in Saint John and Montréal organizing raids on the Maine and Vermont borders, ambitious schemes which in the event came to very little and had no maritime significance. One, however, came close to success. In June 1864 one William Collins, brother of David Collins who had been in Brain's gang on *Chesapeake,* set up a plot to rob the Calais bank. The plot was betrayed by another Collins brother, Reverend John Collins, so that when the robbers appeared, they found themselves under the guns of security men and the raid ended, except for months of legalities involving Collins's credentials as a Confederate officer.

Although another plot was kept a secret until recent years, it now appears that Francis Jones, one of the Calais bank robbers, gave information that CSS *Tallahassee* and CSS *Florida* were to convoy a force of 2,000 men to be joined by 3,000 Confederate sympathizers in Canada to land on unfrequented parts of the Maine coast and conduct a vigorous guerilla campaign as a means of diverting federal troops from the campaign in the South. The plan never got

* Formerly La Hève (Anglicized).

† See chapter notes.

off the ground, but enough evidence was assembled to indicate that something like this was contemplated. For instance, "artists," proving to be Confederates, were captured sketching, or mapping, isolated parts of the coast, and *Tallahassee* did make a raid along the shore in July 1864, in the course of which she captured some thirty vessels off the Connecticut, Massachusetts, and Maine coasts, including *Suliot,* built in Belfast and one of the first California-bound Forty-Niners, *Glenarvon* of Thomaston, and *James Littlefield* of Bangor. *Tallahassee* also raised havoc with the defenseless fishing fleet, destroying some of them in sight of watchers on Matinicus. Short of coal, she put into Halifax briefly and then scuttled back to Wilmington, North Carolina, which she entered safely under fire from Union blockaders. The Navy dispatched sixteen vessels in search of her, no one of which came anywhere near her except for *Pontoosuc,* a gunboat that came just too late to prevent her departure from Halifax.

CSS *Florida,* also supposed to take part in the planned invasion of Maine, made a sortie from Brest, France, along the East Coast in the summer of 1864 but did little damage and was captured by USS *Wachuset* under doubtful legal authority in the neutral harbor of Bahia, Brazil.

Another naval engagement was significant to Maine in that the Union combatant, *Kearsarge,* was launched at the Portsmouth Navy Yard in 1851. She was 201 feet long and registered 1,031 tons. On June 19, 1864, she fought the Confederate *Alabama* off Cherbourg, France.

Alabama was built in England at Liverpool by the Laird yard at the same time as *Florida.* As mentioned earlier, she was known simply as Hull 290 but was clearly a lightly constructed wooden steamer, bark rigged, with enough sail to make her fast under canvas. She had a retracting propeller to eliminate drag so she could use either sail or steam or both.

U.S. Ambassador Charles Francis Adams knew very well that she was destined for the Confederate navy and sent a strong letter to the Queen's Solicitor to have her stopped. That official, however, went insane suddenly and the letter lay neglected for several days, during which *Alabama* sailed on a "trial trip," a trip which ended at Terceira in the Azores. Here she was met by a British ship carrying her armament and ammunition. Guns were mounted; Captain Raphael Semmes, late of *Sumter,* took command; and *Alabama* started on her career of destruction by sinking twelve whalers off the Azores. She then moved to the waters off Nova Scotia where she took eleven ships, including *Lamplighter* of Calais, then *Lafayette* of Freeport en route from New York to Belfast with grain and, incidentally, New York papers accusing Semmes of being a pirate, a charge that he denied by making a long entry in his own journal before he burned *Lafayette.* Captain Semmes went south, capturing and burning United States ships as he went, occasionally sending in one with prisoners; *Baron de Castin* of Castine was one of these. Semmes touched at Martinique, where he was nearly caught by USS *San Jacinto,* and went on to Bianquillas, off the coast of Venezuela, where he coaled from *Agrippina.* He then made a tour of the Caribbean, and had a successful April off the coast of Brazil. One of his early captures was *Louisa Hatch* of Rockland with a cargo of coal. He towed her to Fernando de Noronha, where he took out her cargo and burned her. Later in the month he caught Yarmouth-built *Dorcas Prince,* also loaded with coal, her cargo destined for United States naval vessels in the East Indies. Semmes had no hesitation in burning her. Another Maine victim off the Brazilian coast was *Sea Lark,* built at Trescott. Aboard her was another letter accusing Semmes of piracy, which led him to treat *Sea Lark*'s crew roughly. *John Snow* of Bucksport, *Talisman,* built in Damariscotta, and *Anna F. Schmidt* were three more Maine vessels of the fourteen ships *Alabama* sank in the South Atlantic.

Semmes then ran east to the Cape of Good Hope and caught *Sea Bride* and *Martha Wenzel,* the latter built at East Deering; however, he had to spare her because she was inside the 3-mile limit. A long cruise to the East Indies netted only six victims, one of which was *Emma Jane* of Bath, taken off the coast of India. *Alabama* returned to the South Atlantic with very poor success and in June 1864 put into Cherbourg to refit. USS *Kearsarge,* lying at Flushing, Holland,* was alerted by the American envoy to France that *Alabama* was at Cherbourg. *Kearsarge*'s Captain Winslow at once telegraphed USS *St. Louis* at Lisbon to join him and took *Kearsarge* to Cherbourg where he lay offshore, waiting for *Alabama.* Accounts disagree as to whether Winslow sent in a boat with a challenge to Semmes or whether Semmes regarded *Kearsarge*'s presence as challenge enough. In any case, Semmes sent a message to Winslow: "My intention is to fight the *Kearsarge* as soon as I can make the necessary arrangements. I hope these will not detain me more than until tomorrow evening or after the morrow morning at the furthest. I beg she will not depart before I am ready to go out." Winslow, who had been a roommate of Semmes aboard *Raritan* in the United States Navy before the war, had fought by his side in the Mexican War. Winslow was as zealous a champion of the Union as Semmes was of the Confederacy and had no intention of departing.

At first glance it looked like an even match. Both were wooden ships, about 200 feet long, bark rigged, with twin engines. *Alabama* had six 32-pounders, one 68-pounder, and one 100-pound rifled gun on a pivot. *Kearsarge* carried four 32-pounders, one 28-pound rifled gun, and two 11-inch Dahlgren guns on pivots firing explosive shells. *Kearsarge* carried fourteen more men.

However, a closer look shows that *Kearsarge* had considerable superiority. *Alabama* was foul on the bottom and consequently slow to maneuver. Her crew were mostly British men who had been aboard since she left England, and who had no great zeal for battle. They were tired from a long voyage and despite the many encounters with enemy ships had had little target practice or gun drill. They had sunk one prize by gunfire on their way to Cherbourg and

* Now Vlissingen.

found their powder stale and their marksmanship poor. If *Alabama* did sink *Kearsarge,* other naval vessels would soon be on her trail. She could help the Southern cause very little by fighting the United States Navy. Her mission was not to fight warships but to sink merchantmen. Yet Semmes accepted the challenge, partly out of the same desperate courage that animated the South's last defense in 1864 and partly out of a sense of honor, a romantic reversion to the code *duello.* Finally, the French, seeing that the Union was likely to win the war, would not let *Alabama* lie for long in a French port.

Kearsarge, on the other hand, was clean on the bottom, was recently refitted, had a crew with excellent morale and good training. Winslow had hung chains over the side in the way of the engines and boilers and sheathed over them with boards, so Semmes did not know he was in essence fighting an armored vessel. *Kearsarge* had everything to gain by sinking *Alabama,* for she was indeed a running sore in the Union economy.

Semmes put ashore most of the valuable loot he had accumulated including specie, bonds of bonded vessels, and chronometers. He committed himself to using starboard guns by moving one of his 32-pounders from port to starboard, giving his vessel a bit of a list. At 10:00 A.M. on June 19, a warm, calm day, *Alabama* left Cherbourg in company with the French ironclad *Couronne,* which escorted her beyond French territorial waters. Also present was the English steam yacht *Deerhound,* whose owner was strongly sympathetic with the Confederate cause.

About 7 miles outside Cherbourg the two combatants circled a common point, starboard side to starboard side. *Alabama* fired quickly and inaccurately.

USS *Kearsarge. Peabody Museum of Salem*

Of over 300 shots, only 28 hit *Kearsarge*. Some of the shells failed to explode. One of them, fired early in the battle, buried itself in *Kearsarge*'s sternpost. Had it exploded, it would have blown off her stern and sunk her very quickly. Stale powder, having been long in storage, was a serious handicap. Some of the projectiles struck the chain armor of *Kearsarge* and sank harmlessly. One shell blew a hole in her funnel and another tore off the engineroom hatch. One exploded on the quarterdeck, killing one man and wounding two others.

Kearsarge fired more slowly, Winslow telling his gunners to keep cool and aim carefully. "One hit," he said, "is worth one hundred misses." An 11-inch shell burst in *Alabama*'s engineroom, disabling the pumps and putting out the fires. Shells penetrated the light planking of the topsides and exploded in the 'tween decks, blowing great holes in the upper deck. Leaking badly, *Alabama* tried for the French coast, could not make it, lowered her flag. Winslow ceased fire. *Alabama,* claimed Winslow, fired twice more and ran up her flag again. However, she was sinking fast. Winslow ceased fire and hailed *Deerhound,* urging the yacht to save all she could. *Kearsarge*'s boats were badly damaged, but finally one or two were manned. *Alabama*'s twenty-one wounded were put in their own boats and so rescued. Semmes and forty-one others were picked up by *Deerhound* and taken to England. Other boats in the vicinity picked up what men they could find, and *Kearsarge*'s boats also picked up several. Nine men on *Alabama* were killed in the battle, twenty-one were wounded, and ten more were drowned. Semmes was wounded. Dr. Llewellyn, *Alabama*'s surgeon, was drowned, refusing to take a place in a boat with the wounded. It was said of *Alabama* that she was built in England, armed with English guns, manned by an English crew, and sunk in the English Channel, not really a fitting epitaph for a ship, a crew, and a captain who had done all they could in a lost cause.

The battle wound up the naval part of the Civil War as far as Maine was concerned. The blockade in which Maine men and Maine ships served, tightened. Charleston was besieged and the harbor closed, Fort Fisher was taken, and there were few if any refuges for blockade runners. Two ironclad rams for the Confederacy were built in England, but when Ambassador Adams threatened war, the British navy bought the two ironclads. Another powerful ironclad was built in France, too late to be effective. Ashore, Grant and Sherman bore down hard on the Southern armies, deprived of military supplies by the blockade, and mercifully the Civil War ended.

For Maine the results were devastating. Of the 67,000 men who enlisted in the war, 8,800 did not return. A number of ships were lost to Confederate raiders. More had been sold abroad to exempt them from capture. The shipyards were choked with war contracts. The fishing fleet had been attacked by raiders, many more fishing vessels had been laid up in terror of the Confederate navy, and finally, it was becoming evident that steel and steam were to displace stick and string. Maine was slow to learn that wooden sailing ships had no commercial future, and the peculiar economic conditions of the ensuing fifteen years supported the delusion with the temporary success of the Downeasters.

NOTES

There is no lack of material on the Civil War. The problem lies in trying to shake out what is relevant to Maine. William Hutchinson Rowe in *The Maritime History of Maine* has done an excellent job of this, but his account is brief and can be supplemented from other sources. William Baker's *Maritime History of Bath* has some useful details. Philip Van Duren Stern's *The Confederate Navy* does an excellent job on the commerce destroyers and our relationships with England. Robert Albion's *New England and the Sea,* while not primarily concerned with Maine, is helpful. *A Maine Town in the Civil War* by Vernal Hutchinson is an account of the war in Deer Isle and yields a few interesting naval details, although it deals principally with Deer Islanders in the army. Francis Greene's *History of Boothbay, Southport and Boothbay Harbor* and *Shipping Days of Old Boothbay* are relevant. There are other, general histories of the war, but they largely repeat what is already covered. Mason Philip Smith's *Confederates Down East* gives an excellent and detailed account of the *Caleb Cushing* affair, the *Chesapeake* seizure, and the Calais bank failure. It also explores the daring Confederate plan to invade Maine in 1864.

A symposium at the Maine Maritime Museum in May 1989 included a paper by Kevin Foster on the *Alabama–Kearsarge* battle, principally concerned with the interesting problem of salvaging artifacts from *Alabama.* Present at the symposium was a guest who reported on a rare book written by a seaman on *Kearsarge* for the benefit of a society of surviving members of her crew who met annually in remembrance of their common experience. This book quotes Winslow as saying, "One hit is worth one hundred misses." I believe the entire conference, including discussion periods, was taped.

I personally knew Captain Robert Snowman's grandson and know his daughter. He and the crew of *Archer* at first had no idea they were being captured and afterwards always referred to Read's crew as pirates. Accounts of the *Cushing* affair do not make it clear whether Bibber and Titcomb were deceived, ignorant, confused, or intimidated. In any case, they were not willingly cooperating with the enemy. Bibber's desire to get clear of the *Cushing* was understandable from any point of view.

Archer was returned to her owners and the following year sailed to Chaleur Bay with a nineteen-year-old skipper, Wesley George Pierce.

George Wade, accused of having murdered Schaffer, *Chesapeake's* second engineer, was brought ashore to Queen's Wharf, Halifax, with two other prisoners after *Chesapeake's* recapture. The Halifax sheriff freed all three, but Constable Hutt, bearing a warrant for Wade's arrest, appeared just too late to take Wade in charge. Dr. W. J. Almon, a Southern sympathizer, created a diversion in the crowd and whispered to Wade to jump into a rowboat alongside. Wade jumped, the two oarsmen rowed furiously, Hutt leveled his pistol, Almon seized Wade's gun arm, and both fell overboard together. The crowd cheered. Wade shouted as he was rowed away, "For God's sake, thank the Queen for my liberty." He landed safely at Ketch Harbor and fled the province.

TWENTY-THREE

The Downeasters

JUST AS a unique combination of economic conditions made the clipper ship possible, so a change in those conditions made it obsolete, and a new set of conditions brought about a different kind of vessel, the Downeaster.

After the Civil War, steamers improved rapidly in speed and reliability. They soon took over the North Atlantic packet trade, fortified in Britain by generous mail subsidies, and they also took over the immigrant trade.

In 1855 a railroad across the isthmus of Panama with steamer connections at each end seriously reduced the demand for fast Cape Horn passenger traffic, and the driving of the golden spike in 1869 uniting the east and west coasts of the United States by rail eliminated the Cape Horn passenger traffic entirely. By 1870 steamers were carrying 26 percent of foreign trade, and by 1880 the figure was up to 64 percent.

The opening of the Suez Canal in 1869 opened to steamer traffic the trade to India, the East Indies, and China. The route was far shorter than that around the Cape of Good Hope, and, important for the steamers, the jumps between coaling stations were short. Even if sailing vessels were towed through the canal, the route was impractical for them because the long passage of the Red Sea in either direction was slow and beset with navigational dangers.

However, long voyages far from coaling stations were not practical for steamers. The Cape Horn trade, the transpacific trade, and the transportation of large bulk cargoes across the Indian Ocean were still profitable to sailing vessels.

At the same time that steamers were taking over the high-speed, short-haul routes, a number of long-haul trades in bulk cargoes opened up. California turned from gold mining to agriculture. In 1859, 14,000,000 bushels of wheat were harvested. In 1879, 25,000,000 bushels were grown, and by 1884 the crop had reached 98,000,000 bushels. Most of this crop was exported to England and western Europe and much of it to the eastern United States. With the increase in the harvest, the demand for ships to carry it increased.

YEAR	TONS OF WHEAT EXPORTED
1865	43,302
1871	135,111
1875	359,307
1880	488,089

Ships carrying grain to English or European ports often loaded coal there for San Francisco or South American ports by way of Cape Horn or to the Orient around the Cape of Good Hope; then sailed back to San Francisco in ballast for the next year's crop. Others carried salt and general cargo to the United States and went out to San Francisco with case oil (kerosene in cans), coal, or general cargo. If the California wheat crop was short, a vessel could carry lumber from Puget Sound ports to China, Hawaii, or Australia and return with jute, hemp, hides, sugar, or wool. And as a last and unattractive resort, the Chincha Islands guano trade was still open. The bulk cotton trade from southern United States ports recovered slowly after the Civil War; not until 1879 did cotton exports reach the 1859 level, and then foreign vessels carried half of it.

The conditions, then, called for a sailing vessel that could carry a large bulk cargo with reasonable speed over a great distance at a low cost in construction, maintenance, and manpower. The Downeaster was Maine's answer to the challenge, for Maine had the skilled labor, the shipyards, and much of the timber needed.

A model of *Shenandoah,* built by C. R. Sawyer. Notice the comparatively short ends as compared with *Red Jacket* on page 298, and the double topsails. *Peabody Museum of Salem*

This new type of vessel was about the same length, breadth, and depth as the clipper ship—225 feet long, give or take 25 feet—and was of about the same tonnage as the bigger clippers—2,000 tons. However, she carried half again as much cargo. Her 'midship section had no deadrise; that is, the cross section of the ship was like a flat U rather than like a V. This U section was carried well forward and aft, making the middle of the vessel like a great box. The entrance and run were not nearly as long as on a clipper but still were shapely enough to give the Downeaster a good turn of speed if driven hard. Henry Hall, writing in the 1880 United States census report on *The Shipbuilding Industry in the United States,* says: "The California vessel of today is no longer an extreme clipper, nor is it the bluff freighting ship of 1840, but it is a handsome medium clipper with towering masts and spars, full on the floor, with good bow and a fair run, capable of carrying a great cargo at an excellent rate of speed. The 'midship section (maximum width) is in the center of the length, the ship floats on an even keel, carrying power is 1½ times the register tonnage, and it draws from 20 to 24 feet of water. A few of those built at Thomaston and Bath, Maine, within the last five years out of the profits of the California wheat trade are about 2,000 tons register and carry 3,000 tons of freight."

To carry such a heavy cargo in such a long wooden vessel requires tremendous longitudinal strength. As the vessel is driven hard through the long seas of Cape Horn, she is supported alternately at the ends and in the middle. Massive keel and keelson structure, bound and bolted through and through with iron or bronze, stiffened the backbone. In some vessels—*Henry B. Hyde,* for instance—diagonal metal straps were let into the inside of the frame, although this expensive device was not universal. The planking inside the frames, the ceiling, was edge-nailed and the seams caulked, not only to keep the cargo dry but to wedge the ceiling planks tightly against each other and thus stiffen the whole structure. Under the deckbeams and at the turn of the bilge, the ceiling was made heavier and the deckbeams were supported and braced with hackmatack knees, right-angle braces cut from the trunk and roots of the tree so the grain ran around in a right angle.

Many Downeasters had three decks, though the lower deck was often planked loosely and only at the ends and along the sides. The other two decks, of course, were tightly laid and caulked, not only making them watertight but adding to the longitudinal stiffness of the vessel.

The Downeasters were almost all ship rigged, although there were a few barks. A ship, square rigged on all three masts, is most efficient with a fair wind, and the sailing ship routes were planned to take advantage of easterly trade winds and westerlies in the higher latitudes. The exception was the necessity of beating westward around Cape Horn against the heavy westerlies and an adverse current.

In order to reduce stress and wear and tear on the gear, the yards on a Downeaster were shorter than those on a clipper ship and the sails not so deep from top to bottom. One of the principal devices for reducing manpower was the divided topsail described in detail in the chapter notes. During the earlier years of the century, the topsails had come to be the most used sails on a ship, the first set and the last taken in. In the big clipper ships they had become so deep, so long from top to bottom, that it took a whole watch standing shoulder to shoulder along the yard to reef or furl a topsail in a gale of wind, even more or less confined as it was by buntlines and clew lines. In the Downeaster this deep man-killer was cut into two sails, each only half as deep as the single topsail. With the divided topsail and the shorter yards of the Downeaster, the labor was much reduced.

The labor was further reduced by the elimination of studding sails (stun'sails) except on a very few vessels. The clippers set these sails on extensions of the yards, but it is a labor-intensive operation at best. The need for a large crew was further reduced by winches along the main deck in addition to the anchor windlass on the forecastle and a big capstan for heavy hauling.

Although not as heavily sparred as clippers, the Downeasters usually carried both royals and skysails. The order of squaresails on the mainmast, for instance, starting at the deck, would be (1) course or mainsail, (2) lower topsail, (3) upper topsail, (4) topgallant, (5) royal, (6) skysail. Sometimes another very small, light squaresail, called a moonraker, was set over the skysail in light weather. An awkward four-sided sail set fore-and-aft under the bowsprit in calm weather, called a Jimmy Green, was a chancy rig at best. From the bowsprit on various stays to the foremast were set the foretopmast staysail, and then a succession of jibs to the total number of four or five. On other stays between the masts, staysails were set when the wind was such that they would fill. Basil Lubbock reports that south of 50° south latitude many Downeasters rigged a main spencer, a small gaff-headed fore-and-aft sail of very heavy duck rigged on the mainmast. The throat would, of course, be below the main yard. This was very useful when lying to in heavy weather to steady the vessel and to give her some help in head reaching. It is hard to find a picture of such a sail or of the spencer gaff in his book, but very few pictures were taken of Downeasters below 50° south.

Standards of seamanship and maintenance on a Downeaster were usually very high. Decks were scrubbed white and kept that way. Paint was clean and fresh. Frayed or worn rigging was replaced. Spare sails and spars were carried and promptly used as needed. Mates were very sensitive to the appearance of their ships at all times but especially in port. Yards were squared precisely by lifts and braces, paint work shone, and no paddy's pennants or loose ends were tolerated anywhere. Spars were oiled or varnished. The earlier Downeasters used Russian hemp standing rigging, wormed, parceled, and served: Small stuff was wound in the grooves between the strands, the main line was then wrapped in tarred or painted canvas, and the whole was wound very tightly with marline, a tarred, two-stranded twine laid left-handed; the marline was wound on with a serving mallet so tightly that the tar was squeezed out of it and made a smooth surface to the finished job. The rigging was then set up with deadeyes and lanyards of Russian hemp, the least elastic of natural fibers. In the 1870s, wire rigging set up with turnbuckles came into use.

Lower masts were made up of several pieces mortised together and banded with iron. Other spars were generally of single sticks. However, the "Big Edward," *Edward O'Brien III,* built at Thomaston in 1882, had lower masts of steel.

The wooden Downeasters were covered below the waterline with a layer of felt and sheets of copper. The felt insulated the copper from any iron fastenings in the hull to prevent a galvanic action that would eat up the iron in short order. The copper sheathing poisoned the weed and barnacles that otherwise would grow quickly and reduce the vessel's speed radically. The copper also kept out shipworms, which will quickly eat up a wooden vessel in tropical waters. The British iron vessels were not bothered by worms but fouled up quickly and by the end of a voyage through tropical waters moved slowly. A more complete discussion of the antifouling problem is found in the chapter notes following Chapter 21.

The Downeasters carried more cargo than clippers, with less sail area and smaller crews. The main yard of the clipper *Young America* was 104 feet, while that of the Downeaster *Alfred D. Snow* was 88 feet. *Young America* carried seventy-five men all told, while the Downeaster *A. G. Ropes* had thirty-four including the skipper's family. One would thus expect the Downeasters to be slower. Indeed they were; they made very few voyages from New York to San Francisco under 100 days. However, *M. P. Grace* made the voyage twice in 102 days and averaged 115 days for seven voyages—a record many clippers would be proud of. *A. G. Ropes*'s fastest passages were 104 and 107 days, her average passage being 120 days, and *Henry B. Hyde* once made the passage in 105 days with an average of 124 days.

In 1853 one William Poole, "a notorious and dangerous character," left Portland one jump ahead of the sheriff in the steamer *Isabelle Jewett.* The next day the little 120-foot bark *Grapeshot,* built at Cumberland, just north of Portland, left in pursuit. When *Isabelle Jewett* reached Fayal in the Azores, *Grapeshot* was waiting to arrest Poole.

The Downeaster achieved her speed not by virtue of clipper design but principally by hard driving. True, speed was not the economic factor it had been in clipper ship days, for wheat was not as perishable a cargo as tea. Furthermore, neither the owner of the ship nor the skipper owned the cargo. The owner of the wheat chartered the vessel at an agreed figure per ton, and he might even sell the shipload in the course of the voyage. In a sense, the ship was only a traveling warehouse. Yet skippers and mates were tough competitors. They were proud of their handsome vessels and proud of fast passages. Some of them acquired frightful reputations as hard drivers.

Captain John G. Pendleton of Searsport took his young wife to sea with him in *William H. Connor.* One day in a fresh fair breeze of wind, she came on deck and said, "It's getting awful trembly in the cabin. Wouldn't it be as well to shorten sail?" Before the skipper could answer, the main topgallant sail blew out, leaving nothing but the boltropes, the hardware, and a few rags thrashing in the wind. "Well, my dear," observed the skipper soothingly, "there's the main topgallant sail gone, anyway." His wife went below, perhaps feeling justified, but before eight bells were struck, a new main topgallant sail was bent and drawing, for spare sails were always provided.

Other famous Maine sail carriers* mentioned by Basil Lubbock in *The Downeasters* were Captain Rivers of *A. G. Ropes,* Captain Phineas Pendleton of *Henry B. Hyde,* Captain Eben Curtis of *Tillie E. Starbuck,* Captain Jim Murphy of *Shenandoah,* Captain Zaccheus Allen of *Benjamin F. Packard,* and Captain Dan Nichols of *Wandering Jew.*

To run a big ship of 2,000 tons, 250 feet long, with three or four masts, square rigged, took men of ability and foresight, but it also required strict disciplinarians. The crews, often put aboard by crimps, were sometimes richer in cowboys, waterfront roustabouts, and hobos than in experienced sailormen. Many a tough Down East mate educated his new crew in a great hurry with fist, boot, and belaying pin. When a skipper or mate of this stamp was of a malicious disposition and perhaps stimulated with bad liquor, life for a man before the mast could be hellish.

Felix Reisenberg, one of the few articulate seamen who served before the mast in those days, wrote: "and the figure of the bucko mate, belaying-pins in his short boots and knuckle dusters on his fists, comes back out of the past, not as an adjunct to morbid romance but as a cruel fact. He broke men and killed them on the cruel blue sea without the aid of fire."

The National Seamen's Union of America published in 1885 *The Red Record,* an account of sixty-four cases of cruelty and murder over only seven years in the Cape Horn fleet. In a few cases the captains and mates responsible were punished, but these were the unusual exceptions to "case dismissed for lack of evidence," or "justifiable discipline."

One skipper is reported to have cautioned his mates never to hit a man in the temple with a belaying pin or handspike and when they got him down, to kick him in the legs or above the short ribs; with a short crew, there was no need to disable a man permanently.

One old shellback said, "I'd rather be in hell without claws than aboard of a Yankee ship with the mates down on me."

All skippers and all mates were not like this, of course, although the literature of the time might lead the reader to think so. Captain David Rivers of Thomaston, master of *A. G. Ropes* in 1890, wrote a long letter to a friend in several installments on a voyage from San Francisco to Liverpool. A few excerpts suggest something of his calculated rough behavior.

* A sail carrier in a commercial vessel, fisherman, or yacht is one who does not reef or take in sail until the last minute or a little later.

"The first two weeks at sea is generally the hardest on the Captain as I have a new set of Dagoes to get under discipline and whether I am a good fellow or not, I have to act the part of a tyrant. If a captain undertakes to use this foreign element, which we have in our sailors, half way decent, they will have full charge of the ship in no time. We are thirty-four souls aboard—that is, providing all the sailors possess souls. My family, the mate and the sailmaker are the only Americans; the second mate is a Swede; the third mate Scotch; boatswain, Irish; carpenter, Danish; steward, German; cook, Irish; the balance of the crew of all sorts, even to a Maltese. All of my officers are men of experience and ability. Out of my seventeen able-bodied seamen, there are only four that can do a decent job of rigging, and I have disrated several of those claiming to be able-bodied. . . . The crew I had on my outward passage, just before leaving the ship in port, cut my sails and rigging, knocked holes in the water casks and did other damage that would not be found until they were paid off. These men had been well treated and well fed. So you see we have anarchists way out on the ocean. . . .

"Now in regard to how we spend our time. In addition to sailing, we have made upper and lower mizzentopsails, and repaired several sails. . . . We have scrubbed all the paint work, cleaned and oiled the decks and the tops of the houses, set up [tightened] the fore rigging, repaired all the chafes aloft and at this writing we are pumice-stoning the ship on the outside and tarring the rigging. . . . I am somewhat of a climber and often get up to the skysail yard. There is about $25,000 to $30,000 worth of sails, spars and rigging above the ship's deck and I think these things are worth looking after. When the men suspect the 'old man' is going to see what is done up aloft they do their best to keep out of trouble, for if I find anything wrong there is a calling to account on my arrival on deck, and if you should meet me on one of these occasions you would not consider me much of a saint. . . .

"Yesterday was my 40th birthday and as I had some cigars given to me in 'Frisco and as I do not smoke, I sent my cabin boy forward to treat all hands to two each. They returned many thanks and wished happy returns of the day. Now that looks as though I was a popular and model captain, but I must give you all the facts. Only the day before we had a very heavy squall which carried away some of the sheets and the watch on deck not getting around very lively, I got down on the main deck amongst the men and knocked them helter skelter, and in doing so knocked my thumb out of joint and sprained my ankle in the bout. . . . I have had only one good night's sleep since we arrived in this section (50° south in the South Atlantic). I might take in sail and go to bed and sleep but time is money, and if we are to make time I must keep awake and see that everything moves. Last night the boatswain fell on deck and cut his head so badly that I was called on to perform a surgical operation. Such is the life of a skipper."

The skippers of these vessels, surprisingly, came largely from Searsport and Thomaston. Basil Lubbock lists 149 captains from Searsport, then with a population of about 2,000. To be sure, all were not skippers of Downeasters at the same time and many were skippers of other kinds of vessels. Yet in 1889, seventy-seven Searsport men were in command of American sailing ships and of these, thirty-three were skippers of Cape Horn ships. Command ran in families. The Pendletons had at least fourteen captains. There were twelve Carver captains and seventeen Nichols captains. Often a bright, ambitious boy moved quickly to command. Captain Bert Williams of Thomaston was master of *St. Paul* at the age of twenty-two, and she was no small boat but an 1,824-ton ship, 228 feet long, setting three skysails. John Wallace became master of *J. B. Walker* at nineteen. On his first voyage as master from Baltimore to San Francisco, *J. B. Walker* ran into very heavy weather. Two men fell from aloft, and her main deck and some bow planks were stove in. On the subsequent voyage to Liverpool the fore topmast was carried away in a squall. Young John Wallace continued as captain, however, as long as *J. B. Walker* carried sail.

Often the captain took his wife aboard. It was a rather lonely life for her, but Mrs. Ranlett of Thomaston, wife of the skipper of *Ionian,* found plenty to do on the night of the San Francisco fire. With sparks falling all around the vessel, the skipper broke open a hatch, found a shipment of buckets in the cargo, and he, Mrs. Ranlett, the stewardess, and the officers got a bucket brigade organized so efficiently that they saved the ship. Most of the crew ran for it.

Alice Oliver, also of Thomaston, daughter of Captain David Oliver, brought his vessel to port after the captain's death.

One Thomaston lad cannot pass without mention. Hanson Gregory, as a boy, signed on for cook. His mother, while giving him a crash course in Yankee cuisine, showed him how to make fried pies, dough fried in deep fat. He noticed that the middle was usually raw so suggested that the middle be cut out—and behold, the doughnut.

Although it must be recorded that in many ships at the start of a voyage the scuppers ran red, it must also be recognized that such methods were not universal. Some skippers were highly regarded by their crews. A San Francisco paper in November 1881 noted that when *Frank Pendleton* came in from Yokohama, the crew assisted in making her fast, cleaned up and coiled down, leaving everything shipshape, then lined up on the wharf and gave three cheers for the ship, three for Captain Nichols, and three for the officers. This did not happen very often, but Captain Burgess of *David Crockett,* a clipper that survived to carry grain, is remembered as a strict disciplinarian who with his mates of the same stamp could handle a rough crew without belaying pins or brass knuckles. Captain William J. Lermond was another.

Eighty percent of the Downeasters were built in Maine, and 44 percent were registered in Bath. These almost incredible figures are subject to some doubt over exactly what qualified as a Downeaster and where on the Kennebec River in the Bath customs district certain vessels were built. Lubbock's figures and Fairburn's do not always agree. Nevertheless, it is clear that Maine built by far more wooden oceangoing square-riggers than did any other state, and a large proportion of these were built on the Kennebec. Part of the reason may be that the upper reaches of the Kennebec still supplied white pine and hackmatack. However, most of the big vessels were built of white oak and hard pine imported from Virginia and the Carolinas. Another reason is that Maine had a large number of skilled workmen accustomed to building big vessels and had not been industrialized as much as other states, whose ship carpenters turned to building houses and to factory work and whose capital was invested ashore.

William Fairburn writes: "That Maine after the Civil War was able to continue to build good and profitable wood ships better and more cheaply than any other part of the country (and of the world) was due primarily to the unequaled designers, master builders, and shipwrights of Maine; that Maine could continue to operate such wood vessels and make money in the face of fierce foreign competition was due partly to keen, far-sighted, and well-planned economic management and to the Down-east skippers in command. They continued to the end of sail to be superior in courage, driving power, resourcefulness, frugality, honesty and shrewd trading ability to any other captains who ever sailed the Seven Seas."

The Sewall family of Bath was deeply committed to building Downeasters. From 1854 until 1902, the Sewalls in various combinations (William D. Sewall, Arthur and Edward Sewall, E. & A. Sewall, and Arthur Sewall & Company) built forty-six ships of over 1,000 tons. The Houghton family built seventeen Downeasters during the same period. John McDonald, a gifted designer, was responsible for building twenty of the best of the Downeaster fleet and was responsible for the design and rig of many more. William Rogers between 1854 and 1889 built fifteen ships over 1,000 tons. In Phippsburg, down the river from Bath, Charles V. Minott built ten ships between 1860 and 1893, the last, *Aryan,* being the last wooden square-rigged ship built in Maine—and that means in the world.

In Richmond, T. J. Southard built fourteen ships over 1,000 tons between 1854 and 1884 as well as smaller barks, brigs, and schooners. Thomas J. Southard can stand as an example of the energy, resource, and enthusiasm behind the final rush of wooden shipbuilding on the Kennebec. He was born in Boothbay in 1808, one of twelve children. When he was eleven years old, he walked to Richmond, a two-day hike at least, and signed on a coaster. Then, small as he was—he stood only 5½ feet tall when grown up—he apprenticed himself to a blacksmith. In 1824, when he was twenty-one, he set up his own blacksmith shop and married two years later. In 1836 he took a share in a vessel in payment for her ironwork and by 1840 had built the brig *China,* of which he was managing owner. From then until his death in 1896 he built, either on his own or with his son, thirty-five ships, twelve barks, twelve brigs, and twelve schooners including the clipper *Gauntlet* and the 2,390-ton

Downeaster *Commodore T. H. Allen*. Mr. Southard's efforts were not limited to shipbuilding and managing. He owned a store that sold West India goods, a drugstore, a sawmill, a gristmill, and a cotton mill. He founded a bank, served in the state legislature, and was sheriff of Sagadahoc County.

Although Bath built a great many Downeasters, other Maine towns contributed to the fleet. According to William A. Fairburn, who acknowledges that his figures are incomplete, Kennebunk and Kennebunkport built eighteen big ships, Yarmouth and Freeport built twenty-five between them, and the little village of Waldoboro launched nineteen ships of over 1,000 tons into the eel-rut of the Medomak River between 1854 and 1884, as well as numerous barks, brigs, and schooners. Thomaston is credited with thirty-three big ships, built mostly by Edward O'Brien, who built, owned, and managed eleven of them; one more, *Edward O'Brien III,* "Big Edward," was completed after his death. The Samuel Watts yard in Thomaston launched sixteen, all built to the Watts account. Two of these, *Alfred D. Snow* and *Cyrus Wakefield,* made times to California comparable with those of much-touted clippers. (The comparison will be found in the chapter notes.) Not all these vessels were built in regular yards. Several people might agree to build a vessel, rent a piece of shore property, employ a crew, and build a vessel. When she was completed, the organization might rent another location or dissolve completely. Therefore records are sometimes scanty.

The Camden-Rockport yards built principally schooners and barks, but turned out eleven ships of over 1,000 tons. Among them was *Wandering Jew,* built by Carleton, Norwood. She was one of the few flush-decked ships ever built. She set a record of thirty-three days from Hong Kong to San Francisco. In 1895 she raced *Tam O'Shanter* from Hong Kong to New York. The ships were in sight of each other several times during the passage, sailing side by side with neither gaining an advantage. They arrived in New York on the same day ninety-five days out. The two skippers had to agree that the race was a tie and the time was one to be proud of. In October 1895 *Wandering Jew* was set afire by arsonists in the river above Shanghai, was scuttled, raised, and used as a barge.

Another notable Carleton, Norwood vessel was the four-masted bark *Frederick Billings,* launched in 1885, the largest square-rigged vessel built on Penobscot Bay. She was 282 feet long, registered 2,628 tons, and was only the third four-masted bark built in the United States; later the rig was adopted by Bath builders for their big steel vessels. The *Billings* carried wheat west to Europe and coal east until 1893, when she loaded a cargo of 3,800 tons of nitrate in eight days. It is said that the crew resented harsh treatment and set her afire. The cargo exploded, and in twenty minutes the *Billings* was gone, although all her people were saved.

Twenty-four full-rigged ships over 1,000 tons were built at Belfast. *Hualco,* built in 1856—just in time for the financial panic of 1857—lay at anchor for a year, waiting for a charter. Finally it was given out that she had a charter in

New Orleans. She left in ballast, dropped her pilot, and was sailing down East Penobscot Bay at 8 knots with topgallants set. A member of the crew who had fished in the bay observed to the skipper that he was too close to Saddleback Ledge. The skipper bawled him out in Down East fashion, told the young man to mind his own business and that he, the skipper, would attend to his. Minutes later, *Hualco* struck North Saddleback Ledge, fell off into deep water, and sank abruptly. The crew took to the boats and were home in Belfast before dark.

A number of other towns launched Downeasters. The list extracted from Fairburn will be found in the chapter notes.

The year 1881 was a boom year. From the West Coast, 539 vessels sailed with wheat, of which 154 vessels (or 28 percent) were American. The next year saw only 371 vessels sailing from San Francisco, but 169 (or 46 percent) were American. In the years following these, both the number of ships and the number of American ships dropped off rapidly. This can be attributed partly to the increased size of the vessels, for about the same amount of grain was carried. At about this time Britain began building big iron sailing ships under government subsidy; these could thus be built more cheaply than Maine-built wooden ships. Captain William W. Bates's *American Marine,* quoted in Lubbock's *The Downeasters,* tells us that in the boom years of the grain trade, presumably following 1880, there were 418 American wooden ships and 761 British iron ships carrying grain. A further stimulus to iron ship building at the expense of wood was the policy of the marine insurance companies, particularly Lloyd's, which continued the A-1 rating for iron ships longer than it did for wooden ships. The vessel with the highest rating paid the lowest premium. Also the highest rating earned the highest freight rate, so on two counts the American ships were discriminated against.

As the need grew for bigger and bigger ships, the limit of efficiency in the construction of wooden ships was approached. With massive keel structures and four masts, a wooden ship could be built up to about 2,500 tons and 250 feet in length. Such a vessel was expensive, and to exceed that was pushing the limit. Some did push the limit, but with the increased competition from England in iron vessels, many builders dropped out. According to Lubbock's figures, which if not precisely accurate are at least representative, fifteen big, wooden square-rigged ships were built in Maine in 1882 and the same number in 1883. The next year the number dropped to five, then rose to six in 1885. None were built until 1889, and then no more than three were built in any one year. In 1893 C. V. Minott in Phippsburg built *Aryan* of 2,017 tons, 249 feet long, the last wooden full-rigged ship built anywhere in the world.

Having seen the need for bigger vessels, Arthur Sewall & Co. of Bath built the "Big Four." The first of these was *Rappahannock,* 3,185 tons, the second of that name, launched in 1890 for Samuel B. Sewall. She was rigged as a ship with three skysails, double topsails, and double topgallants. She was an enormous vessel, 287 feet long, her fore and main lower masts 88 and 89 feet long and 38½ inches in diameter. Her main yard was 95 feet long, a prodigious spar. She had a short life. On her first voyage she carried 125,000 cases of kerosene to Japan, the largest cargo ever put aboard a sailing vessel up to that time. She then crossed the Pacific to San Francisco, carried 5,100 tons of wheat to Liverpool in 130 days—not very fast time—and sailed for San Francisco with coal in July 1891. After a rough passage around Cape Horn, 40 days from 50° south in the Atlantic to 50° south in the Pacific, Captain Dickinson found the cargo to be afire from spontaneous combustion. He anchored at Juan Fernandez, put his family and crew ashore, and then tried to fight the fire, but explosions blew the hatches off, and finally blew the ship apart entirely. The crew were all rescued in due course by a Chilean dispatch boat.

In November 1890 Arthur Sewall & Co. launched *Shenandoah,* 3,407 tons, the largest tonnage of any American sailing ship at that time. She was only inches short of 300 feet long and was rigged as a four-masted bark or "shipentine," square rigged on the forward three masts and fore-and-aft rigged on the spanker. She carried a crew of twenty-four forward, thirty-eight all told, and had a steam donkey engine for handling cargo. There was a considerable body of opinion in Bath before she was launched that such a large wooden ship would be cranky, unhandy in heavy seas, and altogether too big. She proved, however, to be a good sea vessel and to "steer like a pilot boat." Her first passage to San Francisco was a respectable 125 days and to Le Havre with 5,628 tons of wheat, 109 days. *Shenandoah* had a narrow escape from spontaneous combustion in a coal cargo, but she was alongside a wharf discharging at San Francisco. The fire was extinguished but not until it had nearly burned through her bow planking. She continued carrying cargoes of coal, grain, and lumber from the West Coast to Europe and Japan until she was laid up for three years in San Francisco Bay, made one more voyage to New York, and was there converted to a barge in 1910. In 1915 she was run down by a steamer and sunk.

Susquehanna, launched in September 1891, was smaller than her sisters, 2,745 tons, 283 feet long. She was rigged as a four-masted bark. She, too, was in the grain and coal trade and made one voyage with sugar from Hawaii to East Coast refineries. In August 1905 she loaded a heavy cargo of chrome ore at Noumea, near New Caledonia, about 900 miles east of Australia. She ran into heavy weather three days after she sailed, broke her back, and sank quickly. The crew took to the boats and eventually reached safety.

Roanoke, the last and the biggest of Sewall's "Big Four," was launched in September 1892. She was 311 feet long, 3,539 tons, with a carrying capacity of 5,400 tons. Her keel was white oak, 16 inches square, in two tiers. Her garboards, planks next to the keel, were 8 inches thick. Her forward three lower masts were over 90 feet long; her main yard, 95 feet. With a fair wind and plenty of it, she was said to be fast; her best day's run was 320 miles. She carried general cargo, case oil, grain, sugar, wine, and salmon from the West

Coast to East Coast and Oriental ports. In 1901 on a voyage from Norfolk to San Francisco, her cargo of coal took fire. The mate crawled below despite the smoke and fumes and located the fire. Water and marble dust were pumped in and the water pumped out with windmills. Captain Amesbury headed for Hawaii where most of the coal was discharged and the fire extinguished, although the vessel was badly damaged. In 1905, loading chrome ore in New Caledonia in company with *Susquehanna, Roanoke* caught fire and burned in spite of the valiant efforts of her crew, of *Susquehanna*'s crew, of the crew of a Norwegian ship nearby, and of the same mate who had located the coal fire.

Thus went the last of the "Big Four," their careers pointing to the conclusion that the limit of size in wooden ships had been exceeded and that the California grain trade was falling into the hands of the British and French iron and steel ships subsidized by their governments.

However, Bath made one more valiant effort to recover an American share of the trade. A British four-masted steel bark, *Kenilworth,* caught fire from a burning warehouse ashore in Porta Costa, California, in August 1889. She was scuttled after having been half filled with water by a fireboat. As she lay on the bottom, she was bought by Arthur Sewall & Co. She was raised, repaired, and used as a means of comparing operating costs and profits between steel and wooden vessels. The conclusion was that future vessels must be of steel.

As soon as *Roanoke* was launched in September 1892, the Sewalls' yard was converted to building steel vessels, and necessary machinery was purchased. To speed up construction, the steel members for a new vessel were

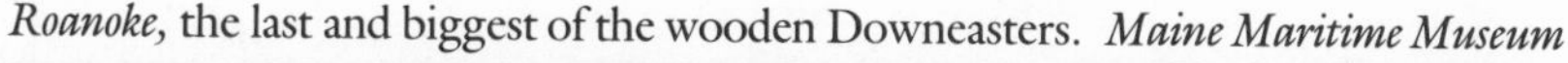

Roanoke, the last and biggest of the wooden Downeasters. *Maine Maritime Museum*

shipped already formed to Bath from Glasgow, and on February 3, 1894, *Dirigo,* America's first steel sailing vessel, was launched. She was essentially a British steel ship, a great steel box, a floating warehouse. However, carrying the conventional rig of a four-masted bark with single topgallants, royals, and skysails, she made good average passages. One drawback was that she could not be sheathed in copper because of galvanic action with the steel, so she fouled rapidly and toward the end of her first voyage to Japan with case oil could do no more than 8 or 9 knots with a fair wind. She was profitably employed carrying grain, case oil, and lumber until sold to a Kentucky firm in 1916 and torpedoed in the English Channel in May 1917.

Hawaii was annexed to the United States in 1897, making the sugar trade "coastwise," a trade from which foreign ships were excluded. With profitable cargoes available in grain, case oil, coal, and now sugar, Sewall built eight more big, steel square-riggers between 1898 and 1902. Their careers were long and in some cases colorful. They may be briefly summarized. *Dirigo* we have already mentioned.

Erskine M. Phelps, 2,998 tons, was built in 1898 after Hawaii joined the United States, adding sugar to the coastwise trades. She carried coal, grain, and sugar until sold as an oil barge in 1913. In 1942 she was taken by the United States Navy to be used as an oil storage tank and in December 1945 was taken out and sunk.

Arthur Sewall, 3,209 tons, was built in 1899. Her rig was unique in that her upper topsail yards were fixed and did not hoist in the usual way. In 1907 she left the Delaware River for Seattle with 4,900 tons of coal and went missing somewhere in the Southern Ocean.

Edward Sewall, 3,206 tons, was also launched in 1899. In February 1910, on a voyage from Newport News to Hawaii, the coal in her forward hold took fire. The heat melted the foot of the steel foremast, which settled 2 feet but fortunately did not slip sideways off its step or it would have gone through the bottom. The fire was finally extinguished, the mast cut off above the melted place, jacked up, and re-stepped. The slack rigging was set up, and the vessel sailed safely to Honolulu. In 1916 she was sold to the Texas Company to carry oil to Argentina and in 1922 to Alaska Packers. She served the salmon fishery until 1936 when she was sold to Japan to be scrapped. *Kauilani,* a smaller steel three-masted bark of 1,520 tons, was also launched in 1899 for the Hawaiian sugar trade. In 1910 she became the Alaska Packers' *Star of Finland.* In 1937 she starred with Gary Cooper in *Souls at Sea.* In 1941 she carried a cargo of lumber from Gray's Harbor, Washington, around Cape Horn to South Africa and then sailed for Sydney, but at the news of Pearl Harbor she put into Hobart, ending there the last commercial voyage of an American-built square-rigged vessel. Yet she seemed immortal. She was taken over by the Army and used as a coal barge during the war. Afterwards she was bought by a Philippine concern and used to carry logs from Mindanao to Manila. In 1936 efforts were initiated to restore her as a museum piece, but she was too far gone.

Above: Dirigo, the first steel Downeaster. *Below:* The *William P. Frye,* last of the steel Downeasters. *Maine Maritime Museum*

Astral, Acme, and *Atlas* were built for the Standard Oil Company in 1900, 1901, and 1902, all practically duplicates of *Edward Sewall*. They were used to carry case oil until sold to Alaska Packers. *Acme* was wrecked in 1918 in the Sea of Japan, and the other two went to Japan in 1935 and 1936 to be scrapped.

William P. Frye was really the last of the steel square-riggers built by Sewall, although launched in 1901 before *Atlas,* which was her twin at 3,374 tons. She carried the usual bulk cargoes of coal, grain, and sugar. On January 27, 1915, with a cargo of grain for Queenstown, she was stopped by the German raider *Prinz Eitel Friedrich*. Her crew was taken off and she was sunk. This touched off a considerable international incident between the United States and German governments when the raider made an American port.

One steel five-masted schooner was built in 1903, and two huge square-riggers were projected but never built. The completion of the Panama Canal in 1914 made the Cape Horn voyage practically obsolete and turned over to steamers and barges the coal, grain, and sugar trades on which Downeasters had flourished.

NOTES

The sources for this chapter are principally William A. Fairburn's *Merchant Sail* (especially Volume V), Basil Lubbock's *The Downeaster,* William A. Baker's *Maritime History of Bath,* and Frederick C. Matthews's two-volume *American Merchant Ships 1850–1900*. In addition, Jacob J. Stahl's *History of Old Broad Bay and Waldoboro* and Aubigne L. Packard's *A Town That Went to Sea* add details on Waldoboro and Thomaston. *Sailing Days on the Penobscot,* by George Wasson and Lincoln Colcord, lists vessels built on Penobscot Bay. My problem is that the figures given by these authorities do not agree, so the figures must all be taken as illustrative of general statements.

The Maine attitude toward efficient moving of cargo is well expressed by a Bath shipbuilder* writing in 1851 and quoted in Fairburn: "We will build only ships that we know are right, that we can stand behind, and that will give satisfaction now and in ten years or more from now; ships that will make money and carry good cargoes at a profit when freight rates get back to normal. We will not throw a ship together in two or three months to please an owner when we know that to build her properly takes twice that time, and we will not build an extremely fine-lined and oversparred ship for the mercantile trade; for ships can be operated only when they make money, and all these sharp and lofty clippers will be laid up when the present boom—which can only last a year or two at the most—has passed. We will build ships that are fast, carry good cargoes, can be operated with moderate-sized crews and low repair bills; ships that on the basis of transporting cargo per ton-mile per year will be so far ahead of the fine-lined overcanvased clipper, with her big crew, big repair bills, and low cargo-carrying

* Fairburn identified this writer as "a leading Bath shipbuilder of Scotch-Canadian stock—canny and experienced in business as well as in the construction and operation of ships. . . ."

capacity, that there can be no comparison drawn whatever in the mind of any business man. We will build ships that may take 130 days instead of 100 to 110 days to reach California, but our ships will carry about one and one half times as much cargo, need a smaller crew, and require much less maintenance expense and a much lower total operating cost. Then our ships will last twice as long as these fine-lined big-sparred clippers, and they will be in their prime when the clippers are either wracked to pieces in unprofitable trade or rotting in idleness."

The size of the vessel grew through the second half of the century to a maximum of about 3,000 tons and 300 feet. However, 2,000 tons and 225 to 250 feet overall is a fair approximation of the typical wooden Downeaster.

A square-rigged vessel needed a fair wind. Matthew Maury, by a study of thousands of logbooks, drew up pilot charts showing what route for what month of the year was likely to be best. In general, a vessel from New York would head south well out in the Atlantic in the westerlies, swing in toward the South American coast in the trade winds, follow the coast south as closely as the westerlies would permit, even passing inside Staten Land through the Strait of Le Maire if the wind served. Then she would have to face up to beating around Cape Horn and come north with the westerlies near Juan Fernandez. She would head far out into the Pacific with the easterly trade winds to avoid the calms along the South and Central American coasts and slide in to San Francisco before the North Pacific westerlies.

Coal, mined both in England and the United States, proved to be a dangerous cargo, for as the voyage progressed, the motion of the vessel shook the coal down so that it packed itself tightly in the hold. With no circulation of air and the dampness of the hold, the coal began to heat spontaneously, sometimes to the point where it caught fire. It was almost impossible to get at the fire because of the poisonous fumes, and water pumped in from above was only occasionally effective, and would stimulate spontaneous combustion elsewhere. The best recourse was to run for port and unload the cargo or scuttle the vessel completely. In 1874 Captain Anderson of *Alaska,* a Downeaster built in Kennebunk in 1867, found his cargo of coal afire off Cape Horn. He ran into Orange Bay on the western side of False Cape Horn and scuttled the vessel in calm water on a smooth bottom. When the fire was extinguished, he pumped the vessel out and continued his voyage to San Francisco.

The following chart is a comparison of a number of voyages of two Thomaston Downeasters with those of five clipper ships. Figures represent length of passage in days. (Chart continues on page 362.)

	TO EQUATOR	E–50°	50° S–50° S	50°–E	E–SF	TOTAL
DOWNEASTER *Alfred D. Snow* 1,987 tons, 232 ft.	20	26	16	20	24	106
DOWNEASTER *Cyrus Wakefield* 2,013 tons, 247 ft.	24	22	18	22	15	101
CLIPPER *David Crockett* 1,679 tons, 219 ft.	20	30	12	20	21	103
CLIPPER *Flying Fish* 1,505 tons, 243 ft.	19	26	9	23	23	100
CLIPPER *Young American* 1,961 tons, 243 ft. Main yard, 104 ft.	19	22	16	22	23	103

	TO EQUATOR	E–50°	50° S–50° S	50°–E	E–SF	TOTAL
CLIPPER *Andrew Jackson* 1,679 tons, 220 ft.	20	23	10	20	16	89
CLIPPER *Flying Cloud* 1,782 tons, 225 ft.	21	26	7	17	18	89
Average, all	20	25.3	11.7	21.4	19.4	97.9
Average, clippers	19.2	25.8	9.6	21.6	19.4	95.6
Average, Downeasters	22	24	17	21	19.5	103.5

Granted that speed is not a fair measure of a vessel's value and that fast passages are usually a matter of luck as well as of good seamanship, apparently Thomaston vessels held their own with the best.

It should further be observed that the Downeasters carried somewhere in the neighborhood of 3,000 tons of cargo, while the clippers carried about 2,000 tons or less. *David Crockett* carried 2,200 tons.

The following Maine towns built Downeasters.

Kennebunk, Kennebunkport	18	Thomaston	33
Saco	6	Rockland	2
Portland, Falmouth, Cape Elizabeth	6	Camden-Rockport	11
Yarmouth	11	Belfast	24
Freeport	14	Searsport	10
Bath area	176	Bucksport	2
Newcastle	3	Bangor	6
Damariscotta	9	Calais	1
Waldoboro	19		

The following chart demonstrates the domination of Bath in building large square-rigged sailing vessels.

	BUILT IN U.S.	BUILT IN MAINE	BUILT IN BATH	% OF U.S. SHIPS BUILT IN BATH
1862–69	21	12	4	19
1870–74	51	34	17	33
1875–79	82	68	28	34
1880–84	56	49	30	54
1885–89	8	8	8	100
1890–94	11	10	8	73
1895–99	4	4	4	100
1900–02	4	4	4	100

If these figures, extracted from Basil Lubbock's book, do not agree with William Fairburn's, I am not unduly distressed. Whether specifically accurate or not, they indicate the trend.

The fates of some Downeasters built in Maine between 1871 and 1875 will illustrate the hazards of the trade and the longevity of the fortunate:

One burned at sea
Eleven were converted to barges

Two were sunk by collisions
One was burned for her metal
Five foundered
One was sold to the government
Eleven were wrecked
One, *Alfred Watts,* was dismasted, and all but two of her crew were washed overboard and drowned or eaten by sharks; two survivors drifted for a month on the derelict before being picked up
One was broken up
One, *Benjamin Sewall,* sailed her last voyage in 1902
One, *Occidental,* sailed her last voyage in 1906
One, *Leading Wind,* was still sailing in 1910
One was abandoned at sea
One, *St. Paul,* was intended for a museum and afloat in 1930
One, *Bohemia,* was bought in 1925 by Cecil B. DeMille for the movie *Yankee Clipper*
One, *Carrie Reed,* was still sailing in 1907
Two others, unknown

Downeasters can be distinguished from clippers at a glance by the double-topsail rig: two narrow topsails instead of one deep topsail. In the clipper ships and in earlier vessels, the lowest yard, the main yard, was more or less permanently fastened to the lower mast just below the doubling where the topmast overlapped it. The topsail yard rested when the sail was furled on the cap of the lower mast above the doubling. When the topsail was to be set, the topsail yard was hoisted to the top of the topmast, and the lower corners, the clews, of the sail were sheeted to the ends of the main yard.

With the divided topsail of the double-topsail rig, the lower mast was made longer, the main yard was made fast lower down, and the lower topsail yard was made fast below the doubling. The lower topsail was set by dropping the sail from the yard and sheeting it to the end of the main yard. The upper topsail yard, when the sail was furled, was on the cap of the lower mast. When it was to be set, the yard was hoisted partway up the topmast and the sail sheeted to the end of the lower topsail yard. Both upper and lower topsails were only half the depth of the old single topsails, hence much easier to subdue and lash up on their respective yards. Also, if the upper topsail yard was lowered, the sail dropped down into the lee of the lower topsail and was much more easily clewed up and made fast. In later years some of the biggest Downeasters were rigged with double topgallants in the same way.

Kenilworth gets a medal for longevity. She carried wheat and sugar for the Sewalls until 1908. She was then bought by Alaska Packers to carry labor and supplies to their canneries in company with nine other big steel sailing vessels, and was named *Star of Scotland.* In 1930 she was sold to be used as a fishing barge in Santa Monica. In 1938 she was bought by a gambling syndicate, her masts taken out, and she was moored 3½ miles offshore and used as a wide-open legal casino under the new name *Rex.* The law finally eliminated this 3-mile loophole, and she was laid up. In 1941 she was found sound and bought by Frank Hillenthal. She was re-rigged as a six-masted schooner with leg-o'-mutton sails and a triangular "squaresail" or raffee on the foremast. The masts, possibly the longest wooden spars ever stepped, were 150-foot sticks of Oregon pine. She was loaded with lumber and sailed from Aberdeen, Washington, to South Africa. She sailed thence in ballast for Paranagua, Brazil, and on November 13, 1942, was sunk by shellfire from a German submarine.

(This information about *Kenilworth* is from *American Neptune* Volume 1, No. 4 and Volume 3, No. 3, July 1943.)

TWENTY-FOUR

The Coasters

HILE MAINE overseas commerce was expanding, while oceangoing sailing vessels were becoming larger and more complicated, and while steamers were proliferating on the bays and rivers of Maine, the coasting trade was also growing. To follow this development, we now look back to the early years of the century.

Two political developments influenced the Maine coasting trade early in the century. The first was the United States Navigation Act of 1817; the second was Maine's separation from Massachusetts. The Navigation Act limited the United States coasting trade to vessels built and owned in the United States, thus eliminating at one stroke all foreign competition. The law is still in force today.

Since the American Revolution there had been agitation in Maine to break away from Massachusetts and to enter the Union as a separate state. This sentiment had grown strong enough in 1816 and 1817 for Massachusetts to call for Maine citizens to vote on the subject, requiring a 5 to 4 majority for separation. After extensive political maneuvering, Maine voters failed to achieve the necessary majority, and the Massachusetts legislature voted against separation. One of the principal objections of Maine coastal people to separation was that under then-existing federal law vessels could voyage to contiguous states without entering or clearing and without port fees. While Maine was part of Massachusetts, Maine coasters could trade freely with New Hampshire, Massachusetts, and Rhode Island. Should Maine become a separate state, even if there were no port fees, Maine coasters could not trade even with Boston without the delay and annoyance of clearing and entering.

Agitation for separation continued, however, and the question assumed national importance when Missouri sought entrance to the Union as a slave state, giving the slave states a majority in the Senate. Senator Rufus King, a Maine man serving as a senator from Massachusetts, convoyed through Congress in March 1819 a law permitting United States coasting vessels to trade without entering or clearing to or from any port from the St. Croix River to

Florida. Maine then voted heavily in favor of separation, Massachusetts assented, and Congress as part of the Missouri Compromise admitted Missouri and Maine to the Union on March 15, 1820. Thus Maine coasters could trade without foreign competition, port fees, or red tape anywhere on the Atlantic coast.

Before Maine became a state, coasters had been very active in carrying lumber, firewood, fish, brick, farm products, lime, and cut stone to Boston to help make up cargoes for overseas trade. They had also visited ports to the westward, bringing back flour, coal, cloth, hardware, tools, and other manufactured goods. As the century advanced, many carried Maine products west, picked up foreign goods in Boston and New York, carried them to Charleston and Savannah, and returned to New York with cotton to load transatlantic packet ships to Liverpool and Le Havre.

Most of these vessels were small, under 100 feet long, and schooner

Western Way, a typical small bay coaster. *Author's collection*

rigged. They were built in large numbers in creeks, harbors, and up the Maine rivers where timber grew near a firm shore with water deep enough for launching. They were, on the average, burdensome little vessels, heavily built and stoutly rigged. Under ordinary circumstances they could beat off a lee shore, but in a gale they could not show enough sail to overcome their leeway and the scend of the sea. The back shore of Cape Cod after a northeaster saw the breakup of many a Maine coaster.

Navigation was primitive—what is known as church-steeple navigation or "barking dog" sailing, where the skipper established his position by knowing the voices of 'longshore dogs. Captain B. J. Willard in the 106-ton schooner *Jerome,* carrying 150 tons of coal from Philadelphia to Portland, tells this story of part of his voyage.

The fog shut down on him off Long Island, so he ran across tide-ridden Block Island Sound at night for Gay Head. He hove to until daylight and then ran up Vineyard Sound, still in the fog, both anchors ready, a man at the foremast head in the hope of seeing over the fog, and another heaving the lead. Breakers on the port bow! Captain Willard luffed the schooner, got a sounding of 8–9 fathoms, then no bottom at 20 fathoms at the next cast. He ran parallel to the breakers and, as the fog scaled up a bit, he saw a wreck on the shore which he recognized as lying just south of Quicks Hole. He then ran off easterly until the lead told him he was near Middle Ground Shoal, felt his way up it with the lead, found a spar buoy on the end of it, and, still in thick fog with the tide running up to 3 knots, "I run down the Sound [Nantucket Sound] on the usual course." After an hour or so at anchor when the wind died, he got underway again after dark with the fog very thick. There is nothing in creation blacker than a foggy night. He kept the foghorn going but heard nothing and saw nothing until a dim glow resolved itself into the lightship, presumably Cross Rip, with no fog bell ringing. When asked why no bell, the lightship crew replied, "What are you running on such a night as this for?" Willard answered, "There are fifty vessels astern and coming up fast." The bell began ringing at once.

As Willard judged it too thick to run for Pollock Rip Channel at night, he took the easier course, still no easy one, around Great Round Shoal and squared away for Portland. The fog broke away the next day as he sailed up the back side of the Cape.

When *Jerome* was some 15 miles north of Highland Light near the tip of Cape Cod, a southerly gale came on with thick rain. Under single-reefed mainsail, foresail, and two jibs he ran on all day and toward dark hauled in to make the land. He thought he was to the westward of Wood Island at the mouth of the Saco River. He hailed a fishing schooner in the dusk to ask the bearing of Wood Island Light. The fisherman asked the bearing of Portland Head. Willard guessed at the bearing of Cape Elizabeth for him, and the fisherman, now out of hearing, waved his arm inshore. Willard stood on toward America, with one of the crew on the peak halyard ready to slack it for a controlled jibe. The situation was certainly tense as it was blowing hard, still thick with rain and mist, getting dark, and he had seen no land since he left Cape Cod. He was rushing on through the murk toward a rocky coast. The lookout hailed, "Breakers," and Captain Willard jibed the vessel over all standing and sailed northerly parallel to the shore. Shortly he came up to Wood Island Light just as the keeper was lighting up. *Jerome,* with the fisherman still following, was now running downwind into the rainy dark for the back shore of Richmond Island. When the lookout heard breakers, Captain Willard luffed sharply, shipping a heavy sea, which filled the waist, but all hands were aft trimming the mainsheet to get the schooner into the wind and no one was washed overboard. The mate wanted to head offshore and heave to for the night. "I told him I was going to Portland, that there was bold water near the Cape [Elizabeth]; I had caught cunners off from every foot of it, and it was safe to go within a schooner's length of the shore. I ran until I thought we ought to see something. I began to think we were running too wide to see shore or lights; but in a few minutes the lookout reported breakers broad off the port bow. I luffed a couple of points and run by the breakers, when opposite the Cape lights [twin lighthouses on Cape Elizabeth], I could just see them through the mist and fog. I run until I judged I was by Broad Cove Rock and Trundys Reef Shoal.

"Then I jibed over to run for Portland Head. The wind dying away some, the fog and mist seemed to be thicker. As I neared up to Portland Head I could hear the rote [surf] on the shore to the south of it. I kept off at once and found it to be Portland Head Light and passed in by very near the Point. Then all sail was put on." They ran out of the fog as they sailed up the harbor and anchored safely.

Captain Willard reports no compass courses, although he had a compass, but for the most part in fog and darkness found his way from Montauk Point to Portland Harbor by watch, lead, and lookout.

Captain Willard's fastest trip was from Portland to Philadelphia and back, with a cargo each way, in ten days; his slowest, twenty-eight days. He left Portland in a northeast snowstorm in January, sailed southeast to be well clear of Cape Cod. A sea broke into the jib and tore it out of its boltropes. In the South Channel the sea was too high to run before it. The next morning both bobstays* parted. The mate with a line around his body went overboard in that wintry sea, fished up the broken stays, and slapped tackles on them. They then ran off under double-reefed foresail. Forty miles off Long Island the wind came northwest with snow squalls in an icy gale. They hove to under a close-reefed mainsail for six days. "The schooner," wrote Captain Willard, "was making good weather and was perfectly tight. The wake to windward broke the heavy combers and we got only light water from them."

The lime trade kept some 200 coasters busy during most of the nineteenth

*These hold the bowsprit down against the pull of the foremast and jibs.

century. A vein of limestone about a mile wide extends from near the site of the Maine State Prison in Thomaston northeasterly to Jamesons Point and Chickawaukie Pond. There are smaller veins northwest and southeast of it, the latter coming out at Ash Point.

Limestone is calcium carbonate, a chemical combination of calcium, oxygen, and carbon dioxide. It is a stable compound formed from the shells of millions of tiny sea creatures ages ago. If limestone is heated nearly to the fusion point, the carbon dioxide is driven off and a compound of calcium and oxygen is left. This is a white powder called quick lime, an apt name, for it combines vigorously with water to produce whitewash or slaked lime, much used in making mortar, plaster, and cement. The chemist describes the reaction thus:

$$CaCO_3 \rightarrow CaO + CO_2$$
$$CaO + H_2O \rightarrow Ca(OH)_2 \blacktriangle$$

The triangle stands for heat. Mixed with water in a bucket, quick lime gets hot enough to boil the water and makes the bucket far too hot to touch. Before Clorox was discovered, fishermen used to put lime on a grounded-out boat with a broom, boiling hot, to clean the weeds from her bottom. Most of the lime, however, was used to make mortar for bricklayers and masons or plaster for house carpenters.

In 1733 William McIntyre was burning limestone on the present site of the Thomaston prison and shipping it to Boston. In the 1740s Samuel Waldo, a hero of Louisbourg, was running two sloops to Boston regularly, carrying lime. After the Revolution, George Ulmer and David Gay were shipping lime from what is now Rockland to New York. When General Henry Knox, artillery officer under Washington, returned to Thomaston after the war and a stint at public service, he ran two schooners and a brig to market with lime and predicted an annual output of 30,000 to 40,000 casks. He was about right, for between 1800 and the embargo in 1807 thirty-five kilns produced 28,000 casks annually. After the War of 1812, during the 1820s, customs officer Hezekiah Prince described the lime trade as "terrible brisk" at 50,000 casks per year. By 1836, 700,000 casks were sent off a year, 100 schooners were employed in carrying lime or firewood, and the business increased from there at an astronomical rate. In 1869 Rockland alone produced 1,131,117 casks.

In the early days the limestone was simply piled on a wood fire. When the limestone was converted to lime, the fire was allowed to go out, and the lime was separated from the ashes, casked, carried to the river in ox carts, and shipped off. Later the limestone was carried to the river, rock kilns were built on the shore, and the lime was burned there. Later, arches of brick or stone were built in the kiln to keep the lime clear of the ashes, and after the Civil War, patent kilns were developed which took in fuel and limestone at the top and from which the finished product was raked out at the bottom. In the 1880s, when wood became scarce and expensive, coal and oil fuels were used.

The industry provided profitable work for a great many people including quarrymen, teamsters, coopers to make the casks, men to tend the kilns, stevedores, shipbuilders, and mariners.

The vessels that carried this prodigious quantity of lime to market—most of it to New York—were small two-masted schooners 60 to 80 feet long, except for a few brigs in the early days and a few barks and three-masted schooners toward the end of the century. They were new, tight vessels in the prime of life, well caulked and frequently pumped, for if water got to the lime, it reacted violently, produced enough heat in the confined space of the hold to set the vessel afire, and swelled enough to open seams and start deckbeams, increasing the leak and hastening destruction by fire and water.

The crew were ever alert for the characteristic smell of heating lime followed by wood smoke. Then the only defense was to get food, water, and blankets on deck, broach a cask of lime, add water to make plaster, and plaster up every crack and seam by which air could get to the fire. Then all sail was set for the nearest protected harbor, which better be not far away. The crew moved ashore and visited the vessel daily to plaster up the source of every wisp of smoke until either the fire was smothered or the swelling lime burst the vessel apart.

One new, tight schooner was launched in Thomaston and loaded with lime casks. She dropped down the river on her way to sea but, overtaken by darkness, anchored. That night a heavy northeast gale with blowing snow struck in. The vessel parted her anchor chains and drove ashore. She pounded on the rocks and started a leak. The lime heated, set her afire, and she burned to the water's edge, a total loss.

The schooner *Herman F. Kimball* was more fortunate. When her cargo took fire off Kittery, her skipper plastered every crack and ran her into the Piscataqua River. For three months she smoldered; an occasional peek through the hatch showed that the fire still burned. After three months, however, it was extinguished, the cargo was taken out, essential repairs were made, and she was sailed home to Thomaston and rebuilt.

Another Thomaston lime schooner gave her crew a far worse time than had the *Kimball*. Bound for Boston, she ran into a gale off Cape Ann and was blown off nearly to the Grand Banks. On her way back toward Boston, she ran into another storm. One of her crew wrote, "Before we knew it, we were back across the Gulf [of Maine] again, sails all gone, cargo afire and the vessel plastered up with a drag [sea anchor] ahead to keep her to the sea." In this difficult situation the writer compares the crew to the Jews rebuilding Jerusalem: " 'Every one with one of his hands wrought in the work and with the other held a weapon.' That's what we did, worked on the drag with one hand and a plastering trowel in the other, smothering the fire . . . and we wasn't doing it on your barn floor either." The main mast burned through below the deck and was prevented only by the rigging from going over the side and prying the deck out of her. At last the crew was picked up 200 miles east of Bermuda and the vessel abandoned.

When a vessel got too loose to carry lime, she went to hauling kiln wood. It took about 30 cords of wood to produce 300 casks of lime, burning three or four days and nights. The cost of the wood was about 30 percent of the cost of the finished product.

You can't sink a vessel loaded with wood. These schooners jammed into the hold every stick that would go in. Then they piled on a deck load 7, 8, or 9 feet high from the foremast almost to the wheel. The helmsmen could see neither over it nor around it, so one of the crew—possibly the only one of the crew—stood on top of the load forward and bellowed instructions aft to the helmsman. The sails were single- or perhaps double-reefed to allow the booms to swing over the deck load, and the main deck of the schooner was sometimes actually under water. The voyages were short and for the most part in protected waters east of Penobscot Bay, so although deck loads were occasionally lost, few wood boats came to grief.

As firewood growing near tidewater or on islands became scarce, wood was brought in from New Brunswick, mostly from the St. John River, on what were called Johnny wood boats. They were built very roughly of native spruce. Their sterns were square across with a rudder hung outboard and their bows almost as square. They were flat bottomed and of shoal draft so they could ground out while loading a cargo. They were two-masted, the foremast right in the bow, with no bowsprit, no jibs, and no topsails. "Wung out," they were quite fast before the wind, but it was slow going to windward. However, they could carry a prodigious quantity of wood.

In the Damariscotta and Sheepscot rivers were built some big, sloop-rigged scows much like the Johnny wood boats but like a punt with a square bow and one big gaff-headed sail on a mast stepped far forward. They, too, were rather crudely built, but style was no consideration nor was seaworthiness particularly important. The object was to float the cordwood to Rockland.

Toward the end of the century, with seagoing steam tugs available, the Rockland-Rockport Lime Company, a conglomerate formed by a number of heretofore independent companies, purchased six big iron barges, each capable of carrying 16,000 casks. These had the advantage of costing nothing while waiting to unload in New York. The tug could bring down a string of loaded barges, anchor them unmanned in New York Harbor, and the next day start back with a string of empties, confident that the first barges would be unloaded when he returned. This ended the lime schooner trade abruptly, and within a few years plywood, concrete, and wallboard largely replaced plaster and lime mortar. The huge quarry holes are all that remain—and the Martin-Marietta cement plant, shipping now by truck.

A lumberman and a seaman are the two figures on the Maine state flag, bearing the motto "Dirigo." Indeed lumber, its cutting, sawing, and delivery, was the leading source of Maine wealth in the nineteenth century. Anyone with the courage to read this book through will remember that from the earliest days of the seventeenth century, masts, clapboards, shooks, and shingles figured, with salt fish, in almost every outward cargo from the coast. After the depression following the War of 1812, Maine lumber ports expanded rapidly; Calais, Machias, Ellsworth, Bangor, Bath, and Portland became the largest. Each of these towns, except Portland, is located on a river running from the forests to the sea. Near the head of navigation for oceangoing vessels the town was established. If there was a fall of water here, as at Calais, Machias, Ellsworth, and Bangor, so much the better. At first water power drove reciprocating saw blades, sometimes several of them, so a log could be sawn into a number of boards at one pass through the mill. About 1850 steam began to be used for the mills, and circular saws were introduced. A Shaker lady spinning wool on her wheel is sometimes given credit for the invention. However, these changes rapidly increased lumber production, and the virgin white pines of inland Maine were carried to ports near and far.

Calais and Machias had special problems, for here the tide rises 20 feet, more or less, leaving wide flats bare at low water. Therefore, vessels had to ground out alongside the wharves and rest on the mud. This called for small vessels strongly constructed with flat bottoms to sustain their weight when loaded. William H. Rowe finds that 272 vessels sailed out of Calais in 1842. In 1860 Calais sawed 85,000,000 feet of long lumber and 115,000,000 laths.

Machias, founded as a lumber town in 1763, was another major producer. A lumber cargo instigated the Battle of Machias in 1775.

Ellsworth in 1853 sent out 35,000,000 feet of sawn lumber and 250,000 box shooks. It is recorded that 159 vessels were owned in town, but that is, of course, no fair measure of Ellsworth's exports.

Bangor, with access to uncounted acres of pine timber fretted with rivers, lakes, and brooks, was the leading lumber port in Maine and, at one time, in the world. In an ordinary year 155,000,000 feet of long lumber would be shipped, and in 1873, the peak year, 245,453,649 feet were shipped. In 1860 there were 3,376 arrivals recorded at the customhouse and, of course, as many departures. Considering that the Penobscot River is frozen for four months of the year, more or less, we are talking about roughly an average of fourteen vessels entering and leaving per day. On a July day in 1860, sixty vessels arrived at Bangor within two hours. It is probable that a large fleet had collected at Fort Point, Castine, Stockton, and Belfast waiting for a flood tide and a fair wind. When it came, every skipper spread his sails.

Unlike the wharves at Calais, Machias, and Ellsworth, frequented mostly by small local schooners, at Bangor one might see every known rig and vessels hailing from exotic ports. Schooners setting square topsails, barks, brigs, and ships were common, their yards swung fore-and-aft as much as possible and cock-billed with one end as low as possible so they didn't lock horns with their neighbors. In later years, after about 1850, three-masted schooners were common, and toward the end of the century, four-masters, with a very occasional five-master, might come up the river.

With any kind of a fair wind, quite large vessels could negotiate the river, although above Bucksport even a fair southerly could turn fluky and call for

A deckload of firewood. *Author's collection*

Primitive steering gear on the deck of *James Webster*. *Author's collection*

instant anchoring. Anchoring was a dangerous expedient, however. As the prevailing wind was southerly in the summer, steam tugs often towed vessels down the river to Fort Point, making up tows of up to thirty vessels lashed three abreast. While it is true that steam vessels must give way to sailing vessels and an anchored vessel must be avoided, in facing a tug towing thirty loaded schooners down a twisty tide-scoured channel, the Law of Superior Tonnage must take over. Also passenger steamers and tugs with barges agitated the river and were not always as polite or law-abiding as the schoonermen expected.

Bangor, besides its wealth of available timber, had another advantage. It was a thriving city with a considerable back-country population of farmers, mill men, lumbermen, and others. Consequently, return cargoes could be carried up to Bangor by vessels returning from a lumber voyage. Coal, flour, pork, rum, molasses, household and manufactured goods of all kinds, were needed and brought in by water.

Lumber cargoes included deals,* planks, boards, and box boards; also shingles, shooks, pilings, staves, laths, pulpwood, and firewood for the hungry kilns of Rockland. Long lumber was usually 16 feet long and loaded through ports cut in the vessel's bow. Before she went to sea, of course, these ports were tightly closed and caulked. Nevertheless, fresh water inevitably saturated the wood around the ports, and here rot often started. Deck loads were added, leaving access to pumps, windlass, and forecastle. If box boards were carried, the deck load was not arranged fore-and-aft, as in long lumber. Box boards are ⅞ inch thick, sawn on two sides only, leaving the rough, uneven bark on two sides. They were laid fore-and-aft up to the rail and then in alternate layers across the vessel, usually winged out over the side, not lashed but secured by occasional nails driven down through the top layer. They apparently were seldom lost.

The deck load might be carried 6 or 8 feet high, leaving the scuppers awash as in the kiln-wooders. The halyards were passed through a block on a chain fast to the deck and belayed at a pin rail above the deck load. The main and foresail were provided with a shallow reef to raise the booms high enough to swing clear. Lifelines were usually rigged between fore and main shrouds.

Thomaston, Damariscotta, Wiscasset, and, to a considerable extent, Bath had been settled early and the timber on their rivers largely cut off and devoted to shipbuilding. Bath imported considerable live oak, white oak, and hard pine from Virginia and Carolina. Portland, like Bangor, imported and distributed many products. Vessels seeking a return cargo could often find a lumber cargo on the Portland wharves brought in by coasters alongshore.

Small towns also cut and shipped lumber in small quantities in small vessels. Cutler, 14 miles from the Canadian border on the Bay of Fundy, might serve as an example. In 1836 a dam was built across Little River at the head of the harbor. A four-saw mill and a lath mill were operated by the tide. Vessels

* Deals are sawn lumber about 3 inches by 9 inches, often resawn at its destination.

Schooner *Endeavour* with a deck load of coal. *Author's collection*

were built here until 1868. Here are a few notes from the diary of Isaac Wilder for 1853 to give the flavor of life in a small Maine coast town.

JANUARY 16, SUN: Schr. *George Gilman* arrived this afternoon from Boston via Portland with hay for me.

18, TUES: Schr. *George Gilman* discharged CMD Co. [Cutler Mill Dam Co.] frte today at Mills.

28, FRI: Schr. *Geo. Gilman* came up from Moose River today where she has loaded for Boston.

29, SAT: Wind moderate and mild all day from WSW. Wilson Randell began duty on board *Geo. Gilman* [a WSW wind would be a headwind out of Cutler].

FEBRUARY 1, TUES: Pleasant clear and mild all day—more breeze N—Middle forenoon Dead calm—Afternoon breeze from WSW. *Gilman* Sailed this morn [with a fair northerly breeze] but came back this evening. [With a headwind and possibly a flood tide, she could not beat down Grand Manan Channel.]

8, TUES: Morn and forenoon cloudy & afternoon pleasant and mild with N winds all day. *Geo. Gilman* sailed today 9 AM—Wm. Cates Schr. *Celt* sailed. Schr. *Augustus* Capt. Blunt Sailed this afternoon—I sent 100 boxes herring on *Augustus* for sale. [This was the fair wind all three vessels had been waiting a week for.]

24, THURS: *Geo. Gilman* arrived this forenoon.

27, SUN: *Ashland* sailed this forenoon 10 o'clock for N.Y.

MARCH 6: The *Gilman* was loaded again and sailed for Boston.

APRIL 8: The *Gilman* was back again in Cutler. Mr. Wilder went to Calais in her, which took a day and a half, laid over in a snowstorm, loaded her for Norwich on April 26 and sailed down the Bay to Lubec that night. The *Ashland* arrived from New York [the voyage having taken from February 27 to April 16, 49 days—a slow trip].

18, MON: Wife confined this day and a daughter was born 5 minutes before 12 AM. Very pleasant with fresh NNE wind.

Ashland and *George Gilman* continued with the same pattern of voyages until,

JUNE 13, MON: Schr. *Ashland* Cast away on Double Headed Shot [an island off Cross Island about 5 miles from Cutler] & in course of day went all to Pieces. Wind fresh SSW and heavy sea—Fog thick this morning but soon cleared away & remained pleasant all day—Went to Machias with Nelson I returned to wreck.

There seems to be no deep regret over *Ashland*'s loss. Apparently it is what one must expect in the coasting trade. Mr. Wilder got her masts and some of her sails and rigging and sold what was left for $157.20.

In August he went up to Eastport in *Elizabeth Ann* for 500 bushels of salt. The brig *Druid* sank, and Wilder saved 2,000 laths. A week later he grounded out the *Gilman* to clean her bottom. In August and September the

Gilman made several trips to Rockland with slab wood for the kilns; the round trip took about a week. In mid-September he went up to Rockland himself in the *Gilman* with kiln wood and collected $1,769 in insurance payoff on *Ashland*. On October 25 it blew a gale, and two ships went ashore at Moose River. With the help of a steamer, he got both vessels off and towed them into Cutler. He put one on the beach and sold her at auction. On Saturday, November 26, his baby daughter Julia was sick. On Monday, November 28, he writes: "Beautiful clear & moderate weather & calm sometimes light Southerly air & eve looking like storm & overcast—Our Babe grew very sick last night and died today at ½ past 11 AM just 7 months & 10 days—Thurlow [a boarder] 1 meal."

Both death and shipwreck seem to have been taken as they come.

Granite was another product of Maine islands which figured briefly in economic and maritime history. Even before the Civil War, granite was in increasing demand for elegant public buildings, monuments, breakwaters, bridges, forts, and lighthouses. Granite from Maine islands was of excellent quality and cheaply available, as it could be shipped in schooners direct from island quarries. Five islands were particularly productive: Vinalhaven; Clark Island, near Tenants Harbor; Hurricane Island, near Vinalhaven; Crotch Island, off Stonington; and Dix Island, in Muscle Ridge Channel. All of these have protected anchorages with deep water close to the shore. Wharves of grout—chunks of refuse stone—were built where schooners and, later, barges could load conveniently.

As early as 1826 a cargo of granite was shipped from Vinalhaven to Massachusetts to build a jail, and before the Civil War there were several quarries on the island. The first federal contract filled on Vinalhaven was for Fiddlers Ledge beacon, which still warns the mariner off Stand-In Point at the western end of Fox Islands Thorofare. Fort Richmond on Staten Island, New York, and Petit Manan Light were built of Vinalhaven granite in the following two years. The State, War, and Navy Department buildings in Washington were built of Maine granite, much of it from Vinalhaven. After the Civil War the demand increased dramatically and included millions of paving stones as well as considerable monumental work calling for artists skilled in cutting out figures of people, animals, and birds. The eagles on the old Pennsylvania Railroad station in New York came from Vinalhaven. One of them was recently brought back to Vinalhaven and now overlooks the main street of that little town with a supercilious stony gaze. Stonecutters were brought in from Ireland, Italy, and Scotland to add to Maine artisans.

The monument to Civil War general Wool in Troy, New York, was shipped from Vinalhaven in a barge in 1879. It weighed 650 tons including the base and was the largest stone quarried up to that time. A defective piece of General Wool's monument still lies by the roadside in the quarry. Some of the stone for the Brooklyn Bridge over New York's East River came from Vinalhaven, providing work for a large crew and 100 yoke of oxen for several years. The larger stones were hauled in galamanders, carts whose two back wheels were 8 or 9 feet in diameter. The wheels straddled the stone, a tackle was chained to the heavy axle, and the stone was raised clear of the ground. A team of eight horses or oxen hauled it to the shore. The galamanders, stone carts, derricks, and most other equipment belonging to the Bodwell Granite Company was painted "Elder Littlefield blue"; no one ever even thought of using any other color.

The Bodwell Company had the contract for the columns in the Cathedral of St. John the Divine in New York. Each was to be a single piece of polished granite 54 feet long and 6 feet in diameter. The first was got out of the ground in April 1899, a stone 64 feet long, 8 feet wide, and 7 feet high weighing 300 tons. It was turned on a huge lathe to the specified dimensions and was being polished when it broke in two. The next two columns also broke on the lathe, so each column was finally made in two pieces, one 40 feet long and the other 20 feet, and they were towed to New York in barges.

The Bodwell Company cut stone for government buildings in Washington and for buildings in Philadelphia, Erie, Jamestown, and Allegheny City in Pennsylvania and in Atlanta, Chicago, St. Louis, Milwaukee, Indianapolis, Brooklyn, New York, Tarrytown, Boston, Fall River, Peabody, Buffalo, and for Ram Island Light in Portland.

Much of the paving stone from Vinalhaven was got out of "motions," exposed ledges of clear stone, by pairs of men working on a contract at a specified price per thousand blocks. Granite is not uniform; it has grain and fault lines along which it splits. A skillful quarryman can get out the blocks with little waste of time or material. Usually granite was quarried by drilling and blasting, but for small pieces they often drove soft, dry pine plugs into the drill holes and poured water on them. The swelling wood split off the piece. Marks of these holes can be seen in old granite foundations and curbstones.

After World War I granite was in diminishing demand. Reinforced concrete and steel were the favored building materials, and asphalt made smoother streets. There was still a demand for curbstones, monuments, and decorative work; but as roads were improved and truck transportation became common, the advantages of being near water diminished and granite was quarried inland. Today thin sheets of polished granite only a centimeter thick are used for curtain walls on buildings, and there is still some used in monuments and trim and for rip-rap on wharves and retaining walls, but except for a small operation on Crotch Island, none is now quarried on Maine islands. The last quarried on Vinalhaven was taken out in 1939.

Dix Island in Muscle Ridge Channel became a quarry almost by accident. An imaginative entrepreneur, Horace Beal, took the island in payment for a debt in 1857 and declared it an excellent site for a suicide. However, he built an elaborate mansion there and after his death, from natural causes, his heirs expanded the quarry, brought in Irish, Scotch, and Swedish workers, and got contracts for several government buildings. In 1874 they had 2,000 workers and more than 80 buildings on the island. Much of their work was ornamental. They employed many skillful artisans who turned out elaborate sculptures, among the simplest of which were the eagles on the Philadelphia post office. However, the demand for craftsmanship in Dix Island granite sagged, and by 1880 the quarries were abandoned. The houses were soon torn down for their material, and all that remains today are cellar holes and grout wharves where schooners once loaded.

Hurricane Island off Vinalhaven was another frenetic, short-lived operation. General Tillson, a Rockland businessman, opened a quarry on the island in 1873 and by 1878 had about 600 Swedish and Italian quarrymen and stonecutters working. A post office was established in 1875 and a school, a town hall, a firehouse, and a jail were built before 1880. A company store supplied material needs. It is said that the ball bearing was invented, or re-invented, on Hurricane Island when an ingenious foreman mounted a derrick on a grooved steel plate over another that matched it and put several well-greased cannonballs between the plates. Didn't she swing some easy!

With the fading demand for stone in the first decade of the twentieth century, business fell off, and by 1910 the quarries were no longer active. The island has now been taken over by the Hurricane Island Outward Bound School, established in the late 1960s by Peter Willauer. The school is committed to teaching people of all ages, conditions, and backgrounds that they can do more than they think they can.

Hurricane Island is well worth a visit, not only for its innovative school but to see the great pieces of rusting quarry machinery and the big fragments of cut and sculptured stone about the abandoned quarries.

Clark Island near Tenants Harbor was getting out stone as early as 1833. By 1850 a map of the island shows a road to a wharf on the eastern point. In 1870 a road led to a wharf at the southwest nub for getting out "fort stone," stone used in building fortifications. In the mid-1870s the island was bought by Milton St. John, like Tillson and Bodwell, a "granite king." He had in 1888–89 fourteen stonecutters, seventy paving cutters, and sixty quarrymen with steam-powered quarry machinery, cutting machines, and polishers. In 1898 Mrs. St. John sold out to the Clark Island Granite Works, but in 1900 she persuaded the town to build a causeway along the bar to the mainland. However, by 1910 the work force numbered only 100 and activity declined—with occasional spurts of energy—until it closed up in the 1930s. In the 1960s one could pick up paving blocks from among the bushes for 20 cents apiece, and now only a huge pile of grout and a granite wharf remain.

Crotch Island off Stonington was the most recently worked of the five principal quarries. It was opened by Job Goss, a stonecutter from Massachusetts, in 1870. By 1880 he had ten stonecutters and at least thirty others living on the island and many more commuting daily from Stonington. About 1900 the Benvenue Company, with quarries on Vinalhaven and Hurricane Island, brought in steam power and pneumatic drills and drilled artesian wells.

"Hundreds" of workers were employed, including skilled stonecutters from the British Isles, Italy, and Scandinavia. Parts of the Boston Museum of Fine Arts and the Manhattan Bridge came from Crotch Island. Business fell off badly in 1910, but in 1913 Crotch Island got out the Rockefeller Bowl, made from a single block 22 feet square and about 6 feet thick, weighing 225 tons. Shaped and smoothed up, it weighed only 50 tons and was shipped to the Rockefeller estate in Tarrytown, New York, in a barge.

Model of schooner *Annie and Reuben* loading granite. *Penobscot Marine Museum*

In 1914 Benvenue sold out to the John L. Goss Corporation, and in 1953 the island was sold again to the Deer Island Granite Corporation. Business was never what it had been, but often a yachtsman bound up the Thorofare would hear the hammer of quarry machinery and see a plume of steam from the little locomotive used to move stone. In the 1960s Crotch Island provided the stone for the grave of President John F. Kennedy in Washington. As late as 1985, summer residents on nearby Deer Isle complained of the howls and screams of stonecutting machinery. In 1990 the granite was being shipped to Rockland by barge and then by truck to Providence, Rhode Island. It would have been much cheaper to ship it all the way to Providence by barge except for the exorbitant cost of unloading by longshoremen in Providence. In 1991 at least some granite was being landed in Stonington and shipped thence by truck.

Many more quarries existed on the coast, from small operations getting paving blocks from motions to quite large operations like those at Webb Cove

Schooner *Thomas H. Lawrence,* one of the last of the terns, carrying pilings to Flushing, Long Island, for the World's Fair in 1939. This was her last successful voyage. *Below:* Captain and Mrs. Trenholm. *Author's collection*

on Deer Isle and Hall Quarry on Mount Desert Island. The chapter notes list many of them.

At first the stone was shipped in small schooners, shoal-draft vessels often with centerboards, which could lie alongside the grout piers either afloat or comfortably grounded out at low water. One of the few that was built especially for the granite trade was *Annie and Reuben,* built by Reuben Hunt in his backyard in Bath in 1891 and for a long time owned by the John L. Goss Corporation. Her foremast was stepped far forward and her mainmast stepped well aft to give her a long hold and deck to stow curbstones and other long pieces. This arrangement, not entirely incidentally, gave her a big foresail, nearly as big as the mainsail, and made her quite fast before the wind. Naamon Hutchinson, who sailed a number of voyages in her, told of one trip home to Stonington from Boston. He ate breakfast at dawn under Charlestown Bridge in Boston and left just ahead of the steamer for Portland. Off Cape Ann the wind struck in strong from the southwest. *Annie and Reuben,* her huge foresail "wung out" on one side and her generous mainsail on the other, flying light, kept pace with the steamer for hours until the steamer swung inshore for Portland. That same night, concluded Mr. Hutchinson, he ate dinner under Green Head in Stonington.

I saw the old schooner in 1938 alongside a pier near the lock in the Charles River basin loaded deep with, presumably, granite. Looking up from my seat in a fragile rowing shell, I hailed the man on deck. After my comment on her minimum freeboard, he added, "She'll go fast when she goes." He was referring not to her sailing ability but to how quickly she would sink with a cargo of granite.

She carried stone and quarry scrap metal until she was sold south in 1943 and foundered off New Jersey. However, long before *Annie and Reuben* went down, barges had taken over the granite and lime trades and reinforced concrete had rendered the quarries obsolete. Coasting under sail was left for a few pulpwood schooners and for "windjammers" carrying passengers.

NOTES

The material on Maine's separation from Massachusetts came from Louis Hatch's *Maine, A History*. It was a great deal more involved than it appears to be from this account, but perhaps we have extracted the most relevant part.

Captain Willard's autobiography—an informal account, certainly—is fascinating. He started as a fisherman, then went coasting, then started a stevedoring business in Portland and became a Portland harbor pilot. He sheds a good deal of light on what was happening alongshore. The account of his voyage up from Montauk to Portland in fog, darkness, rain, and gale would give a modern yachtsman fits. To run down Nantucket Sound at night in the fog with a 2–3-knot tide and to hit the Cross Rip lightship right on the nose one might call luck. But then after a day and a night offshore to make Wood Island Light suggests something more than luck; no one can be that lucky twice. His piloting around Richmond Island, Cape Elizabeth, and Portland Head "by guess and by God" suggests more skill than luck. Other skippers must have been as skillful as Captain Willard, although it is certainly true that a number of them guessed wrong and piled up.

The lime trade is admirably covered in Aubigne Packard's *A Town That Went to Sea,* a history of Thomaston, and in *Quarry and Kiln,* by Roger L. Grindle. Mr. Grindle pays little attention to what happened at sea, but he includes numerous statistics that reflect the tremendous growth and rapid collapse of the trade. John Leavitt's *Wake of the Coasters* and Wasson and Colcord's *Sailing Days on the Penobscot* are very helpful on both the lime and the lumber trades. Gorham Munson's *Penobscot* is interesting but rather inclined toward the romantic and away from the specific.

William Hutchinson Rowe's *Maritime History of Maine* appears to be a source for the authors mentioned above, except, of course, for Wasson and Colcord. Rowe uses some of Wasson's figures and Leavitt uses many of Rowe's. Rowe puts the establishment of steam circular sawmills in 1820. The *Encyclopedia Brittanica* claims the first use of steam and the circular saw came in 1850.

Anchoring in the Penobscot River is still a perilous business as oil barges are towed up and down by night and day. The Law of Superior Tonnage still applies. Another factor more significant 100 years ago than now was that the bottom of the river was deep in waterlogged sawdust and short ends of timber so that an anchor could not get a good bite.

The description of lumber stowage comes from John Leavitt's book. He sailed on lumber schooners himself.

The excerpts from Isaac Wilder's diary come from *Down East to Cutler* by Robert Kord. It appears to have been privately printed. Mr. Kord lives in Cutler. I have not included everything Mr. Wilder wrote, but what I have quoted is just as he wrote it. I have tried to follow the fortunes of *George Gilman* and *Ashland* to give an idea of the small-town coaster's life. I could not escape Julia's short life.

The facts on Vinalhaven quarries came from *Fish Scales and Stone Chips* by Sidney Winslow, which is written mostly from his personal recollections of life on Vinalhaven during the granite years. An article by Norman Drinkwater, Jr., in the September 1963 issue of *Down East* magazine has some information on Dix Island, but Charles McLane's *Islands of the Mid-Maine Coast—Blue Hill and Penobscot Bays* is far more complete, drawing on other writings by Drinkwater. McLane is also very good on Clark Island, Crotch Island, and Hurricane Island. Giles Tod's *Last Sail Down East* tells *Annie and Reuben*'s history. I have often seen her under sail, her big foresail making her easily recognized, even hull down. John Leavitt's *Wake of the Coasters* has an excellent chapter on granite schooners including photographs of most of them and accounts of their lives and losses.

For the record, granite quarries were located at, among other places: Wells, Kennebunkport, Biddeford, Yarmouth, Freeport, Brunswick, Round Pond, Waldoboro, Friendship, Clark Island off Tenants Harbor, Long Cove on Vinalhaven, Spruce Head, St. George, Pleasant Island, Hewett Island, Dix Island, High Island, South Thomaston, Hurricane Island, Gundalow Island, Leadbetter Island, Vinalhaven, Greens Landing at Stonington, Moose Island, Crotch Island, St. Helena Island, Green Island off Stonington, Spruce Island, Bold Island, Stonington, Lincolnville, Belfast, Searsport, Prospect, Frankfort, Brooksville, Sedgwick, Swans Island, Long Island in Blue Hill Bay, Blue Hill, East Blue Hill, Seal Cove on Mount Desert Island, Tremont, Otter

Creek, Hall Quarry, Bar Harbor, Franklin, Sullivan, Milbridge, Hardwood Island, Black Island, Head Harbor Island, Jonesport, Addison, Jonesboro, Bucks Harbor, Red Beach, and Calais.

I have seen evidence of stonecutting on Damariscove and on Black Island off Mount Desert.

Reference to the United States *Coast Pilot,* section A, will locate these towns and islands.

For an authoritative, if fictional, view of an island granite town, read *Speak to the Winds* by Ruth Moore.

TWENTY-FIVE

The Great Schooners

BY GREAT SCHOONERS we mean four-, five-, and six-masted schooners, usually over 700 tons. These were built in the last years of the nineteenth century in response to specific economic needs, as had been the clippers and the Downeasters in their times.

After the Civil War, industry and population expanded very rapidly in the Northeastern states, especially in New England. Cotton, wool, and shoe factories increased in size and number. Their demands for power exceeded the resources of streams and rivers, so they moved to coastal cities where both raw materials and coal were available by sea. Coal was also in high demand for making illuminating gas and then for use in electrical power plants for lighting, power, and trolley lines.

Factory workers, immigrants in increasing numbers, required homes. These houses were built at first of Maine pine, but as this resource dwindled, hard pine from the South was carried north in enormous quantities, not only for building dwellings and factories but for building schooners to bring more lumber north. At the same time a growing demand in the South for ice provided return cargoes. Thus it became profitable to bring coal north from Baltimore, Philadelphia, and Perth Amboy to Fall River, New Bedford, Boston, Salem, and Portland and return with ice, or to bring lumber north from Charleston, Brunswick (Georgia), Jacksonville, and the Gulf ports. When in 1881 the Chesapeake & Ohio Railroad built a line to Newport News and in 1883 the Norfolk & Western reached Chesapeake Bay, Newport News and Norfolk became the great coal ports.

Rather surprisingly, the city of Taunton, Massachusetts, situated on a small river navigable only for barges and small schooners, was an early center for the schooner trade. Here was a locomotive factory, a stove foundry, a silverplate industry, and textile mills. These required quantities of coal, clay, and pig iron, mostly brought in by water and distributed to other mills in Bridgewater, Attleboro, Brockton, and Middleboro. From 1857 to 1888 Sylvanus Staples and William H. Phillips built up a healthy shipping business in small schooners and barges. Coal became increasingly important, and the business expanded to supply Fall River, New Bedford, Boston, and other New England ports. Between 1870 and 1895, forty three-masters and fourteen four-masters were owned in Taunton, not many of which ever saw their home port. Large fleets were also owned in New Haven, Boston, Portland, Bath, and on Cape Cod.

The schooner rig with its fore-and-aft sails had for two centuries been popular for coastal work. It was simple and inexpensive to rig, required only a small crew with very little work aloft, and was efficient going to windward. As demands for moving bulk cargoes increased, two-masted schooners became larger and larger. *Oliver Ames,* built in 1886, 435 tons, was the largest two-master, a two-decked centerboard schooner whose gear was really too heavy to handle. The solution, sought long before *Oliver Ames* was built, was a third mast, at first a short mizzen, but after 1853 the masts were the same height. These three-masters were called terns—nothing to do with birds—because a tern is a group of three. The first terns were awkward, but by the 1870s and 1880s a great many smart sailing terns were built.

Two of the best were *Charles W. Church* and *C. A. White,* designed at Taunton, Massachusetts, by Albert Winslow, and built in Bath in 1884. They were about 800 tons, 180 feet long, 38 feet wide, and 15 feet deep with rather fine ends and some deadrise. They had a quick sheer to keep fo'c's'le and quarterdeck dry when they were loaded, and the stern was a handsome narrow ellipse. They carried big fore- and mainsails, and the mizzen, the aftermost sail, was only slightly bigger. They carried gaff topsails on all three masts and topmast staysails. With masts raked aft and sprung a little forward by taut headstays and with hulls neatly painted in black or green, they were good-looking, able vessels. In the 1870s three-masters grew from 500 tons to 1,100 tons, and in 1880 the first four-master was built, *William L. White.* Between 1880 and 1889 sixty-eight four-masters were built registering up to 2,500 tons. Of these, twenty-eight were built in 1889, and forty-eight were built in Maine.

The schooner rig was especially well adapted for carrying bulk cargoes along the Atlantic coast of the United States. With the coast running more or less northeast and southwest, even more easterly than that to the east of New York, and with the prevailing winds from the southwest in summer and northwest in winter, the schooner's ability to beat to windward was a valuable asset. A good three-master could sail five points, 55° to 60 °, from the wind's eye, whereas a square-rigged vessel could not come within 10° of that heading. A schooner was handier, too, could tack more quickly and in less distance with less loss of headway, so could often sail into harbors where a square-rigger would need a tug. A schooner required far less running and standing rigging, and fewer spars. However, the greatest saving was in manpower. A square-rigged ship might have 200 sheets, halyards, braces, buntlines, and clew lines. To set a main topsail on a square-rigger required handling eleven lines, many at the same time, some of them from aloft. Setting the mainsail on a schooner required handling three lines, all from the deck and all of which could be led to steam winches. A square-rigger on a long ocean voyage required a carpenter, a sailmaker, and at least some men who were good riggers in order to maintain her complicated structure. A schooner on a coastal voyage could have repairs done in port and had less need for skilled seamen. Compare the complements of a clipper, a Downeaster, and a schooner of comparable size:

	CLIPPER SHIP *Sovereign of the Seas*	DOWNEASTER *Henry B. Hyde*	FIVE-MASTER *Nathaniel T. Palmer*
Tonnage	2,421	2,583	2,441
Captain and mates	5	4	2 (plus bosun)
Carpenter	2	1	0
Sailmaker	2	1	0
Donkeyman	–	–	1
Cook, steward, and cabin boy	5	3	2
Seamen	80	24	8
Apprentices	10	–	–
Total people aboard	106	84	10
Tonnage/man	23	76	244

The advent of the steam donkey engine in 1879 reduced the need for manpower and increased speed and efficiency. A schooner with steam power could raise sails and anchor and get underway in half an hour, while a "man hauler" would take half a day. Steam pumps could keep the bilges clear. Steam could heat fo'c's'le and cabin and, in later schooners, provide electricity. It also made practical schooners of ever-increasing size. In 1850 the average collier was of only 150 tons; in 1872 three-masters averaged 500 tons. By the early 1890s, 2,000-ton schooners were common, and after 1900 at least six schooners of over 3,000 tons were built.

In 1888 Albert Winslow designed a big schooner of 1,788 tons for Captain Davis of Somerset, Massachusetts, to be used in overseas trade. Looking at the finished half model, Winslow said she should have five masts. She was built by the Storer yard in Waldoboro, was christened *Gov. Ames,* and was the first five-master built. She was launched with masts stepped and sails bent, taken down the river at once, and soon sailed on her first voyage, in the course of which she lost all her masts. She was re-rigged, and had a very difficult passage around Cape Horn. She carried coal and lumber on the West Coast, to Australia, and to Hawaii and then sailed back around the Horn from Port Townsend to Liverpool with lumber. It was a slow passage, 139 days. Having proved unsuitable for offshore passages, she carried coal north from Norfolk until she was lost in 1910. No other five-master was built until *Nathaniel T. Palmer* in 1898, but after her, fifty-six more were built before the end of schooner construction in 1920.

The first six-master, *George W. Wells,* 2,970 tons, was built by Holly M.

Charles W. Church, an early tern, ready to launch. *Below: Pendleton Sisters,* second of that name, in Penobscot Bay. *Captain W. J. L. Parker*

Eleanor A. Percy, the first six-master built in Bath. *Below: Wyoming* just after her launching, the biggest wooden sailing vessel under American registry. *Maine Maritime Museum*

Bean in Camden for Captain John G. Crowley and launched August 4, 1900. She was followed a few months later by *Eleanor A. Percy,* 3,402 tons, built in Bath by Percy & Small. The next year these two six-masters, the only two in existence, collided off Cape Ann in a summer fog, fortunately without fatal damage to either.

These vessels approached the practical limit for wooden vessels. The *Wells* was 300 feet long and carried 5,000 tons of coal. She could make 15 knots under sail. She sailed from Delaware Breakwater to Havana in six days and from Brunswick, Georgia, to Sandy Hook with railroad ties in four days.

The biggest of the six-masters, the biggest wooden sailing ship to carry cargo under the American flag, was *Wyoming,* built by Percy & Small at Bath in 1909. She registered 3,731 tons, was 329 feet long. Her lower masts were 126 feet long, her topmasts 56 feet. She was planked with 6-inch yellow pine and strapped diagonally with iron inside the planking. To strengthen her longitudinally she had a massive keelson and three decks.

Wyoming spread 12,000 yards of canvas. She carried 6,000 tons of coal and drew 27½ feet of water when fully loaded. Her accommodations forward were declared the equal of officers' accommodations of an earlier day. She had, of course, a steam donkey engine for sails, anchors, and pumps and also steam heat in fo'c's'le and cabin. Her cost is quoted at $190,000.

She was said to be a handy vessel and fast under sail. For all that, she was fragile. On March 11, 1924, she anchored off Chatham to ride out a rising northeaster. The next day wreckage came ashore, but she was never seen again. It is assumed that in the heavy seas she touched bottom and, between her cargo and the sand, was pounded to pieces.

If *Wyoming* closely approached the practical limit for the size of a sailing vessel, the seven-master *Thomas W. Lawson* exceeded it. She was designed by B. B. Crowninshield for Crowell & Thurlow and built of steel in 1902 at Quincy, Massachusetts. She registered 5,218 tons, was 395 feet long, 50 feet wide, 35 feet deep, and drew 25.6 feet of water, too much to lie at most coal wharves. She had three decks and six cargo hatches. Bilge keels were fitted to stiffen her and to moderate her tendency to roll. Her lower masts were steel, 135 feet long, with Oregon pine topmasts 58 feet long. She set 45,000 square feet of sail and required a crew of sixteen. She was too big and too deep for coastal work, too cranky for deep-sea work, and sluggish under sail, loaded or light. She carried case oil from Gulf ports to the Delaware until 1907 and then sailed for England with a cargo of case oil. She anchored in a gale among the reefs of the Scilly Islands on February 17 and capsized that night. There were only two survivors of the seventeen aboard. No other seven-master was built, although there were two other steel schooners—the six-master *William L. Douglas,* built by the same yard as the *Lawson* in 1903, and *Kineo,* a five-master, built in Bath the same year. The *Douglas* was described as "not as bad as the *Lawson*" but was rebuilt in 1912 as a sailing tanker, then cut down to a barge and finally sunk in a collision in 1917. *Kineo* was rebuilt as a motor vessel.

One of the principal owners of coal schooners was William F. Palmer. After graduating from Williams College in 1880 he became a mathematics teacher and then a high school principal in Woonsocket, Rhode Island. Here he met J. G. and J. E. Singleton, wealthy English worsted manufacturers. He then became headmaster of Bristol Academy in Taunton where he met Captain John G. Crowley, studied naval architecture, and designed all but two of his own schooners. He married Mary Convers, whose brother and brother-in-law became large investors. In 1899 when he was a high school principal in Malden, he "dropped out" and in 1900 built two schooners, one of which was *Marie Palmer*. Prominent investors were Captain Lorenzo D. Baker, whose cargo of bananas to Boston had been the start of the United Fruit Company; B. B. Crowninshield, who designed *Thomas W. Lawson;* and James Bliss & Co., ship chandlers, who later supplied the Palmer fleet. *Marie Palmer* paid $316 per share in the first year, 27 percent on the investment, and by 1906 had paid for herself. She was lost in 1909 but had by then earned 127 percent of her cost. Not all schooners were that profitable, but in 1905–06, for example, Palmer schooners paid 11 percent. The Palmer fleet numbered fifteen: two four-masters and thirteen five-masters. Seven were built in Bath, six in Waldoboro, and one each in Rockland and Boston. The last, *Fuller Palmer,* was built in Bath in 1908. All were named for members of the Palmer family or their friends or principal investors. All were painted white and elegantly maintained.

Another owner and manager of schooners was Captain John G. Crowley. At the age of ten he went to sea as a cook. At twenty-one he was a captain. At twenty-two he commanded a four-master, *Mount Hope,* in which he owned shares and was managing owner. He built *George W. Wells,* the first six-master, in 1900; the only seven-master, *Thomas W. Lawson,* in 1902; and the steel six-master *William L. Douglas* in 1903. In 1903 the fleet was incorporated as the Coastwise Transportation Company, based in Boston, and went to barges and steam colliers about 1910.

Peter H. Crowell and Lewis K. Thurlow of Boston operated another fleet, mostly four-masters. They owned sixty-seven different vessels, not all at the same time. J. S. Winslow of Portland owned a large fleet, including a number of Palmer schooners purchased after the death of William F. Palmer in 1909. In 1917 Winslow's schooner fleet was sold to the France and Canada Steamship Company.

Percy & Small in Bath built four-masters and five-masters for Winslow and also five- and six-masters for their own account. They owned at one time 25,000 tons of shipping and moved 400,000 tons of coal a year. Their fleet included the second six-master, *Eleanor A. Percy,* and the huge *Wyoming* built in 1909. Percy & Small's fleet was sold to the France and Canada Steamship Company in 1917, although the shipyard lasted until 1920.

Gardiner G. Deering of Bath built six five-masters and many four-masters to his own account from 1899 to 1920. His last five-master, *Carroll A. Deering,* on her voyage home from South America, grounded off Cape Hatteras in calm weather in January 1921. Those who boarded her found no sign of her crew, and none ever appeared. In 1926 Deering sold out to Crowell & Thurlow.

Schooners were usually financed in shares of 1/64, although half shares were sometimes traded. The captain was expected to own at least one share, and the managing owners owned a number of shares but by no means half the vessel. They owned a few shares in a number of vessels, thus spreading the risk.

The managing owners were responsible for raising the capital in the first place, for seeing that the vessel was properly built, maintained, equipped, supplied, and officered, for arranging charters and managing the finances. Often, particularly in the case of smaller vessels, shares were taken by caulkers, blacksmiths, sailmakers, and other tradesmen in lieu of payment for their services in building the vessel.

The managing owners bargained with the coal shipper for the charter price. A charterer might be a New England wholesale coal dealer or a representative of a mining company. Supply and demand controlled the charter price. At 60 cents a ton a schooner could about break even, barring disaster. The average was 75 to 80 cents per ton, although during the coal strike in 1903 freights soared to $2.00 a ton and fell to 50 cents in the 1907–08 depression. In 1920 coal from Norfolk to Boston was $3.00 per ton and dropped to $1.00 in 1921.

Most of the great schooners were built in Bath but also many in Waldoboro, Thomaston, Rockland, Camden, and Rockport. In these towns there was a tradition of good shipbuilding, an abundance of skilled labor, and money to invest in shipyards. To the westward in Boston, New York, and Philadelphia the skilled shipyard workers of pre-Civil War days had dispersed and capital was going into railroads, mines, and Western lands.

Thirty-four four-masters were built in Maine before 1889. Twenty-six were built in Bath, four in Camden, and one each in Waldoboro and Wiscasset. In 1882 Bath launched more wooden vessels than any other port in the world, although their number was exceeded by builders of iron ships in England and Delaware. In that year Bath had twenty-four vessels under construction, employing 4,000 men. An additional 3,000 officers and men were sailing in Bath-owned vessels.

Of course, these towns built a great many schooners of less than the arbitrary figure of 700 tons, and many other towns from Kittery to Calais built small schooners and even some big four-masters of over 1,000 tons, but none quite equaled the numbers of four-, five-, and six-masters launched by Bath, Waldoboro, Thomaston, Rockland, and Camden-Rockport.

Elizabeth Palmer, built at Bath by Percy & Small in 1903, was typical of the big five-masters of her day. She registered 3,065 tons, was 304 feet long, 48 feet wide, and 28 feet deep. She carried 5,000 tons of coal. She was very heavily built. Her builder said, ". . . we built them with about three times as much timber as they should have to provide for their decay, knowing that there may come a time when one rib in three will have to furnish the strength. . . ." Keel, stem, stern, and frames were of white oak from Virginia and Maryland. Planking was 6-inch yellow pine edge-bolted with bronze and fastened with locust treenails. Bilge clamps—that is, the thick strakes in the ceiling—were 13-by-14-inch yellow pine. The keelson, a heavy structure on top of the floor timbers and frames and bolted through the keel, was six tiers of 14-by-14-inch yellow pine standing, all together, 7 feet high, and there were two sister keelsons of three tiers each to stiffen the vessel against hogging and sagging* as she was supported alternately at the ends and in the middle by seas passing under her. Also, a vessel as long as *Elizabeth Palmer* tended to hog when light because of the great weight of bowsprit, donkey engine, anchors, and chain forward and of her counter aft; loaded, she tended to sag from the weight of the cargo. A lower deck at about the level of the waterline also added to the vessel's stiffness, and so some schooners had three decks.

Elizabeth Palmer's upper deck and house tops were of white pine. Her two anchors weighed about 4½ tons each, and each carried 120 fathoms of 2½-inch chain. She had four hatches 12 feet by 16 feet and three deckhouses, each sunk into the deck. The after house, just forward of the wheel, measured 30 by 32 feet. The captain's cabin was on the starboard side aft, the traditional location on all vessels. Here the captain had all the comforts of home, with a bed, desk, easy chair, dresser, and closet. On the port side was his private bathroom with a tub and running hot water. Forward of the captain's cabin, in the middle of the house, was the main cabin with rooms for mate, guest, and owner opening off it. The dining room, with mate's cabin to port and pantry to starboard, adjoined it. The floors were carpeted and the main cabin and dining room were comfortably furnished, steam heated, and lighted by electricity. There was even a telephone system communicating with all parts of the vessel.

The 'midship house, 20 by 27 feet, aft of the mainmast, accommodated the galley, mess room, and carpenter's shop with rooms for second mate or bosun and steward. The forward house, 28 by 32 feet, housed the engineroom, the crew's quarters, and the engineer's room.

Elizabeth Palmer's masts were of Oregon pine 122 feet long, 30 inches in diameter at the deck, bigger than the lower masts of a ship of the line at Trafalgar. The masts were shipped by rail from the West Coast on three flatcars, the middle car serving merely as a spacer between the end cars supporting the huge spars. The route had to be carefully studied lest it include turns too tight for the three cars. Shipped eight-sided, the masts were finished at the building yard. The topmasts were 60 feet long, the jibboom 78 feet, and the spanker boom 81 feet. The four other booms were 49 feet long. The lower masts, jibboom, spanker boom, and fore topmast were all of Oregon pine, the other spars of Maine spruce. *Elizabeth Palmer* spread 70,000 square feet of sail

* "Hogging" is drooping at the bow and stern, hunched up amidships. "Sagging" is sagging amidships when supported at bow and stern.

in lower sails, jibs, topsails, and topmast staysails. Lower sails were made of 2-0 hard duck, the heaviest cloth that could be sewn together. The standing rigging was wire set up with turnbuckles, although a few vessels were rigged with railroad-car springs to provide a little flexibility under sudden strain.

Such a vessel might be chartered to carry a cargo of coal from Norfolk to Portland. Her captain, mate, engineer, and cook would probably be aboard already, and the captain would sign on eight or ten men as crew. She might sail south light, riding high in the water, designed to sail without ballast. She would head well off to the eastward of Cape Cod to avoid what might become a dangerous lee shore on the outside of the Cape if the wind came easterly, and would beat down Nantucket Sound, anchoring in light airs should the tide be foul. Then down Vineyard Sound she sailed, across to Montauk on the east end of Long Island and off to the south, keeping inside the Gulf Stream.

Schooner *Theoline* loading coal. *Captain W. J. L. Parker*

Arrived off Norfolk, she would anchor and wait her turn to load. The rule was strict. Vessels loaded in the order of arrival. The charter provided for a stated number of days at anchor, after which the charterer paid demurrage of 5 to 10 cents per ton per day. While waiting, the crew unrove running gear, covered sails, and opened hatches. When the vessel's turn came alongside the loading wharf, the coal was dumped down chutes into the open hatches by carloads, a noisy, dirty process. The trimmers had the worst of it. As the hatches were not nearly as wide as the hold, the coal had to be shoveled out to the sides of the vessel. A steel plate was put under the hatch to deflect as much coal as possible to the sides, but men with shovels did the rest for 7 or 8 cents per ton and beer money.

When the vessel was loaded, she was anchored in the roadstead. Hatches were replaced, covered with tarpaulins, and heavily battened down, for if the hatch was stove in, the heavily loaded vessel would quickly go to bottom. The pump was rigged, the vessel washed down thoroughly, rigging rove off, and in some vessels the turnbuckles in the standing rigging were adjusted for the vessel's change in shape. When she was loaded, her bow and stern were raised and her middle sagged with the weight of the cargo.

When a fair wind came, the donkey engine spurted steam as the sails were hoisted—first the spanker and then jigger, mizzen, main, and foresail. The anchor was hove short, broken out, the jibs set and backed to cast her bow in the desired direction, and she was on her way. Topsails and topmast staysails would next be set. After a spell of bad weather, there might be twenty or more big four- and five-masters standing off the Virginia capes together and bearing away to the eastward.

The course lay offshore for Montauk Point, crossing the steamer lanes into Delaware Bay and New York. Constant vigilance was necessary day and night, and especially in thick weather. The captain was constantly on deck, seldom if ever turning in, catching a wink now and then on the settee in his cabin. From Montauk the course lay across to Gay Head on Martha's Vineyard. If the wind came easterly, the skipper might well anchor in Vineyard Haven, Holmese's Hole as it was then called, to wait for a "chance along." If he were caught over Nantucket Shoals with a light headwind, thick fog, or an easterly gale, he might elect to anchor on the shoals and ride it out, both anchor chains out to the bitter end. If he were not drawing too much water and the wind was fair, he might run out through Pollock Rip Channel. If not, he would go out by Great Round Shoal, square away for Highland Light, cross the steamer lanes into Boston and Portsmouth, and raise the twin lights on Cape Elizabeth. It was an anxious voyage, leading through shoal and tide-scoured waters, beset with heavy gales in the winter and with the ever-present risk of collision with steamers and with one of the many other schooners plying the same route and making the same marks. A round trip might be done in two weeks with a fair wind both ways and luck at the loading wharves. In 1892 *King Philip,* a four-master, went from Portsmouth, New Hampshire, to Newport News to Boston in twelve days. The four-master *Frontenac* made a round trip from Boston to Newport News in nine days. *Paul Palmer* ran from Cape Henry to Boston in 59 hours, and in 1907 *George W. Wells* ran the 518 miles from Portland to the Virginia capes, light, in 50 hours, an average of over 10 knots for two days. Usually, however, the round trip took about three weeks: a week running south, a week loading, and a week coming north.

Often a schooner bound south could get a cargo of ice from the Kennebec or Penobscot. In the early years of the nineteenth century some ice was shipped from Maine, particularly when winters in New York and Massachusetts were mild, but not until 1860, an unusually warm winter on the Hudson, was ice a big business in Maine. In that year James L. Cheeseman, the Hudson ice king, came to the Kennebec in February and found ice "15 inches thick and clear as crystal." He cut and shipped 30,000 tons that year. In 1862 he built a permanent icehouse with steam engines for hoisting, and running conveyor belts. He cut 75,000 tons that year. The government began buying quantities of ice for hospitals during the Civil War; 200 to 300 schooner loads were shipped in 1863. In 1868 Cheeseman sold out to Knickerbocker Ice Co., set up twelve new icehouses, and cut 70,000 tons. In the mild winter of 1868–70, 300,000 tons were cut on the Kennebec, requiring 1,000 vessels to carry it. Ice was cut in ensuing years on Merrymeeting Bay, at Phippsburg, Small Point, Sebasco, on the New Meadows River, at Georgetown, Harmons Harbor, Boothbay, and on ponds and lakes wherever it could be moved to tidewater. In 1873–74, another mild winter, 590,000 tons were cut on or near the Kennebec and in 1894, 1,050,000 tons. In 1897 Charles W. Morse of Bath bought the Consolidated Ice Company, which controlled the ice business on the Kennebec, and in the next year bought Knickerbocker and absorbed many other Maine ice companies. In 1899 he combined all these to form the American Ice Company with monopolies in Boston, New York, Philadelphia, and Washington. In 1901 he cut back on Maine ice; no ice was cut for shipping in that year. The high price the company put on ice encouraged the manufacture of mechanically frozen ice, and by 1910 the ice business in Maine was a nostalgic memory.

Cutting ice was a systematic business employing, in 1890, 25,000 men and 10,900 horses on the Kennebec. As soon as the ice froze thick enough to support people, it was scraped clean of snow so the snow would not insulate it and so no melted, slushy snow would get frozen into the ice. Crystal-clear ice without bubbles was considered of the highest quality. As soon as the ice would bear horses, the surface was plowed after every snow and the snow moved onto the shore lest its weight sink the ice. When it was frozen 12 to 14 inches thick, a field was laid out and grooves cut with a team to mark out the blocks. These were deepened and sawn in strips with a whip saw. A canal was opened where the blocks were to be lifted out by cutting "pluggers," blocks wider at the bottom than at the top, and sinking them under the adjoining ice. Then with pikes the long, loose blocks were maneuvered into the canal, onto a conveyor, in lengths several blocks long. As the block came up, a man with a chisel cracked off 4-foot lengths. The ice was skidded into place in layers in the icehouse and insulated with sawdust. It was important to prevent the canal from freezing over at night, so people stood watch to keep it broken up on cold nights.

Cutting ice was a cold and sometimes dangerous job. Men and horses occasionally fell into the icy river. They were usually pulled out quickly but could be carried under the ice by the current. The heavy blocks sometimes took charge. When an icehouse burned, it made a spectacular fire and left a huge stack of ice with no house around it.

As soon as the ice in the river broke up in the spring, schooners and barges came alongside wharves near the icehouses. The blocks were skidded down chutes into the hold and sawdust was shoveled around them. One crew set something of a record by loading 400 tons in one day—and seven crews were working. To move 1,000,000 tons in 1880 took twenty schooners per day. On one day in July 1880 an observer counted 113 schooners in the river at Bath or above; fifteen tugs were occupied in towing schooners and barges up and down the river. On one day in 1898 more than forty-five schooners were anchored at Parkers Flats where the tugs left them, waiting for a fair wind.

Schooners loading ice in West Harbor, Boothbay, in winter. *George I. Hodgdon, Jr.*

In some places ice could be loaded in the winter directly from a pond to the vessel afloat in salt water. From Knickerbocker Pond and West Harbor Pond in Boothbay and from a pond in Sebasco chutes were built to nearby open water. Also ice was carried by rail from a pond in Woolwich to the Kennebec opposite Bath where the river was usually navigable.

The ice went for the most part to Boston, New York, Philadelphia, and Washington. The schooners were unloaded at night to minimize melting, and the ice was carried in ice wagons directly to customers. Little effort was made to store ice in the cities in summer. The schooners were used as floating icehouses. If sales were slow, the charterer had to pay demurrage; however, this was cheaper than building a city icehouse. Cargoes were also carried to Southern and Gulf cities, to Havana, Martinique, Rio de Janeiro, and even to India, although at South American and Oriental ports Maine ice had to compete with Norwegian ice.

Ice was a hard cargo on a vessel. As it melted, fresh water saturated the sawdust and worked down into the bilges, whence it was pumped out. However, the ceiling and timbers of the vessel became saturated with fresh water and were, of course, unventilated. In warm climates especially, this situation promoted rapid rot. To slow this down, many vessels were packed with salt between planking and ceiling. Some claimed this pickled the vessel and preserved it; others claimed that it did more harm than good by keeping the vessel always damp.

Southern hard pine kept many large schooners busy with lumber for dwellings and for factories, whose floors were mostly of hard pine. It came from many ports, among them Wilmington, Charleston, Savannah, Jacksonville, Port Royal, Tampa, Pensacola, Mobile, Pascagoula, and Sabine Pass. Cypress from Appalachicola and Morgan City was carried north for use in interior trim and sash work and for water tanks on the roofs of large buildings where the water pressure was used to operate elevators.

Eberhardt Faber brought cargoes of cedar for pencils to New York from Cedar Keys, Florida. The wood came off the schooner in slabs the exact length of a pencil and half the thickness, for a pencil is made by gluing graphite between two layers of cedar.

Schooners designed for the lumber trade had no hatches in the deck but loaded through ports in the bow, taking floating logs right out of the water. Telephone poles and pilings were loaded thus and the ports caulked. Then deck loads of creosoted railroad ties were often carried. These were covered with boards, but even so, creosote was tracked all over the vessel. Unprotected decks and cabin floors were heavily sanded to absorb the sticky stuff.

Phosphate rock was carried from Florida to fertilizer factories in Baltimore and Arthur Kill, New Jersey. Some of it came to Boothbay where Luther Maddocks had a factory on Spruce Point using the refuse from his pogy factories, phosphate, and bones imported from Argentina.

It is not surprising that the centuries-old trade in lumber, barrel staves, box shooks, and salt fish to Cuba, Demerara, Trinidad, and Jamaica survived from the sixteenth into the twentieth century, but it was dealt a hard blow by the importation of gunny sacks from India to replace boxes and barrels.

Maine-built schooners voyaged to South America, Europe, and the Pacific as well as sailing coastwise. A brisk trade with Argentina came to a peak in the 1880s but lasted until World War I. Many Italians, Germans, and Spaniards emigrated to southern Argentina. No trees grow on the pampas, so they imported spruce, pine, and hard pine for houses and for railroad ties to Buenos Aires and Rosario, sending back wool, hides, beef, and beef bones, the latter for fertilizer and to make bone black, used in refining sugar. Ice was also carried south to Brazil and Argentina. Lumber went to Europe and Britain in schooners, and crude petroleum in oak barrels went to Hamburg, Antwerp, London, and Le Havre. Case oil was carried to northern Europe and to the Mediterranean, to Spain, Italy, Greece, Egypt, and Turkey, for sulphur, salt, marble, rags for paper, lemons, and raisins.

Fish scrap and "tankage" was carried to Europe and Southern ports for fertilizer. Tankage is boiled and dried garbage from cities, not nearly so objectionable a cargo as fish scrap.

Voyages were also made to the West Coast and the Orient—Australia, China, India, Siam—with coal, ice, and lumber. In short, Maine schooners were all over the Earth and the seas thereof.

However, many seamen believed that the schooner rig was ill adapted for offshore work. A schooner is efficient with the wind forward of the beam, but a square-rigger is faster and far more comfortable on long fair-wind passages. There is always the danger in a schooner of an unforeseen jibe, in which the wind gets behind the edge of a winged-out sail and slams it across with terrifying force. Even with a boom tackle rigged forward to prevent the boom from coming over, a jibe can be very awkward. Some deepwater schooners carried a standing yard on the foremast with a squaresail in two halves so it could be set with outhauls to the yardarms and carried lashed in a great sausage forward of the mast when not in use. The barkentine, with conventional squaresails on the foremast, was more efficient, even if men had to go aloft to set and take in the canvas.

The greatest difficulty with the schooner rig offshore was in light weather with a big sea running. Then the tall, heavy sails with heavy gaffs and booms would slam from side to side as the vessel rolled, bringing up on the sheets and peak halyards at each roll with a violent jerk that shook the whole vessel. It was necessary then to lower the sails and wait for enough wind to keep the sails quiet. The steel five-master *Kineo* in January 1905 left Norfolk for Manila with coal. She had to lower sails so often in light airs that she used up all the fresh water she carried for her donkey boiler, which provided steam for the winches. From Manila she went to Australia for a cargo of coal, to Honolulu, thence with sugar back around the Horn to Delaware—a long, long voyage of 205 days, twice the length of a fast square-rigger's passage. Her skipper wrote, "The wear and tear is enormous. . . . There is not a mast hoop left in the ship. She has shot them to pieces. . . . We have lost 14 sails this trip, for the most part while running our 6,000 miles of easting down. Often times the schooner has been obliged to steer N.E. when her course was S.E. and my experience in the *Kineo* off the Horn is a repetition of what the *Gov. Ames* went through and what every other big schooner will go through."

Yet Captain Frank Maguire, after 125 voyages to the River Platte, wrote, "I do not see but a Schr, is as good to go off shore in as a Bark." Captain Lermond in the four-masted Thomaston schooner *Joseph B. Thomas* did so well carrying lumber to England and coal to the Mediterranean that Samuel Watts built the five-master *Washington B. Thomas* in 1908 for overseas work. On her first voyage south for coal she anchored off Old Orchard Beach, Maine, in an easterly gale, dragged ashore on Stratton Island, and broke up. Captain Lermond's wife was drowned, and the disaster discouraged builder and captain from trying again.

An investment in a schooner was no sure thing. Schooners met disaster from going ashore, especially on Nantucket Shoals and the back shore of Cape Cod. Collision with steamers bound in and out of the Chesapeake, the Delaware, New York, Boston, Portsmouth, and Portland was an ever-present danger, and collision with each other was common if not frequent in summer fog and winter snow and vapor. The only two five-masters then afloat, *George W. Wells* and *Eleanor A. Percy,* collided in 1901 in a summer fog. The *Wells* was quite badly damaged and might have been lost had she been loaded.

On September 20, 1905, *Harwood Palmer* was sailing north outside Cape Cod in light airs and thick fog. A steamer's whistle was heard coming nearer with each blast. The *Palmer* blew her horn but the steamer, *Juniata,* apparently unable to hear it, loomed out of the black night. Her bow passed under the *Palmer*'s lofty jibboom, but that great spar, 20½ inches in diameter, cut off the steamer's foremast and wiped out her pilothouse and funnel before it broke off. The bowsprit, 29 by 30 inches, solidly built into the bow structure of the schooner, dug a great gash down the steamer's side, wrecking her starboard staterooms. The schooner's 8,700-pound anchor, carried on the bow, clawed another gash in the steamer. Both vessels anchored to assess the damage and found neither was in danger of sinking. Miraculously, only one person was hurt, a passenger in the steamer. Both vessels were towed to Boston and repaired. The steamer's owners sued the schooner but lost their case. The judge declared that 10 or 11 knots was an immoderate speed for a steamer proceeding at night in a dense fog in frequented waters.

On December 17, 1902, the four-master *Frank A. Palmer* and the five-master *Louise B. Crary* were beating north from Cape Cod in a northwest gale. They split tacks, the *Crary* heading westerly on the starboard tack, the *Palmer* easterly on the port tack. They both tacked hours later and met off Thachers Island, the *Palmer* now on the starboard tack having the right of way. The mate of the *Crary* thought he could cross the *Palmer*'s bow, misjudged her speed, and cut deeply into her side. Both schooners sank. The *Palmer* managed to launch a boat into which fifteen of the twenty-one survivors crowded without food, water, or adequate clothing for December. The freezing gale drove them offshore for three-and-a-half days. Four men died of exposure. One went mad and jumped overboard. The rest were finally picked up on December 21 by the fishing schooner *Manhassett* 45 miles outside the Cape.

In 1921 on a clear night *Singleton Palmer* was run down by the steamer *Apache*. The steamer was traveling at full speed and so deeply cut into the *Palmer* that she filled rapidly and fell over. The crew climbed out on her exposed but sinking side. The mate and one man got off on a hatch cover. A boat from *Apache* came over, rowed around, seemed unable to get the crew off, and went back to the steamer. Twice more the boat came and did nothing. The schooner sank lower, and the captain knew her time was short; then he saw the lights of another steamer. Afterwards he wrote, "Just when it seemed hopeless, I saw the lights of the *Gloucester* coming up. I prayed that there might be some sailors aboard her. In a matter of minutes they had a boat alongside of us, and before we reached the *Gloucester* we saw the *Palmer* go down." The boat from *Apache* picked up the two men on the hatch cover.

The great six-master *Wyoming* was lost off Pollock Rip riding out a gale at anchor. *Dorothy Palmer* broke up on Stone Horse Shoal. *Herbert R. Rawding* anchored in a freezing winter gale in only 6 fathoms of water in Nantucket Sound. She lay to two anchors with 90 fathoms of chain on each, reefed her frozen sails lest she had to get underway. One chain parted, she dragged several miles; she was picked up and towed by a Coast Guard vessel toward Boston. The tow line parted as the gale moderated, and she sailed in.

Many schooners went ashore on the outside of Cape Cod, a dangerous lee shore in an easterly gale. Most of these broke up almost as soon as they struck, for they were fragile vessels, especially if loaded with several thousand tons of coal. Occasionally, one sailing light would be carried far up the beach, be left by the tide high and dry and relatively undamaged. She might eventually be refloated.

Not infrequently in a winter gale a schooner's gear would become iced up. Heavy canvas sails would soak up water and freeze iron-hard. Ice would stiffen and swell ropes so they would not run through blocks. The schooner would run away with her crew, almost out of control, offshore for miles and days, hopefully into the warmer waters of the Gulf Stream where her gear would melt out. In 1902 *Eleazar W. Clark,* on a voyage from Portland to Philadelphia, made Savannah. In the wicked gale of January 12, 1914, *Grace A. Martin* and *Fuller Palmer* were frozen up, overwhelmed, and sunk off Highland Light. *Prescott Palmer* ran off to the south-southeast for several days, losing her second mate overboard. She tried to beat back to Nantucket, was blown off by another gale, and in a sinking condition was sighted by a steamer about 200 miles northwest of Bermuda, and her crew taken off.

The three-master *Annie* was overwhelmed by a waterspout in the Gulf of Mexico, laid flat on her side and sinking. The captain's wife and baby were trapped in the cabin. The wife passed the baby out through a window but could not quite get through it herself. She took off all her clothes, greased herself with engine oil, and was dragged out the window by her husband and the mate just before *Annie* went under.

Charles Merriam went on a voyage in the last five-master, *Edna Hoyt,* in November in the early 1930s. *Edna Hoyt* was heavily loaded with coal bound from Norfolk to Martinique. They ran into a savage 75-knot southwest gale. For a while they ran under nothing but a reefed foresail and forestaysail and then just the forestaysail. Heavy seas swept the decks and beat in a hatch cover, which the mate repaired between seas. The heavily laden vessel made a solid target for the seas, was hit hard, wrenched, and shaken all over. They hung out oil bags and trailed a hawser astern, but heavy seas continued to charge and pound her. "It won't take long if she starts to break up. She can't stand this pounding much longer. Nothing I know of could," said the captain thoughtfully. "There's nothing that you can do. Just step over the side and get it over with as quickly and painlessly as possible. It's happened to thousands and will happen to thousands more." Obviously the stout old schooner survived, but it was a near thing.

However strongly braced and reinforced, however carefully engineered, any structure as big and heavy as a schooner 300 feet long loaded with 4,000 tons of coal cannot remain rigid and watertight. She is necessarily built of short and narrow pieces of flexible wood limited by the size to which trees grow. Heavily loaded, she is not a buoyant bubble floating lightly on the surface, but she is logy, half submerged, only a little less yielding than a half-tide rock, hence likely to be beaten apart by the seas and carried down by the weight of her cargo.

Of the forty-five five-masters built in Maine from 1888 through 1908:

Fifteen foundered, sank at sea
Nine went ashore and were wrecked
Seven were lost by collision
Five were abandoned for old age or unfavorable economic conditions
Four were lost by enemy action in World War I
Three were sold for what they would bring and presumably broken up
One burned
One was converted to a barge

Cora Cressey was moored at Boston and used as a night club, then towed to Bremen to be used as a lobster pound. She was so heavily built that not enough holes could be bored in her to provide sufficient circulation of water for the lobsters, so she now forms one side of a pound built around her. She was partly burned in 1989 when a drifting lobsterboat on fire fouled her.

The average life of a five-master was twelve-and-a-half years; of a six-master, just over thirteen years. Most of the six-masters foundered or were wrecked.

Changing economic conditions, however, did more to eliminate big schooners than did gales and collisions. The railroads transported coal with greater efficiency so that by 1909 Fitchburg, Worcester, Nashua, and other cities about 40 miles inland could buy coal for about the same price by rail as by schooner. Barges had come into greater use. In the 1890s cities south of Cape Cod brought in a great deal of coal by barge.

When more seaworthy barges were built after 1900, coal was carried by barge to Boston and Portland. Finally, steam colliers became profitable. The Reading Railroad built a fleet of fourteen small steamers between 1869 and 1874. Because the same company owned the mine, the railroad, the loading wharves, and the steamers, there was no waiting in line to load, and the vessels could make thirty to thirty-five trips a year against a schooner's fourteen. Also a steamer could be built with longer and wider hatches, which almost eliminated the time and expense of trimming the coal to the sides of the hold.

However, no other coal shippers controlled the shipping-and-loading process. The Atlantic Carriers' Association, an organization of schooner operators founded in 1900, fought to protect the "absolute turn" rule by which vessels were loaded in precisely the order in which they arrived. Sometimes this meant waiting a month or more, and at $240 per day for demurrage, waiting was expensive, especially so for a steamer, which typically had a crew of twenty-five or more men and burned 15 or 20 tons of coal a day at anchor. A big schooner might have a crew of twelve men, all of whom but captain, mate, steward, and engineer could be paid off while the vessel lay idle. A barge could be left at anchor with only two or three men aboard.

Deck view aboard *Cora Cressy,* looking aft. *Maine Maritime Museum*

The break came in 1909 when the Virginia Railway opened a line to carry coal from mines to new loading wharves at Sewall's Point, near Norfolk, Virginia, that could load 36,000 tons a day. This practically eliminated delay in loading and at once made steamers profitable. After 1909 almost no big schooners were built until freight rates soared in the First World War. Bath launched twenty-three schooners over 750 tons in 1908, eleven in 1909, four in 1910, and one in 1912. Waldoboro and Thomaston built none after 1904, Rockland built one in 1909 and then none until 1918, and Camden-Rockport, which had built three in 1904, built one in 1905 and no more until 1919.

Most schooner owners went to barges. These carried big loads; had wide hatches to reduce trimming; were of shallow draft, so they could use wharves schooners and steamers could not; provided quick turnaround for tugs, which could leave a string of empty barges at anchor, pick up a loaded string, and be gone the same day. Barges were less expensive to man, and if they had to wait to load or unload, they could do it cheaply.

Barges were made from cut-down clippers like *David Crockett, Dashing Wave, Expounder,* and *Charter Oak;* from Downeasters like *M. P. Grace, America, A. G. Ropes,* and *Shenandoah;* and from many schooners. They were rigged as "bald headed" schooners, without topmasts or bowsprits and with lower sails to help them on their way with a fair wind. New barges were built in the same way. Bath built sixty-six wooden seagoing barges over 100 tons between 1895 and 1900, twenty-five of them in 1899. Another twenty-five were launched between 1901 and 1908. From then on the size increased, the number decreased, steel barges were built, and 1923 marked the launching of the last wooden schooner-rigged barge.

Although schooners became economically obsolete in 1909, with the wartime increase in freight rates, a number of new ones were built between 1917 and 1920. Bath built thirty-seven over 700 tons, two of them over 2,000 tons; Thomaston built ten; Rockland built eleven smaller schooners; and other Maine towns built several, often smaller than the arbitrary figure we have chosen. Boothbay built ten, ranging from a 400-ton three-master to the 1,600-ton *Bradford E. Jones.* Belfast, Stockton Springs, Bucksport, Bangor, and towns all the way down east to Machias, Eastport, and Calais built three-masters and a few four-masters to take advantage of high freights. In 1916 *Jacob M. Haskell,* a four-master, got $120,000 in freight for a voyage to Africa and $90,000 for the return freight, more than paying for herself. In November 1918 a four-master took 2,000 tons of coal to Brazil at $25 a ton, and another got $50 to $60 a ton for a cargo to the Canary Islands. In 1920 freight on coal from Norfolk to Boston was $3.00 per ton but in 1921 was down to $1.00 per ton, scarcely enough to keep an old schooner sailing.

From 1921 on, no new great schooners were built, but a few of the survivors kept going. In 1927 four- and five-masters carried creosoted railroad ties from Savannah and New Orleans to New York and Boston. *Edna Hoyt,* the last five-master, in 1924 carried rosin to Boston from Brunswick, Georgia, and from Norfolk to Boston. In 1929 she had a cargo of hard pine from Texas to Boston and charters to Venezuela for goat manure, "goatina." In May 1930 she carried fish meal from Eastport to Baltimore and then sailed from Venezuela to Boston with goatina. In 1935 it was barrel shooks from Portland to Barbados, and in 1936 coal from Norfolk to Portland and back to Norfolk for coal to Martinique and then to Venezuela with coal. In 1937 she carried a million feet of lumber from Halifax to Belfast, Ireland, then loaded coal in the Bristol Channel for Venezuela. She ran into a vicious gale in the Bay of Biscay, was towed into Lisbon, was there found unseaworthy and sold for a coal barge.

Edna Hoyt under tow. *Captain W. J. L. Parker.*

Anna R. Heidretter, a four-master, survived until 1942. Built in Bath in 1903 as *Cohasset,* she was in 1909 badly burned, rebuilt, and christened *Anna R. Heidretter.* In 1925 Captain Bennet D. Coleman took command of her and kept her busy carrying coal, lumber, logwood, fertilizer, and what he could get. In 1937 she collided with a steamer but was repaired and kept going. In 1942, with Coleman again in command after a brief effort at retirement, she was caught in a February gale off Hatteras bound north from Haiti with log wood. She had kept well inshore to avoid German submarines, and anchored to ride out the gale. Her anchor chains parted, she came ashore, and broke up. All hands were rescued by the Coast Guard after a long day in the rigging, but Captain Coleman was killed a week later in a taxi accident in New Jersey.

Several vessels laid up in Boothbay Harbor were refitted. *Helen Barnett Gring* carried scratch cargoes until 1940 when she was lost on a reef in the Caribbean. *Reine Marie Stewart* was laid up in Thomaston in the early 1920s but was refitted in 1938. She carried salt, coal, and general cargo until she was sunk by a submarine in 1942.

Sally Persis Noyes, a four-master built in 1918 at Harrington, carried salt and coal until about 1930 when she was laid up at Boothbay Harbor. She was purchased by Robert Royall who renamed her *Constellation* and fitted her up to be used as an expensive cruise ship or a nautical school. In 1936 she went treasure hunting unsuccessfully and was laid up in New York. In 1943 her passenger accommodations were torn out, she was loaded with general cargo, and cleared from New York. She went ashore on a Bermuda reef in July 1943 and was lost.

Herbert R. Rawding, a four-master built in 1919 at Stockton Springs, carried coal, railroad ties, lumber, and salt until 1929, when the vessel, which had cost $190,000 to build, was sold for $1,600. She carried several cargoes of salt and molasses and then was laid up in Boothbay Harbor until 1937. Then she was repaired and re-rigged and kept busy carrying scrap leather, coal, salt, logwood, and goat manure until World War II. She was bought by Intercontinental Steamship Lines, Inc., which owned no steamships and allegedly had a shady record of profiteering. She slipped out of New York, apparently illegally, bound for Africa, but put back for repairs and was laid up until 1945. She was purchased by Captain Rodway for $18,000 and carried a cargo of salt from Turks Island to Newfoundland before the war ended at $18 a ton, bringing $34,000. Then she carried coal from Port Sidney, Nova Scotia, to

Herbert L. Rawding alongside a wharf in New Jersey. Her topmasts have been struck to let her under the Brooklyn Bridge. *Captain W. J. L. Parker*

Newfoundland at $4.00 a ton, bringing in $8,000 for a trip of less than a week. She made one more salt trip, then was cut down to a three-master, her topmasts and jibboom removed, and her masts shortened 12 feet. Two big diesel engines were installed. She was loaded with lumber for Alexandria, then went to Cadiz to load salt for Newfoundland. Off Gibraltar she was found to be badly strained by the vibration of the engines. She leaked copiously, salt clogged the pumps, the crew was taken off by a passing steamer, and the *Rawding* sank in June 1947.

Thus ended the era of the sailing ship in Maine. The last of the abandoned hulks still shows above low water at Boothbay. *Hester* and *Luther Little* decay like unburied corpses beside the idle railroad tracks in Wiscasset. A Deering schooner lies at the head of Robinhood Cove. An effort was made by a misguided romantic to build and employ a wooden schooner, *John F. Leavitt,* but after a series of setbacks she put to sea in December 1979 overloaded with lumber manned by an inexperienced crew, and was lost in a gale, her crew rescued, and with them a film of the whole disaster—now available on video.

NOTES

The most useful resource for this chapter was Captain W. J. Lewis Parker's *The Great Coal Schooners of New England* and his article "To the River" in *The American Neptune,* Volume XXXV, No. 1, January 1975. Furthermore, Captain Parker generously gave me much more information personally. I asked him, "Have you anything to add to your book?" and received several hours of information, reflection, and reminiscence as well as a tour of his museum-quality collection of photographs and artifacts.

William A. Baker's *Maritime History of Bath* included much that Parker had described and added details of towage, of barges, and the ice trade. William Fairburn's *Merchant Sail* gave extensive statistical information and a discussion of the schooner rig's use offshore. It should be added to Fairburn's excellent paragraphs that on the Atlantic coast the northwest and southwest winds are essentially offshore winds so that great seas do not build up and become reinforced by repeated gales as they do, for instance, on the west coast of Ireland or in the Bay of Biscay. The schooner is thus well adapted for use in smooth water with headwinds.

Last Sail Down East, by Giles M. S. Tod, gave specific details on the last days of many of the great schooners and has excellent photographs. William Hutchinson Rowe's *Maritime History of Maine* gives some comparisons of the sizes of crews but, compared to other authorities, is sketchy at best.

The Log of the Skipper's Wife edited by James Balano gives an excellent view of life aboard the four-master *R. W. Hopkins* in 1910. Balano's mother, Dorothea, a graduate of the University of Minnesota, took passage on the schooner, married the skipper Fred Balano, and lived aboard for two years. Her reflection on diet and rheumatism is an example of her alertness to what she saw and her articulate way of keeping a journal.

> I believe their rheumatism results from their extremely high salt intake. Seamen eat salt fish, salt pork, corned beef, and oodles of canned food, which has high sodium content. They breathe salt, bathe in salt, and cover their food with it even when no salt in necessary. . . . [Fred] even says that

when he retires to that illusory and damnable farm, he will salt away his earnings, a layer of one dollar bills, a layer of salt, and so on until the barrel's full and topped with salt.

> Washed clothes till hell won't have it.
>
> Nov. 20, 1911 29°N 34° 35′ W NE trades.
> Fred: Shows what poor luck and bad management will do.
> I: Your management or God's?
> Fred: He and I work together.

Finally, a penetrating analysis of the nautical mind:

Now I understand Fred's unwillingness to talk. He has seen too much and knows too much for landlubbers. They would never understand. . . . Fred despises having himself classified *à la Munchausen.* So he confines his conversation to 'Ayah,' and 'It might be,' and, 'Yes, I was there' while I say 'Is that so' and 'Very interesting,' which used in Spanish conversation, *muy interesante,* means 'How dull.' Seafarers are a distinct tribe, my girl, and now you're one, so take it for what it's worth and glory in its attributes.

Another chronicle, *Last of the 5-Masters,* by Charles Merriam, tells of a voyage from Norfolk to Martinique to Venezuela and back to Tampa in *Edna Hoyt.* Although no date is given, it is probably in the winter of 1935–36. Merriam is a professional writer, excellent on character and atmosphere, and not given to overwriting.

Captain Francis E. Bowker, until recently skipper of *Brilliant* at Mystic Seaport, has written *Atlantic Four-Master, The Story of the Schooner Herbert R. Rawding.* Captain Bowker served as a member of the *Rawding*'s crew and is an experienced seaman; he knows the significance of what he sees. Furthermore, he has researched the schooner's history carefully, so has given an excellent picture of the declining years of the schooner trade.

Harold B. Clifford's *The Boothbay Region, 1906–1960* tells of the flurry of schooner construction in one town during World War I.

In this history we now approach the time within the memory of living people. James Stevens of Goudy and Stevens served on a lumber schooner in his youth and in conversation gave me some of the atmosphere of the time. As a boy I can remember three- and four-masted schooners passing inside Monhegan and in 1938 boarded *Thomas W. Lawrence* outside New Harbor.

TWENTY-SIX

Fishing Under Sail

WHILE COASTING VESSELS were developing from small sloops carrying hay and firewood to great schooners carrying thousands of tons of coal, the fishing industry was also growing. We now outline its growth from the time of the American Revolution where we left it in Chapter 13 to its present state. In 1783 the Maine fisheries were nearly extinct as an economically productive industry. Vessels had been captured by the blockading British or by marauding Tories or had rotted on the shore. Fishermen had fought in the Navy, the Army, or in privateers; many had been wounded, and others returned home crippled or discouraged. Boys had not gained experience at sea as "cut-tails," cooks, or salter's devils. Little capital was available with which to build vessels; and finally, trade with the British West Indies was cut off, and that with the French West Indies was curtailed by laws made to encourage French fishermen. Recovery, therefore, was slow.

However, the Treaty of Paris in 1783 gave Americans more freedom than they had reason to expect from a resentful mother country. American fishermen were granted "unmolested right to take fish of every kind on the Grand Bank and on the other banks of Newfoundland; also in the Gulph of St. Lawrence and at all other places on the sea where the inhabitants of both countries used at any time heretofore to fish." They were also permitted to cure fish ashore on any unsettled place in Nova Scotia, the Magdalen Islands, and Labrador.

England and France paid bounties to their fishermen, and the United States Congress responded in 1789 with a bounty of 5 cents on a quintal of salt fish or barrel of pickled fish exported as a sort of refund on the tariff it had imposed on imported salt and molasses. This was increased to 10 cents in 1790, but with fish at $2.50 a quintal,* the bounty did not make the difference between economic success and disaster.

New England legislators pressed for added help to fishermen. A commit-

*A quintal is 112 pounds.

tee was appointed, including Thomas Jefferson, who wrote a report listing the advantages American fishermen enjoyed over their competitors and the disadvantages under which they labored. In the light of modern standards, a summary of Jefferson's arguments is revealing.

ADVANTAGES

- American fisherman can fish near home so their wives and children can help to cure the fish.
- They can fish in winter, which foreigners cannot do.
- They can use small vessels which require little capital.
- They have able vessels and are excellent seamen so the risk of loss is less.
- Provisions and casks cost them less.

DISADVANTAGES

- They must pay naval and tonnage duties.
- They must pay a tariff on salt.
- The tariffs on rum, sugar, and molasses for which the fish is traded limit their trade where the fish is sold.
- They must pay tariff on imported hooks, lines, leads, sailcloth, rope and twine, and wool for clothes.
- The tariff on the import of foreign fish is ineffective protection against foreign competition.

In response to Jefferson's report, Congress in 1792 set up a new bounty system whereby the bounty was paid to the vessel, not the exporter. A vessel under 20 tons engaged in the cod fishery at least four months during the year was paid a bounty of $1.00 per registered ton of the vessel, three-eighths going to the owner and five-eighths to the crew in proportion to the number of fish each man caught. Vessels of 20 to 30 tons received $1.50 per ton, and those over 30 tons got $2.50 per ton. No vessel was to receive more than $170. These bounties were soon increased 20 percent, providing a maximum of $3.00 per ton, a ceiling of $204, and a practical limit on the size of a fishing vessel of 68 tons if she was to receive the full bounty.

In 1793 Congress permitted fishermen to touch at foreign ports and trade for salt and fishing gear, thus avoiding the tariff on them.

The slow recovery escalated, rather unevenly. After the Revolution about 60 percent of the fish exported went to the West Indies, principally Dutch and Danish colonies, although a review of Chapter 17 suggests that considerable American codfish was consumed on French and British islands. Of the 40 percent exported to Europe, three-quarters was sold in Spain.

All the above figures, the most reliable available, tell little about what happened in Boothbay, Vinalhaven, and Machias. Small boats were certainly built of local timber and fished near home, for in those times codfish, haddock, hake, and cusk were caught even far up the bays. The catch was eaten fresh or salted for winter use locally. As demand for dried and pickled fish for export

An early nineteenth-century home-built fisherman, from an 1882 print in *Harper's Magazine*. *Maine Maritime Museum*

developed in Portland and Boston, larger vessels—still small—were built, and the business gradually expanded.

Machias in 1793 had about 75 tons of vessels and exported 500 quintals of dried fish.

In 1794 there were seven resident taxpayers on Matinicus engaged in fishing, and in 1800 Matinicus sent vessels fishing for herring in the Bay of Fundy. Monhegan was continuously occupied by fishermen, and in 1800 Boothbay was sending a small fleet of vessels fishing in the Bay of Fundy and off Sable Island.

The embargo and the War of 1812 again crippled the fishing industry, and recovery was slowed by the change in laws after the war. Britain held that the War of 1812 nullified the Treaty of Paris of 1783, and the Treaty of Ghent in December 1814 did not mention fishing rights at all. The question was so complicated that the commissioners on both sides agreed to ignore it in their rush to conclude the war. The Americans continued as they had before the war, but the British objected and in June 1815 took eight American fishermen into Halifax, endorsed their papers with prohibition of fishing in British waters, and released them. The United States protested. In 1816 more vessels were seized in the Bay of Fundy, the British claiming that territorial waters extended

3 miles outside a line drawn from "headland to headland." A line from Seal Island off the southwest tip of Nova Scotia to Machias Seal Island off Grand Manan would give Britain control of the whole Bay of Fundy. In 1817 a British naval vessel sent twenty more American vessels into Halifax, and by 1818, as treaty negotiations were started, more vessels were seized.

The Treaty of 1818, the basis of British-American fishing relationships for most of the rest of the century, gave United States fishermen the right to fish off the south, west, and north coasts of Newfoundland, the coast of Labrador, and the Magdalen Islands and to cure and dry fish ashore at unsettled places but forbade United States fishermen to take, cure, or dry fish within 3 miles of any other British possession in North America. American fishermen could enter British ports for wood, water, or shelter and for no other purpose whatsoever. The treaty, however, failed to settle the navigation of the Strait of Canso, which was the route to Chaleur Bay; the purchase of bait and supplies; and the landing or transshipment of fish. Neither did it settle whether the 3-mile limit extended from a line drawn from headland to headland or to the nearest point of mainland.

In 1819 a new bounty law was passed which reflects the United States government's growing emphasis on red tape, paperwork, and formality.

If:

- Three-fourths of a fishing vessel's crew were United States citizens.
- All payment was by shares except the cook, who got wages.
- The vessel was inspected before sailing for her seaworthiness, equipment, and number and nationality of her crew.
- A log was kept and submitted to the Collector after the voyage.
- Arrivals and departures were registered with shore officials.
- Four months were spent in fishing, not necessarily continuous.
- The voyage was for codfish only—no mackerel.

Then:

- Vessels of 5 to 30 tons got a bounty of $3.50 per ton.
- Vessels over 30 tons got $4.00 per ton.
- Vessels over 30 tons with a crew of ten or more fishing three-and-a-half months got $3.50 per ton.
- No vessel was to get more then $360, putting the practical limit for a fishing vessel at 90 tons.

Three-eighths of the bounty was paid to the owner and five-eighths was divided among the crew. This law lasted with modifications until 1866, since which time there has been no bounty.

Recovery of the fishing industry was also hastened by a tariff in 1816 on imported fish of $1.00 per quintal on salt fish, $1.50 per barrel on salt mackerel, $2.00 per barrel on salmon, and $1.00 per barrel on other pickled fish.

Further discussion of the tangled diplomacy over fishing rights will be found in the chapter notes.

The opening of the Erie Canal in 1825 opened a rapidly expanding Western market to dried and pickled fish, and the subsequent increase in population and the expansion of the railroad system stimulated further the demand for fish. By 1840 the United States was using 75 percent of the catch, Europe almost none, and the West Indies, by then supplied largely by Canadian fishermen, were buying only a very small share of the fish caught. However, this expanding domestic market kept demanding more and more fish—salt, pickled, smoked, or canned fish at first and then fresh fish. Professor Raymond McFarland wrote: "It is safe to say that in the half-century between 1830 and 1880 there was not a village bordering on the sea from Kittery to Calais which

Above: The Banks handline cod fishery. *Below:* The Banks trawl-line cod fishery. *George B. Goode, drawings by Elliott Collins*

did not have important fishing interests." The chapter notes support this statement.

In the early days of the nineteenth century, small schooners and pinkies were fitted out in every inhabited harbor, cove, and island community to go to the Banks. These schooners were somewhere in the neighborhood of 50 tons, 50 to 60 feet long, bluff bowed, without topmasts. Arrangements were little different from those of a century before as detailed in Chapter 13. A vessel carried about seven men, sometimes including a boy as cook and "cut-tail." He fished when he could and notched the tail of each fish he caught as a means of keeping count. The owner provided the "great general": the vessel, 120 to 130 hogsheads of salt, barrels of salt clams and salt mackerel for bait, knives, pants for the salter, and nippers. Nippers look like doughnuts made of heavy knitted wool worn like a glove encircling the palm and back of the hand so the cod line does not cut the hand. The "small general" is each man's gear—lines, hooks, leads, boots, barrels, and sea stores paid for by a levy on each member of the crew. On some vessels each man went "on his own hook"—that is, brought aboard his own gear and sea stores for himself consisting of crackers or hard tack, salt port, cornmeal, potatoes, molasses, tea or coffee. Fish was the principal food. "Fish three times a day and a lunch of it before turning in at night," writes Wesley George Pierce, who was there.

When they arrived on the Banks, they anchored and fished over the side of the vessel, each man being allotted a "berth" or space at the rail. The skipper traditionally had the after berth on the starboard side. If the fish were biting well, men fished watch and watch around the clock, each man fishing for four hours, then spending his watch below dressing and salting the fish, eating and sleeping in what time was left, much as Maine fishermen had done for over a century.

The fishermen wore high leather boots with loose tops that could be turned up to cover the thighs, a barvel or apron of oiled canvas, and an oiled hat or sou'wester.

Each man fished two lines, each with two hooks and a 2–5-pound lead, depending on the strength of the tide.

The fish were cleaned, split, salted, and piled in the hold. The salt made pickle, which ran out of the pile into the bilge and was pumped out. The livers were saved in a barrel on deck in which the oil worked out of them. A hole was bored in the side of the barrel near the bottom through which accumulated water could be drained. Eight hundred quintals of fish gave about fifteen barrels of oil.

When all the salt was used and the vessel had a full cargo, she sailed home. The fish were taken ashore, washed, graded, and resalted in hogsheads with first a layer of fish, then a layer of salt, and so on to the top where it was heaped up with salt. The fish soaked for several days in the resulting pickle, then were spread on flakes, wooden frames covered with brush, to dry. At night or in foggy or rainy weather they were piled up and covered. After a week of sunny weather, a salt codfish was a triangle perhaps 3 feet on two sides and half as much on the other, 2 to 4 inches thick, and hard as a board—apparently indestructible. Thoreau wrote from his house where the railroad skirts Walden Pond, "This closed car smells of salt fish, the strong New England and commercial scent, reminding me of the Grand Banks and the fisheries. Who has not seen a salt fish, thoroughly cured for this world, so that nothing can spoil it, and putting the perseverance of the saints to the blush? With which you may sweep or pave the streets, and split your kindlings, and the teamster shelter himself and his lading against sun, wind and rain behind it—and the trader, as a Concord Trader once did, hang it up by his door for a sign when he commences business, until at last his oldest customer cannot tell surely whether it be animal, vegetable, or mineral, and yet it shall be as pure as a snowflake, and if put into a pot and boiled, will come out an excellent dun-fish for a Saturday's dinner."

For this product of two or three months' labor, more or less, the owner got three-eighths of the proceeds and the crew got five-eighths, divided among them in proportion to the number of fish caught by each man, the skipper getting an extra share as well as part of the owner's three-eighths if, as was usual, he was a part owner.

On April 10, 1858, the schooners *Ceylon* and *American Eagle* of Southport sailed for Western Bank off the Nova Scotia coast, the *Eagle* with eight 13-foot dories on her deck. The two vessels anchored on the bank, *Ceylon*'s crew fishing over the side in the conventional way and *American Eagle*'s crew fishing from dories. By June 10, *American Eagle* had 900 quintals of fish stowed below and all her salt was wet. *Ceylon* had only 160 quintals. Captain Reed sailed for home, leaving his dories with *Ceylon,* whose crew landed 600 quintals in Southport on July 1. Other vessels saw the superiority of dory fishing, and soon Maine schooners all down the coast carried dories on deck.

By the 1870s and 1880s, dory handlining had developed a regular pattern. Wesley George Pierce, then a boy of seventeen, shipped on the schooner *Lady Elgin* out of Southport in 1886. *Lady Elgin* was a 72-ton schooner built in East Boothbay in 1883. In March they brought her alongside the wharf from her mooring in the harbor where she had been laid up afloat all winter, took out her ballast of beach rocks, built salt pens in the hold, and put aboard 180 hogsheads of salt. They stowed seventy-five barrels of salt clams for bait. These had been dug and shucked out by Casco Bay fishermen in February and March, salted, barreled, and sold in Portland. Clams were supplemented, in the course of the voyage, by squid caught with a jig like an inverted mushroom, capelin caught with a dip net, bank clams taken from the stomachs of big codfish, and also by Wilson's Petrels. When a little fresh oil was spread on the water, these birds gathered in large numbers and were killed with many-thonged whips. For food stores, seventy-five barrels of water, ten barrels of flour, five barrels of salt beef, one of salt pork, one of sugar, and various vegetables and small stores to last sixteen men for three months were put aboard. The vessel was rigged, sails bent, and fourteen dories lashed on deck, bottom up. The work was done by the crew without pay, although they got lunches and dinners aboard. On April 8 *Lady Elgin* sailed from Boothbay.

Off Monhegan they "thumbed the bucket." The crew stood in a circle holding a bucket, with their thumbs hooked over the rim. The captain, with his back turned, reached behind him and touched one thumb, then counted thumbs around the bucket to a previously agreed number, and so around again. These two men were in the first watch, and so on until all were assigned. Two men were on watch at a time, one at the wheel and one as lookout. They traded places after an hour, and after the next hour, the watch changed. Although four hours on and four off was traditional in the naval and merchant service, fishermen who worked all day found a two-hour watch enough at night. Besides, under ordinary circumstances, two men could handle a fishing schooner.

When they reached the bank, they anchored in 30 to 40 fathoms. The anchor carried 30 to 35 fathoms of chain and 200 fathoms of manila line. Where the chain joined the line, a light line with an empty barrel was attached to float the line and prevent its fouling or being chafed on the bottom. The mainsail was stowed below and a triangular riding sail bent on the mainmast to hold the vessel in the wind at anchor and to balance her under sail when shifting berths. They launched the dories, usually, with a line through a single block aloft to the bow of the dory and another to the stern, each ending in a hook, which was hooked to the bow or stern of the dory.

The crew fished with handlines from the dories, one man to a dory. The dory developed from the shallop, the wherry, and the skiff of the eighteenth century, to a flat-bottomed boat with straight, flaring sides; a pronounced sheer; and a flat, raked stern, very narrow at the bottom and 1 to 2 feet wide at the top. There were usually four sets of frames rigidly constructed so that thwarts were structurally unnecessary and the dories could be stacked one inside the other in two nests, a system without which no schooner could have carried a dory on deck for each man. The dory was lapstrake planked, each plank overlapping the one below it and riveted to it with galvanized boat nails, and further strengthened longitudinally by a stout rail and a stringer running fore-and-aft tying the frames together. Banks dories were 13 or 14 feet on the bottom, about 16 feet overall, but spoken of as 13-foot or 14-foot dories. Each man had in his dory an anchor and rode, a pair of 8-foot oars, two 50-fathom cod lines with 3½-pound leads, snoods and gangings and two hooks, a bait bucket, a baitboard, spare hooks and gangings, a gaff, knife, gobstick, bail scoop, water jug, lunch box, and nippers. The dory had kid-boards, tholepins, a painter, beckets on bow and stern for hoisting her aboard the schooner, and a thwart. Some fishermen carried a compass as well.

The Dekker lead, invented by Eben Dekker of Southport, had a swivel at each end, one end being attached to the line and the other to a 3-foot snood to which the ganging (pronounced "ganjing") was bent. When two hooks were used, each had its own snood and ganging attached to the lead.*

The baitboard was 6 inches wide, extending across the dory aft of the man facing aft. It had slats on it to keep the clams from sliding around and a semicircle cut out of the forward side in which to brace a fish while the hook was being taken out with the gobstick. This was a stick about 2 feet long with a flattened and notched end. When a fish had swallowed bait and hook, the stick was pushed down its throat, was caught on the shank of the hook, and the hook pried out. A gaff was a sharp, unbarbed hook on a short pole for dragging a big fish in over the rail. Kid-boards were removable half-bulkheads, partitions to keep the fish forward of the fisherman or aft of the baitboard and out from underfoot.

The fisherman stood up in the dory, one line in each hand, the lead about a fathom off the bottom, and "jigged" the lines up and down. When he had a fish on one line, he made the other fast, hauled in, gaffed the fish aboard, removed the hook, threw the catch behind the kid-board, rebaited the hook, and threw the hooks and lead clear of the dory. He might then have a fish on his other line. If on to fish, a man had to work hard and fast hauling 30–50-pound cod out of 40 fathoms of water from dawn until about 9:30 A.M.

Then the skipper aboard the schooner fired a gun, or blew a horn or conch shell, and hoisted a basket in the fore rigging as a signal to come aboard. As the doryman came alongside, he passed his painter to the skipper on the starboard side or to the cook on the port side, and pitched his fish aboard with a two-tined fork, counting them aloud. He came aboard, had dinner, went out, and fished until about 3:00 P.M. or until he had 1,700 to 2,000 pounds of fish.

He returned to the vessel, forked out his fish, and the dory was hoisted aboard. He then had supper and went to dressing down.

There were four gangs of three men each on deck and three salters in the hold. The throater cut off the fish's head and threw it overboard, then opened the belly. The gutter tore out the entrails and dropped the liver in a basket. The splitter cut deeply down both sides of the backbone and tore it out so the fish lay flat and then dropped it in a tub of water. After the fish had soaked a while, it was pitched down the hatch, salted, and piled with others, neck to tail.

When the fish were all dressed and salted, all hands had a "mug up" and turned in except for the one man whose turn it was to stand anchor watch. The cook kept tea and coffee always ready on the stove and, for anyone who was hungry, a "shack cupboard" containing bread, canned milk, sugar, doughnuts, and perhaps leftover cake or pie. The shack cupboard was distinct from the locker where the cook kept his regular supplies.

*The snood is the short line from lead to ganging. The ganging is a twisted piece of short line attaching hook to snood.

On a good day a crew might catch thirty-five to forty tubs of fish, a tub holding about 1½ quintals of undressed fish. With reasonably good luck, it might take six to ten weeks to wet all the salt. Then the mainsail was bent and hoisted, the dories nested on deck bottom up and lashed down, the ensign hoisted to the masthead, and the vessel swung off for home.

Each man was paid his share of the crew's five-eighths of the stock, plus five-eighths of the bounty in proportion to the number of fish he caught. On *Lady Elgin*'s 1883 voyage, high line was 6,600 fish, next was 6,000 fish, seventh line out of fourteen was 4,500 fish, low line was 3,000, and the total was 64,000 fish, 1,260 quintals, scuppers awash, a record at Southport.

Dory fishing was more dangerous than fishing from the vessel. A dory properly loaded and handled is a seaworthy boat, floating lightly over the top of any but a big breaking sea. In clear weather, dories fished in sight of each other and the schooner, but there was a danger that in fog, snow, or heavy rain a man could become disoriented and lose track of his vessel or be caught in a sudden heavy squall against which he could not row. He might then find himself adrift for days until he was found by his anxious skipper, picked up by another vessel, or made land. Some never did make it.

The vessel herself was in danger of being caught on a lee shore or in shoal water in a gale. Sable Island and its off-lying bars have caught many fishermen. Also, the routes of transatlantic steamers and big commercial sailing vessels lay right across some of the productive fishing grounds. Finally, in a gale at night or with poor visibility, a schooner might drag her anchor or go adrift and collide with another anchored schooner; then both would be lost. This was particularly true on Georges Bank where, in the shoal water and racing tide, a gale raises a short, steep, breaking sea. One schooner dragging her anchor or parting her cable could take several others down with her.

About 1850, Gloucester fishermen began experimenting with trawls. In 1858 the pinky *Albatross* sailed from Boothbay for the Gulf of St. Lawrence trawling and returned with 900 quintals, a very good fare or catch for a small vessel.

In 1860 the schooner *Island Queen* of Southport took two 18-foot Hampton boats on deck. Each was manned by two men and set three tubs of trawl, about 1,000 fathoms or a mile. Others fished from the deck. The *Queen* returned with 750 quintals. In 1862 *Prima Donna* of Marrs Harbor sailed with five dories, ten men, a skipper, and cook. Besides salt bait they took a 20-fathom herring net to catch fresh bait. Two men went in each dory, one man to haul the trawl and one to take off the fish and coil down the line in the tub. They struck a run of large cod weighing 60 to 70 pounds apiece, wet all their salt in three weeks, sailed home in triumph, and sold the fare for $2.50 a quintal, a good price.

By 1880 Maine trawl fishing hit its peak with about 200 schooners fishing on Georges Bank and about the same number fishing alongshore and on the banks to the eastward.

A trawl consisted of a long ground line, about 300 fathoms, with a 3-foot snood, ganging and hook every fathom. The ground line was coiled down in a tub, each hook baited and laid in carefully. Slivers of mackerel, herring, or pogies were used for bait, either salt or frozen from freezers at Boothbay or Portland. A sliver is half a fish sliced lengthwise close to the backbone. A good man with a sharp knife can hold a mackerel by the head, take a sliver off each side with one stroke, and toss the head, backbone, and entrails overboard in about two seconds.

Two men went in a 15-foot dory, carrying four to six tubs of trawl, two 16-pound anchors, two buoy lines, and two trawl buoys. They fished in 50 fathoms, more or less. The ground line was tied to the buoy line a short distance above the anchor, and anchor, buoy line, and ground line were passed over the side of the dory. When the anchor reached bottom, the buoy was bent on and dropped overboard. One man rowed down the tide or wind, while the other with a stick flipped each hook out of the tub and over the side as the ground line ran out. He was careful to flip the hooks in the right order, or a frightful snarl ensued immediately. At the end of the tub, the ground line was bent onto the ground line of the next tub. At the end of the last tub another anchor, buoy line, and buoy was dropped. The schooner, which had dropped off her dories as she jogged along, now returned and picked up the dories one after the other. After an hour or two, each dory was again dropped near its windward buoy. One man hauled the ground line over a roller or gurdy and passed the fish aft to his dory mate, who unhooked the fish and coiled down the line in the tub. The schooner, which had been jogging around under riding sail, foresail, and jumbo* with the skipper and cook aboard, now picked up her dories, and the fish were pitched aboard, dressed, and salted in the usual way.

In trawl fishing, the method of dividing the income from the voyage is a little different from that of handlining. The owner furnishes the vessel, the dories, the trawl gear, the salt, bait, and stores and receives half of the proceeds. From this he pays the skipper 5 to 7 percent. The crew pays the cook his wages from their half of the proceeds. The rest of the crew's half is divided equally among the crew, including the skipper and cook. This system is essentially the method today.

Mackerel fishing for food was not really significant before 1819. In the fifteen years before that date, only 6,553 barrels were taken in New England. In 1819 alone 5,322 barrels were taken, and in 1831, 66,451 barrels.

In the early days, mackerel for bait were caught by "drailing," dragging a line astern of the vessel as she sailed slowly along. About 1820 the mackerel jig was invented, a hook with a sinker of shiny lead cast around the shank. Shortly after this came the bait mill by which pogies, herring, or whatever is available is ground up and dropped overboard to attract a school of mackerel. The shiny

*Jumbo was the fisherman's name for the big forestaysail, the inner jib, on a sloop or schooner.

jig snatched through the drifting toll bait attracted the fish, which were lofted quickly aboard, slatted off the hook, and the hook flipped overboard again. When a school struck in, a crew caught mackerel as fast as jigs could be hauled in and thrown back.

The mackerel were dressed differently from cod. First the splitter ran his knife vertically down the length of the fish's back close to the backbone. Then the gibber removed the head and entrails, and the flattened fish were soaked for a while to get the blood out. They were then packed in barrels with salt between layers of fish and allowed to settle overnight. The barrels were topped off with fish and headed up. The barrel was then laid on its side, a hole bored in its bilge, filled full with strong pickle, and bunged. The salt mackerel could be sold by the barrel as they came off the vessel, but usually they were sorted, washed, and re-barreled at 200 pounds to the barrel.

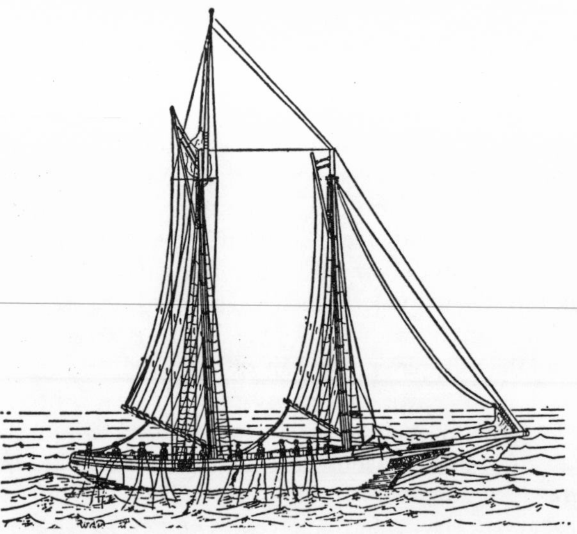

Schooner *Archer* jigging mackerel. *W. G. Pierce, International Marine Publishing Co.*

In 1864 ten Newagen fishermen bought a 100-fathom seine for $2,400 and tried it outside Newagen harbor. They caught all the seine would hold and at $30 a barrel got $8,000 for one afternoon's work. The first seine was made of heavy cotton twine, expensive in wartime. In the 1880s seiners used lighter twine, steam tarred, and set seines 225 fathoms long and 22 fathoms deep. The seine was usually set from a seine boat, a lightly built double-ended boat about 30 feet long propelled by oars, as is soon to be described.

If too many mackerel were landed on deck at one time, they would get soft and spoil on a hot day before they could be dressed. They could not be kept alongside in the seine because sharks and dogfish tore the twine and opened great rents through which the fish escaped, rents which had to be repaired before the seine was set again. Captain Hanson B. Joyce of Swans Island, high-line mackerel killer for several years, devised the pocket. It was a small-mesh net of heavy twine, heavily tarred. It was held out from the vessel's side on booms and the outer edge floated with corks. The inner edge was on the vessel's rail and the middle sunk by a line of leads. The seine was "dried in,"

Above: Setting the seine. *Below:* Pursing the seine. *George B. Goode*

hauled, to the seine boat and the mackerel spilled over the edge into the pocket to be held alive until the vessel's crew were free to dress them. A pocket might hold about 300 barrels of mackerel.

Seining mackerel was an exciting operation. Imagine the schooner cruising, often in company with many others, with one man at the wheel and another at the foremast head on the watch for fish. The seine boat, with the seine flaked down near the stern, tows astern of the schooner, with a dory behind the seine boat. A slick on the water, gannets, gulls, cormorants, or whales suggest the presence of mackerel. Sometimes the lookout can smell a school.

"School-O," shouts the man at the masthead as he sees the ripply patch on the surface made by schooling fish. The crew members haul the seine boat alongside and pile in, getting into oil clothes any way they can, with the skipper usually at the steering oar and nine men rowing, bending the oars, making the light, 28-foot, double-ended seine boat leap through the water. In some boats four men row on the starboard side with long oars and five on the port side with shorter ones, whaleboat style. In others, men row in pairs, as in the illustrations on page 421.

When they get a little ahead of the school, directed by the man at the masthead of the schooner, the steersman shouts, "Give 'em the twine." The seine heaver, the strongest man in the crew, begins heaving the seine over the side as far out as he can heave it. Another passes out the bunt or middle of the net, and a third man passes the corks. The dory, which has been following, picks up the end of the net as the seine boat circles the school and comes back to the dory. The school is now surrounded by a curtain of twine held up at the top by corks and sunk at the bottom by leads and by galvanized iron rings through which runs the purse line.

When the two ends of the seine are joined, the crew pulls furiously on the purse line to gather the bottom of the net like a purse before the fish dive out of it.

The net is then "dried in" to the seine boat as it lies alongside the net while the cook, who was left aboard the schooner, luffs the vessel alongside the seine and takes the corks aboard, thus holding the mackerel in the net between the seine boat and the vessel. As the net is dried in, the fish are forced into a smaller and smaller bag. The water fizzes and sizzles as the fish in the net flip and struggle to get out, flashing blue and green and silver in the water. A dip net with a tackle is then lowered into the net and the fish are bailed out. They thump and drum on the deck and cascade into the scuppers as the bottom of the dip net is opened. When the deck is full, the rest of the fish are spilled into the pocket and all hands go to dressing down, keeping at it day and night until the job is done.

In the 1880s a market for fresh mackerel developed. Schooners from Portland, Southport, Boothbay, Vinalhaven, Deer Isle, and Swans Island joined the large fleet from Gloucester and Boston to sail south in late March. Mackerel began schooling off the Virginia capes about April 1. As soon as a schooner got a school or two so as to have a reasonable fare, she swung off for the Fulton fish market in New York. The first vessel in might get 30 cents a pound for her fish; the last in might not be able to sell her fish at any price. A lucky vessel, as the mackerel came north, might get three trips a week.

Mackerel fishing was a gamble. The fish might be there but might not be schooling. In rough or foggy weather the lookout could not see a school. A school might dive out under the net before it was pursed—a water haul. A gale might swamp the seine boat or force her to tow under or capsize, losing both seine and boat. The price fluctuated more or less unpredictably, although as dealers began shipping fresh mackerel iced in barrels by rail, it fluctuated a little less violently. In some years the mackerel quite unaccountably showed in very small numbers; other years were astonishingly good. In a good year a schooner might pay for her building cost.

The fish came north during the summer, some coming around Cape Cod and into the Gulf of Maine where schools were seined from the Isles of Shoals to Mount Desert Rock. Others worked up the Nova Scotia coast and into Chaleur Bay and the Gulf of St. Lawrence where Maine vessels kept after them.

Some skippers tried "owling," seining at night, locating the fish by the way the water "fired" with phosphorescence. A school showed as a greenish glow underwater. The dory showed a light to guide the seine boat back to it; and when the seine was pursed up, torches were lighted to bring the schooner in. If a squall blew up or fog shut down, it could be a long night in the seine boat.

Although many Maine vessels followed the mackerel, many Maine men went on Gloucester schooners, and the Gloucester models were followed by Maine schooner builders.

Not all Maine fishermen went on long voyages to the Banks for codfish or south for mackerel. Many fished the rich waters of the Maine coast. As the forests were cut off alongshore and the firewood and lumber trades withered, coastal people turned to farming, fishing, and boatbuilding. It was often not easy to tell whether a man with a barn, a hayfield, a big garden, a woodlot, several cows and sheep, a team of oxen, a sloop, and a dory was fisherman or a farmer. He could keep a large family busy at both occupations and build a boat in the winter besides.

Some of these inshore fishermen in pinkies, small schooners, and big sloops fished on Cashes Ledge, Jeffreys Ledge, and the nearby banks, going several days at a time, but a good many fished from dories, peapods, Hampton boats, and small sloops in the bays along the coast. It was possible in the last part of the last century to catch cod and haddock well up the bays in protected waters in spring, summer, and fall. Handlines and trawls were used in the same way they were used offshore. Mackerel were jigged with toll bait, and sometimes when they were tolled up around a sloop, a seine could be set around vessel and school. The head line with the corks was pushed under the vessel with a long oar to let her out of the seine, and then it was dried in.

Weirs for herring, mackerel, and alewives were built in the rivers, as described in the next chapter. Shad, salmon, and mackerel were caught in gill nets, curtains of net hung in the water with corks on the surface and leads on the foot line. The fish swam into the net, tried to turn around to get out, rolled up in the twine, and drowned. Cod nets were set in the same way, only the leads lay on the bottom and the corks did not reach the surface.

Lobsters, once so plentiful that they were spread on the fields by wagon-loads for fertilizer, later were caught in traps, canned, or transported to Portland in well smacks. The lobster industry is the subject of another chapter.

Most of the fish caught by inshore fishermen were brought ashore, salted, and dried. Some were kept for winter provision; others were shipped in schooners to Boston or Portland for domestic consumption or to help make up a cargo for the West Indies or Europe.

While the cod and mackerel fisheries were the most important, both offshore and inshore, herring, menhaden (pogies), and other species were also valuable resources.

Herring caught in seines in the Magdalen Islands were brought home salted, then soaked in pickle, strung on sticks, and hung in rows and rows, tier on tier, in smokehouses. These were built like barns with dirt floors and a slot at the roof tree through which the smoke filtered out. Over the slot was a little secondary roof to keep the rain out. A fire of driftwood was built on the floor and the racks of herring moved up from day to day until the fish were golden in color and thoroughly cured. They were then skinned, boned, and packed in wooden boxes and sold both in the United States and abroad.

Before 1872 "Russian sardines" were imported spiced and pickled in kegs. The Franco-German War cut off this supply, but in 1875 Henry Sellman and Julius Wolff of New York discovered that small herring could be canned in oil to meet the same demand. In 1879 they built a cannery at Eastport, and in 1880 there were five canneries there, as well as at Robbinston, Lubec, Jonesport, Lamoine, and Camden—eighteen canneries in all. As long as the herring held out, sardine canneries increased in efficiency and in numbers, especially after the advent of power-driven sardine carriers.

Herring imported frozen in the winter from Newfoundland were much used as bait either salted or kept frozen in cold-storage plants in Portland and Boothbay. Salmon, shad, and alewives were caught in the rivers and smoked, until overfishing and industrial pollution seriously reduced their numbers.

Pogies, properly menhaden, have been at times an important resource. They are much like herring, but much softer and more oily and of a very unpleasant taste and odor. They are considered unfit for human consumption, although people are said to have eaten them. They travel in enormous schools and in years when they are abundant, sometimes so crowd coves and harbors that they use up the air dissolved in the water and suffocate by the thousands. They are caught in seines and used primarily for oil used in paint. An oil press was built in Blue Hill in 1850, and factories were built there and at Bristol in 1864. In 1866 eleven factories were operating under steam, used to run the hydraulic presses. By 1876 there were eighteen factories, mostly in Bristol, Bremen, and Boothbay.

Maine employed 1,129 men, 29 vessels, 43 steam presses, and capital of $983,000 to produce 2,143,273 barrels of fish oil in a good year. This was fewer men, fewer vessels, less capital, more steam presses, fewer fish, and more oil than all other states combined and says something for Down East efficiency.

In addition to oil at 37 cents per gallon, the residue from the factories was sold at $11.00 a ton for fertilizer and the untreated fish at $1.00 a barrel for bait.

After 1880 the pogies appeared only sporadically, then failed to come at all for a number of years. In the early 1900s the factories were abandoned, and only recently have pogies reappeared.

Halibut grow to enormous size on the Banks and required extra-heavy gear but were caught by dory trawlers in the same way cod were caught. At first halibut were smoked, but later the halibut trawlers iced their catch and sold the fish fresh. Halibut trawling was heavy work, and fighting a 200-pound halibut in a dory was work for two men.

Haddock were thrown away as nuisance fish in the early days, for they did not take salt well. The "discovery" of finnan haddie, smoked haddock, long popular in Scotland and Norway, provided a ready market in New England. With the opening of the fresh-fish market, haddock were iced in the vessel, sold fresh, and were increasingly popular.

Clams, since early Colonial times a ready resource for bait and for the support of the population in hungry times, were dug, shucked out, salted, and barreled in the nineteenth century. They were also sold, both in the shell and more carefully shucked, for the fresh-fish market. In 1889, for instance, 842,349 bushels of clams were sold at 24 cents a bushel, unshucked of course, for all purposes.

The inshore fisherman with a great deal to do on the farm, in the boatshop, and in the woodlot did little winter fishing. In the cold inshore waters, fish and lobsters, if there at all, were inactive. The boat the fisherman used in summer was not suitable for winter work. She might be a dory, perhaps equipped with a sail to help him home with a fair wind, or a peapod. A peapod was a small double-ended rowboat, perhaps 15 feet long. Some were built starting with a heavy board, wide in the middle and tapered toward the ends. Rounded frames were attached, stem and stern pieces bolted on, and the skeleton planked up lapstrake and riveted. Often a centerboard would be built in such a boat, and with a spritsail she would sail to windward and was much easier to row than a dory. Other peapods were carvel planked and built on an oak keel in the same way a vessel was built. An elegant peapod would have each plank running the full length of the boat and fitted precisely to stem and stern. Ordinary pods had butted planks. The fisherman rowed standing up, facing forward with oars crossed in front of him.

Casco Bay fishermen favored the Hampton boat, a rather beamy square-sterned boat that could be either rowed or sailed.

After the Civil War, the builders of the mid-coast developed the Muscongus Bay sloop. At first just a rowboat with a sail and centerboard, it developed into a definite type, almost a miniature of the Gloucester clipper schooners. She was 16 to 25 feet long, sharp forward and flat aft, often with a neat counter. She usually had a centerboard, but drew perhaps 3 feet with the board up, and had lapstrake planking down to the keel, with hollow garboards and a hard turn to the bilge.

The Muscongus Bay sloop had little drag, the keel lying almost parallel to the waterline. She was decked over forward with narrow side decks and a coaming. Her mast was stepped far forward so she could be sailed with mainsail alone when hauling lobster traps or maneuvering among the ledges, but she carried a jib on a bowsprit to give her authority coming home. She was a light boat, lightly constructed, for use in more or less protected waters in spring, summer, and fall.

While the farmer-fishermen of the mid-coast continued to grow in numbers, changes elsewhere began to affect them in the 1880s. The Boston fresh-fish market, developed by the expanding rail network of the Northeast, was growing rapidly, stimulating Boston and Gloucester fishermen to supply it year-round. Schooners became longer, sharper, more heavily canvased, and faster, but not much deeper. Like the Muscongus Bay sloops, they had fine, sharp bows, hard bilges, and little drag. They proved inadequate and unsafe for winter dory trawling on Georges Bank. This shoal rises out of deep water to depths as little as 10 fathoms in many places and to less than 5 fathoms on Cultivater Shoal and Georges Shoal. The tide runs across these shoals at over 2 knots at times. When a long, heavy sea, driven by a gale of wind, rolling out of the Atlantic, meets the shoal water and racing tide, it becomes shorter, steeper, higher, and its advancing face develops a hollow. The crest breaks down the front and is blown out to leeward in long whips and streaks of foam. A winter gale on Georges is a furious sight.

The long, narrow, sharp schooners anchored in these conditions plunged their bows under, reared back violently on their cables, and often broke adrift. Anchored close together over the best fishing spots, a schooner dragging or adrift might foul another and destroy both.

Running before such a sea was equally perilous. As the steep, short sea lifted the schooner's stern, she charged down the steep face and drove her sharp bow deep into the trough. The steep, advancing sea swung her stern around, she broached to, and rolled over as the crest overwhelmed her. Many vessels were lost and many men drowned in these conditions, and among them Maine men who went dory trawling out of Gloucester and Boston. In the one winter of 1879, for instance, 29 schooners and 249 men were lost.

In 1882 Joseph W. Collins, from Islesboro, Maine who had been skipper of Gloucester schooners before he joined the United States Fish Commission, criticized sharply the dangerous design of the clipper schooner, and in 1885,

A clipper schooner overwhelmed on Georges Bank. *George B. Goode*

in collaboration with Dennison Lawlor who built schooners in Chelsea, launched *Grampus,* a considerable improvement. In 1889, the Lawlor-designed *Harry L. Belden* won the Gloucester Fishermen's Race against the best of the Gloucester clipper schooners. It blew hard during that race, but *Harry L. Belden* was wider, deeper, had easier bilges amidships, considerable drag to her keel, and a buoyant, flaring bow. It was a convincing demonstration. The same year, 1889, Edward Burgess designed *Fredonia* on the same principle, and she became the model for many more schooners.

At the same time, George Melville ("Mel") McLain, born in Bremen, Maine, first a dory fisherman, then a skipper of Gloucester schooners, was designing fishing schooners. In 1890 he designed *Senator Lodge* with a little more beam than *Fredonia* and harder bilges amidships to make her a steadier working platform, but she had the deeper draft, drag to the keel, flaring bow, and flat run advocated by Collins, Lawlor, and Burgess. *Senator Lodge* was a very successful vessel, many other schooners being built from her lines.

When more or less regular steamer service came to the mid-coast in the late 1880s and 1890s, the already active fresh-fish market in Boston became available to Maine fishermen. A barrel of iced fish or lobsters could be put aboard the steamer in Friendship or New Harbor or Boothbay, be in Portland the same day, on the night train to Boston, and in the Boston market in the morning.

Anyone fishing for this market then had to meet year-round demand. The

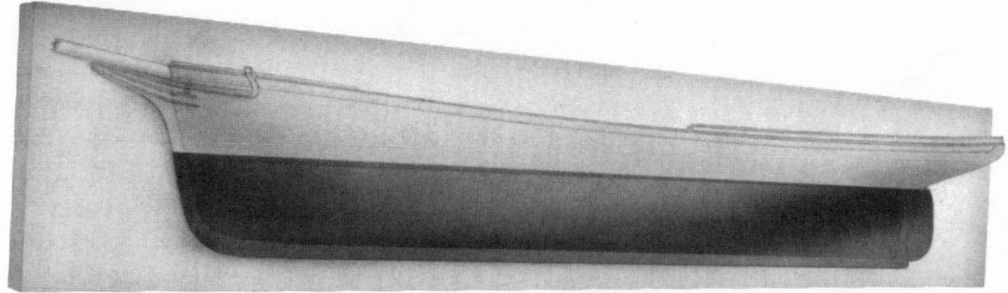

Above: Carrie Knowles, a clipper schooner, and *below,* a Muscongus Bay sloop. *Kathy Bray drawings*

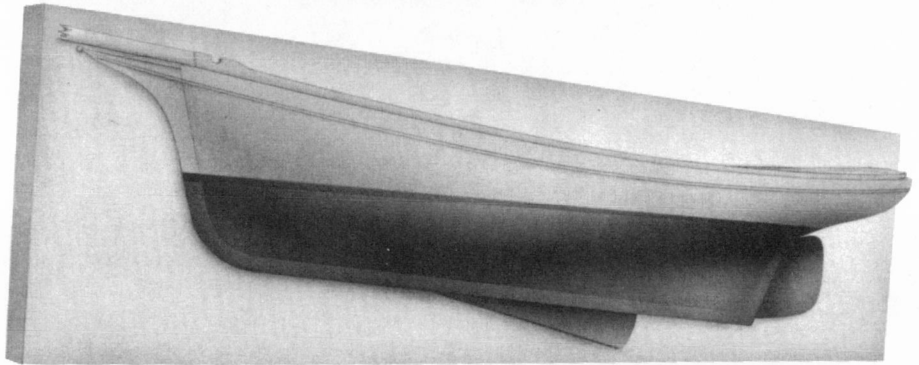

dories, peapods, and Muscongus Bay sloops were not boat enough to face the heavier winds and rougher seas of winter weather, even in coastal waters.

It is probably not assuming too much to speculate that Mel McLain returned to Bremen and discussed with his relative, Robert A. McLain, what made a good winter fisherman. Give her depth enough and beam enough to hold her on her bottom. Give her a high, sharp, flaring bow to cut through a chop and give her buoyancy forward, a flat run to let the water run out from under her easily, and considerable drag to the keel so she will be handy and run well before the wind. She must have sail enough to move her in light weather, with mast far forward so she can be sailed with mainsail alone hauling lobster traps or setting a trawl, and with one or two jibs to help her home. Such a vessel can carry a good cargo of fish and gear, beat off a lee shore, or run in ahead of a gale. She will be fast enough to get her fish in ahead of the market.

A comparison of the McLain sloops and Mel McLain's schooners show the same characteristics. Ralph Stanley of Southwest Harbor, who has built and rebuilt Friendship sloops, believes that Mel McLain actually made the model from which the early Friendship sloops were built.

They were not called Friendship sloops at first, just sloop-boats. Robert A. McLain and his sons Robert E., Alexander, Eugene, and Almond McLain

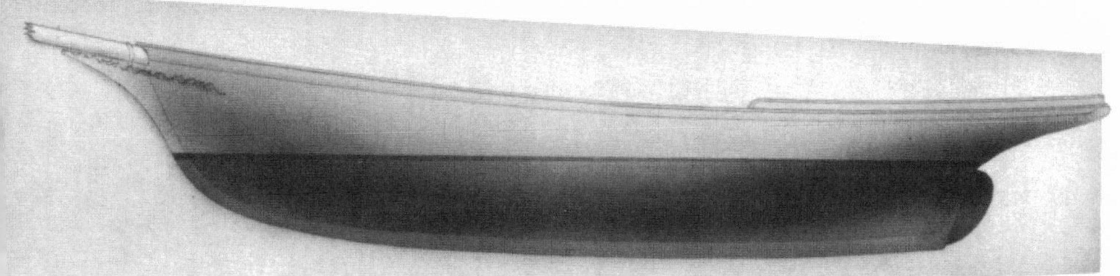

Above: Senator Lodge, designed by Mel McLain, and *below, Estella A,* a Friendship sloop built by Robert McLain. *Kathy Bray drawings*

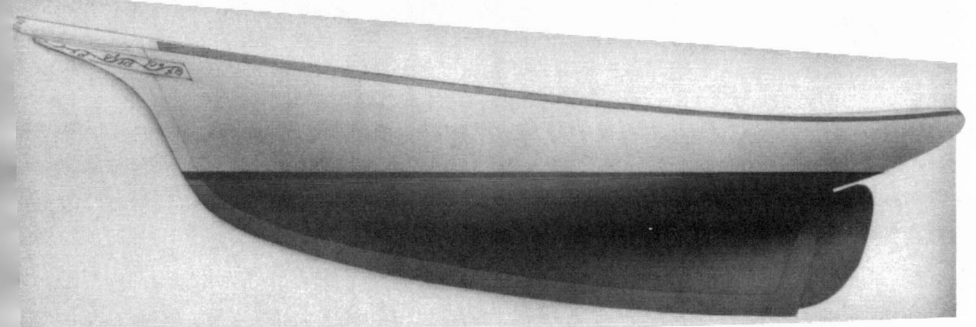

built a considerable number. Also Carters, Collamores, and Priors built sloops on Bremen Long Island.

Wilbur Morse married Mary McLain, sister of Robert A. McLain, and soon got into the trade of building sloops. Most of the McLains built a sloop in the winter, fished in her during spring, summer, and fall, and sold her; then they built another in the winter. But Morse set up as a builder primarily. He moved to Goose River in the town of Friendship where there was a sawmill, and then to the harbor at Friendship. Here with the help of his brother Jonah he built sloops five or six at a time, launching one perhaps every three weeks. The size, model, and standard of construction varied from one sloop to another as the owner wished, but they were all clipper bowed, had a quick sheer, were fast, able, and good-looking. Wilbur Morse called them all Friendship sloops. "A Friendship sloop," he said, "is a sloop built in Friendship by Wilbur Morse." This included, of course, sloops very different from the original McLain model, but the name became attached to these and they were known all up and down the coast as Friendship sloops.

Of course, other people built them, too. Wilbur's brothers Charles and Albion both had boatshops, and Warren Morse on Morses Island with his son Carlton also built many sloops, some of them before the McLains.

As the Gloucester and Essex designers developed round-bowed and knockabout fishing schooners, the Maine sloop builders followed their fashion

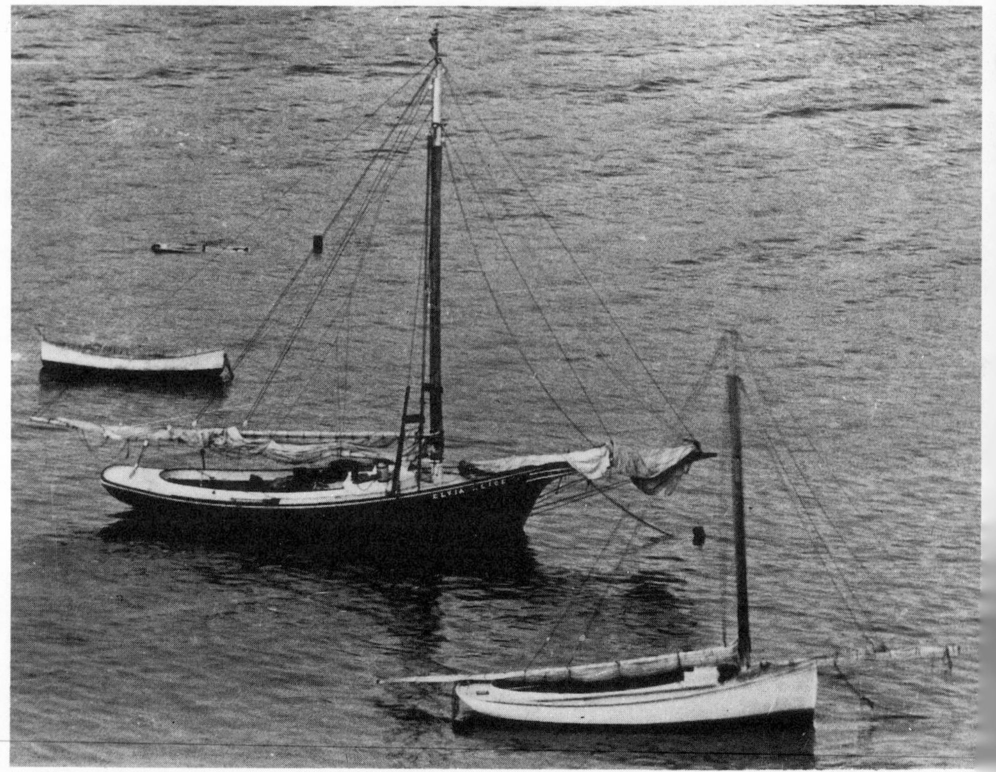

Top to bottom: A peapod, a Friendship sloop, and a Muscongus Bay sloop. *Mariners' Museum*

with round-bowed and knockabout sloops, big, able vessels quite capable of going offshore in winter, carrying a nest of dories on deck. Some were as much as 50 feet long.

With the advent of a reliable marine gasoline engine about 1906, the life of the fisherman, both on the Banks and inshore, changed radically. New methods of fishing and the vessels used for fishing were also changed, and the development of automobile and truck transportation changed every village along the coast.

This, then, was the practical end of commercial sail on the Maine coast. One can romanticize about the loss of wind on canvas, of wooden ships and iron men, of the substitution of the ugly for the beautiful. One must also face the increased production, the increased safety, the increased prosperity of a great many people. Perhaps there is some sort of balance. But what is not quite balanced is a changed attitude on the part of the seafarer. He once struck out across the sea, whether it be for Boston or Cape Horn, prepared by his skill and forethought to use the vessel he was in and whatever winds came his way

Elizabeth Howard, one of the last sailing fishermen built in East Boothbay. *Peabody Museum of Salem*

to move himself and his cargo to its destination. He was subject to whatever came, to gale and calm, to fog and snow and vapor. He could not predict or control it, merely take what advantage he could of it. He was on no schedule. He would arrive when and if he could. He was always in more or less peril, and he knew it.

With an engine, be it steam or gasoline, he became less a sailor, more an operator of a machine, a driver, dependent only on the machine manufactured by others, a machine which dominated the forces of gale and calm, which could bull through what weather came—on schedule. True, disasters occurred when extreme conditions overcame even the forces in the engineroom, but men went to sea to dominate it.

NOTES

Raymond P. McFarland's *A History of the New England Fisheries* is one of the principal sources of this chapter. Published in 1911, it came out at the end of the period of fishing under sail. It is carefully studied, provides many significant statistics, and has excellent descriptions of the methods of the fishermen, for Professor McFarland's father was skipper of a Gloucester schooner. Raymond McFarland's *The Masts of Gloucester* is another authentic and descriptive account.

Going Fishing, by Wesley George Pierce, is another excellent resource. Pierce was a native of Southport, Maine, and went to the Banks and to Chaleur Bay for codfish and mackerel. He later fished out of Gloucester and retired from the sea about 1930 after the advent of the marine engine. He relates his own experiences at sea to the history of the industry admirably.

George Brown Goode's *The Fisheries and the Fishing Industry of the United States,* prepared for the 1880 census, is an excellent and detailed account of the industry at that time with a great many, very instructive illustrations. Volume 8 of the Census of 1880 has a lengthy article by Henry Hall, "The Shipbuilding Industry of the United States." Included is a description of the various fishing vessels up to the clipper schooner but not including, of course, *Harry L. Belden* or *Fredonia* or *Senator Lodge.*

My own book *Friendship Sloops* gives the history and development of that type of inshore fisherman in much greater detail than is found in this chapter.

Albert Cook Church's *American Fishermen* has outstanding photographs of fishermen at work under sail.

James B. Connolly's *Out of Gloucester* and *The Book of the Gloucester Fisherman,* if somewhat fictionalized, are fundamentally accurate descriptions of actual events. "The Race It Blew" in the latter book describes the victory of *Harry L. Belden,* the precursor of *Fredonia, Lottie S. Haskins, Senator Lodge,* and the later schooners that superseded the clipper schooners of the 1870s and 1880s.

Joseph E. Garland's *Down to the Sea* is authoritative, specific, and articulate. The more one knows of the subject, the more interesting this book becomes. The photographs are stunning.

Howard I. Chapelle's *The American Fishing Schooner* has lines, sail plans, dimensions, and biographies of many Gloucester schooners. It is a valuable reference book.

While the Treaty of 1818 was basic to United States-British fishing rights, it raised many problems and caused many disagreements. The principal ones concerned coastal fishing and tariff laws.

The headland-to-headland rule was destroyed by two cases in 1843 and 1844 whereby arbitration decreed that the Bay of Fundy and Chaleur Bay were not British waters. The headland-to-headland rule did not apply to big bays.

The 1854 Reciprocity Treaty gave fishermen of each country freedom to fish in each other's waters but did not apply to rivers and exempted shellfish, salmon, shad, and alewives. Canadian fish were to be admitted to the United States duty free. This lasted until 1866, when it was abrogated. Then the Canadian government issued licenses to American fishermen at a prohibitive rate of $2.00 per ton until 1870. In the summers of 1870 and 1871 American schooners were seized under the Treaty of 1818 for buying bait in Canadian harbors. In 1871 a Joint High Commission met to settle differences between the two countries and permitted American citizens to fish in Canadian waters and Canadians to fish in United States waters north of 39°, roughly Cape May. This permission did not apply to salmon, shad, alewives, and shellfish. Fish and fish oil were to be admitted duty free to both countries. This agreement was to be effective in 1873 for twelve years. In June 1887 the Commission awarded Canada $5.5 million on the basis that the agreement had been more profitable to the United States than to Canada. The Canadian government invested it in improvements to their fisheries, so the United States government was paying the Canadians to improve their competitive position against its own fishermen.

In 1885, when the 1873 agreement ran out, relations were back to the 1818 agreement. Immediately Canada began seizing United States vessels for buying bait. Another commission developed a treaty the Senate refused to ratify, and finally the British government agreed to license American fishing vessels at $1.50 per ton to enter Canadian ports to buy bait and fishing gear, to transship fish, and to ship Canadian crews. If the United States removed its duty on fish and fish oil, licenses would be issued without charge. It was also agreed that American fishing vessels need not enter or clear at Canadian customs offices if there was no communication with the shore.

The United States agreed to this, and the agreement was renewed every two years at least until 1910.

The following statistics support Professor McFarland's statement quoted earlier, "Between 1850 and 1880 there was not a village bordering on the sea from Kittery to Calais which did not have important fishing interests":

• Eastport in 1830 had forty vessels of 60 to 70 tons and 600 men mackerel fishing. Between 1830 and 1868 vessels went to the Magdalen Islands for herring. In 1843 there was a lobster cannery, and in 1850 seven fish firms processed 1,800 quintals of codfish, 3,500 boxes of smoked herring, 12,000 barrels of pickled herring, 300 barrels of mackerel, 3,503 barrels of other pickled fish, 450 barrels of fish oil, and a considerable quantity of canned goods, both fish and vegetables.

• Lubec in 1860 sent eleven vessels to the Magdalen Islands and packed 500,000 boxes of herring.

• Milbridge between 1858 and 1863 packed 100,000 boxes of herring.

• Gouldsboro had a successful hake fishery in Frenchman Bay in the 1850s and 1860s.

• Blue Hill started pogy fishing in 1850. There were 100 fish oil factories between Blue Hill and Gouldsboro in 1863–65.

• Castine imported salt from Cadiz and Liverpool and distributed it to other towns. In 1850, 500 vessels fitted out in Castine.

• Deer Isle in 1840 had thirty vessels, and in 1860–65, fifty boats. During the Civil War, thirty-five schooners were mackerel fishing in the Gulf of St. Lawrence and coasting during the rest of the year.

• Bucksport in 1855 had twenty vessels in the offshore cod fishery, bringing in 20,000 quintals.

• Vinalhaven and North Haven sent vessels to Labrador for cod, to the Magdalen Islands for herring, and had about 130 vessels in 1858.

• Matinicus, in addition to cod fishing, packed 10,000 boxes of herring in 1840.

• Monhegan from 1830 to 1840 was shipping 9,000 quintals of codfish a year in addition to a mackerel fishery.

• Boothbay sent eight to ten vessels a year to Labrador in the 1840s as well as sending others to the Banks and inshore fisheries.

• Wiscasset at the time of the Civil War had thirty to thirty-five Banks fishing vessels as well as an inshore fishery.

• Southport was one of the largest cod and mackerel ports on the coast.

• Georgetown in 1843 packed between 25,000 and 30,000 quintals of codfish.

• Portland was a collection and shipping point for great quantities of Maine fish, packing 45,000 barrels of mackerel in 1841 and 27,000 barrels in 1864.

TWENTY-SEVEN

The Decline of the Fisheries

Helen Miller Gould was the first Gloucester fishing schooner with an auxiliary engine, followed by Mel McLain's *Victor* in 1901 and then by a succession of others. Despite occasional fires and explosions, trouble with stuffing boxes and shaft alignment, and mechanical problems within the engines, it became obvious that power was an advantage. Vessels could get to and from fishing grounds more quickly, especially in calm weather or with headwinds. Furthermore, the expense and weight of a full sailing rig became unnecessary. Topmasts were removed, bowsprits shortened or removed altogether, long main booms and heavy main gaffs were left ashore, and schooners jogged on the banks under riding sail, foresail, and jumbo.

With auxiliary and then full-powered fishing vessels came the beam trawl and then the otter trawl. The beam trawl, imported from British fishermen, was a net hung on a beam that slid along the bottom on skids. An improvement on this was the otter trawl, a long net shaped like a stocking, the mouth held

Otter trawl. *Richard W. Johnson*

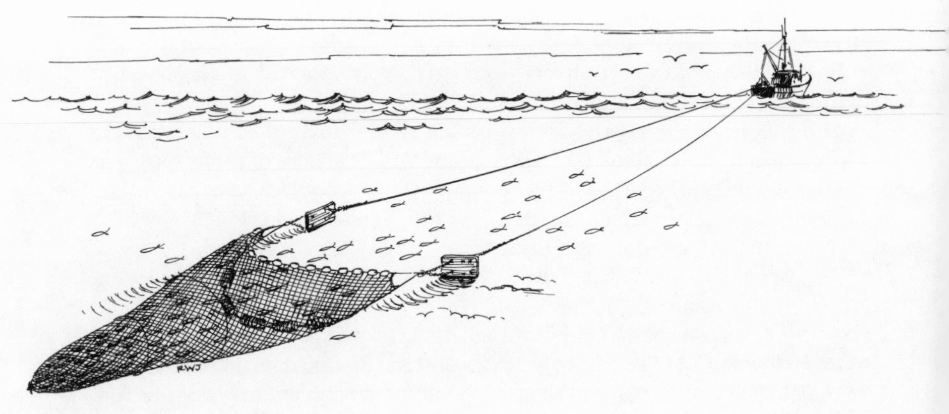

open by heavy oak doors bound with iron; these flew like kites underwater to keep the mouth of the net open. The foot line of the net scraped the bottom, protected by balls or rollers, and the top of the net was held up by floats. The net was towed along the bottom at 2 or 3 knots, fast enough to prevent fish from swimming out ahead of it and not so fast as to raise it off the bottom.

Otter trawling, introduced about 1905, was much easier and more productive than long-line dory trawling and less dangerous. By the 1920s dory trawling, except alongshore by individual fishermen, was obsolete.

Inshore fishing also was radically changed by the introduction of power. Auxiliaries for small boats were at first heavy, one-cylinder, two-cycle make-and-break engines of 5 to 10 horsepower. They were difficult to install on center in existing sloops because the fastenings in the sternpost interfered with the shaft. Installed off center, they made steering awkward, and the propeller was exposed where it would often pick up a pot warp. Such an engine would give a heavy sloop a speed of only 4 or 5 knots in smooth water and would scarcely move her against a head sea.

However, the sloops with engines moved in calm weather, could fish farther from home, and could haul more traps or trawls in a day than could the all-sail sloops. It quickly became obvious that if one were to use power, sail except in emergency was more of a hindrance than a help, and a boat should be designed and built to use an engine efficiently. The transition from sloop to motorboat took place roughly between 1914 and 1920.

Perhaps the reader will find personal recollections of waterfront life in New Harbor in the 1920s and '30s instructive, for New Harbor was more or less typical of many coastal villages.

In the mid-1920s there was only one fully rigged sloop in New Harbor, and she had an auxiliary. There was one little sloop about 23 feet long, her mast cut off a foot above her deck, still with a big cockpit, a cuddy forward, a pretty counter stern, and an engine under a box amidships. Most of the boats, however, had been built as powerboats. They were narrow and very sharp forward, some with torpedo or cruiser sterns. They had big cockpits and a short foredeck. A canvas sprayhood covered the forward half of the cockpit. The engine was amidships under a box, with the exhaust usually going out the port side over the rail. On the starboard side just aft of the engine was a vertical stick with lines attached to the tiller under the afterdeck. Pushing forward on the stick turned the boat to port.

On the stern most boats carried a small sail, either a spritsail or a leg-o'-mutton sail, to keep the boat in the wind when hauling, to steady her in rough water, or because the old man felt good about having a rag of sail aboard. The man with whom I went lobstering one summer about 1930 had quite a big sail aft and a maststep forward. He claimed that if the engine gave up, he could step the mast forward and at least make a "square drift," sail across the wind. He had hauled under sail most of his life.

The engines at first were two-cycle, single-cylinder make-and-break engines built by Knox or Lathrop. The cylinders were large, the flywheels heavy. Oil cups provided lubrication and needed frequent filling, and grease cups were turned down daily. The engine was started by pulling the flywheel up against compression and letting go. She would spin back and usually fire and catch, but sometimes catch in reverse. In coming alongside a wharf, making a mooring, and sometimes in pulling a trap, the fisherman would shut off the engine by opening a knife switch and close it at just the right instant as the flywheel lost momentum to catch it in reverse.

Inshore fisherman of the 1930s. *Author's collection*

Later, in the 1930s, it became common to use retired automobile engines. These usually were installed complete with transmission and run in second gear. They were not built for marine use, were cooled with salt water, and soon rusted out. By the end of the 1930s four-cycle engines built for marine use were common.

With the use of more powerful engines, the hull form developed into that of the modern lobsterboat. The bow became high and widely flaring. The stern became wider, the beam being carried right aft and the run becoming flat in order to prevent the boat from squatting down under the drive of the propeller. The stern was squared off. Instead of the sprayhood, a low house was built forward with a "coop" or shelter for the fisherman, open on the starboard side. The exhaust pipe was often run vertically, uncooled, through the shelter to provide a little heat in winter. A winch was either geared to the engine with a clutch or was belt-run, turning a vertical brass winch head. At first the pot warp was hauled over the side, sometimes over a roller, but later over a davit.

A fisherman's boat was versatile. As a boy, I went one summer with Captain Riley McFarland. We had coffee and cornflakes in his little house on the wharf just after dawn and sculled out to his boat in an 8-foot punt, square-ended with a neat sheer and rocker bottom. He bailed her with a wooden scoop, not dipping the water out but scooting it out.

Aboard the boat, he put on a long apron reaching from his chest to his turned-down boots. I wore oil pants. Both were literally "oil clothes," made of heavy cotton cloth soaked in linseed oil. On warm, damp days they were sticky and had to be pulled apart at the folds.

With the make-and-break engine barking and echoing off the shores, we went down the harbor more or less in company with others and headed offshore to a 10-fathom ridge. We knew when we were there because we could see White Island and Outer Heron Island showing by Pemaquid Point. We had a mackerel net over the ridge, a curtain of tarred net of quite fine mesh, pronounced "mash," with corks on top and leads on the bottom, anchored and buoyed at each end. One of us hauled the corks and the other the leads, flaking down the net in a shallow wooden box with widely flaring sides. Fish would swim into the net, try to turn around, roll up, and drown. Sometimes they tangled the net badly. Occasionally a shark or seal or something big would get rolled up, tear loose, and leave a great hole, called a "Christer." We caught mostly mackerel, some shad, butterfish, and an occasional salmon—not very often. Then we might haul a cod net. This had a larger "mash" and set with its leads on the bottom, its top about 2 fathoms up. We caught codfish, haddock, hake, cusk, and all manner of strange creatures such as skates, monkfish, and things I did not recognize.

We had a line of lobster traps, too, on the ridge, off by the Sunken Ledges, and up along the "back shore." We came up to a trap, cut the engine before we got there, and let the boat's way lift the trap off the bottom. Riley hauled; I was not strong enough then to haul with any speed. He did not haul hastily but swung his shoulders in a steady rhythm and brought the trap dripping to the rail. We threw out the sea urchins—"whore's eggs," he called them—and what weed and trash fish was there. Crabs he dropped on the platform and stomped on, then tossed into the trap for extra bait. Doubtful lobsters he measured with a brass gauge, shorts went over the side, and counters were put in a basket. Then we would start up. I often cranked the engine. It had once had a brass pin on the flywheel which retracted into the wheel when released, but the spring had broken and the pin had been replaced with an oak peg. It was a good idea to get your arm away when you let go, or that peg would come around and rap you—break your arm!

We usually got in around eleven. If it was thick o' fog, as it often was, when it was time to head for home, Riley would steer off into the murk from the last trap and come out at the harbor mouth, every time. I asked if he had a compass. He had one, set it on the engine box, and I watched it turn about a point at every explosion of the engine until it went all the way around. He didn't bother with it. He told me that in the summer there was always a southerly roll under the chop and he steered by that.

When we got in, he weighed his lobsters and put them in his lobster car, a big floating crate about 18 feet by 10 feet, supported by an empty barrel under each corner and held to the end of the wharf. He bought lobsters from other fishermen, too, and sold to a smack from Portland and to summer people who came down the wharf to buy.

We rolled the nets on big reels to dry, and he mended the "Christers" as we rolled them up. Most of the groundfish he sold to the fish firm at the head of the harbor, and others he sold retail to people who came to buy them or to peddlers in pickup trucks.

In the afternoon we set the nets. They were flaked down in the boxes, leads on one side, corks on the other. Riley dropped the net anchor and buoys and headed the boat down the 10-fathom ridge, the net running out as he went. I stood by the box, throwing out each lead and cork as it came. If I missed one or got the wrong one, tangle ensued at once and we had to stop and straighten it out. Riley was a remarkably even-tempered gentleman.

The harbor was much less crowded then than it is now and the boats were smaller, very few over 30 feet, as I remember it. There was a red gasoline barge moored out of the channel. There were at first only two yachts: my father's 28-foot round-bowed sloop and *Lucille,* a small Muscongus Bay sloop built by a local fisherman and sold as a yacht when he turned to power. Later came a Herreshoff sloop and a powerboat, all white paint and varnish—quite elegant.

There were very few summer people around, and they were mostly permanent summer residents in cottages. There was a hotel on the hill and several boardinghouses for summer people. A farmhouse with a big barn was made into a summer hotel and still flourishes.

Once a week we boys heard a whistle and ran for the shore. A freight boat on the Portland–Friendship and Thomaston line, *Myra J. Worcester,* came alongside the stone steamboat wharf. A boy might get 10 cents for unloading freight and carrying it into the freight house on the wharf whence it would be called for by people in wagons and pickups. Some freight came by train to Newcastle. I rode up behind a two-horse team over dirt roads with a storekeeper once. The round trip from New Harbor to Newcastle took all day.

Into the head of the harbor ran a brook from the ice pond. The mud flats were choked with eelgrass in which lived small fish and crabs. We caught cunners and pollock in the harbor and off the rocks. When the eelgrass died in the 1930s and cormorants came in large numbers, the cunners and pollock disappeared.

There were two fish firms in town buying groundfish: cod, hake, haddock, and cusk. The fish were forked up onto the wharf, weighed, and put in high-wheeled carts. They were split and put in hogsheads probably 5 to 6 feet deep; I could not look over the edge of one. They were piled in with alternate layers of salt, and salt was heaped over the top. After soaking in the pickle, they were taken out, spread on flakes covered with chicken wire, and dried by the acre.

A schooner, *William Keene,* came in several times during the summer

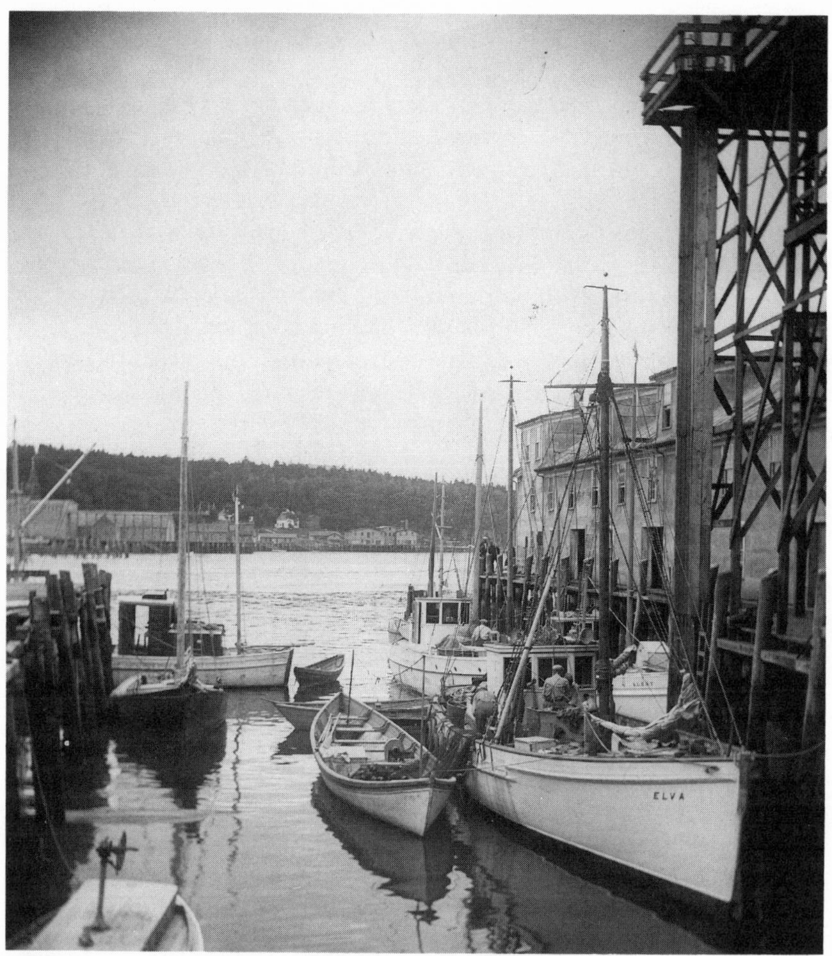

Seiners in Boothbay. *George I. Hodgdon, Jr.*

with salt in bulk. She was a rough little two-master but got around the coast very well.

Most fishermen had a wharf with a fish house where they built and mended traps and stored bait. This was often herring, salted in the fall and winter and pretty strong by summer.

In the spring many fishermen set trawls as described in the previous chapter, baiting with frozen herring from the freezer in Boothbay Harbor and setting from a motorboat. One had to be very quick and accurate flipping out the hooks to avoid a snarl.

There were a few bigger vessels in New Harbor, powerboats about 60 feet long used mostly as seiners. They had high bows, a raised deck forward, under which was a little fo'c's'le. The mast was stepped just aft of the break, with a derrick boom and a gasoline "h'ister" in a box at its foot. The hatch was in the waist about amidships, the pilothouse aft, and the engineroom under and aft of it with a companionway ladder leading down to it. During the summer they cruised slowly, towing a seine boat and with a man aloft looking for schools of mackerel. When they found a school, all but one man went off in the seine boat, which had its own engine, dropped a dory, circled the school, and pursed up the seine as described in the last chapter. The vessel came alongside, the seine was dried into the seine boat, and the fish were bailed onto the deck of the vessel and into her hold using a big dip net and the h'ister, which fired at every revolution under load but only at every three or four revolutions when idling. The fish were taken ashore and sold fresh, as the market for salt mackerel was sagging badly and has since died. Mackerel do not keep well frozen, so other species are now preferred. Some mackerel were and still are sold fresh, and some are used for bait.

Herring were also seined in spring and fall, and to the eastward. Up Muscle Ridge Channel, in Penobscot Bay, and on down east many were caught in weirs. Weirs were more or less circular enclosures of pilings laced with brush, with a long wing set out into a channel where herring ran. The fish swam up with the tide and settled back into the weir. The weir was seined at low water and a carrier boat sent from the sardine factory for the fish. They were often held over a tide to get the feed out of them, as they did not can well if "feedy."

The sardine carriers were slim, handsome, fast vessels, sometimes as much as 70 feet long but usually less, with a mast and h'ister. A sardiner usually carried a pile of salt bags forward of her pilothouse; the salt was scattered on the fish in the hold and sold to fishermen to salt seines, then made of tarred cotton twine.

The lightly salted herring were rushed to the sardine factory and canned at once in oil, mustard, or tomato sauce. When a carrier came in to the sardine factory wharf, the whistle blew and local women lined up at the tables to pack the cans. A conveyor belt took the cans to be filled up with oil, sealed, and pressure cooked. The whole process moved very rapidly. It took less than twenty-four hours, often much less, from weir to can.

Some herring were salted or frozen for bait; and down east in Eastport and across the border in Grand Manan and New Brunswick ports, many were salted and smoked as described in the previous chapter.

Draggers had to work on a reasonably smooth bottom, for rocks would tear or hang up the net. The net was payed out over the vessel's stern as she moved slowly along, and the doors were dropped to spread the net. The doors and the leads on the net's foot took it to bottom. The net was towed by a wire about three times as long as the depth of water for an hour or more—as long as the skipper judged was right—at a speed sufficient to keep the net open and to prevent fish from swimming out of it, but not so fast as to raise it off the bottom. After an hour or so, the net was "hauled back," the doors lifted to the gallows, and the mouth of the net taken over the rail. A strap was passed around the net above the foot of the stocking, called the cod end, and the bag of dripping, squirming fish was hoisted over the rail and swung inboard. A line closing the cod end was tripped, and the whole mass dropped out on deck. The net might then be set again while the crew sorted, dressed, and iced the catch.

Everything on the bottom came up in the net. Not only cod, haddock,

Above: A sardine carrier. *Below:* Dragger hauling back. *Author's collection*

hake, and cusk but lobsters, skates, sculpins, and all manner of trash fish, including many fish too small to keep. These, of course, were drowned or mashed in the net or died on deck before they could be thrown or forked overboard, and so were wasted, except for a few sold for lobster bait.

Local people resented draggers from Massachusetts, saying that they spoiled the feeding and spawning grounds of valuable fish, swept up lobster traps, gill nets, and trawls, and destroyed as much fish as they caught. Laws were made restricting dragging by out-of-state vessels, but nevertheless, dragging was so much easier, safer, and more efficient than dory trawling that it soon replaced dory trawling entirely and was taken up by Maine companies based in Portland and Rockland.

Fish and lobsters from New Harbor were at first shipped by schooner and smack, for the road to the railroad at Newcastle was unpaved and too rough for heavy trucks. Also, the Carlton Bridge at Bath had not been built, so both automobiles and railroad cars had to cross the Kennebec on a ferry. However, with the construction of the bridge, the paving of roads, and the establishment of truck transportation, *William Keene* and the freight boat *Myra J. Worcester* became obsolete, the salt-fish business was discontinued, more and more summer people came in for shorter stays, and the character of the town changed.

New Harbor development was typical of many harbors up and down the coast, yet each was in its own way unique. Boothbay Harbor had several fish-packing firms and its freezer to which offshore fishermen came for bait. East Boothbay was a shipbuilding center, building draggers, seiners, and yachts; the yards were served by a sailmaker, a rigger, and a blacksmith. South Bristol men fished, but many worked in the well-known Gamage yard there. Round Pond had a granite quarry and a pogy factory, abandoned when the pogies left. Friendship concentrated on lobsters and had a boatshop in Hatchet Cove and a quarry on Friendship Long Island. And so it went all up the coast, each town unique yet each having a similar atmosphere of busy people working hard to maintain a way of life many could feel was fading.

World War II changed all this. Many fishermen joined the services, and others gave up fishing to work in shipyards in Boothbay, Camden, Rockland, Southwest Harbor, and other towns building small wooden troop transports, tugs, minesweepers, and barges. Others traveled to Bath to build destroyers or to South Portland to build Liberty ships, a subject covered in Chapter 30. A few continued to fish, getting good prices and contributing substantially to the war effort by supplying necessary food.

After World War II, pressure on the fishery increased tremendously. Since earliest times, fish had been assumed to be an inexhaustible resource. Ten million pounds of fish were exported to Europe, the Canaries, and the West Indies at the end of the seventeenth century, with no depletion evident whatsoever. In 1808, 1,300 schooners from Maine and Massachusetts fished in the Gulf of St. Lawrence and off Labrador with no diminution in the supply. In the 1850s, 1,300 Maine vessels alone, bigger ones now, were cod fishing.

There were still plenty of fish. In 1890 Thomas H. Huxley declared fish an inexhaustible resource and regulation of the fisheries unnecessary and impossible.

In 1911 Professor Raymond McFarland, who had been mackerel fishing commercially with his father, wrote: "The fisherman realizes, as the landsman cannot, that the amount of mackerel in the ocean to be caught is immense—a quantity beyond all possibility of computing; the season's catch may be only 10,000 barrels, yet his knowledge of conditions causes the fisherman to believe that there are millions upon millions of them left untouched—the possibilities of several seasons' work in the future . . . [it is] a truth well known to every mackerel fisherman that the agency of man is the least of the causes to diminish the quantity of mackerel in the ocean—a quantity that in good seasons and in poor seasons is a thousand times greater than the small amount taken by fishermen."

The invention of successful canning techniques and of artificial refrigeration expanded the fresh-fish market in the last decade of the nineteenth century. The use of powered fishing vessels brought in the beam trawl and the otter trawl. Fast freezing further increased the demand. By the mid-1930s salt fish had become an anachronism, and the market for fresh fish was expanding rapidly.

Increased pressure on the supply of fish and depressed prices hurt fishermen badly. Small naval patrol vessels were converted to fishermen. Radar, radio navigation instruments, and depthfinders made navigation and fish finding more precise. More powerful engines and winches meant more time on the banks and bigger, heavier nets and the construction of larger, more efficient stern draggers instead of side draggers. Onboard refrigeration began to replace ice, increasing the fish capacity of a vessel.

The changes might have been very much to the fisherman's advantage, for the United States market for fresh and frozen fish continued to expand. However, foreign countries, impoverished by war and heavily in debt, were seeking exports to strengthen their economies. The Marshall Plan gave them capital to develop their fisheries, and their governments subsidized the construction, repair, and operation of their fleets. Norway, Iceland, and Canada in particular flooded the American market with fresh and frozen fish and with fish sticks. Fish sticks are sawn from frozen blocks of compressed fish—any fish available—and thus provide a market for species formerly considered of no value.

The United States government refused to put a tariff on fish, believing that the expanding American market could absorb both increased American production and foreign fish. It failed to consider the generous foreign subsidies that depressed prices below what unsubsidized American fisherman needed to operate profitably. The State Department believed it more important to keep these democratic countries prosperous, capable of purchasing our exports, and friendly to us, than to take care of American fishermen.

In 1939 United States fishermen supplied 95 percent of the American market; in 1945, 78 percent; in 1948, 71 percent, with a $10,000,000 trade deficit in groundfish. In 1973 the deficit was $295,000,000.

Of course, this heavy fishing by Americans and low prices affected the Maine fisherman, who did not have the capital or the inclination to invest in a larger, more efficient stern trawler with expensive electronic gear and mechanical refrigeration. The only one to profit significantly was the processor, who bought inexpensive foreign fish and sold fish sticks, frozen fillets, and TV dinners on the United States market.

Then in 1961 Russian vessels appeared off the United States coast, to be joined in the next few years by vessels from Poland, East and West Germany, France, Italy, Norway, Greece, Spain, Japan, Romania, Bulgaria, Cuba, Mexico, Venezuela, and Argentina. By 1976 there were 300 foreign vessels fishing between Hatteras and Nova Scotia, most of them on Georges Bank. At first the foreign ships fished for species not sought by Americans, such as herring, but when they had fished out herring, they went for whiting, then other species. This is "pulse" fishing. In 1965 and 1966 the Russians concentrated on haddock.

The average annual American catch of haddock had been about 110 million pounds. In 1965 the total catch of haddock, well over half of it by Russians, was 283 million pounds and in 1966, 161 million pounds. It then dropped off rapidly year by year until in 1974 the catch was down to 6½ million pounds. The haddock fishery on Georges was ruined and haddock nearly extinct. Then they turned to yellow-tailed flounder, and the same course was followed.

In 1950 the International Commission for Northwest Atlantic Fisheries (ICNAF) had been founded to regulate and conserve the fisheries. It set quotas, mesh sizes for nets, and closed areas, but it had no authority, was unable to get quick and reliable information, and proved generally ineffective. Meanwhile, Maine fishermen in 70-foot wooden draggers, some of them twenty years old, faced foreign fleets like that described by Boeri and Gibson in *Tell It Good-bye, Kiddo:*

"Ships of all kinds can be seen sweeping the fishing grounds in every direction: small otter trawlers, purse seiners, medium-sized stern trawlers twice as long as New England's largest fishing boats, and even the larger stern trawler factory ships. Purse seiners and otter trawlers are transferring their catches to 600-foot-long factory ships for processing, while a whole support fleet of oil tankers, fresh water tankers, repair and salvage vessels, tug boats and base ships moves among the vessels of the fishing fleet. And on the perimeter of this fishing armada—which number as many as 100 vessels—and beyond at isolated points of the grounds are reconnaissance vessels which daily report to the fleet command ship such information as type of catch, catch size, water temperature and weather."

A Soviet factory ship could take aboard the catches of four of her smaller fishing vessels and could in one day produce 100,000 pounds of frozen fillets,

300,000 pounds of fish meal, 10,000 pounds of fish oil, and could process in addition 400,000 pounds of herring. This output was transferred to a cargo vessel, which, when loaded, carried over 7,000 tons of fish products back to Russia while the fleet kept fishing.

Not only do the fish have no chance, the small Maine fisherman in his own vessel or fishing aboard a vessel out of Boston or New Bedford cannot possibly compete with the frozen foreign fish imported through Canada or St. Pierre-Miquelon to supply American processors.

An effort was made in 1968 to meet the competition of modern foreign factory ships by building with government support *Seafreeze Atlantic* and then *Seafreeze Pacific*, 295-foot factory ships equipped to freeze fish at sea. They were egregious failures on the East Coast, for they could not afford to pay their crews enough to compensate for the longer voyages. They were both laid up, and *Seafreeze Atlantic* was sent to the West Coast.

With extensive efforts to support ICNAF and protect against the cheating and chicanery of various fleets, the United States, following the lead of Peru, Ecuador, and a growing number of other countries, established in 1976 a 200-mile preferential fishing limit to be enforced by the United States Coast Guard.

Canada responded at once with a 200-mile limit of her own which put the Nova Scotia banks and most of the Grand Banks out of bounds for American fishermen and which overlapped the American limit on Georges Bank. A treaty with Canada which would have shared fishing rights on Georges was negotiated in 1979 but rejected in 1981 in response to vigorous lobbying by American scallopers. Finally the dispute was referred to the World Court, which in October 1984 awarded to Canada the Northeast Peak of Georges and to the United States the southern part. However, the Northeast Peak was by far the richest in cod and haddock, whereas the rest of the bank had been very badly overfished.

The United States government in an effort to bring back the stocks of cod and haddock and other desirable species imposed quotas, closed areas, and limited mesh sizes, but quotas were very difficult to enforce and incidental catches were high. Suppose the quota of cod to have been reached: A vessel dragging for flounder might catch quite a number of cod, and a certain amount of cod would be allowed as incidental catch.

With foreign vessels being phased out—a few were allowed under license and with a quota—-American fishermen went vigorously to work, dragging over the already overfished banks. They used essentially the same old methods and the same old vessels, although a few new steel ones were built by, among others, Goudy and Stevens and by Washburn and Doughty in East Boothbay.

Government help, decreasing annually with budget restrictions, consisted largely in assessment of declining stocks. The Coast Guard was quite unable to enforce the regulations as its budget was cut, too. The fishermen, an independent lot, increased their fishing effort in order to supply a market depressed by imports of high-quality frozen fillets and fish sticks. The fishermen are not unmindful of conservation, but even as they realize the necessity for it, they know very well that what fish they do not catch today will be caught by someone else tomorrow.

Some efforts have been made to improve quality and at the same time improve stocks. One was the construction in 1985 of three long-line steel vessels equipped to fillet and freeze fish at sea. This was an adaptation of the old dory trawl but set from the vessel and hauled over the stern. Gangings were attached to the ground line, baited by machine as the ground line ran out, and stowed on a rack. As the line came in hours later with fish on the hooks, unwanted species and fish too small could be liberated alive. The catch was iced at once and stowed in 50-pound cardboard boxes. The result was an expensive and very high-quality product. However, the experiment failed, as the public declined to pay the price in competition with high-quality imported fish whose fishermen were subsidized by their governments.

A modern stern trawler. *Author's collection*

Otter trawling remains the least expensive and most common way to catch fish, but in the long run it may well be the wrong way. It is not selective, and it tears up the feeding and spawning grounds. No matter what the mesh size in the cod end, the otter trawl, as it slams along the bottom, scoops up everything. If you could sit on the bottom, you might see the wires leading down to the heavy steel-shod doors. If the vessel is towing fast enough, the doors might fly clear of the bottom, but they probably bump and bang along, each stirring up a cloud of mud and sand which streams out behind them. Fish see this as a solid wall and turn inwards. The wings come next, looming through the murk and herding the fish farther in. Then comes the great gaping mouth of the net, the foot line bouncing along the bottom on steel balls or heavy rubber rollers, the top held open by floats. Everything goes in. Everything. It all is washed back to the cod end: mud, rocks, weed on which the fish feed, clams, lobsters, scallops, and fish, both marketable ones and so-called trash fish. Although the mesh at the cod end may be large enough to let young fish out, if a young fish hits the net crosswise, he will never get through. Most likely, a great number of young fish will pile up against the bigger fish and the rocks and mud that get there first. The pressure of the water as the net is towed along mashes the fish hard into the cod end.

When the otter trawl is hauled back and the cod end dumped on deck, the fish caught first are dead, crushed and drowned. The others are dying from the change in pressure as they are pulled up. As the crew clears up the deck, the vessel's wake is littered by dead trash fish forked overboard. The marketable fish are stowed below in ice, the ones first down the hatch mashed under the weight of the iced fish above despite dividing boards put in to take some of the weight. When the vessel leaves the grounds after a week of fishing, she leaves a wide swath of destruction behind her and carries with her a cargo of badly mishandled fish, a product which can with difficulty compete with freshly frozen imported fillets.

As fish stocks go down, fishermen have increased their effort, but by 1989 the groundfish stocks on Georges Bank, as well as the inshore banks closer to the Maine coast like Jeffreys Ledge, Cashes Ledge, and the Fipennies, had been sharply reduced. *National Fisherman* in February 1989 reported stocks of cod, haddock, and yellow-tailed flounder, among others, to be in danger of collapse. One fisherman reported in the same issue that where in recent years he made three trips a month, coming in with 45,000 to 50,000 pounds of fish, he now gets 20,000 to 25,000 pounds. The price of cod has fallen from 80 cents to 50 cents per pound and pollock from 50 cents to between 25 and 40 cents. He, with a number of other fishermen in the same squeeze, is turning toward squid, mackerel, and herring—so-called "underutilized species." Yet 1988 landings of mackerel and butterfish were down, although the supply of squid increased.

A Portland fisherman has just bought a new 130-foot freezer-trawler which, with the one he owns already, he hopes will give him sufficient volume of high-quality squid, mackerel, and butterfish to do his own direct marketing.

Another Portland fisherman is doing the same thing while he is trying to sell his three smaller draggers. They have been dragging on the Grand Banks in summer and doing what they can in the Gulf of Maine in the winter. No one is interested in buying them.

Some of those squeezed out of the groundfish business are going in heavily for scallops and shrimp, and some are moving to Alaska.

Mid-water trawling uses a rig similar to the otter trawl to catch mackerel, herring, and other fish that swim nearer the surface. The net is similar to the otter trawl, stocking-like in shape with its mouth spread by doors and held open by floats and leads. With a fish-finding sonar mounted on the head line, the fisherman knows at what depth the net is fishing, and with his own fish-finding sonar scanning ahead and to each side he can steer his net to catch an optimum number of fish.

Also, purse seiners, now equipped with power blocks to dry in the seines, set enormous seines on schools of pogies to which they are guided by airplane. The fish are pumped out of the net, scaled, stowed directly below, and rushed to a factory to be made into fish oil and fish meal.

With these kinds of pressures on what is clearly no longer an inexhaustible resource, it is evident that the New England fishery is in very serious trouble.

Spencer Apollonio, former Director of the Maine Department of Marine Resources, in an article in the February 1989 issue of *National Fisherman* and in conversation with the writer, suggests that wasteful and destructive otter trawling be phased out and that scientists and fishing management officials, instead of monitoring decreasing stocks, study fish behavior to discover what attracts different species of fish and different sizes of each species in order to determine more selective ways of fishing. Furthermore, some limitations on size and number of vessels, and on size and type of gear should be instituted to give fish stocks a chance to recover.

The bottom of the Gulf of Maine is a highly complex ecosystem to which many different forms of vegetable and animal life contribute. Remove or destroy several parts, and the balance is upset, other parts suffer, and perhaps a new and undesirable equilibrium is established. To hunt cod, haddock, and redfish * nearly to extinction, then to turn as vigorously to mackerel, squid, and butterfish, or to shrimp and scallops, may not be the best way to ensure a continued harvest of fish and a continued livelihood for Maine fishermen.

A start has been made at aquaculture of salmon in New Brunswick waters and off Eastport. In 1989 a small project was started in Toothacher Bay off Swans Island. There are now salmon pens in Taunton Bay, near Bar Harbor, in Georges Harbor, and in Isle au Haut.

Raising salmon in pens is not as easy as at first it may appear. First, fertile eggs must be collected and hatched under properly controlled conditions in a hatchery, and the little salmon, smolts, must be fed and raised in fresh water. When 8 to 10 inches long they undergo changes that fit them to be shifted to a saltwater environment. However, if they are not shifted within two or three weeks after they are ready, they must be held in fresh water for another year.

After they have become acclimated to salt water, they are put in floating pens covered with netting to protect them from gulls, cormorants, or any other bird seeking free lunch, and there they are fed until they are big enough for market. While they are growing, they are likely to contract diseases which spread rapidly in their crowded condition. Also their fecal waste and uneaten

* Redfish is *Sebastes marinus*, also known as rosefish and sometimes sold as ocean perch. It is a small fish usually less than a foot long, red on top and white below. It is caught in otter trawls.

food sinks to the bottom and poisons lobsters, shellfish, and some plants under the pens. To minimize this pollution, pens must be established where there is a strong run of tide and sufficient depth of water under the pens to dilute the poisons. Because the pens must be moored in waters protected from heavy seas, these conditions are not always easy to find. However, the Maine projects seem to be progressing satisfactorily.

NOTES

Sources for this chapter are diverse indeed. Raymond McFarland's *A History of the New England Fisheries* and Wesley George Pierce's *Going Fishing* provide the basic facts on the first part, supplemented by Chip Griffin's *A History of Fishing in the Boothbay Region.* Spencer Apollonio's Tallman Lectures, delivered at Bowdoin College in 1976, just as the 200-mile limit was established, provide statistical data on the decline of the fishery under the pressure of foreign fishing, as does *The Commercial Fisheries of Maine,* by Cyrus Hamlin and John Ordway. This was published in the early 1970s before the 200-mile limit. It deals with declining stocks and increasingly sophisticated technology. *Commercial Fishing Methods,* by John C. Sainsbury, describes in detail the rigging of the stern trawler.

For information on foreign distant-water fishing, William Warner's *Distant Water* is excellent. It is a personal account of his voyages on a number of distant-water ships including British, Russian, Spanish, and Polish. Boeri and Gibson's *Tell It Good-bye, Kiddo,* despite its informal title, is a thorough analysis of the decline of the fishery to 1976. Information on recent years comes from conversations with Spencer Apollonio, David Getchell, formerly editor of *National Fisherman,* and from the files of that invaluable paper.

In addition to this, my own recollections of fishing out of New Harbor as a boy in the 1930s may be useful. I have no written record of these beyond what is published herewith.

TWENTY-EIGHT

Lobstering

IN COLONIAL DAYS lobsters were large, plentiful, and easily caught. They were spread on fields for fertilizer, used for bait, and scorned as poor man's food. A dead lobster decays very rapidly, cannot be salted or dried, and hence had no market.

However, in the early days of the nineteenth century Boston people developed a taste for lobster that could not be met from local supplies, so smacks with wells began transporting live lobsters from Maine. In 1835 Captain John Smith* kept six smacks busy carrying lobsters from Harpswell to Boston, and in 1841 Elisha Oakes of Vinalhaven made ten trips to Boston, with a total of 35,000 lobsters.

In 1850 lobsters could still be picked up in the rockweed at low water, but hoop nets were more efficient. A hoop net was a cone of netting, its circumference extended by an iron hoop—an old wheel tire, for instance—and the apex weighted with a rock. Across the opening was a line to which bait was tied and a bridle attached to a buoy. The net was dropped to the bottom in shoal water. After half an hour or less the fisherman hauled it rapidly to the surface. Lobsters, crabs, cunners, sculpins, and miscellaneous creatures were found in the bottom. With a dozen hoop nets, a boy could make a good start.

Lobstering was not in those times considered work for a full-time fisherman. Old men, boys, and farmers with spare time supplied the smacks. Also, lobstering was not a year-round occupation. In the summer the lobsters were shedding; their shells were soft and were too big for them, so a shedder was half salt water and considered worthless. In winter, conditions were too rugged to go on the water except on an occasional good day. It was assumed, too, that lobsters migrated offshore in winter into the deep water. Inshore fishermen did not have boats suitable for offshore winter fishing.

About 1830 the lobster trap was invented. As the market for lobster increased and the supply diminished, the lath trap came into general use. The

* No relation, so far as I know, to the entrepreneur who cruised the coast in 1614; see Chapter 3.

early ones were about 4 feet long, constructed of spruce bows and slatted with oak or spruce laths. At each end was a funnel of netting called a head. The lobster crawled in through the head but was unlikely to escape through the narrow end of the funnel. Bait was fish heads, cunners, sculpins, herring, alewives, flounders, or whatever a fisherman could find. Fifty traps took about half a barrel of bait and were all a man could tend in a day.

Traps were tended in dories and peapods, the fisherman rowing standing up and looking ahead, with oars crossed. Oarlocks or tholepins were raised above the gunwale for convenience. Some fishermen carried a mast and sail to help them out and back, and as the market improved, larger boats were developed with more or less permanent masts. The Hampton boat of Casco Bay was at first a double-ender, later with a square stern, and rigged with two spritsails. The Muscongus Bay sloop and the Down East Reach boat were other local types.

The lobster market was vastly expanded in the 1840s with the development of canneries. In 1844 William Underwood was canning lobsters in Harpswell. From 1852 to 1857 George Burnham and Samuel Rumery were canning corn and lobsters in Portland. They parted in 1867, Burnham to join with Charles Morrill and Rumery to go with the Portland Packing Company. By 1880 twenty-three coastal factories were canning lobsters, mackerel, clams, salmon, and chowder.

The lobsters, whatever their size, were first boiled and then cooled. The meat from claws and tails was extracted and the bodies were sold for fertilizer or hog feed, or were just dumped off the wharf. The Red Beach Plaster Co. in 1879–80 bought lobster shells from an Eastport factory to use in plaster.

The meat was packed in cans, sealed, boiled for an hour, and a hole punched in the can to let out the air. Then the cans were resealed, boiled two-and-a-half to three hours, cooled, cleaned with acid, painted green to prevent rusting, labeled, and packed in wooden boxes. About half the product was sold in England and Europe.

The cans were made at first by hand and then by machine, soldered up by hand, and a round hole left in the lid. This was soldered up by hand after the can was packed.

In 1880 canneries employed about 800 workers and 1,000 fishermen, but it was still a seasonal business, as shedders were not canned and winter fishing was unprofitable. The peak of cannery production came in about 1870, after which lobsters began to be scarcer and smaller, the market for live lobsters improved, and laws were passed restricting the fishing.

In the 1890s lobsters weighing less than 3 pounds counted only as half a lobster.

George Burnham remembered that in 1854, 1,200 lobsters filled a smack's well; in 1880 it took 7,000 to 8,000 lobsters to fill the same well.

In 1862 lobsters brought from 40 to 50 cents per hundredweight, 4–5-

pound lobsters were considered small, and lobsters under 2 pounds were thrown away. In the 1860s and 1870s a man could do well with 50 to 60 traps. In the 1880s he needed 75 to 90 traps.

In the 1880s the market for live lobsters wanted about 2-pound lobsters, worth 4 or 5 cents to the fisherman. Larger ones were scarce, and smaller ones were sold to the canneries at a penny a pound. A 1-pound can might contain tails and claws of as many as thirty small lobsters.

In 1887 Bristol-area smacks were paying between 3 and 4 cents a pound for market lobsters.

Between 1890 and 1900 hard lobsters were worth 10 cents apiece, and in

Above: Hauling traps from a dory, and *below,* from a sloop. *George B. Goode*

1906 on Trap Day, the January day on which the season opens on Monhegan, lobsters were 25 cents apiece.

Here we see a pattern developing which became familiar in the fishing industry. An abundant creature becomes popular. The price increases. Many fishermen go after it. Techniques improve. The creature becomes scarce. The price goes higher. More fishermen and better techniques press harder on the resource. Prices go up. Effort increases. The resource dwindles, and unless strenuous efforts at conservation are made, the creature becomes, if not extinct, at least so rare as to make its pursuit commercially unprofitable.

By the early 1870s it was evident that conservation laws were needed.

A baby lobster leads a dangerous life, even prenatally. The female mates with the male right after she sheds her shell, when she is soft and vulnerable. If she survives her soft-shell stage, she carries the sperm around within her for nine to twelve months until she lays her greenish-black eggs. From then on, the eggs cling to the underside of her tail, for another ten months. A lobster with a $3\frac{1}{4}$-inch back shell will carry about 10,000 eggs; a $4\frac{1}{2}$-inch lobster will carry 38,000. If she is caught by a Maine lobsterman while she is carrying eggs, he must cut a notch in her tail flipper and let her go. No one is allowed to possess a notched lobster, whether or not she is carrying eggs, for she is now a "breeder."

When the eggs are released, they hatch in one or two days and the baby lobsters, each about $\frac{1}{3}$ inch long, float to the surface and swim about eating plankton and being eaten by everything that eats, as well as being in danger of washing ashore or being ground up by the propellers of eager yachtsmen and busy fishermen. A major oil spill at hatching time, usually summer, would kill all the lobster larvae and the plankton on which they depend and thus wipe out a whole year's production.

After they have molted three times in two to three weeks, the little lobsters—the 1 percent that survive—sink to the bottom, hide among the rocks, and continue to grow. To reach legal size, $3\frac{1}{4}$ inches from the eye socket to the back of the back shell, takes twenty-five molts and five to seven years. The young lobsters eat crabs, snails, worms, mussels, fish, eelgrass, sea squirts, sea urchins, and occasionally each other. If they survive to legal size, 90 percent of them are caught in their first year and of the females, only 2 percent have reached sexual maturity. It is little short of miraculous that any lobsters at all survive.

The first step in conservation, made in 1872, made it illegal to take berried females, lobsters carrying eggs. This was ineffective because the fisherman scraped off the eggs and dropped the lobster in his basket. In 1874, a closed season was established from August 1 to October 15 and a minimum overall length of $10\frac{1}{2}$ inches established. In 1879 lobster canning was prohibited from August 1 to April 1.

In 1885 Maine established a Fisheries Commission, wardens were sent out to enforce the laws, and every fisherman was required to have his name carved or burned on his buoy. Laws forbade bothering other people's traps.

A backward step was taken in 1885 when factories were allowed to use lobsters over 9 inches long in season.

However, during these years the market for live lobsters improved significantly, absorbing most of the 1–2-pound lobsters. Bigger ones were too much for one person to eat at a sitting, and it was rumored that big lobsters are tough. Personal experience belies the charge.

In Canada there was almost no market for live lobsters, and a great many Canadian lobsters were available to the canneries at a low price. By 1885 sixteen of Burnham & Morrill's twenty-one lobster factories had moved to Canada, and by 1892 only eleven lobster factories were left in Maine. In 1895 the 9-inch law was repealed, and that ended lobster canning in Maine.

However, with regular steamer and rail transportation, the market for live lobsters grew rapidly in the cities. Also, the burgeoning summer population of the state increased the demand for live lobsters.

As demand increased and price increased, more people went lobstering. In 1889, 2,000 fishermen caught 25 million pounds of lobsters in 121,000 traps, an average of about 206 pounds per trap and 12,500 pounds per man. In 1898, 3,100 men caught 17.5 million pounds in 156,000 traps, an average of only 112 pounds per trap and 5,645 pounds per man.

In 1897 Francis Herrick, a biologist writing in the *Bulletin of the United States Fish Commission,* predicted coming disaster for the lobster fishery. He declared the law against taking berried females was ineffective, that the minimum size was too low to permit most of the lobsters to spawn even once, and that closed seasons had been ineffective. Raising lobsters in hatcheries was ineffective and too expensive. He recommended a 10½-inch minimum, a requirement that every trap have an escape hatch for short lobsters, and five-year closed seasons on different parts of the coast in rotation. These recommendations were too stringent to gain acceptance.

Closed seasons were abandoned. In 1907 the legal length was made 4¾ inches over the back shell, measured from the eye socket. Like earlier laws, this one was largely ignored by fishermen, who had little respect for biologists and were of an independent nature, to say the least.

In 1915 Herrick pushed for a maximum size limit as well as a minimum, a double-gauge law, to protect the big lobsters which laid more eggs. However, the law was not passed until Depression days, when big lobsters were a liability to dealers.

In 1917 all fishermen were required to have licenses, and wardens were instructed to seize short lobsters and fine those who possessed them, but there were nowhere nearly enough wardens to enforce the law.

In 1932 the legal length was reduced to 3½ inches and in 1933 to 3¹⁄₁₆, with a maximum of 4¾ inches. In 1942 the minimum was raised to 3⅛ inches and in 1957 to 3³⁄₁₆. Catches stayed high.

There has been disagreement lately with Herrick's assumption that because not enough female lobsters reach maturity, not enough lobster eggs and larvae are produced. Robert L. Dow, of the Maine Department of Marine Resources, said that the problem is less in production of eggs and larvae than in the numbers that survive due to conditions of water temperature, salinity, pollution, and predation. Although the minimum gauge size has been increased to 3¼ inches, lobster landings in Maine have held steady at about 20 million pounds a year, with about 8,000 lobstermen fishing about 2 million traps.

The maximum size has now been raised to 5 inches, despite the objections of the biologists. The fishermen claim that the big female lobsters lay many more eggs than small ones and that the big males are active breeders, stalking about the bottom fertilizing every female they find. Biologists deny this attractive scenario of ultra-Babylonian undersea orgies. They do not want an upper limit at all. They observe that very few large females are ever captured and may not even exist. A female lobster can only breed immediately after shedding. If there are large females, they shed very seldom so could breed only at long intervals. Big males cannot mate with small females; indeed, they are more likely to eat a small female shedder than to mate with her. The big male lobsters eat more of the available feed, cannibalize smaller lobsters, and are much more likely to migrate out of state than are smaller lobsters. When they migrate, they move southwest with the prevailing current. New Hampshire and Massachusetts lobstermen are very happy about Maine's double-gauge law and so are the dealers, who promoted the law in the first place and still find big lobsters hard to sell.

After World War II lobster fishermen adopted many war-related improvements. The electronic depthfinder was the first and most useful of these, for with it the fisherman could locate the underwater hills and ledges favored by lobsters without heaving a lead or a length of shafting overboard on a line and listening for the clank when it hit a rock. Radio, both CB and VHF, contributed to his safety. Radar not only helped him to keep out of trouble in the fog and brought him home safely, but if he put a small radar reflector on a buoy, his radar helped him to find his gear. Nylon pot warps are much stronger than sisal and last longer, making it possible to fish six or more traps in a string. Heads knitted of nylon last longer than tarred cotton twine. The hydraulic pot hauler, handier and more powerful than the old rear axle of a car mounted vertically, made hauling quicker, especially in deep water, and with nylon warps made it practical to fish strings. Faster boats with more powerful and reliable high-speed diesel engines enabled a fisherman to tend more traps in a day. Wire traps, introduced about 1970, found slow acceptance, but now their greater durability, lighter weight, and easier stacking have made them generally accepted.

The durability of wire traps, however, has introduced a new problem. A wooden trap, if it is washed into deep water or if the buoy is cut off, soon disintegrates. Worms eat up the laths and sills. However, wire traps keep

Conventional wooden lobster trap. *Author's collection*

Wire trap. *Author's collection*

catching lobsters even after the bait is gone. Lobsters creep in to hide, others come and cannibalize them, and crabs and other creatures that lobsters eat enter the trap, attracting more lobsters. Such a trap could go on fishing for years.

Shortly after wire traps became common, fishermen asked for a solution to this problem of ghost traps. The Maine Department of Marine Resources proposed either that a spruce slat or some other sort of biodegradable panel be included in a wire trap. This became law on January 1, 1990. Also, an escape hatch to let small lobsters out after their free lunch is now required.

The result of these improvements in technique, coupled with a demand that usually exceeds supply, has led to an increasing pressure on the resource. Stand on the shore of Maine almost anywhere, and look out over the water at more pot buoys than you can count. The hunted lobster doesn't have a chance.

The wonder is that despite this pressure, lobster landings have remained more or less stable at a little less than 20 million pounds annually. It is known that some of the offshore lobsters from Georges Banks and other offshore shoals migrate inshore, following the counterclockwise current running north toward Nova Scotia, west to the Maine coast, and southwest along the shore.

These may replenish the Maine lobster population to a considerable extent. In this respect, the double-gauge law may be useful because it keeps all but about a dozen Maine men out of offshore lobstering. If they go off to Cashes Ledge, for instance, where many of the lobsters run over 5 inches, they must sell them in New Hampshire or Massachusetts. However, there is considerable pressure on the offshore lobster population from Massachusetts and Rhode Island

Above: Inshore lobster fisherman. *Below:* Offshore lobster boat used for winter fishing. *Author's collection*

lobstermen as well as from draggers who, although they are after fish, drag up lobsters in their trawls.

If the total catch remains the same despite an increasing number of lobstermen setting more and more traps, perhaps some form of limiting the number of traps and number of fishermen would allow a limited number of fishermen to catch the same number of lobsters as are caught now with fewer traps, hence in less time and with less capital investment and greater profit to those permitted to fish.

In 1984 the Swans Island fishermen embarked on such a project. A legal boundary was drawn around their waters to keep others from encroaching, and each Swans Island fisherman was limited to 500 traps, 600 if he had a sternman. Each year the limit is to be decreased by fifty until 1988. In 1990 the limit was stabilized at 475 traps per boat, whether or not a sternman was carried. The idea is now generally accepted on Swans Island and is enthusiastically supported by many lobstermen who are indeed catching about as many lobsters with fewer traps.

Of course, such a scheme could not work if suddenly more fishermen moved to Swans Island. Some way of limiting the number of fishermen is necessary. In an island community this is done more or less informally. A new lobsterman might not be eagerly welcomed. Indeed, he might find no welcome at all. The same is true on Monhegan and Matinicus, Isle au Haut, and perhaps even on Vinalhaven.

A state law limiting the number of lobster licenses probably would never get off the ground, but with a local trap limit, legally and traditionally enforced boundaries, and the number of fishermen limited as it now is by tradition and local pressure, it might be possible to catch the same number of lobsters with less gear.

If under the present runaway system the lobster is harassed, consider the position of the modern lobsterman in competition with 7,000 men hauling 2,000,000 traps, fighting against Canadian imports which keep prices down, escalating costs of fuel, bait, gear, and bank interest. He must feel almost as badly harassed as the lobster.

The days when a man built his own traps of spruce bows and laths, knitted his own heads of cotton twine, cut out his own buoys from cedar logs, and hauled his fifty traps from a peapod or small sloop, are now long gone. The modern lobsterman is inextricably entangled in a complicated web.

If he is going to be a serious full-time fisherman, he needs a good, fast boat. Many are now built of fiberglass and powered with diesel engines. Equipped with depthfinder, CB and VHF radio, Loran, and radar, his boat bristles with antennae. He will need, too, a hydraulic pot hauler. Then, he will need somewhere near 700 traps. All 700 are not fishing at once; he needs to repair damaged ones and replace lost ones. With line, toggles, and buoys, each trap will cost about $50. He will need some kind of workshop, either at home or on a wharf; a pickup truck to move traps from shop to shore; and some kind of a landing, either a wharf of his own or landing privilege at a co-op or at a friend's wharf. By now he has at least $100,000 invested and is into the bank for a substantial part of it.

He leaves home before daylight. The law prohibits pulling traps more than half an hour before sunrise, but by that time he wants to be where his traps are. He meets other lobstermen, his friends, at coffee in the diner or on the wharf, talks of the weather, prices, bait, rows off aboard his boat, and takes off down the harbor. If there are yachts anchored there, he may go by close to one, rolling it in his wake, just to let the lazy devil know that working men are up and about.

He puts on his oil pants and rubber boots and turns up his radio—some like it hard, some like it loud, and some like it both. He finds his first buoy, gaffs it aboard, flips the warp over the davit and around the wheel of the hauler, and takes in the line, dropping it on the floor of the cockpit. The toggle comes up first—a bottle, either glass or plastic, to float the line, to keep it coming up straight from the bottom so it doesn't foul on rocks or get dragged under by the tide. Then the trap comes dripping to the rail. He hauls it aboard, opens the door, throws out weed, small crabs, sea urchins, stale bait, whatever trash has accumulated. Obviously short lobsters he throws overboard at once; doubtful ones he measures with a gauge authorized by the state; and "counters" he puts in a basket, crate, or barrel, covered to keep the sun off. From a bait barrel he seizes several pogies or redfish racks (what is left of the redfish after a fillet has been taken from each side), runs a long needle through them, threads a line through the eye of the needle, which is on the same end as the point, pulls the needle and line back through, ties the line, and closes the trap. He then revs up his engine, circles around to where he wants the trap, and pushes it overboard, letting the line run out as it came in, being careful not to get a turn around his foot; a man can get twitched overboard thus. And he is off to the next trap. If he has two or more traps on the same line, he will haul, clean, and bait them all, then push off the first one and let the line pull succeeding ones off the stern.

With radio bawling, the squawking CB tuned to other fishermen, he rushes about his day's work, for he may have 500 traps to pull scattered over square miles of ocean. He appears to ignore yachtsmen, although he is aware of them, as he is of other lobstermen, wardens, aircraft, shoals, and even the time of day. He knows when it is time to stop for a lunch and a short rest, although eager ones grab a sandwich between traps.

When the last trap is hauled, he heads for home at high speed, cleaning up his boat on the way, slows in the harbor, slides alongside the buyer's lobster car. The buyer weighs out the catch on his scale, carefully watched, and pays him in cash the established price for the day. This price is established by the trade and influenced by demand, the number of Canadian lobsters available, and the expected catch, although an individual buyer may shade it a little one way or the other.

The lobsterman then fills his fuel tank, buys a tub or two of bait, and goes off to his mooring. He still has damaged traps to repair, his boat to maintain, and such miscellaneous chores to do as he cannot dodge. It has been a day's work.

There is still paperwork to do, too, for the IRS insists on some sort of consistent records from buyer and fisherman.

Some lobstermen take a sternman, whose job is to clean and rebait the traps as they come aboard. Two men can move faster and haul more traps in a day, especially if they fish two or more traps on a string.

Laws entangle the fisherman at every turn. He must have a lobster license, the number burned into every buoy and trap. His buoys must be painted a distinctive color, registered with the state, and a buoy displayed in plain sight on his boat so wardens and everyone else can tell if he is pulling any traps but his own. His boat must be registered with the Coast Guard and the state or documented by the United States and must have a sticker showing he has paid the excise tax in his town. Larger boats must have their numbers in huge characters on the side. He is required to carry life preservers, fire extinguishers, a horn, bell, and distress signals and is subject to inspection by the Coast Guard to be sure he has them and to be ransacked for illegal drugs. He must have a license for his radio and, of course, for his truck. In most harbors he must register his mooring with the harbormaster and in some places get a license and pay a fee.

Beyond all this, there are unwritten "regulations" which he must respect. Legally, he can set his traps anywhere he wants to, but communities have drawn lines between them. Anyone who crosses these lines is likely to have his buoys cut off. Within these lines, it often appears that long-time lobstermen and their families have established "rights" to certain areas. To infringe on these leads to altercations and sometimes buoy cutting. Newcomers usually find it difficult to gain acceptance in the tight community of lobstermen unless they come from a lobstering family or have started as boys with a skiff and a few traps they have made themselves.

On top of all these pressures, what will be the reaction of a man with 500 traps to haul and a bank loan to pay off when he finds someone else has laid a string of six traps across his string and that the two have been entangled by tide and wave actions? Can you wonder that he carries a short, sharp knife under the washboard?

The lobsterman in winter faces all of the difficulties mentioned already and adds more. As water inshore becomes colder, the inshore lobsters become sluggish, burrow into the mud, and hide in the rocky ledges. They eat less and show little interest in bait. Offshore, the deep water is warmer and lobsters are still active. It is possible that some of the inshore lobsters move offshore. In either case, the fisherman now must go from 5 to 10 miles out and set in 200 feet of water or more. The days are short, and one gale often comes right on the heels of another. When the seas are rough, it is hard to find buoys, and if a trap gets caught down as a big sea comes by, either something will part or the sea comes aboard and swamps the boat. Visibility in snow or in "sea smoke"—the vapor rising from the water on a very cold day—shuts down to almost zero, and the cold wind cuts to the bone. A man is lucky if he can haul three days out of seven.

Some fishermen rig for shrimp or scallops in January, February, and the first part of March, using drags or, in the case of shrimp, occasionally wire traps. In some years this is a profitable alternative, but recently the inshore scallops have been few and the supply of shrimp varies widely from year to year.

If you know a lobsterman well enough to ask him why he continues in such a difficult, risky, capital-intensive, labor-intensive occupation, you may find that he does it because he and his family before him have been lobstermen, because he is trapped in it financially by debt, or perhaps because he likes the combination of independence and community that comes with being his own boss in companionship with an elite group of other independent people, or because he likes being on the water. He almost certainly will not say he finds it a good way to get rich. He will call his traps poverty boxes. Yet if he has a good year, if the price is not unduly depressed by Canadian imports, if gales do not wash his traps into deep water or roll them up on the beach in a ball of weed, warp, and buoys, he may make a good living.

NOTES

The best history of the lobster fishery that I have found is *Lobstering and the Maine Coast,* by Kenneth R. Martin and Nathan Lippert. A diverting and picturesque supplement to it is Mike Brown's *The Great Lobster Chase.* James M. Acheson's *The Lobster Gangs of Maine* is a sociological study of the complex web of personal relationships which limit the number of lobstermen in a community and govern far more stringently than laws can do. Cynthia Bourgeault's article "Less is More" in the 1988 *Island Journal* describes the Swans Island experiment. I am grateful to Jay Krause of the Department of Sea and Shore Fisheries for help with the (1989) status of the fishery and to Spencer Apollonio, formerly of the Sea and Shore Fisheries, for recent historical data.

While I did not quote from George Brown Goode's *The Fisheries and the Fishing Industry of the United States,* Section V, I have found it most valuable in showing the situation in 1880. Harold Clifford's *Charlie York,* reminiscences by a Boothbay fisherman, is also both interesting and useful.

I live in a lobstering community. I cannot count the lobster buoys I see from my study window. I sail among them in the summer and occasionally become fouled up in one. The owners are my neighbors. We salute each other on the water and ashore. Although we are not really intimate, for I can never be other than an outsider, I have soaked up a number of impressions, opinions, and attitudes from them which may have found a place in this chapter.

I have tried to answer in the chapter's final paragraph the question of why people go lobstering. Without being unduly sentimental or romantic, I should emphasize what I hinted at when I said that they like to be on the water.

There is a feeling to being afloat with your own boat under you, with work to do that you like to do. A man gains an independence, tempered sharply by the knowledge that he is in a hostile environment. Fog or squall can shut down on him. Gale, ice, or surf on a rocky ledge can overwhelm him, as it has overwhelmed others before him. A turn of line around his ankle, a big sea with a trap or shrimp net caught on bottom, can drown him. Fire and collision are ever-present dangers. Yet amid these perils, he has confidence, a feeling that he and his boat can handle any situation he is likely to meet today. And far in the back of his mind lurks the knowledge that if he is really in trouble, one of his friends will be able to help him, as he is ready to help them.

All this on the North Atlantic Ocean where a bit of horizon is always out there, whence comes the old southerly summer roll. The weather changes, the surface of the sea changes, the islands seem different in different lights, in different seasons. His wake scars the surface for only a moment, yet there is something of which he is a part that always stays the same. He does not talk about these feelings, but some people, seamen, I believe, are deeply moved by them.

TWENTY-NINE

The First World War

THE FOUNDATION of one of Maine's important contributions to World War I was laid long before the war started. Alessandro Fabri, a wealthy summer resident and an amateur radio enthusiast, built a powerful radio transmitting-and-receiving station at his "cottage" in Bar Harbor. In 1912 he received the tenth amateur license issued in the United States. Fabri communicated in Morse code with other American amateurs and in his effort to get greater distance, frequently communicated with ships at sea. One of his frequent contacts was with the North German Lloyd liner *Kronprinzessen Cecilie*. He had made frequent crossings in her and knew her captain and radio operator personally.

In late July 1914 before war was declared, *Kronprinzessen Cecilie* left New York with 1,216 passengers and over $13,000,000 worth of gold and silver bullion to be deposited in German banks. On July 31, two days before she was due to dock in Southampton, England, her radio operator overheard communications between a French naval vessel and the British battle cruiser *Essex* saying that *Cecilie,* "the finest prize ever open to capture," was "close by." Only a few minutes later he received a message from *Cecilie*'s owners in Germany ordering her to return to New York at once.

Captain Polack headed west at 24 knots under forced draft. He drove on through thick fog most of the way, carrying no lights and blowing no whistle, racing to keep ahead of *Essex*. On August 3, 1914, the day on which Britain and Germany went to war, *Cecilie* was off Halifax, still in the fog; and on the morning of August 4 she emerged from the fog of Frenchman Bay and anchored in Bar Harbor.

Why did Captain Polack choose Bar Harbor? With *Essex* he knew not how close astern and with war declared on August 3, the very nearest neutral port was the best and the United States was determinedly neutral. Possibly another British cruiser might guess he was headed for Boston or New York and would wait for him there. He had aboard C. Ledyard Blair, a New York and Bar Harbor yachtsman who knew Frenchman Bay well, and finally, he knew Alessandro Fabri both personally and by radio.

With *Kronprinzessen Cecilie* safely at anchor in Bar Harbor, the passengers were sent back to New York by steamer and train and the bullion was landed under heavy guard. The liner lay in Bar Harbor until November, her crew sumptuously entertained by the Fabris and other wealthy Bar Harbor residents. In November she was taken to East Boston where she lay interned until the United States entered the war in April 1917. She was then taken over by the United States government and used as a troop transport.

As soon as the United States entered the war, Fabri at once donated his 125-foot ketch *Ajax* and his radio station to the Navy. After some hesitation on the part of the Navy—hesitation overcome by Fabri's friend Franklin Roosevelt, then Assistant Secretary of the Navy—Fabri was commissioned an ensign and put in charge of the station. With the assistance and advice of Navy radio personnel, and considerable of Fabri's money, a powerful and state-of-the-art station was built on Otter Cliff, on Mount Desert.

This station received the first word of the Halifax explosion on December 7, 1917, when no other United States station could hear the crippled Halifax station. A hospital ship sailed at once for Halifax. The Otter Cliff station, NBD, regularly received messages from station YN in France, the terminal station for the American Expeditionary Force, and transmitted them to Washington by wire. Reports of submarine attacks were received from ships and sent on. Navy advisories to ships were transmitted. On October 6, 1918, the Otter Cliff station heard POZ in Germany calling station WSL on Long Island. NBD heard POZ clearly and transmitted to Washington Germany's first offer of peace.

After the Armistice, NBD continued to carry a great deal of transatlantic traffic, both commercial and official. So active was the station that a remote transmitter was built at Seawall near Southwest Harbor and the complement of the station was increased to about 200 men. Fabri was promoted to lieutenant and in 1920 was awarded the Navy Cross. The citation reads in part, ". . . it was the most important and efficient station in the world."

Fabri died in 1922, and the station was torn down in 1935 when the land was given to Acadia National Park. Some of the facilities, particularly the RDF station, were moved to Moose Island off Schoodic Point across Frenchman Bay.

Another of Maine's early contributions to the war was in shipbuilding. Although President Wilson was trying valiantly to keep the United States out of the European war, it became obvious that the Navy needed modernizing and strengthening.

The Bath Iron Works Ltd. was in 1914 the nation's foremost builder of destroyers. Founded in 1884 by General T. W. Hyde, the company had built a sound reputation for quality ships, fair dealing, and innovative engineering. The yard had built torpedo boats; destroyers; a number of very large, elegant yachts, some of them square rigged; and the battleship *Georgia*.

All these were powered with reciprocating steam engines. In 1904, anticipating an order for another naval vessel, Charles Wetherbee, superintendent of engineering at the Bath Iron Works, went to England to investigate the Parsons turbine and the Claymore boiler. The Navy, having to choose among the Parsons turbine, the Curtiss turbine, and a reciprocating engine, had three identical scout cruisers built, each with a different power plant. BIW built *Chester,* with Parsons turbines; Fore River Shipyard in Quincy, Massachusetts, built *Salem* with Curtiss turbines and *Birmingham* with reciprocating engines. The specifications called for a speed of 24 knots; *Chester* did 26½ knots. In 1909 the three cruisers raced from Newport to a turning mark off the New Jersey coast and back to New York. *Birmingham*'s engines broke down, and *Chester* beat *Salem* by almost 20 miles. *Chester* was the first turbine-powered vessel in the United States Navy. Before she was delivered, the Iron Works finished *Camden,* the first turbine-powered commercial vessel, and followed her in 1909 with *Belfast,* both built for the Eastern Steamship Company.

In 1909 the newly designed 700-ton destroyers *Flusser* and *Reid* were delivered to the Navy. Their turbine power plants, designed by Charles Wetherbee and built by the Iron Works, drove them at about 34 knots, 6 knots over the specified speed. They were the two fastest vessels in the Navy, although other yards had built 700-ton destroyers.

The Iron Works delivered eight more destroyers before 1915 including *Cassin,* the first of 1,000 tons. In 1915 came another innovation. A turbine operates most efficiently at high speeds, but a propeller at high speeds slips and cavitates excessively. The Iron Works engineered a 10:1 reduction gear whereby the turbine made 4,500 rpm and the propeller 450. The destroyer *Wadsworth,* delivered in 1915, was the first equipped with this gear. She was not only fast but at 30 knots burned 27 percent less fuel than a vessel with direct drive. At 16 knots she burned 45 percent less, thus adding substantially to her cruising radius. Following the success of *Wadsworth,* the Iron Works built two more much like her and then in 1917, *Manley,* the first of the familiar flush-decked four-pipers. During the war, eleven more four-pipers were built at Bath, the number limited by space for only four building ways in the yard.

Bath-built destroyers served as convoy escorts during the war. Afterwards, several were transferred to the Coast Guard during Prohibition to intercept rumrunners, and four were transferred to the British navy in 1940. One of these, *Buchanan,* renamed *Campbeltown,* escorted Murmansk convoys and then was chosen to block the lock gates at Saint-Nazaire, France, in March 1942 to prevent their use by the German battleship *Tirpitz.* Escorted by small MTBs and MLs, and loaded with explosives, *Campbeltown* charged into the harbor at night and rammed herself into the lock. The damage to the lock did not appear to the Germans to be crucial, and the next day they were preparing to move the destroyer out when a delayed-action bomb blew her and the lock gates sky high.

Five of the Bath-built destroyers served in the United States Navy in World War II. *Pruitt, Sicard,* and *Preble,* the last three built, survived until 1946.

Destroyer *Pruitt,* built in 1920, served continuously until 1946. *Bath Iron Works*

During World War I the Iron Works built two yachts, both of which were in naval service. One of these, the 224-foot steel *Winchester,* steam-turbine powered, was first used by her owner, P. W. Rouse, to commute from his Newport cottage to his New York office; in *Winchester* he could beat the trains. He sold her to the Navy when the United States entered the war in 1917. She was used as a patrol boat and as a testing craft for minesweeping gear. After the war she was used as a yacht again until World War II, during which she served in the Canadian navy as a patrol boat and after that was again used as a yacht. She disappeared from *Lloyd's Register* in 1957.

Another yacht was *Isabel,* a 230-foot turbine-powered yacht built for J. N. Willys, manufacturer of the Willys automobile. Before she was finished, the United States entered the war, and Willys sold her to the Navy. She was commissioned a destroyer and did convoy duty in the Western Approaches. After the war she was a tender to the NC flying boats. She was later sent to China as flagship of the Admiral of the Asiatic fleet. She was relieved by *Houston* and was in Manchu on Pearl Harbor Day, fought through the East Indies, and got to Australia where she served as a vessel to train crews in antisubmarine work. She was not scrapped until 1946.

With German merchant ships driven from the seas very early in the war and the British merchant marine largely occupied in war work, there was an increasing demand for merchant shipping. The United States merchant marine carried only 10 percent of the nation's commerce, most of that coastwise. Congress, seeing the need to expand the United States merchant marine rapidly, established in 1916 the United States Shipping Board to form corporations to build, buy, charter, and operate United States merchant ships. At first American yards were reluctant to commit capital to expansion, fearing a short war and a quick collapse of the demand for ships.

However, the Texas Company in 1916 bought the yard of the old New England Company* in Bath and leased the Sewall yard which had built the large steel Downeasters *Dirigo, Erskine M. Phelps, Arthur Sewall, Edward Sewall, William P. Frye,* the five-masted steel schooner *Kineo,* and the three big steel tank barges, the last in 1906. Here the Texas Company built thirty-five steel vessels between 1916 and 1921 including six freighters, fourteen tankers, six tugs, and nine tank barges.

Ten days after the United States entered the war on April 6, 1917, the United States Shipping Board established the Emergency Fleet Corporation to control all merchant ship building, and on July 11, 1917, President Wilson requisitioned all steel vessels under construction. The Texas Company had eight on the ways.

The Emergency Fleet Corporation also planned to have built a number of wooden freighters. General Goethals insisted that all be built to the Ferris design, which was merely a copy of a steel ship and not adapted to wooden construction. Trees to supply the very large timbers this design required no longer grew in Maine, and importation from the West Coast was too expensive. Although some Ferris steamers were built on the Gulf Coast and many on the West Coast, none were built in Maine.

Instead, Maine's yards turned back to the construction of wooden three- and four-masted schooners which could carry freight profitably at the inflated wartime freight rates. Between 1914 and 1920 at least 100 of these vessels were built along the Maine coast: Bath built twenty-seven, as well as nine schooner-rigged barges; Boothbay, fourteen; Newcastle, six; Thomaston, ten; Rockland, nine; Camden-Rockport, ten; Belfast, two; Stockton, five; Bangor region, three; Machias, five; Harrington, six; Milbridge, four; Eastport, one; and Dennysville, two. For a comment on the reliability of these figures, see the chapter notes.

The vessels built early in the war more than paid for themselves, but those not launched until 1920 were, on the whole, losers, as freight rates collapsed after the war. A few vessels operated profitably up until World War II, but most were laid up and eventually abandoned. Their stories have been told in Chapter 25.

At sea the Germans were slow to attack American ships. On January 28, 1915, the German raider *Prinz Eitel Friedrich* sank the Bath-built Downeaster *William P. Frye* in the South Atlantic. The United States was still a neutral country in the European war, but the *Frye* was sunk because her cargo of wheat

*The New England Company built tugs, steamers, and big schooners of wood.

was consigned to "Queenstown, Falmouth, or Plymouth for orders." Plymouth was a fortified town, and as Captain Thierechens interpreted international law, food consigned to a fortified town was contraband. He ordered the grain thrown overboard, but the process was too slow, so he sank the *Frye*.

He took all the crew aboard the *Eitel* and ran for Hampton Roads to put them and other prisoners ashore and to refit. The United States government saw the sinking of the *Frye* as unjustified; the *Frye*'s stockholders called it piracy. The German government had issued a prize order on August 3, 1914, about which Captain Thierechens had not heard, saying that cargoes of food to a fortified port were *not* contraband. The German government agreed to pay for the ship and cargo, although the amount was still being negotiated when the United States entered the war in 1917.

Nevertheless, in spite of the universal agreement that the sinking was unjustified, a wave of sympathy washed over the *Eitel*. No one had been killed or hurt. The crews of the ships the raider had sunk had been well treated. The Germans had admitted they were wrong. The crew of the *Frye* gave eight kegs of beer to the crew of the *Eitel*. The *Literary Digest* proclaimed, "Romance has returned to the merchant marine." Hundreds of letters were written to Captain Thierechens. The *Eitel* was admitted to a dockyard for repairs. When she was ready to leave, Thierechens learned that five British warships were waiting for her outside Chesapeake Bay, so he applied for internment. His application was accepted. Not until May 1915, when 124 Americans were lost on the *Lusitania*, did public opinion turn powerfully against Germany.

After war was declared in April 1917, six German submarines attacked shipping on the East Coast, but few came to Maine waters. One that did was *U-156*. She stopped the fishing schooner *Robert and Richard* 60 miles southeast of Cape Porpoise. The crew were taken aboard the submarine while the schooner was being sunk. The submarine's first officer said he had had a summer home in Maine since 1896 and took the schooner's American flag to fly over it after the war. Another officer had been a towboat captain on the Maine coast. The twenty-three fishermen were released in their five dories, set sails, and headed for the coast. One dory made Kennebunk, and the others were picked up as they approached Portland.

The submarine next was reported off Delaware Bay but returned to Maine and hovered 3 miles off Portland looking for quarry. None appeared, so she went east and torpedoed the Canadian schooner *Dornfontein,* loaded with lumber. The vessel was set afire and the crew freed to row ashore on Grand Manan Island; they were picked up by a patrol boat out of Machias. The schooner burned to the water's edge but, being loaded with lumber, did not sink. She was towed in to Rumery Bay near Eastport.

Then *U-156* rounded Cape Sable and captured the Canadian steam trawler *Triumph*. While the crew of *Triumph* was entertained genially aboard the submarine with brandy and cigars, the German crew put two 3-pounders and ammunition aboard *Triumph,* hoisted the German flag, and, shadowed by the submarine, set out on a voyage of destruction among the fishing fleet on Western Bank. The Canadian crew rowed ashore.

Having wiped out the fishing fleet on the Western and La Have banks, *U-156* went on to the Grand Banks and sank more fishermen. The purpose of attacking fishermen was to interfere with the United States food supply and to divert U.S. naval vessels from European waters. All told, *U-156* sank thirty-four merchant ships and twenty schooners. *Triumph* was scuttled when the submarine was ready to return to Germany.

Other submarines were on the coast, too. Three schooners were sunk by *U-157* in one day off Winter Quarter Shoal lightship between the Virginia capes and Delaware Bay. Two of their captains, Holbrook of *Hattie Dunn* and Gilmore of *Edna,* met aboard the submarine. They had been boyhood friends in St. George, Maine, and had not seen each other for years.

After attacking and decimating the Georges Bank fishing fleet, *U-117* moved south to lay mines off American harbors. The battle cruiser *San Diego* was one of her victims. Altogether, *U-117* sank twenty-one ships. Also, *U-155* attacked fishermen and patrolled off the mid-Atlantic coast; *U-140* and *U-152* operated far to the south of Maine.

Although many fishing vessels were sunk and many more stayed in port for fear of being sunk, it appears that the submarine war on the Atlantic coast was overall a failure for the Germans. America's food supply was not seriously affected, naval units were not drawn away from convoy duty, and no east-bound American troop transports were sunk.

Of course, a great many men from the Maine coast joined the Army and Navy and served with distinction, but their exploits, unless performed near home, are not properly a part of this book.

After the war, freight rates collapsed, building contracts were canceled, and very few new vessels were built. Coastal towns turned to fish, lobsters, and summer people. The Texas Company closed its Bath yard. The Bath Iron Works fell on hard times after they finished the last of the World War I destroyers and the Washington Naval Treaty of 1922 put an end to naval construction. BIW built two 13,000-ton colliers but lost heavily on them because, being bigger than anything built thus far, they required considerable capital investment. Then the Iron Works built six steel lightships. From 1922 to 1944 the yard built two small passenger steamers, *Nobska* and *Islander,* and turbines and condensers for the Eastern Steamship vessels *Boston* and *New York.* Pressed hard for any work at all, the yard built sixteen wooden 58-foot Seawanhaka schooners, one Six-Meter sloop, two wooden express cruisers of 49 and 64 feet, and one 127-foot gasoline-powered steel yacht, *Aras.*

The yard took what work it could get, including repairing paper-mill machinery and rebuilding locomotives. They had a small contract for can buoys and even one for milk cans. In spite of desperate hard work, the Bath Iron Works Ltd. went under in October 1925 and was bought at auction by one Friedburg for $218,100.

It looked like the end of shipbuilding in Bath. Friedburg sold off the machinery and in July 1927 sold the land and buildings to the New England Public Service Company, a subsidiary of Central Maine Power. The property was sold again in 1927 to the Keyes Fibre Company, which planned to use the site for the manufacture of paper plates. This was about as low as a shipyard could sink.

At this point, William S. "Pete" Newell took a hand. He was a man with sound engineering education, broad experience, and immense energy. An MIT graduate and former faculty member, he had been to sea in a four-masted schooner and in a steamer as cadet engineer. He had worked at BIW as a riveter and as a draftsman and with Charles Wetherbee as a designer and engineer. During BIW's last years he was engineering and works manager. After a short spell with Cox & Stevens, he became general manager of New York Shipbuilding Company in Camden, New Jersey. He didn't like it; neither did his wife Caroline, a Bath woman.

On October 1, 1927, backed by Archibald Main, Eugene Thebeau, Wyman of Central Maine Power Co., Frederick H. Low, and especially by Joseph MacDonald, president of Henry Gielow, a distinguished New York naval architect firm, Newell bought back what was left of the Bath Iron Works. He and Joseph MacDonald were disturbed by contracts for large, expensive American yachts going to European firms and believed a rejuvenated Bath Iron Works could build them profitably at a lower price.

On October 1, 1927 the Bath Iron Works Corporation was incorporated and on November 18 signed a contract to build a 240-foot steel diesel yacht, *Vanda,* for Ernest B. Dane of Brookline, Massachusetts. She was to be built on a cost-plus-overhead basis with no margin of profit.

Newell bought machinery from the defunct Cramp yard in Philadelphia on time, hired a work force, and went to it. Before *Vanda* was delivered in April 1929, a diesel tug for the Venezuela Gulf Oil Co. was finished along with three 124-foot trawlers.

On increasingly secure financial foundations, the new Iron Works built a succession of big diesel yachts all well over 100 feet. The biggest and best-known was *Corsair IV,* 343 feet long, 3,080 tons, built for New York financier J. P. Morgan in 1930. A magnificent model of her dominates the hall of the Maine Maritime Museum in Bath. *Corsair* served in the Royal Navy from 1940 until the end of World War II, then became a cruise ship, ran aground, and was lost near Acapulco in 1949 and her machinery incorporated as part of that city's power plant. Most of the other sixteen yachts built before 1932 were later taken over for naval service in World War II.

Besides yachts, the Bath Iron Works built five trawlers and seven Coast Guard cutters, keeping up its reputation for first-class work at a reasonable price. It was ready when naval expansion was started well before World War II.

NOTES

The information on the Bar Harbor radio station is from *The Fabulous Radio NBD,* a pamphlet by Brandon Wentworth. *Down East* magazine for August 1959 has a short piece on *Kronprinzessen Cecilie,* but the pamphlet is more complete.

The Moose Island station has been discontinued and a far more elaborate long-wave station established on Thornton Point in Machias Bay near Cutler.

William A. Baker's *Maritime History of Bath* and Ralph Snow's *Bath Iron Works* have more information on the destroyer program than can be easily digested, but the latter especially is easy reading with considerable picturesque detail.

J. Russell Smith in *The Influence of the Great War Upon Shipping* mentions Goethal's decision.

The figures on the construction of schooners are sadly incomplete. William Fairburn admits that his figures are unreliable. Harold Clifford's *The Boothbay Region 1906–1960* supplements Fairburn to give a figure for Boothbay, and Barbara Dyer's *Grog Ho* does the same for Camden. *Sailing Days on the Penobscot,* by George Wasson and Lincoln Colcord, agrees pretty well with Fairburn but not with others, and it adds places Fairburn does not mention. However, whether one schooner or five schooners more or less were built in one town or another is, for the purposes of this chapter, not especially important. The point is that to fill the shipping needs of the nation, Maine went back to wooden sailing ships.

The story of *Prinz Eitel Friedrich* and *William P. Frye* is in *American Neptune,* Volume XLV, No. 3.

Accounts of the German U-boat cruises come mostly from *When the U-Boats Came to America,* by William Bell Clark, and *German Subs in Yankee Waters,* by Henry J. James.

The story of the collapse and subsequent rise of the Bath Iron Works under William S. "Pete" Newell is a dramatic tale of business administration and relates only tangentially to maritime history. For a fuller account, see Snow's book.

THIRTY

World War II

IN OCTOBER 1934 the Bath Iron Works delivered to the Navy the destroyer *Dewey,* first of a new class of bigger, faster destroyers. Despite efforts to save weight by building the deck structures of aluminum, when overloaded with antiaircraft and antisubmarine weapons and radar antennae for which they were not designed, destroyers of this class were tender. Two were lost in a Pacific typhoon, although *Dewey* herself weathered the same storm.

In 1936 two *Mahan*-class destroyers were built with better, faster turbines. At well over 40 knots *Drayton* and *Lamson* were the fastest destroyers ever built for the United States Navy.

Through the years preceding Pearl Harbor, Bath continued to get contracts for more heavily armed and bigger destroyers, all of which served in World War II. Bath engineers, working with marine architects and engineers at Gibbs & Cox in New York, did much of the design work, especially when Bath was awarded a lead ship, first of her class. Innovation was a specialty at BIW.

Starling Burgess, successful as a yacht designer, one of the most imaginative, if eccentric, men in the profession, worked at Bath with BIW engineers in developing plans for a 285-foot aluminum destroyer of simple V-bottomed design capable of 50 knots. He built a prototype of wood, and when *Drayton* was on speed trials, the prototype literally ran a circle around her. As war came closer, however, the necessity for ships-in-a-hurry and the scarcity of aluminum for aircraft pushed this promising project aside and the Burgess-designed destroyer was never built.

Another of Burgess's designs, the *America*'s Cup defender *Ranger,* was built at Bath for Harold S. Vanderbilt. We will tell her story in the next chapter.

By 1938 the Bath Iron Works Corporation was on solid financial ground, but the need for capital improvements to meet increased production led Pete Newell and his staff to "go public," and to sell stock in the corporation.

In 1940, seeing the need for space to prefabricate parts of vessels, the

Harding plant was built in West Bath. Pete Newell's son John was largely responsible for this project.

The Bath yard was expanded from six building ways to eight. A large building was built for preassembling sections of vessels and then having them lifted into place with a crane and welded together. Plans were standardized so a gang could concentrate on one section—say, the bow of a destroyer—and, when it was done, start another identical bow for another identical ship rather than shift from one task to another. With production thus streamlined, in spite of increases in the size of vessels, the Iron Works built thirty-one 2,100-ton

USS *Drayton*—at 43 knots, one of the fastest destroyers built for the United States Navy. *Douglas photo, George I. Hodgdon, Jr.*

destroyers, twenty destroyers of 2,200 tons, and thirty-one of 2,250 tons. Machinery was standardized among different manufacturers, and with the designs standardized not only from vessel to vessel but from yard to yard, the time for building a destroyer was rapidly cut. The first 2,100-ton destroyer built in 1941 took 1,354,000 man-hours; the last, built in 1943, took 990,000. The last 2,250-ton vessel was built in 677,262 man-hours. The time from keel-laying to delivery was cut from 700 days to 210 days.

USS *Nicholas* on her builder's trials. Radar and AA armament has not been installed. Built in 1942, she served through World War II, the Korean War, and the Vietnam War. *Douglas photo, author's collection*

A Liberty ship fitting out at the West Yard in Portland. *Maine Maritime Museum*

In 1943 and 1944 the Iron Works was delivering twenty-one destroyers a year, one every seventeen days. The yard built eighty-three destroyers, four 11,750-ton cargo vessels, and one yacht from January 1, 1939, to December 31, 1945.

Bath-built destroyers served in all parts of the world, from Guadalcanal to Normandy and back to the Pacific. Bath destroyers were present in Tokyo Bay at the Japanese surrender. Several went on to serve off Korea and Vietnam.

The building of merchant ships was another of Maine's contributions to victory at sea in World War II. Congress recognized in the 1930s that the United States was carrying very little of its own commerce and needed a viable merchant marine both for peacetime commerce and as a naval auxiliary. In 1936 it established the U.S. Maritime Commission to bring this about by the construction and chartering of vessels, by subsidies for building and operating vessels, and by crew-training schools.

When in 1940 the submarine war escalated and Britain was losing ships at an alarming rate, the British sent a commission under R. C. Thompson to the United States to contract for sixty 10,000-ton freighters of shoal draft and comparatively narrow beam so they could use small British harbors less likely to be attacked by Hitler's bombers.

To speed production and to keep the ships simple to operate, they were to have Scotch fire-tube boilers with triple-expansion reciprocating engines, a simple power plant familiar to British marine engineers. Because sufficient coal was available in Britain for a round-trip voyage to a United States port, they were to burn coal. Henry J. Kaiser's Todd Shipyards agreed to build the ships but had no yards available in which to do it. The Bath Iron Works was busy with destroyers and had two Maritime Commission merchant ships on the ways, but Pete Newell, through his association with Gibbs & Cox, who were redesigning the British plans for welded construction, suggested to Kaiser that South Portland would be an ideal site and that the Bath Iron Works Corporation could build the yard and thirty of the ships. Accordingly, the Todd-Bath Iron Works Corporation was established.

R. C. Thompson returned to England with the new plans and contracts. His ship was torpedoed en route, but he threw his briefcase with the plans into a lifeboat, climbed in after them, and arrived safely. On December 20, 1940, the British government signed the contract for sixty ships with Todd Shipyards. Work started at once on the South Portland yard and on one in Richmond, California.

The South Portland site, what came to be known as the East Yard, was unique in having a solid rock ledge under about 20 feet of sand and mud. A coffer dam was built to keep out the harbor water, and the sand and mud was excavated. Building ways for seven ships were set up so the vessels could be built in basins below sea level, the basins flooded, and the ships floated out instead of being launched in the usual way. This meant that with the ships below the surrounding shore, materials could move downhill from fabricating shop to ship. Workers were more or less protected from wind and weather, and ships could be built level rather than inclined toward the water. Furthermore, no launching ways or elaborate launching cradle need be built. With the basin flooded, the completed hull would be floated off the keel blocks and towed out to the fitting-out pier. With the gates closed and the basin pumped out, a new keel could be laid on the same blocks at once.

Work was started on January 3, 1941, and pushed forward night and day. In four weeks the coffer dam was built. Before the end of April, the sand and mud had been excavated. In May 1941 the first keel was laid. The administration building was finished in June. In July, six more keels were laid, and the plate shop was ready. The machine shop was ready in September. In February 1941 a free school for welders had been established, and its graduates were put to work at once. On December 20, 1941, the first two ships were floated and towed to the new 1,000-foot fitting-out pier. In February 1942 the first ship, *Ocean Liberty,* sailed from Portland for Britain fully loaded, and on November 18, 1942, the thirtieth ship, *Ocean Glory,* sailed.

These vessels, called the Ocean class, were stout ships, among the first ships to have their plating welded together, although the plating was still riveted to the frames. Unlike welded ships from other yards, none of these broke in half or developed serious cracks. Eleven were bombed, torpedoed, or sunk by shellfire. Three went ashore, one was sold to China and one to the U.S.S.R., and fourteen survived, to be scrapped in the 1960s. *Ocean Rider* took a torpedo in her forward hold but survived. *Ocean Glory,* loaded with gasoline, was set afire at the invasion of Sicily and was sunk by an Allied destroyer; "but anyone seeing the pounding she got before she went down would get an awful lot of confidence in welded jobs," wrote her skipper.

Ocean Faith, loaded with ammunition, was hit by a bomb in her forward hold and set afire. Her crew boldly attacked the fire and put it out, only to find 20 feet of water in the hold. This they pumped out by hand, and they limped into a port, where a patch was fitted over the leak. The patch came adrift, but they pumped their way to their destination and delivered their cargo.

The speed with which these ships were built was also impressive. In World War I, four months had been a record-breaking time for the construction of a 10,000-ton freighter. South Portland's fastest time for building the Ocean-class ships from keel-laying to delivery was ninety-seven days, fifty-eight days from keel-laying to launching. It was expected that it would take twenty-four months to build the thirty ships, but the job was done in twenty-two-and-a-half months, after a slow start in a yard still under construction.

This kind of quality and speed could not have been accomplished without a committed work force. Workers often traveled 40 or 50 miles each way to work in the yard, and most of them knew nothing of building steel ships. A few experienced men, mostly foremen or leading men, were brought from Bath, but all the rest had to be trained or learn on the job.

In the spring of 1941, with the East Yard already building ships for

Britain, it became obvious to the Maritime Commission that the United States was soon going to need a great many more ships very soon. The Commission favored the C-2 and C-3 cargo ships, for they were bigger than the Ocean class, and faster. However, they were also turbine powered and far more complicated to build and operate. With ships being torpedoed at an increasing rate, rapid production was essential. Therefore the Commission settled on the Liberty ship, much like the Ocean class.

The Liberty ship was a great steel box 441 feet long, 57 feet wide, the same as the Ocean ships. Like them she was driven by a triple-expansion reciprocating steam engine, but steam came from an oil-fired water-tube boiler. There were a few other differences: The Liberty ships had one house amidships where the crew lived. They had solid bulwarks to protect deck cargo, instead of chain rails, and they carried masts instead of kingposts for handling cargo. A CO_2 fire-fighting system was included because the boilers were oil fired, and hatch covers were of wood to serve as liferafts.

Equipment was whittled to a minimum. No forced ventilation was provided in living spaces or cargo holds. A fathometer was included, to help the navigator because degaussing to protect against magnetic mines rendered a magnetic compass useless and gyro compasses were not available. Anchor chains were reduced from two of 240 fathoms to one of 135 fathoms and one of 75 fathoms. Some Liberty ships were sent to sea with only one anchor. The heavy, vertical door from the shaft alley to the engineroom, which penetrated a watertight bulkhead, was omitted to retain the bulkhead's integrity because oilers often left the door open and enginerooms had been flooded through the vulnerable shaft alley. Oilers thus had to go on deck and descend aft of the bulkhead to oil the shaft, such a nuisance that the shaft was not always properly lubricated. In later vessels a small hinged door was included.

To build some of these ships, Newell was asked to establish a new yard in South Portland next to the already active East Yard. Although up to his ears in destroyer production at Bath and building for the British in South Portland, he agreed, and the South Portland Shipbuilding Corporation was established on April 28, 1941, the management consisting of the same men who were running the East Yard under the name of the Todd-Bath Iron Works Corporation.

Construction started immediately on a new yard with four building ways from which ships would be launched in the conventional manner. The four ways were built and ships were under construction on them when the Maritime Commission demanded in October 1941 that the yard be expanded to six ways. This decision slowed production on the ships because material for the new ways had to be carried across the existing ways and the construction of the ships interfered with construction of the new facilities. And there were other difficulties, too. The Harding plant in West Bath could not do the fabrication for destroyers in Bath, seven British Ocean ships in the East Yard, and now six Liberty ships in the West Yard. Progress was slow; steel backed up in the storage yard in Portland. Congressmen investigated the slowdown and found or professed to find culpable financial irregularities, nepotism, and ineffective supervision in the West Yard. There is no doubt that the rapid expansion led to stretching the management too thin and that divided responsibility among the Maritime Commission, the Bath Iron Works Corporation, the Todd-Bath Iron Works Corporation, and the South Portland Shipbuilding Corporation led to confusion, even though the three corporations were run by the same people at the top. Also, the rapid expansion led to the employment of inexperienced supervisors and a great many workers with no knowledge of steel ship building. By early 1942 the situation at the West Yard was at best a tangled one.

The Maritime Commission took over with a heavy hand. It appointed Karl E. Klitgaard deputy president of the South Portland yard and took the land between the East Yard and the West Yard by eminent domain, dispossessing 140 homeowners, to build storage, fabricating, and preassembly facilities. Also they ran a railroad spur along South Portland's shore. These decisions enraged South Portland residents and their representative in Congress, who continued to stir the pot, bringing to the surface unfavorable comparisons with California yards.

Klitgaard moved decisively, replaced many of the inefficient supervisors, hustled production of the fabrication shop, and developed preassembly techniques whereby whole sections of a ship could be built in the shop, lifted into place by cranes, and welded together. This meant that more people could work on a ship at the same time. While 710 people worked on a ship in South Portland, in Oregon, where the preassembly method was followed, 2,400 men worked on one ship. Also the work went more quickly because workers could get at the sections of a ship more easily, did not have to weld over their heads or in so many tight and awkward places. Even pipefitting and wiring could be done before the sections were welded in place.

Klitgaard also had to deal with labor troubles because the Bath Iron Works was under an independent union, the East Yard was under CIO, and the West Yard was under AF of L. Each labor organization was trying to recruit the two yards not under its flag, which led to a strike in the West Yard in October 1942 and in the East Yard in November. Klitgaard was at a serious disadvantage because he had jurisdiction over only the West Yard.

In November 1942 the last Ocean freighter was delivered. The British sold the East Yard to the Maritime Commission, and the two yards were merged under a new entity, the New England Shipbuilding Corporation.

Under unified management, with its own fabrication and preassembly shops, with construction of the West Yard completed, the railroad spur operating, and with improved and now more experienced management, production picked up. By the end of its production in May 1945, the West Yard had built 112 Liberty ships and the average man-hours per ship had dropped from 996,400 hours to 410,000. The East Yard built 30 Ocean-class freighters and

132 Liberty ships with even fewer average man-hours per ship than in the West Yard.

Man-hours is a term used by accountants, but at least half our readers will be interested to note that a great many of those hours may be attributed to women. Beginning in September 1942 if not before, women were working as burners and tackers, cutting steel plate with oxyacetylene torches and tack-welding plates in position, and later as welders, pipefitters, and in other trades, including crane operators. Of the 20,000 people employed at the East and West Yards, at least 3,700 were women.

In the final accounting, the South Portland yard kept up with the Todd yard in California. The thirty Ocean ships were delivered in twenty-two-and-a-half months, one-and-a-half months ahead of schedule. South Portland's average time to build a ship was 124 days, four days better than California's 128. South Portland's fastest time from keel-laying to delivery was ninety-seven days, only one day ahead of California's, but certainly not behind.

There was also a need for wooden vessels, and Maine's smaller yards experienced in wooden ship building responded quickly. Under the Maritime Commission, yards at South Freeport, South Gardiner, Camden, and Belfast built 134-foot, 1,500-ton wooden barges, and at least eighteen other yards were active with Navy contracts. The chapter notes show a summary of wooden vessels built by these yards, from 10-foot pine skiffs classified as workboats to oceangoing minesweepers, transports, and patrol boats.

Men and women who worked in these yards may disagree heartily with these figures, declaring the Maine wooden boat effort much understated. These people are undoubtedly correct, for they were there—joining the timbers, spiling the planks, driving the fastenings, and caulking the seams. The above figures came from fragmentary records but serve to show that Maine's smaller wooden yards were very actively engaged in America's war effort and deserve their shares of the victory. Some of their vessels, seven APCs from Camden and one from Damariscotta, were taken through the Panama Canal to Bora Bora, Samoa, Fiji, New Caledonia, and Sydney. These vessels then operated along the New Guinea coast, supporting progressive island invasions.

Enemy activity started along the Maine coast well before Pearl Harbor, although from what is known about German plots, they were inept and failed to gain any support from Germany. They centered around the activities of Bruno D. Lever* and Harold W. Coffin. The latter was a reserve officer in Army Intelligence working for the power company in Bangor.

In the spring of 1940, two University of Maine radio amateurs intercepted a German broadcast ordering German agents to prepare to carry out a prearranged program. They reported this to the intelligence office in Bangor. Shortly afterwards the electric company got a call from Gustav Jensen* for

*This is a fictitious name used by Coffin. It is not the name by which the man was known in Maine. See the chapter notes.

underground service to his newly built house in the woods, close to the junction of Route 1 and the road down to Hancock Point and with access to deep water at Kilkenny Cove on the Skillings River. Jensen claimed to be a third-generation Norwegian with a German wife and a nine-year-old son. Coffin could see no reason for expensive underground service to Jensen's cottage except concealment, became suspicious, and kept an eye on the place. He found nothing conclusive but noticed that Jensen had his name on both sides of his mailbox although the mailman always left the mail southbound and all the other boxes had names on the north side only. Could it be for the benefit of someone coming up from the shore? Twice in the ensuing summer a seaplane landed on the Skillings River near Jensen's and two men walked up to Jensen's cabin. Jensen explored the river, dug clams, and shot ducks. Mrs.

A wooden coastal transport of a type built by many Maine yards during World War II. *George I. Hodgdon, Jr.*

A non-magnetic minesweeper built during the Korean War. *George I. Hodgdon, Jr.*

Jensen in an Ellsworth market was quoted as saying, in 1940, "My sister knows der Fuehrer and der Fuehrer says. . . ." The boy refused to salute the American flag in school. Such "evidence" is inconclusive, but in tense times arouses suspicion.

Then in July 1940 Bruno D. Lever visited Jensen and drove to Ellsworth with him to take a driving test for a Maine license. Lever said he was an officer in the Luftwaffe and showed an identification card to prove it. Coffin checked up on Lever and found he had told a Boston couple that he had been in the German army in World War I, had graduated from Heidelberg University, had done post-graduate work in the United States, and was an expert telegrapher. A nurse said she had been impressed with his knowledge of bacteriology and botany. He claimed to be working for a company that bought old quarry machinery for junk.

The ever-suspicious Coffin with his intelligence unit in Bangor considered what sort of activity the Germans might be planning for the Maine coast—probably not a full-scale invasion. They might, however, be looking for a place through which to introduce spies or saboteurs and perhaps a base from which to supply submarines. Such a place, reasoned the intelligence people, would have to be isolated, have access to deep water, proximity to a paved road leading to bus or railroad connections, a wharf, a building for storage and residence, and German sympathizers nearby. Few places west of Schoodic afforded isolation and a wharf. However, at Lang's quarry on Pleasant Bay on the east side of Cape Split in the town of South Addison, these considerations were met, and there Coffin found Bruno D. Lever.

The quarry had been established in 1905 by Lang, a German stonecutter and monument maker with a shop in Brooklyn, as a source of black granite for his business. Lang abandoned the granite project but in 1911 tried again, without success. In 1931 he bought an old three-masted schooner, *Dorothy,* and used her masts to replace his ancient derricks, then scuttled her for a breakwater. He brought in quarry machinery, and a crew of German stonecutters with their families. They built a big cutting shed and a tight administration building. Coffin was called in to set up electric service. However, the granite project still was a loser.

Lang got an RFC loan in 1938, it was foreclosed in 1939, and Lang sold the quarry in 1940 to whomever Lever represented—at one time a New York firm, at another a Philadelphia firm. Lever had a telephone installed and the electric power increased to handle an electric winch on the derrick.

Local people grew suspicious of the German families living there in 1940 and called the State Police. Lever told them his name was Kirk and boasted of his Scotch-Irish ancestry.

In mid-September 1940 the schooner *Rebecca R. Douglas* took 400 tons of scrap from the quarry to Jersey City, and on September 26 the schooner *Anna Sophia,* which had once belonged to Lang and was owned in 1940 by the C & S Navigation Company, came in to load scrap. The C & S Navigation

Company was as mysterious as Kirk / Lever and the two companies said to own the quarry. *Anna Sophia* had a large crew of Germans, a diesel engine, a coppered bottom, and an Oriental cook who was an avid photographer. On September 29 the immigration officials came to inspect the cook's papers, but *Anna Sophia* had left—without the scrap. On October 20 she sailed from Philadelphia for La Guaira, loaded with dynamite.

On October 28, 1940, Lever ordered the power turned off, to be turned on again in the spring, and disappeared, having made no progress organizing a Fifth Column in the Jonesport region.

Coffin suspected Lever was organizing a German "cell" as a base for submarines and saboteurs.

In March 1942, after Pearl Harbor, when the United States was at war with the Nazis, Coffin returned to Cape Split and found a resident German, one of Lang's former quarry workers, building a boat.

Later in the spring a crew of Germans from the Lane Lifeboat & Davit Co. of Flushing, Long Island, appeared, claiming to have taken over from the illusory Philadelphia salvage company, and prepared to remove the rest of the useless quarry machinery. A United States combat team patrolled the area, and one of its members was fired on. Immediate search revealed nothing suspicious but a carbon electrode in the cabin of the wrecked schooner. On August 14, 1942, Coffin visited the quarry with the combat team and found lobster traps with buoys painted red, white, and black—German colors. He speculated that they might be used to buoy a channel up the bay for a submarine; no one was working hard at lobstering or quarrying.

A few nights before, a submarine had been sighted off Big Nash Island and the Navy had "established a good contact," a phrase meaning that they rather thought they had sunk it. Coffin visited Big Nash Island a day or so later and found pieces of cork and asphalt, used to line submarines. Naval Intelligence told Coffin that it confirmed the report of successful action with a German submarine.

The Aircraft Warning Service at Cape Split had reported flash signals from east of Big Nash Island, and lighthouse keepers at Nash Island and Moose Peak had reported the sound of diesel engines.

On another night, Naval Intelligence predicted a submarine would appear, and indeed, one surfaced about 10 miles from Nash Island. Jeep patrols watched Lang's quarry carefully but saw no signals.

In February 1943 the quarry was inspected again. It was deserted, the crane was gone, the machine shop bare, the buildings locked, the houses deserted, and no boat in sight. In the cabin of the schooner the Combat Patrol found several cans of electrodes such as might be used in a projector to focus a high-intensity narrow beam through a window in the schooner's cabin. That seemed to close the action at Lang's quarry. If it was a plot to establish a German base of sorts, it was very clumsily done and, so far as is known, accomplished very little, but it does suggest some enemy action. However, see the chapter notes for another view of the matter.

More definite was the activity at Hancock Point, near Jensen's house. On November 29, 1944, a German submarine lay all day on the bottom on Cod Ledge about 2 miles off Otter Cliff on Mount Desert Island. After dark it surfaced, crept in by Egg Rock, and close to midnight set ashore two men in a rubber boat on the west shore of Hancock Point. It was snowing lightly.

Harvard Hodgkins, high school student, Eagle Scout, son of a deputy sheriff, was driving down Hancock Point alone, coming home from a dance. He met two men coming toward him dressed in city clothes and carrying suitcases. He drove by them far enough so they could not see that he had stopped and followed their tracks back to where they had come up to the road from the shore through the brush.

In the morning he and his father followed the tracks to the shore, found a rubber boat, and notified the FBI. The Germans were trailed to New York, their contacts identified, and all were captured. Coffin assumes that they had spent the night at Jensen's.

Even before war was declared, steps were taken to guard Portland. Antiaircraft guns and searchlights were set up, Coast Artillery battalions brought in to man guns, and minefields laid. After Pearl Harbor, antisubmarine nets, booms, and barriers were set up, and a Harbor Entrance Control Post was established at Fort Williams to identify all vessels and inspect suspicious ones. The Navy took over the Maine State Pier and the Grand Trunk Railway pier. A destroyer base for the Atlantic fleet was established around USS *Prairie State* in the outer harbor, and the battleships *New York* and *Texas* anchored there. In May 1941 when word came that *Bismarck* was at sea, both battleships sailed, although neither was capable of facing a pocket battleship. *Bismarck* was faster and more heavily armed than either.

During the summer of 1941, escort vessels left Portland to convoy the cruiser *Augusta* carrying President Roosevelt to Newfoundland to meet with Churchill and sign the Atlantic Charter.

On September 6, 1941, the day after the destroyer *Greer* was torpedoed, sixteen destroyers departed from Portland bound east.

After war was declared in December, soldiers were stationed to patrol the beaches west of Cape Elizabeth on foot with combat teams and patrol battalions at strategic points. Liaison was established among the Coast Guard, Customs and Immigration, Sea and Shore Fisheries, the State Police, the Army, and the Navy. Inshore patrol bases were established at Portland, Rockland, and Bar Harbor. Observation posts were established at Cape Elizabeth, Jewell Island, Bailey Island, and Cape Small, with sonobuoys and underwater sound loops to record the "signatures" of passing vessels. A chain of aircraft warning posts was set up and manned by civilians to report suspicious occurrences. Picket boats patrolled Portland Harbor and inshore waters. Lighthouses and lifesaving stations were made observation posts. Security guards at Bath and South Portland shipyards were enlisted in the Coast Guard Reserve so they could carry weapons and arrest possible saboteurs. The FBI urged trusted civilians alongshore to report suspicious circumstances. Dimout was enforced alongshore and blackout exercises practiced. Civil defense volunteers carried out air-raid and disaster drills. Anyone who had business on or near the water was required to get an I.D. card, file a float plan, be in by dark, and identify himself on demand. The coast of Maine was alerted and mobilized.

A little farther offshore there was more activity. In response to a great many sinkings within sight of the coast, many yachtsmen not qualified for regular Navy or Coast Guard service volunteered to patrol the coast. The Navy was at first unresponsive, believing a yacht could be of little service. On March 5, 1942, Commodore Alfred Stanford of the Cruising Club of America offered the Navy thirty auxiliary sailing yachts of 50 to 90 feet, with crews. By April 27 he could offer seventy seagoing yachts and a hundred smaller ones. On May 4 the Coast Guard Auxiliary took over the vessels they could use, equipped them with 50-caliber machineguns and the larger, faster ones with four 300-pound depth charges each. They were each to patrol an area 15 miles square along the 50-fathom curve to "observe and report actions and activities of all hostile submarine, surface, or air forces and to attack and destroy enemy submarines when armament permits."

By August 25 the First Naval District had on patrol fifty-one sailing yachts from 50 to 75 feet in length, including the schooners *Blue Goose, Grenadier,* and *Primrose IV,* the ketch *Tioga,* and the yawl *Rose,* all well-known ocean racing vessels. They and others patrolled offshore from Grand Manan Island across the Bay of Fundy, off Georges Bank, and on down the coast during the rough, cold winter of 1942–43. Thirty to forty yachts were at sea in the First Naval District at any one time from September 1942 to September 1943. They sank no submarines, although two subs were sighted by patrolling yachts off Montauk in September 1942.

In January 1943 their numbers were reduced, as new 83-foot Coast Guard boats became available, and almost all of the "Hooligan Navy" was retired by October 1943.

Although the yacht patrols did little execution, made few reports, and rescued only a few crews of torpedoed vessels, they proved very valuable in training in small-boat work Coast Guard and Navy personnel sent to supplement and stiffen yacht crews. These men distinguished themselves in landing craft later in the war.

The Civil Air Patrol volunteered with their own light planes for the same sort of coastal patrol work. Unarmed at first, later the planes that could carry them were fitted with a depth charge and a demolition bomb. They flew from bases in Portland and in Trenton, near Bar Harbor. On August 24, 1942, thirty-five members with six planes reported to the Bar Harbor airport at Trenton to find wretched accommodations, a hangar with a dirt floor and leaky roof, and almost no shop facilities. Eleven days later they began patrolling from Quoddy Head to Port Clyde. They flew their own planes, bought their own gasoline although the government gave them a mileage allowance, took no draft deferment. They flew in some very dirty weather, made emergency deliveries, and escorted Boston–Halifax convoys. Two men were lost when a CAP plane crashed off Petit Manan on February 2, 1943. Another plane reported the crash, and help was rushed from Bar Harbor, but it came too late. The men died of exposure. However, ten days later, on February 12, a Navy observation plane from the Naval Air Station in Brunswick crashed in Blue Hill Bay. An alert Civil Air Patrol pilot reported the crash and circled a survivor, who swam ashore on Goose Rock off Newbury Neck. Help was rushed to the scene by land, and the man was rescued and revived.

Altogether, flying over the East Coast, the Civil Air Patrol between March 5, 1942, and September 1943 flew 5,684 convoy missions, reported 173 submarines, 91 vessels in distress, and rafts or lifeboats with 363 survivors. One of the principal values of the CAP proved to be in training boys as mechanics and pilots. As soon as they became eighteen, they moved directly into the Air Force and Ferry Command where they did good work.

Fishing vessels were given radios to report submarines, but this idea proved less rewarding than its proponents hoped. Fishermen were out to catch fish, not to fight wars. Some of them may have been slow to report submarines, fearing that if they used their radios, they would be shelled. In the First Naval District only twenty reports of submarines were received from offshore fishermen.

All through 1942 and 1943 the beaches were patrolled and the shore watched. There were numerous false alarms here. A stranded lobster buoy was identified as a mine or bomb by an inexperienced patrolman and occasioned enough alarm to get into official reports. On a cold February night a young soldier from the corn country was patrolling the beach south of the mouth of the Saco River. Ice was coming down the river with the tide, piling up on the shore and being tumbled about by the sea, making strange creaks, groans, and pops. The soldier interpreted some of these noises as an attempt to land enemy troops, and fired. Another patrolman north of the river mouth heard the same noises and when he heard the shot, fired back. Reinforcements were rushed to both sides of the river, but fortunately the "battle" was terminated before anyone was hurt.

Of course, Navy and Coast Guard ships and planes patrolled waters off Maine assiduously and made many attacks on submarine sonar and radar contacts. Many of the reports were false alarms.

A lady on Aircraft Warning Service watch at South Bristol reported a submarine in Johns Bay which on investigation by the Damariscove Coast Guard turned out to be blackfish.

Another very convincing report proved to be a fisherman towing a load of brush for his fish weir. The Bailey Island station reported puffs of steam or smoke arising from the sea and proceeding in an easterly direction; it turne out to be a whale.

The Cashes Ledge buoy was reported as a submarine by a commerci aircraft.

A submarine was reported in Passamaquoddy Bay. Portland called R. Peacock, owner of the Peacock Canning Co. in Lubec, who sent out tw unarmed sardiners to investigate. He sent two because if it was a submarine, would doubtless fire on the nearest sardiner to prevent her using her radi The second sardiner could report the situation on her radio, at least for a sho time. They went out without hesitation, Mr. Peacock himself on the fir sardiner, but the submarine proved to be a tree adrift with one branch stickin up.

On July 15, 1942, a submarine was reported about 15 miles east-south east of Cape Elizabeth. Patrol boats *W-78* and *W-80* made what they reporte as a definite contact, but the official evaluation of the Harbor Entrance Com mand Post reads:

> Alas their azdics did but ping
> A school of blackfish on a fling.

Many reports received this sort of negative evaluation. The Navy would nc admit the presence of a submarine unless a piece of it was brought in. Ther were many reports, most of which no doubt were whales, blackfish, ledge buoys seen through fog or darkness, plain hallucination, wishful thinking, o instrument error. It is not at all unlikely, however, that some of these case were indeed enemy submarines that escaped. The inexperience of the su hunters and the frequent communication problems that often extended th time from the sighting of a conning tower to the arrival of a plane or destroye could have enabled the submarine under the command of a skillful skipper t slide away or hide on the rocky bottom.

For instance, on July 14, 1942, *CGC-655* sighted a submarine off Tw Bush Light. Her radio was out of order, but she followed the submarine fo 40 minutes before she lost it.

On July 30 the watch at the lifesaving station at Damariscove reporte the sound of a diesel engine at night. No fishermen were allowed out at night and while the sound could have come from a fisherman caught out or a nava vessel out of position, it could have come from a submarine.

On September 6, 1942, an Army plane saw a submarine on the surfac about 5 miles south-southeast of the Portland Sea Buoy. Patrol boat *YMS-3* rushed to the scene, saw a whale, but later got a good contact, dropped dept bombs, and saw an oil slick. Surely the presence of a whale does not eliminat the very strong likelihood of a submarine's having been in the vicinity.

Captain Alexander Moffat, USNR (ret.), in *A Navy Maverick Comes o Age,* his memoirs of his service in World War II, reports a conversation hel in the late summer of 1943: "They think German subs have landed a fev trained saboteurs on the coast of Maine, destination unknown. We know, o course, that subs have been attacking convoys further offshore, but they've never attacked shipping near the coast. Intelligence assumes this is only because they don't want to attract attention to their landing operations. So far these agents have escaped capture." Moffat was at this time in command of Northern Ship Lane Patrol out of Boston.

On June 28, 1944, a periscope was seen between Belfast and Islesboro headed southwest at about 7 knots. By the time a boat arrived from Rockland, it was gone.

On July 5, 1944, the Coast Guard boat *Ilex,* towing a lighter, got a strong contact northwest of Mount Desert Rock. However, though *Ilex* could not attack with the lighter in tow, she hesitated to let the lighter go adrift, followed the sub for quite a long time, and finally gave up.

On August 6 an Army plane saw a submarine on the surface east of Matinicus Rock.

On July 2, 1944, a fisherman saw a wake southeast of Great Duck Island, followed it for some time, and reported by radio. A patrol vessel rushed out, got a sound contact, and depth-charged it, with no result. The patrol vessel decided it had attacked a pinnacle rock, searched farther, and got no contact. Ledges do not make a wake. It seems not unlikely that the submarine's skipper knew of the rock and used it. Or maybe he was just lucky.

Turn to harder evidence yet. On June 5, 1942, fourteen fishermen from two fishing vessels sunk by a submarine were brought into Southwest Harbor. On June 22, 1942, the Bailey Island observation post reported a submarine on the surface bound east. About 2:15 it was seen again off East Brown Cow. The commander of the 155mm battery on Sabino Head saw it, drew a bead on it, was about to fire, when the destroyer command in Portland ordered him not to fire because if he missed, the submarine might elude the destroyer *McCalla* coming full speed. The submarine submerged. *McCalla* got a good contact at 6:15 and dropped depth charges. At 6:43 the submarine was depth-charged again 7 miles east of Halfway Rock and again at 7:25 southwest of Seguin. A quantity of oil came to the surface, and the next day bodies of German seamen came ashore on Small Point.

On June 16 the steamer *Port Nicholson* was torpedoed in a Boston–Halifax convoy 50 miles southeast of Cashes Ledge.

As mentioned before, in August 1942 a submarine was sighted and attacked off Nash Island. Colonel Coffin found cork and asphalt lining on Big Nash Island which Navy Intelligence accepted as being from a German submarine.

One June 13, 1944, the Portland fishing vessel *Lark* was fired on by a submarine 30 miles SxE ½ E of Cape Sable. The crew abandoned ship in dories, leaving the skipper and cook aboard, and stayed in the dories all night. In the morning the skipper picked up the crew and headed for Nova Scotia. The skipper reported holes in the pilothouse big enough to put your fist through.

On the night of July 2, 1944, the blimp *K-11* came down in the water southwest of Mount Desert Rock, with the loss of seven of her eleven crew. The survivors were brought to the Bar Harbor base and the blimp, still afloat, was towed in and beached on Little Cranberry Island. Technicians found holes in the fabric where bullets, presumably 40mm, had entered the bag aft of the car and come out through the top of the bag amidships. Nevertheless, the crash was officially caused by "pilot error."

On August 22, 1944, the steamer *James Miller* was torpedoed southeast of Grand Manan near Gannet Rock and subsequently ran ashore.

On December 3, 1944, the steamer *Cornwallis* was torpedoed between Mount Desert Rock and Isle au Haut. The crew saw the submarine before the torpedo was fired.

We have already described the landing of two enemy agents from a submarine in November 1944 on Hancock Point.

To sum it up, the likelihood seems to be that the Gulf of Maine was a very busy place during World War II. Enemy submarines certainly did come into Maine coastal waters at various times during the war. Defense forces were on the hair trigger to attack and doubtless harassed whales, blackfish, schools of mackerel, and even deep currents of warm or cold water, and they responded to anomalies in their instruments. Therefore the Navy was very reluctant to evaluate a report of a submarine without very convincing evidence.

Furthermore, the Navy did not report submarine sinkings in the Gulf of Maine or anywhere else, believing that the disappearance of a submarine without trace or comment would be most damaging to the morale of surviving submarine crews.

Colonel Coffin summed up the situation thus: "As the war progressed and our antisubmarine technique improved, the Germans ventured inshore between Cape Cod and Cape Sable less frequently. Once they were inside the Gulf of Maine, their chances of getting out again in this life were poor."

The Coast Guard was, of course, active during the war with a number of patrol and picket boats as well as smaller craft. They maintained port security, kept buoys in repair and on station, and manned lighthouses and lifesaving stations. The light stations and lifesaving stations were valuable lookout and listening posts and they also served their original purpose, for there were at least two notable wrecks during that time on the Maine coast. The trawler *Georgetown* went ashore on Strattons Island off Old Orchard, and on September 14, 1944, in a heavy gale described as a hurricane, the American freighter *Hartwilson,* 3,078 tons, ran ashore on Bantam Rock, a half-tide ledge a mile outside Damariscove Island. The surfboat from Damariscove responded at once and was nearby at 0800 but because of the heavy sea and shoal water could not get close enough to take off the crew. Lifeboats from Burnt Island and the Kennebec and a naval vessel arrived as *Hartwilson* began to break up. The freighter's crew drifted a line attached to a life ring to leeward which was picked up by the naval vessel, but the Kennebec lifeboat got her propeller tangled in it and was slammed against the naval vessel.

A modern guided-missile frigate built at Bath. *Bath Iron Works*

After dark, at 6:35 pm, the cutter *Ilex* arrived, took station to windward, and at 7:22 pumped out oil and launched a small boat, which shot a line aboard what was left of the freighter and hauled aboard the crew, one at a time. The chart still shows a wreck on the rock, but careful inspection on a calm day showed no sign of it.

In the last months of the war, activity on the coast subsided somewhat. The German submarine bases had been captured, and Germany was much too busy defending herself in Europe to spend energy on Maine. After VE Day all attention shifted to Japan. When the news of Japan's surrender hit Maine on the afternoon of September 1, 1945, joy was unconfined. Gasoline rationing was off at once. People careered around tight curves in our narrow roads, slammed over the bumps, drove through towns with horn buttons clamped down, and in an excess of enthusiasm set fire to two four-masted coasting schooners laid up in the mud at Boothbay Harbor. As their masts fell and the embers died out in the rising tide, the very last remnants of an era died, too. The sun rose on a new world.

NOTES

I have drawn heavily again on Ralph Snow's *Bath Iron Works* for detailed information on the destroyer program at Bath. Also, I worked as a rigger's helper in the Iron Works during the summer of 1943 and saw something of how the work went on. It was fast. There was a launching about twice a month and with no great fanfare. The commitment of men and women who traveled 30 or 40 miles from home over rough roads in all weather with tires and gasoline rationed was impressive. I heard a number of reflections on it. Some of these were wryly humorous, meant to be taken with a twist

TYPE BUILT FOR NAV

NAME OF BUILDER	Submarine S.S.	Torpedo Testing Barge	Destroyers, Various D.D.	Coastal Mine-sweeper AMC	Coastal Transport APC	Patrol Vessel YP	Rescue-Tug ATR	Covered Lighter YF	Motor Launch ML	Picket Boat	Buoy Boat	Yawl	Workboat	Plane Re-arming Boat
Steel														
NAVY YARD	71	3												
BATH IRON WORKS			64											
NEW ENGLAND SHIPBDG. CO.														
TODD BATH IRON														
Wood														
BRISTOL YACHT BUILDING CO.				3	4	2								
CAMDEN SHIPBDG & M.R. CO.				2	11		12							
GRAY BOATS, INC.								7						
HENRY R. HINCKLEY														
HODGDON & GOUDY & STEVENS				2	10									
MAINE BOAT YARDS ASSOC., INC.									4					
HARRY G. MARR				2	5									
MOUNT DESERT BOAT YARD, INC.											25	3	90	
S. B. NORTON & SON											10			52
REED BROTHERS											10			30
RICE BROTHERS CORP.														
FRANK L. SAMPLE, JR., INC.							6							
SNOW SHIPYARDS, INC.				10										
SOUTHWEST BOAT CORP.												6		
STONINGTON DEER ISLE YACHT BASIN														
WEBBERS COVE BOAT YARD										5				
WALDOBORO SHIPYARD, INC.														
BELFAST SHIPBUILDING CORP.														
CASCO SHIPBUILDING CORP.														
RICHMOND SHIPBUILDING CORP.														

SUMMARY OF VESSELS BUILT IN MAINE FOR U.S. GOVERNMENT

(from December 7, 1941, to July 14, 1945 inclusive)

								TYPE BUILT FOR ARMY							BUILT FOR MARITIME COMMISSION		
Motor Mine-sweeper, YMS	Net Laying Ship	Ocean Jug Auxiliary ATA	Salvage Vessel ARS	Plane Personnel Boat	Surf Boat	18′ Lifeboat	Harbor Tug YTL	20′ Motor Cargo Boat	26′ Motor Mine Tow Yawl	38′ Cabin Picket Boat	46′ Motor Tow Boat	65′ Freight	114′ Freight & Passenger	140′ Freight & Passenger	Steel Steam Vessel C2.S.Al	Steel Steam Vessel Liberty	Wood Freight Barge
															2		
																234	
																30	
																	4
								9	317	93	46						
	4	2	2														
				20		42				2							
											19	2	4	2			
					30												
						4	4										
																	2
																	4
																	3

of lemon and aimed at the few who were not pulling their weight.

Pete Newell was taking a Navy expediter on an inspection tour of the yard. After climbing over half a dozen ways, inspecting the plate shop, the machine shop, and probably the rigging loft, the expediter asked, "How many men are working here, Mr. Newell?" Pete replied, "About half of them." About one who quit work early: "He got dirty on company time, so he washes up on company time."

One day as I was splicing in life nettings and sewing servings on the deck of a destroyer, a man with a hammer stopped to watch. "What gang are you in?" he asked.

"Riggers," I announced proudly, for the riggers were one of the elite trades. "What are you?"

"I'm an outside machinist, but I don't do any work. I found a place down under the ship where I can sleep all day. I didn't do anything yesterday, and as soon as the timekeeper sees me carrying this hammer, I'll go back down there and sleep the rest of today."

On the way home, I repeated the conversation to the man I rode with, a lobsterman perhaps forty-five years old who would not be drafted and who gave up a profitable business lobstering to drive 80 miles round trip every day in order to win a war that needed winning. He made no patriotic speech, but he felt deeply what he said: "I'd be ashamed to come so far and do so little."

For the story on the South Portland yards, read Frederic C. Lane's *Ships for Victory*. It includes the whole Maritime Commission's story, so one must pick out the parts relevant to Maine. In addition to a factual, if brief, account of the building of the two yards, Lane deals at some length with the inefficient management of the two yards. While the facts he gives about the financial irregularities are undoubtedly true, and Snow in *Bath Iron Works* admits as much, he does not explain why these things happened, leaving the reader to believe that the management was seeking unreasonable financial gain. Snow, defending Newell, adds to Lane's story enough to indicate that most of the inefficiency and extra expense came from the sudden rapid expansion of the three shipyards, including the one at Bath, with inexperienced engineers, supervisors, and bureaucrats, seasoned with a dash of politics. *Portland Ships Are Good Ships*, by Herbert G. Jones, is principally devoted to supporting its title. However, the facts it states are impressive, regardless of what it leaves out.

The facts on the construction of wooden vessels are hard to assemble, but the following table is a fair estimate. Incomplete figures from one source fail to support incomplete figures from another.

The accounts of the Lang's quarry plot and the Hancock Point landing as well as many of the subsequent details on coastal defense came from an unpublished manuscript by Colonel Harold W. Coffin in the archives at the University of Maine at Orono. Coffin worked for the electric company in Bangor and was active in the intelligence division of the Army Reserve. When the reserve was called up, he was assigned to Portland as Harbor Defense Intelligence Officer, from which position he kept track of activities from Kittery to Calais. His account is highly factual and makes fascinating reading. He tells us that Jensen and Lever are fictitious names, not the names by which the men were known in Maine.

Other material came from the War Diary, Northern Group, in the archives at the National Records Center in Waltham, Massachusetts. There is a great deal of uninformative routine in these reports, but one occasionally washes out a nugget. Volume 6 of Admiral Morison's *History of United States Naval Operations in World War II* gave a good account of the yacht patrol, the Civil Air Patrol, and the actions of fishermen along the coast.

There is a great deal of work to be done by professional historians and local chroniclers in assembling and organizing the wealth of scattered information on activities in Maine during World War II. It should be done while there are people still living who remember those days. Mr. E. Farnham Butler of Mount Desert told me that on the occasion of a visit to the Mount Desert patrol headquarters he saw a map recording a "good contact" off Mount Desert Rock. A "good contact" usually meant a submarine sunk or probably sunk. Mr. Butler also spoke of Mr. Watson Lunt's experience. Mr. Lunt, son of the man who supervised antisubmarine activity in New England during the war, was a naval officer on NATO maneuvers in the Mediterranean. His opposite number, a West German who had been on submarines during the war, described the Frenchman Bay area in detail, recited the characteristics of lights and buoys, and reported that he knew of about eighty spies and saboteurs who had been landed on the Maine coast. How many of them, if any, landed on Hancock Point or at Lang's quarry we do not know.

A Navy Maverick Comes of Age 1939–1945, by Captain Alexander Moffat, USNR (ret.), recounts his experiences as commander of Northern Ship Lane Patrol and as commander of the Bar Harbor naval station. The account is straightforward and factual. It mentions names, dates, and places. I knew the late Captain Moffat personally, and I have no doubt that his book can be relied upon. His account of the loss and salvage of the blimp *K-11* is detailed.

The Navy's published account of German submarine losses in *U.S. Submarine Losses in World War II* includes none in the Gulf of Maine, but a conspicuous footnote declares the figures incomplete.

THIRTY-ONE

Vacationland

IN 1858 ROBERT CARTER, a New York journalist, with three friends chartered a fishing sloop in Boston and cruised down east to Mount Desert Island. Carter's fascinating account of the first yachting cruise on the Maine coast, if we except Samuel de Champlain's and Captain John Smith's, mentions only one summer hotel and one other yacht.

The hotel was the Appledore House on Appledore Island, one of the Isles of Shoals. It was established in 1848 by Thomas Laighton, a member of the New Hampshire legislature who had run for governor and been defeated by foul means. He vowed never to set foot on the continent of North America again, became keeper of White Island Light, and then moved to Appledore. By 1858 he had a four-story building—Carter says five stories—125 feet long with rooms for eighty guests. By 1860 he and his sons had expanded to accommodate 300. In the course of a few years the Laightons acquired row-boats and whaleboats in which their guests could row, sail, or go fishing. Laighton dammed up a cove for a swimming pool, built a tennis court, and later built a gas plant so he could light the hotel in the latest style. He maintained a fast schooner to bring his guests to the island and later added a steamer. His guest list was impressive. It included, among many others, Henry D. Thoreau, James Russell Lowell, Franklin Pierce (later President of the United States), Thomas Bailey Aldrich, Nathaniel Hawthorne, Henry Ward Beecher, Sarah Orne Jewett, and Harriet Beecher Stowe. Other arts than literature were represented. The internationally recognized violinist Ole Bull was a visitor. Artists Ellen Robbins and J. Appleton Brown were frequent guests. Thomas Laighton's daughter Celia married Levi Thaxter and became a popular poet in her day. She was also a skillful gardener and wrote *My Island Garden,* illustrated by Childe Hassam, another regular guest at the hotel.

In 1872 John R. Poor bought adjacent Star Island, built the Oceanic Hotel, and advertised it widely. In 1874 he promoted a race for the finest and fastest yachts of his day from the Isles of Shoals around Boon Island and back. The schooner *America* won, the same schooner that in 1851 had crossed the

Atlantic to beat Britain's fastest yachts and brought back the cup still called *America*'s Cup. She was owned in 1874 by the notorious General Ben Butler, hated governor of New Orleans during the Civil War. The race attracted a large spectator fleet, some of whose owners, crews, and guests were rather a wild crowd, driving the more staid guests at the Oceanic over to Appledore.

The next year Poor arranged another race, in the course of which the judges transferred from one committee boat to another and changed the finish line without informing the contestants. All but Butler in *America* and Rufus Hatch in *Resolute* sailed away in protest. *America* beat *Resolute* in a race-off for the silver punch bowl. Later in 1875 the Oceanic burned. Poor rebuilt it but later in the year sold it to Oscar Laighton, surviving son of Thomas, and both hotels did very well for several years.

In the 1890s, however, business fell off. There were too many hotels easily accessible on the mainland. After 1900, when people began to drive directly to mainland hotels by automobile, Laighton was just making it. Thomas Elliott, a guest at the Oceanic, approached the manager, proposing to bring out a group of Unitarians who wanted to use the Oceanic for religious gatherings. Oscar Laighton, suspicious, asked what a Unitarian was. On being assured that Unitarians were indeed a respectable religious group, he consented. The next year Unitarians filled the Oceanic to the rafters and overflowed to Appledore. Shortly afterwards, Laighton sold Star Island and the Oceanic to the Unitarians, who still own it.

In 1914 the Appledore House burned and the island reverted to poison ivy, gulls, and a few cottages. It is now occupied by an oceanography research station and summer school, run by Cornell University and the University of New Hampshire.

All along the coast during the last decades of the century, other hotels were established. The Marshall House at York, the prominent hotel on Bald Head Cliff in Ogunquit, the complex of hotels and amusement parks at Old Orchard, and the Black Point Inn at Prouts Neck are but a few of the links of a chain that extended through the islands off Portland—Peaks, Diamond, and Chebeague—to the Allequipa House at Small Point, Sebasco Lodge at Sebasco, Grey Gables at Harmon's Harbor, and on to Boothbay.

At Boothbay, where there was easy steamer connection with the railroad at Bath, the increase in summer visitors was impressive.

As early as 1839, a Maine Gazetteer stated, "Boothbay is a fine watering place, and many visit it, in summer months, for health or pleasure. Here may be found all the enjoyments of sea air and bathing, fishing and fowling, ocean and island scenery, for which Nahant in Massachusetts Bay is justly celebrated." Until some time after the Civil War, most visitors boarded with private families or camped out. In 1870 several Bates College professors, including the president of the college, and other Lewiston residents bought Squirrel Island in Boothbay Harbor and incorporated themselves as the Squirrel Island Association, a corporation that still exists. Fourteen cottages were built in 1870. In 1871 a new landing, a store, a bowling alley, and a sidewalk were added. In 1877 a summer post office was established, in 1881 a chapel was built, and in 1882 a hotel. This was expanded to become the Squirrel Inn in 1894 with accommodations for 200 guests. The inn burned in 1962, one of the most spectacular fires the region has ever seen.

In 1904 Boothbay town water was piped across to Squirrel Island from Spruce Point. The first attempts failed because the channel was so deep that the pipe, being payed out from the stern of a boat, broke of its own weight. Luther Maddocks, an ingenious entrepreneur of Boothbay and a principal advocate of town water, suggested that the pipe be laid in a wooden trough with just enough buoyancy to float it, the trough to be built in sections as the sections of pipe were joined together and laid in it. When the trough and pipe reached the island, it was connected to the water system, then connected at the Spruce Point end, and the valve was opened. When the pipe filled with water, it weighed enough to sink and so lowered itself neatly to the bottom, undamaged.

In 1906 Squirrel Island had 115 cottages and 910 summer inhabitants. The cottages, most of which still stand, were large, and in many cases ornate with tower rooms, broad screened porches, hardwood floors, and wicker furniture. They were lighted with kerosene lamps, and cooking was done in a back kitchen on a kerosene or wood stove. Families came in the spring on the steamer from Augusta or Bath, which landed them, their trunks, and perhaps a cook, a maid, and a governess, on the island wharf. They moved in for the summer. They fished, rowed, swam, sailed, played tennis and baseball, walked, painted pictures, read good books, and attended an island church. They lived simply, bought at the island store, and had milk, eggs, fish, and vegetables delivered daily by a man who rowed over from Damariscove Island in a dory. It was a self-contained summer community.

Now, on the other end of the twentieth century, Squirrel Island has electricity and telephone service to the mainland. There is no longer a general store on the island, and no one rows over from Damariscove with milk and eggs. Islanders shop at a Boothbay supermarket via a ferry which makes scheduled trips several times a day. However, the Association still owns the island and tries to maintain the tradition of simplicity by forbidding the use of automobiles on the island.

In 1876 the Mouse Island Association was incorporated, and in the next year a hotel was built there. In 1878 the Capitol Island House was established by John Sidney, who had, according to Francis Greene, "all the charms of the wild Indian and all the vices of tame civilization." However, the island flourished as a summer resort and in 1906 had an association and thirty cottages. It still has a hotel and many more cottages.

Southport had six or seven hotels, numerous cottages and boardinghouses, and a summer church, All Saints By the Sea, in 1906. It now has more cottages and a number of motels, two of which are descended from old hotels with still a touch of the grace and leisure they reflected.

The Isle of Springs in 1877 had an association, nine cottages, and a hotel.

The mainland had also a considerable summer establishment with hotels, boardinghouses, and cottages at West Harbor, Boothbay Harbor, Spruce Point, Bayville, East Boothbay, and Ocean Point. These centers have all expanded since the early days.

By 1915 the summer population of the Boothbay region was 32,954. After World War I the growth accelerated further. Route 1 was paved east in the late '20s. The Carlton Bridge at Bath in 1927 made access by automobile and train much easier. In 1932 a new bridge was built at Wiscasset, and renewed in 1983. Route I-95 was opened to high-speed limited-access traffic from Kittery to Portland in 1947 and was pushed on from there through the next ten years. The high-level bridge at Kittery was built in 1972.

The Depression slowed growth, but before World War II it began to recover. Although rail and steamer service was cut off after World War II, automobile traffic increased incredibly. The pattern changed from that of the early days, when visitors came to stay in a gracious hotel or boardinghouse for a week or more or in a cottage for all summer, to one, two, or maybe three nights in a motel shack. Instead of sailing, rowing, fishing off the rocks or from a dory, tennis, walking, and perhaps a clambake on the shore, most of the modern tourists take a half-day trip in a power excursion boat, where they listen to an electronic voice, spend a half day in gift shops, eat in a fast-food restaurant, and look at television. If the next day is foggy, they move on. The number of cottages has vastly increased, driving real estate values, especially of shore property, to astronomical heights. Many of these cottages are occupied by families who come for the summer, but an increasing number are rented for one or two weeks or a month and occupied sporadically. Most of the hotels are gone now, either burned or torn down, rendered obsolete by the motels; and boardinghouses are now bed-and-breakfast establishments.

Recently, many condominiums have been built along the shore and are occupied on a time-share basis for short periods during the summer. Many of these condominiums remain unsold.

East of Boothbay along the mid-coast, development has been less explosive. Christmas Cove had its Holly Inn on the isthmus between the Cove and the Thread of Life, affording views on both sides and cool breezes on hot days. It and another hotel near the head of the harbor were popular for years. Many cottages were built, and the Holly Inn, after burning and being rebuilt several times, was given up. The other hotel became part of Coveside Marina and cottages, for practical purposes a motel. The Christmas Cove community consists now, as it has for years, mostly of cottages.

New Harbor, Round Pond, Friendship, Port Clyde, and Tenants Harbor are active lobstering harbors, the demand for shore property and services not yet having driven out the lobstermen.

The Samoset at Rockland was a famous hotel and is still a vacation resort, somewhat modified to fit current lifestyle.

Camden is another town that, like Boothbay, has been profoundly affected by summer people. Formerly a mill and shipbuilding town, in the late 1880s it attracted the attention of a number of wealthy families. The first cottage was built in 1878 by Edward F. Dillingham, followed by Watsons, Cyrus Curtis, and others. Attracted by the impressive views of the Camden Hills, the sheltered harbor, and good steamer connections with Boston via Rockland and a trolley line, later directly by steamer, summer people built large, elegant summer homes. Transients were accommodated at the gracious Whitehall Hotel. Large and beautifully furnished steam yachts of summer residents lay in Camden Harbor and were joined by equally elegant visitors. *Corsair, Robador, Apache, Lotus Land,* and Curtis's *Lyndonia* frequently anchored there. Dr. Seth Milliken's 85-foot yawl *Thistle* was a visitor. An old photograph shows a barkentine, four big schooner-yachts with two topmasts and spoon bows, several big racing sloops, one small steam yacht, and one coasting schooner.

Mr. Curtis bought land on the harbor and built the handsome yacht club, which still stands. A separate building was built for the comfort of yacht captains, chauffeurs, and stenographers who might have to wait for their employers.

About 1928, feeling the need for a fairly fast, safe class racing boat for young people, Mr. Watson sent Mr. Carney Andrews to Turku, Finland, to look at a racing class there called the HAI boats, HAJ in Swedish, pronounced "high," meaning "shark." These were long-ended sloops about 32 feet overall with a big high-aspect mainsail. The rig was redesigned on a smaller scale, and about fifteen were built in Finland and sent to Camden. Others came later until there was a class of twenty-six, called in this country Finn boats. Four or five were still sailing in 1989. Other small boats were raced, too—Dark Harbor 12-footers and 17s, both designed by B. B. Crowninshield.

Camden, despite this influx of summer people, maintained its Knox Woolen Mill and a boatyard, after H. M. Bean sold out his big yard in 1906. A number of coasting schooners were built here during World War I, and in World War II the Camden Shipbuilding & Marine Railway built minesweepers, barges, troop transports, and tugs. After the war it built yachts for a while, but foreign competition and fiberglass led to the establishment on the same site of Wayfarer Marine, entirely devoted to an enormous maintenance, repair, and charter business. Camden, Rockport, and Rockland became bases for a large windjammer fleet, as described in Chapter 32.

The fine old cottages still stand, some of them still occupied by families that have come summer after summer for generations, but the pressure of motels and real-estate development is increasing.

Islesboro was "discovered" by another group of wealthy people in the early years of the century, and one Smith built the exclusive Islesboro Inn. A number of elegant cottages were constructed, and the summer population was said to consist of a stronger solution of the Social Register than that of any other resort on the coast. Small-boat racing, of Dark Harbor 12s and 17s, was very popular, and big yachts of New York and Philadelphia millionaires often lay in Gilkeys Harbor. The Depression hit Islesboro hard, and the loss of steamer service was a real blow until the Maine Department of Transportation put on the ferry *Everett Libby,* running from Lincolnville Beach. Islesboro still flourishes on a somewhat diluted level.

North Haven and the north shore of Vinalhaven experienced similar development, mostly by wealthy Massachusetts people. Elegant cottages and small-boat racing were the rule. Much of the old atmosphere can be felt by anyone sailing through Fox Islands Thorofare, especially if a fleet of North Haven dinghies is encountered racing around the buoys off the town.

The towns east of the Penobscot River developed more slowly and less extravagantly than Boothbay and Camden while there was steamer service. Smaller, more modest cottages, hotels like Gray's Inn, now Bucks Harbor Inn, at South Brooksville, and boardinghouses like Hiram Blake's on Cape Rosier, accommodated "summer boarders." There was considerable small-boat racing in Dark Harbor 12s and Manchester 17s at Bucks Harbor, but many of the cottagers were independent people who sailed, rowed, and cruised in small, simple craft, in an unostentatious way.

Castine, situated on the Bagaduce River, what Commodore Saltonstall had called in 1779 "that damned tide-hole," developed more slowly. Its stately homes recalling its Loyalist background and its nineteenth-century commercial prosperity, and the presence of Maine Maritime Academy, make it unique. Still, it too developed its summer cottages, class racing, and its yacht yard.

The towns along Eggemoggin Reach—Sargentville, Sedgwick, and Brooklin—attracted few and simple summer residents compared to towns west of the Penobscot River. Deer Isle, after the construction of the Deer Isle–Sedgwick bridge in 1939, developed in much the same way. Stonington on the south end of the island remained until World War II a busy granite town. It was and is a base for lobstermen fishing the productive waters between Deer Isle and Isle au Haut and it remains a distribution center for Deer Isle. Consequently, Stonington never developed as Boothbay Harbor and Camden did, but even today retains much of its commercial atmosphere.

Blue Hill, at the head of protected Blue Hill Bay and with an excellent harbor, changed from a small but flourishing commercial town into a center for vacationers and yachtsmen. It remained a distribution center for the towns on the peninsula to the south of it without losing its dignified character.

Bar Harbor and Mount Desert Island, however, developed somewhat more in the style of Boothbay and Camden, although it could not be said to have followed them.

When Robert Carter visited Mount Desert in 1858 there were no summer homes on the island and only two inns, one at Southwest Harbor and one at Somesville. He stayed with the postmaster in Bar Harbor and reported that "of late years it [Mount Desert Island] has become attractive to artists and summer loungers, but it needs the hand of cultivated taste."

First, from about 1844 to 1870, came the artists, campers, hunters, and college students on vacation. Then vacationing families boarded with local people.

By 1870 there was a regular stage from Bangor and two steamers a week from Portland. The Maine Central Railroad built a spur from Bangor to Mount Desert Ferry in Hancock which connected with a steamer to Bar Harbor, and daily steamer service was established from Rockland. Mount Desert developed rapidly.

Local people expanded their houses to accommodate boarders and soon built hotels. Some summer people, after several years as "mealers"—people who lived in the hotel or boardinghouse and took their meals there—built simple cottages and became "hauled mealers," who "lived out" and came to meals at the hotel. Then they became independent cottagers. As more summer people came and bought up the picturesque shore property, hotel guests found they could not get to the shore, and the hotel business fell off. By 1880 the cottages on the Bar Harbor side of the island were much larger and more luxurious than the early people could have imagined.

In 1880 Northeast Harbor had no summer places at all. A party of Harvard students, including the son of the college's president, Charles W. Eliot, camped on the uninhabited shore of Somes Sound. His glowing report to his father suggested a summer place at Northeast Harbor. Mr. Eliot came, saw, bought, and built. About the same time Bishop Doane of Albany, New York, who boarded at Squire Kimball's, bought land and built. Later came Dr. Gilman, president of Johns Hopkins University. Other plain livers and high thinkers joined them, including Dr. Francis G. Peabody and, in this century, Admiral Samuel Eliot Morison. A Mr. Savage built the Asticou Inn at the head of the harbor, named after an Indian chief whose encounter with the Jesuits had led to their settling briefly on Mount Desert as narrated in Chapter 4. The Asticou Inn and the Kimball House still stand. Yachtsmen were attracted to Northeast Harbor, the second-best harbor on the island, and raced in the sheltered waters of Great Harbor between the Cranberry Islands and Mount Desert, as early as 1900.

With the tremendous increase in the number of small cruising boats on the coast, Northeast Harbor has now built a marina with finger piers, has buoyed off a narrow channel, dredged out mud flats, and peppered the harbor with moorings. All summer it is a crowded and busy scene.

Southwest Harbor began its growth about 1882 but grew much more slowly. It was a commercial harbor, home port for a considerable fishing and boatbuilding industry. The cottagers who settled here were considerably more restrained in lifestyle than were those at Northeast Harbor, Seal Harbor, and Bar Harbor. Now, however, with the phenomenal growth of the Hinckley boatyard on the Manset side, Southwest Harbor seems to have caught up, or been caught up. Its harbor is now crowded with yacht moorings, to the near exclusion of fishermen, and the shores once encumbered with lobster traps, net reels, and launching ways are being built up and "landscaped." A town ordinance forbids storing boats on the shore now.

Somesville had a well-known hotel for years, the Somes House, but it is gone now. The town's very pretty harbor is crowded, and efforts are being made to keep large vessels out lest they pollute the water.

Bar Harbor was the first harbor to attract summer people and for a time was a name to conjure up glamorous images. By 1880 the town, then called Eden, had, according to one historian, a roster of summer residents that seemed to have been compiled very cautiously from the Social Register and Dun & Bradstreet. In those happy pre-income-tax days when people with money made no effort to hide it, huge "cottages" were built and an appropriate summer establishment maintained. A proper cottage required a gardener, a coachman, and a second man outside. Inside there were a cook, two waitresses, two chambermaids, and another cook to cook for the servants. There were ninety or more of such cottages built on the south and west sides of the island. Not until 1915 were automobiles permitted on the island, so the people drove about in carriages, put on elaborate parties, raced 17s, called B-boats on Mount Desert, and 50-foot Bar Harbor 30s on Frenchman Bay and paddled canoes gently among the nearby islands. Great steam yachts and elegantly maintained schooners lay in the harbor. The United States Navy visited the harbor annually, the New York Yacht Club often included Bar Harbor on its summer cruise, bringing no yacht smaller than a New York 30, which is over 40 feet overall. British and Italian naval vessels were also occasional visitors. Any such visit was the opportunity for a series of glittering receptions.

With the distraction of World War I, followed by the income tax, the Depression, then World War II, and finally the great fire of 1947, which burned over the eastern part of the island and wiped out many of the surviving estates, Bar Harbor was left as it is today, a more or less ordinary town having a deep harbor with poor holding ground and a persistent roll frequented by a few yachts and many tourists attracted by the faded glamour of former days and by the beauties of Acadia National Park.*

Across Frenchman Bay on Grindstone Neck in Winter Harbor is a summer settlement laid out in 1892 with something of the Bar Harbor aura. It was dominated by the Grindstone Inn from whose spacious porches one could enjoy a magnificent view of the Mount Desert hills. Below the inn in Sand Cove was a small but elegant yacht club which used to maintain a racing class of sloops about 30 feet long. In 1956 the inn burned. The cottages still stand and the yacht club still maintains a landing and moorings, but the glamour is gone.

East from Winter Harbor, summer development has been slow. It is a

*In 1916 Congress established Sieur De Monts National Park on land donated by the Rockefeller family. In 1919 it was named Lafayette National Park and the name changed to Acadia National Park in 1929. Since its establishment, it has been expanded and developed to double its original size.

long drive from Boston, even with modern roads, really too far for a weekend visit. Route 1 lies well back from the shore. The peninsulas are long, the roads rough. There are few motels. The few small towns are devoted largely to lobstering and are in no hurry to attract summer people. However, a few people who like isolation and a simple life are coming in quietly.

Some of the islands have been affected by the rush of vacationers. Small inshore islands have been bought by individuals or families, who have built cottages and landings. They are in search of privacy. Larger islands like the islands in Casco Bay off Portland, Chebeague, Islesboro, Vinalhaven, Swans Island, and the Cranberry Islands off Mount Desert have attracted summer people in somewhat the same way as have mainland towns, but the pace is less frenetic because one must take a ferry to get to the island, the ferry cannot carry many cars, and without a car, one feels less pressed.

The offshore islands are much less affected. Damariscove is owned by the Nature Conservancy. Monhegan, because of its isolation and picturesque quality, was early an attraction to artists and still is; Rockwell Kent and Jamie Wyeth will serve as examples. The Island Inn and the Monhegan House still flourish, and there are one or two boardinghouses. Now, however, excursion boats from Boothbay, New Harbor, and Port Clyde daily flood the island with tourists. The land on Matinicus is largely owned by a few summer people, but the shore property in the harbor is held by fishermen who don't want to let it go. There is almost no summer "development," which suits both fishermen and summer people. Monhegan horrifies them. Isle au Haut is mostly Acadia National Park. It is served by a mailboat that carries few people and no cars. Except for a campground maintained by the park at Duck Harbor, for which one must make reservations months in advance, there is no place for visitors to stay. A few people own summer homes, enjoy them quietly, and say little about the island. Many yachts visit but seldom stay long.

Frenchboro Long Island is a fishing community with only very occasional ferry connection. An effort is being made to keep the elementary school active and the working population up, but there are almost no summer people.

Great Wass Island and many of the islands near it are owned by the Nature Conservancy.

The Roque Island group is owned exclusively by the Gardner-Monks family and seems unlikely to change. There is a family farm on the north side of the island, but most of the island is wild. Cross Island is at present occupied only by a station of the Hurricane Island Outward Bound School, which owns 20 acres of the island; the rest is a wildlife refuge. Much of the island was cut over for pulp some years ago and is a tangle of fallen and overgrown timber. Development is most unlikely.

Thus we see some of the coast, the hard-to-reach eastern part, largely undeveloped. A man on the wharf at Cape Split said to me as I climbed the weedy ladder from the lobster car below, "This isn't the end of the world, but you can see it from here."

The coast west of the Schoodic Peninsula, especially the section west of the Penobscot River within a four-hour drive from Boston on the Maine Turnpike, is heavily populated and, if anything, overdeveloped in regions near principal towns. West of Portland the development came earlier and, one hopes, has reached its peak.

Our license plate proclaims us Vacationland, and that we had better be.

N O T E S

Robert Carter's *A Summer Cruise on the Coast of New England* deserves much more attention than we give it here. Carter was an observant journalist interested in marine biology, geology, people, and the weather. Further information on Appledore came from Oscar Laighton's *Ninety Years at the Isles of Shoals,* essentially the biography of the Appledore House. The account of the 1874–75 yacht races is from *America* by Charles Boswell.

Louis C. Hatch's *Maine, A History* lists a number of summer establishments on the coast. I have not included them all, for the important point is simply that many existed. My father and I between us visited those mentioned.

Francis B. Greene's *History of Boothbay* and Harold Clifford's supplement to it provide most of the history of the Boothbay region. The story of the Squirrel Island water pipe is told at greater length in Luther Maddock's autobiography, *Looking Backward,* published by the Southport [Maine] Historical Society. Mr. Maddocks was an entrepreneur of unexampled energy and ingenuity and has no hesitation in describing his achievements.

The facts on Camden and Islesboro come through the kindness of William Pattison, since the early years of the century a resident of Camden. He kindly loaned me a rare copy of *Glimpses of Camden* and of Barbara Dyer's *Vintage Views of Camden.* From the photographs in this book, one can deduce something of the early days of the century. Mr. Pattison also arranged to have me talk with Angie Ferris, Stillman Kelley, and Lewis and Sally Iselin, who remember clearly the early days of this century in Penobscot Bay.

I saw the latter part of the development of the smaller towns on Penobscot Bay and Deer Isle just before the steamers were discontinued in 1934 and afterwards. The distance over the road from Boston is what saved them from what Boothbay, Camden, and Mount Desert experienced. The latter, of course, was served by railroad and steamer.

The information on Mount Desert came from *Mount Desert, the Most Beautiful Island in the World,* by Sargent Collier and Tom Horgan, from George E. Street's *Mount Desert—A History,* published in 1905, and from *Radio NBD,* by Wentworth. Admiral Morison's *The Story of Mount Desert Island* is a very short treatment of the subject, with considerable emphasis on yachting. Most important was a half day with Mr. E. Farnham Butler, founder of the Mount Desert Yacht Yard, whose recollections are indeed illuminating. It is to be regretted that everything he said could not be included.

The accounts of the offshore islands come from personal experience and information assembled through fifty years of research for *A Cruising Guide to the New England Coast*.

If the chapter's final sentence seems a bit cryptic, consider it in the light of the collapse of Maine seaborne commerce, of the lime, granite, and lumber industries, of the struggling shipbuilding industry, and the sadly depleted fishing industry. Without the Portsmouth–Kittery bridge and the Maine Turnpike, coastal Maine would be in hard shape.

THIRTY-TWO

Yachting and Yacht Builders

ANY SUMMER RESIDENTS in coastal Maine came because it is one of the world's most interesting coasts on which to sail. Protected bays, open ocean, coves and harbors, islands and ledges, and enough fog to make it challenging attracted yachtsmen from the early days, and many of their yachts were built in Maine.

From earliest times one may speculate that fishermen and professional seamen enjoyed a good reaching breeze. Certainly, when opportunity offered, they raced, and a race was often a feature of a Fourth of July celebration. We know that Wilbur and Charles Morse built a number of sloops as yachts in the last years of the last century, yachts used for daysailing and "rough it" cruising by boys, young people, and eccentric old men. We may remember that Captain Charlie Barr of the *America*'s Cup defender *Columbia* in 1899 beat Thomas Lipton's first *Shamrock* with a crew from Deer Isle.

However, as a part of formal maritime history, we might begin by looking at the really big steel yachts, owned by the country's millionaires. In Maine, these were built principally by the Bath Iron Works. Their first was *Eleanor,* built in 1894 for W. A. Slater, whose fortune was made in the textile business. He wanted a yacht in which he could cruise comfortably around the world, and in 1893 that meant Cape Horn. Slater was not a man to skimp on any aspect of a vessel. With the advice of his paid skipper, Captain Scott, Slater had the Iron Works build a 220-foot vessel, rigged as a bark with topgallants but no royals on fore- and mainmast. *Eleanor*'s triple-expansion steam engine would drive her at 12 knots under ordinary conditions. She carried enough coal for 4,000 miles under steam alone. The luxury of her appointments was staggering. Ralph Snow, in his history of the Bath Iron Works, devotes two large, closely written pages to what amounts to a list of elegances, from the comfortable fo'c's'le for thirty hands and small private staterooms for servants, to the main saloon, "dominated by a large mahogany table with carved sides and legs, and by a rich cut-glass Tiffany hanging lamp. Around the sides of the compartment, divans 'upholstered in a delicate shade of plush' offered haven to the weary traveller. . . . the walls of the saloon were graced with oil painting valued at no less than $60,000 and the floor was covered with valuable Persia carpets." The owner's cabin was equally ostentatious, with steam heat, speak ing tubes communicating with captain and engineer, and electric bells t summon servants. Similar cabins without the speaking tubes were provide for guests. *Eleanor* carried on deck and on davits not only two lifeboats but 28-foot gig, a 20-foot dinghy, a 25-foot naphtha launch, and Mr. Slater's 2(foot catboat in which he could sail about in the protected waters of foreig harbors.

Eleanor did, indeed, sail around the world, from 1894 to 1896, passin through the Suez Canal and the Strait of Magellan from west to east. Sh served Slater for several more years, was sold to Mr. James Martinez-Cardoz in 1900 and then to the railroad tycoon James J. Hill. She served in Worl War I as a convoy escort and after the war was sold to a Greek shipping firm an island steamer. In 1948 she was still afloat.

We deal with *Eleanor* at such length because in many ways she was cha acteristic of the quality demanded by open-handed millionaires.

Following *Eleanor,* in 1896 came the 136-foot *Peregrine* for Euger Tomkins on an only slightly more modest scale. In 1899, *Aphrodite* was bui for Colonel Oliver H. Payne. He had chartered *Eleanor* for a season and wante something even better. *Aphrodite* was bark-rigged, 330 feet overall, with 3,500-horsepower triple-expansion steam engine to drive her at 17 knots, an with appointments to match *Eleanor*'s. The 170-foot *Virginia* followed i 1899, and the 182-foot *Pantooset* in 1902. The 224-foot *Winchester,* for P. W Rouse in 1916, and the 229-foot *Isabel.* for J. N. Willys in 1917, were bot purchased by the Navy during World War I. They carried no sails, but we turbine powered, and both were built for speed, which they attained. The histories have been related in Chapter 29.

The Iron Works also built sailing yachts. The first, *Defiance,* built in 191 to defend the *America*'s Cup, was a 92-foot sloop, designed by George Owe with steel frames and keel, planked with mahogany and ceiled with fir, t woodwork being subcontracted to Hodgdon Brothers in East Boothbay. Sh was a handsome vessel, but because of dissension* within the syndicate sh never even approached her potential in races with *Resolute* and *Vanitie*. Th Cup race was postponed until 1920 because of World War I, and long befo *Resolute* faced *Shamrock IV*, *Defiance* had been scrapped. In 1924 the Bath Irc Works Ltd. built their last steel luxury yacht, *Aras*.

Eager for any work to keep the crew busy, the Iron Works built for Fran Paine a wooden Six-Meter yacht in 1924. In 1925 sixteen 58-foot woode Seawanhaka-class schooners and two wooden power yachts were built, an with these the Bath Iron Works Ltd. went under.

* The biography of *Defiance,* with an account of the disagreements within the syndicate and of relations with George Owen, is published in *WoodenBoat* magazine, September/October 199 See the Bibliography.

Pete Newell and his associates chartered the new Bath Iron Works Corporation in 1927 on the premise that they could build quality steel yachts for a price competitive with German yards.* Their first was 240-foot *Vanda* for Ernest B. Dane in 1927. She was followed by seventeen more yachts before the end of 1931, ranging in size from J. P. Morgan's 343-foot *Corsair* to C.

Above: Bark-rigged steam yacht *Aphrodite*. *Below:* Launching of J. P. Morgan's *Corsair*. *Bath Iron Works*

* See Chapter 29.

Hayward Murphy's 106-foot *Althea*. Only one of these was rigged with sails and most were diesel powered, but the tradition of unbounded luxury was maintained. Almost all served in the Navy during the war in some capacity—stripped, of course, of luxury fittings—and few returned to yachting after the war, for the tradition of golden-age yachting was fast expiring among millionaires.

The only two sailing yachts built by the Bath Iron Works Corporation before World War II were *Black Douglas* and *Ranger*. The former was a three-masted schooner, 150 feet long, built in 1930 for Robert Roebling, grandson of the architect of the Brooklyn Bridge and connected with the wire-rope business. Rigged as a staysail schooner and equipped with a diesel auxiliary, she sailed around the world. She was bought into the Navy during the war. Her masts were removed and she was armed and used as an antisubmarine patrol boat. She was used by the U.S. Fish and Wildlife Service and the U.S. Bureau of Fisheries after the war until 1960, when she was re-rigged as a three-masted schooner and used as a charter yacht in the Caribbean. Now she is a private yacht again with *Aquarius* across her stern.

Ranger, the last J-boat to defend the *America*'s Cup, was designed by Starling Burgess and Olin Stephens for Harold S. Vanderbilt and built in 1937. *Ranger*'s hull was of steel, her plating riveted to the frames and faired absolutely perfectly without a bulge or hollow anywhere and smooth as glass. She was launched, rigged, and towed down the Kennebec, bound for Marblehead. Off Seguin that night she met a choppy sea, and someone on deck heard a *"spung"* from aloft. Whatever had parted put a greater strain on her remaining bar shrouds. So carefully were the strains calculated to reduce weight aloft that shroud after shroud let go during the night as an extra strain came on it, and at last the 165-foot duralumin mast, unsupported above the lower spreaders, folded over and collapsed. Within three weeks a new mast was built, and *Ranger* showed her quality. She won every qualifying race she entered and swept the challenger, *Endeavour II,* in four straight races. On the New York Yacht Club cruise she raced with the four other surviving J-boats and won almost every race. All told, she finished thirty-four races and won thirty-two during the one year of her sailing life, 1937. She was scrapped in 1941, and so ended the era of unrestrained luxury in yachting. No longer was it said of a gentleman's yacht, "If you have to ask what it costs, you can't afford it."

Long before World War II, emphasis had begun to shift toward smaller yachts that could be handled by amateur crews, perhaps with the help of an experienced paid captain and a foredeck hand or two. A gentleman desirous of owning a yacht would probably go to a naval architect like John Alden, Winthrop Warner, George Owen, Philip Rhodes, William Hand, S.S. Crocker, or Sparkman & Stephens—there were others—and explain what he wanted the boat for and where he intended to use her. The architect designed the boat to fit the customer's taste and needs, discussed the design with him at length, and solicited bids from builders in whom he had confidence. A builder was then selected and the hull built. It was expected that a gentleman interested in yachting would want a substantial vessel, something in the 40–60-foot range at least. The schooner rig was very popular, but many yawls and a few ketches were built. Most of the designs showed a relationship with fisherman ancestors, with round or clipper bows and neatly rounded counters. They carried a great deal of sail compared to modern yachts and were of comparatively large displacement. Teak decks, teak and mahogany trim varnished brilliantly, pol-

Ranger, last of the big J-boats to defend *America*'s Cup. *Bath Iron Works*

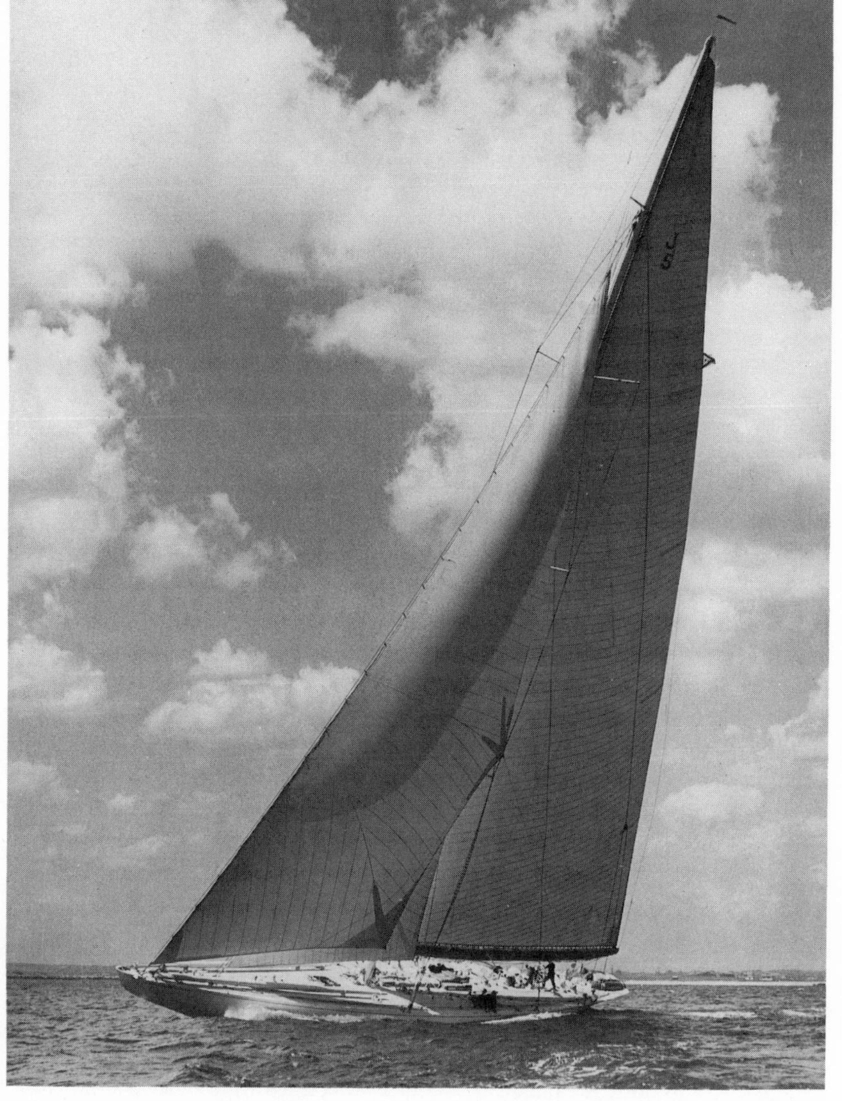

ished brass, and snowy cotton sails were considered proper for a gentleman's yacht. On vessels under about 75 feet a captain and steward were employed to live aboard during the season, maintain the yacht in sparkling condition, airing sails each sunny day, wiping down varnish, polishing brass, and, of course, hosting the ensign, private signal, and yacht club burgee at 8:00 A.M. and lowering them before the echo of the yacht club's sunset gun died away. The steward, besides helping the captain with the grubbier jobs, was responsible for cooking and cleaning up below and for keeping the yacht supplied with food and drink should the owner appear and wish to go to sea.

When the owner was aboard, of course, he was in command, but the captain did as much of the piloting, steering, sail handling, and anchor work as the owner wished him to do. The captain also had the usually unstated responsibility of keeping the yacht off the bottom and out of trouble. This sometimes called for considerable tact.

The steward was cook, waiter, dishwasher, and general cleaner-upper. The late George Peabody Gardner, Harvard 1910, successful businessman, owner of Roque Island and typical of the best of the gentleman-yachtsmen of the 1930s and '40s, describes his lifestyle aboard his 50-foot yawl *Glide* in his book, *Ready About*:

> A typical day's eating schedule on the *Glide* would be approximately as follows:
>
> Breakfast usually at anchor, about 7:30. Fresh berries or bananas, if possible; if not, fresh or frozen orange juice; dry cereal, whatever kind appeals; scrambled eggs and bacon, or kippered herring. (Eggs are scrambled because Minot won't eat any other kind.) Or if no eggs then pancakes, particularly if there are fresh blueberries to mix in the batter; this is a specialty of the *Glide*. And no matter what else there is for breakfast, there is always ready at hand some English marmalade.
>
> Mid-morning snack about 11:30. V-8 or tomato juice if the day is warm, or hot consommé or chicken broth if it is cold; in either case with wheatmeal biscuits or the equivalent.
>
> Lunch underway about 1:00. Usually a hot chowder if by any chance Oscar [professional skipper and cook] has built one, or if there is any left over from the previous day—second-day chowder being always the best. (A chowder, mind you, is never "made" or "cooked"—it is always "built" or "fashioned." Those nondescript affairs in which tomatoes play such an important part, and which in certain benighted regions masquerade under the name of chowder, may be "made" or "cooked," for all I know or care.) Or the soup may be a Philadelphia pepper-pot, or vegetable beef broth, chicken noodle, or pea—whatever seems appropriate. Cold meat, cheese (avoiding the processed kind if possible), salad, and instant coffee. The salad is made up of whatever vegetables happen to be on hand, with a dressing prepared by the skipper—me. This varies somewhat with the mood, but the ingredients are usually a small amount of wine vinegar, a good deal of the best Italian olive oil, salt, pepper, and mustard, a sprinkling of herb mixture and dash of onion—but easy on the onion because of Minot's stomach. Then comes a good tossing and turning of the whole thing, a process which almost takes care of itself if the boat is jumping about enough.
>
> Afternoon tea just as soon as we have dropped anchor, or even before, if we are late getting into port. A China tea, of course, sweetened with honey and no cream.

Nearly all of my companions seem to like tea—if not for breakfast, as I do, certainly when anchored after a wet cold day. Some of them have even been known to put a dash of rum or Bourbon in theirs. Along with the tea we have biscuits or toast, and jam—strawberry, or cherry, or blackberry.

Dinner hour depends upon when we get in, but is never before we have spruced up a bit and had our cocktails, be they Martinis, rare Bourbon, or Scotch. With the cocktails, olives, but only the super-colossal kind—just plain colossal won't do at all—and furthermore, not stuffed; nuts of various kinds; sardines, cheese, smoked whale-meat—very good, by the way—smoked salmon, spratts, pâté de foie gras. Seldom, if ever, caviar. In my opinion, this delicacy has to be very fresh to be rewarding.

For dinner perhaps a green turtle soup, with our own sherry added; juicily cooked fried chicken, as only Oscar can do it (or steak when we can get a good one); new boiled potatoes, fresh string beans, cranberry sauce. The sherbet glasses (our euphemistic name for wine glasses) are on the table and it is decided to fill them from the bottle of Montrachet that was thoughtfully put on ice earlier by the skipper or one of his companions. For dessert, brandied peaches and cream—once in a while, if we think the "brandied" fruit has been misnamed and needs a little boosting, just a teeny extra dollop of something might be added!—Bourbon biscuits, and coffee or Sanka.

At risk of spending altogether too much time talking about the pleasures of the table, I would also mention that we make a practice of using good china, stainless-steel cutlery, and proper glasses. Most of the latter are of the unbreakable kind and, like the china, are inherited from the *Rose*.* We have plastic plates as well and some exceptionally serviceable plastic bowls that can be used with impunity on deck as well as below. But whether fine china or plastic is the choice, dishes are always carefully washed in very hot water, wiped, and promptly stowed away; not, as on some boats, swished in salt water and tossed into the sink, ready for the next meal.

Lest the reader conclude that the gentleman yachtsman did nothing but eat and drink, we include this account of a crossing of the Bay of Fundy from Cape Sable to Roque Island. Oscar, paid skipper and cook, was ashore in a hospital as a result of an accident. Gardner had three friends for crew. Mr. Gardner writes:

We found the whistle off Seal Island [Cape Sable, the southwest corner of Nova Scotia] without difficulty and put the *Glide* on her course for Libby Island, Maine. A nice fair breeze, and after lunch we hoisted the spinnaker and began clocking off the miles. Our troubles, we thought, were now over. What a kick it gave us to enjoy a fine wind and a moderately smooth sea, even if the skies were overcast and the sea rather greasy-looking.

By evening the wind had freshened considerably, so much so that when we took in the spinnaker, under which we had been doing eight knots or better by the Kenyon speedometer log, we were soon going just as fast without it. We sighted what we thought was a buoy but which turned out to be Lurcher Lightship. We passed it at 6:50 P.M. although we had not figured on passing it until 8 P.M. at the earliest. This

* *Rose* was a 65-foot marconi-rigged yawl built for Gardner. She was loaned to the Navy for the yacht patrol in 1942 and stranded on Peaked Hill Bar off Cape Cod. The crew was rescued, and *Rose* sailed off by herself, intercepted a convoy, and was sunk by gunfire.

plainly showed what the tides can do in that region; our usually accurate log was off b seven miles.

Just before dark—we were approaching the Bay of Fundy—it began to rain an to blow even harder. We decided it would be wise to take down the mainsail whil there was still light, especially as at the rate we were going we might come up on Libb before dawn. Soon we were going as fast under forestaysail and mizzen as we had bee with spinnaker and mainsail.

By then the rain was lashing us and the sea was really angry. All around us was wild confusion of whitecapped waves, a colossal stampede of maddened white horse rearing, galloping, and tumbling. To look behind was truly terrifying. Seas came roa ing toward us, threatening to break over our stern and overwhelm us with tons c water. Time after time it seemed nothing short of miraculous that those enormou waves instead of engulfing us would merely raise our stern skyward and then continu on their mad career.

It became a constant fear that we would not be able to check the wide swings c our bow in time to prevent the *Glide*'s broaching to and being rolled over and smoth ered by those frenzied waves. To steer a straight course was impossible. In vain w hoped the cloudbursts of rain would knock down the sea and moderate the wind. Onc we caught a distant glimpse of a bobbing light of some fishing boat; except for that w were very much alone.

Dumpy and I were on deck until midnight. Shortly before then the four of us wit some difficulty had taken in the mizzen, and under forestaysail alone we still we logging eight knots. At one stage, when the sea was roaring loudest, Dumpy leane toward me and shouted: "Maybe the boys at the Somerset Club, after their broile salmon with *sauce verte,* have something on us after all."

At midnight Jimmy and Bill Cox took over. Conditions were then so bad that th thought of life jackets had been forced into my mind. In my entire cruising experienc I had never had occasion to don one, but it seemed clear that this was rapidly becomin an occasion for which a life jacket was designed, if ever. . . .

A little later, while I was hanging on in my bunk, trying to doze, I heard shou from Jim on deck. He and Bill had picked up a fog signal and feared we might be clo aboard. I withstood the impulse to rush on deck in scant attire, taking time to cloth myself fully before going up to face the highly disagreeable elements and the ne complication.

There were three possibilities. The sound might have been from Machias Se Island. In that case we were all right if we kept it to starboard; if to port—oh, oh! C from Libby, for which we were aiming but which we had no desire to come up on i pitch darkness; Libby was no place to make a landing at the rate we were going. Or might have been Moose Peak, in which case we were well off our course and facin plenty of trouble on either side. . . .

After a while we no longer heard the fog signal. . . . There was no sense in runnin a needless risk, so we gybed over and backtracked on our course as closely as possible

When daylight began to dawn and we had a hundred yards or more of visibilit we turned back on our course and soon picked up the sound once more. This time w were able to assure ourselves that it definitely came from Libby. As things turned ou we still had some way to go, and it was actually over an hour before we saw the loo of Libby. Here we went in close, laid our course for the bell off The Brothers, and fro The Brothers we could see clearly enough not to worry any more. Soon we were c

> Great Head [Roque Island]; a few minutes more and we were tying up at our own mooring at Roque. Never did the call from the bow, "All secure, Captain!" sound sweeter. . . .
>
> Off came the oilskins, off peeled the wet clothes! Down went a slug of Bourbon!—then hot coffee—a sizzling steak!
>
> And so to bunks.

Anyone who will cross the Bay of Fundy in rain and fog at night in a gale of wind without Loran, radar, or radio direction finder is a man of skill and courage.

Gentlemen's yachts in Boothbay Harbor. *George I. Hodgdon, Jr.*

Such vessels as *Rose* and *Glide* were built and finished with great care, their construction often overseen by the owner's hired skipper. Furthermore, the builder's reputation was on the line with the designer, the owner, and the yachting fraternity, whose members inspected each others' yachts rather critically. Also, the owners, unlike the owners of the big steam yachts, did not adopt a "cost-is-no-consideration" attitude. They expected the architect to keep the cost down as much as possible. Thus the architects shopped around for good builders who could do yacht work at modest prices, and this brought them to the Maine coast.

John Alden as early as 1906 had Wilbur Morse of Friendship, the builder of many Friendship sloops for Maine fishermen, build a 33-foot gaff topsail sloop, *Aimee,* for one of his clients. Before the United States entered World War I, Alden had used the Adams, Hodgdon Brothers, and Rice Brothers yards in East Boothbay, and F. F. Pendleton's yard in Woolwich for a total of twelve yachts, the largest being the 72-foot schooner *Jeanette,* built by Hodgdon Brothers in 1912. Most of the twelve were in the 40–60-foot rang although Rice Brothers built eleven 26-foot Stamford knockabouts in 191 These, however, could scarcely be classed as real yachts in those days.

In 1906 Hodgdon Brothers built the 53-foot schooner *Clione* for B. Crowninshield and, before World War II, thirty-seven others for George Owe John Alden, Tams, Crowninshield, and Bowes & Mower.

Yacht building was, of course, interrupted during World War I, b picked up rapidly in the 1920s. Yachting was spreading rapidly down t social ladder. Owning a yacht and yachting like a gentleman was expensiv but owning a yacht was a status symbol as well as a pleasure. More and mo of the growing upper middle class got into it in the 1920s and 1930s.

Rather strangely, the designers found that good boats could be built le expensively in Maine than in Massachusetts, Connecticut, or New York. Ce tainly living is no cheaper in Maine than to the westward in terms of foo clothes, and fuel, although taxes then may have been somewhat less. Howeve Maine yards had been building fishing vessels for generations and had a po ulation of skilled craftsmen who were used to putting up a vessel quickl efficiently, and strongly. Yacht finish was not learned in the building of fishe men, but when business was slow in a Maine winter many Maine carpente went to Massachusetts yards like Simms' or Lawley's, or to Herreshoff's Rhode Island or to City Island in New York, and worked on yachts the Maine men were much in demand, for they did good work quickly and soo acquired the knack of working to yacht standards. Paul Luke, later founder his own yard in East Boothbay, developed much of his skill in cabinet work rebuilding the cabins of the big schooner-yacht *Dauntless* in Perth Ambo New Jersey. Goudy and Stevens in East Boothbay sent down a crew to spe most of the winter on that job.

As an example of Maine prices, compare F. F. Pendleton's bid on 67-foot yawl designed in 1934 by Philip L. Rhodes with those of four othe

Minneford Yacht Yard	$34,500
Jacobson & Peterson	33,400
M. M. Davis & Sons	26,200
George F. Lawley & Sons	25,500
F. F. Pendleton	22,000

Note the great spread in bid prices. Perhaps some of the high bidders were n very hungry. It is interesting, too, to look at some of the costs on which M Pendleton based his bids:

Planking	5,000 bf $150 / 1,000, delivered	$800
Oak	8,000 bf $60 / 1,000, delivered	480
Teak deck	1,950 bf .40 / bf	780
Spars		1,000
Lead keel	2,800 lb cast & delivered	1,400
Anchors	125 lb and 175 lb	105
Chain	35 fathoms ½″ BBB	100

Standing rigging (material only)	100
11 winches	265
Steering gear w / 32″ wheel	200

East Boothbay in the years between the wars built a great many yachts for well-known designers. Most of these yachts were beautifully finished and elegantly appointed for individual discriminating yachtsmen. Three yards dominate the small town.

Hodgdon Brothers, with a family tradition of commercial shipbuilding going back at least to 1819, turned to yacht building about 1905. Between then and World War I, they built forty-one wooden yachts to designs by Owen, Crowninshield, Alden, and others. Among these was *Quill II,* a 38-foot yawl that became a tradition on Penobscot Bay. Neat and well finished as she was in every detail on deck, she exceeded that standard below with a neatly built-in galley, a dresser with carved doors, a fiddle rail supported by turned posts, and drawers with dovetailed joints. The 72-foot *Dorello II,* designed by Owen, and the rugged schooner *Black Duck,* built for Alexander Forbes of Naushon, are notable.

During the war, Hodgdon built two 110-foot sub-chasers for the Navy but kept on with yacht work. Between 1919 and 1940 the yard launched ninety yachts for designers William Hand, John Alden, Starling Burgess, George Owen, and Sparkman & Stephens. Among these were eight yachts over 70 feet long, including the 127-foot schooner *Zodiac.* In addition the yard built the 87-foot arctic-exploration schooner *Bowdoin,* for the late Donald MacMillan. Rebuilt, *Bowdoin* is still sailing under the flag of the Maine Maritime Academy. Hodgdon also built a small fleet of 21-foot sloops called Christmas Cove sloops for the yacht club at Christmas Cove on Rutherford Island, Bristol.

During World War II and again during the Korean War, Hodgdon Brothers joined Goudy and Stevens to build naval vessels, but continued to build yachts of more modest size and finish.

In 1957 George I. Hodgdon, Jr., took over the yard and built fifty-three more boats of generally smaller sizes. In 1966 he sold the yard to the Tillotson Corporation and moved to Linekin Bay where he continues to build fine wooden boats, usually one at a time, with a smaller crew. Recently his son Tim has taken over the yard and presided over the finishing of the 87-foot *Yorel.* According to *Maine Boats and Harbors* magazine, "Comments have been made to the effect that *Yorel* might easily be the finest wooden power yacht ever built in Maine."

Goudy and Stevens was established in a small barn up the hill from the original Hodgdon Brothers yard in 1920 by Wallace Goudy and J. Arthur Stevens. They started with small boats, built a 47-foot excursion boat in 1924, and bought the Adams yard on the shore. Here they quickly got into yacht work with several powerboats and, in the next few years, built eighteen 43-foot Alden schooners. In 1929 they built *Sartatia,* a 53-foot schooner, and

Pinafore, last of seventeen Alden 43s built by Goudy and Stevens. *Goudy and Stevens*

went on to build between three and eight yachts each year until World War II. In 1945 they were building yachts again, launching eleven in that year ranging from Alden's ketch *Malabar XIII* to a succession of 21-foot Boothbay Harbor One-Design racing sloops.

In 1950 they were again into war work, building minesweepers. Then they varied wooden yacht work with small steel workboats and between 1959 and 1961 built forty-two stock Boothbay 33 powerboats, no longer in the luxury tradition of the 1920s. In 1963 Goudy and Stevens built their most famous yacht, the 106-foot replica of *America* for the Schaefer Brewing Company. Although much like Commodore John Cox Stevens's original *America* outside, she had modern machinery and conveniences below. In 1967 they built their first big steel dragger. In 1969 the three-masted steel schooner *Sea Star* was built for Laurance Rockefeller, and with her, the yard converted to building big steel fishermen and took over the old Hodgdon yard for yacht storage, maintenance, and repair. George I. Hodgdon started a smaller yard at the head of Linekin Bay.

Rice Brothers was also building yachts and got into steel construction early, varying yachts with a number of steel lightships. In 1926 they built the 125-foot steel schooner *Starling,* a fleet of 30-foot A-boats for Northeast Harbor owners, and a number of fast powerboats—including engines.

Harvey Gamage across the river in South Bristol built fifteen Alden 43s as well as a number of 30-foot Malabar Juniors. Nicholas Blaisdell & Son of Woolwich also built nine Malabar Juniors.

Charles Morse in Thomaston had built several big round-bowed sloops for fishermen, either with or without bowsprit, following the trend of Gloucester fishing schooners. In 1908 he built the first round-bowed knockabout fishing sloop, *Harvey A,* 40 feet overall. She was very successful and was followed by several others including *Pennesewassee* and *Lowell Boys*. The best known was *Lizzie M,* built in 1917 for Tom Martelock. When fishing under sail became obsolete, these sloops were converted into highly successful yachts. Morse, influenced by the Gloucester schooners and by the success of his round-bowed sloops, built the 60-foot schooner *Lloyd W. Berry*. As a yacht she was a great success, so successful that John Alden went down to Thomaston in search of a

Replica of *America,* built by Goudy and Stevens in 1967. *Goudy and Stevens*

Sea Star, last of the big sailing yachts built in East Boothbay. *Boutilier photo*

Lion's Whelp, a luxury motoryacht of the 1960s. *Goudy and Stevens*

big fishing sloop or small schooner he could modify as a yacht. Morse at first would have nothing to do with Mr. Alden or his project but, as Alden was leaving, called him back and eventually agreed to build *Malabar I* in 1921. Morse and Alden got on very well after this success, and Morse built *Malabar II, III, IV,* and *V* as well as over thirty other yachts for Alden before World War II, mostly in the 40–60-foot range.

I. L. Snow's yard in Rockland and Camden Shipbuilding & Dry Dock also built a few large gentlemen's yachts.

Mount Desert Island was a yachting center rather separate from the rest of the coast. As the wealthy people established cottages at Bar Harbor, they brought their luxury yachts with them, and others joined them from time to time. As early as 1871 Harvard president Charles Eliot had saluted seven Eastern Yacht Club yachts from Marblehead off Schooner Head. By the mid-1880s many big, handsome sailing and steam yachts anchored in Bar Harbor. In the 1890s Bar Harbor 30s, about 50 feet overall, were racing as a class in Frenchman Bay.

In 1914 six Eastern Yacht Club 17-footers designed by Edwin A. Boardman, known as A-boats, were raced at Northeast Harbor. The A fleet increased after World War I as more of the original Lawley-built A-boats were brought up, and in 1926 Rice Brothers in East Boothbay built twenty-five more from the same plans. They raced in diminishing numbers until 1971, and a few are still afloat.

In the early 1920s a number of Manchester 17s were established in Bar Harbor, Northeast Harbor, Islesboro, North Haven, Camden, and Sorrento as a racing class and known as B-boats in Mount Desert waters. Manchester 15s, Alden O-boats, MDIs designed by Ralph Winslow, and in 1929 a fleet of Swedish 30-Square-Meter boats designed by Manfred Curry in Germany made Mount Desert Island the biggest yachting center east of Marblehead. Before World War II, in 1938, the establishment of the International class with fourteen sloops built in Norway and designed by Bjarne Aas of Frederikstad put the "big boat" cap on Mount Desert racing. These 33-foot, fast, handsome vessels are no toys. The class is indeed international, and regattas are still held annually with representatives from many states and countries.

After the war the Luders 16 became popular, followed by a number of other classes including Bullseyes (Herreshoff 12½s), Mercurys, Huskies, and Brutal Beasts, in varying numbers at different times. Now J-boats, not the great J-boats of *America*'s Cup racing but a series of smaller, fast cruising-racing boats, are an important part of the Northeast Harbor fleet.

Most of these racing boats were built elsewhere, but there are several yards on the island, the best known of which is The Hinckley Company (formerly Henry R. Hinckley Inc.) at Manset. In 1932 as a young man Henry Hinckley took over the management of a small service yard owned by his father in Manset. During the 1930s, assisted by Cliff Rich of Bass Harbor, he built a number of small powerboats and, just before World War II, six yawls for the Naval Academy and several Islander-class sloops for Sparkman & Stephens.

During the war the yard built about 500 powerboats and afterwards built about 100 Hinckley Sou'westers from an Alden design, twenty Sou'wester Juniors, and twenty or thirty Hinckley 21s followed by the Hinckley 36, the Owens cutter, and the Pilot 35. These were all wooden stock boats.

When fiberglass boats began to displace wooden construction, Hinckley at first finished off Beetle-built fiberglass powerboat hulls from South Dartmouth, Massachusetts, and undertook to repair fiberglass boats as needed, but in 1960 built the first Tripp-designed Bermuda 40, a highly successful design. By 1991, 203 hulls had been turned out of that mold. Other models followed, and now the Hinckley yard offers the 40-, 42-, 51-, and 59-foot auxiliaries and 39-foot and 42-foot powerboats.

These boats are all built to very high standards of construction and are neatly finished out in a less ornate style than that of the 1920s. The sailing vessels are available as sloops or yawls. Accommodation plans can be varied somewhat to suit the owner's needs and such amenities as running hot water, showers, and mechanical refrigeration provided. Hinckley yachts

A Hinckley Bermuda 40, one of the most popular modern cruising-racing yachts. *Henry Hinckley, Inc.*

A contemporary production fiberglass yacht.

have been all over the world and have done well in numerous ocean races.

In recent years the firm has developed an active storage, repair, and maintenance service and a busy brokerage and chartering division. Their float is busy all summer with new yachts fitting out, charter boats coming in or out, and transients in need of help. A base at Bass Harbor has been established to take off some of the pressure.

E. Farnham Butler established the Mt. Desert Yacht Yard at the head of Somes Sound before World War II at first to provide storage and repair facilities for racing boats and to build a small boat or two in the winter. During the war the yard expanded to build three Naval Academy yawls and a number of buoy boats and workboats.

After the war, Butler designed and built three Maine Coast yawls—lovely boats of a conventional design. A study of construction and maintenance costs led him to the conclusion that these costs were directly proportional to displacement; hence, any way of reducing weight was economically desirable. In 1950 Cyrus Hamlin, an innovative naval architect, had adapted the old fisherman method of strip building to modern craft. Butler took it up, building a boat without frames from 1-inch square strips of cedar, each glued to the one below and nailed through two into the third. Strengthened by bulkheads, deck and floor timbers, the boat was practically one piece, very strong, and most unlikely to leak. Having found the method successful, he then developed the Controversy design with a reverse sheer. The thinking here is that in a yacht,

Reverse-sheer *Constellation* leading a conventional Maine Coast Yawl, *Snowflake*. *E. Farnham Butler*

room amidships, particularly headroom, light below, and buoyancy when heeled are highly desirable. With buoyant forward sections and freeboard amidships, she will not soak her cockpit crew unduly. Strip built, she will be light, hence economical to build and maintain, and without the usual frames and ceiling will gain space below. Butler designed and built the 31-foot *Controversy* and sisters of different sizes in 1952 and 1953. He also developed the Amphibi-Con, a 25-foot Controversy type small enough and light enough to be carried on a trailer yet fast, able, and comfortable enough for cruising. One was sailed to Labrador and brought home from Newfoundland on a trailer. In the late 1950s, with the coming of fiberglass and the pressure of foreign competition, Mt. Desert Yacht Yard, with many other Maine yards, specialized in storage, maintenance, and repair work.

At the same time as expensive gentlemen's yachts were being built and sailed on the coast, a subculture developed of people who liked cruising, had strictly limited budgets and a modest lifestyle. These people bought fishing sloops rendered obsolete by gasoline engines, extended the cuddy to make a small cabin, built in bunks, tied down a small Shipmate woodstove or a two-burner alcohol or kerosene stove, and pushed off, towing a punt, skiff, dory, or peapod instead of a varnished cedar tender.

They carried water in gallon jugs and made do without a head. Most took pleasure and no little pride in maintaining their boats themselves and learning to do what rigging, engine work, and carpentry became necessary. When bottoms fouled with weed in mid-season, they grounded out on the tide alongside a wharf, slapped on a coat of quick lime boiling hot with an old broom, and later perhaps a quick coat of copper paint. Small brass and little varnish was the rule.

These sailors dressed in work clothes with a long-billed swordfisherman's cap and, in wet weather, the sticky oil clothes of the fisherman. They ate fish they caught, what they could buy at local stores, and simple canned goods—beans and corned beef hash. They slept in sleeping bags on camp mattresses. Ashore they were students, teachers, college professors, small-business men, artists of one sort or another; afloat they saw themselves as competent seamen with profound respect for fishermen and a large contempt for the ostentation of yachtsmen.

When the fishermen's sloops gave up, these low-profile cruising people had built small sloops and yawls, usually less than 35 feet, which the yacht builders often built alongside a larger boat to use short ends of time and materials. A market for these boats developed, of which designers took advantage. Alden developed the Malabar Junior, a sloop about 29 feet long. The Owens cutter and the Amphibi-Con were mentioned earlier. These could be built as stock boats, with many built from the same molds and patterns, and could be put together quickly and comparatively inexpensively. Finish was ordinarily plain and neat but varied, of course, from yard to yard.

Any account of yachting on the Maine coast would be incomplete without mention of the phenomenal development of the Friendship sloop as a yacht. Anyone cruising the coast from Kittery to Mount Desert is almost certain to see one of these handsome sloops, like a memory of a past era, slashing through the afternoon chop or running for a quiet harbor at day's end.

When fishing under sail became obsolete after World War I, many Friendship sloops were laid up and soon rotted out in the sun and rain. Some were converted to yachts, but most yachtsmen were uncomfortable with a main boom extending well over the counter and a long widow-maker of a bowsprit. Consequently, they cut off the mainsail at the first reef band and shortened the bowsprit to balance the rig. They found the sloop thus cut down slow and logy in ordinary summer weather, so sought other yachts. By 1960 there were very few Friendship sloops surviving and almost none had been built in recent years.

In 1960 Bernard Mackenzie of Scituate, Massachusetts, in a cut-down and rebuilt Charles Morse sloop, *Voyager,* won the Boston Power Squadron "bang and go back" race, running before a fresh easterly for which a single reef was about right. Delighted with the performance of a Friendship sloop against modern boats, with the assistance of John Gould, Carlton Simmons, Herold

Jones, and other Friendship residents, he founded the Friendship Sloop Society, dedicated to preserving the heritage and traditions of the Friendship sloop. Fourteen sloops appeared for the first homecoming race in 1961 at Friendship. A regatta has been held every year since. Now 250 sloops are registered with the Society, most of them built since 1950 and many built by their owners. Lash Brothers in Hatchet Cove, Friendship, built six and Philip J. Nichols of Round Pond built four. McKie Roth in Edgecomb and James Rockefeller on Bald Mountain each built three. Ralph Stanley in Southwest Harbor built several and rebuilt several more. In 1969 Jarvis Newman built a 25-foot sloop of fiberglass, the first of a whole generation. In the same year Bruno & Stillman in Newington, New Hampshire, started a series of 30-foot fiberglass Friendships on an altered design. Passamaquoddy Yachts in Eastport built a fiberglass version of one of McKie Roth's sloops. In 1974 Newman produced a larger 31-foot sloop from the rebuilt *Dictator*. She has been very successful.

The Friendship Sloop Society is active, conducting regattas at New London and Marblehead as well as the principal one, which has now moved from Friendship to Boothbay. You can't get away from Friendship sloops in New England.

Powerboats also became popular in the 1920s and 1930s. Chris-Craft, Elco, and other builders turned out stock craft on designs usually showing commercial ancestry. They were comfortably appointed, modestly powered according to modern standards, and sometimes quite good-looking.

With the fiberglass revolution in the late 1950s, everything changed. At first the fiberglass yacht looked like the greatest discovery since the birchbark canoe. Inexpensive to build, not subject to rot, unlikely to leak either through deck or bottom, cheap to maintain, and light in weight, fiberglass boats became the fashion. However, they effected profound changes in American yachting which soon became visible on the Maine coast.

Fiberglass boats are made in hollow molds the shape of the outside of the boat. First a "plug" is built to exactly the shape of the proposed boat. Around this is built a mold of fiberglass. The inside of the mold is waxed, then sprayed with gelcoat. Then layers of 'glass cloth are laid inside the gelcoat and each layer soaked with a chemical resin and allowed to harden. The boat is lifted out of the mold, ballast is either put into a hollow keel or bolted on, bulkheads and interior work are installed, and a deck, popped out of another mold, is bolted and 'glassed on. The engine and rigging are installed, and away she goes, presumably never to leak and never to need painting.

In this process the most expensive parts are building the plugs and molds for hull and deck. To recover these costs the builder must sell a considerable number of identical boats. He must have a sales department, an advertising program, a financing system to persuade the public that his particular model is the safest, fastest, easiest to handle, most comfortable, and least expensive yacht on the market.

Many of the fiberglass boats are sold in boat shows to customers who have no tradition of sailing behind them and who have had little saltwater experience. The prospective customer mounts a set of steps alongside the boat, is asked to take off his shoes to prevent scarring the fine fiberglass finish (an impressive gesture) and shown the carpeted cabin with six bunks, a "teak and holly" plywood sole, a cramped head with a shower, a neat, compact little galley with stainless-steel sink and a gas stove with oven, a mechanical refrigerator, electric lights, and full headroom. The engine? Oh yes. Tucked away under the cockpit with quarter-berths partitioned off on each side. Storage space for sea bags, oil clothes, wet sails, anchors and rode? Hard to find. Place to spread out a chart without getting in the cook's way? Seldom does the inexperienced prospect think of that. How does she sail? The prospect is shown a colorful brochure with a picture of the boat going fast under sail, heeling just enough to be fun. Seldom does such a buyer insist on trying the boat out under sail. He is told that if he puts down a payment at the show, he will get a substantial discount and suddenly, with the down payment, he will become a captain.

This selling campaign aimed at the inexperienced brought changes in design. The "discovery" that cost was proportional to displacement, the emphasis on speed—or apparent speed—and the emphasis on accommodations led to short-ended, broad-beamed, shallow hulls with excessive freeboard and cabin height. To keep such a boat on her feet, she was short rigged, ballasted with a short, deep fin keel, and, because the keel was short, steered with a detached rudder supported, if at all, with a short skeg. Being very light, these boats seem quite fast in moderate breezes in smooth water, especially racing against each other.

Despite its advantages, fiberglass as a construction material has revealed a few weaknesses. The outer gelcoat is not always impervious; water gets in through tiny pinholes, causes unsightly blisters, and causes the 'glass layers beneath to separate. This involves expensive refinishing. Also, a fiberglass boat is not entirely without maintenance costs. Rigging and engine are subject to the same maintenance problems as those of wooden yachts, although modern stainless-steel rigging and better-engineered diesel engines have reduced these problems. The bottom of a fiberglass yacht needs the same antifouling treatment as that of any other boat, and the topsides, unless vigorously washed and waxed, become dull and unattractive. Brightwork, of course, being wood, requires sandpaper, elbow grease, and varnish. The modern boat is usually equipped with winches which require attention, and electronics need careful maintenance.

Of course, the preceding paragraphs are grossly unfair to many experienced and capable yachtsmen, to designers who have developed really excellent and handsome fiberglass yachts, and to responsible builders who build and sell with restraint. The number of rugged fiberglass boats in the Bermuda Race, the Fastnet Race, the BOC transatlantic and 'round-the-world races, attests to

Yorel, a modern elegant wooden yacht built by Hodgdon Yachts in 1989. *George I. Hodgdon, Jr.*

their quality. Hal Roth's experiences running ashore in *Whisper* on Tierra del Fuego and north of Australia demonstrate the punishment a well-built fiberglass hull can absorb. Nevertheless, we see a great many under-rigged, high-charged little production yachts on the coast.

When wooden boats became almost obsolete because of the scarcity of good lumber and the expense of skilled labor, Maine building yards sought ways to survive. Some have hung on to building wooden boats of very high quality at high prices for the few who believe that wood is still the best material for a boat. Among respected wooden boat builders are Joel White in Brooklin, Ralph Stanley in Southwest Harbor, the late Malcolm Brewer and the late Elmer Collemer, both in Camden, J. O. Brown in North Haven, Winfield Lash in Friendship, the late J. Ervin Jones in East Boothbay and his surviving son, and George Hodgdon and his son Tim, also in East Boothbay. Others to the westward built or are building in York, Kennebunk, Falmouth Foreside, and Bailey Island. And there are a good many more.

These builders do not build many boats. They work alone or have small crews of older men who like to build wooden boats and younger ones eager to learn. Most of them take on considerable storage and repair work to keep their crews and provide regular income.

A little wooden boat building is done by alternative education schools. Lance Lee started the Apprenticeshop in association with the Maine Maritime Museum in Bath and built, among other vessels, the small Tancook Whaler

Vernon Langille. He moved to Rockport, where he established a new Apprenticeshop building interesting foreign types of boats as well as traditional Maine types. The Bath Apprenticeshop still builds and restores boats at the museum. WoodenBoat School in Brooklin has a Friendship sloop under construction in 1991, and its students have built a wide variety of small boats. The Washington County Vocational-Technical College runs an Apprenticeshop at Eastport, and there is the Landing School at Kennebunkport. However, even with all these builders and schools put together, not many wooden boats are built compared to the number of fiberglass production boats turned out nationwide.

Another response to the fiberglass revolution was that of Paul E. Luke of East Boothbay. He worked for Goudy and Stevens in his youth and in 1933 set up a small shop in which he built small boats, repaired larger ones, and built several sloops designed by Winthrop Warner. Warner was so pleased with Luke's quality that he had another sloop built for himself by Luke. Needing more space in which to build a 48-foot motorsailer to Warner's design, Luke bought land on Linekin Bay, rafted his shop to the new site, and built the boat. Until World War II he built "gold-platers" for Warner, C. Raymond Hunt, K. Aage Nielsen, and other prominent designers. After the war, during which he worked for the Navy, for Frank L. Sample, Inc., and for the Bath Iron Works, he returned to yacht work and built between forty and fifty fine wooden yachts in the 30–50-foot range for Nielsen, Alden, Garden, Sparkman & Stephens, Luders, Hunt, McCurdy & Rhodes, and others.

By 1969 it was becoming clear that the future of wooden boat building was dim indeed. The choices were (1) to stay with wood, building a very few first-class boats for the diminishing few who wanted wooden boats or (2) to go into production fiberglass, like Hinckley, involving heavy capital investment and a sales program, or (3) to go into aluminum. Luke chose the last alternative because although it involved considerable capital, it avoided the monotony of production work and meant building individual boats for individual designers and owners who valued high-quality work.

While his last wooden boat, *Kumari*, was under construction for McCurdy & Rhodes, Luke visited yards in Michigan and City Island, New York, that were building aluminum boats and learned the problems involved in forming and welding aluminum. He went several times to Holland and to Germany to visit the yards of Abeking & Rasmussen and to purchase the necessary machinery to work aluminum into compound curves. He returned with a contract to build another McCurdy & Rhodes vessel, the 48-foot aluminum *Sea Swallow*, for Oscar Straus. Luke lined up his crew, which had just finished *Kumari*, and said, "You are good wooden boat builders." He touched each on the shoulder with an aluminum rod and added, "And now you are good aluminum boat builders." *Sea Swallow* was launched in 1969. Since then, they have proved he was right. Luke's yard has built twenty-five aluminum boats to designs by the country's best-known designers for the most discriminating yachtsmen. At least until 1991 no other yard in Maine has built aluminum yachts, except for Paul Luke's son John. John Luke founded North Atlantic Industries in East Boothbay and builds hard-chined aluminum lobsterboats and motoryachts either to his own design or that of another architect.

In the last few years the competition with European yards for the very few aluminum yachts being built has led Paul Luke's yard into specializing in feathering propellers, stoves and cabin heaters, three-part Herreshoff storm anchors, and such deck hardware as ventilators, winches, and blocks. Paul's son Frank, who now runs the yard, has taken on storage and repair work to supplement the production of accessories.

Alacrity, a modern aluminum yacht built by Paul Luke for Dr. George Clowes. *Boutilier photo*

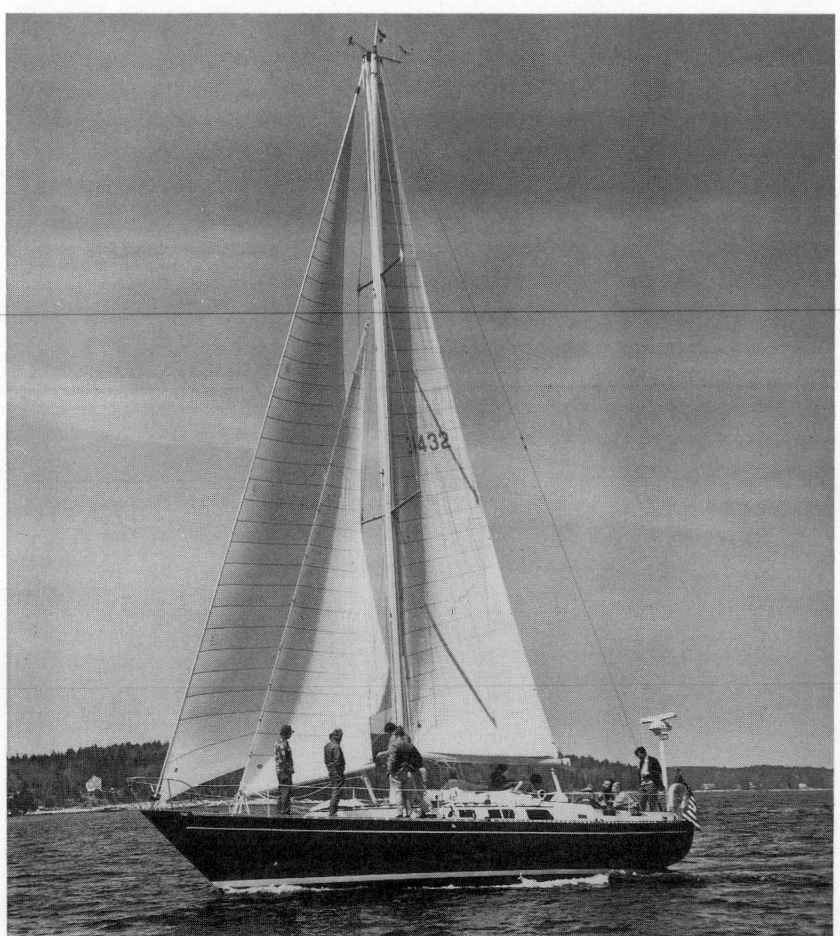

There has recently developed competition from Japan, Taiwan, and Korea in fiberglass boats, which can be built well and less expensively in the Orient than they can in the United States. This has led most Maine yards into storage, repair, and maintenance work. Billings Marine in Stonington, Wayfarer Marine in Camden, and Goudy and Stevens, Deerfoot Sample, and the Boothbay Region Boatyard in Boothbay will serve to illustrate a trend widespread from Mount Desert to Kittery.

With the rapid increase in the number of small yachts has come an advance in navigational devices. The Maine coast used to be avoided by the timorous because of its frequent summer fogs which obliged the navigator unacquainted with the coast to lie at anchor often for days. With the coming of Loran-C and radar, which can be carried on very small cruising boats, fog has few terrors—especially for the foolhardy who believe that electronics are infallible. Thus there are many more yachts on the Maine coast than there were fifteen years ago. Harbors are now peppered with moorings, marinas with finger piers have been established at such popular harbors as Kittery, Kennebunkport, Portland, South Freeport, Boothbay, Camden, and Northeast Harbor, and open coves that have never been considered as harbors are now crowded.

Numerous party-boats are eager to accommodate the vacationer who wants to sail or fish in Maine waters but who cannot own a boat. Since Robert Carter chartered a fishing sloop in 1858 with skipper and cook, party-boating has been part of a Maine summer. Fishermen on off days took sailing parties, and in the more popular harbors, some skippers made a summer's business of sailing parties. Friendship sloops, with their roomy cockpits, stable hulls, and good looks, were and are ideal for this business. In 1991 Friendship sloops are sailing parties from Perkins Cove, Boothbay, Friendship, Tenants Harbor, Rockland, Camden, Northeast Harbor, and Bar Harbor, and there may be others from year to year.

In 1936 Captain Frank Swift, an artist and a steamship man, applied the principle of the Western dude ranch to the schooner trade. He chartered the 54-foot coasting schooner *Mabel,* hired Captain Shepard of Deer Isle to go as skipper and Shepard's wife to go as cook. He signed on three passengers who paid for the opportunity to haul anchor, hoist and take in sail, trim sheets, and perhaps to get a trick at the wheel. The business started slowly, but as the idea caught on, Swift chartered more schooners—easily available, for there was no other work for them—and at one time had as many as nine. In 1961 he sold the business to Jim Nesbit and in 1969 he sold to Les Bex. Meanwhile, other skippers have entered the trade, and the "windjammer" business is booming.

Most of the old schooners built in the last century have now been retired from old age and pushed aside by increasingly stringent Coast Guard safety regulations, although several have been extensively rebuilt and still sail. A number of new vessels have been built especially for the trade. *Mary Day, Bill of Rights, Harvey Gamage,* and *Appledore II* were built by Harvey Gamage in South Bristol. They are fine, able vessels, comfortable within limits, and hand-

One of the first "windjammers," *Annie Kimball,* 1938. *Author's collection*

The skipper at the wheel of *Clinton,* an early "windjammer." *Author's collection*

some, although not noted for speed. *Shenandoah,* a topsail schooner with square fore topsail built by Gamage on the lines of an 1812 privateer, is very hard to catch with sheets started. Doug and Linda Lee and John Foss at North End Shipyard in Rockland built *Heritage. Roseway* and *Timberwind* were used as pilot schooners before they entered the passenger business, and *Adventure* was a high-line Gloucester fisherman, fast and handy with Captain Jim Sharp at the wheel. She is now being rebuilt as a museum piece by the city of Gloucester.

Heritage, a modern "windjammer" schooner built by Douglas Lee at North End Shipyard in Rockland and commanded by her builder. *Ed Glasser photo, Douglas Lee*

The biggest and most impressive of the fleet was *Victory Chimes,* a 132-foot three-masted schooner built as a "ram" for use in the Chesapeake and Delaware bays. She is just the size and almost the shape of the smallest lock on the Chesapeake–Delaware Canal. Captain Frederick Boyd Guild of Castine, who had been mate on big coasters, been fishing, and sailed parties in the big Friendship sloop *Georgie C. Bowden* and in the schooner *Alice Wentworth,* bought *Victory Chimes* as she lay on the bottom of Rockland Harbor in 1959, fixed her up all spit and polish, brass and varnish, employed a crew of nine, and carried forty-six passengers in the grand manner. It was always a delight to sail alongside her, to behold Captain Guild standing on the quarterdeck, his wife Janet at the wheel, and to see him ceremoniously raise his hat to us.

Captain Guild sold *Victory Chimes* about 1986 to a man who was going to use her on Lake Superior; he sold her to Domino's Pizza. Her name was changed to *Domino Effect*. She has been extensively rebuilt and was seen on the coast in the summers of 1989 and 1990 and was sailing passengers in 1991. She is again for sale.

These schooners usually make one-week trips, leaving Rockland or Camden on Monday morning, sailing east through the Thorofares or Eggemoggin Reach, usually making some harbor on Mount Desert. On the way west they may visit Isle au Haut, Matinicus, or Vinalhaven; Stonington, Brooklin, Castine, and Pulpit Harbor are popular anchorages. Usually they have a clambake ashore on an island, returning to home port Saturday morning in time for the crew to clean up and reprovision for receiving a new group of passengers Sunday afternoon. The food is said to be excellent and plentiful on these vessels. The music of guitar and accordion supports enthusiastic song on many cruises. Even if the weather is thick and wet, people seem to have a good time together on the water and return to the same vessel year after year.

Once each season, usually early in the summer, a number of schooners cruise to the westward, converging on Boothbay Harbor for Windjammer Day. They sail up the harbor together and anchor off the town, escorted by a horde of local small craft and excursion boats with the Coast Guard watching over them. Usually a naval vessel is present. There is a parade ashore, a concert, the crowning of Miss Windjammer, and a high old time. Later in the summer they rendezvous in Brooklin on Eggemoggin Reach, and an annual schooner race is held off Camden.

Recently the fleet has grown far beyond those listed here, and others join each year.

NOTES

The accounts and descriptions of Bath Iron Works yachts comes largely from Ralph Snow's *The First 100 Years,* although part of the story of the loss of *Ranger*'s first mast is from my recollection of a crew member's story of the event.

From here on, the chapter has been assembled from *John G. Alden and His Yacht Designs,* by Robert Carrick and Richard Henderson, and from personal interviews with James Stevens of Goudy and Stevens, George I. Hodgdon, Jr., of Hodgdon's Yachts, Paul E. Luke, E. Farnham Butler, and Robert Hinckley. Some help came from George P. Gardner's *Ready About,* from my own recollections, from bits out of Harold Clifford's *The Boothbay Region 1906–1960,* from the *Boothbay Register, Nautical Quarterly No. 8,* from research done previously for my book *Friendship Sloops,* from recollections of William Pattison, Angie Lewis, Stillman Kelley, and Lewis Iselin, all of Camden.

There is very little on power yachts. Most of those I have seen on the coast are stock boats. They are doubtless as carefully engineered and constructed as sailing yachts and are fitted up as nicely. Personally, I have had little experience with them, and that experience has not endeared them to me. Inexcusably but understandably, I have slighted them.

The fiberglass revolution I have watched, and I have several times visited the Hinckley yard in Manset. It is an impressive exhibit in quality work. However, it is the exception, not the rule. A visit to any boat show or marina or repair yard will support most of the statements herein.

The disclaimer at the bottom of page 525 I mean seriously, for certainly there are well-designed and well-built fiberglass boats.

As a party-boat skipper myself and an acquaintance of other party-boat skippers I have acquired much of the information and all of the prejudices in the last part of the chapter. Harry W. Smith's *Windjammers of the Maine Coast* provided specific facts on individual vessels.

The term "windjammer" needs explanation. In the last days of sail, steamboat men referred to square-rigged cargo vessels rather scornfully as windjammers. Count Luckner, in his account of his World War I experiences, uses the word in this context. When commercial sailing vessels disappeared from the seas and the cruise schooners multiplied on the coast, the word was resurrected and given a romantic connotation. Now it refers specifically to coasting schooner types that carry passengers. My Friendship sloop in the modern sense is not a windjammer. The term "tall ships," to apply to sailing vessels, particularly square-rigged vessels, has been lifted from John Masefield's "Sea Fever" and has a far more romantic ancestry than "windjammer."

In 1991 these "windjammer" schooners were sailing out of Camden and Rockland: *American Eagle, Isaac H. Evans, Lewis R. French, Heritage, Domino Effect, Summertime, Mary Day, Roseway, Stephen Taber, J & E. Riggin, Timberwind, Nathaniel Bowditch;* and the ketch *Angelique*. This list is not necessarily complete.

THIRTY-THREE

History Hot Off the Stove

HISTORY HOT OFF THE STOVE is difficult to write and probably unreliable. Just as a good chowder is better the second day when its fish, salt pork, and onions have had a chance to get acquainted with its potatoes, so the events in a history need time to settle into proper relation with one another. Nevertheless, here are some thoughts about the ingredients of 1992 history.

The Maine coast fisherman is living in the industry's period of transition between a time of abundance and a time when the resource, the fish stocks, must be maintained at a sustainable yield. The fisherman is surrounded by troubles physical, economic, and political. His principal problem is that there are now not enough fish.

In 1977, the Magnuson Act established a 200-mile limit and practically banished foreign fishermen from American coastal waters. American fishermen, including, of course, Maine fishermen, at once built more and bigger vessels to increase their catches. Canada also established a 200-mile limit which overlapped that of the United States. The dispute was submitted to the World Court, which in 1984 established the Hague Line, giving Canada the Northeast Peak of Georges Bank and Brown's Bank, very productive grounds on which United States vessels had fished.

The loss of these grounds came at the same time that the effects of overfishing began to reduce catches significantly. New England landings of groundfish—that is, cod, haddock, cusk, hake, flounder, and other bottom-dwelling fish—dropped from about 375 million pounds in 1984 to about 240 million pounds in 1989. Overfishing continues, and landings decrease.

The federal government under the Magnuson Act sought to prevent continued overfishing and give the fish populations, particularly cod and haddock, a chance to recover by regulating the mesh size of trawl nets and by establishing quotas on the amount of each species that could be landed. These methods were only marginally effective, and overfishing continued. The regulations were established under the Department of Commerce through the National Marine Fisheries Service. In addition, regional councils were established consisting of fishermen, dealers, scientists, lawyers, and government people to make policies relevant to each region. The result appears to be confusion confounded as the National Marine Fisheries Service tries to regulate the fisheries in order to protect the resource while the councils—particularly, for our consideration, the New England Council—deadlock in their efforts to protect the fishermen and the fish simultaneously.

In 1991 the deadlock appeared to have broken when the Conservation Law Foundation of New England sued the Department of Commerce for permitting overfishing. The court accepted a consent decree requiring the New England Council to produce a draft plan by March 1, 1992 to double the population of cod within five years and of haddock within ten years and to produce a final plan by September 1, 1992. Should the Council fail to do so, the Department of Commerce through the National Marine Fisheries Service is required to do so.

In order to move the process along, Congressman Gerry Studds of Massachusetts has introduced a Groundfish Restoration Act which, if passed, should satisfy the court decree. It includes, among other things, provisions hitherto indignantly rejected by fishermen, such as a moratorium on new licenses, followed by a plan for restricted access—that is, limiting the number of fishermen or fishing vessels. It also includes quotas on the weight of fish landed per trip, restrictions on the number of days spent at sea, and area closings where large numbers of small fish are found to congregate. The result of all this thus far has been for the individual fisherman increased effort resulting in catches of fewer and smaller fish, and a distressing uncertainty about the future. Already some fishermen have been forced out; and if the fishing effort is to be restricted as sharply as is contemplated, many more will be eliminated.

One alternative is to concentrate on underutilized species. The most promising of these may be mackerel. There appears to be plenty of mackerel but no market for them. Mackerel do not keep for long on ice, and they do not freeze well. Formerly, large numbers of mackerel were salted in barrels, but salt mackerel are not popular now when other fish can be kept frozen. Some mackerel are sold fresh in the United States, and foreign vessels take many in joint ventures with American fishermen; but if a strong domestic market could be developed, the mackerel fishery would prosper.

Another underutilized species is dogfish. The biomass of dogfish and their cousins, the skates, has more than doubled over the 1968–1989 average. Furthermore, as the populations of cod and haddock decreased, the number of young cod and haddock eaten by the increasing number of dogfish may have become significant. And the dogfish ate food which the young cod and haddock would have eaten. Consequently, a fishery directed at dogfish and skates would help to increase the cod and haddock supply and would occupy profitably vessels squeezed out of the conventional fishery.

Some fishermen have made a beginning by catching large numbers of dogfish in gill nets set on the bottom. The fish are sold to a dealer who sends the fins and tails to Japan for soup, the backs to England for the fish-and-chips shops, and the bellies to Germany. The rest of the creature goes to Washington, Maine, where it is ground up into a horrible gravy and composted with sawdust to produce an effective and nearly odorless fertilizer.

Skate wings are used for lobster bait in America and are frozen and shipped to Europe as a delicacy.

The only objection to concentrating on this fishery is the fragility of the stock. Dogfish produce only six to fifteen "pups" a year, born alive, and skates produce only about two progeny per year. Consequently, a very heavy fishing effort can quickly reduce the biomass below critical levels. Landings of dogfish in New England increased 218 percent in 1990 to 14,300 metric tons, and landings of skate increased 71 percent to 6,600 metric tons. Provincetown, Massachusetts, is a center for this fishery.

The harvesting of sea urchins by divers wearing scuba gear has recently become a viable industry. Dealers pay about 40 cents per pound for urchins on the wharf. The creatures are shipped by air. Within two days of their leaving Penobscot Bay, they are consumed in Japan as a delicacy.

Another problem the fisherman faces is that of safety. Fishing is dangerous. The sea is a hostile environment. Fishing gear is heavy, and the machinery to operate it is powerful. Almost every issue of *National Fisherman* includes accounts of disasters, from a lobsterman's being dragged overboard by a turn of pot warp around his foot, to capsizings and sinkings of big vessels with the loss of many or all of the crews. In an effort to protect fishermen and to save lives, the Coast Guard in 1991, after a long period of uncertainty, revised the safety regulations. In small boats operating near the coast, life preservers, fire extinguishers, flares, a horn, a bell, and an immersion suit are required. An EPIRB, an emergency position-indicating radio beacon, is required on most fishing boats. This is a radio which, when activated either by hand or by floating free from a sinking vessel, broadcasts a distress signal that is picked up by a satellite and relayed to the Coast Guard. Larger boats operating farther offshore must carry life rafts, specified navigational equipment, radio equipment, radar, radar reflector, Loran, or a satellite navigational system. Furthermore, there are strict specifications concerning hull design and construction, rigging, pumps, first aid, electrical equipment, ventilation, fuel systems, and more. All this is expensive, and its installation and use consume time and space.

Marketing fish is also something of a problem. In 1991 three of the principal fish companies left Maine. Willard & Daggett of Portland sold out for lack of fish. The company's president, Kenneth Tonneson, said that eighteen vessels are now landing what one vessel brought in before 1984. F. J. O'Hara & Sons of Rockland was convicted of price manipulation and of misrepresenting Canadian fish as of American origin, and sold its processing plant to Oak Island Fisheries. The General Seafoods plant in Rockland was closed and its shipyard sold to O'Hara to service his few vessels still on the East Coast and fishing out of Gloucester. Other vessels were sent to Alaska. At several harbors alongshore, like Boothbay Harbor, New Harbor, and Stonington, groundfish are bought and trucked either to dealers or to the Portland Fish Exchange where fish from each vessel are displayed and auctioned.

Thus the Maine fisherman, whether working in a small boat close inshore or in an 80-foot dragger on the offshore grounds, is facing decreased stocks of fish, uncertain laws to restrict the fishery, heavy and still uncertain expenses for safety equipment, and a shaky market.

Aquaculture is another recent development influencing the coastal economy, as mentioned in Chapter 27. Salmon pens have proliferated in Passamaquoddy Bay, where strong tides and sheltered waters favor them. However, they are not without drawbacks. The uneaten feed and fecal residue rot and pollute the water, and the antibiotics with which the salmon are treated to prevent disease may be creating unknown effects on indigenous fish. The meshes of the nets confining the fish get fouled with weed and prevent proper circulation of water, and where there is any local stock of salmon at all, salmon escaped from the pens genetically corrupt local fish. Nevertheless, the project at Toothacher Bay off Swans Island is being expanded. Two pens have been established at Allen Island in Muscongus Bay, and two pens for sea trout have been moored on the west side of Frenchboro Long Island, all of which are said to be doing well. The Peacock sardine factory in Lubec is now processing some salmon, and there is talk of a processing plant either at Bass Harbor or on Swans Island to deal with the Swans Island and Frenchboro fish.

The shrimp and scallop fisheries, like the groundfish fishery, are about to be regulated to preserve the stock but are at present marginally profitable.

Although lobster landings were at a record high in 1990 and are expected to be nearly as good in 1991, this is partly the result of increased effort and efficiency and may very well be at the expense of the breeding stock. In 1987 the legal length for a lobster was 3 3/16 inches, measured from the eye socket to the back of the shell on the creature's back. This was increased to 3 7/32 inches in 1988 and to 3 1/4 inches in 1989. In 1991 it was to go to 3 9/32 inches, but this increase was deferred and the gauge remains at 3 1/4 inches minimum and 5 inches maximum.

For a while there was concern that restaurants and markets were importing live lobsters from Canada, where the legal limit is 3 3/16 inches, to the detriment of the Maine product. However, this practice is now illegal and may perhaps be compensated for by Canadian factories which buy some American lobsters. The tails are frozen, the claw meat is canned, and the leg and body meat is made into paste and canned.

While the supply of lobsters has been good for the last two years, the price has been low. The average price paid to the New England lobsterman was $2.54 per pound in 1990, down steadily from $3.10 in 1987. While this is a low price, many lobstermen sold their catch at a much lower average price. In the summer, when the lobsters shed, the price dropped well below $2.00, and in the last two summers the nation's chilly economic climate has sharply reduced the number of lobster-hungry tourists who visit the coast. Higher prices prevail in the fall and early winter when the shedders have hardened up, the weather is windy and cold, and traps are set far offshore. Only the really serious lobstermen in big, rugged boats set traps then, and even they cannot haul more than two or three times a week. The smaller boats cannot profit by the higher winter prices.

Some people thought that when the Portland Fish Exchange began to accept lobsters for auction, the price would rise. However, the Exchange has no way to store live lobsters, so for practical purposes only local lobstermen could sell there. Also, the dealers, although much maligned as gougers, provide a valuable service. They pay cash on the spot for a man's catch, sell fuel and bait and often marine supplies, and the local lobster car and the wharf above it serve as a gathering place and news exchange for the fleet.

The lobsterman, already hard pressed by uncertainty and low prices, finds the cost of a lobster license has been raised and a surcharge laid on top of that to fund a plan to publicize Maine lobster widely with a view to expanding the market. It is now practical to ship live lobsters by air anywhere in the United States in chilled cardboard boxes insulated with styrofoam and moistened with gel-paks. The European market is now available by air, and live lobsters can even be sent to Japan. When they get as far as Hawaii, the lobsters are put in aerated saltwater tanks for a few days of R&R, given a good lunch, and repacked for the rest of the trip.

Lobstermen are affected as the fishermen are, by uncertainty over new rules to protect the stock and to ensure that a large enough population of lobsters will survive to provide a sustainable yield. These rules may involve limiting the number of licenses issued, possibly limiting the number of traps that can be set by one man or one boat, possibly instituting closed seasons. Also, the 3¼-inch gauge may be moved up 1/32 inch a year because only about 20 percent of the lobsters have reached sexual maturity at 3¼ inches. As it is now, almost all the lobsters that have become legal the previous summer have been caught by January, leaving very few to breed. It is remarkable that lobsters are as plentiful as they are.

The uncertainty affecting fishermen and lobstermen is reflected in the boatbuilding business. No one is going to borrow money to build a boat if he is about to find that limited access to fishing and lobstering is going to eliminate boats built after a certain date, a date not yet given; or if his catch will be so limited that he cannot pay for his new boat.

In order to finance a new boat to the tune of something over six figures, most fishermen must go to the bank. In view of the same uncertainty about limited entry, limited catches, and safety requirements, banks are reluctant to make loans without a substantial down payment of 25 to 50 percent, thus limiting the orders made to boatyards. The result is that yards that have been building fishing vessels are turning to building yachts. Hulls designed as lobsterboats and fishermen have all the characteristics of speed, seaworthiness, stability, and comfort desired in a yacht and can be finished out with every conceivable luxury. Duffy & Duffy and Flye Point Marine in Brooklin, Holland's Boat Shop in Belfast, Jarvis Newman, Inc. and Pettegrow in Manset will serve as examples. Duffy & Duffy reports that 80 percent of the fiberglass boats they have delivered recently have been yachts. Pettegrow says that 90 percent of their business is in 40- to 60-foot yachts. All the builders mentioned have built yachts on lobsterboat hulls, but now with the depressed economy and the luxury tax on yachts costing over $100,000, the yacht market has slowed nearly to a standstill. Duffy & Duffy employed forty-eight people in 1989 and in 1991 is able to keep only twenty. Jarvis Newman, Inc. reports a 60-percent drop in sales. In August 1991, Holland had seven boats on order but six were on hold.

The two bigger yards building steel vessels also have their troubles. Washburn & Doughty in East Boothbay used to be constantly busy building steel fishing vessels from 40 to 200 feet long. In 1991 they have recently launched a tug, are building a ferryboat, and will lay the keel for the 175-foot steel full-rigged school ship *Discovery* as soon as her sponsors raise the necessary money. Goudy and Stevens, also in East Boothbay, are finishing up their second oil skimmer* with no other steel vessel under construction. According to Joel Stevens, there are enough good steel fishing vessels available. During the good times between the establishment of the 200-mile limit in 1977 and the establishment of the Hague Line in 1984, a number of fine steel fishing vessels were built. As catches became smaller and restrictions tighter, some owners dropped out and sold their boats to those who were able to stay in. These vessels were built to be depreciated over twenty-five or thirty years and are still in excellent condition. The future in steel ship building, says Stevens, lies in the environmental field: vessels like oil skimmers and research vessels.

Yacht yards are suffering, too. The Hinckley Company, Inc. in Manset has several yachts to build in the winter of 1991–92, some, it is said, for foreign owners, but is turning more to storage, maintenance, and repair work. Paul E. Luke, Inc. in East Boothbay, builder of many elegant aluminum yachts, has had nothing to build for several years and is taking storage and repair work while keeping up work on feathering propellers, anchors, and stoves. Padebco in Round Pond has several small boats to build but is heavily into storage and repair . . . and so it goes.

Some boatyard owners, appalled at the taxes on shore property, have moved their yards back into the woods. They float the boats onto big trailers with hydraulic arms to support the boats, tow them to yards far from the water, and set them down for storage and maintenance work. Many boat owners, both commercial fishermen and yacht owners, hire the trailers to transport their boats to their own backyards where they can work on them

*An oil skimmer is a vessel over 100 feet long with doors in the bow which open to scoop up floating oil after an oil spill. The first one was named *Valdez Star*. This one is *Shearwater*.

themselves. Some build a plastic shelter around the boat which, on a sunny winter day, becomes warm enough to work in without mittens. All of these developments are hard on heavily taxed shoreside boatyards.

In the midst of all these efforts to conserve marine resources and still make a living stands the environmentalist with as legitimate a concern as the fisherman and the boatbuilder. The Maine coast is unique. The loss of its purity, its beauty, its wildlife, its culture would be the state's loss, the nation's loss, and the world's loss. What is being done to preserve it?

Islands are being bought up and preserved. Many island owners protect their islands as bird and animal refuges by actively discouraging visitors and by putting conservation easements on their deeds through the Maine Coast Heritage Trust. The Nature Conservancy owns over fifty islands, including such big ones as Damariscove off Boothbay, White Island and Bradbury Island in Penobscot Bay, and Great Wass Island off Jonesport. The Nature Conservancy tries hard to protect wildlife on their islands, but in order to promote their fundraising program to buy more islands, they do not want to prohibit visitors; they do, however, prohibit camping. The Maine Audubon Society is doing the same thing with other islands. Other organizations like the Friends of Nature control a few islands. The State of Maine, through the Bureau of Public Lands, the Bureau of Parks and Recreation, and the Department of Fisheries and Wildlife, manages others. Most of these islands are open to visitors under certain conditions and at specified times. The federal government through Acadia National Park owns some islands, notably most of Isle au Haut, and holds easements on others. Finally, the Island Institute is actively engaged in patrolling and protecting the coast. One of their principal tools is the Maine Island Trail Association, founded by David Getchell for kayakers, canoeists, oarsmen, and sailors of small boats. The Association has laid out a trail from Portland to Machias with sixty-eight island locations on which members have permission to camp. The Association is insistent that its 2,200 members use the islands with respect, protect them against fire and pollution, leave each island cleaner than they found it, and especially avoid disturbing wildlife. They are urged to report people who would violate the islands. Thus far, the project has been highly successful. People who paddle, row, and sail small boats are close enough to land and water to admire and protect the unique island ecology.

Environmentalists have interests, too. The Mammal Protection Act, which prohibits harming or harrassing seals, whales, and porpoises, was promoted by environmentalists. Now they are trying to reduce the killing of porpoises in gill nets and on longlines set for swordfish and tuna.

Pollution is another environmental concern. In "the old days," if you did not want something, you threw it to hell overboard. Either it sank out of sight and out of mind, or it soon disintegrated or was eaten by gulls. However, with the coming of indestructible plastics after World War II and with the enormous increase in the number of people throwing things to hell overboard, the water grew foul. Rafts of seaweed would include milk jugs, oil jugs, plastic plates, and beer-can yokes. Ten miles offshore one might meet a fleet of foam cups, perhaps thrown to hell overboard off Cape Cod, heading buoyantly for island shore or harbor down east.

The matter was publicized, laws were made, dumpsters were provided at landings, and the littering was suddenly and drastically reduced although not eliminated. Vessels are now required to have holding tanks. Overboard discharge of raw sewage is prohibited. There is no longer a long streamer of empty bottles, trash, and garbage floating down the tide from Monhegan. The law now forbids throwing overboard anything not biodegradable and anything biodegradable that will not pass through a 1-inch screen.

In 1990 Casco Bay was declared a "national estuary" and received two million dollars of federal money to plan ways to clean up its pollution from cities, towns, and paper mills. Overboard discharge of untreated sewage is now prohibited all along the Maine coast, and vigorous efforts are being made to clean up polluted rivers so that clam flats now closed can be reopened.

The few inhabited islands have a particular problem in disposing of sewage and solid waste, and an even greater problem in maintaining a viable community. The islands off Portland Harbor, serviced by ferries, are almost suburban in character already, but severe restrictions have been put on their further development. Monhegan, the seat of a vigorous and profitable lobster fishery from January to June and of an active summer community from June until early fall, seems in little immediate danger of collapsing; but its culture is under considerable pressure from day trippers, especially on a sunny August Sunday.

Matinicus, another profitable lobstering community, has different problems. Well over half the island, some say as much as 80 percent, is owned by summer people, and their taxes support the small school and pay much of the town expenses—for waste disposal, among other things. Should the landowners go in for tree farming, for instance, to reduce taxes, the community might not be able to support itself. If they lose the school, families with children would have to move ashore, and the community might well collapse, as Criehaven did. The population is not growing, as Matinicus lobstermen do not encourage newcomers.

Swans Island and Frenchboro, on the other hand, are aggressively seeking new year-round settlers, the aquaculture projects being one way of providing jobs for them. Isle au Haut, largely owned by Acadia National Park, has a decreasing number of winter residents and is heavily dependent on Stonington.

Several scientific communities in Maine are working to find out more about coastal ecology and how to preserve it. Cornell University and the University of New Hampshire maintain an oceanography and marine biology laboratory on Appledore Island in the Isles of Shoals off Portsmouth, New Hamphire. The College of the Atlantic at Bar Harbor is studying the ecology of eastern Maine. The University of Maine maintains a laboratory and aquaculture reasearch center on the Damariscotta River at the Darling Center. The Department of Marine Resources and the Maine Fish and Wildlife Service research the ecology of the Gulf of Maine with particular concern for its economic future. Their laboratories are at Boothbay Harbor.

The picture thus far presented of the Maine coast in 1992 is kaleidoscopic, its pieces all clearly related, yet their connections constantly changing and not always obvious. As an attempt to see what several aspects of the coast really look like, let us conclude with a summer day at the shore.

Early in the still dawn, lobsterboats are at work. Some are big, offshore boats with high-speed diesel engines, two men working out straight, hauling the first of the day's 500 traps in strings of six, mentally keeping count of the catch to see if it is going to pay for bait, fuel, bank loan, taxes and leave a share for them. Others will be alone in smaller boats, hauling as busily, perhaps hurrying to get ashore in time for an eight-hour job. Maybe we will see a boy or an old man in an outboard skiff hauling thirty or forty traps in the protected waters of the bay and perhaps, but unlikely, someone in a peapod hauling a few because he wouldn't feel right without traps in the water.

As the sun gets up, the yachts whose bare masts have been crowding the harbors begin to appear. While the early wind is light, most will be under power, steaming along to "get somewhere" with little concern for the manner of their going. As the southwest breeze comes in they may set sail, and most will shut off their engines when well clear of the harbor.

An excursion boat appears, a motor vessel perhaps 60 feet long, the lower deck enclosed in glass, the upper deck exposed to sun and wind. People sit in rows facing forward, and the skipper, looking official in a peaked cap with white top, through a public address system names the islands, identifies houses of distinguished residents, and heads for a ledge inhabited occasionally by seals. This stirs some of the passengers to action with cameras and binoculars. The seals, embarrassed, slip into the water to stare curiously at the tourists.

A sailing party-boat beats down the harbor, a Friendship sloop perhaps or a schooner, her cockpit crowded with people who have never been sailing and consider it a dangerous adventure but are willing to try.

"This boat can't tip over, can it, Captain?" asks one.

"Only once," replies the devilish skipper, and leaves the questioner to think that one over. Maybe—often—there will be a passenger aboard who has had a yacht of his own and wants once more to feel the lift of the ground swell and hear the wind in taut sailcloth.

Near the head of the bay the bright sails of Turnabouts blossom, a class of boys and girls from the yacht club learning the feel of the tiller, the trim of sheet and centerboard, and the terror of an unforeseen jibe.

A fleet of racing boats lines up for a start hard on the starboard tack, hitting the line on the gun, the windward boat gaining fast on the crowd in the dirty air to leeward. Power yachts, excursion boats, and ferries try to avoid the race with varying success, kicking up wakes and arousing wrath.

It may breeze up pretty fresh in the afternoon but few will reef. Most will motor under jib—some just motor.

As the sun gets low and the breeze slacks off, the party fishing boats that left before dawn will come roaring in at the high speeds they need to get to offshore fishing grounds. They are followed by clouds of gulls. It is often suggested that crews wait to dress their catch until they get near home so people can see the gulls and know that the trip has been successful.

Here comes a commercial fisherman, a dragger, otter boards on the gallows, the big net on a roller astern, hoping the price will be high enough to make his meager catch pay.

An outboard shatters the afternoon, towing a waterskier at frightening speed. Far offshore, away on the horizon, the sun catches a gleam of white where the Nova Scotia ferry from Portland is heading for Yarmouth. Bright patches of color mark two youths on windsurfers. They are dressed in wetsuits and skillfully lean into the wind, guiding their delicate craft with their weight.

A parade of yachts under blooming red and yellow and blue spinnakers comes up from the westward before the last of the breeze. They round up, douse sail, and motor to moorings off the yacht club. Maybe one eccentric skipper sails up the harbor and luffs up to his mooring, but most know they have to run their engines for some time during the day to keep the ice cubes cold and the hot water hot. What better time than when entering or leaving port? Anyway, with a big jib set, you can't see anything to leeward, and quick tacks are awkward.

As the sun sets over calm water, a windjammer carrying passengers comes in, pushed by a diesel engine in the yawlboat with her main and foresail set. Her foresail comes in, she rounds up, the anchor splashes. A hand carries a riding light forward to hang in the fore rigging, and all hands go below for dinner, leaving the mainsail set in the gathering dark.

Maybe twice a summer a small tanker comes in to fill dockside tanks with fuel, a Coast Guard picket boat occasionally stops a yacht for inspection or tears by at high speed, blue light flashing, on a rescue mission. Buoy boats change government buoys, taking them ashore for repair and painting.

It has been a long time since David Ingram walked the coast, since Champlain shivered on St. Croix Island, since Waymouth and Captain John Smith saw a new continent, rich beyond their imagining. Today we sail a coast made richer by the people of nearly 500 years. Here they fished, settled, fought and traded. Their shallops, sloops, pinks, and schooners sailed these waters. Brigs, barks, and clipper ships were launched into the rivers we sail today. The great Downeasters, the finest square-riggers ever built, set skysails off Seguin and Monhegan. Unwieldly coal schooners hove-to for tugs off Portland Head. Destroyers poured out of the Kennebec like hornets. Through it all, fishermen hauled codfish, herring, and lobsters over their rails to feed a nation.

Now our summer bays are white with the sails of yachts. Our coast is no longer the new, unmarred coast of John Smith. For us each island, point, and headland is more than a landmark on the chart. It is a monument to all of the people who have lived here before us.

NOTES

Much of the material in this chapter came from the issues of *National Fisherman* for 1990 and 1991. Also I talked at length with Philip Conkling of the Island Institute in Rockland, with Jay Krouse of the Department of Marine Resources in Boothbay Harbor, with Joel Stevens of Goudy and Stevens in East Boothbay, with Paul E. Luke, my neighbor in East Boothbay, and with Rusty Kort of Boothbay Harbor; he is the fisherman catching dogfish.

NOAA Technical Memorandum NMFS—F / NEC 86, which gives the status of Fish Resources off New England, and "A Summary of Maine Lobster Laws and Regulations," by Kevin H. Kelley, published by the Department of Marine Resources, are both very helpful. *Commercial Fisheries News,* published monthly in Stonington, adds a dimension to *National Fisherman*.

The concluding imaginative picture of a day on the coast in largely the product of my own observation. Perhaps it has no place in the final chapter of a history. It is here, however, to show the juxtaposition of Vacationland and what remains of the traditional fisherman's life. I have not included the chaotic situation ashore. Imagination staggers.

Bibliography

Abbott, John S. C. *History of Maine.* B. B. Russell, Boston; 1875. Has Thevet's account.

Acheson, James M. *The Lobster Gangs of Maine.* University Press of New England, Hanover, New Hampshire; 1988.

Albion, Robert G. *Forests and Sea Power.* Archon Books, Hamden, Connecticut; 1965.

———. *Rise of the New York Port.* Scribners, New York; 1939.

———, et al. *New England and the Sea.* Wesleyan University Press for the Marine Historical Association Inc., Mystic, Connecticut; 1972.

———, and Jennie Barnes Pope. *Sea Lanes in Wartime; The American Experience 1775–1942.* W. W. Norton, New York; 1942.

Allen, Gardner Wild. *Massachusetts Privateers of the Revolution.* Massachusetts Historical Society, Boston; 1927.

Andrews, Charles M. *The Colonial Period of American History,* three volumes Yale University Press, New Haven, Connecticut; 1934.

Apollonio, Spencer. *Tallman Lectures,* delivered at Bowdoin College 1976. In Special Collection room, Bowdoin College Library, Brunswick, Maine.

Baker, William A. *Colonial Vessels.* Barre Publishing Company, Barre, Massachusetts; 1962.

———. *Maritime History of Bath, Maine and of the Kennebec Region.* Marine Research Society of Bath, 1973. Available from Maine Maritime Museum, Bath, Maine.

———. *Sloops and Shallops.* Barre Publishing Company, Barre, Massachusetts; 1966. Reprinted by University of South Carolina Press, Columbia, South Carolina; 1989.

Balano, James. *The Log of the Skipper's Wife.* Down East Books, Camden, Maine; 1979.

Baxter, James Phinney. "A Lost Manuscript." Proceedings of the Maine Historical Society, Series 2, Volume 2. An address read before the Society, December 18, 1890; also " Sir John Moore at Castine." Maine Historical Society, Portland, Maine.

———. *Pioneers of France in New England.* Joel Munsell's Sons, Albany, New York; 1891.

———. *Sir Ferdinando Gorges and the Province of Maine.* Prince Society, Boston; 1890.

———, ed. *Documentary History of the State of Maine.* Volume 3. Maine Historical Society, Portland, Maine; 1884. This includes the Trelawney papers.

Beck, Horace P. *The American Indian as a Sea Fighter in Colonial Times.* Marine Historical Association, Mystic, Connecticut; 1959.

Bigelow, Henry B., and William C. Schroeder. *Fishes of the Gulf of Maine.* Fishing Bulletin, Volume 53, No. 74, Fish and Wildlife Service, U.S. Government Printing Office; 1953.

Blanchard, Fessenden S. *Sailboat Classes of North America.* Doubleday, New York; 1963.

Boeri, David, and James Gibson. *Tell It Good-bye, Kiddo, The Decline of the New England Offshore Fishery.* International Marine Publishing Co., Camden, Maine; 1976.

Bolton, Charles Knowles. *The Real Founders of New England.* F. W. Faxon, Boston; 1929.

Boswell, Charles. *The America, The Story of the World's Most Famous Yacht.* David McKay Co., Inc., New York; 1967.

Bowker, Captain Francis E. *Atlantic Four-Master, The Story of the Schooner Herbert L. Rawding.* Mystic Seaport Museum, Mystic, Connecticut; 1986.

Bradford, William. *Of Plimoth Plantation,* Boston 1856. There are numerous reprints, one by Samuel Eliot Morison, Knopf, New York; 1952.

Brereton, John. *A Brief and True Relation of the Discovery of the North Part of Virginia.* London; 1602. Reprinted in Collections of the Massachusetts Historical Society, Third Series, Volume 8, Little & Brown, Boston; 1843.

Brooks, Robert C. Unpublished manuscript on the Battle of Machias. In author's possession and mine.

Brown, Alexander. *The Genesis of the United States.* Houghton Mifflin, Boston and New York; 1890.

Brown, Mike. *The Great Lobster Chase.* International Marine Publishing Co., Camden, Maine; 1985.

Bruce, Erroll. *Challenge to Poseidon.* Hutchinson & Co., London; 1956.

Burrage, Henry S., DD. *Early English and French Voyages, Chiefly from Hakluyt.* Scribners, New York, 1906. Includes Brereton's account of Gosnold.

———. *Gorges and the Grant of the Province of Maine. Portland, Maine; 1923.* Printed for the state of Maine.

———. *Maine at Louisbourg.* Burleigh & Flint, Augusta, Maine; 1910.

Calvert, Mary R. *Dawn Over the Kennebec.* Twin City Printery, Lewiston, Maine; 1983.

Carrick, Robert W., and Richard Henderson. *John G. Alden and His Yacht Designs.* International Marine Publishing Co., Camden, Maine; 1983.

Carter, Robert. *A Summer Cruise on the Coast of New England.* New Hampshire Publishing Co., Somersworth, New Hampshire; 1969.

Champlain, Samuel de. *Voyages of Samuel de Champlain.* Translated from the French by Charles Pomeroy Otis, PhD, with historical illustrations and a memoir by the Reverend Edmund F. Shafter, A.M. The Prince Society, Boston; 1878–82. Volume VII.

———. *The Works of Samuel de Champlain.* Edited and translated by Biggar, The Champlain Society, Toronto; 1922. This gives English and French texts on facing pages.

———. *Samuel Champlain.* His narrative of his Maine cruises. Printed by John Wilson & Sons for the Prince Society, Boston; 1878.

Chapelle, Howard I. *History of the American Sailing Navy,* W. W. Norton, New York; 1949.

———. *The American Fishing Schooners 1825–1935.* W. W. Norton, New York; 1973.

———. *The Search for Speed Under Sail.* W. W. Norton, New York; 1967.

Chapman, Leonard B. "The Mast Industry of Old Falmouth." Proceedings of the Maine Historical Society, Series 2, Volume 7. An address read before the Society, April 24, 1896.

Church, Albert Cook. *American Fishermen.* W. W. Norton, New York; 1940.

Churchill, Winston. *History of the English Speaking People.* Dodd, Mead & Co., New York; 1957. Four volumes.

Clark, Captain Arthur. *The Clipper Ship Era.* Putnam, New York; 1910.

Clark, William B. *When the U-Boats Came to America.* Little, Brown, Boston; 1929.

Clifford, Harold. *Charlie York.* International Marine Publishing Co., Camden, Maine; 1974.

———. *The Boothbay Region 1906–1961.* Cumberland Press, Freeport, Maine; 1961.

Codman, John, II. *Arnold's Expedition to Quebec.* MacMillan, London; 1901.

Coffin, Harold W. *World War II Hits the Maine Coast.* Unpublished manuscript in special collections of library at University of Maine at Orono.

Coffin, Robert P. T. *Book of Uncles.* MacMillan, New York; 1942.

Collier, Sargent F., and Tom Horgan. *Mount Desert, The Most Beautiful Island in the World.* Houghton Mifflin, Boston; 1952.

Connolly, James B. *Out of Gloucester.* Scribners, New York; 1903.

———. *The Book of the Gloucester Fishermen.* John Day Company, New York; 1927.

Cutler, Carl. *Greyhounds of the Sea.* G. P. Putnam, New York; 1930.

Daniels, Josephus. *Our Navy at War.* George H. Doran Co., New York; 1922.

Dayton, Fred Ewing. *Steamboat Days.* Tudor Publishing Co., New York; 1939.

DeGolyer, E., ed. *Across Aboriginal America: The Journey of Three Englishmen Across Texas in 1568.* Peripatetic Press, El Paso, Texas; 1947. Reprint of Ingram's narrative from first edition of Hakluyt.

Dodds, James, and James Moore. *Building the Wooden Fighting Ship.* Facts on File, Inc., New York; 1984.

Donald, David, ed. *Divided We Fought.* MacMillan, New York; 1952.

Dow, George F. *Slave Ships and Slavery.* Marine Research Society, Salem, Massachusetts; 1927.

Drisko, George W. *Narrative of the Town of Machias.* Press of the Republican, Machias, Maine; 1904.

Duncan, Roger F. *Friendship Sloops.* International Marine Publishing Co., Camden, Maine; 1985.

———, and John P. Ware. *A Cruising Guide to the New England Coast.* G. P. Putnam's Sons, New York; 1990.

Dyer, Barbara F. *Vintage Views of Camden, Maine.* Camden Printing Co., Camden, Maine; 1987.

———. *Grog Ho.* Courier-Gazette, Rockland, Maine; 1984.

Esterly, Diana. *Early One Design Sailboats.* Scribners, New York; 1979.

Fairburn, William Armstrong. *Merchant Sail.* Fairburn Marine Educational Foundation, Center Lovell, Maine; 1945–55. Five volumes.

Fassett, Frederick T. *The Shipbuilding Business in the United States of America.* Society of Naval Architects and Engineers, New York; 1948.

Faulkner, Alaric and Gretchen. *The French at Pentagoet, 1635–1674.* Maine Historic Preservation Commission, Augusta, Maine, and the New Brunswick Museum; 1987.

Fell, Barry. *America B.C.* Quadrangle Books, New York; 1976

Flood, Charles Bracelen. *Rise and Fight Again.* Dodd, Mead & Co.,New York; 1976.

Forester, C. S. *The Age of Fighting Sail.* Doubleday, Garden City, New York; 1956.

———. *The Captain From Connecticut.* Sun Dial Press, Garden City, New York; 1945.

Fowler, William A., Jr. *Rebels Under Sail.* Scribners, New York; 1976.

Gardner, George P. *Ready About.* A. S. Barnes, New York; 1959

Garland, Joseph E. *Down to the Sea.* David R. Godine, Boston; 1983.

Goode, George Brown, et al. *The Fisheries and Fishing Industries of the United States.* Volume 5, 1880 Census Report, Washington, D.C.

Gould, Edward K. *British and Tory Marauders on the Penobscot.* Rockland, Maine; 1932.

Gould, Nathan. "Falmouth Neck in the Revolution." Proceedings of the Maine Historical Society, Series 2, Volume 8. Maine Historical Society, Portland, Maine.

Greene, Francis B. *History of Boothbay, Southport and Boothbay Harbor, Maine.* Loring, Short & Harmon, Portland; 1906. Republished by the Boothbay Region Historical Society, Boothbay, Maine.

Griffin, Carl R. III. *A History of Fishing in the Boothbay Region.* Unpublished master's thesis in the Boothbay Harbor Library, Boothbay Harbor, Maine.

———, and Alaric Faulkner. *Coming of Age on Damariscove Island, Maine.* Northeast Folklore Society, University of Maine, Orono, Maine; 1980.

Grindle, Roger L. *Quarry and Kiln, The Story of Maine's Lime Industry.* Rockland Courier-Gazette, Rockland, Maine; 1971.

———. *Tombstones and Paving Blocks.* Courier of Maine, Rockland, Maine; 1977.

Hahn, Harold M. *The Colonial Schooner.* Naval Institute Press, Annapolis, Maryland; 1981.

Hakluyt, Richard. *The Principal Navigations and Voiages, and Discoveries of the English Nation.* London; 1589—and subsequent editions. An edition published for the Hakluyt Society and Peabody Museum at University Press, Cambridge, England; 1965. Facsimile.

Hall, Henry. "Report on the Shipbuilding Industry of the United States." In *Report of the Tenth Census,* Volume 8, 1884.

Hamlin, Cyrus, and John Ordway. *The Commercial Fisheries of Maine.* Maine Sea Grant Bulletin No. 5, Ocean Research Co., Kennebunk, Maine. No publication date (early 1970s).

Hatch, Louis C. *Maine, A History.* New Hampshire Publishing Co., Somersworth, New Hampshire; 1974. A facsimile of the 1919 edition.

Hosmer, George L. *A Historical Sketch of the Town of Deer Isle, Maine.* Fort Hill Press, Boston; 1905.

Howe, Octavius T., and Frederick C. Matthews. *American Clipper Ships.* Marine Research Society, Salem, Massachusetts; 1926. Two volumes.

Hubbard, William. *A Narrative of the Indian Wars in New England From The First Planting Thereof in 1607 to the year 1677.* Facsimile reprint of 1864 edition, with notes by Samuel Drake. Heritage Books, Bowie, Maryland; 1990.

Humiston, Fred. *Windjammers and Walking Beams.* Blue Water Books, Portland, Maine; 1968.

Hutchinson, Vernal. *A Maine Town in the Civil War.* Bond-Wheelwright, Freeport, Maine; 1957.

Island Institute. *Island Journal,* Volume 5. Island Institute, Rockland, Maine; 1988.

James, Henry J. *German Subs in Yankee Waters.* Gotham Press, New York; 1940.

Jenness, John Scribner. *The Isles of Shoals, An Historical Sketch.* Second edition. Hurd & Houghton, New York; 1875.

Johnston, John. *History of Bristol and Bremen in the State of Maine Including the Pemaquid Settlement.* Joel Munsell, Albany, New York; 1873.

Jones, Herbert G. *Portland Ships Are Good Ships.* Machigonne Press, Portland, Maine; 1945.

Josselyn, John. *An Account of Two Voyages to New England.* London, 1674. Edited and introduced by Paul J. Lindholdt, University Press of New England, Hanover, New Hampshire; 1988.

Kellogg, Elijah. *The Fisher Boys of Pleasant Cove.* Lee & Shepard, Boston; 1874, 1902.

Kershaw, Gordon E. *The Kennebec Proprietors.* Maine Historical Society / New Hampshire Publishing Co., Somersworth, New Hampshire; 1975.

Ketchum, Richard M., and Bruce Catton, ed. *American Heritage Picture History of the Civil War.* American Heritage Publishing Company, New York; 1960.

Kevitt, C. B. *General Solomon Lovell and the Penobscot Expedition.* Norfolk County Development and Tourist Council and Weymouth Historical Commission, Weymouth, Massachusetts; 1976.

Kilby, William Henry. *Eastport and Passamaquoddy.* Edward E. Sheal Co., Eastport, Maine; 1888.

Kord, Robert. *Down East to Cutler.* Tan Books and Publishers, Inc., Rockford, Illinois; 1985. For information, call Robert Kord, Cutler, Maine.

Laighton, Oscar. *Ninety Years at the Isles of Shoals.* Andover, Massachusetts; 1929.

Lane, Frederic C. *Ships for Victory, A History of Shipbuilding Under the U.S. Maritime Commission.* Johns Hopkins Press, Baltimore; 1951.

Lang, Steven, and Peter H. Spectre. *On the Hawser, A Tugboat Album.* Down East Books, Camden; 1980.

Lavery, Brian. *Arming and Fitting of English Ships of War 1600–1815.* Naval Institute Press, Annapolis, Maryland; 1987.

Leavitt, John F. *Wake of the Coasters.* Wesleyan University Press, Middletown, Connecticut; 1970. For Marine Historical Association, Mystic, Connecticut.

Letcher, John. *Self Contained Navigation with H.O. 208.* International Marine Publishing Co., Camden, Maine; 1977.

Lever, D'Arcy. *The Young Sea Officer's Sheet Anchor.* Edward W. Sweetman Co., New York; 1963. A facsimile of the second edition, published in 1819.

Lincoln, Waldo. *The Province Snow "Prince of Orange."* Press of Charles Hamilton, Worcester, Massachusetts; 1901. Proceedings of the American Antiquarian Society, April 24, 1901.

Long, Charles A. E. *Matinicus Isle, Its Story and Its People.* Lewiston Journal Print Shop; 1926.

Lubbock, Basil. *The Downeasters.* Dover Publications, New York; 1987. Originally published by Brown, Son & Ferguson Ltd., Glasgow; 1929.

Maddocks, Luther. *Looking Backward.* Southport Historical Society, Southport, Maine; 1987.

Manning, Samuel F. *New England Masts and the King's Broad Arrow.* Thomas Murphy, Kennebunk, Maine; 1979.

Marine Research Society, ed. *The Pirates Own Book.* Marine Research Society, Salem, Massachusetts; 1924.

Martin, Kenneth R. *Whalemen and Whaleships of Maine.* Harpswell Press, Brunswick, Maine; 1975. For Marine Research Society of Bath, Maine.

———, and Nathan Lipfert. *Lobstering and the Maine Coast.* Maine Maritime Museum, Bath, Maine; 1985.

Matthews, Frederick C. *American Merchant Ships 1850–1900.* Two volumes. Dover Publications Inc., New York; 1987. Originally published by Marine Research Society, Salem, Massachusetts; 1930, 1931.

McFarland, Raymond. *A History of the New England Fisheries.* D. Appleton Co., New York; 1911. For University of Pennsylvania.

———. *The Masts of Gloucester.* W. W. Norton, New York; 1937.

McLane, Charles. *Islands of the Mid-Maine Coast—Blue Hill and Penobscot Bays.* Kennebec River Press, Woolwich, Maine; 1982.

———. *Islands of the Mid-Maine Coast—Mount Desert to Machias.* Kennebec River Press, Falmouth, Maine; 1989.

McLennan, J. S. *Louisbourg From Its Foundation to Its Fall.* The Book Room Ltd., Halifax, Nova Scotia; 1979. Reprinted 1983. First printed McMillan & Co. Ltd., London; 1918.

Meltzer, Michael. *The World of the Small Commercial Fisherman.* Dover Publications Inc., New York; 1980.

Merriam, Charles. *Last of the 5-Masters.* Claude Kendall, Inc., New York; 1936.

Millar, John F. *American Ships of the Colonial and Revolutionary Periods.* W. W. Norton, New York; 1978.

Moffat, Alexander W. *A Navy Maverick Comes of Age 1939–1945* Wesleyan University Press, Middletown, Connecticut; 1977.

Moody, Edward C. *From Agamenticus, Gorgeana and York.* York Publishing Co., York, Maine; 1914.

Moore, Ruth. *Speak to the Winds.* William Morrow, New York; 1956.

Morison, Samuel Eliot. *History of United States Naval Operations In World War II.* Volumes 6 and 10. Little, Brown, Boston; 1947.

———. *Maritime History of Massachusetts.* Houghton Mifflin, Boston; 1921.

———. *Oxford History of the American People.* Oxford University Press, New York; 1965.

———. *Samuel de Champlain, Father of New France.* Little, Brown & Company, Boston; 1972.

———. *The European Discovery of America, The Northern Voyages A.D. 500–1600.* Oxford University Press, New York; 1971.

———. *The Story of Mount Desert Island.* Atlantic Little, Brown, Boston; 1960.

Moulton, Augustus F. *Portland By The Sea.* Katahdin Publishing Co., Augusta, Maine; 1926.

Munson, Gorham. *Penobscot, Down East Paradise.* J. B. Lippincott Co., Philadelphia and New York; 1959.

Nordblok, A. B. *The Lore of Ships.* Gothenburg, Sweden; 1975. A number of authors and illustrators contributed.

O'Brien, John. "Exertions of the O'Brien Family." Proceedings of the Maine Historical Society, Series 2, Volume 2, pp. 246–249. Maine Historical Society, Portland, Maine.

Packard, Aubigne L. *A Town That Went To Sea.* Falmouth Publishing House, Portland, Maine; 1950.

Paine, Ralph D. *Joshua Barney.* The Century Co., New York; 1924.

Pares, William. *Yankees and Creoles.* Harvard University Press, Cambridge, Massachusetts; 1956.

Parker, Arlita Dodge. *Pemaquid.* Macdonald & Evans, Boston; 1925.

Parker, Captain W. J. Lewis. *The Great Coal Schooners of New England 1870–1909.* Marine Historical Association, Mystic, Connecticut; 1948.

Parkman, Francis. *A Half-Century of Conflict,* Volumes I and II. Little, Brown & Co., Boston; 1898.

———. *Count Frontenac and New France.* Little, Brown, Boston; 1898.

———. *Pioneers of France in the New World.* Little, Brown & Company, Boston; 1898.

———. *The Old Regime in Canada.* Little, Brown & Company, Boston; 1898.

Parks, George Bruner. *Richard Hakluyt and the English Voyages.* American Geographical Society, New York; 1928.

Peabody, Robert E. *Log of the Grand Turks.* Houghton Mifflin, Boston; 1926.

Phillips-Birt, Douglas. *A History of Seamanship.* Doubleday, Garden City, New York; 1971.

Picking, Sherwood. *Sea Fight Off Monhegan.* Machigonne Press, Portland, Maine; 1941.

Pierce, Wesley George. *Going Fishing.* International Marine Publishing Co., Camden, Maine, 1989. First published by the Marine Historical Society, Salem, Massachusetts; 1934.

Portland, City of. *Portland.* Greater Portland Landmarks, Inc., Portland, Maine; 1972.

Potter, E. B., and Nimitz, Chester W. *Sea Power.* Prentice-Hall, Englewood, New Jersey; 1960.

Pratt, Fletcher. *The Navy.* Garden City Publishing Co., Garden City, New York; 1941.

Proper, Ida Sedgewick. *Monhegan, The Cradle of New England.* Southworth Press, Portland, Maine; 1930.

Reynolds, Erminie S., and Kenneth R. Martin. *"A Singleness of Purpose," The Skolfields and Their Ships,* Maine Maritime Museum, Bath, Maine; 1987.

Rice, George W. *Shipping Days of Old Boothbay.* New England History Press and Boothbay Region Historical Society, Boothbay Harbor, Maine; 1984.

Richardson, John M., *Steamboat Lore of the Penobscot,* Courier-Gazette, Rockland, Maine; 1971. Fifth edition.

Roberts, Kenneth. *Arundel.* Doubleday, Garden City, New York; 1947.

———. *Captain Caution.* Doubleday, Garden City, New York; 1934.

———. *The Lively Lady.* Doubleday, Garden City, New York; 1931.

Robinson, Reuel. *History of Camden and Rockport.* Camden Publishing Co., Camden, Maine; 1907.

Rolde, Neil. *Sir William Pepperrell of Colonial New England.* Harpswell Press, Brunswick, Maine; 1982.

Rosier, James. *A True Relation of the Most Prosperous Voyage Made This Present Year, 1605, by Captain George Waymouth In the Discovery of the North Part of Virginia.* London; 1605. Reprinted in *Rosier's Relation of Waymouth's Voyage to the Coast of Maine in 1605.* With introduction and notes by Henry S. Burrage, DD. Gorges Society, Portland, Maine; 1887. Also in Massachusetts Historical Society Collections, Series 3, Volume 8, Little and Brown, Boston; 1843.

Roth, Hal. *Always a Distant Anchorage.* W. W. Norton, New York; 1988.

———. *Two Against Cape Horn.* W. W. Norton, New York; 1978.

Rowe, William Hutchinson. *The Maritime History of Maine.* W. W. Norton, New York; 1948.

Sabine, Lorenzo. *Report on the Principal Fisheries of the American Seas.* Part of the annual report of Thomas Corwin, 1852, Secretary of the Treasury, second session of the 32nd Congress. Robert Armstrong, Washington, D.C.; 1853.

Sainsbury, John C. *Commercial Fishing Methods.* Fishing News (Books) Ltd., West Byfleet, Surrey, England; 1971, 1975. Written for the University of Rhode Island.

Shay, Frank H. *American Sea Songs and Chanteys.* W. W. Norton, New York; 1948.

Smith, Bradford. *Captain John Smith, His Life and Legend.* J. B. Lippincott, Philadephia and New York; 1953.

Smith, Captain John. *Works.* Edited by Edward Arber. English Scholars Library, Birmingham, England; 1884. Also an edition with introduction by A. G. Bradley, J. Grant, Edinburgh; 1910.

Smith, Harry W. *Windjammers of the Maine Coast.* Down East Books, Camden, Maine; 1983.

Smith, J. Russell. *The Influence of the Great War Upon Shipping.* Oxford University Press, New York; 1919.

Smith, Mason Philip. *Confederates Down East.* Provincial Press, Portland, Maine; 1985.

Snow, Ralph L. *Bath Iron Works, The First Hundred Years.* Maine Maritime Museum, Bath, Maine; 1987.

Stahl, Jacob Jasper. *History of Old Broad Bay and Waldoborough.* Bond Wheelwright Co., Portland, Maine; 1956.

Stanley, Ralph. Unpublished manuscript on John Manchester, John Bunker, and *Falmouth Packet.* In my possession.

Stern, Philip V. *The Confederate Navy, A Pictorial History.* Doubleday, Garden City, New York; 1962.

Street, George E. *Mount Desert, A History.* Houghton Mifflin, Cambridge, Massachusetts; 1905.

Talbot, George F. "Capture of the *Margaretta.*" Collection of Maine Historical Society, Series 2, Volume 2, p. 2 ff.

Thompson, Lawrence. *The Navy Hunts CGR 3070.* Doubleday Doran, Garden City, New York; 1944.

Thoreau, Henry D. *Walden.* W. W. Norton, New York; 1951.

Tillinghast, William H., and Harry E. Barnes. *Ploetz Manual of Universal History.* Houghton Mifflin, Boston; 1925.

Tod, Giles M. S. *Last Sail Down East.* Barre Publishers, Barre, Massachusetts; 1965.

Tuchman, Barbara W. *The First Salute.* Alfred A. Knopf, New York; 1988.

Tucker, Captain Daniel. "Capt. Daniel Tucker in the Revolution." An autobiographical sketch with prefatory remarks by Rev. E. C. Cummings. Read before the Maine Historical Society, February 4, 1897. Proceedings of the Maine Historical Society, Series 2, Volume 8, pp. 225–257.

Tulley, John A. *The British Navy in the American Revolution.* University of South Carolina Press, Columbia, South Carolina; 1987.

United States Navy. *U.S. Submarine Losses in World War II.* U.S. Navy, Washington; 1946. Contains a table of Axis losses but is incomplete.

Unwin, Rayner. *The Defeat of John Hawkins.* Allen & Unwin, London; 1961.

Villiers, Alan. *The Way of a Ship.* Charles Scribner's Sons, New York; 1953, 1970.

Warner, William. *Distant Water, The Fate of the North Atlantic Fisherman.* Atlantic Little, Brown, Boston; 1983.

Wasson, George S., and Lincoln Colcord. *Sailing Days on the Penobscot.* Marine Research Society, Salem, Massachusetts; 1932.

Wentworth, Brandon. *The Fabulous Radio NDB.* Beech Hill Publishing Co., Southwest Harbor, Maine; 1984.

Williard, Captain B. J. *Life History and Adventures of Capt. B. J. Williard.* Lakeside Press, Portland, Maine; 1895.

Williamson, Joseph. "Sir John Moore at Castine." Proceedings of the Maine Historical Society, Series 2, Volume 2, p. 203 ff.

Williamson, William D. *History of the State of Maine from its First Discovery A.D. 1602 to the Separation, A.D. 1820.* This book is referred to as *History of Maine* in various chapter notes. Glazier Masters & Co., Hallowell, Maine; 1832.

Willison, George F. *Saints and Strangers.* Reynal & Hitchcock, New York; 1945.

Winslow, Sidney L. *Fish Scales and Stone Chips.* Machigonne Press, Portland, Maine; 1952.

No author given. *Casco Bay Steamboat Album.* Down East Enterprise, Camden, Maine; 1969.

No author given. *Glimpses of Camden.* John R. Prescott, Newtonville, Massachusetts.

No author given. *Kennebec–Boothbay Harbor Steamboat Album.* Down East Books, Camden, Maine; 1971.

Periodicals

Bergeson, Lloyd. "The Tragedy of *Defiance.*" *WoodenBoat,* Number 102, pp. 62–81.

Carlton, William C. "Masts and the King's Navy." *New England Quarterly,* Volume 12, Number 1.

Churchill, Edwin A. "The Historiography of the *Margaretta* Affair, Or, How Not to Let the Facts Interfere With a Good Story." *Maine Historical Society Quarterly,* Fall 1975, pp. 60–74.

Drinkwater, Norman, Jr. "The Stone Age of Dix Island." *Down East,* Volume 10, Number 2, pp. 43–47.

Hall, Phyllis A. "Sinking of *William P. Frye.*" *American Neptune,* Volume 45, Number 3.

Lyman, John. "The Last Voyage of the *Star of Scotland,*" *American Neptune,* Volume 3, Number 3, p. 266.

———. "Register Tonnage and its Measurement." *American Neptune,* Volume 5, Number 3, pp. 223–234.

———. "The *Star of Scotland* ex-*Kenilworth.*" *American Neptune,* Vol. 1, No. 4, pp. 333–344.

Marsh, Nim. "Hinckley." *Nautical Quarterly,* Number 8, pp. 2–25, 117–118.

Parker, Captain W. J. Lewis. "To the River." *American Neptune,* Volume 35, Number 1, pp. 5–19.

Stevens, James. "The Families Who've Made Shipbuilding History." *The Boothbay Register,* Volume 100, Number 52, pp. 6–7.

Villiers, Captain Alan. "How We Sailed *Mayflower II* to America." *National Geographic,* Volume 112, Number 5, pp. 627–674.

———. "We're Coming Over on the *Mayflower.*" *National Geographic,* Volume 111, Number 5, pp. 708–728.

Note: A study of any issue of *National Fisherman,* published in Camden, Maine, will shed light on the current landings of fish, the prices, and methods of fishing.

Index